**CULINARY CLAIMS**

Indigenous Restaurant Politics in Canada

**Food for Thought
Food for Pleasure
Food for Change**

*Series Editors*

Jayeeta (Jo) Sharma (Toronto)
H. Rosi Song (Durham)
Robert Davidson (Toronto)

*Editorial Advisory Board*

Cristiana Bastos (Lisbon)
Shyon Baumann (Toronto)
Daniel Bender (Toronto)
Andrea Borghini (Milan)
Miranda Brown (Michigan)
Sidney Cheung (Hong Kong)
Simone Cinotto (Gastronomic Sciences)
Tracey Deutsch (Minnesota)
Jean Duruz (South Australia)
Rebecca Earle (Warwick)
Beth Forrest (Culinary Institute of America)
Michael Innis-Jiménez (Alabama)
Alice Julier (Chatham)
Lindsay Kelley (New South Wales)
Zeynep Kiliç (Alaska)
Mustafa Koç (Toronto Metropolitan)
Charles Levkoe (Lakehead)
Ken Macdonald (Toronto)
Raúl Matta (Göttingen)
Massimo Montinari (Bologna)
Fabio Parasecoli (New York)
Jeffrey Pilcher (Toronto)
Elaine Power (Queen's)
Signe Rousseau (Cape Town)
Kyla D. Tompkins (Pomona)

# CULINARY CLAIMS

*Indigenous Restaurant Politics in Canada*

L. SASHA GORA

UNIVERSITY OF TORONTO PRESS
Toronto  Buffalo  London

© University of Toronto Press 2025
Toronto Buffalo London
utorontopress.com

ISBN 978-1-4875-4474-4 (cloth)    ISBN 978-1-4875-4476-8 (EPUB)
ISBN 978-1-4875-4475-1 (paper)    ISBN 978-1-4875-4478-2 (PDF)

**Library and Archives Canada Cataloguing in Publication**

Title: Culinary claims : Indigenous restaurant politics in Canada / L. Sasha Gora.
Names: Gora, L. Sasha, author.
Description: Includes bibliographical references and index.
Identifiers: Canadiana (print) 20240419197 | Canadiana (ebook) 20240419243 | ISBN 9781487544744 (cloth) | ISBN 9781487544751 (paper) | ISBN 9781487544768 (EPUB) | ISBN 9781487544782 (PDF)
Subjects: LCSH: Indigenous peoples – Food – Canada. | LCSH: Restaurants – Political aspects – Canada. | LCSH: Restaurants – Social aspects – Canada.
Classification: LCC E98.F7 G67 2025 | DDC 641.59297/071 – dc23

Cover design: Mark Rutledge
Cover image: Adrian Stimson, *Iini Sookumapii: Guess Who's Coming to Dinner?* (detail), 2019, mixed-media installation, dimensions variable, commissioned by the Toronto Biennial of Art, photo by Triple Threat, courtesy of the Toronto Biennial of Art.

We wish to acknowledge the land on which the University of Toronto Press operates. This land is the traditional territory of the Wendat, the Anishnaabeg, the Haudenosaunee, the Métis, and the Mississaugas of the Credit First Nation.

University of Toronto Press acknowledges the financial support of the Government of Canada, the Canada Council for the Arts, and the Ontario Arts Council, an agency of the Government of Ontario, for its publishing activities.

 Canada Council for the Arts   Conseil des Arts du Canada

 ONTARIO ARTS COUNCIL
CONSEIL DES ARTS DE L'ONTARIO
an Ontario government agency
un organisme du gouvernement de l'Ontario

Funded by the Government of Canada   Financé par le gouvernement du Canada

*To the best-looking Blake*

# Contents

*List of Illustrations*   ix

*Preface*   xi

Introduction: You Are Welcome   3

1  Agricultural Flagpoles   29

2  From Trains to Tundra   64

3  Restaurants and Representation   87

4  An Edible Exhibition   116

5  One Address, Three Restaurants   143

6  A Meal for a Chief   172

7  Culinary Resurgence   191

8  Seal Tartare   212

9  Where the Beaver and Buffalo Roam   237

10  Salmon and the F-Word   260

Conclusion: The North   285

*Acknowledgments*   307

*Notes*   313

*Bibliography*   391

*Index*   447

## Illustrations

1.1 "Two Aboriginal women reading a Canada's Food Guide posted in the Community Health Workers Training Program, Coqualeetza, British Columbia" 35
1.2 Sonny Assu, *Breakfast Series*, 2006 42
1.3 Sonny Assu, *Treaty Flakes*, 2006 43
1.4 "Buffalo bones gathered from the Prairies," c. 1880–90 47
1.5 "Bannock baking contest, Flin Flon Trout Festival" 48
1.6 "Trappers Festival, bannock baking," 1963 49
1.7 Lisa Myers, *Blueprints – Garden River Bridge*, 2015 53
2.1 Front and back cover of La Toundra restaurant menu, 1967 66
2.2 "Cuisine Canadienne" section of La Toundra restaurant menu, 1967 67
2.3 "La Toundra" section of La Toundra restaurant menu, 1967 68
2.4 "International Cuisine" section of La Toundra restaurant menu, 1967 69
2.5 "Expo 67 Canada Pavilion – Inuit mural for its restaurant La Toundra," 18 October 1967 71
2.6 "Whale meat shipment at North Toronto Station," c. 1916–19 75
2.7 "Indian Room menu" 76
4.1 Front of "Muckamuck Restaurant: Northwest Coast Native Indian food," c. 1975 117
4.2 Back of "Muckamuck Restaurant: Northwest Coast Native Indian food," c. 1975 118

4.3  Edward S. Curtis, "Nootka method of spearing," 1915   126
4.4  Sean Griffin, "Muckamuck strike opening," 2 June 1978   132
4.5  Sean Griffin, "Muckamuck restaurant strike begins," 4 June 1978   132
4.6  Sean Griffin, "Muckamuck strikers march, downtown Vancouver," 12 August 1978   133
4.7  Dana Claxton in collaboration with Sean Griffin, *Muckamuck Strike Then and Now*, 2018   139
4.8  ReMatriate Collective, *YOURS FOR INDIGENOUS SOVEREIGNTY,*, 2018   141
5.1  "Liliget Feast House interior," 2006   163
5.2  "Liliget Feast House menu," 2006   165
7.1  "NishDish," 2019   204
9.1  Kent Monkman, *The Rise and Fall of Civilization*, 2015   246
9.2  Kent Monkman, *Les Castors du Roi*, 2011   247
10.1  Lawrence Paul Yuxweluptun, *Fish Farmers They Have Sea Lice*, 2014   270
10.2  "Little Miss Chief smoked salmon label"   283
11.1  AA Bronson, *A Public Apology to Siksika Nation*, and Adrian Stimson, *Iini Sookumapii: Guess Who's Coming to Dinner?*, 2019   293
11.2  Adrian Stimson, *Iini Sookumapii: Guess Who's Coming to Dinner?*, 2019   294
11.3  Adrian Stimson, *Iini Sookumapii: Guess Who's Coming to Dinner?* (detail), 2019   295

# Preface

The meal began with "Mejillons con Fresas Y Pipa": a soup of mussels and green strawberries strained to be as fluid as water and crowned with coconut foam. Local ingredients, tropical ingredients. I was embarking on a twelve-course tasting menu at Intimo in Panama City, the capital of a slender country that couples two continents (although one local told me she grew up believing they are one). Having been born and raised in the lands now called Canada, in Panama I felt as if I was on the continent's furthest edge. I was somewhere I considered south and yet this soup with coconut made me think of the north.

What is north and what is south depends on both geography and culture, but while dining at Intimo I was surprised to be confronted by the north. It was not the aggressive air conditioning; rather, it was the restaurant's cookbook collection, fanned behind the bar like décor. My stool granted a view of the open kitchen, of its shelves of books and booze: *Fäviken* by Magnus Nilsson (named after the restaurant he ran in northern Sweden for over a decade), Copenhagen-based René Redzepi's famed *NOMA: Time and Place in Nordic Cuisine*, and another tome from the Danish capital: *Relæ: A Book of Ideas* by Christian F. Puglisi. Why look north? What can a chef working with tropical ingredients glean from a Nordic cookbook? I may give the impression that I can give a tidy definition of what or where the north is, but my concern here is something else. It is about how place is imagined through food. And unlike the "empty" landscapes that Lawren Harris and other settler

Canadian artists, including the Group of Seven, famously painted – razor-sharp glaciers and wind-swept trees – my understanding of place is one inhabited by people. So, to revise my question: how are place and the peoples of a particular place imagined through food?

*Culinary Claims: Indigenous Restaurant Politics in Canada* looks north to chronicle a cultural shift in representations of Indigenous foodways, the changing relationship between cuisine and place, and the textures of this – the tastes – in a settler colonial state. More specifically, it stories the emergence of Indigenous cuisines in urban restaurants across Canada. Plants and animals trespass borders. Cuisines do too. And so to study such culinary changes, to consider how the local is knotted with the global, I cross the Atlantic to weigh what is Nordic fare and its international influence. That said, the Nordic is less of a subject and more of a context, a distant backdrop. This book also travels to Canada's southern neighbour, the United States, to better chart the role that restaurants play in Indigenous resurgence beyond colonial lines. It wends south to understand the north, venturing to California, and via this mussel and green strawberry soup, to Panama. The lands it depicts are urban, have ripe appetites, and are hungry for stories that better represent their histories, peoples, and foods.

**CULINARY CLAIMS**

Indigenous Restaurant Politics in Canada

# Introduction: You Are Welcome

In July 2015 Toronto hosted the XVII Pan American Games. A year before, the *Globe and Mail*, Canada's national newspaper, published an opinion piece by the Games' chairman and former Ontario premier, David Peterson. With the tone and volume of a pep rally, Peterson wanted Toronto to feel excited, really excited, because "Never before has Canada hosted a multi-sport event of this size."[1] His promises were as large as the competition itself. "These games will change lives for the better," Peterson vowed.[2] The stakes soared equally high: "the world will be watching as we showcase this region and its incredible diversity and talents."[3] The article mentioned spectators, from the United States to Brazil, and the excitement that Peterson was confident "all Canadians" would feel. However, it did not note any First Nations.

Now based southwest of Toronto, near Brantford, Ontario, the traditional territory of the Mississaugas of the Credit embraces Canada's largest city. The land was signed over to the British Crown in the 1787 Toronto Purchase and then clarified in 1805 in Treaty No. 13.[4] Terrain stretching from Ashbridges Bay to Etobicoke Creek – the 250,808 acres that encompass the city's core – went for ten shillings, the equivalent of $60 Canadian in 2010, plus 2,000 gun flints, 120 mirrors, 96 gallons of rum, 24 laced hats, 24 brass kettles, and a bale of flowered flannel.[5] In 1986 then-Chief Maurice LaForme filed a land claim, which, finally, in 2010, the Government of Canada settled for $145 million, a fairer estimate of the tract's worth.[6]

Like Peterson, this Ojibwa First Nation saw the Pan Am Games as an opportunity. But instead of imagining the sporting event as a chance to market the city, province, and country, it was a chance to raise awareness of Toronto's original inhabitants. And they did so with food. The Mississaugas of the Credit collaborated with Toronto-based chef David Wolfman – a member of the Xaxli'p First Nation – on the You Are Welcome Food Truck: *Gii Daa Namegoon*. "Food is universal and it brings people together from all different cultural backgrounds," explained then-Chief Bryan LaForme. "We are honoured to officially welcome people to our traditional territory this summer and invite everyone to taste delicious Aboriginal dishes."[7] You are welcome, however, carries a double meaning. On the one hand, it welcomes athletes, their entourages, and other visitors. "Welcome to Toronto," it conveys. On the other, it speaks directly to Torontonians. It says "You are welcome" in the sense of accepting the gratitude of those who, and those who do not, acknowledge the Mississaugas of the Credit as the city's traditional residents. The truck, in short, was equally concerned with laying claim to land as it was with welcoming people. It leveraged food as a way of narrating Toronto's Indigenous past alongside its present and future.

Enthusiastic with their praise, journalists described the food truck as "a First Nations welcome to Toronto" and "a good cause."[8] Curious appetites ran through these articles, but the attendant politics were missing.[9] Instead of detailing reasons for the limited opportunities to eat Indigenous fare, they present such cuisines as novel, as something new to try. But absence always shadows presence. By aiming to create awareness of Toronto's ongoing Indigenous present, the truck also exposed the extent to which the city has attempted to erase its history. Wolfman and the Mississaugas of the Credit's 2015 food truck thus staged a culinary counternarrative to settler accounts of Toronto, exemplifying the range of something as everyday as food and its power to both claim and reclaim cultural and political ties to land. How what we eat stories where we eat.

There are over eight thousand restaurants in Toronto.[10] If you count all food-serving establishments – the likes of bakeries and bars, take-out counters and food courts – that number is even higher.¹¹ But the year Toronto hosted the Pan Am games, only one offered Indigenous fare: Tea-n-Bannock. Then in 2016 the Pow Wow Cafe opened, and in 2017 two more: NishDish Marketeria and Kūkŭm Kitchen. Why are there so few Indigenous eateries in Toronto, as well as the rest of Canada? And how does this Toronto tale relate to changes in global restaurant culture? Beyond places to grab a bite, restaurants are venues for exchange. *Culinary Claims* is, therefore, a cultural history of representations of Indigenous foodways in restaurants across Canada and how these depictions have transformed in relation to the ebb and flow of political and global culinary shifts.

To study food is to study how it is rooted in, or transcends, place. It is to study land, and how land is worked and transformed, imagined and represented, bought, sold, won and lost, whom it belongs to, and who belongs to it. "Food is land."¹² It enacts relationships, a point the Anishinaabekwe activist Winona LaDuke animates. "Food for us comes from our relatives whether they have wings or fins or roots," she says. "That is how we consider food. Food has a culture. It has a history. It has a story. It has relationships."¹³ Culinary encounters are intimate; they dissolve boundaries between food and feed, between bodies and environments. To study food, then, is also to study relations. And it is to study power: who has the power to define what is food, where it comes from, and how it gets to the table. Literary scholar Margery Fee poses the question: "How does literature claim land?"¹⁴ I ask: how does food claim land? At its most abstract level, *Culinary Claims* is about the relationship between food and land in a settler colonial state; at its most concrete, it's about how Indigenous restaurants resist, revise, and represent that relationship.

Eating is one of the most direct ways we interact with environments – both near and far – by literally digesting them. Food, thus, bridges self-identity with place-identity to the point that, as geographers David Bell and Gill Valentine synthesize, "what we eat (and where, and why) signals, as the aphorism says, who we are."¹⁵ Departing from this claim, historian Nicolas P. Maffei summarizes that global food studies typically focus on two processes: "the blending of local food cultures, and resistance through reassertion of the local."[16] This book turns its attention to the latter and unpacks the politics of the "local" in a settler society.[17] Fashions in food evolve to reflect changing relationships to nature and place. Sociologist Jean-Pierre Poulain diagnoses modern food as delocalized – separated from climate constraints and geographical origins.[18] The response to this is relocalization.[19] The return to place-based eating practices echoes historians Matthias Middell and Katja Naumann's description of "globalization as a dialectical process of de- and re-territorialization."[20] What qualifies as local is not straightforward, nor is it static. Local foods shift based on the migration of people, plants, and animals, as well as fluctuations in climate, oscillations in environments. It is also a matter of who can define what is local, and thus a question of power.

But place is as much about imagination as it is about geography. Place taught cultural critic Rebecca Solnit how to write. It also taught her that "*place* is problematic, implying a discrete entity, something you could put a fence around."[21] Sometimes this is true, other times not. "What we mean by *place*," she says, "is a crossroads, a particular point of intersection of forces coming from many directions and distances."[22] As much as food nurtures a sense of connection, it also incites disconnect and erects fences. Food divides as much as it unites. Historian Donna Gabaccia makes clear that "Eating habits both symbolize and mark the boundaries of cultures."[23] Food builds borders, constructs difference, and polices value. It is central for making and negotiating identity, for claiming and reclaiming. In Canada food has been a tool of colonial control and cultural assimilation. The limited presence of Indigenous restaurants reflects this. The Canada I write about, the one that is imagined through celebrated and forbidden foods, shared meals and exclusive entry-by-invitation-only affairs, is this intersection of forces – a chaotic conjunction of ideas and a competition of definitions. Names in English and French, in Ojibway and Cree, in Franglais and Chinook Jargon all at once.

A medium for sharing and for exchange, food builds relationships – with what you eat and whom you eat it with. It, thus, plays a central role in efforts made by Indigenous communities across the country, continent, and world to reclaim languages and traditions, and to practise sovereignty. Indigenous governance scholars Taiaiake Alfred and Jeff Corntassel, for example, include "Decolonize Your Diet" as one of five "Indigenous Pathways of Action and Freedom."[24] Whether at a pop event or at a brick and mortar restaurant, Indigenous chefs, like David Wolfman, are leveraging food to reclaim a contemporary presence. Food is fuel. It fires cultural revitalization and political resurgence.

*Culinary Claims* is about Canada, but one could tell a similar story in Aotearoa New Zealand, Mexico, or even Panama. Each of these histories is, of course, distinct. The Indigenous food movement in Canada frames itself around reconciliation, whereas the one in the United States rallies around revitalization. It confronts different regulations and political structures. But both movements aim to reclaim Indigenous cultures through food, restore relations, and defend the rights to self-determination. "Indigenous food sovereignty represents a movement," writes Swampy Cree scholar Tabitha Robin, "one where we are re-defining our food systems and revitalizing our culture, one that is political and dynamic and hard."[25] *Culinary Claims* asks: What role do restaurants play in this movement?

## A New Nordic

The rise of Indigenous restaurants overlaps and intersects with broader shifts. Although no longer new, the new Nordic food movement tapped into an increasing curiosity about the genealogy of ingredients and a refreshed appetite for local foods. Taste is ever changing, as are the values that mandate taste. There is a continual evolution of which foods are valued and why. Early Canadian settlers were dependent on Indigenous foodways but, then, imported animals – cows and chickens, pigs and sheep – and transplanted

Europe's reverence of wheat to North America. But as more people have become aware of the ills of global food systems – which make people, plants, and animals sick, soil and water too – the appeal of local and wild foods has grown.

Because of its focus on foraged flora in northern climates, I argue that the new Nordic food movement has been particularly influential in Canada and indicative of a revival of Indigenous ingredients. In 2003 chef René Redzepi, together with Claus Meyer, opened Noma in Copenhagen. A portmanteau of the Danish words *nordisk* (Nordic) and *mad* (food), it won first place in *Restaurant Magazine*'s Best Restaurant in the World competition in 2010. Previously, restaurants that stuck to the rules of classic French cuisine or experimented with molecular gastronomy dominated the list. Never before had a Nordic restaurant attracted such attention, and Noma's ascent revamped Copenhagen into a high-end culinary destination overnight.

I turn to the new Nordic food movement in Chapter 3 and its global significance for international dining and, therefore, perceptions of local cuisines. What matters here is that Noma built its reputation by cooking ingredients that are "native" to the region. For example, journalist Frank Bruni writes that Redzepi is "omnivorous in his exoticism, but restrictive in his geography. If the Nordic region doesn't yield it, Mr. Redzepi doesn't serve it, with rare exceptions [coffee, say, or chocolate]."[26] His headline says it all: "Nordic Chef Explores Backyard."[27] Although tomatoes are banned, potatoes are embraced, despite both originating in the Americas. How and why has the potato "gone Native" in a Nordic context?[28] This question is not my concern; however, raising it reveals the fluctuating categories of food and how cuisines are continually evolving. Noma makes it clear that it does not serve traditional Nordic fare; rather, it serves an interpretation. Nordic restaurant cuisine may not overlap with historic regional diets; rather, it provides insight into how chefs like Redzepi construct Nordic gastronomic heritage, which ingredients are allowed to take part, and how such culinary formulas spill out to the rest of the world, as the cookbooks in Panama City's Intimo reveal. Food, after all, expresses how a region imagines its geography and how it defines its history and heritage, its present and future.

Cuisines are entangled with cultural hierarchies and, traditionally, French cuisine has claimed the throne. France has long been associated with abundance, whereas Nordic countries have been imagined as lands of scarcity. However, Noma challenged this narrative and tilted the apex of fine dining by promoting ingredients that were previously not thought of as restaurant fare, the likes of beach grasses and bugs. Noma further localized fine dining, a tendency that was already simmering thanks to nouvelle cuisine in the 1970s. This influence bursts beyond the Nordic region. Hardie Grant Books, an Australian publisher, has released titles like *The New Nordic: Scandinavian Cuisine through the Seasons* and *Nordic Light: Lighter, Everyday Eating from a Scandinavian Kitchen*. What appeal does a Nordic cookbook have for an Australian audience or, say, a Panamanian one? What principles behind the movement apply to other climates and ingredients? And how have representations of Indigenous food cultures changed in light of global culinary changes that celebrate local and seasonal eating? To study how restaurants in Canada stage Indigenous cuisines, I frame my research in the context of major shifts in international dining culture, which the new Nordic food movement exemplifies. Doing so addresses the local, national, and international forces shaping what people eat. This connects with issues that stretch beyond national borders, the likes of food security and sovereignty, Indigenous rights and resurgence.

Central to the arguments in *Culinary Claims* is that more Indigenous restaurants continue to open. Recent examples include Mi'kmaw chef Norma Condo's Miqmak Catering Indigenous Kitchen in Montreal, Quebec, and Anishinaabe chef Gerry Brandon's L'Autochtone Taverne Américaine in Haileybury, Ontario – both of which opened in 2019.[29] In 2020 Mohawk chef Tawnya Brant launched Yawékon, a lunch restaurant and catering business, in Ohswé:ken, Ontario, on Six Nations of the Grand River.[30] That same year, Dean Herkert, a Manitoba Métis Federation member, opened Bistro on Notre Dame in Winnipeg. Curtis Red-Rokk Cardinal, a member of Whitefish Lake First Nations in Alberta, started selling bannock out of his backpack at pow wows around Edmonton in 2010, which sparked his catering business Tee Pee Treats. In 2021, it expanded to offer take-out and delivery and, now, seasonal seating. In 2022 Ojibwa chef Zach Keeshig debuted the weekend-only, reservations-essential Naagan in Owen Sound, Ontario, which presents a nine-course tasting menu, and, in Winnipeg, Manoomin opened in the Wyndham Garden Airport Hotel with Jennifer Ballantyne, of the Opaskwayak Cree Nation, as its chef. In 2023 Suzette Foucault opened Manitou Bistro in Renfrew, Ontario, on National Indigenous Peoples Day.[31] This book – a cultural history of the representation of Indigenous cuisines in restaurants in Canada – contextualizes the increase in Indigenous restaurants and adds texture to this history. Studying early examples adds to the movement's historiography and combats the erasure of the contributions made by early Indigenous restaurateurs.

In order for me to avoid being the one who determines which restaurants may call themselves Indigenous, an eatery must actively identify as Indigenous in its name, advertisements, or motto.[32] Contemporary accounts often collapse Indigenous foods into either a singular image of bannock, a quick flatbread, or a romanticized imagined past of hunting and gathering. Perhaps, this is why it is still relevant to ask what an Indigenous restaurant is and what makes it Indigenous. I focus on what restaurants serve (and are allowed to), but also consider the environments from which these foods come. And I steer clear of stereotypes like this bannock versus hunter-gatherer binary. These extremes are examples of what novelist Chimamanda Adichie calls "the single story." As Americanist Psyche Williams-Forson summarizes, "the single story is the one that popular culture has delivered time and time again. It is the story that places people – particularly those considered 'other' – in a box that is manageable and relatively comprehensible. It is the default place in which the speaker, writer, performer, and activist must remain so that sense can be made of them."[33] *Culinary Claims* avoids telling a single story. It avoids a single voice and embraces the messiness of defining any cuisine, especially those that have been actively suppressed by colonialism. An Indigenous restaurant is not just one thing, and *Culinary Claims* maps the many stories that Indigenous eateries across Canada have told over time. But despite its focus on restaurants, this book is more than just the study of lunch and dinner (and sometimes breakfast). It explores the politics of urban restaurantscapes across Canada and situates these examples within a transnational context.

Conceptually, *Culinary Claims* is about interchanges between wild plants and introduced animals, the domesticated and the rogue, Indigenous foodways and Canadian regulations, chefs and customers. It employs restaurants to write about the history of social and political issues regarding cultural representation. It looks at Indigenous influences on Canadian foodways and the rise of Indigenous restaurants and narrates this entangled history to engage with questions about how changes in food preferences reflect larger social, cultural, and environmental shifts. I discuss historical and contemporary representations of Indigenous cuisines and how they have been changing in light of the relocalization of foodways. Noma exemplifies fine dining's relocalization and has set a new international standard. Although the new Nordic food movement has been globally influential, it is especially relevant in a northern country like Canada that shares similarities in climate. But in Canada to talk about local food is to talk about land, power, and settler colonialism. In response, *Culinary Claims* traces the presence and the absence of Indigenous restaurants in Canada's cultural landscape.

## A Home on Native Land

Toronto's identity as a multicultural city is recent, but the city is now a transnational buffet of dim-sum, Jamaican beef patties, and roti. The St. Lawrence Market doubles as an encyclopaedia of Eastern European mustards and Italian-American sandwiches. Downtown Toronto has two Chinatowns, and I lived on the outskirts of Chinatown East, a few blocks from Greektown and a short streetcar ride west of Little India. I grew up snacking on *dou sha bao*, Greek fries, and fresh sugarcane juice. Like many settler Canadians, I learned about my family's history through food – from Polish *pączki* and Icelandic *vínarterta* to my granddad's beef and barley stew his Gaelic-speaking mother taught him to make.

I understood the world's geography because of what I ate, but it took me much longer to learn about Turtle Island. I ate *puposas* years before I learned about pemmican, not to mention fiddleheads or sweetgrass, oolichan or seal (as meat and not a cute plush toy).

I am a fourth-generation settler. Every morning in school I had to sing the national anthem, and by the time I started high school, classmates had changed the words: "Our home *on* Native land," they sang. A "Native Studies" class introduced me to Victoria Freeman's *Distant Relations: How My Ancestors Colonized North America*, which encouraged me to ask the same. This class was in Toronto – from the Mohawk word *Tkaronto* – the traditional land of the Huron-Wendat, the Seneca, and the Mississaugas of the Credit. *Culinary Claims* is part of a growing body of scholarship that is committed to rethinking Canada, to telling different stories, and it uses food to do so. It is also about reconciling the foods I grew up eating with ones that tell the country's history more critically and inclusively. Foods that reveal rather than erase Indigenous histories.

Why does this past matter? Personal history frames the researcher, the storyteller. It frames why someone is telling a story and their ability to do so. In order to apply an "Indigenous research paradigm," the scholars Tabitha Robin, Jaime Cidro, Michael Anthony Hart, and Stéphane McLachlan underline the importance of "situating yourself in your research – describing who you are and how you came to be."[34] They cite Kathy Absolon and Cam Willett's fittingly titled paper, "Aboriginal Research: Berry Picking and Hunting in the 21st Century," which posits: "Location of self in writing and research is integral to issues of accountability."[35]

Cree-Métis scholar Deanne Reder agrees. Positionality, she writes, emphasizes "that all knowledge is generated from particular positions, that there is no unbiased, neutral position possible."[36] It is, thus, an ethical decision to frame this project personally. To tell my story as opposed to seeking to speak for others. Here I take my cue from postcolonial theorist Trịnh Thị Minh Hà's notion of "speaking nearby" rather than "speaking about." She describes this as "A speaking that reflects on itself and can come very close to a subject without, however, seizing or claiming it."[37] This follows the same beat as the "personal turn" in food studies.[38] By locating myself, I recognize the "place-based responsibilities" I have inherited as a guest on the lands where I was born and raised.[39]

In Winnipeg, Audrey Logan, who appears in Chapter 1, showed me around a permaculture garden she planted to secure her own food. Before we toured the community of plants, we sat down, shared coffee from a thermos, and chatted about my research. "What are you going to do with this knowledge?" she asked, her eyes locked with mine. Her question reminded me of the writer Thomas King. "Stories are wondrous things," he says.[40] He also warns that they are dangerous. "For once a story is told, it cannot be called back. Once told, it is loose in the world. So you have to be careful with the stories you tell," he cautions, "And you have to watch out for the stories that you are told."[41] Stories are powerful. And sharing them comes with great responsibility. "Humans cannot live without stories," argues the literary scholar Stephen Greenblatt. "We surround ourselves with them; we make them up in our sleep; we tell them to our children; we pay to have them told to us."[42] Because stories are necessary and because they are powerful, they require prudence. And as I have learned from the environmental historian Dolly Jørgensen, "narratives are always time-dependent," which is to say that it matters where our stories start and where they end.[43]

*Culinary Claims* presents a story. "It is," to quote the environmental historian Bathsheba Demuth, "like any history, not the story but a story."[44] Stories speak of the specific, as well as the general. In her comparison of Sky Woman to Eve, Potawatomi ethnobotanist Robin Wall Kimmerer sums up: "Same species, same earth, different stories. Like Creation stories everywhere, cosmologies are a source of identity and orientation to the world. They tell us who we are."[45] Reflecting on Eve's exile from Eden, Kimmerer recites ethnobiologist Gary Nabhan's call for "res-story-ation," or as Kimmerer writes, "our relationship with land cannot heal until we hear it in stories."[46] Following this advice, *Culinary Claims* is not only an act of storytelling but also an act of storymaking. When I requested an interview with the Anishinaabe and Algonquin chef Johl Whiteduck Ringuette, he said yes, with a catch. "I would be interested in a trade of information with you," he replied.⁴⁷ He reminded me of the importance of sharing stories, of circulating research, and what we learn from both. Stories illuminate connections and transmit culture.⁴⁸

The history of restaurants in Canada is a history of migration.⁴⁹ It tells stories of sailing settlers – and the plants and animals they brought with them – of displaced Indigenous communities and their fight to maintain relationships to their ancestral lands, and the culinary knowledge and traditions of generations of migrants. Stories of people from around the world eating for a sense of place, a sense of home. And the history of North America as a whole is a history of migration and displacement – stories that range from voluntary travel to forced relocation and exiled flight.⁵⁰ But stories also add up to much more than the sum of their parts. They harden, shift shape, acquire power, and write laws. They amplify some voices and erase others. This is what the Cree literary and Indigenous studies scholar Dallas Hunt and the Cree and Saulteuax political science scholar Gina Starblanket call "storying." The term sketches "the ways in which narratives, or spoken and written accounts, come alive and function as important political tools."⁵¹ I return to their work in Chapter 1, but here I wish to illuminate how storying underlines King's observations that stories are as dangerous as they are wondrous. Echoing this, Hunt and Starblanket reveal "how settler colonialism narrates itself into being through processes of storytelling."⁵² Their collaborative scholarship offers an invitation to become aware of these histories, these stories, and how they structure imaginaries, institutions, and interactions, which is shorthand for life and death.

Although *Culinary Claims* unfolds across the lands that are now called Canada, it tells stories that expand and defy national borders. It also problematizes and unsettles the border between Canada and the United States, which King addresses in *The Inconvenient Indian: A Curious Account of Native People in Canada*. "While the line that divides the two countries is a political reality, and while the border affects bands and tribes in a variety of ways," he says, "I would have found it impossible to talk about the one without talking about the other. For most Aboriginal people, that line doesn't exist. It is a figment of someone else's imagination."⁵³

*Culinary Claims* questions and crosses this settler border. The Conclusion turns to the United States, and throughout my focus on Canada I keep King's words in mind.

## Table Manners

A dish is an assemblage of ingredients that reflects and constructs time and space, seasons and place, cultures and traditions. Food materializes debates about what is fit to eat. It is embodied – political, discursive, economic. Culture codes materials into ingredients. It is, thus, culture that turns edibles into food, not edibility alone. A cuisine is a particular cooking style, a term that comes from Latin. Tellingly, French, Italian, and German have one word for both kitchen and cuisine (*la cuisine*, *la cucina*, and *die Küche*). Gastronomy comes from Greek, *gastro* meaning stomach and *onomy* the body of knowledge that governs the stomach. Gastronomy focuses on eating food and cuisine on preparing it. I follow sociologist Priscilla Parkhurst Ferguson's lead that cuisine is "the code that brings food into the social order. As dining socializes eating, so cuisine formalizes cooking."[54] Gastronomy, in contrast, favours taste, erudite eaters, and the perspective of those at the table as opposed to those in the kitchen.[55] I prioritize cuisine because it includes the labour – symbolic and physical – of turning animals and plants into food.

Cuisine encompasses how people cook and eat, when, where, with whom, and how. Zona Spray, an Arctic cuisine specialist, recounts food writer Giuliano Bugialli's five criteria for defining a cuisine: "1) indigenous food stuffs 2) a specific heat source 3) unique cooking methods and preserving techniques 4) specialized cooking implements and preserving equipment or tools 5) a distinctive flavoring or seasoning base giving all foods a unified taste."[56] That said, I do not discuss food as food, meaning how it tastes or what it does nutritionally; instead, I approach food as a site of cultural negotiation. As a cultural symbol. I consider what food does emotionally, how it represents land and territory, traditions and social tensions. How food enacts power.

*Culinary Claims* does not study what people in Canada eat per se. Nor does it study health and nutrition. Instead, it focuses on restaurant culture. It studies menus as cultural texts to reflect on how eateries represent culinary cultures. Restaurant menus tell stories. They stage narratives and are culinary ambassadors of social orders that require particular forms of literacy.[57] A menu holds things in relation with other things, and by things I mean flora and fauna.[58] *Culinary Claims* details how restaurants interact with larger political and social forces – what I call restaurant politics – and their role as venues for cultural representation. The history of Indigenous restaurants in Canada narrates a broader story about how food mediates relationships between peoples and places.

To track the evolution of the representation of Indigenous foodways in Canada, *Culinary Claims* focuses on the period from 1967 to 2017. But it also jumps back to the late nineteenth century and first half of the twentieth. It concentrates on urban Canada, but does not cover all provinces. Nor does it venture to the three territories, all gaps that deserve further attention. Although important, I do not discuss restaurants on reserves, another point for future scholarship. This book is an urban food cultural history. Despite employing these divisionary terms, I recognize their flaws and agree with Leanne Betasamosake Simpson, a Michi Saagiig Nishnaabeg scholar, who contests this separation. Recognizing how the settler colonial distinction reinforces division between reserve and urban communities, she writes, "Reserves are colonial constructs, as are urban communities."[59] Simpson emphasizes that "Cities have become sites of tremendous activism and resistance and of artistic, cultural, and linguistic revival and regeneration, and this comes from the land."[60] My focus on the urban understands cities as an integrated part of these relationships with land.

*Culinary Claims* is not exhaustive, nor is it encyclopaedic. It does not name every Indigenous restaurant, past and present. It is not a list, but a story. It is not a detailed description of Indigenous foods and food practices, nor is it a restaurant or food reference guide. It is, rather, a critical contemplation about food's meanings and the role restaurants play in staging cultural experiences. It is about restaurant politics. Its aim is not to study Indigenous cuisines and foodways. It is a work of food cultural history that demonstrates how both settler and Indigenous communities use foods – and restaurants as venues for their representation – to claim land, culture, and history. In other words, *Culinary Claims* does not represent a definitive history. Just as an ingredient is never the same – some apples, for example, scream sour, while others stay sweet, some succumb to the touch of a finger and others hold onto their crispness – a restaurant's dishes are always in flux. I thus embrace this variability and adaptability, this complexity, in the historical narratives I craft.

*Culinary Claims* depicts the power dynamics of cross-cultural encounters of eating in restaurants. It weaves individual restaurant histories together with themes such as culinary exchange, Indigenous sovereignty, and the politics of "authenticity." Furthermore, it examines the history of Indigenous restaurants in Canada from an interdisciplinary perspective. I employ a narrative voice that fuses the scholarly and the popular, the empirical and the subjective. I aspire to bring more awareness to earlier restaurant examples and to contextualize their role in the representation of Indigenous foodways. Likewise, instead of focusing on what Indigenous foods are, I attend to how contemporary renditions of Canadian cuisine imagine the history of Indigenous food cultures and, thus, the country's culinary heritage, especially now that local ingredients are in vogue.

Indigenous restaurants have come and gone since the 1970s, and yet there is little cultural memory of them. By revisiting these restaurants, I uncover stories about how land is imagined and who is part of this storytelling. I also track how these stories have shifted shape. The quality of a restaurant's food obviously affects its ability to survive, but what matters more for this book are its stories. To think about where food comes from and how it links people and places. *Culinary Claims*, in part, is about restaurants, but it is also about the narratives surrounding these restaurants – culinary discourse and restaurant politics. It, therefore, takes up how mainstream Canadian media has reported, which is to say has storied, Indigenous eateries.

Since the release of the Truth and Reconciliation Commission's 2015 report on Indian residential schools, the Canadian government is confronting the ongoing legacies of what the report calls cultural genocide. The year 2017 marked 150 years since Canadian Confederation, for which the federal and provincial governments threw celebratory parties. Another two years later, in 2019, the National Inquiry into Missing and Murdered Indigenous Women and Girls released *Reclaiming Power and Place*, which further pressed the urgency of reconciliation. And then on 28 May 2021, a headline announced: "Canada: remains of 215 children found at Indigenous residential school site" – 215 unmarked graves at Kamloops Indian School in British Columbia.[61] This headline confirmed what survivors had been saying for decades, and the discovery of these unmarked graves "is a condemning reminder of the horrific consequences of an ongoing genocide."[62] The residential school system enacted terrible abuse. Food, too, played a part. *Culinary Claims* contemplates food's role in residential schools, as well as cultural imperialism at large.

Political scientist Sam Grey and geographer Lenore Newman describe cuisine as "an important, overlooked lens" in food sovereignty scholarship.[63] They discuss the Andes and the Pacific Northwest, yet do not mention restaurants, a notable gap, considering that restaurants are where cuisines largely live today. Turning to another settler colonial Commonwealth country, anthropologist Carolyn Morris has studied the representation of Māori foodways in cookbooks, as well as the absence of Māori restaurants in Aotearoa New Zealand.[64] She attributes this absence to "the lack of a Māori clientele on account of economic status and the availability of culturally marked food in other venues, and the lack of a Pākehā clientele because of the perceived unpalatability of Māori food."[65] There are similarities between Aotearoa New Zealand and Canada. For example, Morris identifies ingredients – such as crayfish and sweet potatoes – that Pākehā (non-Māori) settlers have embraced, ingredients that are classified as either Māori or Pākehā, which is akin to Canada. Maple syrup, for instance, can be Indigenous and/or Canadian. Where my study parts ways from Morris's, however, is in its historiography. Morris reviews three Māori restaurants, one that opened in 1999, one in the mid-1980s, and one in 2003, arguing that the reasons they closed are representative of the Māoris' refusal to be assimilated. In contrast, *Culinary Claims* establishes a larger history of Indigenous restaurants in Canada to map how they represent political and social changes and how chefs use food to reclaim a contemporary cultural presence.

Drawing from discussions with colleagues, Morris's understanding is that the situation of "Native Americans and Australian Aborigines is similar to that of Māori, in that few if any restaurants sell their cuisine."[66] Instead, national cuisines adopt and appropriate what they like – claiming their preferred ingredients as their culinary building blocks and discarding the rest.[67] But this does not account for change. The restaurant that a Māori political activist ran created "the potentially disturbing confrontation with an uneasy colonial history."[68] This may have been true of earlier Indigenous restaurants, especially in the 1970s and 1980s, but I believe contemporary eateries, particularly ones that have opened since 2015, are spaces in which settler diners are becoming more comfortable with the discomfort required in confronting Canadian colonialism. This demonstrates how Indigenous restaurants – and the stories they serve – have evolved over nearly five decades and further illustrates what I mean by restaurant politics.

To piece together the history of how Canada's restaurant landscape has represented Indigenous foodways, I have consulted historical and contemporary menus, cookbooks, and recipes, conducted semi-structured qualitative interviews and oral histories with restaurateurs and chefs, and practised participant-observation, mostly front-of-house, but occasionally in the kitchen too. No matter how long the meal, restaurant experiences are ephemeral. Recipes, and therefore cookbooks, are more durable. Some restaurants leave a paper trail and others almost no traces at all. Sometimes menus survive, doubling as archives, but other times they're lost to appetites past. Primary sources about restaurants, especially Indigenous ones, are typically scarce. To compensate, I have combed through newspaper, magazine, and online reviews. In the absence of detailed histories about restaurants in Canada, print media take up the slack. That said, newspapers, for example, are colonial archives.[69] Critics judge Indigenous restaurants from a settler colonial point of view – a limitation I keep in mind. I parse menus from contemporary restaurants, as well as menus from ones that closed decades ago. But menus change – chefs grow bored and customers, too. Ingredient prices rise and fall. Tastes change. Or a global health pandemic crashes into the industry, closing many eateries and transforming others into take-out joints. This means that the contemporary restaurant menus I write about might already be, in some ways, historic. This book is, thus, a dizzying chronicle of restaurant openings and closings, of beginnings and endings. To date, there has been little discussion of restaurants in Canada, let alone Indigenous ones. *Culinary Claims* is a beginning, and I aim for it to encourage more scholars to give restaurants the attention they deserve.

One part narrative analysis and one part visual study, *Culinary Claims* brings together food studies and cultural history and uses archival, oral history, and visual methodologies to illuminate the politics that restaurants represent and enact. It is an interdisciplinary study of the emergence of Indigenous cuisine as a distinct style of dining in tandem with the negotiations restaurants make with pre-existing imaginations of Indigenous fare while defying those imaginations. By focusing on representations of Indigenous foodways and contemporary urban food culture, it seeks to contribute to understandings of Canadian colonialism. *Culinary Claims* reflects seven years of research, spread across archives, art collections, and conversations with chefs and restaurateurs. Using open-ended interview techniques, I attuned my listening to the ways in which restaurant spaces negotiate and amplify practices of sharing memories and stories. My strategy for seeking interviews was to identify restaurateurs based on historical and contemporary media coverage. As anyone who has traced Joni Mitchell's lyrics by drawing a map of Canada knows, the country is big. And travel is expensive. These limitations meant I focused on a handful of cities based on their archive collections, Indigenous restaurant histories, and contemporary food scenes: Vancouver, Winnipeg, Toronto, Ottawa, and Montreal. I acknowledge the shortcomings in this geography and its inability to speak on behalf of all regions.

For places I could not travel to, I further relied on archival material, ranging from newspaper accounts to government reports and from cookbooks and recipes to online reviews and photographs.

To complement these sources, I have pulled together literature from food studies, history, Indigenous studies, settler colonial studies, and the environmental humanities. *Culinary Claims* joins a body of scholarship that reads food socially, politically, and culturally.[70] Following *Northern Bounty: A Celebration of Canadian Cuisine* and *What's to Eat? Entrées in Canadian Food History*, the edited volume *Edible Histories, Cultural Politics: Towards a Canadian Food History* is the most thorough attempt to compile a national food history that includes some mention of Indigenous foodways.[71] I, however, aim to bring a discussion of representations of Indigenous and Canadian foodways into dialogue with international culinary changes. Lenore Newman's *Speaking in Cod Tongues: A Canadian Culinary Journey* acknowledges Indigenous restaurants but is a survey rather than a study.[72] *Culinary Claims*, in contrast, contributes to widening the scholarly discussion of restaurants in Canada, how they represent Indigenous cuisines, and the knots and tangles of the negotiations and politics of such representations. My goal is not to provide a comprehensive history of Indigenous restaurants, but instead to offer a starting point for understanding how stories about food – as staged by restaurants – have played a critical role in cultural representations. Furthermore, the ten chapters do not intend to tell these stories comprehensively but instead to develop a critical historical approach toward decoding restaurants and the politics they represent and enact.

## Reading Restaurants

Restaurants are so naturalized that their histories often go unnoticed. In the history of eating out, the restaurant, however, is just one model. Others are taverns and inns, guesthouses and cafés, teahouses and cookshops. What differentiates one from another includes fixed or unfixed mealtimes, individual versus group tables, set prices, the range of foods – from no options to many – and who may request a table. "Although restaurants might seem an inevitable part of urban civilization," historian Paul Freedman makes clear, "most prosperous, commercial societies in the past managed quite well without them."[73] A restaurant is not a given.

Restaurants go back to the eighteenth century, but eating out has a much longer and wide-reaching history.[74] Pompeii hosted a lively "street food" scene and there are records from as early as 1000 CE of dining options in imperial China.[75] But the word restaurant emerged in eighteenth-century Paris. Historian Rebecca Spang traces the first restaurants to places peddling consommé, a healthful soup. "In the last twenty years of the Old Regime," writes Spang, "one went to a restaurant (or, as they were more commonly called, a 'restaurateur's room') to drink restorative bouillons, as one went to a café to drink coffee."[76] By the 1820s, "restaurateur's rooms" had evolved into what we recognize as restaurants today.[77] But until the mid- to late nineteenth century, restaurants were a Parisian phenomenon.

Over time, restaurants have served diverse people with distinct needs: hungry travellers with nowhere else to eat; elite socialites keen to entertain; workers in need of lunch; bachelors without kitchens; and families on the road. Restaurants are sites of business and of leisure. Somewhere between public and private, restaurants are places to eat – often intimate ones – as well as places to be seen eating. This makes them venues for distinction and social performance. Some eateries maintain the status quo, having upheld, for example, racial, gender, and socioeconomic segregation, policing who can dine where and with whom. Others have challenged such divisions, pushing to expand who can claim a seat at the table.[78]

Before there were restaurants in North America, there were taverns, inns, and boarding houses where (mostly) men could drink and travellers could fuel on food, and even spend the night. When Upper Canada was only ten years old, in 1809, it already had 108 taverns.[79] Writing about this period, historian Julia Roberts defines a tavern as "a building that was open to the public (and, for travellers, open at all hours), licensed to sell spirituous and fermented liquor by small measure (by the glass, gill, half-pint, or pint), and had the facilities to provide food, lodging, and stabling."[80] In the nineteenth century, alcohol first and foremost defined a tavern. Drink came before food, thirst before hunger. But the genre of drinking establishments spilled beyond the tavern; there were also beer-houses, shops, and illegal drinking houses. At taverns, food played a supporting rather than a starring role. Options were limited and meals hearty, often of the bread, butter, and salt pork trinity. Mostly settler-travellers took their meals in inns and taverns.[81] Restaurants introduced greater choice than what an inn's or tavern's kitchen could provision.

Richard Dulong opened Auberge Saint-Gabriel in Montreal in 1754, and in 1769 it received the first liquor licence in North America.[82] But as its name makes clear, its main occupation was that of an inn. Toronto's oldest tavern is the Wheatsheaf, which opened in 1849 on King Street at the corner of Bathurst.[83] The history of restaurants in Canada dates to around the end of the nineteenth century.[84] The 1891 census clocked 891 restaurant keepers, which was the first year that restaurant was a separate category of employment and not partnered with hotels and boarding houses.[85] There were 228 restaurants in Quebec, 203 in Ontario, and 173 in Nova Scotia, largely in urban areas.[86] The 1911 census listed 2,720 restaurant keepers who employed 7,283 workers, the majority of them male and foreign born.[87] In 1928, the Canadian Restaurant Association was founded, and since then, the industry has continued to grow.

In her study about fast food in Canada, sociologist Ester Reiter discusses restaurants up to the First World War, the industry's expansion around the Second World War, and then rapid growth in the 1950s and 1960s. She outlines how eating – an activity that once took place in the home – migrated to the public sphere and became an industry of its own. "There were two major phases to this process," she writes; "the first was the development of restaurants as separate eating establishments, and their growing patronage by people away from home at mealtimes."[88] The development of the fast food industry marks the second phase. Even at the beginning of the twentieth century, Canada lacked the population density that a restaurant market requires.[89] As immigration grew, so did urbanization, and by the 1930s Canadian cities had sufficient populations to fuel an industry. That said, demand and the number of people who could afford to eat out remained limited.[90] This changed after the Second World War. Previously, restaurants met the needs of those on the road in search for a meal. But now they provided an alternative for families who usually cooked and ate at home.[91] Eating out became more and more popular, especially around the late 1960s and early 1970s.[92]

As of 2018, Canada had nearly 97,000 restaurants, caterers, and bars, with more than 37,700 in Ontario alone.[93] The industry employed 7 per cent of the country's workforce – 1.2 million people – and made up 4 per cent of its GDP. Per day, Canadians made 22 million visits to restaurants, out of which 9.1 million were in Ontario.[94] In the past two hundred years, restaurants in North America have ranged from exclusive and expensive to democratic and cheap, and from venues to celebrate special occasions to a spot close to work to grab a quick lunch. Just as restaurant fashions have changed over time, so too has the word's meaning.

## Words, Worlds, and Maps

Originating in the nineteenth century, the children's rhyme "Sticks and stones may break my bones, but words will never break me" changes now and then, and in 1981 the rock band The Who sang "But names can never down you." Donna Haraway, however, suggests otherwise. Names matter. Words matter. Names can down you and words can break you. To borrow Haraway's, "It matters what matters we use to think other matters with; it matters what stories we tell to tell other stories with; it matters what knots knot knots, what thoughts think thoughts, what descriptions describe descriptions, what ties tie ties. It matters what stories make worlds, what worlds make stories."[95] And it matters which worlds make laws. Because words build worlds, it matters which words we use.

I use Indigenous to refer to First Nation, Inuit, and Métis people, and purposely capitalize it. Here I take the lead from sociologist Michael Yellow Bird, an enrolled member of the Mandan, Hidatsa, and Arikara tribes from North Dakota, who writes: "'Indigenous Peoples' and 'First Nations Peoples' are capitalized because they are used as proper nouns (particular persons) and signify the cultural heterogeneity and political sovereignty of these groups."[96] Indigenous is a multivocal term. And it is a relational one that colonialism defines. As Alfred and Corntassel make clear, "Indigenousness is an identity constructed, shaped and lived in the politicized context of contemporary colonialism."[97] Making a similar point, Mohawk anthropologist Audra Simpson outlines how the term marks when "people left their own spaces of self-definition and *became* 'Indigenous.'"[98] Because of this, as much as possible, I refer to specific nations and communities.[99] But because Indigenous is broad, I also use it to differentiate between First Peoples and Canadian settlers. With settlers, I refer to all non-Indigenous Canadians.

Like words, capitalization matters. So do accents as well as italics, which emphasize foreignness.[100] Despite its canonization, I do not refer to the "new" world. I use Turtle Island interchangeably with North America, a term that originates in the Haudenosaunee creation story – the Tsi Kiontonhwentsison – about Sky Woman.[101] There are many versions with various twists and turns, but each one uses the term Turtle Island to reclaim North America based on traditional Indigenous names. Moreover, the performance artist Guillermo Gómez Peña rightly points out that "America is a continent, not a country."[102] And yet, Michael Twitty uses the word America "because the term 'United States' conveys politics but no dreams."[103] Following convention, I use American to refer to the people, places, and particularities (and dreams) of the United States.

Equally as important as the power of language is gender. Kitchens exaggerate gender performances.[104] Although the professional cooking world is slowly shedding its macho reputation, many restaurants have been designed to keep women out. Analysing the role of gender in Indigenous restaurants, and those who have been marketed to look Indigenous, is beyond this book's scope. Nonetheless, I want to gesture to the fact that the history of cooking has largely been a history of women, but the history of professional cooking looks different. Although many male chefs wax poetic about their mother's or grandmother's cooking, the professional culinary world is still predominantly a boy's club.

So why have there been so few Indigenous restaurants in Canada? Chapter 1 responds to this question by unpacking colonial culinary narratives. It surveys the role that food has played in the Canadian colonial project in tandem with what drove traditional foods off the menu to lay the groundwork for historicizing the representation of Indigenous foodways in restaurants. Even though government policies actively sought to weaken and break Indigenous foodways, Canada drew on the visualization of such foodways to construct and market its own identity and cuisine. This is exemplified by train menus that visually dress up typical Euro-Canadian fare with romantic paintings and photographs of imagined Indigenous life. Then, in 1967, as the country celebrated its centennial, Indigenous foods were back on the menu, but this time as Canadian, which is the subject of Chapter 2.

Chapter 3 takes up eateries in Canada at large and fleshes out the three time periods of Indigenous restaurants I define: 1971 to 1996, 1997 to 2014, and 2015 to the present. In 1971, the first Indigenous-themed restaurant opened in urban Canada; in 1996, the last residential school closed; and in 2015, the Truth and Reconciliation Commission of Canada released its report concluding that Indian residential schools committed cultural genocide. Schools separated Indigenous bodies – children's bodies – from the land, including the traditional foodways that anchor relationships to plants, animals, and places. They violently interrupted how knowledge – including culinary knowledge – passes from one generation to the next in Indigenous families, communities, and nations. This is why 1996 marked a significant breaking point, as did the year the Truth and Reconciliation Commission of Canada concluded.

These restaurant periods are also in dialogue with Kiowa chef Lois Ellen Frank's historicization of Native American foodways. She identifies four periods stateside, which also spill into Canada. The first is ancestral, pre-contact foodways. The second is first-contact foodways, encompassing when Indigenous diets began to incorporate plants and animals that colonists introduced, such as sheep. The third is the commodity food period, also known as the government-issue period, which represents the introduction of reservations and a growing dependence on rations from the government, the likes of bannock and frybread. The final period she calls "New Native American cuisine." This portrays the present, in which chefs are reinterpreting Indigenous foods, reclaiming ingredients, and revitalizing connections between physical and cultural health.[105] Matching these periods with restaurants, 1971 to 1996 represents first-contact foodways in tandem with the commodity food period; 1997 to 2014 begins to move away from commodity foods toward a period of revitalization, which defines 2015 to the present. That said, my periodization aims to summarize major sociocultural changes – and thus culinary shifts – without overstating the difference from one year to the next.

Starting with Chapter 4, the chapters that follow spotlight specific restaurants. Chapters 4 and 5 map Vancouver's first Indigenous eateries. Moving east, Chapter 6 discusses early Indigenous restaurants in the Rockies and on the Prairies. Chapter 7 turns to Toronto to review its past and present eateries by charting how some claim dishes and others reclaim Indigenous ingredients. This introduces the fact that in many instances Indigenous restaurants may serve similar dishes to those found in farm-to-table Canadian restaurants, but their ingredients narrate different stories.

The last three chapters pair restaurants with issues such as regulations, hunting and aquaculture, what is game to eat and for whom, and sovereignty. Taking direction from Mary Douglas, I argue that eating is a way of ordering a culture's environment, of tabulating plants and animals as edible or not.[106] Chapter 8 stays in Toronto to discuss what happens when seal does – and does not – have a place on the menu. It starts from "Seal tartare" – Kūkŭm Kitchen's signature dish – by reviewing how it represents the continuation of a half-century-long debate over sealing. Chapter 9 serves meat as its main, considering conflicting imaginations of the edible, which is to say what is "game" to eat. It travels from Wakefield, Quebec, to Ottawa, Ontario, and then back to Winnipeg, Manitoba, to ask questions about hunting and edibility, restaurants and regulations. This showcases the tensions – and politics – in defining restaurant fare. This chapter also asks: why do Indigenous restaurants continue to close? Before moving to the Conclusion, Chapter 10 returns to Vancouver to profile Salmon n' Bannock. It unpacks "Indian candy" and discusses culinary adaptation and how salmon became celebrated as an iconic, pan-Canadian food. It also ponders "the f-word" and whether farmed salmon can hold the same symbolic meaning as wild. All of these chapters couple restaurants with clusters of ideas about Canada's culinary landscape, asking who is able to partake, in what role, and on what terms. Together they compose a history of the representation of Indigenous foodways in Canada and add up to an argument about how old ingredients are telling new stories about the relationship between food and land, people and politics.

Tailgating these restaurant histories, the Conclusion puts the previous chapters in dialogue with culinary changes around the world. It compares Indigenous eateries in the United States and Canada to map differences and similarities in how restaurants represent Indigenous foodways. Returning to the question of why there are so few Indigenous restaurants, I conclude by focusing on human-plant relations, contemporary restaurant politics, and Indigenous revival. Through readings of material and visual culture – from restaurant interiors to their menus, dishes, and reviews – *Culinary Claims* asserts that restaurants not only represent politics and identities but also shape and enact them.

chapter one

# Agricultural Flagpoles

Stretching from the local to the global and from the regional to the national, plates stage cuisines. They also map them, drawing connections between eating and ecology, between cookery and culture. "There is no chef without a homeland," writes Michael Twitty, "your plate is your flag."[1] Cooking is testimony to a chef's and even to a culture's relationship to its environments, near and far. That there has been minimal visibility of Indigenous cuisines in restaurants in Canada does not reflect their dynamism or diversity. Rather, it reflects how Canadian cuisine has appropriated some elements of Indigenous foodways while suppressing others. This is what food studies scholar Kelly Donati terms "gastro nullius" – "the denial of Aboriginal gastronomic cultures."[2] Cuisine is but one scale. A larger one is agriculture, and settler colonialism has coded some relationships to land as "labour" and others as "nature." Unpacking this binary, this chapter outlines the "erase and replace" cultural imperative that drove Indigenous foods off the menu.

Before I can answer why there are so few Indigenous restaurants in Canada, I must first consider food production – the laws that govern hunting and fishing, foraging and agriculture. By spotlighting the entanglement between food and colonialism, this chapter provides the context for *Culinary Claims*' discussion of restaurants and the settler colonial contexts they embody. Imperialism is cultural. Recognizing this, I centre the cultural imperialist aspects of the Canadian colonial project. More specifically, I take up how

Indigenous ingredients "disappeared" only for images of Indigenous peoples to emerge as aesthetic relics of an imagined past.

## To Plant a Seed, to Wave a Flag

The Mississaugas of the Credit's emblem features an eagle with its wings spread wide. Three flames frame the eagle and, below, its claws reach toward a long pipe. At a 2018 event celebrating the heritage of Toronto's Humber River, Elder Gary Sault welcomed the crowd with song and dance. Between performances, he put his drum down, leaned back on a camping chair, and walked me through the emblem and "the dish with one spoon." The ceremonial pipe symbolizes the sealing of a peace treaty and the dish with one spoon views the land of what is now called Southern Ontario, which both the Mississaugas and the Haudenosaunee call home, as one territory. A single dish they share with only one spoon. Sault showed me a purple and white Wampum belt, a historic replica. "Each white shape represents an area," he explained, "where people could hunt and fish." Carolyn King, a former chief of the Mississaugas of the Credit, glanced down at the belt and then up at me. "It is all about food," she said.[3] Her statement rings just as true for the eighteenth- and nineteenth-century history Sault spoke of as it does now.

Being able to access land means being able to access food. "The goal of Indian Affairs," King tells me, "was to change us, to make us farmers." King grew up on a farm populated with cows and chickens, pigs and grain – all cash crops. Farming was a means to make money, but her family also kept a garden where they grew food for themselves. Their garden grew plants and their farm crops. Thomas Pecore Weso, a member of the Menominee Indian Nation of Wisconsin, makes a similar point. "Agriculture is for personal gain," he writes, "cultivation is for subsistence."[4] This difference, he explains, distinguishes Indigenous traditions from European ones. King's family farm conformed to Euro-Canadian agricultural standards, whereas their garden followed Indigenous practices, such as planting the three sisters. "Together these plants –

corn, beans, and squash – feed the people, feed the land, and feed our imaginations, telling us how we might live," writes Kimmerer.[5]

As the word itself gives away, agriculture is cultural. "People invent agriculture," argues environmental historian Donald Worster, "that is, they choose some plants to eat, cultivating and breeding them, while ignoring others."[6] Many plants are edible, but it is the process of selecting them that transforms them into food. The same is true of animals, which is to say culture codes some flora and fauna as food, while rejecting others. American studies scholar Frieda Knobloch begins *The Culture of Wilderness: Agriculture as Colonization in the American West* with a claim. "Colonization is an agricultural act," she asserts. "It is also an agricultural idea."[7] The word colony comes from the Latin *colonus*, which means farmer.[8] Agriculture requires land and is a means of claiming territory. This is as true for the United States, the country she writes about, as it is for Canada. This is not to overlook Indigenous agricultural practices, but instead to contextualize European approaches to colonial expansion. Applying Knobloch's work to North America at large, activist Zoe Matties believes that to understand how the continent's modern food systems continue their ties to settler colonialism one must understand the interconnection between agriculture and colonization.[9] Canada's food system is rooted in the colonization of Indigenous foodways. And this is not confined to the past. Large-scale infrastructure projects together with the contamination of traditional foods, such as fish, with pollutants like mercury, lead, and polychlorinated biphenyls (PCBs) represent the ongoing colonization of Indigenous foodways.[10]

In North America agriculture cannot be separated from settler colonialism, its aims, history, and ongoing present. Potawatomi philosopher Kyle Powys Whyte offers a reminder of its overarching goal. "Settler colonialism," he writes, "refers to complex social processes in which at least one society seeks to move permanently onto the terrestrial, aquatic, and aerial places lived in by one or more other societies who already derive economic vitality, cultural flourishing, and political self-determination from the relationships they have established with the plants, animals, physical entities, and ecosystems of those places."[11] Whyte's definition includes the land and all the species that live from, off, and with it. Settler colonialism's aim is to replace one native with another: the "erase and replace" ethos. In Canada, this means resetting the clock so that the country's history begins with Europeans, erasing Indigenous peoples and denying their culinary presence, an example of "settler time."[12]

Importantly, Whyte refers to processes. As historian Patrick Wolfe makes clear, settler colonialism in not an event, it is a structure.[13] A structure about land. Wolfe identifies that "the primary motive for elimination is not race (or religion, ethnicity, grade of civilization, etc.) but access to territory."[14] Settlers gain access to land and claim said land by initiating new relationships with the native flora and fauna, often as natural resources, as well as by introducing new species. Audra Simpson enlists trees as a metaphor. "Indigenous lands and bodies were Western sovereignty's (supposed) *terra nullius* and tabula rasa – their lands, their bodies and then minds were to be cleared, like a forest for planting and emplacing others here."[15] A certain species of tree, or even a cow, serves as a flagpole in claiming someone else's land. Colonists saw Turtle Island according to the vocabularies of the European landscapes that they had left behind on the other side of the Atlantic.

Agriculture, contends the environmental historian Michael D. Wise, has been a primary lens through which North Americans have learned to see land and what counts as labour.[16] This introduces the first of four myths he identifies as buttressing "the imperatives of settler colonialism and white supremacy."[17] The myth that Indigenous peoples did not practise agriculture, that the land was "naked."[18] The other three are that they were predominantly hunters, usually hungry, and, because of this perpetual hunger, "did not care about flavor and therefore never developed taste or cuisine."[19] But he recognizes that myth does not quite fit as the right label. This is because settler colonialism relied on these as facts rather than fables, incorporating them into its very struture, an example of what Hunt and Starblanket call "storying."

Taking commercial pastoralism as his example, Wolfe writes that this expansive practice eats its way through Indigenous territory, reimagining native flora and fauna as dwindling resources, and, thus, restricting modes of Indigenous reproduction.[20] Land not only grows food, it also grows cultures and worldviews. It is for this reason that Leanne Betasamosake Simpson advocates thinking "of dispossession in more complex terms than just land loss."[21] To lose land is to risk losing culture. The foods the land grows and the knowledge to prepare them. Settlers propagated conflicting interpretations of land across Turtle Island. "In the settler mind," Kimmerer writes, "land was property, real estate, capital, or natural resources. But to our people, it was everything: identity, the connection to our ancestors, the home of our nonhuman kinfolk, our pharmacy, our library, the source of all that sustained us."[22] Agriculture, the purposeful practice of growing particular plants, operates differently in these worldviews.

Having studied agriculture's role in the colonization of western Canada, historian Sarah Carter argues that the standard reason for its failure was identified as a lack of interest or ability by Indigenous peoples, but the evidence proves otherwise: Government policies hindered agriculture on reserves.[23] One example is an 1881 amendment to the Indian Act. In 1876 Canada first passed the Indian Act ("An Act to amend and consolidate the laws respecting Indians"), which granted the federal government great power over Indigenous life, from governance and cultural practices to health care and education. To discourage competition for settler farmers, the 1881 amendment restricted First Nations on the Prairies from practising commercial agriculture.[24] Police even fined settlers for purchasing potatoes from Indigenous farmers and, occasionally, arrested others.[25]

Agriculture also ties into what Amy Kaplan calls "manifest domesticity." In contrast to the common separation between the foreign and domestic spheres, domestic discourse – tending plants and animals and making dinner – has an imperial reach.[26] The home, and especially its kitchen, plays an important role in imperial expansion, and, as Carter shows in her study of Canada's Prairie West, white women became essential symbols and "civilizing" agents.[27] In turn, Euro-Canadian farming practices promoted gendered labour among Indigenous communities.

American studies scholar Christina Gish Hill argues that this disenfranchised "women by coercing men to farm using Western techniques."[28]

Colonization also impacts seed sovereignty. Seeds relay cultural and historical knowledge, mirroring their communities of origin and, sometimes, transmitting religious beliefs. "It is reasonable, therefore, that seeds be treated as the cultural legacy and sacred entities that they are," writes Gish Hill, "and, like other ancestors, cared for in traditional ways."[29] From cultural kin to commodity, colonial agricultural practices across Turtle Island introduced value systems for seeds. In addition to planting flags, settlers spread the seeds of their homelands. These seeds went from orbiting in relationships of reciprocal responsibility to individual ownership.

## "Sad ol' Mush"

In addition to using treaties and reserves to restrict where Indigenous nations could hunt and fish, gather and graze, the Canadian government whittled down traditional foodways through the Indian residential school system. Assigning reserves to marginal locations – in terms of geography as well as politics and economics – coerced "dependence on imported, processed Western foods which tended to be much higher in fat, carbohydrates, and sugar, and lowered [Indigenous] consumption of fruits and vegetables, relative to traditional subsistence diets."[30] So-called commodity foods replaced traditional staples – an example of "dietary assimilation" and "milk colonialism" (Figure 1.1).[31] Indigenous communities did not historically consume animal milk, but colonial beliefs about nutrition ignored this. Ironically, as well as tragically, because of food shortages some parents reluctantly sent their children to residential school.[32] A collaboration between the federal government and Christian churches, residential schools further enforced dependency on foreign foods by serving staples that aligned with their mission of forced assimilation. To become Canadian one had to eat like one.

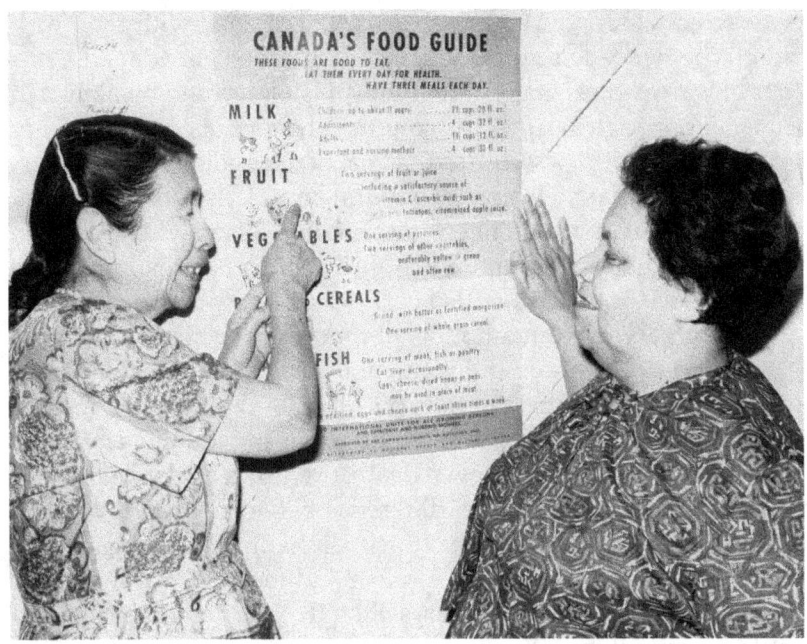

Figure 1.1. "Two Aboriginal women reading a Canada's Food Guide posted in the Community Health Workers Training Program, Coqualeetza, British Columbia," n.d., accession number 1983–120 NPC, item number 4322469, Library and Archives Canada.

From 1831 to 1996, 130 schools operated across Canada. The Catholic Church ran three-fifths – the majority. The Anglican Church operated one-quarter and the Presbyterian and United Churches the rest. Around 150,000 children were forced to attend. The first residential school opened in 1831: the Mohawk Institute in Brantford, Ontario. Missionaries had run earlier ones; however, starting in the 1830s such schools became part of federal policy. Fuelled by a belief in forced assimilation, Canada's Indian Act was in synch with efforts in the United States best summarized by Richard H. Pratt's 1892 speech at Carlisle Indian School, the first American boarding school for Native children. "Kill the Indian in him, and save the Man," declared Pratt.[33]

Residential schools featured foods that aligned with their mission. Whether called mush or gruel, oatmeal or porridge, the history of warm bowls of ground grain spills far beyond breakfast. In Canada, porridge narrates the country's history of enforced Indigenous assimilation, which was the goal of its residential school system. Porridge maps a history of cultural imperialism, of attempts at dietary assimilation, and of efforts to replace bison with beef, corn with wheat, and turn hundreds of Indigenous nations into Canadian citizens. But porridge also narrates a history of resistance.

Schools served scant amounts of food of poor quality, the likes of watered-down gruel. In his memoir *Indian School Days*, Anishnaabe writer Basil Johnston calls porridge "sad ol' mush."[34] Survivors recount insufficient portions and pronounced hunger that led to severe malnutrition and even death, examples of "food abuse."[35] Survivors also relay a sharp difference between what they ate – rotten meat, thin soups, and "thick slices of bread spread with lard" – and what staff ate – fresh fish and meat, butter and jam.[36] There were even cases of schools selling their farm produce to local settlers, while students went hungry.[37] One survivor was forced to eat "porridge with worms," then beaten when she refused.[38] Historian Ian Mosby further reports that the Canadian government performed nutrition and medical experiments in residential schools.[39] Taking advantage of the pupils' hunger, scientists tested out diet theories, further de-culturing the bodies of Indigenous children.

Students were forbidden to speak their mother tongues, having to communicate in English or French, languages they often did not know. Hair was cut and Christian names replaced Indigenous ones. Until the 1950s, days were divided between lessons and labour. Girls cooked, cleaned, and sewed. Boys were responsible for agricultural work and carpentry. This was to train students for blue-collar employment but also to contribute to school finances. In addition to forced labour, thousands of children experienced abuse and died. Justice Murray Sinclair, the chair of the Truth and Reconciliation Commission, estimates that at least six thousand children lost their lives, but, because of poor record keeping, the full number is unknown.[40] Not all deaths were reported, and many children were classified as missing.

Numbers feel abstract. They simplify in order to organize, to represent. On 28 May 2021 a headline revealed proof that residential schools were also graveyards; the remains of 215 children were found at Kamloops Indian School in British Columbia.[41] This headline confirmed what survivors had long reported. It also posed a question: Are there more? Less than one month later, another headline answered: "Canada discovers 751 unmarked graves at former residential school." A number three times larger than last month's news, this time from Saskatchewan's Marieval Indian School. Then, one day before Canada Day, the Lower Kootenay Band in BC found 182 unmarked graves at St. Eugene's Mission School. The question repeats: Are there more? How many more?

As should be clear, the residential school system enacted horrific abuse. And food played a part. This is because food is just as much about culture as it is about nutrition. Residential schools fed Indigenous children culturally coded dishes to turn them into Canadians. This returns to Simpson's argument about how dispossession is more than land loss. It is to lose relationships that bodies have to land through food. "We have to think of *expansive dispossession*," Simpson writes, "as a gendered removal of our bodies and minds from our nation and place-based grounded normativities."[42] This also exposes how eating connects to larger landscapes. If a plate is a chef's flag, then its boundaries matter, where they begin and end. "The edge of the plate," notes writer Priya Basil, "is like a border emphasising the specificity of a choice, the relations, traditions and dispositions that influence it."[43] To eat is to express roots and routes. It is to wave your flag.

How did residential schools use food to assimilate pupils? An 1893 menu from the Qu' Appelle North West Territories Industrial School, for example, lists oatmeal or cornmeal porridge with tea and bread, but butter only for "working pupils and those not in robust health."[44] This was breakfast four days a week. The other days "all the pupils receive butter and cheese." For lunch the menu promises soup, meat, or fish with vegetables and bread with hot tea for "weak children and those working outside," and for dinner "meat for the working pupils and hashed meat and vegetables for the rest." But what menus listed schools did not necessarily serve. According to survivor George Manuel, "Every Indian student smelled of hunger."[45]

Born in 1929 into the Chippewas of Nawash Unceded First Nation, Basil Johnston lived with his family until he was ten. Then, an Indian agent took him and his sister to schools in Spanish, Ontario, one for boys and the other for girls. It was at St. Peter Claver School, Canada's only Jesuit-run school, where Johnston ate "sad ol' mush." Another Ontario school, the first to open in Canada – Brantford Mohawk Institute – was even nicknamed "the Mush Hole."[46] Johnston calls his fellow students "inmates of Spanish."[47] "We were 'wards of the Crown,'" he says, "not citizens of Canada."[48] The school sentenced its inmates to work. The boys produced food, but could not always eat the fruits of their labour. Johnston recalls boys who slaughtered chickens only for the meat to go to hospital kitchens and not to their own plates.[49] However, in the summer they picked blueberries, which they exchanged for pocket money "to relieve our hunger during the coming winter by bread-lard-candy trading."[50] Seven jawbreakers bought a slice of bread, five a spoonful of lard.[51]

Every morning at 7:25 a.m., the boys entered the refectory and, in total silence, took their seats. "In the middle were two platters of porridge," recounts Johnston, "which, owing to its indifferent preparation, was referred to as 'mush' by the boys."[52] The table was a tableau of sixteen slices of bread, a round dish of eight spoons of lard, and a large jug of milk. "It was mush, mush, mush," continues Johnston, "sometimes lumpy, sometimes watery, with monotonous regularity every Monday, Wednesday, Friday and Saturday. The boys would have vastly preferred the Boston baked beans that, along with a spoonful of butter, were served on Tuesdays, Thursdays and Sundays … Not until we had said grace – 'Bless this mush,' some boys said in secret, 'I hope it doesn't kill us' – could we begin."[53] Unlike Goldilocks, who found porridge that was "just right," Johnston relays many a complaint about "sad ol' mush." In the nineteenth-century British fairy tale *Goldilocks and the Three Bears*, the blonde protagonist visits the home of three bears. With them gone, she helps herself to their porridge. The first bowl is "too hot," the second "too cold." But "this porridge is just right," she sings about the third. Despite the dominance of mush at St. Peter Claver, the boys never warmed to it. No bowl tasted right. However, Johnston describes the quantity as "just enough food to blunt the sharp edge of hunger for three or four hours, never enough to dispel hunger completely until the next meal."[54] Complaints about porridge also appear in Richard Wagamese's novel *Indian Horse*. Saul Indian Horse describes "oatmeal mush" as "lumpy tasteless porridge" accompanied by dry toast and "watery powdered milk."[55]

In addition to Goldilocks, porridge appears in Charles Dickens's *Oliver Twist*, first published as a serial from 1837 to 1839 and, later, assembled as a book. In a famous mealtime scene at the parish workhouse, Oliver shuffles to the front of the dining room with his empty bowl in his hands. "Please, sir, I want some more," he shyly requests. "What?" belches the master. Oliver repeats himself. "More?" repeats the roar. Oliver drops his bowl and runs. Although he did not receive more, he did dare to ask. Complaints about sad ol' mush were important. This is because food was one of the few acceptable things to criticize. "Food was the one abiding complaint because the abiding condition was hunger, physical and emotional," explains Johnston. "Food, or the lack of it, was something that the boys could point to as a cause of their suffering; the other was far too abstract."[56] Tucked behind these culinary protests were larger grievances. To object that they sipped on "barley or pea broth" while staff feasted on "roasts of beef and pork ... was ... a protest against abuse and maltreatment."[57] Food translates more serious complaints. As Johnston unpacks the linguistic coding: "To say 'This mush is too salty,' or 'Why'd we have to have raw carrots? Why can't we have a sandwich once in a while?' was quite acceptable; it was a complaint that the prefects could tolerate. Saying that so-and-so prefects had no feelings would have been regarded as a statement tantamount to biting the hand that fed ... So the boys took out on the peas, barley, mush and onions what they could not take out on the prefects. And yet they would not have dared, as Oliver Twist had once dared, to ask for more."[58] His "Please, sir" reference recognizes the limits of their complaints.

One day, four "mystery" women appeared just in time for dinner. Because the school only admitted boys, the sight of women was out of the ordinary. The women scribbled notes while the boys ate. "Next to the mush was a bowl with eggs ... and there was butter again, instead of lard," Johnston describes. "Some boys rubbed their eyes. They couldn't believe what they beheld. Was it an illusion?"[59] One boy asked the women what they were doing. "We're here to inspect the food," one woman answered.[60] "About time," sighed the boys. But then nothing happened: "No police came to the school to investigate, as the boys had fully anticipated."[61] Months later a report arrived. "While we were in your school we heard many complaints about the food," wrote the women, "but that is to expected from ... boys who know nothing or care little about the nutritional value of food and who would prefer to subsist on candies, cookies, chocolate bars, hot dogs and soda pop."[62] The boys reacted with acute disappointment: "Throughout the school there was sense of betrayal and helpless bitterness directed at the new cook, at the women, at the prefects and at the priests."[63] This returns to their status as wards of the Crown. The report reflects the paternalistic relationship the school had with students, undermining their complaints and knowledge, neglecting their hunger.

Food was at the core of the Indian residential school system: from forcing the students to produce food, to then withholding it from them, rationing their servings, and even experimenting with their diets. Johnston's memoir applauds the children for leveraging food as a means of resistance: stealing snacks and hoarding leftovers, sneaking out to forage, and even running away.[64] Like the railways, which the second part of this chapter details, the schools were part of the imperialist Canadian project to wash away Turtle Island's Indigenous histories. To yank and pluck and sever Indigenous traditions as if they were weeds.

It eventually became obvious that these schools were ineffective in advancing assimilation, and in 1969 the Department of Indian Affairs decided to phase them out. The last school closed in 1996: Gordon Indian Residential School in Punnichy, Saskatchewan. Twelve years later, then Prime Minister Stephen Harper issued a public apology, and, organized by the parties of the

Indian Residential Schools Settlement Agreement, the Truth and Reconciliation Commission of Canada was founded. The "Food: 'Always Hungry'" subsection of its final report confirms that "no school was doing a good feeding job."[65] In 2020 the government announced plans to designate two former schools – Nova Scotia's Shubenacadie and Manitoba's Portage La Prairie – as national historic sites. What were once sites of assimilation are now sites of commemoration, sites where lives and culture were lost, but where this loss is now remembered.

The mouth is a gateway. It secures passage to the continuation of one culture or the enforcement of another. Eating is a means of acquiring nutrients. If you weaken a community's food supply, you weaken its strength. Efforts to restrict Indigenous communities' abilities to procure their own food cultivated a growing dependency on "commodity foods." As Sam Grey and public policy scholar Raj Patel write, "Through adoption of a Westernized diet, the colonial supplants the traditional in the most literal sense, with non-nutrient-dense, industrial foods deculturing people from the inside out."[66] This demonstrates that eating is not only about energy, but also about cultural continuity. It also connects to the periods of restaurants I define. It was exactly cultural continuity that the residential school system attacked. Speaking about gastronomy, Grey and Newman envision it as a frontier and "thus define culinary colonialism as the extension of settler jurisdiction over, and exploitation, of Indigenous gastronomy."[67] Because food takes such a central role in processes of settler colonialism, I argue that cuisine is an essential part of the colonial project.

## A Pot of Land

Five boxes of cereal narrate the history of how settler food cultures have transformed Indigenous ones. Their bright colours and cheerful graphics are familiar to anyone who grew up watching American cartoons. At first glance, they are playful and comforting, triggering memories of sugary childhood mornings. But the text reveals that these cold cereals are not familiar at all. What

42   Culinary Claims

Figure 1.2. Sonny Assu, *Breakfast Series*, 2006, digital print, foam-core, 12 x 7 x 3 inches each, image courtesy of the artist and the Equinox Gallery, photo by Chris Meier, image © Sonny Assu.

looks like *Frosted Flakes* is *Frosted Treaty Flakes*. Instead of *Froot Loops* there is *Salmon Loops*; *Bannock Pops* instead of *Corn Pops*. Not actually breakfast, this is a 2006 artwork by Sonny Assu (Figure 1.2).

Assu grew up in suburban Vancouver. When he was eight, he learned he was Ligwilda'xw of the Kwakwaka'wakw Nations. Working across a range of media, Assu crafts stories about lived Indigenous experiences in a settler colonial state. *Breakfast Series* comments on the history of commodity foods. The Seattle Art Museum acquired the work, and as one of its curators writes: "The cereal boxes and their contents become a metaphor for the unhealthy government commodity food forced upon Natives and First Nations, and that took the place of the healthy diet of fish, seafood, venison, berries, and wild greens that indigenous people thrived upon for thousands of years."[68] Assu's Tony the Tiger, depicted in the formline style typical of Pacific Northwest Indigenous art, makes it clear that commodity foods are ensnared in larger land disputes (Figure 1.3). In addition to "Nutritional Facts," the box lists Member Nations, Total Land, and 100% "GOVERNMENT

Figure 1.3. Sonny Assu, *Treaty Flakes*, 2006, digital print, foam-core, 12 x 7 x 3 inches, image courtesy of the artist and the Equinox Gallery, photo by Chris Meier, image © Sonny Assu.

BS." Also illustrated in formline style, Toucan Sam of *Froot Loops* fame chirps: "Now Bursting with even more delicious Salmon Flavor!" *Salmon Crisp* contains coho, pink, chinook, chum, and sockeye, and expresses environmental concerns. *Bannock Pops* spotlights nutrition and boasts: "FRY BREAD CHLORESTORAL SO TASTY!" *Lucky Beads* advertises a "FREE POT OF LAND IN EVERY BOX."

Assu pairs irony with politics. He describes the series as having a sense of humour, "But there's also political conversation behind all five cereal boxes."[69] Beyond the politics of treaties and land claims, *Breakfast Series* represents the characteristics of mass-produced grocery store commodities. From Texas to Alaska and from British Columbia to Nova Scotia, one finds the same cereal brands in the same supermarkets. A shelf of *Lucky Charms* reveals little about what season it is and which region one is in. This type of culinary commodification is homogeneous, placeless. Breakfast as business.

The introduction of commodity foods goes hand-in-hand with the goal of residential schools to replace Indigenous traditions with Euro-Canadian homogeneity. Some Indigenous children dodged residential school, only to be shipped off to foster care instead. The government practice that began in the late 1950s of removing children from Indigenous homes and placing them in foster or adoptive care with, largely, settler families was named the "Sixties Scoop" by researcher Patrick Johnston in 1983.[70] Audrey Logan, a Nehiyaw (Cree)/Métis woman, is a Sixties Scoop survivor. Today the Winnipeg-based Elder runs a permaculture garden on the property of Klinic, a community health centre. She took over the garden in 2014, transforming it into a community of self-sufficient plants. "The plants here know how to find water," she tells me, "whereas, the ones in the store are too dependent."[71] But Logan is dependent on these plants. "This isn't a project. It is how I can secure my food," she clarifies. When we met in 2016, she used her cane to point out different herbs and vegetables among the tangles of leaves: purple basil and apple mint, black raspberries and sweet potatoes, squash from an eight-hundred-year-old seed. Logan is on disability insurance, for which she receives a meagre daily food allowance of four dollars. Some people call her a medicine woman. "I am a grower of food," she corrects them.

The garden is also a means to reclaim knowledge. Logan's approach returns to what Gish Hill writes about seeds: "Seeds are relatives, ancestors, and sacred entities. They are also archives. They hold genetic knowledge, breeding knowledge, knowledge of the appropriate ways to live in relationship with the broader ecosystem."[72] We walked around the garden with chef, activist, and radio producer Anna Sigrithur. As Logan recounted the efforts it took to reconnect with her ancestral knowledge of plants, we paused. "The history of food and what we grow on the land is political," affirmed Sigrithur.[73]

A Ukrainian family raised Logan after she was adopted. They had a farm and, because they had lived through the Dirty Thirties, were suspicious of food marketing. They only trusted what they grew and picked, preserved and pickled. Shadowing memories of her foster mother fermenting vegetables, Logan recounts an awareness of "how food was manipulated and used to control people." She also remembers growing up thinking these vegetables were, like her foster family, from Europe. Squash, potatoes, and beans. She did not know that, like her, they were from Turtle Island. Years later Logan spent time with an aunt in northern Manitoba, learning to trap and forage. Such knowledge is not about food alone; it is about the continuation of culture, about landscape literacy. Thomas Pecore Weso remembers family stories about how his grandmother would guide his aunts to pick apples, with which they made jams and jellies. Preparing fruit preserves doubles as a means of preserving cultural and family knowledge, of passing on "traditions of survival."[74]

Because the Canadian state separated Logan from her family, gathering food knowledge and stories about plants was not easy. It took time. There was, and still is, confusion. "People had to hide their traditions, and so now are confused about what was there pre-contact," she says. They were also punished for remembering. Logan recounts walking around a First Nation in Saskatchewan.

A plant caught her attention. "What's this?" she asked her host. Logan was taken by his pause. He mumbled something about residential school; how he was told this was the devil's plant. He remembered something he had been forced to forget. "There is a lot of angst now," Logan explains, "because people are doing what they were not allowed to do." Foods that were once forbidden have become fads.

Beyond food's role as a weapon to capture Indigenous lands, it was an incentive for colonial expansion. And it was a yardstick with which to calculate colonial gains. "Colonizers measured the success of colonial enterprise," historian Julia Roberts reveals, "in part, through the dinners they consumed."[75] To rule well is to eat well. Historian Lizzie Collingham makes the case that "Britain's quest for foodstuffs gave rise to the British Empire."[76] Her story begins with Newfoundland codfish and claims that when the British set sail in the sixteenth century they were in search of food.[77] Imperialism diversified the British pantry. And its colonies fed the empire's appetites.

Colonization through food worked in two ways. The first was to remove existing Indigenous food sources, such as agricultural and hunting lands, as well as animals like the bison, to which Chapter 9 returns (Figure 1.4).[78] This confirms Alfred and Corntassel's argument that "Contemporary settlers follow the mandate provided for them by their imperial forefathers' colonial legacy, not by attempting to eradicate the physical signs of Indigenous peoples as human *bodies*, but by trying to eradicate their existence as *peoples* through the erasure of the histories and geographies that provide the foundation for Indigenous cultural identities and sense of self."[79] The second was to replace them with European systems that, in addition to producing edible commodities like wheat and pigs, also produced new symbolic values.[80] The history of colonial agriculture in Canada, and the rest of the Americas, is one of expansion. It rewrote the land's history to obscure where plants came from. It recategorized squash and potatoes and beans as Canadian. Logan had to unlearn this history in order to relearn how to care for plants so that these plants would feed and, therefore, take care of her.

Figure 1.4. "Buffalo bones gathered from the Prairies," c. 1880–90, accession number 1971–270 NPC, item number 3193117, Library and Archives Canada, Ottawa.

## Can't Buy Me Bread

The settler colonial project redesigned the land to grow Europe's agricultural staple and bread's main ingredient: wheat. Like "sad ol' mush," bannock narrates a larger history of cultural and culinary assimilation. The versions are countless, but the list of ingredients always begins with flour. Next comes a leavening agent, usually baking powder (although Blackfoot and Aleut recipes use yeast).[81] Then comes salt, sugar or another sweetener like honey or maple syrup, fat of some sort – lard or butter, shortening or oil – and a liquid that moistens and turns the mix into dough: water, milk, or water mixed with milk powder. "Hunter's Bannock" throws in

48   Culinary Claims

Figure 1.5. "Bannock baking contest, Flin Flon Trout Festival," n.d., CH 0267, government photographs, GR10030, SA-2-57, ZZ-12-2-6-1, Archives of Manitoba.

an egg or two for extra protein.[82] Bannock can be pan-fried, deep-fried, cooked on a griddle, baked in an oven, or roped around a stick and toasted over a campfire (Figures 1.5 and 1.6).[83] Bannock is dense and heavy when baked, and fluffy and light when fried. The latter type is called frybread.[84] Both are a blank slate. Bannock is anything a cook wants it to be. You can sweeten it with cinnamon and blueberry jam or make it a savoury meal with flaked fish and fresh herbs.[85]

But whether fried or baked, bannock is a commodity food that settler governments introduced.[86] It, therefore, represents the imperial weight of wheat, indexing flour's history of dispossession and violence. None of bannock's ingredients are indigenous to Turtle Island. Europeans brought wheat to the Americas in 1602.[87] Historian Kyla Wazana Tompkins couples wheat with Kaplan's concept of imperial domesticity.[88] Bannock's geography now spans regions that grow wheat alongside ones that cannot, including north of the tree line.[89]

Figure 1.6. "Trappers Festival, bannock baking," 1963, CH0267, government photographs, GR0201, 63-744, CV-24-166-2, Archives of Manitoba.

Edited by Jo Marie Powers and Anita Stewart, *Northern Bounty: A Celebration of Canadian Cuisine* mentions bannock six times, three times in settler contexts and three in Indigenous ones.[90] The story goes that bannock originated in Scotland and came to Canada as part of the fur trade.[91] Its etymology backs this up: the word comes from the Old English *bannuc*, of Celtic origin. However, unlike in Scotland – where bannock is made with oats and barley and, often, indistinguishable from oatcakes – in Canada it is made of wheat flour.

There are also lesser-known examples of "pre-contact bannock." On National Indigenous Peoples Days in 2001, then-Aboriginal Affairs Manager of the Kamloops Forest Region, Michael Blackstock, published seventeen recipes. "In precontact times, bannock was made from natural substances gathered from the woods: flour from roots (like cattails), corn, nut meal and ground plant bulbs (like cama bulbs), natural leavening agents and a sweet syrup made from the sap of trees," he details. "Some rolled the dough in sand then pit-cooked it. When it was done, they brushed the sand off and ate the bread. Some groups baked the bannock in clay or rock ovens. Other groups wrapped the dough around sticks and toasted it over an open fire."[92] All these varieties share one name. Blackstock includes a recipe for pit-cooked or steamed black tree lichen called "Secwepemc lichen bannock," contributed by Elder Mary Thomas from the Neskonlith Band.[93] But what happened to these earlier versions? And what were their Indigenous names? That these distinct versions now all gather under the English word bannock further points to wheat's role in the "erase and replace" colonial project. Bannock has assimilated and obscured other culinary histories.

Bannock is polarizing. On the one hand, it crosses regional and tribal borders. On the other, it is a survival food, a memento of the introduction of reserves, commodity foods, and government rations.[94] Having to make something out of nothing. Like all bread, bannock is more than the sum of its parts. It transforms flour and water into food that will alleviate hunger. Chef David Wolfman distinguishes between traditional and cultural foods, arguing that bannock is a cultural food, representing what people eat, but not a traditional one, which represents historic foodways. These categories are not mutually exclusive. A food can be both cultural and traditional. Furthermore, a cultural food can become traditional and a traditional food can go out of fashion and lose its status as cultural.

Although some Indigenous chefs embrace it, others decry it, faulting it for a health crisis. Poet Heid E. Erdrich, a member of the Turtle Mountain Band of Ojibway, writes: "Fry bread was treaty ration food made of the flour and lard many indigenous people waited for – and starved for – when provisions did not arrive from governments that demanded we stop hunting and start eating the colonial diet. Yet, even with the conflicting history, we love fry bread."[95] Her cookbook's title, *Original Local: Indigenous Foods,*

*Stories and Recipes from the Upper Midwest*, reclaims the mantra of the local food movement. In this context, original means much more. Mary Kate Dennis and Tabitha Robin compile an inventory for "Indigenous foods," which spans labels like traditional, country, wild, cultural, and original. "The use of the word original foods is deliberate," they write, "and part of the resurgence of land and political-based activity regarding the history of a colonized food system."[96] When Erdrich started collecting recipes, she pledged not to include frybread, but later made an exception for "bangs."[97] Her "Pumpkin bangs" recipe calls for white and whole-wheat flour, salt, baking powder, and water, allspice, pumpkin puree, and honey.[98] She recommends frying discs of dough – "bangs" – in either coconut or sunflower oil. That this recipe comes with a disclaimer is telling.

Choctaw historian Devon Mihesuah is sceptical about frybread's status as a survival food: "Whose survival?" she asks.[99] This debate is what the Cherokee anthropologist Courtney Lewis terms "the frybread wars."[100] After having launched a line of merchandise, from bumper stickers to T-shirts, with a red line crossing out the word "frybread," Mihesuah was "assailed by frybread fans as 'anti-Indian' and 'not really Indian.'"[101] In response, she consulted historical records to confirm that there are no government reports verifying the legend that "Navajo women fried their flour rations in lard."[102] The archival material she read conjured "reminders of sickness and death – not of survival."[103] Nonetheless, Mihesuah recognizes frybread's duality and that "it is not surprising that one Native might declare that frybread is sickening and is not a traditional food, while another cannot name a single food their tribe ate historically, and still asserts 'I'm Navajo: frybread and mutton are my speciality.'"[104] She also sees that the celebration of frybread as "traditional" takes advantage of the loss of knowledge about tribal foodways.[105] This is what gifts frybread power. As memories of other foods have faded, people remember frybread as traditional – an example of what Monica Cyr and Joyce Slater term "neo-traditional foods."[106]

Not only has frybread come to symbolize "survivance," it also cultivates a sense of solidarity.[107] Chrystos, a Menominee poet, expresses a similar sentiment in "Really Delicious Fry Bread." The poem wraps up: "We love fry bread in memory of the women / who, thrown off their land / with death in every dawn / & starvation in their children's eyes / made this food / so we'd all survive / Each tender bite honours our ancestors / who despite the greatest genocide / in world history / kept on / & kept on / So we could share bannock this morning / and love."[108] This is an example of frybread as a recipe for survival, of how the past peppers the foods of the present.

## A Country and Its Railway

Food was at the heart of surviving residential school. It was also crucial for running away from it. Lisa Myers, an Anishinaabe artist, musician, chef, curator, scholar, and member of Beausoleil First Nation, has been making art with wild blueberries since 2010. She uses berries as a dye for printmaking and performances. Trained at Stratford Chefs School, Myers cooks as an artistic research method, a critical means of inquiry. Her interest in printing with blueberries comes from reflections on how one consumes stories just as one consumes food, and for her, the blueberries represent a family story of survival. In 2009 Myers walked 250 kilometres from Sault Ste. Marie to Espanola, Ontario. The eleven-day walk retraced her maternal grandfather Vance Essaunce's route when he ran away from the Shingwauk Residential School, around 1919–20.[109] He grazed on blueberries that grew wild next to the train tracks he followed home, a story that informed Myers's *Along the Tracks* project. She documents visual fragments of the journey – blurry views of the family on a railroad bridge and close-ups of freshwater waves – overlaid with an audio recording of her grandfather recalling his escape.

In Myers's series – *Blueprints* (2012–15) (Figure 1.7) – she renders blueberries into an anthocyanin pigment, with which she prints maps. Mapping is never neutral. A map reflects the spatial boundaries of power. "Through straining the berries and encouraging absorption into wood and paper materials the pigment maps its

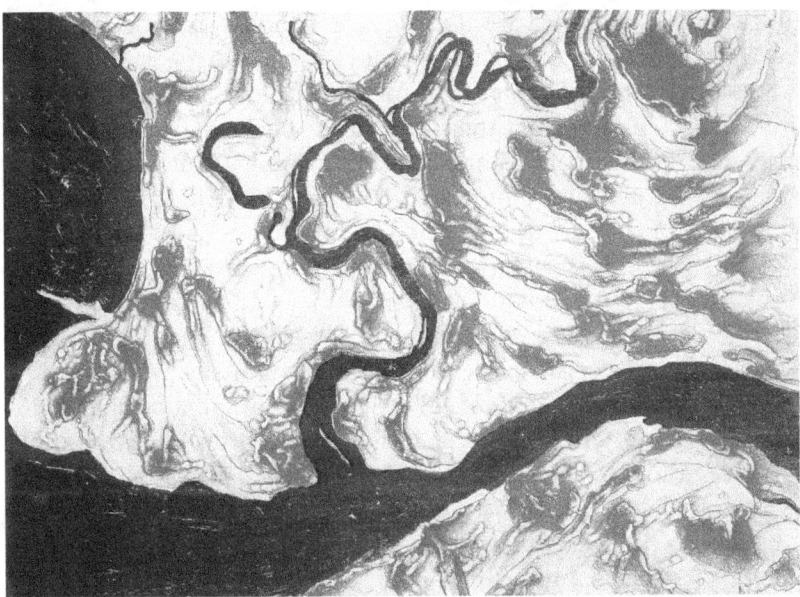

Figure 1.7. Lisa Myers, *Blueprints – Garden River Bridge*, 2015, blueberry ink, screen print, 30 x 22 inches, image courtesy of Lisa Myers.

own forms," Myers writes, "and the metaphor of straining and absorbing recalls ways to survive through trauma, displacement and oppression."[110] Consisting of two maps with four prints, *Blueprints* range from abstract puddles of blueberry ink to intricate traces of symmetrical tracks and loose flows of water. Critic Maya Wilson-Sanchez describes the series as appropriating "the language of mapping in order to reconsider a family story and demonstrate a personal way of relating to space."[111] Visually layering information about a targeted place, Geographic Information Systems (GIS) is used for resource extraction. But Myers appropriates its language, turning it into a form of mimicry that challenges the very practice that divides and fractures landscapes.

*Blueprints* maps where Myers's grandfather crossed two railroad bridges and traversed Garden River – the location of the Garden River First Nation Reserve – and, then, the Mississagi River, where he was welcomed by its members to eat with them. His first meal since having run away.[112] *Blueprints* is concerned with food and place. In many ways, it is impossible to separate the two, and, for Myers, the same holds true for food, land, and stories. The three inform each other. Every ingredient leads back to land, the politics that map land and the stories that imagine it. Train tracks inevitably lead to stories about trains. And in Canada, trains expose that despite colonial attempts to erase Indigenous foodways and cultures, there is a history of appropriating them in an effort to construct a Canadian national identity.

The use of Indigenous imagery to sell Canada begins with a railroad, two oceans, and the dream to transform the land in between into one nation. In 1871 British Columbia became Canada's sixth province. Just shy of four years after Confederation, the Dominion of Canada courted BC by promising to build a railway to the Pacific.[113] "It would be longer than any line yet built – almost one thousand miles longer than the first American road to the Pacific," says author Pierre Berton, "which the United States, with a population of almost forty million, had only just managed to complete."[114] Canada's population at the time was three and a half million. Alexander Mackenzie, the Liberal party leader in 1871 and in opposition to John A. Macdonald's ruling Tories, called the railway proposal "an act of insane recklessness."[115] Politics stalled the process, and construction began only ten years later.

To secure the land on which to build the tracks, Canada hurried to abolish Indigenous title to land. Between 1871 and 1877 the government signed Numbered Treaties 1 through 7. Construction commenced in 1881, and by 1883 the vast majority of Indigenous peoples were on reserves and, thus, under the government's control.[116] Historian James Daschuk asserts that, in support of their efforts to clear the land, Canadian officials took advantage of food shortages, which is what he calls the politics of starvation. "To the hungry indigenous population," Daschuk writes, "this meant that officials quickly turned the food crisis into a means to control them to facilitate construction of the railway and opening of the country to agrarian settlement."[117] It is for this reason that Tabitha Robin frames Canadian colonization at large as "the hunger project."[118] Hunger is something that can be crafted and designed. And

Canada has manipulated hunger as a means of isolating Indigenous communities on reserves and inducing them to sign treaties.

Ironically, clearing the land by using some people's hunger created an opportunity to satisfy the mother country's appetite. A few years after Confederation, when John A. Macdonald passed the Homestead Act in 1872, British investors funnelled millions into plans to construct the railway in hope that Canada would feed Britain, that its Dominion – especially the Prairies – would become its breadbasket.[119] After four years of construction, the last spike was driven in on 7 November 1885 in Craigellachie, BC. The Canadian Pacific Railway (CPR) did not connect a nation: it created one. But the role of Indigenous peoples in this nation was up for debate. On the one hand, they were sectioned off on reserves, a classic out-of-sight, out-of-mind scenario. On the other, they now appeared in paintings as Canada mined for visual material with which to build an identity of its own.

Accompanying the tracks, the CPR constructed a series of grand hotels designed to mimic European chateaus. Traversing the country, examples include Quebec City's Château Frontenac (1893); the Banff Springs Hotel (1888), named after Canada's oldest national park; Victoria's The Empress (1908); Calgary's Palliser Hotel (1914); and Toronto's Royal York (1929). Names featuring words like Château, Empress, and Royal speak to the ambitious architectural style.[120] The grandeur of these hotels – connected to one another by railway – celebrated Canada's transition from a colony to a nation.

A good room, be it on a train or in a hotel, comes with the option of board. The Canadian Pacific Railway cars and hotels provided various dining options, including train station lunch counters, on-board restaurant wagons, and hotel dining rooms. The menus that survive archive their dishes.[121] The visual graphics are shorthand for how this young country was positioning itself, and these menus tell stories that seasoned Canadian Pacific Railway meals. By proposing a sequence of dishes, a menu knits a narrative that ties them together. Addressing restaurants in Western Canada from 1880 to 1920, including CPR dining cars and rooms, historian Kesia Kvill argues, "Canadian identity was, by far, the most common meal on the menu."[122] In transit and in cities, the CPR crafted menus that sold stories about the land it connected and crossed. And these menus visually referenced Indigenous cultures in an effort to claim them as Canadian – an example of "settler replacement narratives."[123]

In English there are separate words for menu and map, but in French they share only one: *la carte*. Like a map, a menu drafts lines with which to imagine the space of the nation.[124] Restaurant menus map borders. They chart cuisines. They draw lines between what is on and off the table and establish boundaries of edibility. Cultural studies scholar Lily Cho discusses how menus and nations overlap, writing: "The *carte*, the map, the menu, remains with us as one of the primary means by which food is represented, textualized, as a metonym of the boundaries of the nation."[125] By presenting a repertoire of dishes, menus represent a time and place. They also contribute to that time and place's construction.

Like other CPR menus, "Before the Canadian Pacific" unfolds in three parts.[126] The formula consists of a coloured illustration or photograph on the cover that sets the scene. A double-sided page listing dishes follows. The menu, then, concludes with text captioning the cover's opening scene. This one is undated, but is likely from the 1940s.[127] The cover captures a horse suspended mid-jump with a storybook "Indian" on its back. I use this word to cite Daniel Francis's *The Imaginary Indian: The Image of the Indian in Canadian Culture*. Published in 1992, the book begins by asserting: "Indians, as we think we know them, do not exist … when Columbus arrived in America there were a large number of different and distinct indigenous cultures, but there were no Indians. The Indian is the invention of the European."[128] Francis uses "Indian" to refer to "the image of Native people held by non-Natives" and Native or Aboriginals when "referring to the actual people."[129] This is a reminder that Indigenous is a relational term. Following Francis's distinction, the "Before the Canadian Pacific" menu depicts an "Indian." With a bow and arrow in his hands, he is about to shoot a hefty bison. The hunter is shirtless, but wears feathers in his hair. Behind him, other men hunt. This image is not particularly unique. The bison (commonly, albeit incorrectly, called buffalo) hunt is a popular painting motif. It is a typical example of the romanticized "Indian." Man and animal in "nature."[130]

Referring to the 1880s, the back states that "Before the Canadian Pacific" this is how the Plains looked. "Building the railroad across this unsettled, unproductive continent was the supreme test of the growing nation's courage, its vision, and its resources." This is a hyperbolic, flag-waving text. "Think of Canada without Vancouver and Victoria!" it exclaims. "Without Winnipeg?" As the text attests: "Without transportation, Canada's boundless acres had no value." This equates transportation with land, ignoring the history of transit via waterways. "By binding together her widely-scattered peoples, by uncovering the wealth of the prairies, by opening the highway from the Orient to Europe," the text wraps up, "the Canadian Pacific laid the foundation of Canada's greatness." It never directly addresses the cover image. Nor does it mention the people who lived across these lands before European colonization. Instead, the image represents a "before" that was "unsettled" and "unproductive." The Canadian Pacific Railway takes credit for the "after." Such an image, such a story, matches the CPR's larger work to advertise the Canadian west to settlers and then physically escort them there.[131] In tune with larger marketing campaigns, this narrative paints the lands the railway tracks as ones of unparalleled opportunity, and, as Hunt and Starblanket point out in their unspooling of such settler colonial storying, here opportunity "is entangled with capitalist logics, promising newcomers the ability to accumulate wealth and property."[132] It promises "empty" land spilling across an expansive geography. This image – this promise – of the "Last Best West" aimed to lure prospective immigrants to the Canadian prairies.

This storying, however, changes beats when you open the menu to browse its dishes. The left side is titled "Mid-Day" and the right "A la Carte." Although the dishes are rather standard (the likes of omelettes, chicken, and roast beef), some ingredients highlight their geographical provenance. There is "Okanagan celery," "Broiled Lake Superior trout, Maitre d'hotel," and "Filet of Lake Superior whitefish, horly, tomato sauce."[133] There are also "British Columbia potatoes," "Individual Canadian comb or strained honey," and "Canadian cheddar." The dishes allege their geographical origins based on region (Okanagan), province (British Columbia), and country (Canada). These markers cover a vast geography. Lake Superior, the largest of the Great Lakes, located in Ontario, Minnesota, and Wisconsin, is more than two thousand kilometres away from the Okanagan Valley. Despite the menu's attempt to affix dishes to the lands of Canada, there is a disconnect between the menu's illustration and its food. One could imagine the same dishes with any number of covers, like a portrait of a grand hotel or quaint country house. The illustration adds value. The image goes beyond the text. An "Indian" on horseback suggests food other than Canadian cheddar. The illustration contrasts with the dishes. There is nothing that ties "Sliced Hawaiian pineapple with hot biscuit" to bison hunting.

Similarly, a portrait of a Chief decorates a 1943 CPR menu. Unlike the "Before the Canadian Pacific" menu, which puts the illustration to narrative use to represent a "before," this menu features an ornamental painting. The words "An Indian Chief" appear in blue cursive. The artist is "N. de Grandmaison."[134] Born into a noble Moscow family in 1892, Nicholas Raphael de Grandmaison studied art in London and Paris before moving to Canada in 1923. Art historian Gloria Jane Bell writes about similar colonial artworks by Europeans who journeyed to Canada, describing them as "complex negotiators between colonialist and colonized … [that] embody a multiplicity of desires and agendas that move through time."[135] A single painting can convey conflicting aims. Despite Grandmaison's romantic rendering of "An Indian Chief," the portrait can be read as having been flatteringly painted, as well as having been employed in a visual culture that supported settler colonialism. "An Indian Chief" is but one of many examples of colonial imaginations. Bell's analysis starts from the literary scholar Beth Fowkes Tobin, who writes: "Drawings and paintings are sites where the tensions and contradictions of colonist doctrines and practices are negotiated, more or less successfully, on an aesthetic level."[136] Therefore, the artworks adorning the CPR menus are more than ornamental even when they are employed as decoration.

"An Indian Chief" is a portrait; nonetheless, the menu does not say whose. It is more concerned with representing a culture as opposed to an individual. Scott Manning Stevens, an Indigenous studies scholar and citizen of the Akwesasne Mohawk nation, writes about the visual language of empire. The menu decorates itself with a painting that does "not attempt to place the peoples represented in an individuated narrative; rather they present the normative European viewer with a collection of specimens meant to be metonymically representative of a larger population of ethnic Others."[137] Images like "An Indian Chief" reflect the culture of the time, which drew from a tradition of imagining Indigenous peoples with ink, oil paints, and pastels. A tradition of anchoring them to the past.

The popularity of this genre of image far exceeded menus, and the legacy of such tropes lives on today. On the one hand, these artworks were rose-tinted, idealistic renderings that simultaneously marvelled at and mourned cultures that settlers believed were disappearing. The "vanishing Indian" myth gave artists a sense of urgency. Overlooking the problems with this assumption, some artists, especially those in the nineteenth century, believed they were saving visual bits and pieces of endangered cultures. Artists working in the twentieth century inherited this style linked to a belief in the vanishing "Indian." As in the case of the "Before the Canadian Pacific" menu, such artworks furthered a political agenda of expansion and settlement, expressed in the proclamation that before European colonization "Canada's boundless acres had no value." The CPR menu exemplifies a tendency of settler colonialism that Wolfe identifies. Physically, settler society needed land with which to establish its own territory. "On the symbolic level, however," as Wolfe points out, "settler society subsequently sought to recuperate indigeneity in order to express its differences – and, accordingly, its independence – from the mother country."[138] These CPR menus belong to a moment when Canada was aiming to craft a separate identity from Britain. To do so, Canada looked for visual inspiration among the Indigenous communities it was trying to assimilate and erase. The CPR menus also illustrate historian Bill Parenteau's observation that, starting in the nineteenth century, North America was reimagining wilderness. Instead of the "barrier to civilization" it had been in the past, wilderness became positive, desirable, even "a foundation of national character."[139] Railroads promoted this idea of wilderness while also escorting tourists in their "search for authentic wilderness experiences," ones that rebranded Indigenous culture as an attraction.[140]

Moving from dining cars to dining rooms, the Royal York Hotel's 20 August 1956 menu reproduced J.D. Kelly's painting *The Toronto Purchase*.[141] Aboard the *HMS Seneca* on Lake Ontario, a group of clean-shaven men in ornate jackets huddle around a table. A British flag doubles as a tablecloth. One man holds a quill. Another stands in front of a man in a feather headdress. The dense cluster of feathers signifies that he is the Chief, but one can only glimpse a sliver of his profile. This menu fetes the British imperial roots of what would become Canada's largest city. It describes the painting as portraying "one of the most important incidents in the early history of Ontario – the purchase from the Mississauga Indians of the present-day site of Toronto." It details some of the items that were exchanged, including "a wealth of articles dear to hearts of the Indians." The last paragraph reads: "Since its founding in 1793, Toronto has continued to live up to its Indian name, meaning 'a place of meeting.' A great convention, trading and manufacturing city, it now attracts people from all over the world – to meet at the Royal York Hotel." This text attempts to create a genealogy for Toronto's "Indian" heritage, as expressed by its name, as a way of legitimizing and marketing the hotel's commercial activities. It does not, however, reveal from which language the name descends.[142]

Once again, the dishes are typical for 1950s high-end hotel fare. The only ones that indicate a geographical connection are the "Grilled Northern Lake trout," "Baked Canadian cured ham with spinach, wine sauce," "Roast Ontario capon with dressing, red currant jelly," and "Canadian cheese with crackers." Others include the likes of a "Bavarian tart," "Grilled sirloin steak," and "Grilled halibut steak, sweet potato butter." The menu visually leverages *The Toronto Purchase* to distinguish itself from its continental predecessors and to claim the region's history of Indigenous trade for the hotel and for the city.

A 1959 CPR breakfast menu moves from painting and illustration to colour photography.[143] A diptych, the top image captures men on horseback. The horses are as colourfully decorated as the men's headdresses. The bottom photograph exhibits a typical Rocky Mountains landscape: rushing water in a blur of white, turquoise, and muddy blue; snow-capped mountains; jagged rocks; and, tall, bushy trees. In the top image, rough mountaintops peek out from behind the foliage; however, this picture is most concerned with representing people. The second, in contrast, is concerned with representing place: an "empty" landscape, *terra nullius*. The back cover provides further context and a location: "Indian Days at Banff," at Bow Falls. It also describes what the men are doing: "Every summer at Banff tribal sports and contests are held during a four-day period known as 'Indian Days.' Chiefs and braves compete on sturdy mountain ponies in the traditional tribal contests. Squaws exhibit intricate bead work, moccasins, gauntlets and exquisite designs in quills."[144] The 1959 "Indian Days" menu differs from "Before the Canadian Pacific" in that it refers to an actual event and thus actual people. "Before the Canadian Pacific" stages a scene that was likely painted from the artist's imagination. In contrast, Banff's "Indian Days" took place in 1889, 1894, and 1897, and then annually from 1907 to 1976.[145]

Indigenous studies scholar Laurie Meijer Drees calls Banff Indian Days Canada's version of Buffalo Bill's Wild West show.[146] Courtney W. Mason, a rural livelihoods and sustainable communities scholar, argues that the festival's visuals contributed to a discourse that "supported pre-colonial images that exoticized and temporalized local Indigenous cultures."[147] This discourse confined Indigenous peoples to a bygone era, which the photograph adorning the CPR menu captures.[148] Although this 1959 menu visualized Indigenous peoples, it did so in a manner that restricted them to the past. Another example of settler time.

Despite the festival's romanticism, as witnessed on the CPR menu and in the organizers' policing of costumes,[149] it was an opportunity for encounters between Canadian settlers, tourists, and the local Indigenous population: predominantly the Nakoda. The festival exhibited an active presence of Indigenous life in Banff.

It served as a temporal contact zone, a concept I later return to, at a time of tightened segregation. Following the Northwest Resistance in 1885, the Canadian government introduced the "pass system," which restricted and controlled Indigenous movement and mobility, requiring an authorized travel document to leave and return to a reserve. Its aim was to prevent large gatherings. So although it was highly regulated, Banff Indian Days was more than a tourist spectacle. "The events provided a popular arena," Drees argues, "where Indian-White relations could be openly expressed, negotiated and, most importantly, manipulated."[150] It afforded the Nakoda the chance to have agency in their representation. Despite the government's efforts to assimilate Indigenous peoples and fashion them into Canadians, settlers and tourists were eager to see "Indians" in bright feather headdresses.

The Banff Indian Days became an important source of income for the Nakoda, as well as other local Indigenous communities, including the Cree, Siksika, and Pikunni.[151] Participants were paid, as well as gifted the likes of candy and cigarettes.[152] They were also fed: starting in the 1920s, participants received bison. Dinner doubled as a tourist performance, where men carved the meat and handed out portions to the participating families. But despite this spectacle for Banff visitors, families did not always consume the bison. After their performances, organizers gave them beef.[153] Why butcher bison only to eat beef? Never mind that it had been more than a generation since the Nakoda had hunted bison, this is the image, the story, that settlers and tourists wanted. Furthermore, the Nakoda traditionally hunted in the mountains, which means bison was not a central part of their cuisine.[154] The Banff Indian Days festival was a staged performance of ethnicity by means of food, but it was also a way for the Nakoda to secure food. This was especially important during the years of the pass system, since it restricted access to game.

Although bison did not represent Nakoda foodways, it did meet visitors' expectations of an "authentic Indian" meal. The choice of bison is also ironic. Returning to Daschuk's account of how Canadian officials took advantage of hunger among Indigenous communities in their efforts to construct the railroad, he writes how "bovine tuberculosis had spread to the human population through ingestion of infected bison and introduced domestic cattle" even before the sickness became widespread in the 1880s.[155] A shortage of bison, as well as contaminated bison meat and beef, played a role in what Dashuk calls "clearing the plains" of both Indigenous peoples and their foods.

The Banff Indian Days festival aimed to present Indigenous culture despite the government's assimilation efforts. This points to another layer of CPR menus. Despite their romanticism and contradictory agendas, these menus, consciously or not, recognize the presence of Indigenous peoples. As Drees synthesizes: "The Indian Days provided a form for the differentiation of Indian from White culture at a time when these distinctions were beginning to disappear."[156] Although these images were by no means accurate portrayals of Indigenous cultures, they did go against the trend of assimilation as a process of erasure. Participating in the festival gave the Nakoda a degree of agency in their self-representation, whereas, on the printed railway menu, their image was reduced to decoration, painted or photographed by settlers for other settlers. This, however, changed the year of Canada's centennial; in 1967 Indigenous ingredients were on the menu.

chapter two

# From Trains to Tundra

In 1967 Canada celebrated its centennial by throwing a six-month party of an exposition. And at this expo of a birthday party, references to Indigenous peoples and lands were no longer solely visual: the food now also proclaimed a connection. In 1962 the Paris-based Bureau des Expositions selected Montreal as the host of an international exposition and, one year later, announced the theme: "Man and his World." Running from 26 April to 29 October, and attracting more than fifty million visitors, the cultural agenda of the 1967 International and Universal Exposition (Expo 67) was twofold: it applauded the country's centennial while proving, even flexing, that Canada had matured into a cohesive nation, the country the Pacific Railway menus had rallied for.[1] Expo 67 also modelled the country's new flag to the world. Raised two years prior for the first time on Parliament Hill, on 15 February 1965, the red and white maple leaf solved Canada's "flag problem," just in time for its centennial.

Like all good celebrations, Expo 67 served food. It boasted seventy-three restaurants, seventy-six snack bars, forty-six food shops, and over five hundred vending machines.[2] As the program advertised, "of the more than 15,000 friendly people there daily to greet you, more than half are employed in services related to Expo-Restaurants Division."[3] This was big business. Maurice Novek, the head of Expo 67's Restaurant Division, wrote in his welcoming note that "it is anticipated that the combined sales of food and beverages on the site will be in excess of 80 million dollars."[4]

Among its sixty-two national pavilions, Expo 67's restaurants both staged and saluted the cuisines of the nations they represented. La Toundra (The Tundra) was one of two housed in the Canadian Government Pavilion. The other restaurant was The Buffet, but La Toundra was clearly the main event. Claude Sauvé, of the Château Laurier, oversaw the restaurant, and Raymond Waleau, who formerly directed food operations at the Queen Elizabeth Hotel in Montreal, was the maître d'.[5] The Canadian Government Pavilion occupied a column in the Expo 67 Restaurant Division's Program with seven of its eight paragraphs detailing La Toundra and only the last surveying The Buffet.[6] The names also reflect an asymmetry of excitement. Whereas La Toundra conjures up romantic images of a Northern landscape, The Buffet could not be more nondescript.

Complementing the national pavilion, smaller ones represented Canadian regions. Nova Scotia, New Brunswick, Prince Edward Island, and Newfoundland shared the Atlantic Provinces Pavilion; Manitoba, Saskatchewan, Alberta, and British Columbia the Western Provinces Pavilion; and Ontario and Quebec each had their own. Taking Expo 67 as its case study, this chapter addresses the tensions between the categories of "Canadian" and "Indigenous" while gesturing toward the growing politicization of Indigenous peoples in Canada, which Chapters 4 and 5 then take up.

## "Cuisine Canadienne"

La Toundra's menu is split into three sections: *Cuisine Canadienne*, *La Toundra*, and International Cuisine (Figures 2.1, 2.2, 2.3, and 2.4).[7] The typography suggests that *La Toundra* is a continuation of *Cuisine Canadienne*, an additional set of options for those wanting to sample dishes representing the host nation. *La Toundra* is also the only section that does not include the word cuisine.[8] Rather eclectic, it features the likes of "Beaver tail broth," "Braised maple sugar cured ham," and "Snails Bourguignonne."

Before announcing the dishes, the menu spotlights drawings of people and animals. Sketched in ink, the illustrations are

Figure 2.1. Front and back cover of La Toundra restaurant menu, 1967, 47 x 20 cm, M2004.156.2 / B1.1, box 3. Fonds Gilberte Christin de Cardaillac, McCord Museum.

**FRITTONERIES**
Crudités du Potager .50
Jus rafraîchis de Niagara .30
Terrine de l'Habitant .70
Perles Noires de Nipissing 3.00
Coquillages de l'Atlantique (en saison) 1.75

**CHAUDRONNÉES**
Soupe aux Pois de Mère Caron .40
Oignons et Concombres .40
Consommé en Gelée .40

**NIBBLES AND MORSELS**
Fresh and Crisp .50
Chilled Niagara Juice .30
Settler's Posset .70
Black Pearls of Lake Nipissing 3.00
Oysters and Clams from Atlantic Shores (in season) 1.75

**STEAMING CROCKS**
Pea Soup de Mère Caron .40
Onion and Cucumber .40
Jellied Consommé .40

## CUISINE CANADIENNE

**PROVENDES**

Côte de Boeuf de l'Ouest
Tranche succulente de boeuf rassi et rôti à point avec flocons de raifort frais. 4.75

Jambon braisé au Sucre d'Érable
Préparé et servi à la façon traditionnelle des Laurentides. 2.90

Kee Wee Sen des Ojibways
Ce poisson délicieux a fait le régal de générations de braves Ojibways. Selon la légende, il a sauvé la tribu menacée de famine. 2.75

Caneton Okanagan
Rôti entier au four et aromatisé au fumet délicat de pommes fraîches.
Pour un ou plusieurs 3.50 par personne

Doré au four Outaouais
Cuit patiemment comme au Bon Vieux Temps et fileté à votre table 5.00 pour deux

Tourtière des Ursulines
Porc frais haché avec oignons émincés et aromates cuit au four dans une pâte croustillante. 2.50

Régal du Stampede
Un généreux morceau de filet de boeuf gentil dans sa parure de gros sel selon une vieille recette des vachers. Pour deux ou plus 6.50 par personne

**Pour Compléter**
Blé d'Inde au beurre    Betteraves marinées    Picorins
Croquette de Riz sauvage
Salade Verte de Saison assaisonnée Cidre et Crème

**SUCRÉES ET ODORANTS**
Sélection de Fromages Canadiens prêts à point .75
Tartes et Gâteaux frais du four. Douceurs .60
Crème Glacée au Sirop d'Érable .40
Crêpes Ville-Marie 1.75 par personne
Fruits Frais et Baies en saison .60
Breuvages frais ou fraîchement infusés .20

**HEARTY FARES**

Roast Rib of Western Beef
Tender slices of the finest aged beef with shredded fresh Horseradish 4.75

Braised Maple Sugar Cured Ham
Prepared and served in the traditional Laurentian manner 2.90

Ojibway Kee Wee Sen
This delectable fish as enjoyed by generations of Ojibways braves. According to legend, Kee Wee Sen saved the tribe from starvation 2.75

Duckling Okanagan
Oven roasted in casserole and delicately flavoured with apples
For one or more 3.50 per person

Baked Doré Outaouais
Prepared whole in the manner of yesterday and filleted at your table 5.00 for two

Tourtière des Ursulines
A savoury combination of minced pork, chopped onion and herbs, baked in a golden pie crust 2.50

Stampede Favourite
Hearty piece of beef tenderloin appetizingly broiled in coarse salt according to an ancient cattlemen's recipe.
For two or more 6.50 per person

**To Complement**
Buttered Corn    Marinated Beets    Picorns
Wild Rice Fritters
Green Salad of the Season Cream and Cider Dressing

**DAINTY AND PIQUANT**
Fine Selection of Canadian Cheeses .75
Old Fashioned Baked Pies, Tarts, Cakes, Sweetmeats .60
Maple Ice Cream .40    Crêpes Ville-Marie 1.75 per person
Fresh Fruits and Berries of the Season .60
Freshly Brewed or Chilled Beverage .20

Figure 2.2. "Cuisine Canadienne" section of La Toundra restaurant menu, 1967, 47 × 20 cm, M2004.156.2 / B1.1, box 3. Fonds Gilberte Christin de Cardaillac, McCord Museum.

68   Culinary Claims

Figure 2.3. "La Toundra" section of La Toundra restaurant menu, 1967, 47 x 20 cm, M2004.156.2 / B1.1, box 3. Fonds Gilberte Christin de Cardaillac, McCord Museum.

## LES PETITES ENTRÉES

Les Escargots Bourguignonne 1.30
L'Assiette de Hors-d'Oeuvre 1.00
Le Buisson de Crevettes 1.70
La Coupe de Fruits Rafraîchis .60
Le Pâté de Foie .70
Le Saumon fumé 1.30

## LES CRÈMES ET CONSOMMÉS

Le Velouté de Champignons .60
Le Consommé double au Xérès .50
La Vichyssoise glacée .60

# INTERNATIONAL CUISINE

## LES ENTRÉES MAJEURES

**L'Omelette de la Forêt Noire**
Mélange d'oeufs frais battus et de fameuses saucisses fumées en tranches 2.00

**Le Vol au Vent aux Fruits de Mer**
Fameuse recette combinant les crustacés, flétan et doré avec une sauce au vin blanc servie dans un vol-au-vent croustillant 2.50

**Les Côtelettes de Porc Hochelaga**
Adaptation moderne d'une recette typiquement centenaire qui rehausse le tout de cannelle et girofle 3.00

**Le Poulet Sauté Chasseur**
Tendre volaille colorée dans le poêlon et servie avec la sauce chasseur 2.75

**Le Homard Canadien à la Nage**
Dégusté de par le monde, ce homard canadien est mijoté dans un court-bouillon aromatisé. Ou bien grillé 5.00 la livre

**L'Entrecôte Grillée Maître d'Hôtel**
Coupe de choix dans la longe rassise à point, avec beurre maître d'hôtel 4.75

**Le Filet Mignon Béarnaise**
Tranche de filet de boeuf sélectionné avec soin, accompagnée de sauce béarnaise 5.75

## ENTREMETS

Haricots Verts Sautés    Petits Pois à la Française
Pommes de terre Frites
Salade César (pour deux ou plus) .75

## ISSUES

Pâtisseries Miniatures et Gâteaux .60
Variété de Crèmes glacées et Sorbets .40    Coupe Jacques .55
Crêpes Suzette 1.75    Cerises Centenaire 1.25
Café Filtre .50    Demi-Tasse .30

## SAVOURY APPETIZERS

Snails Bourguignonne 1.30
Hors d'Oeuvre Platter 1.00
Chilled Shrimp Cocktail 1.70
Fresh Fruit Cup .60
Pâté de Foie .70
Smoked Salmon 1.30

## BROTHS AND VELOUTES

Cream of Mushroom .60
Sherry Consommé double .50
Cold Vichyssoise .60

## ENTREES

**Black Forest Omelette**
A blend of lightly beaten eggs and slices of smoked sausage 2.00

**Seafood Vol au Vent**
Renowned recipe combining crustaceans, Halibut and Dore with wine sauce in a flanky Vol au Vent 2.50

**Pork Chops Hochelaga**
Modern adaptation of a Century old recipe where braised pork chops are enhanced by cinnamon and cloves 3.00

**Chicken Saute Chasseur**
Half of a plump chicken lightly sautéed and served with wine and mushroom sauce 2.75

**Canadian Lobster a la Nage**
World famous Canadian Lobster simmered in a wine flavored aromatic court bouillon. Or grilled 5.00 per lb.

**Grilled Sirloin Steak Maitre d'Hotel**
Slice of the choicest aged sirloin broiled to your taste 4.75

**Filet of Beef Bearnaise**
Well marbled choice cut of the finest filet of Prairie beef accompanied by Bearnaise sauce. 5.75

## GARNISHES

Buttered Green Beans    French Peas
Deep Fried Potatoes
Caesar Salad (for two or more) .75

## DESSERTS

Miniature Pastries and Cakes .60
Variety of Ice Cream and Sherbets .40    Coupe Jacques .55
Crêpes Suzette 1.75    Cherries Centennial 1.25
Café Filtre .50    Demi Tasse .30

Figure 2.4. "International Cuisine" section of La Toundra restaurant menu, 1967, 47 x 20 cm, M2004.156.2 / B1.1, box 3. Fonds Gilberte Christin de Cardaillac, McCord Museum.

simplistic: thin outlines filled in roughly, only here and there. The menu comes in a legal-size envelope and features three figures. The middle one – with shoulder-length hair gathered in clusters as stiff as dreadlocks – towers over the others. The style is loose and clunky, the illustrations dark black and earthy brown. The front page, which is narrow and doubles in width when opened, spotlights the figure from the envelope's right. The three menus each fill one double-sized page. The pages listing *Cuisine Canadienne* depict figures hunting a blob of an animal on one side. On the other, two people sport more hair and delicate features compared to the menu's cover. They stand side-by-side with figures carrying hunting equipment on their backs. The International Cuisine page is the only one to not depict people. Instead, three birds with decorative feathers and exceptionally long necks twist their heads to look down at the "Entrees."

The menu's graphics continue in a similar style to La Toundra's décor, albeit messier. The Expo 67 organizers commissioned two Inuit artists from Cape Dorset, Elijah Pudlat and Kumukuluk Saggiak, to create site-specific wall murals and sculptures for the Canadian Pavilion's restaurant (Figure 2.5). Architect and design scholar Rhona Richman Kenneally describes the mural as a "narrative of everyday life in far-northern Canada"[9] Unlike the menu, these wall figures featured clean lines.[10] Populating a "sea-green" wall, the figures relate thematically to the drawings on the menu, but the styles differ. Although not overly detailed, tidy strokes outline their faces.

In addition to these "magnificent murals, hand-carved by skilled Eskimos,"[11] the Expo 67 program preserves details about the décor: "carvings and tapestries, hand-woven table linen, ceramic dishes and lamps, and special hand-crafted metal utensils all decorate the exquisite main dining room 'La Toundra' … while such authentic touches as seats upholstered in Sealskin and carpeting patterned and woven to resemble '*Lichen[,]*' that sparse mossy undergrowth of the Northern regions, add to the glamour."[12] An advertisement in the *Gazette* painted the restaurant as "swank eskimo-styled … perfect for the foot-weary sightseer."[13] The same attention was paid to the waiters, who donned "Eskimo-inspired costumes with rough Whalebone stitching."[14] Another review described the

Figure 2.5. "Expo 67 Canada Pavilion – Inuit mural for its restaurant La Toundra," 18 October 1967, Montreal, Quebec, accession number 1970-019 NPC, item number 3354431, Library and Archives Canada.

uniforms as "high Arctic style: soft tan jackets with black turtleneck sweaters."[15]

Coming to the food, Kenneally suggests that one would assume that a national pavilion's restaurant would serve what is commonly found in the country's eateries and home kitchens.[16] "Yet the appearance and menu of La Toundra point, quite distinctly, to the culture of the original inhabitants of the Canadian landscape ... the décor, design of the menu ... and, to quite a large extent, the food were cast in First Nation and Inuit tropes."[17] Simply put, La Toundra was an unfamiliar environment for the majority of its Canadian patrons.[18]

Even though Expo 67 predates Canada's 1969 Official Languages Act, which legislated bilingualism, the menu is in French and English. The first pages announce *Cuisine Canadienne* and then *La Toundra*, subtitles that appear only in French. However, the left-hand page lists the dishes in French, in brown, and the right-hand one in English, in black. French represents Canadian cuisine and English international. This is, perhaps, to reflect Montreal's majority language, but it could also be seen as elevating Canadian fare by aligning it with the cuisine of France, which has long held a superior reputation to that of Britain.

Each of the menu's three sections abides by a similar structure, but the names differ. They include two categories of appetizers, a small plate and a soup, one of mains, and one of desserts. The *Cuisine Canadienne* and *La Toundra* category names read like dramatic prose. "Nibbles and Morsels," "Steaming Crocks," "Hearty Fares," and "Dainty and Piquant" for *Cuisine Canadienne*, and "From Icy Streams and Lakes," "Bubbling Kettles," "Sustaining and Fortifying," and "Katimavik Treats" (which means "meeting place" in Inuktitut, although the menu does not disclose this) for *La Toundra*. International Cuisine employs more common names that bore in comparison – "Savoury Appetizers," "Broths and Veloutes," "Entrees," and "Desserts."

"For Expo 67, Canada, our host country has set a magnificent table," the program says, "offering three distinct choices of cuisine, Canadian, Arctic and International, with guests selecting from any one or combining all three."[19] From new and novel to safe and familiar, these differences illustrate La Toundra's range of options. From the same menu, one can have vastly different culinary experiences. International Cuisine is European or Western fare. Some of the dishes emphasize national products – Canadian lobster and Prairie beef – but the dishes are standard and predictable, with the likes of a "Black Forest omelette," "Filet of beef béarnaise," and "Grilled shrimp cocktail." On the contrary, the less common dishes – including "Beaver tail broth" and "Kelalugak beluga casserole" – appear under *La*

*Toundra*. The menu, thus, categorized its most unusual offerings as Arctic fare.

All three sections list sides. Under "To complement" on the *Cuisine Canadienne* menu, they include "Buttered corn," "Wild rice fritters," and "Marinated beets." International Cuisine lists "Garnishes" and includes "Caesar salad," "Deep fried potatoes," and "Buttered green beans." *La Toundra* does not feature an additional heading and only provides two options: "Parsleyed potatoes" or "Fiddleheads." Although fiddleheads – the coiled fronds of any young fern and, more specifically, those of the ostrich fern – have been eaten for centuries, their history as a restaurant vegetable is more recent.[20] Historian Paul Freedman writes about how New York City's Four Seasons featured them as a seasonal special when it opened in 1959.[21] This moneyed restaurant made Freedman's list of "ten restaurants that changed America" because it pioneered the idea of seasonality in high-end American dining, at the same time as offering a menu that challenged French culinary domination.[22] Although contemporary North American diners expect seasonal offerings today, in 1959 this would have been "startling."[23]

Fiddleheads are as seasonal as a vegetable can be. They can only be harvested for a couple of weeks in the spring. And fiddleheads testify to how far ahead of the curve the Four Seasons was in establishing a seasonal North American menu, since they were not seen in other restaurants until the 1990s.[24] For La Toundra to have peddled fiddleheads in 1967 was equally novel. The Quebec Pavilion's Restaurant also featured them, and the Atlantic Provinces Pavilion offered them as an accompaniment to Winnipeg Goldeyes. Specializing, unsurprisingly, in seafood, the Atlantic Provinces restaurant served pan-broiled "Ilkalu" – Arctic char – also classifying this dish as part of Atlantic Canada's culinary repertoire.[25] The presence of Indigenous foods in both the national and provincial pavilions demonstrates how Canadian cuisine on an international stage claimed Indigenous ingredients as its own. Expo 67 storied Indigenous foods as Canadian, enacting how menus map lands and their plants and animals, and exemplifying restaurant politics. Coming back to Hunt and Starblanket, Expo 67's La Toundra performed the settler story of Indigenous fare.

Names aimed to further tether La Toundra's food to Canada, like "Tourtiere des Ursulines," which references Quebec City's Ursuline Monastery.[26] However, the menu assumes familiarity with these names. It also references Canadian geography, sometimes specific and other times vague: "Chilled Niagara juice," "Black pearls of Lake Nipissing," "Oysters and clams from Atlantic shores," "Roast rib of western beef," "Duckling Okanagan," and "Frobisher chowder." This geography attempts to establish a pedigree for "Canadian" dishes.

One- or two-sentence descriptions accompany the mains. In some instances, they matter-of-factly present uncommon foods, like "Kelalugak Beluga Casserole." "The hearty flavour of Beluga whale meat prepared in the fashion of today," the menu explains. Kelalugak means beluga whale, which renders the name repetitive. It is not clear what is "the fashion of today," but, more importantly, whale is not popular in Canada. But, La Toundra's maître d' had hoped otherwise, having boasted, "No new discovery has emerged in the food world since the development of the Cornish hen. With the introduction of the Arctic whale, Canada may create a culinary revolution at Expo."[27] Furthering this agenda, the official Expo 67 program highlights only one dish in bold font: "Muktuk" (whale skin and blubber).[28] "An Eskimo delicacy. One of the unique dishes you can enjoy in the Canadian Pavilion Restaurant."[29] Despite various efforts, whale did not catch on (Figure 2.6).

Although the menu includes whale and beaver, it excludes seal, which is an important protein in Canada – one that Chapter 8 addresses. Curiously, seal was absent at Expo 67 as a Canadian food, but did appear as Québécois: The Quebec Pavilion's Restaurant served "Seal dumplings from Ungava with pernod sauce."[30] And although not on the menu, La Toundra's chairs were upholstered in sealskin.[31]

A separate menu lists drinks. The same figures bookend four pages of options. From cocktails and scotch to gin and rye and from vodka and "rhum" to "port/sherry vermouth" and cognac and from beer to soft drinks, it repeats the usual suspects that dominate hotel bars.[32] However, the final page presents four "Speciality Drinks": the "Atlantic Cooler" is "as refreshing as a sea breeze. Long and Cool." The "Cariboo" is "The Trappers'

From Trains to Tundra  75

Figure 2.6. "Whale meat shipment at North Toronto Station," c. 1916–19, item 1939, fonds 1244, City of Toronto Archives.

favorite in days gone by. A Potent combination of Spirits and Wine." There is also the "Red River," which is "Not to be underestimated. As Hearty and Robust as Western Hospitality." And, finally, "If you are sound of Health and Spirit" then the "Coast to Coast" "is for you." Appearing in this order, these four drinks double as a map that begins with the Atlantic's sea breeze, follows the trail of trappers on the hunt for caribou, floats west toward the Red River, and ends by connecting one coast to the other.

Before La Toundra, in the 1950s Montreal had a "popular dining and cocktail lounge" that did the same, even if it was only by name: the Indian Room (Figure 2.7).[33] A 1961 review indexed its broad offerings, none of which had Indigenous origins: "Lamb Shashlike Caucasian served on a flaming sword," "Rib steak," "Roast beef," "East India chicken or shrimp curry," "Chopped liver," "Marinated herring," and "excellent desserts," such as "Banana flambee" or "Crepes suzettes."[34] "Smoked salmon" was the exception.

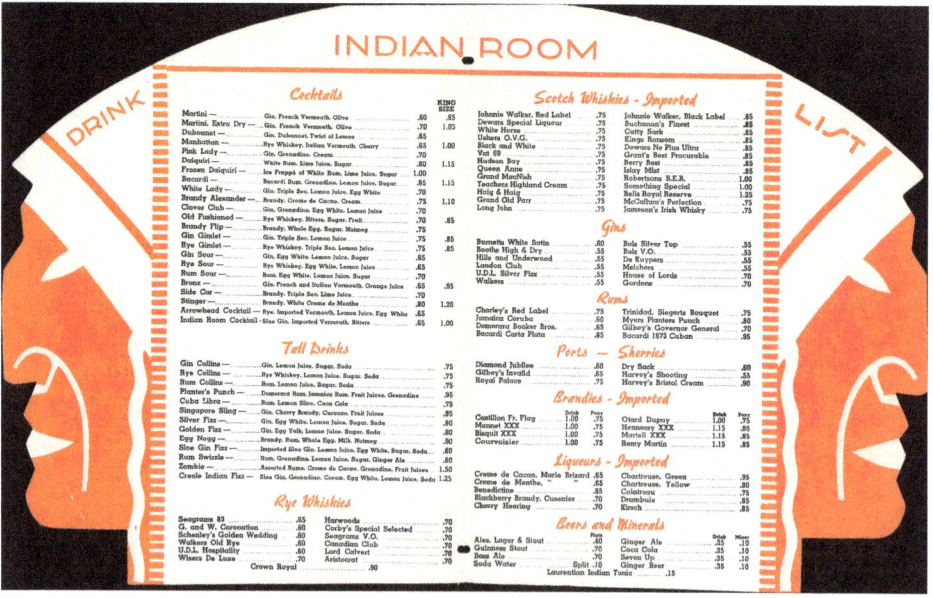

Figure 2.7. "Indian Room menu," n.d., C285/B1, 1, Menus, Restaurants montréalais (1951–), Fonds Gilberte Christin de Cardaillac, McCord Museum.

The Indian Room, however, attracted more press about its music than its food. The eatery-club hybrid mined imaginations of Indigenous culture for its name, as well as its visual identity. A 1951 advertisement in the *Gazette* describes "the remarkably unusual Mosaic Mural adorning the lobby entrance of the Indian Room: Full Blood Blackfoot Indian executed in genuine Italian Mosaics, from an original painting from life."[35] A red and white drinks menu is shaped like a Chief's profile, only to list classic cocktails like the Manhattan and Rum Sour. But it does, albeit problematically, catalogue a couple of drinks that match the eatery's name: the "Arrowhead Cocktail" (rye, vermouth, lemon juice, egg white) and the "Creole Indian Fizz" (sloe gin, grenadine, cream, egg white, lemon juice, soda).[36] Assigning names like "Arrowhead" and "Creole Indian" to the likes of vermouth and gin is clearly questionable, considering alcohol's colonial history in Canada. But compared to the Indian Room, La Toundra found inspiration not only in romanticized aesthetics but also in Indigenous ingredients.

By June 1967, La Toundra was "rapidly gaining a reputation as a great place to eat."[37] Yet it is difficult to know what the average diner made of its food. How many Canadians ordered whale? It is also hard to say if the quality of the food was fit for a queen, but it was served to one. Queen Elizabeth II, Canada's head of state, was Prime Minister Lester B. Pearson's guest of honour at a state luncheon at La Toundra on 3 July 1967.[38] The luncheon menu has not survived, so one can only wonder if Her Royal Majesty snacked on whale, sipped on beaver tail broth, or sampled the "Pork chops Hochelaga." The menu describes the latter as a "Modern adaptation of a century old recipe where braised pork chops are enhanced by cinnamon and cloves." What the menu does not reveal is that Hochelaga was the name of the sixteenth-century Iroquoian village on the St. Lawrence in what is present-day Montreal. Environmental historian William Cronon calls the pig "one of history's great imperial animals."[39] In New England, Montreal's neighbour, he writes that pigs "became both the agents and the emblems for a European colonialism that was systematically reorganizing Indian ecological relationships."[40] "Pork chops Hochelaga" is an example of how La Toundra used Indigenous history, names, and tropes to solidify and celebrate a Canadian identity, one that it, in turn, served to its queen.[41] But unlike the Canadian Pacific Railway menus, La Toundra not only used visual references to Indigenous culture to sell a Canadian experience, it also served Canadian identity both on its menu and on its plates.

The Expo 67 program enlisted a different style from La Toundra's menu. Four illustrations decorate its cover, including one of a couple locked in conversation while a waiter flambés a dish tableside (perhaps the "Paillard de bison flambé"). The illustrations are urban, colourful, and detailed – a world away from the scenes decorating La Toundra's menu. However, in the program La Toundra figures appear in a full-page advertisement, which ends with "La Toundra. Unforgettable. Like every part of the Canadian Pavilion."[42] This has proven true. Because Expo 67 celebrated Canada's centennial, it was the country's coming-out: a "hive of activity where Canadians sought to represent their nation to the world."[43] The national version of a sweet sixteen, or bat mitzvah. It was a culinary manifesto, an edible declaration of the country's independent identity.[44] Expo 67 branded Canada as a modern Northern nation, and it signified a shift: La Toundra's menu claimed Indigenous ingredients as Canadian.

Although La Toundra was a pop-up restaurant of sorts, its name is still in use. The former Canadian pavilion – now La Toundra Hall – continues to stand in Montreal's Parc Jean-Drapeau and is available to rent as an event space. Expo 67 has also lived on in interpretations of Indigenous foods. Lisa Myers unspools this legacy. In 2011 she organized the graduate exhibition *Best Before* in Toronto, which featured works by five artists – KC Adams (nêhiyaw/Anishinaabe/British), Keesic Douglas (Ojibway from the Rama First Nation), Peter Morin (from the Tahltan Nation), Suzanne Morrissette (Métis), and Cheryl L'Hirondelle (of Métis/Cree descent) – based on family or community recipes. In Myers's accompanying thesis, "Best Before: Recipes and Food in Contemporary Aboriginal Art," she writes, "Their use of food engages the politics of place in relation to colonial history, which acknowledges the presence and absence of traditional food memory in their lived experience."⁴⁵ The exhibition highlighted food as a way of negotiating belonging, relationships to place, and identity.

Like You Are Welcome, *Best Before* carries a double meaning. It commonly means the date before which a perishable food is good, which is to say safe to eat. Beyond food, it suggests nostalgia for the past. Myers merges both meanings. "*Best Before* refers to the way recipes can encapsulate the secrets of food preparation, relationships and memories," she writes, "while also invoking the idea that someone made the best food *before*."⁴⁶ A comparison of the present to the past also characterizes attempts to define Indigenous cuisines.

Myers first noticed the emergence of something called "Aboriginal cuisine" in relation to Expo 67. She summarizes that "The Tundra represented an emergence of Aboriginal cuisine interwoven into an example of national Canadian cuisine at an international forum."⁴⁷ Not only did this national restaurant propose a definition of Canadian cuisine, it also offered a blueprint for Indigenous cuisine(s). However, the emergence of "Aboriginal cuisine," Myers argues, "obscures underlying Indigenous issues of land and identity."⁴⁸ The same is true of La Toundra's menu. The restaurant served dishes that showcased the diversity of Canada's landscapes. It appropriated Indigenous ingredients in an effort to piece together and present a national cuisine. Myers expounds further on La Toundra's representation of Arctic fare: "In Canada, the term 'Aboriginal cuisine' contributes to the construction of nationalism whereby indigenous foods, cookbooks and menus give a sense of pride about the country's bounty, and inform cultural identity."⁴⁹ Critically analysing how the Canadian colonial framework aims to construct "Indigenous cuisine," she highlights that the key indicator is "the use of ingredients derived from an indigenous source that has strong associations with the land, wild meat, or wild edible plants ... this cuisine and these ingredients generate romantic notions of traditional, pre-contact food sources that imply a sense of authenticity in regards to food and identity."⁵⁰ This differs from commodity foods and Assu's cereal boxes. Instead of reserve rations, Myers points to the role of pre-contact ingredients in characterizing how Canada imagines Indigenous cuisine. This definition looks to the past and flirts with nostalgia.

La Toundra's décor, menu, and costumes romantically imagined Northern life. Just as the Canadian Pacific Railway menus showcased Francis's imaginary "Indian," La Toundra's dishes did too. Take for instance the description of "Ojibway Kee Wee Sen": "This delectable fish as enjoyed by generations of Ojibway braves. According to legend, Kee Wee Sen saved the tribe from starvation." Featured on the *Cuisine Canadienne* menu, it reads like a haiku, only to skip important details. What kind of fish? How is it prepared? Instead, the menu allots its few sentences to chronicling a brave tale of diverted starvation. It prioritizes a heroic tale over a practical description.

Returning to best before's multiple meanings, La Toundra represented a "before" Arctic. It was around the time of Expo 67 that Canadian government policy was radically transforming Inuit life. Yet, La Toundra exhibited an era before these changes, an era before forced relocations in the High Arctic. An era of spears instead of rifles, wild meat instead of store-bought, commodity foods, dog sleds instead of snowmobiles, igloos instead of trailer homes. La Toundra celebrated these characteristics of Northern living as distinct from southern Canadian cities like Montreal. At the same time, the Canadian government was further colonizing life in the North to mimic that in the South.[51] Having moved from visuals alone to visuals in tandem with edibles, Expo 67's La Toundra romantically imagined Indigenous ingredients and dishes as belonging to the national pantry, and thus signified a shift in the history of the representation of Indigenous foodways in Canada.

## An Eatery Called "Ethnic"

Expo 67 coincided with a revived interest in ethnicity, and as the next chapter unpacks, national and ethnic identities frame cuisines. Traditionally, French restaurants have been simply restaurants, or classified as fine dining. Majority culture restaurants are restaurants, whereas minority ones are forced to wear the label "ethnic."

On the one hand, this adjective is meaningless because everyone has an ethnicity. On the other, it materializes how the ethnicities of some cultures are normative. In short, labelling an eatery "ethnic" naturalizes certain cuisines and exoticizes others. Ethnic as category is steeped in power dynamics, the privilege of the dominant for some and the burden of difference for others. In discussing the rise and fall of "ethnic" as a category in American cuisine, food studies scholar Krishnendu Ray concludes that "Ethnicity is not a thing. It is a relationship of domination and the very grounds on which the dominated have successfully pushed back."[52] Ethnicity implies a level of separation, food that is unfamiliar.

Although Indigenous peoples are the original inhabitants of the lands now called Canada, their nations and communities are minorities in relation to the majority settler population. According to this criterion, Indigenous cuisines count as "ethnic" in the sense that they represent the foodways of minority cultures, even if those foodways have been affected by the majority culture and, additionally, even if those foodways represent the country's First Peoples. Just as eateries are venues for encountering national cuisines, they are, to borrow the words of feminist theorist bell hooks, venues for eating the cuisines of those marked as other. Her text – "eating the other" – is based on metaphor, but her discussion lends itself to food.[53] It supports Expo 67's idea that you can travel the world with your mouth. Folklorist Lucy Long calls this culinary tourism, which she defines as "the intentional, exploratory participation in the foodways of an other."[54] It is difference that defines culinary tourism. The appetite for a cuisine, however, has little to do with the acceptance of its culture. In his discussion of how immigrants co-produce taste, Ray references Ghassan Hage's term "multiculturalism without migrants" to point to "the international circulation of gastronomic conceptions rather than the circulation of migrants."[55] Culinary tourism, therefore, can divorce a cuisine from its culture, including tastes while excluding the people crafting those tastes.

Some restaurants tell stories about faraway places. Others share tales about what is at their doorstep. Expo 67's eateries did both. The same is true of restaurants in Canadian cities. A Polish restaurant, for example, speaks about "the old country," but also about those who left it, when, and why, and the dishes they brought. These stories suggest food's potential to taste as if it comes from somewhere specific. They cast food in the role of transmitting how a place looks, smells, and tastes, and how cooks remember these sensory souvenirs.[56] As sociologists Shun Lu and Gary Alan Fine write, "Ethnic food validates the self, as dining out is identity work."[57] Eating "ethnic" food becomes a shared symbol that unites and makes sense of the diverse cultural fragments that stitch together North American culture. This distinguishes the culinary politics of eating out in a multicultural, settler colonial context.

As venues for representation, restaurants claim a cultural presence. Writing about Chinese Latino restaurants in New York City, anthropologist Lok Siu explains that the United States' racial framework assumes Chinese Latinos to be one or the other, which renders the complexity of their cultural identity invisible. However, restaurants give them visibility which, Siu writes, "boldly announce[s] their existence by claiming a distinct ethnic cuisine and cultural space within the urban landscape."[58] Restaurant signs, menus, and dishes – culinary materialities – are the means by which a culture gains a physical presence.

In his study of North American restaurants, cultural geographer Wilbur Zelinsky concludes that audience, in part, determines whether or not a restaurant is considered ethnic. "A Mexican café in an all-Mexican section of San Antonio, Texas," he says, "would not qualify unless it went to the trouble of advertising its menu to attract persons from afar, but a restaurant offering Mexican specialities in Edmonton, Alberta would qualify almost automatically."[59] Audience matters. It defines the position of a restaurant for "insiders" versus that of an "ethnic" restaurant for "outsiders." These categories also determine who feels welcome – and even safe – dining where. Weso, for example, remembers eating out with his family in Wisconsin, usually at diners. "We traded stories with other Menominee families about which diners were friendly to Indian customers and which were not."[60]

Although they are "ethnic" in the sense of representing a minority population within Canada, Indigenous restaurants are unique.

According to Zelinksy's distinction, if Indigenous restaurants target customers outside of Indigenous communities, then they can be understood as "ethnic" restaurants, but if they cater to their own communities they are not. In the former case, Indigenous restaurants might serve as a potential gateway for the Canadian settler majority culture to sample Indigenous dishes and, thus, cultures.

However, Indigenous restaurants are positioned differently from those opened by immigrant minority cultures. This is because Indigenous restaurants represent a distinct experience of displacement. Lily Cho writes about the agency of menus and how, in the instance of Chinese menus in Canada, they can be read as countercultural texts. These menus, which the next chapter further explains, need "to be read as informed by the dislocations of colonialism as well as the continuing difficulties of negotiating the assertion of otherness within a predominantly white cultural space and within the legacy of dislocation."[61] Cho writes about the "other" in the racialized context of settler colonialism. What about the native? Indigenous history in Canada is also dislocated by colonialism. The dynamics of this dislocation are distinct from those of racialized immigrants, yet Indigenous restaurants also negotiate "the assertion of otherness within a predominantly white cultural space."[62] In addition to a history of displacement, Indigenous restaurants represent a history of erasure. Instead of portraying a minority culture that moved to Canada, Indigenous foodways – including their misrepresentation on menus like La Toundra's – expose the cultures that were violently displaced. But La Toundra was not an Indigenous restaurant; instead, it was a settler culinary tale that, nonetheless, was influential in defining Indigenous fare. An example of settler storying.

## Dead or Alive

The illustrations on the Canadian Pacific Railway's and La Toundra's menus are examples of what Thomas King calls "Dead Indians." His terminology encompasses Francis's imaginary "Indians," but King delineates it further, distinguishing between "Live,"

"Dead," and "Legal." Trained as a historian, he uses a methodology that "draws more on storytelling techniques than historiography,"[63] which hints at how to interpret these categories. King's terms blend tongue-in-cheek humour with deep-cutting criticism. What distinguishes "Live Indians" from "Dead" and "Legal" ones? "All Native people living in North America today are Live Indians," King explains.[64] He cites Lakota scholar Vine Deloria's 1969 manifesto *Custer Died for Your Sins*, which argues, "Our foremost plight is our transparency."[65] King writes, "Deloria might as well have said that Indians are invisible."[66] He further explains: "North Americans certainly *see* contemporary Native people. They just don't *see* us as Indians."[67] Deloria and King both imply that what people see are imaginations. This is why representation matters.

King's definition of "Dead Indians" summons Wolfe's concept of "repressive authenticity": when Indigeneity is determined externally rather than internally.[68] When settler colonists define and measure Indigeneity. "Dead Indians" are the ones non-Indigenous people do see. They are, in King's words, "Garden of Eden-variety Indians. Pure, Noble, Innocent. Perfectly authentic. Jean-Jacques Rousseau Indians."[69] The single story "Indians." The settler story "Indians." The Canadian Pacific Railway menu "Indians," leisurely hunting on horseback and then eating bison, rather than beef, at Banff's Indian Days. In contrast, Live Indians embody those not allowed to participate because their outfits do not obey the organizer's regulations. "Live Indians are fallen Indians, modern, contemporary copies," says King, "not authentic Indians at all, Indians by biological association only."[70] And all Legal Indians are Live Indians, but not all Live Indians are Legal Indians. "Legal Indians" are the ones the Canadian and US governments recognize as Indigenous. "Government Indians, if you like," King spells out.[71] Historians Allyson Stevenson and Cheryl Troupe offer further context: the Canadian government introduced "the legal fiction 'Indian'" vis-à-vis a "group of laws that created a racialized system of oppression."[72] "Legal fiction 'Indians,'" if you like.

But two years after Expo 67, in 1969, the Canadian government proposed to do away with, to eliminate and erase, "Legal Indians." Pierre Elliott Trudeau's Liberals, elected in 1968, introduced a White Paper, formally titled the "Statement of the Government of Canada on Indian Policy, 1969," which aimed to abolish the Indian Act and all previous nation-to-nation agreements. This translated as terminating all treaties, eliminating legal Indian status, and relocating the responsibility for Indigenous peoples from the Canadian federal government to the provinces. "White Paper liberalism," sums up historian Sarah Nickel, "ignored the legacy of colonialism, failed to consider the unique nature of Indigenous rights, and assumed the infallible legitimacy of the Canadian state in defining, granting, or retracting Indigenous rights."[73] In a nutshell, despite its good – albeit paternalistic – intentions, the White Paper completely rejected Indigenous nationhood.

In the late 1960s Indigenous activism across the country was already simmering, but the White Paper turned up the temperature to a boil. In 1970, Jean Chrétien, the White Paper's architect, withdrew it. The White Paper was not, as Nickel makes clear, the only factor at work in the growing politicization of Indigenous nations during this period. Nonetheless, it further mobilized support for pan-Indigenous activism and unity across the country that would challenge Canada's settler colonial storying in the decades to come.[74] Given this background, Expo 67 reflects an important transition. As La Toundra demonstrates, Canada cast Indigenous peoples as an attraction, as no longer "vanishing." In a country that was aspiring toward multiculturalism, this emerging identity assigned Indigenous nations the new status as a minority.

King published *The Inconvenient Indian* in 2012 and tidied up the continent's relationship with Indigenous peoples into the three categories he defines: "North America loves the Dead Indian and ignores the Live Indian, North America *hates* the Legal Indian."[75] His distinction between "Dead" and "Live" Indians is supposed to ruffle feathers by calling out inimical stereotypes. He intends to disrupt the conversation, not to set these categories in stone. He treats them not as categories per se, but instead as a provocation, and even a theory about North American colonial history. Furthermore, the three overlap. King argues against seeing "Dead" and "Live" Indians in binary terms. The two can occupy the same space and time.[76] King aims to render the power struggle between self-representation and the stricture of societal expectations and stereotypes visible. The power struggles behind cultural representation. Who designs a menu and who decorates it. Or, in the case of one Vancouver restaurant, who gets their name on a burger and who gets to name the burgers. Leaving behind trains and tundra, the next chapter contextualizes how Expo 67's "Canadian" eatery inherited and then influenced the country's restaurant scene, eventually leading toward restaurants that were not Indigenous-inspired but Indigenous-led.

chapter three

# Restaurants and Representation

The Tomahawk Barbeque is a ten-minute drive from Stanley Park's Brockton Point. This corner of Vancouver's famed park is an outdoor museum. It displays nine totem poles and is British Columbia's most visited tourist attraction.[1] From here, you cross the Lions Gate Bridge, suspended above the Burrard Inlet, a coastal fjord that separates downtown Vancouver from its North and West shores. Since 1926 the Tomahawk Barbeque has been a North shore culinary fixture, one that even precedes the bridge. "North Vancouver's Tomahawk Barbeque has survived the Great Depression, a world war, the fast-food revolution, the diet craze, progress, regress, life, death and dry rot," says a 2016 review.[2] The restaurant, too, is a museum of sorts: a "souvenir-cum-Indian-artifact collection."[3] Two totem poles – the Thunderbird on the left and a human on the right – dressed in yellow and green, red, white, and black flank its entrance. Totem poles recount stories, honour legends, celebrate culture, and express artistic mastery, and here they set the mood for the food that waits inside.

Born in England, Chick Chamberlain immigrated to Canada in 1903. In 1926 he opened the Tomahawk Barbeque as a drive-in, the city's first.[4] Its original location was on Marine Drive, a strip that has since become a shopping mall. It moved to its current location in 1960. Chuck Chamberlain inherited the Tomahawk from his parents and continues to run it. As the restaurant alleges, the food is not its only appeal: "One of the main attractions ... is the outstanding collection of North Shore and West Coast Indian artifacts ... Chick Chamberlain began collecting interesting handcrafted artifacts from the Indians themselves about 80 years ago, when most people thought they were worthless. Now they are indeed of great historical value."[5] Because the restaurant opened on the eve of the Great Depression, many locals were cash poor and paid for their food with carvings or crafts instead, from cooking utensils and totem poles to masks and drums.[6] But the Tomahawk's pride in its artifact collection also tells a larger story of how the value of Indigenous material culture has changed in Canada: a shift from "worthless" to "of great historical value." Moreover, carvings and crafts that were a currency with which to purchase a meal have become examples of "art by appropriation" rather than "art by intention."[7]

The restaurant's name, too, is an artifact of sorts. Scott Manning Stevens places the tomahawk "in the category of what ethnohistorian Laurier Turgeon titles 'intercultural objects.'"[8] The tomahawk is a hybrid object. Despite metalwork's European or settler production, Stevens charts its "overdetermined level of symbolism within the context of American Indian culture."[9] Because of this symbolism, the tomahawk radiates "an aura of referents" and is an example par excellence "for such an overdetermined concept as 'Indian savagery.'"[10] By naming itself after this intercultural object, the restaurant frames both the material artifacts it exhibits and the food it serves.

## "Skookum Chief Burger"

The Tomahawk's menu is "basic meat and potatoes."[11] Typical diner fare. All the usual "greasy spoon" suspects appear: bacon and cheddar omelettes and BLT sandwiches, meat loaf and Caesar salad.[12] But the hamburgers stand out. The Tomahawk is proud of its burgers, each "named after some of the Indian chiefs Chick had known over the years, a sort of memorial to his friends: Skookum Chief, Chief Capilano, Chief Raven, Chief Dominic Charlie, Chief August Jack."[13] The "Skookum Chief burger," for example, is a tower of lettuce, onion, tomato, an organic beef patty, a free-run egg, Yukon-style bacon, a wiener, and Tomahawk special sauce. The burgers are popular. "Ever since the 1920s," boasts one review, "the Tomahawk ... has served burgers which have been rated the best in Canada."[14]

Chuck Chamberlin explains that his father "was enthralled by Indians. My Dad referred to them as Hollywood Indians, but in England that is all he saw."[15] He became involved in the community and, according to one report, even served on the local band council – "the first white man to do so."[16] A portrait of Chief Simon Baker, who had a burger named after him while he was still alive, hangs in the restaurant. His namesake burger dresses a beef patty with Yukon-style bacon, sautéed mushrooms, and aged cheddar. "When a Chief passed away we named a burger after him," Chamberlain says. "It might sound like nothing to you or [me], but it was quite an honour to them."[17]

Just like pigs, cattle have an imperial history. Incorporated as a city in 1886, Vancouver borrows its name from the British Royal Navy officer Captain George Vancouver (1757–1798). Coincidentally, he introduced cattle to Hawaii in 1793. Writing about cows, sheep, and horses, historian John Ryan states: "These animals, with their many uses in agriculture, labor, warfare, as food sources, and even as the ultimate sources of certain diseases, became a vanguard of colonialism. Cattle multiplied even when colonists did not."[18] Cows trample, tromp, trespass, and graze. They monopolize meadows and grass. In addition to meat, they provide milk for a vast range of foods that some people can stomach but others can't.[19] Cows consume water, grass, and other plants and then, through their waste, spread pathogens and seeds. Therefore, they helped shape and conquer landscapes, and were central to the transformations of the Pacific, the Prairies, and beyond in the late eighteenth and early nineteenth centuries.[20] Settler animals. Cows also represented land ownership models and animals as property. A burger is not just a burger. Another ingredient that seasons the patty is this entangled history of animals, land, and real estate.

Not all Tomahawk burgers are named after Chiefs. Nor are they all beef. The menu also offers the "Seaburger" (cod), "Veggie burger" (black bean and brown rice), "Tomahawk totem burger" (chicken), the "Tomahawk pow wow" (wiener slices, bacon, and Tomahawk special sauce), and the "Potlatch deluxe" (also with wiener slices and special sauce). In 1885 the Government of Canada passed legislation banning the potlatch that was in effect until 1951.[21] A gift-giving feast marking major personal and political events, such as births and weddings, the Pacific Northwest potlatch tradition further reveals the connection between food and power, culture and politics. Even if the Tomahawk named their burger after the ban was lifted and as a symbol of recognition, the "Potlatch deluxe" feels like an odd name. It doesn't quite fit, like too stiff a leaf of lettuce or too thick a slice of onion that slides off the patty, escaping the bun. Similar to Banff's Indian Days, the history of the potlatch ban was coupled with an ongoing settler fascination with Indigenous cultures. An example of when cultural appropriation becomes culinary appropriation.

A 2017 video celebrating the Tomahawk's ninety-one years begins with Chamberlain unlocking the restaurant, switching on the lights, and picking up a pile of paper headdresses. It ends with a Caucasian family of five celebrating, having become Canadian citizens. The youngest wears a headdress. The camera zooms in on the middle sister, a paper menu in her hands. More cartoonish in style compared to the one on La Toundra's menu, the figure on the Tomahawk's is bare chested and dressed in a loincloth. A single feather peeks out from his long hair. He holds a hamburger in one hand and a soda in the other. Despite the Tomahawk's history as a community meeting place and its displays of West Coast Indigenous visual culture, it perpetuates images of King's "Dead Indian."

"The Tomahawk Restaurant," according to a 2016 review, "has an unmediated relationship with its history."[22] The critic compares eating there to watching Looney Tunes and considering the warning to the viewer that the cartoons do not reflect the studio's views today. "Just like Warner Bros.," he writes, "Tomahawk has decided not to temper or shy away from these relics; they coexist with the rest of the artifacts to paint a richer and more accurate picture of where we have come from to get where we are today."[23] The question, however, remains how customers interpret the décor. Looney Tunes opens with a disclaimer. The Tomahawk does not. Another review describes the Tomahawk as "a kitschy diner ... most notable for its brunch line-ups and typical colonial appropriation of First Nations cultural imagery."[24] *The Canadian Encyclopedia* defines cultural appropriation as "the use of a people's traditional dress, music, cuisine, knowledge and other aspects of their culture, without their approval, by members of a different culture."[25] To clarify that this debate is about more than names, it continues: "Cultural appropriation often reflects a racialized power imbalance between two cultures, the taking of culture – rather than the consensual sharing of it – which often, in turn, involves exploitation of one group over another."[26] Cultural appropriation, including culinary appropriation, is about power. Recognizing – and debating – the dynamics of cooking and eating another culture's food is important because, as Krishnendu Ray argues, "it engages with the question of power in the making of a culture."[27]

Beyond who has the right to represent a culture, there is the question of who profits from it, which is to say who makes money. It is not only a question of who gets to use someone else's culture. A story from south of the border provides an example. In 2016, Chicago-based Aloha Poke Co. was granted a federal trademark for "Aloha Poke."[28] Two years later the company sent cease-and-desist letters to Aloha Poke Stop in Anchorage, Alaska, owned by a Native Hawaiian family, demanding that it change its name. Food writer Soleil Ho summarizes Hawaiian activist Kalamaokaaina Niheu's response to this case: "Hawaiians, for nearly a century until 1987, were forbidden from using their native language in schools. To have a mainland corporation trademark native Hawaiians' own words, in 2018, feels like more of the same silencing, but with an ironic twist: this time, their language is something to be commodified rather than erased."[29] "Erase and replace" has become "copy and commodify." This echoes a similar progression to what has happened in Canada. Efforts to deny Indigenous cultures have evolved into efforts to sell them. And alongside appropriation, a second word emerges in these debates: authenticity.

## Authenticity and Other Fables

The *Oxford English Dictionary* defines authentic as 1) "of undisputed origin and not a copy: genuine," and 2) "made or done in the traditional or original way, or in a way that faithfully resembles the original."[30] For the latter, it gives the example of a "restaurant [that] serves authentic Italian meals." But what makes an Italian meal authentic? Is it the ingredients, the cooking techniques, or the people? When writing about foods associated with particular places, authenticity comes up as a measure of value; however, the concept is more complex than its dictionary definition suggests.

The idea of authentic food assumes, first, that a dish can be consistently the same.[31] This does not account for variations in preparation styles or taste preferences. Second, it expects that a dish, not to mention an ingredient, does not change over time. Third, it marries food to ethnicity, to blood and soil, a dangerous tie that gifts nationality far too much agency and racist beliefs an easy place to hide.[32] So if authenticity is a rigid – not to mention potentially violent – concept that does not capture nuance, why is it a popular way to judge food? Addressing its role in rating restaurants, sociologists Josée Johnston and Shyon Baumann argue, "authenticity is socially constructed, and is not inherent to particular foods."[33] Instead, authenticity is relational. Here, as often is the case, the idea of the other is paramount. For some foods to be authentic, others have to be inauthentic, and for the former they identify five criteria: "Food is understood as authentic when it has geographic specificity, is 'simple,' has a personal connection, can be linked to a historical tradition, or has 'ethnic' connections."[34]

Fine dining has changed tones. Gone are the days when one needed a famous name or a secret phone number to secure a reservation at one of the world's best restaurants. Today anyone who has a high enough limit on their credit card and fast enough fingers can book a table online for one of the world's best Michelin-starred restaurants. But in this more democratic dining world, as Johnston and Baumann argue, there still needs to be a system of measurement to rate some restaurant experiences higher than others. Foodies no longer fancy traditional, buttoned-up snobbery. And yet with less stiffness, they can still distinguish "a symbolic boundary" between foods that are worthy and those that are not. "This is precisely what the focus on authenticity and exoticism achieves," they explain.[35] Michelin stars represent one side of the restaurant world, the one where guests are willing to pay high prices. The name of Guy Fieri's television show "Diners, Drive-Ins and Dives" represents the other side: where enthusiastic eaters compete to find an under-the-radar joint serving great food at low prices, a so-called "hole-in-the-wall." Race also plays a role in this distinction. This spectrum adheres to the idea that French restaurants are expensive and so-called "ethnic" restaurants are not.

Asian-American studies scholar Robert Ji-Song Ku provides another answer to why authenticity is a popular measure with which to judge food. Despite considering the concept "troubled, troubling, and troublesome,"[36] he recognizes that it is convenient. "To believe in authenticity," he writes, "is to rely on transcendental means to answer questions posed by a reality deemed untidy and undesirable."[37] In a nutshell, Ku argues, authenticity is a "coping mechanism." It simplifies a complex world and provides a structure, a set of rules to follow.

But beyond its potential dangers, authenticity is too narrow a concept to apply to the hybrid and messy business that is turning flora and fauna into food. Folklorist Regina Bendix argues that because the term has become popular, it now means little. "'Authentic' means original, genuine, or unaltered," she writes, "but the semantic domain the term invokes has grown so broad and elusive that one is tempted to place it in the catalogue of 'plastic words' devised by language philosopher Uwe Pörksen – words that have come to mean so much that they really mean very little while nonetheless signalling importance and power."[38] This is the paradox of authenticity. Even though what it means is not clear, it still wields great authority.[39]

For the 2016 You Are Welcome food truck at the Toronto Pan Am Games, chef David Wolfman cooked four dishes: "Curried elk pastry," "Nish kabobs (venison kabobs with birch, balsamic glaze)," "Smoked turkey chilli," and "Wild blueberry bannock." While the Mississaugas of the Credit wanted to raise awareness of their traditional territory, Wolfman wished to promote Indigenous ingredients.[40] Although not a restaurateur, Wolfman has been at the forefront of Indigenous cuisine since having started a catering company specializing in "Aboriginal Fusion back then – Indigenous Fusion these days" in the 1990s.[41]

When the *Toronto Food Trucks* website covered the You Are Welcome Food Truck, one reader did not like the menu. Where are "the scone dogs, pizza scone, hamburger soup and INDIAN TACOS!' Don't go all gourmet," she rallied.[42] Only the bannock earned her approval. She wanted the greatest hits of reservation and pow wow cooking. A food truck, however, is not a restaurant. Both sell vittles from a selected list of options for a set price, but mobility sets them apart. The You Are Welcome food truck, moreover, was a project and not a business, and its food was free. Running a restaurant, in comparison, is risky. It requires capital and commitment and comes with great uncertainty. The median lifespan of a restaurant in the western United States is 4.25 years, and for restaurants with five employees or less, that number drops to 3.75 years.[43] Additionally, around 17 per cent of restaurants fail in their first year.[44] Because opening a restaurant requires more red tape and more risk, for some chefs a catering business or a food truck is a means to an end: a layover en route to a brick-and-mortar restaurant.[45]

But the You Are Welcome Food Truck's aim was something else: it was to culturally reclaim its land. Carolyn King was the elected Chief of the Mississaugas of the Credit from 1997 to 1999 and, today, is their cultural ambassador. Three years after the Pan Am Games, she described the food truck as a "soft" project, an educational awareness venture to teach whose land Toronto is on – and an expensive one. "We lobbied up, showed up, and paid up," she told me. The cost of participation was around $3 million, half of which the nation paid and half of which they raised through sponsorship.[46] The 2010 Vancouver Winter Olympics had set a precedent, and so the Mississaugas hired the same support.[47] But some visitors were confused, commenting that it was nice to see the First

Nations presence, while others asked: "What does it mean you are the host First Nation?" The Mississaugas' involvement was not without pushback. "Sporting is all about sponsorship. It isn't conclusive to recognition," King says.[48] Although the food truck did not have to make money, it still wrestled with its shadow, with corporate influence, and the politics of sponsorship.[49]

But with the You Are Welcome food truck, Wolfman could focus on what he wanted to cook instead of having to sell it. He describes his cooking as "Indigenous Fusion: Traditional Foods with a Modern Twist." This modern twist also applies to the context in which he cooks and not just the food he prepares. Similarly, Lois Ellen Frank describes her recipes as having "an Ancestral twist."[50] It is not just the food that matters, but what the food represents, and how it connects people, land, and stories. Why does Wolfman define his cooking as Indigenous fusion? And what makes cuisine fusion?

## Add to Taste

National and regional borders frame a dish's geographical and cultural coordinates: French or Provençal, Chinese or Sichuan. Other than global dishes – like fried chicken, which belongs to too many cultures to attribute to just one – and globalized ones – such as California rolls and French fries, which, despite their names, are eaten the world over – a cuisine anchors itself in a specific geography. Even if its ingredients come from all over, a dish is always from somewhere.

To fuse is, therefore, to redraw the map, to reinterpret place, and sometimes even to subdue it. Fusion takes various shapes and stems from various impulses: to add, to substitute, to integrate, or to compromise and accommodate. The first, to add, is credited to curiosity or creativity. To borrow a flavour married to one cuisine and graft it onto a dish from elsewhere, the likes of "Green tea crème brûlée," is a Japanese "twist" on a French classic. The second impulse is to substitute, because an ingredient is either unavailable or undesirable. If you are making a stir-fry and do not have, say,

Chinese black vinegar, you might reach for balsamic instead. The third is to integrate. Beef short ribs bathed in soy sauce, rice wine, sesame oil, and sugar, seared on a grill, blanketed in kimchi salsa, and wrapped in a tortilla: the "Korean taco" was born in Los Angeles.[51] Korean barbecue in corn tortillas tells the story of a city with large Korean and Mexican populations, a city where cultures spill from one neighbourhood to the next. This diversification of fusion models a familiarity with a broad range of cuisines. Familiarity, however, does not always equal acceptance. The fourth, and last, impulse is to compromise and accommodate, often to gain culinary confirmation. It is to add cream cheese and imitation crab to a makizushi sushi roll, name it after California, and serve it to those who prefer cooked seafood to raw.

A chef's capacity to fuse – and to be celebrated for bending the geography of the cuisine they cook – differs based on cultural positioning. Chef Joyce Goldstein considers Austrian chef Wolfgang Puck's Chinois the first fusion restaurant in the United States.[52] Opened in Santa Monica in 1983, it was hailed by critics and diners as a creative sensation. The restaurant continues to operate today, mixing Californian ingredients, Chinese culinary traditions, and French techniques. In contrast to Puck's Euro-American-Asian fusion, Goldstein cites the late Los Angeles-based critic Jonathan Gold's review of chefs preparing the likes of Korean tacos as having "identified a new breed of chefs in LA – Asian Americans who grow up with their family's native cuisine set against the city's multicultural landscapes."[53] "These chefs," she summarizes, "approach Western cooking with a novel mind-set, which he called 'fusion from the other side.'"[54] "From the other side" identifies one side as normative, as business as usual, and the second as "other." But this report also points to a turning of the tables on who can engage in fusion.

In her study of the absence of Māori restaurants in Aotearoa New Zealand, Carolyn Morris argues, "Only the dominant can fuse food: similar practices in dominated foodways are regarded as degradation. As such, the ability to fuse, rather than to be fused, can be read as a sign of culinary and cultural power."[55] Western chefs, like Puck, borrow from non-Western cuisines, but the recognition of Korean-American-Latino fusion signifies a shift. Lok Siu observes that in the 1990s fusion implied the combination of Asian and European influences (usually Japanese and Chinese with French), but "the fusion of today has a broader reference, one that includes both Asian and Latino influences."[56] Morris's critique, however, indicates that the broadening of fusion does not yet extend to Indigenous chefs in Aotearoa New Zealand. Although its range of diversity has expanded, fusion still carries cultural baggage. It continues to adhere primarily to Western cultures' culinary codes, to the grand dame that is French cuisine.

Fusion is a passé trend, pronounce Annto Melasniemi and Rikrit Tiravanija. As the title of their 2019 cookery volume *Bastard Cookbook: The Odious Smell of Truth* declares, they align with a label that aims to dissolve national boundaries and to disobey culinary patrilineage. Melasniemi, from Finland, is a musician turned restaurateur, Tiravanija a Thai artist. At an art event in Stockholm, Tiravanija "bastardized" Swedish meatballs by lacing them with curry paste – an example of what art historian Jörn Schafaff calls "reverse assimilation."[57] For Melasniemi, fusion and bastard cooking differ in that "fusion cooking tries to present a kind of caricature of two nations' cuisines combined, but to preserve each of their 'essential' qualities at the same time."[58] He suggests that bastard cooking tries "to get rid of the sanctity of 'nationalism' altogether."[59] Melasniemi attributes fusion to the late 1990s and early 2000s, and insists that bastard cooking is a more serious commitment to equitable synergy. Hybridization welcomes it when distinct forces collaborate and prompt something new. This echoes food historians Alberto Capatti and Massimo Montanari's conviction that identity is defined by exchange.[60]

Wolfman calls his cooking Indigenous fusion.[61] What about creole? Geographer Lenore Newman dedicates a chapter of *Speaking in Cod Tongues* to "Canadian creole." Because the country is multicultural, she argues, Canadian creole expresses itself "most often as either a recipe from somewhere else reimagined with Canadian ingredients or as a Canadian recipe reimagined with ingredients from elsewhere."[62] Newman asserts, together with political scientist Sam Grey, that creolization is the final stage of "gastronomic multiculturalism."[63] The first stage is the suppression of subaltern cuisines, the second authenticity-seeking plurality, and the third creolization, which is to say convergence. This model demonstrates the progression of food from "different," "exotic," or even unpalatable to a staple in the multicultural Canadian pantry.

How does creole cooking differ from fusion? Returning to the United States, historian Donna Gabaccia, too, employs a three-step model to discuss the development from what she terms "colonial creole" to "ethnic enclave eating" to "contemporary creoles."[64] Fusion best matches ethnic enclave eating in that it attempts to eat across a cuisine's borders while retaining a distinct category. Creole cooking, on the other hand, blurs these borders. Fusion is then a mix and creole a merger.

Whether nationalized or labelled fusion, bastard, or creole, the practices of adding, substituting, integrating, and compromising or accommodating are part of any cuisine's development. Early fusion was a conscious effort to mix and match culturally distinctive ingredients, flavours, and techniques. Contemporary fusion, melting-pot fusion, and Canadian creole, I argue, emerge when cultures mix and match and meld. In comparison to bastard cooking, creole reflects assimilation, often based on the majority culture's terms. Bastard cooking, in contrast, seeks to challenge the power dynamics that lead to "melting-pot" assimilation or "tokenism" fusion.

Wolfman lives in Toronto, a city where nearly half the inhabitants were not born in Canada. Fusion food in Canada's metropolis, like Los Angeles' Korean tacos, mirrors the city's demographics.[65] Take, for instance, the Hungary Thai in Kensington Market, which hawks Hungarian and Thai options alongside dishes of spring rolls *and* cabbage rolls, schnitzel *and* pad thai side by side.[66] The restaurant is less interested in creating new dishes. Instead it is committed to serving the greatest hits of both cuisines on the same plate. One street east is Rasta Pasta, which is named after its signature dish: "soft fluffy gnocchi, sautéed in Alfredo or marinara sauce and served with Jamaica's national dish, ackee & saltfish."[67] Fusion seasons Toronto's culinary culture. Despite cooking in a creole city, Wolfman's cuisine is very much fusion, one that keeps its Indigenous roots intact.

But as an Indigenous chef, does Wolfman's fusion come from adding, substituting, integrating, or accommodating Indigenous cuisine or elements of all four? A member of the Xaxli'p Nation in Lillooet, BC, Wolfman grew up in Toronto's Regent Park neighbourhood. He markets himself as an expert in Indigenous food and culinary arts; both matter. "To be clear, my recipes are not about making a meal out of whatever you can gather on a walk in the bush or about eating only those foods that were available in North America before the lost Spaniards reached the so-called New World in the fifteenth century – new to whom?" he says. "My recipes are about taking the essence of indigenous ingredients and putting it under the spotlight. I blend the traditional with modern tastes."[68] Wolfman doesn't seek to be an authority – let alone the authority – on Indigenous cuisines. Instead, his cooking highlights Indigenous ingredients while preparing them with the techniques of the contemporary culinary arts.

Wolfman's "Curried elk pastry" for the You Are Welcome Food Truck demonstrates this synthesis. Elk is traditional game hunted not just for food but also for tools and clothing. By enveloping elk meat in puff pastry – *pâte feuilletée*, which originated on the other side of the Atlantic and is made with wheat flour and probably too much butter, lard, or vegetable shortening – Wolfman fuses distinct culinary traditions together. He presents a traditional Indigenous ingredient in a non-traditional way. This sparks the question: does "Indigenous fusion" aim to connect or accommodate? Wolfman's cooking seems to encompass both. On the one hand, he connects diverse flavours to garner a broad appeal. On the other, his cooking is accommodating. He strives to convince people to try new ingredients by cooking them in familiar ways. Beyond culinary techniques, his recipes borrow from other parts of the world. "Smoked turkey chili," for example, combines ingredients indigenous to Turtle Island – turkey, pinto beans, and tomatoes – with pantry items that originate elsewhere, like olive oil, white wine vinegar, and yogurt.[69] Unlike other Indigenous chefs, Wolfman does not restrict himself to a pre-contact pantry. His cooking is based in a specific region, but not limited to it. Wolfman's "Nish kabobs" tell a similar story. Slang for Anishinaabe, nish is the Ojibway word for people. He marinates deer medallions in a bath of birch syrup, lime juice, soya sauce, balsamic vinegar, and olive oil, which he spikes with peppercorns, rosemary, thyme, garlic, Dijon mustard, and brown sugar. He then grills the venison and slathers it with a glaze.

Wolfman made the You Are Welcome recipes available online, so more people are able to experience the food. His aunt taught him "that the stories shared with you are given to you to share. They're not given to you to keep ... So a recipe I give you, it's not a secret recipe ... You're going to take it and add your own things to it and share it with other people and so on. It stays alive that way."[70] Like recipes, stories are to pass on, to share. And through cultural continuity, one generation hands recipes down to the next. Wolfman emphasizes that "it's not your job to keep the story – it's your job to share the story."[71] To share is to season and it is the people, Wolfman says, who season the food. "People say, 'What kind of herbs did native people use?' but when I talk to elders they always say that herbs were for medicine ... I did a lecture ... and they said, 'so the food was bland,' but that is not what I said. I said the emphasis was more on the feast; the actual gathering of people together, the sharing."[72] In addition to the physical aspects – food transfers nutrients, alleviates hunger, and gives pleasure – Wolfman's approach stresses how food brings people together. It symbolizes the feast. It materializes the gathering. It establishes relations.

## The World on a Menu

Despite its décor and even its name, the Tomahawk, unlike the You Are Welcome food truck, is not Indigenous. In June 2017, a CBC News article pointed out the absence of Indigenous restaurants. "Wander down restaurant row in any of Canada's major cities and you'll see a culinary mosaic of international offerings. But there's a culture that's been notably absent, until now," begins the article.[73] The text accentuates the last two words: until now. "A new surge of Indigenous restaurants opening across the country," journalist Eli

Glasner continues, "has chefs finding innovative ways to serve up First Nations inspired selections."[74] A companion map catalogues fifteen restaurants: four in British Columbia (Painted Pony Cafe in Kamloops, Kekuli Cafe in Merritt and Westbank,[75] the Thunderbird Cafe in Whistler, and Salmon n' Bannock in Vancouver); one in Alberta (Native Delights in Edmonton); one in Saskatchewan (Wanusekwin Heritage Park Bistro in Saskatoon); two in Manitoba (Cookem Daisey's and Feast Cafe Bistro in Winnipeg); four in Ontario (Kokom's Bannock Shack in Dryden and Kūkŭm, Tea-n-Bannock, and NishDish in Toronto); one in Quebec (Nikosi Bistro in Wakefield); and one in Nova Scotia (Kiju's on Membertou First Nation).[76] Comprehensive but not complete, the map missed Toronto's Pow Wow Cafe and Wendake, Quebec's La Traite, as well as Montreal's Roundhouse Café and Wendake's La Sagamité. Nonetheless, it makes clear just how few Indigenous restaurants there were in 2017.

The CBC article suggests that Indigenous restaurants are new, which this book demonstrates is not the case. More Indigenous restaurants are now opening, but how do they differ from earlier ones? Is the food different? The stories? And why are more opening now? But I also ask: Why does the media continually package Indigenous restaurants as new? Why were earlier ones forgotten?

Glasner was not the first to note this absence. Over fifty years prior, in December 1975, the *Winnipeg Free Press* reviewed *Parsley, Sage and Cynthia Wine*: "the only existing, fairly comprehensive critique of Winnipeg restaurants, it is being touted as THE guide to local cuisine, a sort of flat-lands Michelin."[77] Commissioned by Manitoba's tourism minister, it sold four thousand copies in two days. Journalist Ted Allan summarized Cynthia Wine's culinary inventory: "Greek, German, Indonesian, French, Hungarian, Italian, East Indian, Northern Chinese, Peking Chinese and Canton Chinese, Japanese, Jewish, Mexican, Portuguese, Polish, Ukrainian and even (do not be afraid …) Transylvanian."[78] He distinguished between Northern, Peking, and Canton Chinese, reflecting an awareness of regional cuisines. But closer to home, Allan repeats Wine's acknowledgment of an important gap: "She bemoans the absence of native restaurants: 'The number of Metis and Canadian

Indian people in Winnipeg is large and to have found not even one permanent outlet for their food in Winnipeg is a sad commentary on the extent to which the native peoples' culture has been overwhelmed.'"[79] "Overwhelmed" understates the history of the attempted erasure of Indigenous foodways in Canada.

Although Wine laments Winnipeg's lack of Indigenous restaurants, Allan's review takes a U-turn. "The Indian and Metis Friendship Centre used to serve a sumptuous rabbit stew and bannock," he adds in parenthesis, "but it's probably just as well that no ersatz native restaurants have leaped into the vacuum. An Ojibway friend once passed on an authentic recipe for a moose nose preparation which began: 'Toss two hot rocks into a pot ...' Good hot rocks are probably as difficult to come by as moose noses."[80] By these comments, Allan suggests that if an Indigenous restaurant is not going to serve the "authentic" thing, it might as well not bother. His imagination of Indigenous food lives in the past – another example of repressive authenticity and settler storying. Allan assumes the Indian and Métis Friendship Centre would have only utilized historic culinary techniques. Did it make its sumptuous rabbit stew by first tossing two hot rocks into a pot? His commentary remains rooted in the romanticized imagery of the Canadian Pacific Railway menus. Never mind that bannock is the result of colonial contact, Allan more or less dismisses Wine's wish that Winnipeg had an Indigenous restaurant. To the contrary, I argue that restaurants are important venues of cultural negotiation and culinary assertion. The chapters that follow look at Canada's culinary landscape by questioning the stories behind restaurants and their menus and by charting how eateries have constructed, presented, and interpreted Indigenous cuisines over time.

Menus can be timeless, or even out of time. A winter menu peddling asparagus, a spring vegetable, goes against time, disobeying the seasons. Such contradictions render menus curious and complex. Early restaurants, from at least the 1770s, employed menus. Unlike earlier eating establishments, menus accommodate individual choice. Instead of eating what everyone else did and at the same fixed time, as was the practice at a table d'hôte, menus facilitated individual orders, allowing diners to distinguish their meal from their dining companion's. This advances sociologist Georg Simmel's notion that the origin of individual choice is the shared meal.[81] Like a playbill, early menus announced the food, whereas those that emerged around the 1770s offered various options and, thus, the means to differentiate.[82]

Menus catalogue what a restaurant offers, as well as archive what it once did. A menu relies on text, and sometimes images and illustrations, to communicate what the kitchen can prepare, and to manage customers' expectations. Because a meal is time-based and temporal – and sometimes theatrical, unfolding in numerous acts – a menu is the textual trace of a restaurant's dishes. If restaurants represent contemporary foodways, defining the styles of their times, then the menu (or the lack thereof) is its record. Menus thus represent larger shifts in what people eat, how, and why. In the words of critic Patric Kuh, "Restaurants have the ability to frame the historically momentous within the confines of their windows."[83] Menus track changes in price, availability, and preference.

Although restaurants reflect particular times, early menus were often out of time, and sometimes even out of place, overcoming seasonal time to flaunt raspberries in winter and French fish in California. Today, many contemporary menus – in Canada and beyond – shadow the seasons, aiming to represent a specific time and place. Locally anchored food in a globalized world. Dining fashions went from transcending the local to resisting the global, an attempt to distinguish a menu's fare in a world where one can eat Korean BBQ in Los Angeles, Cairo, and Seoul.

Just like the word restaurant, *haute cuisine* – or fine dining – has meant different things at different times. The *grande cuisine* period began around the time of the French Revolution, and later evolved into *cuisine classique*, which is associated with the French chef George Auguste Escoffier (1846–1935), who codified much of traditional French fare. *Nouvelle cuisine* then interrupted *cuisine classique*'s dominance. Emerging in the 1960s, it emphasized fresher ingredients, lighter sauces. "The movement began from within," write Latin American studies scholar Sarah Portnoy and historian Jeffrey Pilcher, "as revolutions often do."[84] Its protagonist was French chef Paul Bocuse (1926–2018), who gently modernized French food for a new century, more of a simmer and less of a boil. The French chef Joël Robuchon (1945–2018), whom writer Adam Gopnik describes as "rooted unashamedly in the classic techniques of the French restaurant kitchen,"[85] represents the *post-nouvelle* era. Fine dining used to mean French. "The global presence of Robuchon's cooking, what has been called 'the planetary turn,' came to be a paradoxical one," writes Gopnik. "French chefs went out to colonize the world – and soon found the world colonizing, or even abandoning French cuisine."[86] He uses colonize as a metaphor; however, opening a high-end French restaurant in Bangkok involves soft power: the capital to navigate foreign licences and building contracts, as well as the power to attract the local and international elite to a foreign-owned establishment. What matters is that, during Robuchon's career, cuisine changed: the "once-hegemonic influence" of French cuisine began to wane.[87]

The history of cuisine, like all histories, is not linear. Beginnings, as well as endings, are messy. By summarizing this history, I do not wish to simplify it.[88] Instead, my purpose is to contextualize North American restaurants and where they have looked for inspiration. Up until the 1970s, the answer was always the same: France. But in 1971, Alice Waters opened Chez Panisse in Berkeley, California, and, ironically, her rendition of a French provincial restaurant represents the emergence of California cuisine. As Waters narrates, Chez Panisse "began with our doing the very best we could do with French recipes and California ingredients, and has evolved into what I like to think of as a celebration of the very finest of our regional food products."[89] The debate continues about how to categorize Chez Panisse, but, labels aside, the restaurant unquestionably changed North American dining culture. Geographer Julie Guthman credits Waters with pioneering California's take on *nouvelle cuisine*.[90] California set the model for the rest of the continent, Canada included. The history of Chez Panisse and the California food revolution is entangled with the fall of French cuisine's reign. The 1959 opening of New York City's the Four Seasons Restaurant – the first restaurant in the United States to offer fine dining that wasn't French – foreshadowed what was to come.[91]

Risking redundancy, it is impossible to overstate Chez Panisse's influence and what Guthman calls "the Alice Waters diaspora."[92] These chefs left the Bay Area for other kitchens, bringing with them ingredient-based menus and an obsession with quality produce. Detailed descriptions and lists of ingredients – the likes of "Frisée salad with baked goat cheese, figs and almonds" – came to replace dish names. Chez Panisse cast the mould for contemporary North American restaurants peddling seasonal and local fare. Waters started naming the farmers she worked with, listing them on her menus like the credits in a film. But she was far from the first to do so. "Nothing, in fact, could have been older," says Kuh.[93] The practice of adorning dishes with regional place-names – the likes of "Boston baked beans" – is older than the Republic itself. "Even if one takes the practice of using place-names simply for their promotional value," Kuh continues, "it dates at least as far back as the nineteenth century, when Maine oysters, Maryland terrapin soup, and canvasback duck from the Chesapeake marshes were important component parts of ... '5th Avenue cuisine circa 1895.'"[94] Listing American ingredients might not have been novel, but it seemed original when it re-emerged in California in the late 1970s. Waters taught Americans to see their foodways on their own terms. No longer just copying and pasting the food of France, she adapted its culinary techniques to taste California in a new way. Other chefs then followed suit by looking at their edible landscapes through a culinary lens of their own.

The next two globally influential developments took place on the other side of the Atlantic: molecular gastronomy, as exemplified by Ferran Adrià's el Bulli in Catalonia, Spain, which closed in 2011, and new Nordic cuisine, engineered by Danish chef René Redzepi (who worked at el Bulli in 1999). In many ways, Redzepi's Noma is a marriage between molecular gastronomy's exacting techniques – more at home in a laboratory than in a kitchen – and the gospel of local, sustainable, and seasonal eating. Standing on the shoulders of both culinary movements, Redzepi reinvented Nordic cuisine. He vernacularized fine dining.[95] His contemporary imagination of Nordic cuisine emphasized "raw materials" rarely identified as food. It further localized it, shifted the hierarchy, and dethroned a high-end, universal cuisine that had started using local ingredients but still largely drew from the French repertoire. Redzepi took Waters's torch of local and seasonal eating in golden California and ran with it in the icier Nordic region. To attempt to contour the seismic scale of Noma's influence risks coming off as hyperbolic. And yet what Noma pinned on its menu crashed against and rippled through the world of fine dining and was nothing short of a culinary reformation.

The writer Rune Skyum-Nielsen chronicles early reactions to Noma in the restaurant's first English-language cookbook: "The rest of the Danish restaurant world laughed at Noma's gastronomic concept," he details. "Even some of René's closest allies in the profession poured scorn on this insubstantial vision and gave the restaurant nicknames like 'Blubber Restaurant,' the 'Whale Penis' and the 'Seal-Fucker.' Messing about with traditional Nordic food and raw materials was not the thing done. It was ridiculous." Seven years after opening, Noma's effort to "mess about" with "raw materials" (a term that replaces the word ingredient in its vocabulary) and "traditional Nordic food" was no longer considered ridiculous. Noma was now considered the zenith of gastronomy, the place to dine to experience contemporary haute cuisine.[96]

As Intimo in Panama City previewed, the relevance of the new Nordic food movement stretches far beyond its region. For other northern environments, its influence is that much more pronounced. At the 2019 Dublin Gastronomy Symposium, the executive chef of Chapter One, a Michelin-starred restaurant, claimed: "The best thing to happen to Irish food, and young Irish chefs, was the Nordic food trend – it taught chefs to use what is on your doorstep." "Using what is on your doorstep" might sound obvious, but it is not. After all, canned food was once rare and elite. "Using what is on your doorstep" had become globally influential.

But in a settler colonial context, eating at your doorstep is complicated. Teresa M. Mares and Devon G. Peña confront this in their discussion of what they rename the "AlterNative" food movement. "[S]hould we not also consider," they ask, "how a call to eat locally invokes spaces that have been settled, colonized, ruptured, and remade through complex processes of human movement and environmental history making?"[97] What does local mean when colonialism has radically shifted and suppressed foodways? What does the new Nordic food movement mean for Canada? And what makes a restaurant Canadian? Despite La Toundra's proposal of a national cuisine at Expo 67, Canadian cuisine did not begin to appear in restaurants until several decades later. There were budding signs in the late 1980s, but 1995 was a turning point. That year the pan-Canadian restaurant Canoe opened in Toronto, and *Northern Bounty* was published. Edited by Jo Marie Powers, the founder of Taste Canada, and Anita Stewart, the founder of Food Day Canada, and the outcome of a 1993 conference, the book has patriotic undertones. It aimed to define the country's cuisine, while cheering it on. The introduction makes this clear: "Our book *Northern Bounty* is a flag-waving exploration of Canadian cuisine, and a turning point in our collective awareness of it."[98] Its name is complimentary, painting an image of a lush land.

Among a collection of complementary chapters, food writer Eve Johnson's contribution sticks out. In "Historical Influences on West Coast Cooking," she writes: "Call it the 'Alice Waters–Chez Panisse' effect. But here's the paradox for you: our interest in fresh, local food comes from the new orthodoxy of the international food world. It comes from *Bon Appétit* and *Gourmet*, from the sudden shifts in North American understanding that made it okay to think and talk about food as something more than fuel. If you'd like a convenient date for the revolution in Vancouver, try 1980, when Granville Island Market opened ... Now, here's the real puzzling part. Why did it take so long for us to show this level of interest in our own food?"[99] Geography and history alone do not determine what people eat. Global trends shift tastes. This shift exhibits Waters's influence on chefs in other regions and countries to cultivate their own ingredients, their own cuisines. It was an international shift in the value of food, from south of the border, that created an interest in local food, not the bounty itself. And it was a restaurant in California that sparked this renewed interest in Canada. "From the beginning," Johnson continues, "the urban West Coast was able to by-pass the dependence on local food that might have led us to develop a distinct culinary tradition. We could eat what we wanted, and unfortunately, that meant British colonial food – the food you get when you take the natural conservatism of British cooking and put it in an environment in which fears for cultural survival run high."[100] Settlers attuned their appetites to their culinary habits, and even fears, rather than to availability, channelling conservatism as a conscious strategy to express and maintain a dominant cultural identity in a foreign environment. It was a sign of power – and distinction – not to eat the foods they were surrounded by.

Twenty-two years after *Northern Bounty*, Lenore Newman published her survey of Canadian food. The title of her 2017 *Speaking in Cod Tongues* is spelled out on its cover in a skinny black font with foods performing the work of letters. Saskatoon berries form the P, lobster the A, a fiddlehead the G, rhubarb the I, a Montreal bagel the O, cod the T, and salmon the U. *Speaking in Cod Tongues* serves this wild food as Canadian, while previewing one of Newman's central arguments: "Nationally, Canadian cuisine is heavily steeped in the use of wild and seasonal foods."[101] Whereas Johnson stresses the importance of international food trends in the renewed interest in local ingredients, Newman accepts this as the norm. This gestures toward a shift in thinking about local food in Canada, as well as Canadian food, that took place between 1995 and 2017.

How did restaurants represent this shift? Rosanna Caira's *Northern Bounty* contribution maps "The Evolution of Canadian Cuisine in Restaurants." Addressing the mid-1980s to 1990s, she writes: "In a matter of a decade, restaurateurs across the country have learned to sing the culinary praise of Canada. A mere decade ago, the chances of a restaurant promoting *Canadian* cuisine would have been not only unlikely, but highly improbable."[102] Most eateries would have never even thought that a thing called Canadian cuisine existed. Once a question and not a category, this changed in the 1990s when chefs began to cook what they called Canadian cuisine. Distinct from restaurants that combined food from elsewhere with North American staples – the likes of Chinese and Canadian restaurants serving stir-fried beef in the company of French fries, which Cho archives[103] – these new establishments looked to the wild in search of Canadian fare. Toronto's Canoe, opened in 1995, peddles pan-Canadian cuisine and is an influential example.[104]

Returning to how *la carte* signifies both a menu and a map, restaurants are spaces to construct, imagine, and represent national cuisines. The plate is a chef's flag, as Twitty phrases it. By the 1990s the romanticized visuals chronicled in Chapter 1 were gone. The Indigenous images, names, and places largely disappeared, but the ingredients, like Pacific salmon and fiddleheads, stayed. Caira's definition of Canadian cuisine, however, overlooks Indigenous influences. She writes: "Because Canada is a relatively young country that has opened its arms to various cultures from all over the world, a distinctly Canadian cuisine has never really emerged. Though initially much of our culinary heritage was shaped by British and French traditions, the influx of immigrants over the past four decades has left a strong culinary imprint."[105] But what about Indigenous imprints? Similarly, *Northern Bounty*'s conclusion mentions Indigenous ingredients, but not peoples. While some chapters credit Indigenous origins, others ignore them, continuing the narrative that Canada carries on European culinary traditions. Although *Northern Bounty* includes an essay about traditional native plant foods in BC, the book's only Indigenous contributor is Bertha Skye from the Ahtahkakoop Cree Nation in Saskatchewan.[106]

As Expo 67 exemplified, tourism is decisive in staging Canadian cuisine. Six years after, the *Ottawa Citizen* reported on the "Eat Canadian campaign," explaining that it "is based on the theory that tourists want to know they are in a foreign country experiencing something different."[107] An appetite for the local when options are increasingly global. The campaign, a collaboration between the Canadian Restaurant Association (CRA) and the federal trade department's travel industry branch, believed that "tourists – particularly the 36 million-plus Americans who visit Canada each year – should go home smacking their lips over more memorable meals than Kentucky fried chicken in Ottawa and New York cut steak in Alberta."[108] The campaign asserted that Canada has its own culinary canon distinct from the United States. And it wanted Americans to taste it: "We don't want them to eat the same food as they eat at home, but to go back saying 'Gee, that Canadian food is good.'"[109]

But what was Canadian food in 1973? The article cites Nova Scotia chowder, Winnipeg goldeye, poached British Columbia salmon, Ontario fruit and vegetables, and a medley of dishes from Quebec: pea soup, maple syrup pie, and *tourtière*, its famous meat pie. According to the campaign, "There has not been enough interest in developing Canadian identity in food and services."[110] Durrell Kent, then CRA's general manager, saw game as deserving a spot on menus, and the article mentions moose steaks: "Canada is known as an outdoors country, but it's illegal to serve game in a restaurant." Kent suggests "the commercial raising of buffalo and perhaps deer and moose, to provide game meat without raising the ire of conservationists. Wild game would remain taboo."[111] Meat is Chapter 9's main dish, but here I wish to emphasize the campaign's efforts to reframe restaurant ingredients as Canadian, similar to La Toundra. With funding from the federal government, the Canadian Restaurant Association debuted "clip-on cards for menus to advertise 'CanaDay' specials" in July 1973, drawing attention to the Canadian provenance of the ingredients on their plates. The restaurant industry sells food with a side of identity – culinary branding – and Canada was still in search of its brand. But one cannot talk about local foods or Canadian foods or what new Nordic means in Canada, I argue, without considering Indigenous foodways.

### Repair, Recuperate, Reconcile

Menus are contracts and restaurants hosts. They welcome guests and mount cultural experiences. They host stories, foods, and transactions. Restaurants are sites of cultural conflict, as well as accommodation. To read a menu from an Indigenous restaurant is to read more than the dishes on offer. It is to read how an Indigenous restaurant culturally negotiates its place in a settler-dominated city. It is to read the dishes as stories about Indigenous traditions, histories, and resistance, as examples of Indigenous resurgence. I assert that a menu, like the restaurant itself, is an example of what literary scholar Mary Louise Pratt terms a contact zone.[112] She coined the term "to refer to social spaces where cultures meet, clash, and grapple with each other, often in contexts of highly asymmetrical relations of power, such as colonialism, slavery, or their aftermaths as they are lived out in many parts of the world today."[113] Contact zones are spaces of colonial encounters, interactions, and negotiations. Spaces to establish relations and then to re-establish them. But these encounters are not equal. Power relations govern contact zones.[114] They are not removed from prevailing social and racial hierarchies, but they do provide spaces to forge new encounters and to renegotiate relations, to cook and eat back. Restaurants are contact zones. They are venues for cultural negotiation. This is especially true for Indigenous restaurants in a settler colonial, Canadian context.

The word restaurant shares its linguistic roots with the verb "to repair" or "recuperate."[115] The definition from the 1835 edition of the *Dictionnaire de L'Académie Française* reads: "RESTAURANT, adj., that which restores or repairs strength. *restorative remedy. restorative portion. restorative food.*"[116] Before it became a place to eat, a restaurant was a healthful and healing broth. Reconciliation, too, is based on restoration. If food was a tool of coercion and assimilation, as the Truth and Reconciliation Commission's report proves, then food is also a tool of resistance, restoration, and reconciliation. Of resurgence. Like a good broth, reconciliation is multi-layered. A broth may be mostly water, but seasoning it is an art. What separates a bad broth from a good one includes the individual quality of bones and vegetables – how fatty a bone, how shrivelled an onion, or how bossy a garlic clove – and how these flavours merge to become more than the sum of their parts. There is no one definitive recipe, and the role of time is of equal importance to the ingredients.

To reconcile means to bring something back, to make something whole again. It means to heal, but also to harmonize, to "restore friendly relations," or to settle a quarrel. The TRC's official mandate begins with "There is an emerging and compelling desire to put the events of the past behind us so that we can work towards a stronger and healthier future."[117] Although it does not define reconciliation, this description emphasizes recognizing, coping with, and overcoming the past. The rest of the mandate is: "The truth telling and reconciliation process as part of an overall holistic and comprehensive response to the Indian Residential School legacy is a sincere indication and acknowledgement of the injustices and harms experienced by Aboriginal people and the need for continued healing. This is a profound commitment to establishing new relationships embedded in mutual recognition and respect that will forge a brighter future."[118] Although the commission narrowed in on the Indian residential school system, its findings address Canada's history of settler colonialism at large. Furthermore, it makes clear that reconciliation is the responsibility of all Canadians, not only residential school survivors, their families and communities, as well as the school's former employees, but also "the people of Canada."[119]

When Ojibway Anishinaabe Justice Murray Sinclair, the commission's chairman, presented the final report, he announced that he was hopeful that the country was at the threshold of a new era:[120] the so-called Truth and Reconciliation era. But as Simpson makes clear, reconciliation is a state-controlled process.[121] In dialogue with Simpson, Billy-Ray Belcourt, a poet and literary scholar from Driftpile Cree Nation, calls reconciliation "an affective mess" that happens "at the expense of more radical projects like decolonization."[122] "Reconciliation," as Eve Tuck and Wayne Yang point out, "is about rescuing settler normalcy, about rescuing a settler future."[123] Decolonization destabilizes a settler-led perspective to centre Indigenous ones. Colonization started with land and so decolonization must also start with land.

Jeff Corntassel considers reconciliation one of three examples of what he calls "the politics of distraction." The other two are rights and resources. Instead, he prioritizes resurgence. "Processes of reconciliation," Corntassel writes, "are merely reinscribing the status quo; counter to reconciliation, *resurgence* takes the emphasis away from state frameworks of 'forgive and forget' back to re-localized, community-centered actions premised on reconnecting with land, culture and community."[124] Reconciliation only goes so far and yet,

I argue, has the potential to create awareness about not just cultural resurgence but political resurgence too.

Of the ninety-four Calls to Action, numbers 13 to 17 address language. The first calls "upon the federal government to acknowledge that Aboriginal rights include Aboriginal language rights."[125] One of the limits of reconciliation is that the word is English, a colonial language.[126] Reconciliation came from Latin to Late Middle English, via Old French: "from Latin re- 'back' (also expressing intensive force) + concilare 'bring together.'"[127] By suggesting that restaurants are venues for reconciliation, I do not imply that it is the responsibility of Indigenous chefs to reconcile. Instead, I argue that restaurants are contact zones that can host conversations about resurgence that can unsettle, that can decolonize. Consciously or not, Indigenous restaurants are expressions of and agents in shaping how Indigenous peoples are popularly represented in Canada. But beyond reconciliation, Indigenous restaurants are acts of resurgence. They reconnect Indigenous peoples with land and culture through food, and share stories about this reconnection through the dishes they serve. This also recalls the periods I define. The residential school system further suppressed Indigenous culinary knowledge by removing children from their families, cultures, and lands. The restaurants that have opened, first, since the last school closed and, second, after the Truth and Reconciliation Commission, thus, operate in different political landscapes.

Indigenous restaurants are diverse in terms of what they serve, the stories they tell, and the cultures they represent, as well as their staff, ingredients, prices, interiors and design, and customers. Indigenous ingredients and décor, or at least what have been imagined as such, have also been used in other eateries, such as the Tomahawk and Expo 67. Therefore, I focus on self-identified Indigenous restaurants in urban centres, namely Vancouver, Winnipeg, Edmonton, Toronto, and Ottawa. Although there have been Indigenous restaurants on reserves at least since the mid-1890s,[128] this book focuses on urban restaurants, as they are more explicitly venues for cultural negotiation and confrontations between Indigenous chefs and ingredients and Canadian settlers and regulations. There is no single blueprint for an Indigenous restaurant.

I loosely organize Indigenous restaurants in Canada according to three time periods. The first is 1971–96: from when Muckamuck opened in Vancouver to the end of the Indian residential school system. The second is 1997–2014: post-residential school, but pre-Truth and Reconciliation Commission. The third and final period is 2015 to the present: restaurants that have opened since the Truth and Reconciliation Commission published its final report. The following chapters give examples from all three periods, highlighting the various versions of Indigenous cuisines these restaurants construct.

Instead of ranking dishes in terms of authenticity, *Culinary Claims* focuses on the stories they tell. Stories of entangled histories of conflicts between food and land. Nor do I seek to offer a concrete definition of Indigenous cuisines. How does one even begin to summarize the cooking styles of a continent with vast geographical and cultural differences? Does one look only at what people cook and eat at home, or are restaurants the ultimate platform for defining cuisine? Can one understand Indigenous cuisines only with pre-contact ingredients, and ignore the influence of centuries of contact? That I have been switching back and forth between singular and plural is my way of avoiding having to attempt to define the diversity in historic and contemporary Indigenous foodways across Turtle Island. Instead, I am interested in how restaurants in Canada imagine and represent Indigenous cuisines and how these imaginations have changed based on social, political, and cultural shifts. I look at Indigenous restaurants as spaces of cultural representation and negotiation. As contact zones. As a medium for cooking back and for broadcasting counter narratives. As entanglements of ingredients and techniques and labour that claim and reclaim Indigenous plants, animals, dishes, and culture.

Although I discuss many restaurants, there are many others I do not, such as Miqmak Catering Indigenous Kitchen, Montreal's first year-round Indigenous restaurant opened by Mi'kmaw chef Norma Condo on 29 June 2019, Kelowna's Red Fox Club, which closed in 2020 after five years, casino restaurants like Calgary's Little Chief Hotel Restaurant on the Tsuut'ina Nation, and the long-running Kekuli Cafe in Merritt and Westbank, BC, which first opened in 2005.¹²⁹ Therefore, the chapters that follow are not a complete chronology, but rather an assemblage of restaurants, menus, and chefs that narrate various interpretations of what makes a restaurant Indigenous and how such restaurants negotiate their positions in the Canadian culinary landscape. How they speak back to settler stories.

chapter four

# An Edible Exhibition

"Sun dried chopped seaweed," "Indian style smoked salmon," and "Cold raspberry soup." The front of the postcard-size menu showcases baskets and bowls decorated with carvings, shaped like animals, and bursting with bread, fish, and greens (Figure 4.1).[1] One cradles fiddleheads and corn. The photograph's back lists the Muckamuck Restaurant's menu from circa 1975 (Figure 4.2): "Northwest Coast Native Indian Food" introduces this Vancouver restaurant. At Expo 67, fiddleheads represented Canada; here, they typify "Northwest Coast Native Indian Food." The "Indian bannock bread" is "baked fresh daily." The menu also lists a "Wind and sun dried salmon appetizer" and salmon barbecued over open alder fires. There are oolichans and trout. With salmon prepared multiple ways, three other fish, and four kinds of shellfish, seafood dominates the Muckamuck's brief menu. But the restaurant's representation of Northwest Coast Native Food also calls on duck, rabbit, and "meats."

The same year that Alice Waters launched Chez Panisse, 1971, the Muckamuck Restaurant opened in Vancouver.[2] It was one of the first Indigenous-themed restaurants in urban Canada, if not the first. Muckamuck was popular, licensed, open seven days a week, and located at 1724 Davie Street. In fact, the history of Indigenous restaurants in Vancouver begins with this one address. Two blocks from Stanley Park, 1724 Davie Street consecutively housed three different restaurants – first the Muckamuck, from 1971 to

An Edible Exhibition 117

Figure 4.1. Front of "Muckamuck Restaurant: Northwest Coast Native Indian food," c. 1975, AM1519-: 2011-045.1, box: 632-A-02, Pamphlet Collection, City of Vancouver Archives.

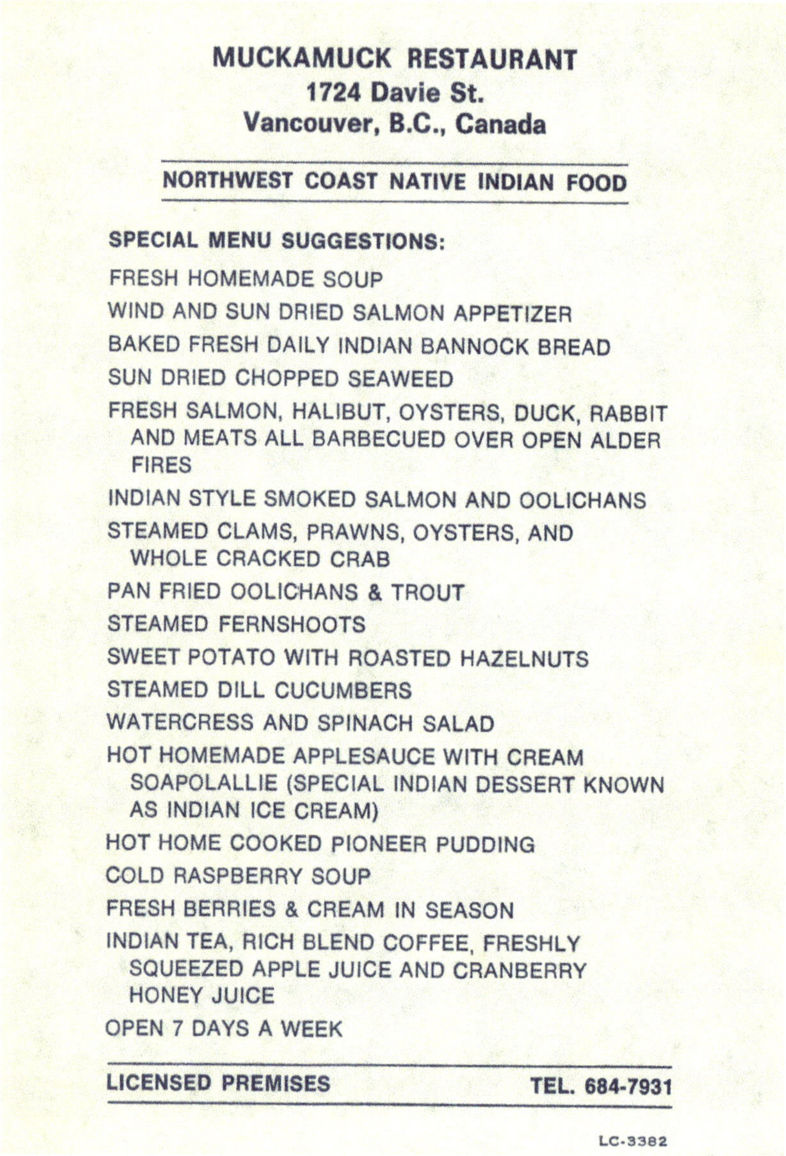

**MUCKAMUCK RESTAURANT**
1724 Davie St.
Vancouver, B.C., Canada

NORTHWEST COAST NATIVE INDIAN FOOD

**SPECIAL MENU SUGGESTIONS:**
FRESH HOMEMADE SOUP
WIND AND SUN DRIED SALMON APPETIZER
BAKED FRESH DAILY INDIAN BANNOCK BREAD
SUN DRIED CHOPPED SEAWEED
FRESH SALMON, HALIBUT, OYSTERS, DUCK, RABBIT AND MEATS ALL BARBECUED OVER OPEN ALDER FIRES
INDIAN STYLE SMOKED SALMON AND OOLICHANS
STEAMED CLAMS, PRAWNS, OYSTERS, AND WHOLE CRACKED CRAB
PAN FRIED OOLICHANS & TROUT
STEAMED FERNSHOOTS
SWEET POTATO WITH ROASTED HAZELNUTS
STEAMED DILL CUCUMBERS
WATERCRESS AND SPINACH SALAD
HOT HOMEMADE APPLESAUCE WITH CREAM SOAPOLALLIE (SPECIAL INDIAN DESSERT KNOWN AS INDIAN ICE CREAM)
HOT HOME COOKED PIONEER PUDDING
COLD RASPBERRY SOUP
FRESH BERRIES & CREAM IN SEASON
INDIAN TEA, RICH BLEND COFFEE, FRESHLY SQUEEZED APPLE JUICE AND CRANBERRY HONEY JUICE
OPEN 7 DAYS A WEEK

**LICENSED PREMISES**    **TEL. 684-7931**

LC-3382

Figure 4.2. Back of "Muckamuck Restaurant: Northwest Coast Native Indian food," c. 1975, AM1519-: 2011-045.1, box: 632-A-02, Pamphlet Collection, City of Vancouver Archives.

1981, then the Quilicum, which opened in 1985, and the Liliget Feast House, from 1995 to 2007. A condo building now stands at the same address, a typical Vancouver story.

Unlike the Quilicum and the Liliget Feast House, Muckamuck was not Indigenous-owned. However, it marketed itself as Indigenous. As educator Janet Mary Nicol reveals, "Three white American owners, Jane Erickson, Teresa Bjornson and Doug Christmas [sic][,] also had investments in art galleries and other restaurants in California and British Columbia."[3] Although the owners were settlers, the restaurant hired Indigenous staff. Similar to La Toundra, Muckamuck was a Canadian imagination of Indigenous food cultures. Why did "three white American owners" open the Muckamuck? "Muck-a-Muck House started as an art gallery," a July 1972 *Ottawa Journal* article reports, "but soon turned into a work of culinary art."[4] Teresa Bjornson helped transform what was the Ace Gallery's basement into a "unique" restaurant.[5] "We just wanted to get some things together for an exhibit of Indian foods," she explained.[6] The idea was to serve "Indian food" to patrons, showcasing ingredients and relatively unknown dishes. But the gallery ran into issues with the Vancouver licensing department, and so "From there it was a short step to turning the basement into a restaurant."[7]

For its first couple of years it was called the Muck-a-Muck House.[8] Summarizing its history in 1974, the *Gazette* recounted that Erickson and Bjornson were both "amateur cooks," and reported their ages (twenty-eight and twenty-five) and, curiously, their relationship status ("single").[9] Although Chrismas owned the Ace Gallery, his name does not appear in these articles.[10] He stayed behind the scenes and described Erickson as the Muckamuck's "liaison between the white and Indian communities."[11] Nonetheless, Chrismas owned 51 per cent of the restaurant; and as one article put it, "The Muckamuck workers hardly knew what he looked like until they decided to join a union."[12] In any case, the gallery came first, then the idea for an "Indian foods" exhibition, and finally, its institutionalization as a restaurant.

The word "muckamuck" comes from nineteenth-century Chinook Jargon – also called Chinook Wawa – a mix of Indigenous languages, including Nuu-chah-nulth, Lower Chinook, and Salishan, with English and French.[13] *The Canadian Encyclopedia* translates muckamuck as a lot of food. Press coverage in the 1970s provided a range of definitions; one article wrote that it meant "food in the Chinook tongue."[14] The *Oxford English Dictionary* identifies muckamuck as shorthand for "high muck-a-muck," meaning "A person of great importance or self-importance."[15] "Highmuckymuck" possibly refers to "someone who sits at head table."[16] Just like the staged outdoor photograph of Muckamuck dishes, the restaurant's name aims to signify its "Nativeness."

Before the restaurant could open, Bjornson and Erickson had to define the food it would serve: "Indian food." As the *Ottawa Journal* explains, "The first problem was lack of information about traditional Indian foods and cooking methods. 'Not many of the local Indian people keep up the traditional cooking,' said Miss Bjornson. 'We went through the whole province trying to get recipes typical of many tribes.' Traditional cooking implements were also in short supply. 'They don't make them any more … Things like boiling baskets are almost extinct.'"[17] Bjornson suggested that it was a choice for Indigenous communities not to "keep up" traditional cooking, thus overlooking the history of regulations enforcing assimilation and restricting the continuity of Indigenous foodways. She matter-of-factly announced: "Many of the original Indian dishes just aren't done these days."[18] In addition to playing the part of culinary researchers on reserves, Bjornson and Erickson consulted an anthropologist and botanist at the University of British Columbia and read "a detailed old report of American Indian ethnology."[19]

The press viewed the Muckamuck's decision to hire Indigenous staff, "Indian women and young men given to wearing headbands or broad-rimmed hats with feathers,"[20] as a commitment to "authenticity." It omitted the attendant power dynamic between white owners – those writing the paycheques and drafting the menu – and Indigenous employees working for an hourly wage. Beyond lending the Muckamuck an air of "authenticity," hiring Indigenous staff provided economic benefits. Management hired employees through the Canada Manpower Training Program, "offering to 'train' First Nations people to work in the restaurant and in return, received 75 per cent of the trainee's wages from the government."[21]

In addition to knowing which ingredients to use, sourcing them was a challenge. "Dried meat and dried fish were too difficult to come by," said Bjornson.[22] In 1972 the restaurant did not have a menu; instead, it listed dishes on a blackboard. It did demand that its ingredients were local, including berries like salmonberries, salal, wild blueberries, black currants, and elderberries. What the restaurant was not able to gather or pick, it purchased from "local Indians," including fish. However, it quickly became aware of how regulations determine what is on the menu. Bjornson explained, "We know of a man who could supply us with all the mountain goat we could eat – but we're not allowed to serve it."[23] In 1972, Muck-a-Muck House was only allowed to sell venison from Norway, which it couldn't afford.

Government regulations affected not only what was on the plate but also the plate itself. "Naturally we wanted wooden dishes and big serving bowls, in the traditional style. But the department of health said no way – wood is frowned upon because it can't be thoroughly cleaned," said Bjornson.[24] This led one review to conclude: "So Muck-a-Muck House is a little more like an ordinary restaurant and a little less traditional."[25] Either the regulations changed or the restaurant ignored them, because in 1975 helpings were "lavishly arrayed in large wood bowls individually created by Indian woodcarvers."[26] These are the vessels the 1975 menu depicts. By 1977 the wooden bowls were off the table (again or still), but goat was now on it. Restaurant critic James Barber crowned the goat ribs one of his favourite dishes: "the finest, gamiest tasting chops – the taste of smoke, rosemary, a wild night in the forest, it's dark and 'we've only just got the fire going.' Me Tarzan. You Jane …"[27] His performative praise is over the top, typical of cultural stereotypes in restaurant reviews at the time.

By 1975 the Muckamuck had a printed menu, either for diners or marketing or both. It is not organized strictly according to European or North American culinary codes, which is to say category headings like appetizer, main, or dessert. However, the dishes appear in this sequence. It does not provide details beyond dish names. Nor does the photograph supply information about what the dishes include. You may assume the ingredients are from the Northwest coast, where the photograph captures them outside, but the menu does not confirm their provenance. How is the "Watercress and spinach salad" dressed? Do the "Pan fried oolichans" come with a side, or should one perhaps order "Sweet potato with roasted hazelnuts" or "Steamed dill cucumbers"? What are "Hot home cooked pioneer pudding" and "Indian tea"?[28] This menu needs a server. It is the server's task to announce the soup of the day, the available meats, and what Indian tea is. What is clear, however, is that Muckamuck's menu positions these dishes as "Northwest Coast Native Indian Food." The categorization of "Native" dominates their culinary details.

Early press emphasized the restaurant's story over its food, but in 1975 critic Sheila McCook prioritized its cooking. Her review made it into a handful of newspapers and unveils who the Muckamuck attracted: "Diners whose taste buds venture beyond ketchup and mayonnaise; whose idea of restaurant elegance is more exotic than white linen and chandeliers; who don't reel back when presented salmon head, tail and belly."[29] She ranked the soups – duck, salmon, and clam chowder – "superb starting points for any meal." Labelling the vegetable repertoire "familiar and exotic," she listed "roasted hazelnuts, steamed fernshoots, dill carrots and cucumber, corn on the cob, boiled onions." Out of the bunch, fernshoots – also known as fiddleheads – presumably portray the "exotic."

Another dish McCook considered exotic enough to spell out to readers was made from soapberries. It appeared on the 1975 menu as "Hot homemade applesauce with cream soapolallie (special Indian dessert known as Indian ice cream)." She compared them to huckleberries, describing how they are "whipped up with sugar into a tasty froth."[30] On their own, soapberries are bitter; sugar tames them, sweetening them into dessert. McCook also says that "There's juniper berry tea for those who like to polish off their meal with authenticity. For those who don't, there's wine and beer."[31] This answers what Indian tea is, but also reveals the value of authenticity for critics, as well as the restaurant's ability to accommodate a diner's thirst for wine. In addition to the 1975 menu, other dishes came and went: the likes of pickled burdock root, juniper duck, herring eggs, and barbecued oysters that are "quite different to normal restaurant food."[32]

Some ingredients like "grease" were pushed off the menu. "Grease is extracted from oolichan, a fish, and offered as a side dish for those preferring their soup authentic, if oily," explained McCook. "It's optional, as is the sun-dried seaweed, to be sprinkled on food for a flavorful, salty effect."[33] To make this seasoning optional is to compromise. It is to cater to cultural expectations. Oolichan, a smelt-like fish also known as candlefish, raises the issue of who can stomach what and how to navigate discrepancies between one diner's delicious and another's disgusting. One review spells out the decision to offer grease on the side: "Why not offer their customers a nice authentic soup flavored with the grease rendered from the oily little fish called the oolichan? No, their Indian cook warned them. They wouldn't like it. Oh yes, the two white women said, they would. So the cook made the soup with the oolichan grease and the women took a spoonful and they've never tried its sharp fishy flavor again."[34] As most Muckamuck diners would have been unfamiliar with grease, to make it a side allowed the curious to try it without treading too far outside their culinary comfort zones.

McCook's review also points to the important role servers play. In addition to taking orders and escorting dishes to the tables, they act as ambassadors. This is not true of all restaurants, but when a menu is sparse or a dish unfamiliar, it is the server's job to mediate. To take on the role of a culinary guide, an interlocutor between chefs and customers, between kitchen and table. As McCook wrote, "Almost everyone who comes to the Muck-a-Muck has questions to ask and the employees, all Indians, take the time to explain how each dish is cooked, what it tastes like, even how to eat it. They assist in making choices from the menu, encouraging the adventurous while steering more timid diners toward the European-like dishes."[35] In addition to interpreting the menu, the servers educated diners about Northwest Coast Native cuisine.

For many, the Muckamuck was a novel experience. A 1984 article, published in Ottawa, Montreal, and Calgary newspapers and titled "Come to the Muckamuck: It Means Food. *Real Canadian* Food" (original italics), acknowledged the need to explain to readers what this was. "The Muckamuck's menu is Indian," it wrote. "Not the Prairie's pemmican or stewed rabbit or wild rice. But Pacific Northwest Indian: barbecued salmon, smoked black Alaska cod, whole cracked crab, scallops in the shell, watercress salad, fried bread and mountain huckleberry preserves."[36] In addition to their research, Bjornson and Erickson relied on their staff's knowledge. Mary Wilson, from the Haida Nation, was the restaurant's first chef.[37] Having previously worked on fishing boats and at Vancouver's Hotel Georgia, at the Muckamuck she consulted the menu and introduced Bjornson and Erickson to salmon soup and oolichan grease.[38] As Bjornson summarizes, "We always wanted things super authentic, but Mary Wilson said it just wouldn't be practical to serve bear fat or seal grease."[39] It was Wilson who encouraged them to offer grease on the side, which was perhaps also an effort to shield her culinary culture from those who would dismiss it as an acquired taste.

McCook, in conclusion, recommended the Muckamuck. In addition to her own approval, she chronicled other endorsements: "The Muck-a-Muck is 'one of the most interesting restaurants in Vancouver,' according to Anne Hardy, in the book 'Where to Eat in Canada, 1974/75,' and 'highly recommended' in Chuck Davis's 'Guide to Vancouver.'"[40] More importantly, McCook stressed that diners approved. She also indicated "Indian groups" have granted it their support.[41] Another article repeated this sentiment: "the restaurant is genuine enough that the Union of B.C. Indian Chiefs meeting in Vancouver recently held a dinner at the Muckamuck and pronounced themselves pleased."[42] Reviewers valued that Indigenous diners also appreciated the Muckamuck. This made it on to their list of criteria by which they pronounced the restaurant "authentic," suggesting that the Muckamuck targeted both "insiders" and those unfamiliar with this cuisine and thus "outsiders," to whom the restaurant would register as "ethnic."

## Gone Fishing

Three years before McCook's review, in 1972, the Muckamuck ran an advertisement in the *Vancouver Sun*.[43] On the bottom left side of the page is a photograph of a man with shoulder-length hair perched barefoot on two rocks. He wears a knitted coat, and his gaze follows his left arm as he studies where his fishing spear breaks the water. Waves ripple in the background, and, to the fisherman's left, text promotes the restaurant. Spelled in capital letters, the first paragraph is in Chinook Jargon, the second in English: "Food house offering North West Coast Indian Food. Much is Rare and is going. Open now." A third paragraph reads, "All foods prepared and served by North West Coast Indian People." The advertisement stresses the identity of the restaurant's employees rather than its owners, and stages a cultural context for experiencing a Muckamuck meal. As reviews reveal, diners ate it up. One proclaimed, "Everybody is West coast Indian – cooks, waitresses, waiters, everybody."[44]

This 1972 advertisement does not disclose the photographer; however, the Muckamuck has not been the only one to use it. The United States Department of Agriculture's Forest Service includes it on its website with the caption "Alsea fisherman."[45] And the Government of Canada features it on its "First Nations in Canada" page.[46] Without a caption, the photograph appears next to the subsection "The Hudson's Bay Company." According to the CBC, it shows a Nootka (and not Alsea) man spearfishing on Vancouver Island.[47] Once again, the photographer's name is missing, but it was no other than the famed American Edward S. Curtis. He took this image in 1915 for Volume 11 – "The Nootka. The Haida" – of his magnum opus *The North American Indian* (Figure 4.3).[48]

Financed by the banker J. Pierpont Morgan, Curtis published his twenty-volume series between 1907 and 1930.[49] Theodore Roosevelt penned the foreword and praised the project as "a real asset in American achievement."[50] Despite this celebration, Americanist Mick Gidley describes the central flaw in Curtis's approach: he hammed up "the 'primitive' otherness" of his subjects, typifying "the fraught and complex history of 'white' endeavors to represent Native life."[51] Curtis's photographs were romanticized imaginations of Indigenous life, what Francis called imaginary "Indians" and King dead ones.[52] This is not to overlook the agency of those posing, but Curtis's staged re-enactments of pre-contact life tell

Figure 4.3. Edward S. Curtis, "Nootka method of spearing," from *The North American Indian*, 1915, Charles Deering McCormick Library of Special Collections, Northwestern University Libraries.

more about Curtis himself than the people in front of his camera. Nonetheless, different eras have looked at his work through the distinct lenses of their times, a timeline that English studies scholar Mathilde Arrivé summarizes: "applauded in the 1910s, they were neglected in the 1920s, literally forgotten between 1930 and 1960, showered with praise in the 1970s, repudiated in the 1980s and ultimately collected and widely exhibited from the 1990s onward."[53] The 1970s revival of Indigenous culture pushed Curtis to centre stage: he was now considered "a defender of Native rights and even an icon of resistance and a counterculture hero."[54] And this was the wave of meaning that the Muckamuck advertisement was hoping to ride.

In addition to Indigenous revival, the renewed popularity of Curtis's catalogue in the 1970s also tapped into the period's interest in so-called primitive art. The term emerged at the beginning of the twentieth century and by mid-century had achieved both acceptance and popularity, as exemplified by its monetary value and even a museum of its own in New York City.[55] Similar to labels like "ethnic" and "authentic," "primitive" is relational and does not exist in isolation. "This is a category created for their circulation, exhibition and consumption outside their original habitats," writes anthropologist Fred Meyers about objects branded "primitive."[56] It is telling that the Muckamuck assigned to a staged 1915 photograph the task of representing Northwest Coast Indian culture and its foods in 1972. The image circles back to the Muckamuck's original idea to present an "exhibition of Indian foods." To exhibit foods disconnects their display from their everyday edibility.

Aligned with the advertisement's text, Curtis's photograph frames a man fishing as his community always had. The image hangs out of time, suggesting continuity and the reign of tradition, but by 1915 there were strict laws regulating BC's booming fishing industry. This confirms Mark Cronlund Anderson and Carmen L. Robertson's argument that "the press throughout Canadian history has cast Aboriginals as mired in an unprogressive and non-evolving past, as if they exist outside linear time."[57] The image centres settler time.

Today it is illegal to spearfish in the Vancouver metropolitan area as well as on Vancouver Island.[58] The 1888 fisheries regulations specified that "Indians shall, at all times, have liberty to fish for the purpose of providing food for themselves but not for sale, barter or traffic, by any means other than with drift nets, or spearing."[59] These regulations allowed fishing for subsistence only. Such laws furthered the Canadian government's efforts to control and constrict Indigenous people. "This initiative formed part of the underlying logic behind prohibiting the spearing of salmon," explains Bill Paranteau, "which was seen by Fishery and Indian Affairs officers as part of the wandering life characterized by indolence and vice."[60] The Muckamuck's 1972 advertisement pictures an imagined past rather than the fishing conditions and laws of the time. As part of 1970s ethnic revival, the Muckamuck's employment of Curtis's photograph was a celebratory gesture of Northwest Indigenous culture. Yet, reminiscent of the Canadian Pacific Railway menus, it was a romanticized one.

## The Line

With ten tables "similar to large picnic tables," the Muckamuck was mid-sized. Because it did not take reservations, diners frequently queued.[61] Despite its basement location, the restaurant was bright. Fascinatingly, one review pointed out that many customers mistook it as Japanese: "This is because the cedar dining tables are at a low level over scooped-out wells where diners dangle their feet."[62] Although the first Japanese restaurant in Canada only opened in 1955 – the House of Fuji-Matsui in Toronto – by the Muckamuck's time customers were more familiar with Japanese restaurant décor than "Native."[63] How, then, did this one look? Small stones carpeted the floor, outfitting the Muckamuck with a beachy atmosphere layered over a soundtrack that alternated between "Indian chants and country."[64] Fir trunks stood tall like totem poles.[65] Cans emptied of salmon and filled with sand served as ashtrays, contributing to the "lost-in-the-forest picknicky" atmosphere.[66] Ceremonial blankets draped the walls, which McCook described as ancient "magnificent, colorful wall hangings."[67] The rest of the restaurant dressed in "subdued, natural colors." Partially visible from the dining area, the kitchen provided further visuals: cooks "slowly turning their fish, meat and fowl over alderwood cinders."[68]

From its food to its décor, the words unique and unusual surface again and again. In 1974 the *National Post* called the Muckamuck "Delicious and highly unusual, even to the smoked salmon bellies and raspberry soup."[69] In 1975 McCook stressed, "The décor is unusual and attractive."[70] A couple of years later, the *Ottawa Journal* hailed the Muckamuck "an unusual place."[71] Despite being overwhelmed by the "gargantuan" portions and having ordered too much – salad, clam chowder, barbecued salmon, and the "hot, spicy, and potent" "Indian answer to Irish coffee" – the critic concluded his review positively: "A different and thoroughly enjoyable evening."[72]

News of the Muckamuck travelled south of the border.[73] Robert Trumbull, then chief *New York Times* Canada correspondent, recommended it in 1977 – particularly, its barbecued rabbit and Dungeness crab. "Tops as a personal favourite," he exclaimed.[74] In 1978, the *Atlanta Constitution* shared a bannock recipe – "an excellent complement to fish or rich foods" – from a reader who had sampled it at this "unique and delightful Indian restaurant in Vancouver."[75] In the 1970s, it was not every day that a restaurant in Canada made it into American newspapers, but one columnist and regular was not pleased about this international praise. Complaining of frequent line-ups, James Barber blamed them on when "Time magazine discovered the Muckamuck and all those expense accounts from Toronto, Chicago and Los Angeles went and told all the other expense accounts."[76] Despite the lines, Barber crowned the Muckamuck "the sort of restaurant we can all be proud of, without Time Magazine's accolades."[77]

When the *Minneapolis Star* published a profile of the Muckamuck in July 1978, the restaurant was temporarily closed because of "labour problems."[78] The article did not elaborate; instead, it focused on how the Muckamuck had popularized "Chinook food" and shared three recipes from Bjornson and Erickson: "Muckamuck watercress and spinach salad," "Muckamuck's baked whole wheat bannock," and "Muckamuck clam chowder" (which, surprisingly, calls for canned clams).[79] This suggests that, labour problems or not, the Muckamuck was worth visiting, or at least its recipes were worth preparing at home.

A photograph on 12 August 1978 records a protest, where Debbie Mearns, then president of the Vancouver Indian Centre, walks together with Christina Prince, the strike leader.[80] Behind them Ethel Gardner carries a sign with a photograph of Doug Chrismas and the word "Joker." To her left a protestor carries the sign: "Walk the Muckamuck Walk. Sign a 1st Contract SORWUC Local." SORWUC stands for the Service, Office, and Retail Workers' Union of Canada, "an independent, grassroots, socialist-feminist union,"[81] and was the union the Muckamuck staff joined. As one former employee explained, "racial issues emerged when employees realized that the owners were getting rich off Native culture."[82]

A 1980 profile in another Minneapolis paper – the *Tribune* – further detailed the "labour problems." Journalist Catherine Watson summarized that Indigenous employees went on strike after a quarrel over scheduling, wages, and the right to unionize.[83] She reported that the Muckamuck closed the moment the strike began and remained shuttered for seven months. It then reopened with new employees, also Native Americans, but without having settled the dispute. Quoting the union's vice president, Muggs Sigurgeirson, Watson surveys the employees' chief complaint: "that 'Native American culture was being exploited to make money,' while Native American employees were not benefitting sufficiently."[84] In an effort to report both sides, Watson quoted the Muckamuck's manager, Suzzy Selbst, who claimed that the union "exploits the native peoples by living off their problems."[85] The *Minneapolis Tribune* informed potential American diners what to expect should they show up: "The restaurant is still open, the strike is still officially on … But the restaurant's advertising doesn't indicate this … out-of-town visitors, drawn by curiosity and the restaurant's reputation, are likely to be surprised."[86] The review did not advise against eating at the Muckamuck; instead, it informed tourists of what they might encounter, leaving it to them to decide whether or not to cross the line.

Janet Mary Nicol was a "regular on the Muckamuck picket line."[87] In a 1997 article she quotes union organizer Ethel Gardner, a Stó:lō member of the Skwah First Nation, as declaring, "being in a union is the only way we can guarantee that our rights as workers will be respected."[88] Through an employment agency, Gardner got a job in the cold kitchen, making drinks and salads.[89] As she recounts, the working conditions were questionable. "The cook was charged for getting the soup burnt and I was fined for leaving the bannock out overnight," she remembers.[90] Gardner voiced additional complaints: "Breaks were few, if any ... Employees were suspended two weeks at a time for not attending ... [staff] meetings, even if it was their day off."[91] In addition to the usual grievances associated with restaurant work, Gardner disclosed: "We are also told that we must wear Native jewellery and if not we are badgered about not being proud of our culture."[92] This repeats the kind of clothing regulations that the Banff Indian Days had enforced. According to the Muckamuck's management, it was not enough for Indigenous people to work at the restaurant, they had to dress in a way that performed and flaunted their Indigeneity, as defined by the settler owners.

Gardner informed the employment agency that she wanted to quit, but a counsellor suggested she join a union, recommending the SORWUC. She did exactly that. As Nicol writes, employees specifically selected it, "a feminist union ... formed with a primary goal to organize women in industries neglected by trade unions."[93] On 21 and 23 February and 29 March 1978, SORWUC "launched charges of unfair labour practices on behalf" of Muckamuck's employees. Gardner was fired 23 February.[94] After the union's certification in March, Christina Prince fleshed out the racialized tensions at work: "management had told workers they 'should be happy' to have a job because of their race."[95] Eighteen of the twenty-one employees joined the union, the majority of which voted to strike, and the picket line formed on 1 June 1978 (Figures 4.4, 4.5, and 4.6).[96]

In addition to rallying for better working conditions and wages, the picket line drew attention to issues related to Indigenous civil rights, which take on an accent of their own in Vancouver. Unlike

Figure 4.4. Sean Griffin, "Muckamuck strike opening," 2 June 1978, Pacific Tribune Photograph Collection, MSC160-378_15, Simon Fraser University Digitized Collections.

Figure 4.5. Sean Griffin, "Muckamuck restaurant strike begins," 4 June 1978, Pacific Tribune Photograph Collection, MSC160-380_2A, Simon Fraser University Digitized Collections.

Figure 4.6. Sean Griffin, "Muckamuck strikers march, downtown Vancouver," 12 August 1978, Pacific Tribune Photograph Collection, MSC160-396_03, Simon Fraser University Digitized Collections.

other regions in Canada, treaties are limited in British Columbia.[97] The strike lasted a total of three years. Picketers confronted potential diners, as the *Minneapolis Tribune* article had warned. As at all picket lines, the decision to cross was an ethical one. Gardner recalls the reaction of one woman she handed a leaflet to: "[She] stopped on her tracks, mouth dropped, and eyes big, exclaimed, after reading a few words or sentences of the leaflet, 'I don't believe it! Is this true? If it is, we can't eat here!' I reassured her that it was true, and let her know that she would be confronted with another leaflet inside. She went to another restaurant."[98] Business suffered, and diners who did cross the line no longer had to wait for a table at what had once been a bustling restaurant.

As interpretations of Curtis's photographs in the 1970s championed the revival of Native American culture, despites its shortcomings, the Muckamuck is also connected to this wider revival. The 1970s marked a "Native American Renaissance," particularly in the field of literature but, also, in culture and political activism. Thanks to Chrismas, Andy Warhol ate at the Muckamuck. In 1976 Chrismas threw "a spectacular Indian banquet" in the artist's honour.[99] Warhol was in town to exhibit new work. From November 1976 to March 1977, *Andy Warhol: The American Indian Series* was on view, first at the Ace Gallery in Vancouver and then in Los Angeles.[100] Spotlighting Oglala Lakota Russell Means, the American Indian Movement's first director, Warhol crafted a series of prints, posters, paintings, and drawings in his signature bright colours. Because he wished to visit the University of British Columbia's Museum of Anthropology, Chrismas asked Haida sculptor Bill Reid to give Warhol a tour, which he did.[101] Reporting on the occasion, the *Vancouver Sun* wrote: "The dignified, soft-spoken Reid and the aging *neif* share a common interest: Warhol collects Northcoast Indian art, 'because I have always liked it.'"[102]

In 1978, the constellation of Chrismas, Warhol, and Means acquired a new meaning. Around the beginning of the strike, Chrismas invited Means to Vancouver to meet with Muckamuck employees, and Means gave them the advice of forming a co-op to buy out the owners and make the restaurant their own.[103] However, they did not have the funds to do so. Assuming the role of negotiator, Means bolstered the Muckamuck and the Indigenous strike-breakers, as well as those on the picket line. One paper reported SORWUC's account of Means's role "There was a telegram in support of the scabs in the window of the Muckamuck from Russell Means … The strikers did not feel Means was against them as he pointed his fingers at the owners and said *You treat these people properly.*"[104] The outcome of the strike and the restaurant's closure prove otherwise, but Means's involvement also connects the Muckamuck to the American Indian Movement.

Nickel sketches out the conventional timeline of Red Power – a "decade-long Indian activist movement" in the United States: its beginning was the 1969 occupation of Alcatraz by the pan-Indigenous group Indians of All Tribes and its end the 1978 Long Walk in July.[105] But this timeline shortens and simplifies. "This limited temporal and geographic definition of Red Power," asserts Nickel, "ignores the ways in which radical ideologies and people moved across borders and reshaped the movement."[106] Furthermore, its timeline is less important than its aims, which were tribal sovereignty, self-determination, and the recognition of treaty rights, aims that crossed the Canada–United States border to unite Indigenous activists beyond nation-state lines.

Four and a half months into the strike, in October 1978, Chrismas and Erickson debuted a new business on Davie Street where the Ace Gallery had been: Chilcotin Bar Seven. By now, Bjornson had sold her shares "because she was upset by the accusations of racism."[107] The Muckamuck was closed at this point, but this new eatery also bore an Indigenous name. It called itself after BC's Chilcotin region, which, in turn, is named after the Tsilhqot'in (Chilcotin): "people of the red river."[108] The name did not preview the menu, and Chilcotin Bar Seven sparked headlines like "Cowboys lasso Muckamuck" and "Muckamuck goes cowboy in bid to beat strike."[109] In the former article, the *Vancouver Sun* published a theatrical opening: "The clump of cowboy boots has replaced the sound of moccasins on pebbles. It could be called Showdown on Davie, but it's not your typical late-night Western. In this case, the Indians are on strike."[110] More than seventy picketers raised their voices at the opening, drawing further attention to the strike, as well as to the cultural insensitivity of opening a cowboy-themed restaurant in the midst of a strike led by Indigenous employees. In their defence, Erickson explained that they had always viewed the Muckamuck as a British Columbia restaurant, but it was impossible to serve beef because the Muckamuck specialized in "authentic Indian fare."[111] This recalls Banff Indian Days' demand for bison over beef. The picketers were not amused. An article in the *Times Colonist* adduced a SORWUC spokesperson who "accused the owners of hiring mostly non-native workers, clad in cowboy shirts and boots, and hanging cow hides on the walls 'in an attempt to dispel the image of the original Muckamuck.'"[112] A *S.O.R.W.U.C. Newsletter* issue called the décor "quite tacky – pink lights, red walls and a cowboy atmosphere that reminds one picketer of howdy-doody."[113] Like a mechanical bull ride, Chilcotin Bar Seven did not last long.

The Muckamuck reopened in December 1978 with new employees. As Gardner mentioned, management fought back with its own leaflet, as well as editorials, including one penned by four Muckamuck employees, cook Florence Differ included, which the *Richmond Review* published. "To say that we were being exploited is so far from the truth. As a matter of fact, we are proud to be native and proud to be part of Muckamuck, that serves Indian food, whereby the general public have an opportunity to enjoy some of our superb native food," the four wrote.[114] Additionally, they pointed out that the Muckamuck sources many ingredients from Indigenous people – from soapberries to herring eggs and from oolichan grease to smoked salmon – and the strike wreaked financial losses on these producers. "If we destroy Muckamuck," the editorial concluded, "we only destroy ourselves."[115] This demonstrates the strike's complex layers. To some, it was confusing to witness Indigenous employees both in the restaurant and on the picket line, making it unclear whom to support.

A week after Chilcotin Bar Seven opened, the *Vancouver Sun*'s business writer, Eleanor Boyle, penned a controversial opinion piece claiming that "Both sides' failing victimize Muckamuck." Boyle argued that the Muckamuck is undeniably using "the culture to make money … But so are the Indian workers at the restaurant using their Indian-ness to make money, 'exploiting' their own culture."[116] This repeated the Muckamuck manager's critique. Boyle argued that the Muckamuck "should also be spared from crucifixion for hundreds of years of Canadian neglect of native people."[117] On behalf of the striking employees, Prince penned a response, asserting that their complaint was not that the "owners are using the culture to make money," but instead that the employees were "constantly being reminded that the owners have done a lot for natives."[118] Directly responding to Boyle, Prince wrote: "It's true native people have been exploited for hundreds of years, but there's no desire or intention on our part to have the Muckamuck owners 'crucified' for it."[119] What started as a dispute over working conditions quickly became a larger debate about responsibility and the ongoing legacies of colonialism.

The Muckamuck strike aligned with other issues related to Indigenous rights. For example, in December 1978 Debbie Mearns delivered a speech at a public demonstration, stating: "The Muckamuck strikers deserve a lot of respect from us. They have never been against the idea of a gourmet-Indian food restaurant ... What those workers ask for is simply to be treated as any other workers in the industry."[120] Aligning the strikers with the wider community, she argued: "we all must become involved or we'll continue to be pushed around."[121] Her words underlined how the strike reflected Indigenous peoples' access to Canada's labour sector and the challenges they faced, including negative stereotypes that were harnessed to justify exploitative working conditions. The strike is also a reminder of how colonial threats to Indigenous food sovereignty are what created a need for wage labour in the first place.

As Mearns's speech demonstrates, news about the strike travelled beyond the culinary world. The Union of BC Indian Chiefs leant their voice to the debate, siding with the strikers because the "problems being experienced here by our people are the same problems we have been experiencing all over B.C. for 100 years. The owners of the Muckamuck exploit our resources – Indian work, Indian culture, Indian foods – yet refuse to treat our people fairly."[122] Erickson responded with a "sad heart."[123] In a letter addressed to the president of the BC Indian Chiefs' Union, George Manuel, Erickson wrote that the Muckamuck prioritized Indigenous peoples, but "was not a company whose purpose was to provide donations to the Indian community."[124] She lamented that the owners of a "Japanese-owned French restaurant" near the Muckamuck were not accused of exploiting French culture. "It is very possible to respect, admire and emulate a culture without exploiting it" she stressed.[125] Her comparison reveals that she thought of Indigenous cuisine as another "ethnic" cuisine, as opposed to taking into consideration the complexities of commercially selling a cuisine that the Canadian government has actively suppressed in its effort to enforce assimilation. This overlooks how Indigenous restaurants in Canada are discursively distinct from others serving culturally specific cuisines.

From a heated television debate and charges of violence – including raw eggs, a black eye, and an incident with a crowbar – to missed hearings, late paycheques, and temporary picketing bans, Muckamuck's three-year strike has too many details to repeat here. That both owners, Chrismas and Erickson, were living in California only made the strike a knottier, transnational affair. In 1980 the *Vancouver Sun* proclaimed it "the longest-running strike in Vancouver"[126] and the *Province* called it "the ugliest strike in B.C. history."[127] Because of the strike, Erickson concluded that the restaurant no longer wished "to be directly involved with native culture in BC to the degree of commitment required in the past."[128] The Muckamuck closed for good in 1981, and SORWUC shut down its picket line. A final legal ruling lingered for another two years. On 1 March 1983, the Labour Relations Board concluded that Muckamuck management had not bargained in good faith and owed the union $10,000.[129] However, because Chrismas and Erickson no longer held assets in BC, SORWUC never received this compensation. It later disbanded in 1986.[130] In the end, SORWUC did not negotiate a contract with the Muckamuck, but the strike did draw attention to working conditions at the restaurant, especially regarding the politics of cultural representation in restaurants.

## "Yours for Indian Self-Determination"

The month the strike began, the *Union of B.C. Indian Chiefs Newsletter* published a letter by Gardner rallying for support. She contextualized her experience at the Muckamuck in relation to colonial history: "We are part of the renewed struggle of Native people to gain the rights and respect denied us since Captain Cook landed here."[131] Workers wanted more input in "the menu planning of the cuisine,"[132] but Gardner's primary complaint wasn't about the restaurant as such, but about its abuse of power. In the July–August issue of *Kinesis*, Gardner elaborated that she and other employees were proud of the image of Native culture the Muckamuck projected, "but the owners are exploiting both our culture and our people in order to make exorbitant profits."[133] She claimed the issue was not that the owners were white but that they marketed the restaurant to suggest otherwise.[134] Despite the illusion that the Muckamuck represented progress for Indigenous peoples in the commercial restaurant sector, it maintained unequal power

An Edible Exhibition 139

Figure 4.7. Dana Claxton in collaboration with Sean Griffin, *Muckamuck Strike Then and Now*, 2018, photographic mural, courtesy of the artist.

relations between those in charge and those providing labour, between settler owners and Indigenous employees.

In 1980 Gardner co-signed a letter published in *Kinesis* with what had become the picketers' sign-off: "Yours for Indian Self Determination."[135] In 2018 these same words swaddled the Morris and Helen Belkin Gallery at the University of British Columbia. The 1978 "Muckamuck strikers march, downtown Vancouver" image (Figure 4.4), taken by Sean Griffin, belongs to the photograph collection of the *Pacific Tribune*, the Communist Party of Canada's weekly newspaper. Lakota artist Dana Claxton revisited this photograph in the 2018 exhibition *Beginning with the Seventies: Collective Acts* (Figure 4.7). Claxton used the 1978 image as a base for a photo mural that traversed the gallery's wall. She digitally edited it to add members of the ReMatriate Collective. In the slight gap that separated the protestors holding the "Walk the Muckamuck Walk" and "Joker" signs, Claxton's 2018 reimagining features two women captured in mid-stride. The photograph is black and white, except for a series of colourful stripes orbiting one woman's skirt – a rainbow of pale pinks and blues and a band of green – and Debbie Mearn's blue belt buckle. By injecting colour, Claxton visually connects the women and, thus, two generations of activists. As the title suggests, *Muckamuck Strike Then and Now* recovers the strike's history to assert its continual relevance.

The ReMatriate Collective also developed a work in dialogue with the SORWUC's Muckamuck strike. Formed in 2015, the ReMatriate Collective's name plays on the word repatriation. In the exhibition's words, "An important process of decolonization, the etymology of the word repatriation reflects non-Indigenous concepts and relationships to belongings, place, land and ownership. ReMatriate challenges this framework by re-centering Indigenous matriarchs, womxn, non-gender binary and Two-Spirited individuals."[136] Beyond the art world, the term is important for Indigenous food sovereignty – a concept Chapter 8 spotlights. From Akwesasne and now based in California, Rowen White is a seed keeper who runs Sierra Seeds. She uses rematriation to frame her quest for seed sovereignty. Rematriation means "bringing these seeds home again."[137] From seeds to art, rematriation seeks to rewrite power relations and centralize Indigenous worldviews. For the 2018 exhibition, the ReMatriate Collective's red-on-red appliqué banner wrapped around the gallery's south side, spelling out in capital letters the words that double as its title: "Yours for Indigenous sovereignty, [sic]." These words framed the exhibition and cast the gallery as witness, as ally (Figure 4.8).[138] To conclude Muckamuck's history, these words also summarized its picket line: a battle for self-representation. A fight for Indigenous sovereignty. This history of one restaurant in Vancouver in the 1970s attests to the power of restaurants in general to represent a culture and the complexities this takes on in a settler colonial state. It also illuminates the politics of Indigenous restaurants in Canada.

Sovereignty is about power. The Muckamuck reinforced a structure that favoured its settler owners over its Indigenous staff. Despite its abuses of power, the Muckamuck constitutes an important early example of an Indigenous restaurant and played a central role in shaping Indigenous restaurant fare and

Figure 4.8. ReMatriate Collective, *YOURS FOR INDIGENOUS SOVEREIGNTY,*, 2018, appliqué banner, Collection of the Morris and Helen Belkin Art Gallery, University of British Columbia, purchased with support from the Canada Council for the Arts, Rachel Topham Photography.

décor. It is certainly no coincidence that Muckamuck belongs to the same period in which North Americans developed appetites for unique culinary experiences shaped around local ingredients, as championed by Chez Panisse, as well as a revitalized interest in Indigenous cultures, as exemplified by Curtis's photographs, alongside the Red Power movement's growing political activism.

The Muckamuck accommodated distinct agendas: those of the owners (largely financial) and those of the employees (also financial, but, more importantly, concerned with the stakes of cultural representation). The battle for "Indian self-determination" ultimately led to the downfall of this settler-owned restaurant. Nonetheless, it was an early ambassador of Pacific Northwest Indigenous cuisine. The crowds who lined up before the strike granted recognition of "Northwest Coast Native Indian Food" as a worthy part of the city and, as the widespread reviews attest, the country, and even the continent's restaurantscape. Indigenous food at 1724 Davie Street did not end with the Muckamuck, and the next example in the history of Indigenous restaurants in Vancouver, the Quilicum, inched closer to the goal of Indigenous self-determination.

chapter five

# One Address, Three Restaurants

Two years after the Muckamuck closed, new owners converted the building's main floor into a grocery store while the basement restaurant continued to gather dust.[1] The following year, Malcolm McSporran, an architectural designer, toured its kitchen and saw that much of its equipment remained.[2] After having planned the Indian Education Centre, McSporran was courting the idea of "re-opening a new Indian restaurant."[3] He largely worked with First Nation communities, and one newspaper reported: "His grandmother was native, but he doesn't consider himself Indian."[4] Another mentioned that he was married to a Navajo anthropologist.[5]

Before McSporran could go ahead, he had to settle the $10,000 fine that loomed over the property. The BC Labour Board, however, ruled that, since this was a new company, it was not responsible for the fine.[6] Together with former Muckamuck employees-turned-strikers Art Bolton and Bonnie Thorne, McSporran reopened Vancouver's only Indigenous restaurant, bestowing on it a new name: the Quilicum. Before joining the Muckamuck, Thorne, who is Nootka and from the Nuu-Chah-Nulth Nation, was part of the "training staff in the restaurant which operated out of the Vancouver Indian Centre."[7] Bolton, an artist specializing in wooden masks, jewellery, and prints, crafted some of the Quilicum's serving vessels. The Quilicum sold one hundred $1,000 shares, 98 per cent of which Bolton, Thorne, and McSporran held.[8] Like the

Muckamuck, the Quilicum received federal government support. But unlike its predecessor, it was partly Indigenous-owned.

The Quilicum opened on 6 May 1985.[9] Also a Chinook Jargon word, Quilicum means "return of the people."[10] A restaurant's name is its calling card; it introduces how it positions itself and narrates its food. Quilicum doubled as a metaphor. As one review exclaimed, "The Quilicum has risen from the ashes of a bitter and lengthy labor dispute that closed down the old Muckamuck."[11] To return is to recover, to revive. Decades before Canada's reconciliation era, this name foretells restoration and resurgence. The name takes back the restaurant and reclaims it for its Indigenous staff and now co-owners. It also relays a political meaning. As Thorne explained, they selected a Chinook Jargon term so people "don't think the restaurant belongs to only one nation."[12] Like the Muckamuck, the Quilicum prioritized local, Northwest Coast Indigenous foods, but in a language that did not favour one culture over another. In line with growing pan-Indigenous solidarity and unity, the restaurant aimed to represent a community of nations.

Although its thirteen employees were not unionized, the Quilicum received SORWUC's blessing nonetheless.[13] Yet memories of the picket line haunted 1724 Davie Street. The new name could not instantly resurrect a property weighted down by the ghosts of headlines past. A 1985 review recounts visiting on a Tuesday and finding only one other table occupied. "[M]anagement admitted they sometimes close an hour early because of slow business. Pity! The Quilicum offers good traditional food in a unique atmosphere," it lamented.[14] Reflecting on the nearly empty restaurant in tandem with its new name, the review concluded: "It's a prophecy that remains unfilled."[15] However, later reviews reveal that the prophecy eventually did come true. Business picked up, and so did complimentary reviews.

In many ways the Quilicum carried on from where the Muckamuck had left off and peddled a similar menu. A former Muckamuck cook, George Ross from Lax-kw'alaams First Nation, was the first to lead its kitchen. Ross, a relative of Bolton's, had logged time working in San Francisco and Los Angeles, but credits his grandmother with having taught him to "cook Indian food," which is what he liked best.[16] This meant preparing fresh ingredients over "an open fire with real alderwood – not just the chips."[17] He seasoned dishes with fire, steam, and herbs, explaining: "Everything I do is in the old ways and is part of my Tsimshian heritage."[18]

Like the Muckamuck, the Quilicum offered fare that was hard to find elsewhere in Vancouver: herring eggs from Haida Gwaii,[19] barbecued caribou (a Vancouver supplier had a connection to Inuit raising caribou),[20] and fiddleheads.[21] Goat, once again, was on the menu.[22] There was also "duck with juniper berries," "clam fritters," and "Alaska black cod."[23] The Quilicum's version of the Muckamuck's spinach and watercress dish went by the name "Wild man of the woods salad."[24] Diners generally preferred the water-based dishes to land-based ones. One review declared the Quilicum's caribou stew "for the adventurous."[25] Another reported, "A note in the visitors book warns against the caribou stew, and I suspect it's good advice."[26] The Quilicum's salmon, however, was consistently a hit.

There were still smoked oolichans, which Thorne nicknamed "Indian peanuts."[27] But nearly two decades after the Muckamuck opened, oolichan grease was as divisive as ever. A 1990 *Seattle Times* review recommended: "Everyone should try oolichan grease at least once."[28] It described oolichan as once "the bottom line for Native American cooking": something to dip bannock and fish in, or mix with berries, or to even cure a cough. That said, one critic thought it tasted like "melted butter, albeit with a fishy aftertaste," and another that it tasted like "smoked motor oil."[29] Beyond oolichan grease, this recommendation left an aftertaste. By calling it "the bottom line for Native American cooking," it imagined a single cuisine that flattened Turtle Island's culinary diversity.

The Quilicum encouraged sampling and grazing, and offered "the Potlatch platter" for two or three to share a nibble of "almost everything" for $24.95.[30] It played the restaurant's greatest hits, from salmon and barbecued oysters to prawns and smoked cod and, even, caribou.[31] Unlike the Tomahawk, with its mismatched marriage of "golden grilled wiener slices" and the name "Potlatch Deluxe," the Quilicum's platter offered a taste of pre-contact ingredients. A history lesson about the Northwest Coast, its land

and waters and peoples, the foods they produce and cultures they represent.

To end the meal, the Quilicum offered "Indian ice cream." The June 1985 edition of the *Province's Magazine* even included the restaurant in its Vancouver ice cream guide, listed next to Baskin Robbins and Italian joints with names like Venezia Gelati.[32] The Quilicum earned positive accolades from diners and reviewers. One critic claimed its bannock might even be the best bread in Vancouver.[33] Another agreed, ranking the bannock alone "Reason enough for a visit."[34] She also considered the poached halibut "one of the best pieces of fish" she had ever tried. Other than the caribou stew and the polarizing oolichan grease, the Quilicum's menu landed well with critics.

The food, however, was only one part of representing Indigenous culinary cultures. The restaurant's personality also came from how it served its dishes, leaving this last critic to conclude, "The food is very good at the Quilicum, but what helps make the experience is the long-house atmosphere, little touches like the fresh greenery, the fantastic Indian art."[35] She was just as impressed by the prawns in the shell as she was by their vessel: a "traditional Indian serving bowl" that Bolton had carved.[36] From the food to the décor, another review observed, "There's little difference between the Quilicum and the old Muckamuck. It's a cozy, scent-filled space, giving the impression of an old post-and-beam longhouse."[37] Once again, the walls doubled as a gallery, showcasing "Native Indian paintings, carvings and prints from Potlatch Arts."[38] In the background "Indian music plays … and the air is fragrant with smoke from open cooking fires."[39] One change was that the new owners balanced fir planks across the gravel, making walks to and from tables smoother.[40] Surely what was a practical addition one review painted more romantically: "A narrow wooden path runs through it, like a stream through the woods."[41] Diners were as enamoured with the atmosphere as with the food.

The label of unique lived on, demonstrating that even though the Quilicum was not the city's first Indigenous restaurant, it was still novel. The *San Francisco Examiner* called it "one of the most unusual restaurants in North America."[42] Writing for the *Vancouver*

*Sun*, Eve Johnson claimed, "Quilicum Native Indian restaurant has a sense of place so strong that it's a bit disconcerting."[43] She continued: "It has an integrity and coherence that makes anyone else claiming to serve regional food look like a Johnny-come-lately."[44] In 1994 the *Atlanta Constitution* trumpeted it "the most offbeat ethnic restaurant in town," serving "dishes straight from the recipe books of Canada's West Coast Indians," which is ironic, considering that there were few such cookery books at the time.[45] It also classified it as "ethnic," thus distinguishing it from mainstream Canadian eateries.

Similar to Banff's Indian Days, the Quilicum facilitated contact between Indigenous peoples and settlers and tourists. A 1987 *Philadelphia Inquirer* review alleged, "It can be difficult for tourists to speak with the Indians. We managed to talk with some briefly one evening at Quilicum."[46] This desire is complex and multifaceted. On one hand, some diners sought out the Quilicum as a place to encounter Indigenous peoples. On the other, these encounters were loaded with expectations and, often, cultural stereotypes. As the review continued, "We learned later, though, that the entrepreneurial Indians who owned the restaurant were uncommon in both their openness and, judging by the crowd that evening, their affluence."[47] Setting aside these biases, the review points out the importance in considering who could afford to eat at the Quilicum. Even with Indigenous co-owners, the restaurant was limited in the extent to which it could represent Northwest Coast cultures and to whom. Nonetheless, this review's author wished to interact with Indigenous peoples and not just representations of their cultures.

In 1994 the *Philadelphia Inquirer* published another article endorsing the Quilicum, but this time it suggested that Indigenous cultures and, therefore, peoples were gaining more of a spotlight: "The first thread traces back to the original settlers – not the English, but the native North Americans, the Indian tribes of the Northwest. Their life and culture can be seen not only in museums but also – thanks to a revival in recent years – in art, carving, weaving, jewelry, and other crafts ... There's even a restaurant called Quilicum, serving only Northwest native Indian cuisine."[48] This points to the renewed presence of Indigenous culture in Vancouver – to urban

Indigenous revival. Instead of representing Indigenous culture of years past – the kind Curtis staged in his rose-tinted photographs – the Quilicum provided a platform for Indigenous cultures to claim a contemporary presence and, thus, refuse settler time.

In her 1989 review, Anishinaabe educator Priscilla Hewitt applauded "Bonnie and Art" for their efforts. "Again, in keeping with the Native perspective, they have managed to maximize the strengths of their individual selves, which in turn impacts on their family life and then has a positive effect on our community," she writes. "Our people can be justifiably proud of their endeavours."[49] Hewitt underscores that the restaurant did more than serve food: it created jobs, empowered the community, and exercised self-representation, all adhering to Indigenous values while setting an example for future culinary activism.

McSporran's name had disappeared in later reviews, obscuring his involvement. In 1987 the *San Francisco Examiner* identified Bolton and Thorne as "the native Canadian owners."[50] Either way, in 1990, the *Province* claimed that the Quilicum was "remarkably the only full-service native restaurant in Vancouver,"[51] airing an expectation that Indigenous restaurants should have taken off by now.[52] In June 1991, the *Financial Post Magazine* introduced the Quilicum with the phrase: "Only in British Columbia."[53] What does this say about the restaurant landscape in the rest of Canada? That Vancouver continued to host only one Indigenous restaurant testified that Indigenous entrepreneurs continued to face barriers in entering the industry. It also shows that even though the general presence and awareness of Indigenous culture was growing, the mainstream appetite for Indigenous fare remained limited. Nevertheless, the Quilicum marked an important shift: from an Indigenous restaurant owned by settlers to one with Indigenous co-owners.

## Another City, Another Expo

The laudatory Muckamuck and Quilicum reviews imply that Vancouver was a recognized dining destination. But in 1994 the

*Philadelphia Inquirer* confessed, "it wasn't too many years ago that the hotel restaurant scene in Vancouver was considered something of a joke. But the 1980s – helped considerably by the 1986 World's Fair – changed that forever."[54] Just like Expo 67 in Montreal, Vancouver's 1986 Expo promoted Indigenous fare. But unlike in Montreal, the Vancouver menu was Indigenous-authored and not just inspired – a moment of self-representation rather than of settler storying. The *Los Angeles Times* surveyed its culinary options – caribou and musk ox, Arctic char and Arctic whitefish, blueberry and cranberry ice cream – further demonstrating the importance of events like fairs and sporting competitions in staging place-based cuisines.[55]

One year after the Quilicum resurrected 1724 Davie Street, Canada hosted its second World's Fair: the 1986 Exposition on Transportation and Communication in Vancouver, also known as Expo 86. Unlike Expo 67, this was a special category exposition.[56] But like its predecessor, it celebrated a centenary: Vancouver's one-hundredth birthday. Incorporated on 6 April 1886, Vancouver opened Expo 86 one century later. Running from May to October, it welcomed millions of visitors. Just as in Montreal, Vancouver's Expo 86 granted a ticket "to eat and drink your way around the world."[57] Yet, according to one paper, "some of the best food will be from B.C.'s own backyard." Published a few months prior to the opening, this preview whetted appetites by boasting, "The First Nation Restaurant will be serving genuine B.C. Native Indian cuisine," meaning a menu of "barbecued salmon, buffalo steak and caribou stew."[58] Expo 67 had La Toundra. Expo 86 had the First Nation Restaurant. However, this eatery framed its food as Indigenous, rather than Canadian – a tension that surfaces again and again both in this book and in the history of the representation of Indigenous foodways at large.

Twenty-three-year-old Wet'suwet'en chef Andrew George Jr. took the reins as the First Nation Restaurant's head grill cook one year after graduating from Vancouver Vocational Institute's culinary training program.[59] He paid for his tuition by cooking part-time at the Vancouver Indian Friendship Centre. At culinary school, he recalls jabs from his classmates; "Indians can't cook," some growled.[60] But cook he did and it was at the Quilicum where he learned to "cook professionally on a wood-burning grill and to prepare many Native dishes characteristic of the Pacific Northwest – wood-barbecued salmon, oysters, rabbit, caribou, smoked eulachons, steamed smoked Alaska black cod, crab in the shell, wild rice, seaweed and rice, crisp watercress salad, whipped soapalillie, cold raspberry soup."[61] This shows the culinary opportunities the Quilicum provided for young Indigenous chefs like George Jr.

Despite the taunts George suffered in culinary school, a 2007 profile looks back with a different take, writing "He didn't know it at the time, but what started out as an obstacle for George – his aboriginal heritage – would soon serve him well."[62] Exhibiting Indigenous heritage was Expo 86's First Nation Restaurant's aim. The restaurant was Bob Hall's idea. In an interview, Hall, a member of Skowkale First Nation from Sardis in the Fraser River Valley, recounted that a few bands had tossed around the idea of a joint pavilion. But the idea never materialized. Instead, Hall partnered with Gunnar Vogel, originally from West Germany, of Ambassador Industries. As the First Nation Restaurant Inc.'s co-owner and manager, Hall was "the only native Indian concessionaire at Expo."[63]

A few days before its opening, a newspaper reported that Hall had "struggled for years to set up an authentic Northwest Coast Indian food restaurant at the fair."[64] The article prints his portrait, a light moustache framing his upper lip, with the caption: "BOB HALL it wasn't easy." Three years earlier, in 1983, he had proposed an Indigenous restaurant to Expo chairman Jimmy Pattison. "I think he was honest with me – he said, 'When you've got the money on the table come back and see me.'"[65] Come back he did. Even before Expo opened, Hall beamed confidence: "It's an excellent opportunity for us to share our traditional food – I know it's going to work."[66]

Although Hall was set on Expo 86 including an Indigenous eatery, he did not have a background in the restaurant sector. "I have done all kinds of things – consulting in Indian government, band management, funding sources, financial investment and sawmill management," he sums up.[67] In 1979 he started the

American Indian Resource Corporation; one year later, he became the manager of Fort Nelson Indian Band. According to his local paper, the *Chilliwack Progress*, "Hall has accumulated a good deal of business knowledge since the days in the early 1970s when he was dismissed by some non-Indians as a radical 'red power' advocate. A lot has changed since those days some 15 years ago."[68] This narrative suggests that Hall had to shed his "radical" beliefs to make it in business and open an Indigenous eatery at Vancouver's World's Fair. It also implies that demanding an Indigenous presence at an international event was not a form of activism, which *Culinary Claims* contests. A core debate at the time was the question of whether Indigenous activists should work with the state or independent of it. Either way, the politics of refusal and the assertion of self-representation take on shapes of all kinds, and for Hall this meant claiming a seat at the table at Canada's World Fair.

Unlike at Expo 67, in 1986 the Indigenous restaurant was not attached to the Canada pavilion. In fact, the Canada pavilion was the only one off site, accessible with the newly constructed Skytrain.[69] The Folk Life Pavilion hosting the First Nation Restaurant was "tucked away in the eastern corner of the fairgrounds ... a tranquil spot that features cedar buildings, one of the few patches of grass on the site and wooden boardwalk instead of cement sidewalk."[70] The Expo Centre, Folklife, Yukon and Northwest Territories pavilions, and the Chinese pavilion shared this corner. One review describes the First Nation Restaurant as "somewhat out of the way."[71] Another recommends the Folklife Complex for those longing "for a touch of green and the smell of cedar. The site itself is grassroots stuff – folk singing, square dancing, native arts and crafts and, of course, dining native style."[72] It ends by describing the Folklife Complex as "an alternative to the more commercial aspects of Expo."[73]

Neighbouring the 230-seat First Nation Restaurant, Hall managed "a northwest native Indian art gallery" peddling "arts and crafts of 23 B.C. tribal groups," including four-metre totem poles and Cowichan sweaters.[74] Both the art and the food drew crowds. Open from 10 a.m. to 10 p.m., which was later extended to midnight, the First Nation Restaurant was casual – a "buffeteria."[75]

One review labelled its spread as "unusual fast food."[76] Diners lined up with plastic trays, which led one newspaper to claim, "it was hard to believe that the First Nation menu at Expo dates back hundreds of years. But they really do serve authentic northwest coast Indian food. There's also a dash of the Prairies thrown in, unless they want us to believe the buffalo roamed this side of the Rockies."[77] This review balances a can't-fool-me attitude with a hunger for "authentic" food that recalls the settler gaze behind Banff's Indian Days. Recalling Wolfe's "repressive authenticity," this review flexes the critic's authority by reinforcing the false settler binary between pre- and post-contact.

Diners filled their trays with "Indian-style salmon jerky for $2.95," "Salmon barbecued over a pit and served with corn on the cob and a baked potato" for $8.25, "Northwest coast seafood soup for $2.95," and "chopped buffalo steak for $4.95."[78] The "buffalo steak" was actually a burger – ground bison "topped with onions and gravy, served with thick-cut fries and carrots." Two writers conclude that "sometimes they overcook it, leaving the patty with too little of that gamey, robust taste of real buffalo."[79] Another called it "passable."[80] To make up for the burger, one review details "a dollop of dill-flavored mayonnaise" accompanying the "thick, juicy, and charcoal-grilled" salmon steak sandwich, pronouncing it "The best single take-out 'dish.'"[81]

Reviews documented the First Nation Restaurant's hits and what critics considered its misses. In addition to the seafood soup, there was venison stew, but one reporter was far from impressed: "You'd be hard-pressed to tell the difference between First Nation's soup and stew. Both the $5.75 venison stew and the $2.95 West Coast seafood soup are thin. The stew at least has a lip-smacking taste. That can't be said for the meagre and milky soup, with its skimpy bits of seafood."[82] But, the salmon was "superb." Another noted, "Of course the salmon is fresh and it's broiled to perfection, using a combination of cherrywood, applewood and alder. It's a toss up as to which the First Nation Restaurant is better known for – their salmon or their deep fried bannock bread."[83] The same review, however, dismissed the salads and desserts as "uninspiring."[84]

The bannock consistently attracted praise. The *Province*, the same paper that questioned the bison burger's historical geography, recommended "sparing a buck for the bannock bread." But, once again, it debated its "authenticity," writing: "This deep-fried creation is just a relative of the real thing. They didn't have fat fryers two hundred years ago, after all, but these crispy-crusted critters are an addictive treat."[85] What "the real thing" was it does not say. Nonetheless, it convinces readers that the First Nation Restaurant's bannock is a must. Another paper concurred, even titling its review "First Nations' does its bannock right." "When the restaurant first opened," it reports, "it was thought a local bakery could ship them the dough and they would deep fry it. None of the bakery products lived up [sic] the President and partial owner, Bob Hall's expectations, so he set out with his crew to develop this tasty offering himself."[86] A tasty offering requiring five hundred pounds of flour a day.

Bannock made it into a California paper. Describing lunch at the First Nation Restaurant for the *Santa Cruz Sentinel*, Barbara Burklo was charmed by bannock "in the form of round, puffy rolls." She requested the recipe, only to learn there wasn't one: "The bread is made by the Salish, a Canadian Indian tribe, and, the restaurateur told me it's basically made from a biscuit dough and deep fried. Served with any wild berry jam, it is delicious."[87] She recounts her efforts to recreate it at home, using her "favorite and fairly rich biscuit dough," which cooked too quickly on the outside and too slowly on the inside. As a backup plan, she "turned to a commercial biscuit mix," which resulted in a "treat."[88]

The First Nation Restaurant caught the attention of a reporter from the *Arizona Republic*. In her Expo 86 write-up, she chronicles "Musk ox, two kinds of bannock, soapalallie berries" as "just a few of the new foods we found at Expo 86."[89] After listing Greek honey balls, Bavarian liver dumplings, and "*sate* (sah-tay)," she informs readers that she "bypassed most of the foreign foods in favor of a taste of Canada." This critic describes bannock as "a food of the Salish Indians that resembles Arizona's Indian fry bread in taste and texture, but not in shape: it looks like a minifootball."[90] Although she calls bannock new, she was already familiar with fry bread.

Soapalallie berries, however, were new for her. The First Nation Restaurant sold "Indian ice cream" for $1.95.[91] When she placed her order, the "friendly counterman" asked if she had tried it before and then fed her a spoonful because "'Most people don't like it.' Small wonder. The fluffy white whip has a weird flavor. Soap? Still, it deserved more of a chance than just a spoonful, so we ordered it … It has a bitter aftertaste, and we could not finish it all. But how often does one get to try soapalallie berries?"[92] Although not a fan, she did not regret trying it, valuing the chance to sample a food she considered a novelty. Similarly, another paper warned that the soapberry ice cream is "an item to really beware of." Describing it as "a delectable-looking mound of whipped berries," two reporters outline how "We dived in with spoons flying but our preconceived notions of sweet ice cream were destroyed instantly."[93] They conclude that this "favorite traditional Indian treat" is "definitely an acquired taste."[94] A taste that stalled their spoons mid-air, suspended between mouth and bowl.

Another attraction at the First Nation Restaurant was the opportunity to interact with Elders, echoing reviews of the Quilicum. An article published in the *Edmonton Journal* three months before Expo 86 previewed how "Guests can not only feast on Pacific salmon and buffalo steaks, but will also be treated to tales that unravel native traditions as elder tribe members share their stories of long ago."[95] This repeats Banff's Indian Days' assumption – that Indigenous culture belongs to a time "long ago" as opposed to the present. That the restaurant was assigned to the Folklife area further gave away the expectation of its living-history-museum character. One review recommends "pausing to admire the weavers, or a Haida carving a totem pole" on your way to the First Nation Restaurant.[96] A sort of appetizer for the eyes. However, a local paper wrote that Hall had invited twenty-five Coast Salish Elders "to come and talk about past and present traditions to the visitors from around the globe."[97] Although some visitors might have expected stories from another time, the restaurant's organizer aimed to represent contemporary Indigenous life. Two reporters recorded that they "sorely missed the Coast Salish elders, who occasionally gather in a corner to relate tales of olden times in B.C. … But on both our visits, they were absent. They would have made up for the dessert."[98] Although they were underwhelmed by the "Indian ice cream," they were hungry for stories about Indigenous culture.

Hall considered the First Nation Restaurant and art gallery as "'It' as far as a native Indian presence at EXPO 86 is concerned."[99] However, the Northwest Territories restaurant hawked similar dishes. It was also an abundance of ice. Neighbouring the colourful Yukon Pavilion, "reminiscent of the frontier spirit," the Northwest Territories Pavilion was all angles and glass – ice blue in colour and "igloo" in theme.[100] Its restaurant, appropriately titled Icicles, cooled drinks with rough "pieces of a Resolute iceberg believed to date back to the last ice age."[101] In addition to chilling drinks with names like "Bushpilot Caesar, permafrost and ptarmigan fluff," "Iceberg alley" (vodka, liqueurs, and 7-Up) and "Iceflow" (vodka and milk) with "10,000-year-old Arctic ice chunks," the 250-seat restaurant sold "tiny white-chocolate polar bears (75 cents each)."[102] An icy taste of the north.

A more formal affair compared to the First Nation Restaurant's buffeteria, the menu at Icicles touted "Arctic fish chowder ($3.25)," "a muskox burger (a bestseller at $6.75) and a caribou steak ($11.50), pleasantly milder than beef," and "paper-thin slices of smoked Arctic char with bannock bread."[103] Icicles also hooked the *Arizona Republic*'s attention, which detailed how the building "in chilly shades of grey" was "designed to look like a vast iceberg" and that its menu assembled "reindeer ragout, Arctic fish chowder, tundra burgers and raisin bannock with cranberry preserves."[104] Equating it with a small buffalo in its looks, the critic sampled the musk ox and reindeer alongside the Arctic char and Northern white fish – "all nicely charboiled" with "Canadian wild rice" and "squares of bannock" tagging along as sides. The musk ox she proclaimed "similar to beef, but very chewy" and the reindeer "quite tender, with a strong but not unpleasant taste."[105] But the bannock at Icicles was distinct – "a wheat bread totally different from the puffy oval Salish bannock served at First Nation and also different from the bannock of the American Colonists, which was made of cornmeal."[106] Although short, the review's bannock catalogue gestures toward regional cuisines rather than a singular monolith.

In other provincial offerings, the Saskatchewan Pavilion hosted the 210-seat Harvest Restaurant, peddling "traditional Prairie fowl supper or roast beef or turkey."[107] Like the First Nation Restaurant, buffalo burgers were on offer at Harvest.[108] Alberta, considered by one reporter to boast "the funkiest pavilion architecturally," had "the most original menu" to match: "air-dried buffalo meat, reindeer cutlets in blueberry sauce, roast pheasant, wild mushroom, vol-au-vent and French onion soup with Alberta beef."[109] The Indigenous influences at these restaurants are obvious. British Columbia and Ontario entertained pavilion restaurants; however, "Regrettably, neither France nor Quebec is providing examples of its cuisine."[110] Once again, an eatery represented the host nation: The Canada Pavilion housed the 350-seat Prow Restaurant. This time "Seafood, fettuccini with salmon, and caviar champagne velouté" were on the menu, similar fare to the Norway Pavilion's "Hot and cold Scandinavian buffet of salmon, lobster, roast reindeer, herring, and other delicacies."[111] In addition to endorsing the reindeer and musk ox at Icicles and the barbecued salmon and caribou stew at the First Nation Restaurant, the *St. Louis Post-Dispatch* praised the Quilicum, honouring it as "One Vancouver restaurant that shouldn't be missed."[112] Whether on the Expo grounds or in the city centre, this paper persuaded American tourists to seek out an Indigenous meal.

## A Second Restaurant in Town

When Expo 86 wrapped up, Hall had the chance to continue renting the building, but despite believing that "A fine native Indian dining restaurant would go well in Vancouver," he never opened one.[113] And although it was not fine dining, a second Indigenous eatery eventually did open. In 1991 George Jr., from Expo 86 and the Quilicum, opened a restaurant of his own. He named it Toody Ni Grill and Catering Company after the Wet'suwet'en land where he grew up – Toody Ni meaning "Where the Hill Faces the River."[114]

Unlike the Quilicum, George Jr.'s catering business-cum-eatery was a tenant in an already existing cultural institution.

The restaurant shared an address with the Vancouver Aboriginal Friendship Centre (then called the Vancouver Indian Friendship Centre) at 1607 East Hastings. George Jr.'s first cookbook describes East Hastings Street as "not-always-friendly."[115] It was also here that he worked while attending culinary school. "I made 2.35 an hour cooking hamburgers and fries," George Jr. remembers.[116] Around this time, in 1984, a local paper recommended the Vancouver Indian Centre's "famous buffalo burger" for "the adventurous."[117] For George, Toody Ni was a return to where he cooked when he was starting his culinary career, as well as a new beginning.

Toody Ni differed from the Muckamuck and the Quilicum in that it was not a standalone restaurant. In its dedication to promoting Indigenous culture, which it did with cuisine, its aims were an extension of the Friendship Centre's. As its name gives away, Toody Ni also solicited catering, a model that other Indigenous restaurants in Canada would later employ. Some press reports present Toody Ni as a restaurant, but others classify it as a catering company.[118]

In culinary school George dreamed of opening a restaurant: "a first-class one featuring the foods of the Aboriginal Peoples of Canada's Pacific Northwest."[119] After years of cooking toward this dream, he spent another year planning, "raising money without government support," and finding a location.[120] Toody Ni opened in summer 1991.[121] To mark the occasion, the Friendship Centre threw a grand party in its gymnasium with guests and speakers, drummers and dancers. Platter after platter came out of the kitchen, "for truly this was a feast that featured Native cuisine with a Pacific Northwest flavour."[122] The feast included three hundred trout that George Jr. caught with his cousin, for which he had driven sixteen hours to Telkwa. He packed them in ice, drove back to Vancouver, and grilled them for Toody Ni's first guests, letting the fire brand them with flavour.[123]

Compared to Vancouver's other Indigenous restaurants, Toody Ni aimed to attract Indigenous diners. For example, a 1992 advertisement in *Windspeaker*, "North America's Leading Native Newspaper," drew attention to Toody Ni, "Specializing In Native &

Continental Cuisine For All Occasions."[124] Based in Edmonton, the paper provided "information primarily to Native people of Alberta and Saskatchewan," and so news about this Vancouver restaurant had travelled to the Prairies.[125] Its customer base also travelled, extending beyond Indigenous diners to provide "both Canadian and Native fare."[126]

Reviews were solid and business quickly grew, and so in 1991 Vancouver hosted two Indigenous restaurants for the first time. Although both traded in similar ingredients, Toody Ni highlighted "comfort food." "We started out very basic, you know, doing buffalo burgers and all that other stuff," George Jr. recollects. "But when we got into catering we did a lot of traditional foods."[127] A reminder that a catering menu is not always a facsimile of a restaurant's and that comfort is not necessarily a synonym for simple. One dish that was a customer favourite was the "rich and delicious" "Seafood Chowder Toody Ni."[128] It melts together bacon fat or butter with onion, celery and garlic, potato, carrot, and green pepper, clams, salmon, and red snapper, and is then flooded with cream.

The locations of the Quilicum and Toody Ni also set them apart – the Quilicum trafficked more in tourists and Toody Ni in locals. However, this distinction was far from absolute.[129] And just like the Quilicum, Toody Ni caught the press's attention. Thinking that world leaders might experience culinary homesickness during the 1993 Vancouver Summit, the *Province Preview* published a checklist for the food it imagined Presidents Clinton, Yeltsin, and company might crave. From a Russian café to bakeries slinging home-made pie, it includes what the reporter calls a "When in Rome" offering: "Maybe our guests would like to try some authentic local specialities, such as alder-smoked salmon and bannock bread. The two places that spring to mind for the best in native Indian cuisine are Quilicum … and the Toody-Ni."[130] The city's two Indigenous restaurants were now considered culinary delegates of Vancouver.

Toody Ni caught David Wolfman's attention, and George started a new training regimen the same year he opened his restaurant. Previously, his education had versed him in haute cuisine's sauces and how a knife chops and slices so that he would be able to hold his own in a kitchen, and, eventually, run one of his own. This new regimen, in contrast, was training for a competition: the Culinary Olympics in Frankfurt, Germany. A "mystery diner" at Toody Ni, "who remains unidentified to this day," recommended George Jr. to the organizers of a Canadian Native Haute Cuisine Team, the first ever Indigenous team to compete at the Culinary Olympics.[131] In the middle of dinner service, the phone rang. It was Wolfman, the team's captain, offering George Jr. a spot as "Second Cook."[132] George Jr. was one of five Indigenous chefs to fly to Frankfurt the following year.

But the team was regional rather than national. There was also a Team Canada, composed of seven chefs. "Taking as their inspiration native culture and Canada's 125th birthday," one newspaper reports, "the team made a dessert display of poured sugar coloured like stained glass. It depicted an Indian in a canoe harvesting wild rice. Another dessert featured an Indian headdress with feathers of chocolate and marzipan."[133] Accounts of the Canadian Native Haute Cuisine at the Culinary Olympics tend to leave out Team Canada's spread. Yet, I argue for reading these teams in relation to one another. The year an Indigenous team competed in the Culinary Olympics for the first time, the national team was melting chocolate and sculpting marzipan into the feathers of an "Indian headdress." In many ways, the 1992 Culinary Olympics fused together the culinary representations at Montreal's Expo 67 and Vancouver's Expo 86. One team, the Native one, cooked to represent themselves. The other team, the Canadian one, looked for Indigenous inspiration to represent Canada. Team Canada brought home medals, but not quite as many as the Canadian Native Haute Cuisine Team: six gold and one silver compared to the Native Team's seven gold and two silver. According to *Anishinabek News*, the gold medals prove "that traditional Native food and cooking methods stand the test of time and palate."[134] The competition secured the culinary talents of contemporary Indigenous chefs.

The timing of the Culinary Olympics was significant, taking place two years after the Oka Crisis – a tense land dispute between, first, the Mohawk and the Quebec town of Oka and, then, Indigenous peoples and the Canadian government at large. Also known as the Kanehsatà:ke Resistance, the conflict broadcast ongoing and unresolved tensions between Indigenous nations and the Canadian state. "I think that the reason that we put [the team] together was because at the [time] there was a lot of ... difficulty between Aboriginal and non-Aboriginal [people] in Canada," explains one of its co-organizers, Montreal-based Danielle Medina. "Also there was a saying that the ... two cultures [Aboriginal and non-Aboriginal] are two parallels that will never meet," she continued. "So if you look at the logo of the Aboriginal [Haute] Cuisine [team], it [represents] the two parallel[s] crossing each other in the form of a tipi [and] underneath was a [cooking] pot, because we [felt] that it is through food that you discover and understand a culture better."[135] George's summary backs this up: "It was more than a competition. It was a statement ... Cause right up to about 1960, Aboriginal people weren't even allowed in a lot of restaurants."[136] This returns to eateries – and the culinary world at large – as spaces that either uphold or challenge the status quo and the politics that they enact.

George Jr. returned from the Culinary Olympics a star. However, one year later, in 1993, he closed Toody Ni and moved back to Burns Lake to care for his father.[137] Around the same time that his father suffered two strokes, which was George Jr.'s call home, a paper reports that Toody Ni was experiencing financial difficulties because of "a poor location."[138] Back in the Lakes District, "because he couldn't find work as a chef anywhere between Prince George and Prince Rupert," he accepted a job with the BC Ministry of Forests.[139] "Everyone said I was overqualified. I think the Olympics scared them all off," George Jr. confessed.[140] However, he never hung up his chef whites and continued to keep one foot in the culinary world, working as an instructor and consultant. In 1997 he published his first cookbook. While preparing for the Culinary Olympics, George Jr. met Robert Gairns, an Ontario-based Métis writer working as the Canadian Native Haute Cuisine Team's communications advisor. Following George Jr.'s success at the Culinary Olympics, Gairns asked him if he was interested in penning a cookbook.[141] Doubleday published *Feast! Canadian Native Cuisine for All Seasons* in 1997.[142] The title pays homage to "the traditional

Wet'suwet'en feast, *denii ne'aas*, which means 'people coming together.'"[143] To add to the title's cheerful exclamation mark, local press celebrated the cookbook as the "first-of-its-kind."[144] As this one newspaper says: "*Feast!* is the first all-Native cookbook written by Native chef, and the book's publisher, Doubleday of New York, is convinced it has a best-seller on its hands."[145] Another local paper hailed the cookbook as "Glitzy, but not too gourmet."[146] Vancouver's next Indigenous restaurant – the Liliget Feast House – would also mark the end of its culinary contribution to the city with a cookbook.

## From Platter to Feast

While the Quilicum was indexing ways to prepare salmon and George Jr. was turning the Vancouver Indian Friendship Centre into a restaurant, Dolly Watts was running a catering company outside of the Museum of Anthropology at the University of British Columbia: Just Like Grandma's Bannock.[147] At the age of forty-nine, Watts enrolled at UBC and, at fifty-seven, launched her catering company.[148] That same year, 1992, she graduated with a degree in anthropology, and had plans to continue studying. She filled the time in between by baking bannock, which rerouted her on a culinary path. Her company grew out of a one-time fundraiser for the museum's Native youth education program.[149] "We were brainstorming and I said, 'What about selling bannock?' 'What's that?' the kids asked."[150] They quickly sold out, and raised enough funds for a field trip. The museum, where she worked as a tour guide, encouraged her to regularly set up shop.[151] "We made it in the museum's staffroom and you could smell it everywhere," chuckles Watts.[152] A fundraiser became a food cart, then a catering company, and, finally, a restaurant.

Sometime between 1994 and 1995, the Quilicum closed. In 1995 the *Vancouver Sun* announced that Watts would reopen it as the Liliget Feast House.[153] A Gitk'san word, liliget means "where people feast."[154] Parting ways from the Muckamuck and Quilicum, both Chinook Jargon names, and similar to Toody Ni, Watts named her restaurant in her language, thus aligning it with her First Nation. This identifies her restaurant with her specific culture and, therefore, cuisine, rather than carrying on the pan-Indigenous take that Vancouver's first two Indigenous eateries established.

Unlike the Muckamuck and Quilicum, the Liliget Feast House was fully Indigenous-owned, making Watts's acquisition of this forty-nine-seat eatery an important milestone. I asked her if she had eaten at the Quilicum: "No," she replied. "My son found the restaurant space and told me about it. It wasn't in good shape." A United Airlines pilot, he also fronted her the money.[155] The restaurant cost $130,000 to acquire and renovate.[156] At the age of sixty, Watts took on this ambitious new project and ran the restaurant for twelve years. The Liliget Feast House opened its doors at the end of August 1995 and became, in the words of her daughter Annie Watts, "the world's only Native American fine dining establishment at the time."[157]

Why did the Quilicum close? A closure is often quieter than an opening. Despite its many reviews, the Quilicum's ending left fewer marks.[158] Watts's memory of her son stumbling upon the restaurant varies in one article, which states, "In 1995, an old friend passed away from cancer and left behind a restaurant … the longhouse setting provided an excellent ambience for Watts' dream restaurant … but she wasn't completely sure at first. 'She was my friend, and she ran a restaurant here for 10 years. I didn't feel good about renting it right away,' Watts said."[159] Alongside the address, the Liliget Feast House shared its predecessors' décor. Indigenous art dressed the walls and diners had to flip up the cedar tabletops to swing their legs beneath (Figure 5.1). Reviews boasted about the architect: the celebrated Canadian Arthur Erickson, who was known for the post-and-beam Museum of Anthropology and, coincidentally, was also involved as a consultant for Expo 67's Canada Pavilion.[160] A server summed up the interior as Erickson's "idea of an Indian longhouse, without having ever seen one."[161] Erickson's name is curiously absent from the Muckamuck and Quilicum reviews; nonetheless, he designed the original restaurant space in the early 1970s.[162]

In 2001 the *Vancouver Sun* carried on the comparison between the restaurant's interior and Japanese aesthetics, a similarity first

Figure 5.1. "Liliget Feast House interior," 2006, Vancouver, British Columbia, image courtesy of www.foodgps.com.

observed in the 1970s: "the atmosphere is near mystical with heavy cedar posts and an almost Japanese, sparse beauty."[163] A couple of years earlier – and on the other side of the world – the *Sydney Morning Herald* not only recommended the Liliget Feast House but also specified that its décor was "inspired by the atmosphere of a Salish Coast Longhouse."[164] Gone were sweeping terms like "Indian" and "Native," marking a shift in both representation and awareness.

Some dishes were similar to what came before: fern shoots and crab cakes, wood-roasted salmon and duck, steamed herring roe and pan-fried oolichans, bannock and "magic berries, or sopalali, whipped into a delicious mousse."[165] Liliget Feast House also plated dishes in carved cedar and alder bowls, and employed similar cooking techniques: "We grill most everything over fire," explained Watts. "We use alder wood so that everything we cook tastes so much like the food we used to eat in our villages."[166] Unfortunately, the Quilicum's menus have not survived in public records; however, in comparison to the Muckamuck's, Liliget Feast House presented its dishes in a more maximalist fashion. Detailed descriptions replaced minimalist names. In 2005 the *Vancouver Sun* published a cross between an endorsement and a menu called "Canadian content." "What food could be more indigenous than that of our first nations?" it asks, before listing dishes such as "Crisp kelp on steamed rice with oolichan oil," "Wind-dried salmon with drawn butter," and "Steamed herring roe with drawn or garlic butter."[167]

Liliget further distinguished itself from the Muckamuck and Quilicum by peddling bison – "Alder-grilled buffalo smoky" with wild blueberry sauce.[168] This decision stretched Liliget's geography beyond the Pacific Northwest coast and east towards the Great Plains where bison once roamed in grand numbers and, recently, have started to return.[169] The "Buffalo smokies" also circle back to the beginning of Watts's culinary career, when she served this "hugely popular" dish outside the Museum of Anthropology.[170] The restaurant's version was more upscale, but the idea came from a customer's question: "Why don't you make a sandwich with the bannock?" "We called it a ban-wich," Watts laughs.[171] A drive she took outside of Vancouver inspired her to seek out bison. "I saw buffalo on a field. I couldn't believe it."[172] This prompted her research and she found a place in Vancouver that sold bison meat.

Instead of the "Potlatch platter," Watts offered the "Liliget feast platter," which spotlighted her famous "Buffalo smokies" in addition to the likes of alder-grilled sockeye salmon, mussels and Pacific oysters, venison and duck breast, sweet potatoes with hazelnuts and fiddleheads, wild rice medley and wild blueberry sauce (Figure 5.2).[173] By 2005 the platter cost $49.95 before tax and tip, and $53.95 in 2006.[174] A 2006 menu captures another version that included "Crispy calamari," "Sweet potato tarts topped with pecans," and "Savory rhubarb sauce."[175] With dishes like "Crab cakes with corn salsa," "Clam fritters served with sweet and sour sauce," and "Stuffed jalapenos with cream cheese," the Liliget Feast House served hybrid dishes that one might call fusion, which recalls Chapter 3.

# RESTAURANT MENU

*Liliget Feast House & Catering*

## Starters

RECOMMENDED WINES
NK'MIP CELLARS
**Merlot or Chardonnay**

Complimentary Basket of Bannock with Smoked Salmon-Cream Cheese Spread
Recommended Beer: Granville Island Kitsilano Maple Cream Ale .......... $4.95
Crab Cakes with Corn Salsa ...................................................... $7.95
Smoked Oolicans with a Lemon Wedge ........................................ $8.95
Wind Dried Salmon with Drawn Butter......................................... $6.95
Clam Fritters served with Sweet and Sour Sauce ............................. $6.95

2004 BC Gold Komochi Konbu Iron Chef Challenge

## Main Entrees

Gold Medal Winner BC Iron Chef Dolly Watts

Where Magazine

Winner "Best Ethnic Cuisine" 2002

National Aboriginal Achievement Award

Winner "Business & Commerce" 2001

Aboriginal Tourism BC

Award Winner "Excellence in Customer Service" 2006

Supernatural White Owl Family Crest

**Feast Platter for Two:** Alder Grilled Marinated Duck Breast, Marinated Venison Strips, Buffalo Smokies, Poached Half-Smoked Wild Salmon and Crispy Calamari. Served with Sweet Potato Tarts topped with Pecans, Wild Rice Medley, Seasonal Vegetables, Savory Rhubarb Sauce and Dill Sauce $53.95 (Platter for One $26.95)

**Alder Grilled Marinated Venison Chops:** Served with Sautéed Onions, Mashed Russet Potatoes, Seasonal Vegetables and Savory Rhubarb Sauce $23.95

**Alder Grilled Marinated Wild Salmon:** Served with Wild Rice Medley, Seasonal Vegetables and Dill Sauce $21.95

**Poached Half-Smoked Wild Salmon:** Served with Wild Rice Medley, Seasonal Vegetables, Sweet Raspberry Onion Garnish and Dill Sauce $22.95

**Vegetarian Platter for One:** Wild Rice Medley topped with Crisp Kelp, Sweet Potato Tart topped with Pecans, Spinach Quiche Tart, Stuffed Jalapenos with Cream Cheese, Potato with Cheddar Cheese Perogies and Steamed Seasonal Vegetables $23.95

**Alder Grilled Buffalo Smoky:** Served with Mashed Russet Potatoes, Seasonal Vegetables and Savory Rhubarb Sauce $14.95

Prices do not include applicable taxes or gratuity.

Figure 5.2. "Liliget Feast House menu," 2006, Vancouver, British Columbia, image courtesy of Annie Watts.

The restaurant attracted "local regulars, out-of-town tourists, and celebrities alike."[176] The "Feast platter" was expensive, but Watts also provided more affordable dishes. In 2001 she launched the "traditional favourites" lunch hour, which offered a buffalo burger with a beverage and dessert for $10. "It should be good for local Aboriginal people," Watts clarified. "They crave stuff like that. They only get it when there's a powwow."[177] Similar to later examples in Toronto, Liliget identified an urban demand for pow wow fare. Her menu moved away from traditional ingredients only and made room for contemporary tastes.

Once again, the restaurant at 1724 Davie Street pleased diners and drew positive reviews. The year the Liliget Feast House opened, in 1995, Jurgen Goethe crowned it "Best native Indian" in the *Vancouver Sun*, although one is left wondering about its competition.[178] The 2006 menu also listed some of the Liliget Feast House's awards, including "Gold Medal Winner, BC Iron Chef Dolly Watts" and the "2004 BC Gold Komochi Konbu Iron Chef Challenge."[179] In 2002 Liliget Feast House won *Where Magazine*'s "Best Ethnic Cuisine" title. Despite headlines like "Canadian content," the press continued to classify Liliget Feast House as "ethnic," subconsciously ranking it at a lower position in the hierarchy of eating out. To recall Chapter 2, a restaurant receives carte blanche to cook as its kitchen pleases, whereas the "ethnic" label calls on a menu to represent not just the chef's point of view but their culture at large.

Reviews continued to frame Liliget Feast House as unique, just as earlier ones had done for the Muckamuck and Quilicum. A 1999 *Pacific Rim Magazine* article concluded, "Liliget provides a stimulating dining experience that is a little bit different from a typical night out."[180] In 1996 the *New York Times* recommended it, a prestigious endorsement, writing, "Wind-dried salmon and pan-fried oolichans ... are some of the unusual choices."[181] These reviews did more than just praise the Liliget Feast House; they also persuaded readers to walk down the stairs to give it a try. For instance, a 2003 *Globe and Mail* article stated, "I walk by almost daily but have never bothered to visit. I've been intrigued by the concept – Liliget is the proud, lone practitioner of Pacific Northwest native cuisine, whatever that might mean. But the entrance, just a small narrow doorway on Davie Street, never seems to promise much."[182] The critic was delighted when she finally descended the stairs, reinforcing the reviewer's role in convincing diners to try a restaurant. Her initial hesitancy reveals that even a professional critic was not sure about trudging down to a basement restaurant to eat "whatever" Pacific Northwest native cuisine was.

In 2001 Watts received a National Aboriginal Achievement Award for Business and Commerce. An *Edmonton Journal* article celebrating the winners introduced her with: "There will never be a market for indigenous food in a restaurant setting in Canada. Wrong. If you want to know just how wrong, talk to Dolly Watts."[183] She was not only running a successful business; Watts was also proof that Indigenous fare crafted by Indigenous chefs belongs in Canada's restaurant landscape.

Reviews praised Watts's cooking, but she was not the only one in the kitchen. The restaurant was a family affair. Her daughter Cynthia helped at the food cart.[184] Marina, Watts's granddaughter, also worked there.[185] Before joining her mom at the Liliget, Annie Watts had waited tables, which sparked her interest in becoming a chef. She enrolled at Malaspina College on Vancouver Island, earning a culinary arts degree. In addition to planning the menus and designing the restaurant's promotional material, Annie cooked part time.[186] Beyond Watts's family, most of the staff were Indigenous.[187]

Dolly Watts grew up in Kitwanga, a village in central BC. When she was ten, she was sent to Alberni Residential School (1891–1973), located on Nuu-chah-nulth land on Vancouver Island, over one thousand kilometres south from her family home.[188] Ironically, one article describes this school as where she reaped her first culinary success.[189] Instead of characterizing Watts's experience at residential school as traumatic, this article sees it as part of her culinary education, as part of the beginning of her CV. "Recruited to fill in for an absent breakfast cook, she sidestepped the daily fried eggs by lining muffin tins with baked bacon rashers, filling them with eggs and milk and finishing them in the oven."[190] Another article reports, "while at school she earned pocket money making desserts for the teachers."[191] Watts did not cook because she wanted to. "We had no choice," she told me. "There were no adult workers, only four adult supervisors for 150 girls. We did the work."[192] She had to scrub staircases and cook meals. "Most of the food we got was left over from stores. We got potatoes and cabbage. Every morning we got porridge. No toast. No milk."[193] No bannock.

When Watts moved to Vancouver years later, she "didn't see bannock."[194] It was her mother's she missed most. "Mom never gave me instructions about cooking. But I followed her around the house … watching her cook." Her mother made bannock every morning for breakfast, with yeast instead of baking powder. "She didn't deep-fry it," Watts remembers. "She would fry it on the stove. It was so good. It was really flat, but in the oil it would rise." Decades later, Watts made bannock the same way in Vancouver, frying it in about an inch of oil and selling it, first, from her food cart and, then, at her restaurant.

A 2008 article, published the year after Watts closed the Liliget Feast House, romanticized her childhood while also taking into account how traditional Gitk'san foodways had changed. Titled "Nature's Supermarket," the article by journalist Mia Stainsby opens with: "When you grow up in the country, you're on a guest list to the free store: nature's supermarket. Dolly Watts of the Gitk'san First Nation had a further advantage. She inherited thousands of years of tradition and knew her way around the store better than most consumers of wild edible foods."[195] This paints a picture of abundance. It also marks the mainstream media's growing interest in Indigenous ingredients. "We had all the game we wanted, all the salmon we wanted," recalls Watts. She spent her childhood foraging for bulbs, berries, and bark, wild rhubarb, tubers, and hemlock sap, water lily roots, fiddleheads, and fireweed.[196] Ingredients that Stainsby identifies as "only found in high-end restaurants these days."[197] In contrast to these wild foods, Watts recalls, "The real change was when baloney came around and my mom bought some for variety. We thought it was like steak. We didn't know what we had been eating was expensive, good quality food."[198] This account represents a shift in value of both wild and commodity foods. In 2008 wild foods had been elevated to fancy restaurant fare – the kind Noma was crafting its reputation with – but when Watts was growing up in the late 1930s and early 1940s, baloney was as sophisticated as steak.[199] These foods had swapped places. Gourmet restaurants had returned to the land in search of wilder ingredients years after the Canadian government had restocked Indigenous kitchens with bagged flour and processed meat.

Despite its success, in 2004 a journalist published Watts's plan to sell the restaurant.[200] Watts remembers it differently: "There was the question of when we should quit. I was in my 70s and all of a sudden we got word to move out. The whole block had been sold."[201] She used this opportunity to retire. In March 2007 the *Vancouver Sun* announced that Watts had sold the Liliget Feast House to a condo developer, which ends the story of 1724 Davie Street, but not of Indigenous restaurants in Vancouver.[202] After a twelve-year run, longer than either the Muckamuck or the Quilicum, the legacy of the Liliget Feast House lives on in *Where People Feast: An Indigenous People's Cookbook*.[203] One critic called it "one of only a few North American aboriginal cookbooks available."[204] It won the Gourmand Award for Best Local Cuisine Book (Canada). As one review claimed, "Long before the idea of a 100-mile diet popped into our heads, the First Nations people who lived here were already walking the walk."[205] By serving dishes inspired by her childhood as well as her personal taste, the Liliget Feast House represented Watts and her culture, beaming her culinary point of view and, thus, further expanding the register of Indigenous restaurant menus in Canada.

## 1724 Davie Street

In answering the question of why there are so few Indigenous restaurants, it is important to ask why earlier ones closed. The labour dispute forced the Muckamuck to shut its doors, an illness did the same to the Quilicum, the combination of a family illness and financial difficulties closed Toddy Ni, and the sale of the building to a condo developer put an end to the Liliget Feast House. In Chapter 10, I revisit Vancouver by discussing Salmon n' Bannock, which opened in 2010. But, first I distil the city's history of Indigenous restaurants from 1971 to 2007 into a few observations. Minus the gaps between the Muckamuck and the Quilicum (four years), then between the Quilicum and Liliget Feast House, and the two years between the Liliget Feast House and Salmon n' Bannock, the history of Indigenous restaurants in Vancouver has the most continuity in Canada.

The Muckamuck was non-Indigenous-owned (two women ran it and a man co-owned it), the Quilicum was Indigenous co-owned (by two men and one woman), and the Liliget was Indigenous-owned, just like Toody Ni. Would Watts have opened the Liliget Feast House if it were not for the space she inherited from the Quilicum? Would the Quilicum's concept – a restaurant named after the return of the people – have developed without the Muckamuck and the solidarity that the staff forged on the picket line? In many ways 1724 Davie Street is one story with three chapters. The Muckamuck and Quilicum broke in Vancouver's diners, who were then ready for Watts to open a restaurant with contemporary Indigenous fare that challenged textbook stereotypes. Together these restaurants tell a story about the evolution of Indigenous restaurants – and their reception – in Vancouver.

As this history shows, Indigenous restaurants are not new. However, because of changes in the relationships between Indigenous peoples, the government, and Canadian society at large, contemporary restaurants occupy different political and cultural landscapes. When the Muckamuck opened in the 1970s, residential schools were still serving "sad ol' mush" to kill the "Indian" to save the child. Watts opened the Liliget Feast House in 1995, one year after the last residential school in BC – St. Mary's Mission – closed, and one year before the last one in the country.[206] The Muckamuck and Quilicum belong to the first period of Indigenous restaurants I identify: 1971 to 1996. The twelve years the Liliget Feast House operated straddle this period with the one that follows, 1997 to 2014: after the residential school period, but before the Truth and Reconciliation era. Indigenous restaurants shadow the politics of each period they belong to as well as shape.

Unlike the CPR dining cars and hotels, Expo 67's La Toundra, and the Tomahawk, the Liliget Feast House presented an Indigenous interpretation of dining, not someone else's imagination, an act of culinary self-determination. Following the dispute between the Muckamuck and its staff, those who resurrected the restaurant as the Quilicum continued to serve similar dishes but with distinct stories. The biggest change between the two was ownership and, thus, who had the power to tell whose stories. The Quilicum voiced a different story with the same food: one promoting an awareness of Indigenous culture on Indigenous peoples' terms. Toody Ni did the same. The Liliget Feast House inherited the Quilicum's space but not its menu. Watts served some dishes in the tune of the Muckamuck and Quilicum – "Sweet potatoes with hazelnuts" and "Alder-grilled sockeye salmon" – but also others in an entirely different key, the likes of "Buffalo smokies" and "Clam fritters with sweet and sour sauce." After years of Vancouverites eating Indigenous fare more reminiscent of a historic ethnographic study than a contemporary cookbook, the Liliget Feast House affirmed just how diverse Indigenous cuisines are. How did this history in Vancouver compare to culinary developments in other cities? I now turn east to Winnipeg, back west to the heavily trafficked highway between Calgary and Banff, followed by a short stop in Edmonton, and then to Saskatchewan.

chapter six

# A Meal for a Chief

Vancouver was not the only Canadian city to host an Indigenous restaurant in the 1980s. In 1981, the year the Muckamuck closed, Bungees opened in Winnipeg on 28 September. The following year the *Financial Post Magazine* called it "Canada's only native restaurant."[1] Four years before, in 1977, Mary Richard, then director of Winnipeg's Indian and Métis Friendship Centre, Yvonne Monkman, the principal of Little Ones' School, and Joy Fedorick, the assistant director of Youth Action Project, had already registered the name of the business.[2] The Manitoba government supported the idea of an Indigenous restaurant, but, as historians Kimberley Moore and Janis Thiessen illuminate, this had less to do with championing culinary creativity and more to do with the racist assumption that the restaurant, on one hand, "would be a 'crime prevention' project" and, on the other, a training program for people "who need to learn to work."[3] Despite the province's support, it did not offer any funds and Richard and Monkman took out a private loan.[4]

Named after "the first Indians to settle the Red River country" and outfitted to resemble a cabin, Bungees had a menu spanning "Salteaux soup" (buffalo consommé with garlic, sunflower seeds, and fiddleheads), "Crêpes stuffed with pickerel cheeks," and "Smoked sturgeon with bannock" – all "exotic" according to the *Financial Post Magazine*.[5] Fiddleheads – spring's maze of a vegetable – have played a supporting role in representations of Indigenous cuisines, from La Toundra in Montreal to the Muckamuck and

Quilicum in Vancouver. However, unlike the West Coast's first Indigenous eateries, traces of Bungees are faint, comparable to foraging for greens in a maelstrom of green. A fiddlehead fern snakes itself into a tight spiral, looking more like an endless loop than a vegetable with a clear top and tail. Compared to Vancouver, the beginnings and endings of Winnipeg's first Indigenous restaurant, likewise, are difficult to spot and separate.

In 1984, 236 Edmonton Street was remodelled and renamed, becoming the Teepee Restaurant and Lounge.[6] In 1985, Regina's *Leader-Post* published a picture of Richard alongside the headline "Native women obstructed in business community." This article was less concerned about the Teepee's fare and, instead, narrowed its focus on the structural obstacles hindering Indigenous entrepreneurs, in general, and women, in particular. Revisiting the question of why there have been so few Indigenous restaurants in Canada, the first attempts in Winnipeg point toward the racial intolerance and hostility that restaurateurs endured. Alongside fiddleheads, racial discrimination is a perennial theme that threads together the first urban Indigenous eateries.

Dressed in plaid, Richard poses in front of one of the eatery's booths. Neatly cut logs of wood and an abstract landscape painting line the wall – an interior that fulfils expectations of a cabin atmosphere. Reporting on a Winnipeg conference tackling "the problems Indian and Metis women face in the business world," the article quotes Richard on the challenges she has encountered. "Overcoming that negative stereotype is very hard," she stresses.[7] That Richard flags derogatory stereotypes only further underscores the perpetual power of settler storying. At the time the Teepee opened, hostile and racist stereotypes of Indigenous peoples hovered over the businesses they opened and ran. And because of gender discrimination, this especially hit women. Indigenous business owners were not seen as legitimate.

The following month the *Financial Post* again reported on the Teepee, repeating its emphasis on entrepreneurship, but, this time, disclosing more of its history. "About five years ago, Richard and partner Yvonne Black, who had worked together at a Winnipeg social-service agency, set up the downtown Teepee Restaurant," the newspaper recorded.[8] Why did Bungees change its name to the Teepee? And why did it change its décor? Questions aside, what is clear is that running an Indigenous restaurant was not easy. This article reported that Richard's success "has helped to encourage other native people, particularly women, to attempt the plunge."[9] And yet the word plunge suggests less an optimistic endorsement and more a cautious "best of luck." Richard, at the time, was also a director of the Winnipeg-based Native Economic Development Program. Job creation was central to her decision to open a restaurant, which trained around sixty people and regularly employed thirteen.[10]

Tailgating the 1969 White Paper, as Chapter 2 outlined, Indigenous activism across the country continued to pick up speed. Historians Allyson Stevenson and Cheryl Troupe draw a direct line between kitchen tables and formal social and political organization. Although their study spotlights Saskatchewan, its concerns ripple across the provinces. "Excluded from the patriarchal male-dominated organizations that did not represent their interests or concerns," they explain, "Indigenous women across Canada began politically organizing along gendered lines."[11] Canadian colonialism rewrote the script for gender across the lands it claimed, reassigning power to replicate the roles the government subscribed to. This clashed with the many matriarchal and matrilineal societies across Turtle Island, which credited motherhood as a source of both social and political power.[12] Colonization, in a nutshell, weakened the power of Indigenous women. Written in the tune of Euro-Canadian patriarchy, the Indian Act explicitly disadvantaged Indigenous women, as exemplified by its privileging of male lines of descent. The gendered experiences of colonialism thus shaped the forms in which Indigenous women resisted and organized. This resistance casts everyday acts – especially ones that stitch together food, labour, and care – as a genre of activism. To open a restaurant not only claimed a cultural presence, but also amplified a social and political Indigenous voice in a settler-majority urban space – another instance of restaurant politics.

The saying prophesies that success depends on "location, location, location," and the Teepee's was good: downtown and around the corner from the Royal Winnipeg Ballet. "It was visible," Richard said, "and I was sort of hoping it would take away the Main St. image. It creates a whole new area where native people haven't been involved at all."[13] Richard's hope returns to how her restaurant had to shed settler storying and stereotypes in order to be taken seriously. But it also gestures toward the city's racial segregation. Main Street in Winnipeg's North End, a neighbourhood I return to in Chapter 9's summary of contemporary Indigenous eateries in the city, is an example of food apartheid – a system that divides those who have access to a profusion of nutritious food from those who do not. A textbook case, Main Street has a large Indigenous population yet few grocery stores. This is to say that Richard identified negative cultural stereotypes as one of the biggest obstacles hindering Indigenous women, and men, from pursuing independent, business ventures, and Main Street, tragically, is haunted by structural racism. As Richard's quote makes clear, the Teepee was a powerful venue for projecting an image of Indigenous life that went beyond the legacy of misinformed stereotypes. It was a culinary – and cultural – intervention. In 1987 Ming Court restaurant, which first opened in another part of Winnipeg in 1979, had moved to 236 Edmonton Street.[14] Winnipeg's first stint of hosting Indigenous restaurants, a period that had started in 1981, had already ended. In contrast, this chapter – which groups together the first eateries to spawn in Manitoba, Alberta, and Saskatchewan in the 1980s and 1990s – now roves back west from the Prairies to the Rocky Mountains to pen the biography of a long-lasting Indigenous eatery: Chief Chiniki.

## "Chief Chiniki Salad"

A location, especially one with "a commanding view of mountains," can sell a restaurant, and Chief Chiniki Restaurant in Alberta, which also opened in 1981, flaunted both the location and the view.[15] Although *Culinary Claims* focuses on urban restaurants rather than ones on reserves, Chief Chiniki is an exception. It differs from other examples because of its location on the highly frequented stretch of the Trans-Canada highway thirty minutes outside of Calgary and en route to Banff. Perched on the Morley turnoff, it attracted urbanites retreating from the city for a day or two, often with skis strapped to their cars. A 24 July 1981 advertisement in the *Calgary Herald* announced its opening: "When the Chiniquary Band of Indians at Morley decided to commemorate the life of Chief John Chiniki, they chose a unique form of memorial – the first native Indian restaurant in Alberta."[16] Chief John Chiniki, who died in 1906, had signed Treaty Number Seven at Blackfoot Crossing in 1877, and over a century later the Nakoda First Nation nominated this "fitting building," constructed from natural wood, in his honour.[17] Other early eateries chose names that flagged words in Indigenous languages or symbols of Indigeneity. In contrast, Chief Chiniki paid homage to one individual, adding his name as a historic marker on the drive from Calgary to Banff. The eatery – and therefore the memorial – was a success, and by 1989, the *Calgary Herald* declared Chief Chiniki Restaurant a "must for out-of-towners."[18]

Chief Frank Powderface hatched the idea together with Nakoda Elders. Unlike how the Tomahawk slapped the names of chiefs onto their hamburgers, this entire restaurant commemorated a historic leader, casting its name as a tribute, a eulogy. Chief Chiniki Restaurant was also an act of self-representation. "The band felt that this would provide employment for native people, and keep money on the reserve," reported the *Calgary Herald*, "as many of the reserve's residents enjoy eating out and had to travel some distance to do this."[19] The restaurant would allow them to eat "native dishes on home territory" on their own terms, identifying a local demand. After opening in 1981 with Helen Houle as its chef, Chief Chiniki Restaurant quickly became a "hub for Morley reserve elders and mountain tourists alike."[20] Tourists were welcome to drop by for a bite, but it was not them alone the restaurant sought to attract. Chief Chiniki was, first and foremost, a community restaurant, catering to the appetites of locals.

In some ways Chief Chiniki was also a sequel to Banff's Indian Days, which is to say it served as a contact zone between the Chiniquary band, a Nakoda nation (formerly known as the Stoney), on their home territory and Calgarians and travellers touring to or from Banff. But this time, these encounters were on the Nakoda's terms. Historically, government policies severed Indigenous reserves from settler cities and aimed to patrol a hard border between them, as exemplified by the pass system in western Canada. But these policies also limited the lands Indigenous peoples could access and how, while cutting them off from economic opportunities. Sarah Carter documents an instance in 1885 when "one Indian agent urged the citizens of Calgary not to purchase anything from Aboriginal people or hire them, since this would help keep them out of the town."[21] By inviting settlers and tourists alike to the table, Chief Chiniki Restaurant challenged the ongoing legacies of historical segregation without catering to settler expectations.

Unlike at Banff's Indian Days, at Chief Chiniki Restaurant the Nakoda were no longer forced to perform settler imaginations of Indigeneity. They could now dress how they wanted and cook what they pleased. Not only did this now include bison, which this time was their choice, but it was the main dish. In 1981 the restaurant vaunted its "variety of native dishes, all authentically Indian, served with freshly baked bannock and crisp salads."[22] Akin to how the menus at Vancouver's Indigenous restaurants catalogue salmon, Chief Chiniki offered lessons in the culinary lives of bison: "Slow roasted buffalo," "Buffalo burgers," "Buffalo stew," and "Charcoal broiled buffalo steaks," "all made from the meat of buffalo raised on the reserve and federally inspected."[23] A tableau of the Plains' animal protagonist. Chapter 8 attends to "federally inspected" meats, but here I am interested in what the menu as a whole says and how it shifted over time. Beyond bison, Chief Chiniki provided game meat and fish according to availability, such as elk, moose, deer, rabbit, trout, and whitefish. There were also "traditionally Canadian dishes" like fish and chips, homemade pies, sandwiches, and the usual meat trio of pork, chicken, and beef.[24] A 1984 advertisement even promised caribou.[25] The restaurant did not serve alcohol.

After having driven by Chief Chiniki "a million times," in 1987 Kathy Richardier finally pulled over at the Morley turnoff. "The thing is, it's about 65 kilometres west of Calgary, or about a half-hour drive on the Trans-Canada and, on the way to skiing, it's too close to stop," she justified.[26] She wasn't the only one: "Everyone who has driven to and from the mountains has glimpsed the Chief Chiniki – it's the only thing there."[27] As she reported for the *Calgary Herald*, she was happy to have tried its speciality: bison meat that the "Stoneys raise." "Buffalo meat is good, at least the way these people (all Indians as far as we could ascertain) prepare it. It is mild and, to us, tasted more like beef than anything else we were familiar with, but was also more flavorful," she said.[28] She was most impressed with the "Chief Chiniki salad," which came with Italian dressing: "It did Chief Chiniki proud," she praised, describing "a generous and most attractive arrangement" of ham, turkey, beef, "real bacon … still hot from the pan," romaine and iceberg lettuce, red cabbage, and radishes.[29] She "devoured every morsel." But why did the salad wear Chief Chiniki's name? Had it been his favourite? As the next chapter contends, naming this salad after Chief Chiniki, like the restaurant itself, was an act of claiming. The name grafts value, similar to the Canadian Pacific Railway's history of adorning its menus with images worlds away from its European-inspired dishes. But Richardier doesn't consider the connections between the restaurant dishes and their names. "Our food was much what we expected – plain, but, on the whole, prepared with care, priced very reasonably and served by pleasant people," she concludes her review.[30] "Plain" undercuts the kitchen, only for the word "but" to soften her verdict and elevate it to an endorsement.

Echoing the history of international expos and events as culinary stages, the Chiniki Band renovated the restaurant's grounds in time for the 1988 Calgary Olympics, and added a gift shop.[31] In the Olympics they saw an opportunity to promote themselves, akin to what the Mississaugas saw decades later in Toronto's Pan Am Games. By 1995 Chief Chiniki Restaurant's most popular dish was an "Indian taco": a pile of frybread, buffalo meat, tomatoes, lettuce, and cheese.[32] Now with Tom Yorke heading the kitchen, the eatery had "put a lot of effort into redesigning the menu to meet increased tourist demand for native cuisine."[33] However, this overlooks the appetites of its Indigenous customers. The *Calgary Herald* listed the updates, which do not sound too different from the previous fare: "the new menu prominently features buffalo, but in updated ways, including everything from ground buffalo steak with eggs for breakfast to buffalo steak, stew and even gigantic buffalo burgers."[34] Like earlier reviews, it makes sure to flag that the bison comes from the nearby reserve.

## The Other Side of Hospitality

One year after Chief Chiniki, a second Indigenous eatery opened in Alberta: Tribes Restaurant in Edmonton at 8006 103rd Street. On 4 August 1982, an *Edmonton Journal* advertorial pronounced it "the only restaurant west of Winnipeg specializing in native Indian foods, representing both plains and costal delicacies."[35] This overlooked Chief Chiniki. But it also reveals that the singularity of Indigenous eateries was a unique marketing feature. "One of Edmonton's newest restaurants, Tribes, offers North America's oldest cuisine – native Indian," boasted the ad. Instead of flaunting the novelty of Indigenous cuisine, it reframes it as the continent's original fare. This aligns with efforts across Turtle Island at the time to topple settler storying and to challenge its narratives of Indigenous erasure. Eric Shirt of Saddle Lake Cree Nation was the owner and manager behind Tribes. He "chose the Indian theme because there was no such restaurant in Edmonton – 'and there's no reason there shouldn't be.'"[36] According to Shirt, Indigenous fare deserved a spot in Canada's restaurantscape. A band-owned company, Saddle Lake Investments Ltd., owned a quarter of the restaurant, and Shirt the rest.[37] Tribe's logo was a man hunting a bison on horseback, feathers fastened to his hair.

Halibut and "salmon grilled on alderwood" represented "Coastal Indian" fare. Rabbit, whitefish, and bison – the likes of "Marinated buffalo stew" and "Buffalo on a bun" – portrayed "Plains Indian food." The menu also included bannock, "Sweet potatoes with roasted hazelnuts" (a dish the Muckamuck had also served), "Saskatoon and gooseberry pie," "Smoked salmon chips," "Johnnycake with hot spicy sauce," "Alderwood-cooked duck with black currant sauce," and "Juniper duck baked in salt marinated cabbage served with wild rice."[38] "Rabbit or buffalo liver shish kebobs" entailed "more exotic items." Beyond the Indigenous pantry, there was a New York cut sirloin steak. Despite the advertorial having categorized "Buffalo liver shish kebobs" as "exotic," Shirt stressed the familiarity of Tribe's ingredients. "He points out that many of the foods in common use are North American in origin and were introduced to European settlers by the Indians," reports one review. "As a result, many of the items on the menu are well known to all Canadians."[39] Shirt purposely used his menu to expose the Indigenous pedigree of what had become "Canadian" ingredients. This tension surfaces again and again, and is a point that the next chapter further unpacks.

With three floors boasting ninety seats, Tribes was large. It had an adjoining bar with a separate name: Fort Whoop Up. Beyond making bannock and bison available in the city, Tribes helped to "round out Edmonton's selection of restaurants offering ethnic specialities and could be a real treat for anyone visiting from Europe."[40] This returns to its insistence on making space for Indigenous cuisines in Canadian cities. Yet, the critic classified Tribes as "ethnic." As a first-time restaurateur, Shirt encountered the usual snags in opening a business, but considered training staff his greatest challenge: "There are lots of native people out there who want to work, but not too many who have restaurant experience," he said. Despite this need, "Governments were unwilling to help through any of their job-training programs so that training was conducted at the restaurant's expense."[41] Shirt was not able to access government support as the Muckamuck had. This files another structural obstacle for Indigenous restaurateurs. Shirt was on his own.

Like the two restaurants in Winnipeg, Tribes has left faint traces, a few newspaper clippings here and there. In October 1991, the *Edmonton Journal* published two articles about Indigenous cuisine, one proclaiming it "the year of the native coffee table cookbook" and the other that despite "a new-found interest in native cooking" among publishers, "Edmonton diners have yet to sustain an authentic Canadian Indian and Metis restaurant."[42] Opening an Indigenous restaurant was one thing, and keeping it open another. The article continued: "The only real attempt at the cuisine in Edmonton was Tribes ... a venture that died soon after its opening."[43] Reflecting on why no one has tried to open an Indigenous eatery in Edmonton since, the journalist consulted the Provincial Museum of Alberta's ethnology curator, Pat McCormack, who believes "prospective native restaurateurs find it difficult to satisfy both sophisticated diners and those seeking a purely traditional approach."[44] Here, "sophisticated" appetites clash with what is coded as traditional, rendering the two incompatible. McCormack also points out "the difficulty in obtaining wild food on a regular basis," and, therefore, prescribes offering alder-smoked buffalo together with Caesar salad. "It is possible to be both authentic and popular," he believes.[45] "Maybe offering native foods from a number of regions," McCormack speculates, "would be a better approach for a restaurant."[46] But Tribes did exactly this, purveying salmon and clams, which represented Canadian coastal regions, alongside a classic New York cut sirloin steak. This nearly replicates McCormack's formula – the seafood plays the role of the buffalo and the New York steak that of the Caesar salad. And yet, the lifespan of Tribes was still short.

In contrast, Chief Chiniki has been Alberta's longest running Indigenous restaurant and an example of a culinary business that has achieved success in tandem with endurance. Although it stuck to comfort food, its menu evolved to include a "Trappers breakfast" (eggs with ham, bacon, sausage, toast, and hash browns), "Elders breakfast special" (a slimmer portion with hash browns, toast, or pancakes), "Prairie soup" (with buffalo, barley, and vegetables), "Pow wow buffalo burger," and a "Bulgogi burger."[47] By referencing a Korean dish, the "Bulgogi burger" hybridizes a Prairie classic and takes a similar approach as the Liliget Feast House by flirting with culinary fusion.

However, in 2016, one critic was not impressed with Chief Chiniki Restaurant. He wanted more, signalling a shift in culinary expectations. Unlike nearly twenty years earlier, a salad with freshly fried bacon was no longer enough to sate a critic. Synthesizing his meal for CBC News, John Gilchrist brands Chief Chiniki as "one of those essential TransCanada pitstop places."[48] A must on any drive across the country for at least a cup of coffee and the view. He lists the "Chiniki bannock taco," "Chiniki poutine," and the "'Rez dog': a hot dog on fry bread topped with chili," only to then sound his disappointment, calling the menu "basic": "the kind you can find at a ballpark or a lounge."[49] "Unfortunately, I think little has been done to include First Nations cuisine. They've got the bannock, the bison, but that's not enough these days," he says, before proceeding to prescribe what he thinks the kitchen should cook: venison, trout, and Saskatoon syrup rather than maple on the pancakes.[50] His use of "these days" acknowledges how diner expectations have changed, representing how enthusiastic eaters have become what philosopher Lisa Heldke terms "food adventurers," which is another way to say "cultural food colonizers."[51] As a critic, he expected Chief Chiniki's menu to perform to his expectations of Indigenous fare.

Restaurants represent the power dynamics behind negotiating what chefs want to serve and what customers want to eat. Tourism belongs to the hospitality industry, and it is telling that the words hospitality and hostility share a root. "Hospitality often holds hands with its brother word *hostility*," writes Priya Basil. "Both are birthed from *ghos-ti*, their ancient Indo-European root, which meant host, guest and stranger."[52] Basil's description echoes Jacques Derrida's concept of "hostipitality." In reading this interdependency, he asserts that hospitality "carries its own contradiction" and that it "allows itself to be parasitized by its opposite."[53] For Derrida, "the undesirable guest" represents hostility – hospitality's opposite. Restaurants are entangled with these tensions.

Gilchrist's comments flex a restaurant critic's position of power: he believes that he is able to determine what "a First Nations dining experience" is. His interpretation makes room for bannock, but emphasizes pre-contact ingredients without clearly acknowledging their Indigenous origins. His review de-Indigenizes maple syrup, exemplifying its largely forgotten pre-contact history.[54] Although Indigenous staff crafted the menu and cooked the food, for him it was not "Indigenous" enough. After eating a "Bison burger on bannock," which was "just fine," he gave the restaurant a six out of ten, summarizing it as "a lost opportunity because, again, it is right on the TransCanada and you can get all of these people coming in for real, Canadian First Nations cuisine."[55] Here the word "real" performs the same work as the word authentic. Gilchrist described his burger as leaving "the Native realm when you add on cheddar and lettuce, tomato, onions, and pickles. It is nothing special. And certainly again, it is not much of a First Nations dining experience."[56] This limits Indigenous fare to pre-contact ingredients, although bannock, made with wheat flour, seems to get a pass even if cheddar cheese does not. It recalls Morris's observation that "The demand that foods (and cultures) meet the criteria of exoticness/authenticity is one of the practices through which the ethnic other is kept firmly in their culinary and cultural place."[57] Gilchrist's advice to serve only "real, Canadian First Nations cuisine" once again exemplifies Wolfe's concept of "repressive authenticity." This represents a conflict between the restaurant's dishes and the diner's expectations of what an Indigenous menu can include.

In between the "Chief Chiniki salad" and the demand for "real, Canadian First Nations cuisine," the restaurant went up in flames. In August 2012 Chief Chiniki burned to the ground. No sooner than the building turned to ash, talk to rebuild began.[58] Four convictions, a two-year federal prison sentence for arson, three years, over three million dollars, and a $1.8-million-dollar insurance claim later, Chiniki Restaurant reopened in July 2015.[59] This time, however, the band decided to lease the restaurant to a tenant, because, in the words of band CEO Lindsay Blackett, it was "not financially viable" to run it itself.[60] Nonetheless, the Stoney Nakoda Nation continued to value the restaurant. As one Elder stated, "It's pretty important that it's reopening again because, obviously, at one point in time it was a landmark for tourists as well as the community."[61] Reopening would also create job opportunities and a venue for Chiniki Community College culinary students to gain experience, similar to how George Jr. had trained at the Quilicum. As Blackett said, "It's got great significance and pride for the Chiniki First Nation people and Stoney Nation."[62] But in spring 2017, not quite a year and a half after its reopening, it closed. A sign announced that a cultural centre would open that summer.[63] It did reopen as the Chiniki Cultural Centre and Stones Restaurant, but then, less than one year later, in July 2018, it closed again. That November a paper reported, "It's unclear when it will reopen and the website no longer exists."[64]

Even with its three-year closure and a one-year gap between the restaurant and the cultural centre complex, Chief Chiniki Restaurant's history spans 1981 to 2018, by far the longest example in the history of Indigenous restaurants in Canada and an impressive feat for any restaurant. It also stretches across the three time periods I distinguish: 1971 to 1996, ending with the closure of Canada's last residential school, 1997 to 2014, the post-residential school and pre–Truth and Reconciliation period, and 2015 to the present. Chief Chiniki simultaneously exemplifies but also defies this classification. It best represents the period in which it first opened, and by the time it rebuilt and entered the post–Truth and Reconciliation period, its menu continued to tell diverse stories about what Indigenous food is and for whom, but without the politics of reconciliation. Chief Chiniki's menu did adapt over time, but so did Canadians' expectations of Indigenous restaurants.

## To Pull a Rabbit Out of a Pot

Returning from the Rockies to the Prairies, Saskatchewan's capital hosted an Indigenous restaurant at the same time that travellers were pulling off the Trans-Canada Highway for the food and views at Chief Chiniki's. A 1999 article profiled the recently renovated eatery at the Landmark Inn: "Regina's original First Nation restaurant."[65] Taking in its décor, Kirk Harrison, the food services manager, points to "the Indian-made art … and the pottery," and exclaims, "There's a new look in the restaurant."[66] Describing the menu as matching the décor, the article makes clear that "it's meant for everyone, not just natives." This assumes the range of voices with which a menu speaks, sharing a language with some diners and extending a translation to others.

Three years earlier, the Ochapowace Band had bought the Landmark Inn. In addition to adding "a First Nation theme suite," they renovated the restaurant's booths and updated the artworks and menu.[67] In turn, they physically transformed the Landmark Inn to represent an Indigenous culinary perspective and to match its menu, on which the likes of "wa-poss stew" (rabbit stew) starred. "No other place in Regina serves that," it boasted.[68]

Decades before this $1-million Indigenous makeover, 4150 Alberta Street had hosted an inn in the 1960s. A photograph from around 1975 captures a curly font advertising the property's original name: "Golden West Inn." Squat rows of stacked rooms typical of post-war roadside motels flank the sign.[69] By 1977 it had a new name: the Landmark Inn.[70] In addition to rooms, in the 1980s the Inn entertained events that ranged from big band concerts to how-to-quit-smoking workshops.[71] Then, in the words of a 1990 headline, the inn became the "latest victim of [the] economy."[72] The hotel went into receivership and its financial difficulty snowballed into fraud. Shady deals that passed around the hotel in the early 1990s culminated in several accounts of fraud for siphoning "immigrant investors' money" that later ended up in court.[73] A few years after these deals and before these court cases, the Ochapowace Band purchased the Landmark Inn for 2.2 million dollars.[74]

When the Band acquired the inn in 1996, it had one Indigenous employee. But by 1999 around 45 of its 120 full- and part-time employees were Indigenous. Similar to Chief Chiniki, for the Ochapowace Band the restaurant was an opportunity to offer "good entry-level jobs to native people that they can use as stepping stones to other jobs."[75] Moreover, as Lester Henry, the general manager, says, "the band made 'the decision to use First Nation's ownership as part of marketing strategy and use it to our advantage.'"[76] This explains the 1999 decision to give the menu a makeover, something the front desk manager, Larry Pratt, considered an "improvement. I've tried some of these [dishes]. I like wild meat myself. A lot of non–First Nations people who haven't had a chance to experience First Nations cuisine would be quite surprised."[77] Novelty assisted in lassoing a settler interest in the menu.

"It may seem strange," the *Regina Sun* reports, "that a non-native such as Harrison is making such dishes, but he has had a lot of experience as a chef."[78] This observation points to two things. First, it identifies a connection between a chef's ethnicity and the food they cook. Second, and most important for the history of Indigenous restaurants in Canada, it hints at an awareness that one must acknowledge – and even justify – who is cooking which culture's food, which is to say Indigenous restaurant politics. After mentioning that Harrison is not Indigenous, the article lists his credentials for cooking Native food: he worked at multiple country inns across Manitoba, and "Besides, he says, he also grew up in a rural area of Manitoba and cooked such things as rabbit stew at home."[79] Although this recognizes cultural ownership of certain dishes, it also illustrates how "Wa-poss stew" can signify an Indigenous dish and the same ingredients under a different name, "Rabbit stew," can signify a settler one.

Bannock accompanies the "wa-poss stew." Other dishes on the menu are "Venison loin chops served with wild mushroom sauce and saskatoon berry sauce" and "Flatlander fusilli" – a pasta dish smothered in a sauce of "lean bison simmered in red wine, wild mushrooms, tomatoes and green onions, finished with cream and served with garlic toast."[80] This selection reveals the spirit of eating in the late 1990s, when fat was bad (making it worth mentioning that the bison is lean) and carbohydrates good (pasta with a side of bread). Venison, rabbit, and bison: once again, "wild" meats represent Indigenous foodways. As the article's title sums up: "His Menu Is a Bit 'Wild.'" But these "wild" meats also pose a challenge: "The cooking techniques have to change somewhat to make the wild game tasty and tender ... It's a lot of moist cooking needing lower temperatures, so you adjust your cooking time," says Harrison.[81]

The Landmark Inn's menu replicates Prairies landscapes and promotes Saskatchewan ingredients like wild rice from La Ronge, including wild rice flour, Saskatoon berries from Keeler, and bison, of course. Harrison reports that the menu aims to "reflect the Cree and Assiniboin cultures" but also branches out to include smoked salmon. As Harrison states, "I'm happy we're going to appeal to hotel guests and people from Regina looking for something different and unique."[82] Options for all and another example of a restaurant called unique. Bologna also makes an appearance. One of the top-selling breakfasts is "George's Special" – fried bologna, fried eggs, fried mashed potatoes, and "fried bread" named for a regular from northern Saskatchewan. Typical of a hotel restaurant, the Landmark Inn opens at 7 a.m. and closes at 10 p.m. seven days a week, long hours to accommodate the inn's 186 rooms.[83]

A few months later, in December 1999, Regina's *Leader-Post* covered the inn's "grand reopening ... repackaged with what the menu calls 'First Nations Cuisine.'"[84] The quotation marks around "First Nations Cuisine" flag the term's novelty for the newspaper, but also its curiosity. "About time we say. There are enough pizza and Chinese food and hamburger restaurants in this town that diners could do with some variety."[85] This recalls "food adventuring" – a settler demand for a plurality of culinary options. Confronted with the choice of bison fusilli, bison burgers, baked salmon, "Bullet soup" ("basically meatball soup"), and "Indian tacos," the reporter "was very pleased by the bison skewers and wild rice, while our supper companion spoke well of the rabbit stew."[86] For a short review, the praise was long: "There are, of course, other items on the menu, like lasagna and ribs, but it seems to us that the big story here is the historical context."[87] The menu storied the business as a whole. Complimentary to how the Ochapowace First Nation reimagined the hotel, the reporter writes: "The redecorated lobby looks great and could not, ever, ever be mistaken for a generic, plastic 'chain' hotel."[88] He then ends with a prophecy: "We have seen the future and it might just be businesses like this."[89] This review applauds the Landmark for breaking up the city's culinary monopoly and dime-a-dozen hotels. But as the following chapters show, the emergence of more Indigenous-owned restaurants has not been such a straightforward story. New ones open only for earlier ones to close.

The Landmark's Inn time as Indigenous-run was short-lived. Two years after this laudatory review, the hotel closed with a bill of "$1 million in unpaid federal and municipal taxes."[90] The general manager, Warren Berg, informed employees on 15 October

2001, writing, "It is with both sadness and hesitation that on behalf of the Ochapowace First Nation and myself ... I must inform you that the hotel will be ceasing daily operations as of 5 p.m. Oct. 22."[91] At that point seventy of the hotel's employees were Indigenous.[92] Denton George, then the Ochapowace Chief, blamed the business's closure on this debt, stating: "It is a situation where Revenue Canada is always threatening to seize our accounts and it's hard to operate any kind of business when Revenue Canada is after you."[93] The Ochapowace Band sold the Inn and its four-acre lot to a property-development company on 2 January 2002.[94] That same January the company knocked down the hotel and commenced construction work on a shopping complex. Vacating 4150 Albert Street, Shopper's Landmark Mall now stands where the Inn once served wild rice, Saskatoon berries, and bison. The property hosted a hotel for thirty-nine years and an Indigenous restaurant for two. The lot is now a strip mall outfitted with a drugstore and dentist's office, and its current culinary tenant is Prairie Donair – a takeout joint peddling fast food, from Greek gyro and its namesake Donair wraps to naan bread, poutine, nachos, and basmati rice platters.

But in 2016 "Rabbit pot pie" was once again on the menu in Saskatchewan, this time just north of Saskatoon at Wanuskewin Heritage Park's restaurant.[95] That same year, its "Rabbit stew" was endorsed in the popular travel guide DK Eyewitness Travel's Canada edition.[96] And one year earlier, CBC shared a recipe from its chef Ryan Young for "Rabbit braised in muskeg tea" – a steaming swirl of onion and garlic, carrots and celery and, of course, chunks of rabbit in muskeg tea.[97]

A sacred site and gathering place, Wanuskewin translates from Plains Cree as "seeking peace of mind."[98] In 1983, Wanuskewin Heritage Park became a provincial heritage site and, four years later, a national one. Its public trails and visitor centre, which houses a "cafeteria-style" restaurant, followed in 1992.[99] That spring, on 11 May, the Wanuskewin announced the appointment of Delbert Bear to the position of restaurant manager in the *Star-Phoenix*. Painting his previous management experience as of "journeyman calibre," the profile detailed that "His genuine love for the business and sensitivity to Plains Indian Culture will reflect in the quality of service and food."[100] He had honed his skills at a restaurant in Prince Albert and, on the side, taught cooking courses. But the announcement also underlined the heritage park's economic significance alongside its cultural and historical import. "As a major tourist attraction," it said, "it is expected to put as much as $12.7M directly into the Saskatchewan economy."[101] The draw for tourists is the park's "6000 year old archaeological discoveries." But in November 1992, a classified ad solicited applications for a restaurant manager, one expected to have "knowledge of Native food cuisine."[102] And, somewhat ironically, in October 1993 the Wanuskewin Heritage Park took out an ad in the *Star-Phoenix* to run a "Thank You Dairy Producers," from which they received $37,500 toward the development of its restaurant.[103]

In 2019, Wanuskewin welcomed bison back, and its work only continues; it is now working toward applying for UNESCO World Heritage status – which would make it the first site in the province of Saskatchewan to receive such recognition. The Park describes itself as "A living reminder of Indigenous peoples' sacred relationship with the land." Three kilometres north of Saskatoon and west of the South Saskatchewan River, it showcases pre-contact life for the Indigenous communities of the Northern Plains in tandem with the connections between the site and contemporary Indigenous cultures. After fifteen years of planning and three years of renovation, in 2020 it debuted its revamped cultural centre, which spans art galleries and a gift shop, event spaces and a restaurant. Jenni Lasard, a citizen of the Métis Nation in Saskatchewan, ran Wanuskewin Heritage Park's kitchen as its first female executive chef, and continues her work as a culinary consultant.[104] In 2005, she had opened a restaurant of her own – New Ground Café in the small farming town of Birch Hills, Saskatchewan – but sold its century-old brick building after nearly eight years to move to Saskatoon, where she continued her catering business until 2019. In September 2021, Cree Doug Hyndford became Wanuskewin's executive chef. It was a return, as a decade earlier he had run the site's kitchen.[105] Keeping time with the museum's hours, the eighty-seat restaurant is open from 11 a.m. to 4 p.m.

From Manitoba to Alberta and then to the province they flank, Saskatchewan, the eateries this chapter has compiled demonstrate the start-and-stop dynamic of Indigenous restaurants. Wanuskewin, although important, is a historic site first, a visitor centre second, and a restaurant third, which is to say that it is the vastness of its timeline – a history as capacious as the Plains themselves – and the depths of its cultural significance that primarily attract visitors. Although Chief Chiniki contributed to Alberta's culinary scene for decades and is, thus, an example of a successful Indigenous-run restaurant, the short-lived attempts in Winnipeg, Edmonton, and Regina demonstrate how, despite an increasing interest in Indigenous fare in urban settings, many of these earlier eateries have been forgotten. The next two chapters travel further east, mapping the emergence of Indigenous restaurants in Canada's largest city.

chapter seven

# Culinary Resurgence

In 2017, the year Canada celebrated 150 years of Confederation, its largest city had the highest number of Indigenous restaurants in the country: a total of four. Even though it has more nicknames – T.O., the 6, Toronto the good, Hogtown, and the Big Smoke – compared to the rest of Canada, no other city has hosted more Indigenous restaurants simultaneously. But before this, three others had come and gone. Duke Redbird, an Anishinaabe poet and journalist from Saugeen First Nation, opened the Eureka Continuum at 205 Richmond Street West in 2000. A decade later, in 2012, settler pastor Enso Miller opened Tea-n-Bannock in the East End, at the edge of Little India. One year earlier, chef Aaron Joseph Bear Robe, from the Siksika Nation, opened Keriwa Cafe in Parkdale, a neighbourhood with Canada's largest Tibetan community. It closed in 2013. Caterer Shawn Adler opened the Pow Wow Cafe in October 2016 in Kensington Market, a historically Jewish district next door to one of Toronto's Chinatowns. Also a caterer, Johl Whiteduck Ringuette opened NishDish Marketeria in April 2017 in Koreatown. Joseph Shawana, from the Wikwemikong Unceded Reserve on Manitoulin Island, opened Kūkŭm Kitchen in May 2017, in the mid-town neighbourhood of Davisville. Three out of four opened after the Truth and Reconciliation Commission, and each one tells a singular story about historic foodways, their contemporary reinterpretations, and Indigenous resurgence. This chapter begins by surveying Toronto's first two Indigenous restaurants, neither of which made it to Canada's Centennial, before analysing the politics with which these restaurants claim dishes and reclaim ingredients.

The Eureka Continuum neighboured a billiard bar in Toronto's Entertainment District – the Coloured Stone – that Redbird had opened in 1993 with Ron LeBlanc,[1] together with Diana Robinson. Management had assigned miscellaneous "experiments" to its backroom, which spanned a café, a tea house, and a dance club, and, starting in 2000, the space hosted "a restaurant serving native fare such as bison, caribou, caramelized salmon and bannock."[2] Art, antiques, and soapstone carvings adorned the restaurant, and candles illuminated it.[3] "Traditionally, there was no 'native' cuisine as such," Redbird said in an interview: "Our menu is an evolution, an updating of old recipes."[4] A new take on the old. The restaurant cast traditional foodways as a muse rather than a rulebook.

The Eureka Continuum was Indigenous owned, but not exclusively staffed. Its chef, Nwang Tharchen from Tibet, cooked up "Crispy wild rice risotto cakes," "Smoked caribou sausages with spicy black beans," and "Bison and frites." Dishes more elaborate than what Redbird had grown up eating, but ones inspired by a "traditional native food" pantry – the likes of fish and berries, caribou and deer, fiddleheads and squash. The *Toronto Star* published a recipe for one of its hits, "Caramelized salmon," which calls for soy sauce, honey, cider vinegar, brown sugar, and pineapple chutney with jalapeño pepper and red onion, a sure contender for what Wolfman calls Indigenous fusion.[5] "The whole idea throughout the native community," outlined Redbird, "is to share and the climate in Canada today is one in which people want to know about and participate in our culture."[6] Redbird suggests that Torontonians were open to trying Indigenous-inspired foods at the beginning of the 2000s. Curiosity whetted the city's appetite. Nonetheless, the restaurant closed in 2002 when a new landlord increased the rent.[7]

Three years later, in 2005, the twelfth annual Canadian Aboriginal Festival took over the city's main sports stadium. Set up on the Rogers Centre's sprawling field was a "makeshift 'restaurant'" named Origins.[8] Brian Skye, the son of Bertha Skye, who was a member of the Native Team at the 1992 Culinary Olympics alongside Wolfman and George Jr., served as this sixty-seat pop-up eatery's executive chef. At the time, Skye was running a catering company based on pre-contact ingredients, among other gigs such as writing plays and substitute teaching. The restaurant's name, as Skye reveals, was "inspired by the origin of aboriginal foods."[9] Offering "fancy food with pricetags to match," its menu spanned "Pheasant consommé with wild rice," "Venison rib steak with rosemary-thyme sauce," "Rabbit saddle stuffed with sage bread dressing," and "Smoked duck breast with orange honey sauce."[10] At previous editions of this annual happening, vendors peddled "powwow food – bison burgers, Navajo tacos, fry bread and wild boar sausages," but as the *Toronto Star* notes, "the festival decided to step things up this year with Origins restaurant."[11] The paper highlights the pleasure in the contrast between the place and the plate. "There's something deliciously disconcerting about enjoying native haute cuisine in an empty sports stadium in Toronto instead of in the colourful chaos of an outdoor powwow," it wrote.[12] However, Skye challenged these labels. When asked to "elaborate on native haute cuisine," he replied: "It's just food to me – good food."[13]

Like La Toundra, Origins was an eatery accompanying an event, a restaurant with a defined and temporal timeline. However, its menu previewed the next Indigenous restaurant Toronto would welcome. In August 2011 chef Aaron Joseph Bear Robe opened the Keriwa Cafe at 1690 Queen Street West. In what had become a familiar pattern, many reviews – from the *Chicago Tribune* to the *National Post* and from the *Globe and Mail* to *Toronto Life* – mistakenly crowned it Toronto's first Indigenous restaurant.[14] Only *Now Magazine*, Toronto's free weekly, clarified it was the city's second.[15]

After one month in business, the *Globe and Mail* dubbed the Keriwa "the hottest table in town."[16] Bear Robe's father is Blackfoot, his mother Nova Scotian, and he grew up in the Siksika Nation in Alberta. At the age of eleven, he moved to Calgary, an hour and a half west.[17] Bear Robe was a fine-dining veteran. When he relocated to Ontario as an adult, he put in time at a handful of prestigious restaurants, including Michael Städtlander's Eigensinn Farm outside of Toronto – a protagonist in the history of high-end farm-to-table dining in Canada – before opening the Keriwa Cafe.[18]

Bear Robe's menu frequently changed. The dishes shared stories about where he and his parents are from, as well as about Toronto. Plated on mix-matched china, the restaurant served "Roasted Brussels sprouts with bacon bits, pear, and maple syrup"[19] and "Bison short ribs with pommes puree with Thunder Oak gouda, celeriac salsa verde, and pickled Ontario peaches."[20] From ribs to brisket and ravioli to pemmican, Keriwa's menu majored in bison, which it ordered from Alberta.[21] "Bison pemmican pierogies with juniper berries and crème fraiche" encapsulated the Prairies' history and present; Manitoba has large Polish and Ukrainian populations.[22] Alongside bison, the menu peddled "Roast chicken with baby artichokes, shaved fennel slaw, and house-made bread bits." One critic was particularly impressed with the "Spiced chicken with chopped tomatoes and a tamale packed with mealy corn filling," an ode to the Indigenous backbones of Latin American cuisines.[23]

After bison, the menu's minor was in whitefish, which starred in dishes like "Lake Huron whitefish wrapped in bacon and doused in pickled sea asparagus foraged from Nova Scotia salt marshes" and, another Eastern European tribute, "Smoked Lake Huron whitefish with buckwheat blinis, horseradish crème fraiche and pea shoots."[24] Keriwa poured only Canadian wines.[25] And its dessert menu rotated the likes of "Flourless chocolate cake" and "Buckwheat plum cake."[26] It sourced its ingredients from local farmers and suppliers.[27] It also dabbled in brunch, a meal that doubles as a competitive sport in Toronto, offering poached eggs with "sweet browned butter" hollandaise.[28] Its food came at a price: $107 for dinner for two plus tax in one review in 2011,[29] and $175, including tip and wine, in another.[30]

The décor hinted at Bear Robe's family's Blackfoot history. This was less of a shout and more of a whisper. "The only signs of Bear Robe's heritage," recounted one review, "are ... a buckskin robe that once belonged to the chef's grandmother ... photographs of a First Nation brave ... and a giant silver-eagle feather ... paying homage to the word 'keriwa,' which means eagle in Algonquin."[31] The tone suggests that the reviewer had perhaps anticipated more of a shout. Similarly, the restaurant's name was not a direct reference to his heritage. Instead, it acknowledges the eatery's coordinates.

The Algonquin name – keriwa – recognizes an Indigenous language of the lands now called Ontario. Another article chronicled a "whalebone-shaped dreamcatcher of cutout metal with hanging feathers and beads" and, on another wall, "a collage, a patchwork quilt of birch-bark squares."[32] Swatches of Navajo blankets padded the benches.[33]

"When I journey to Queen West ...," began the *National Post*'s 2011 review, "I expect some form of history lesson. Instead, I have a welcome culture shock."[34] Other than expecting one, it is not clear if the critic desired a history lesson. And yet she did travel with "a list of the best-known items on the traditional aboriginal menu." Instead of letting the menu teach her about "traditional" victuals, she packed a list of her own. Pemmican – a pressed mixture of dried meat, fat, and, often, berries – was on the top. Her review then detours into a lecture. The British army stashed pemmican as iron rations during the Boer War, she writes. Although she calls it "the Cree, the Plains people's claim to global influence," she parallels this with pemmican's non-Indigenous history, calling it "the lifesaver for Lewis and Clark as they opened up the West for Canadian fur traders."[35] Documentary data aside, what did she make of its taste? "This pemmican is gentrified to please the pickiest tastebuds – strips of bison soaked in a rich, faintly fruity mahogany sauce, as suave as teriyaki," she exclaimed.[36] By selecting the word gentrification as opposed to, say, hybridization, she adorns the Keriwa Cafe with an additional association. Parkdale – traditionally a working-class neighbourhood that is a popular arrival destination for newcomers – has long been at the forefront of gentrification debates in Toronto, a further layer in restaurant politics.[37]

Beyond the "gentrified" pemmican, how did diners understand the Keriwa Cafe? One review recommended it to those wanting "to taste Canadian cuisine in an authentic space,"[38] which frames the restaurant as Canadian, rather than Indigenous. In 2012, *enRoute* listed Keriwa Cafe at number eight on its prestigious top-ten list of Canada's Best New Restaurants: "Keriwa's seasonal-minded menu draws First Nations techniques and unspoiled tastes of the Canadian landscape into an urban context," it chronicled. "Canadian head-to-tail cooking with a history: a real dream catcher."[39] Once again, the restaurant was claimed and, thus, celebrated as Canadian. A 2015 *Food & Wine* article recommends the Keriwa Cafe, but calls Bear Robe "Aborigine," a notable error.[40] *Toronto Life* ranked the Keriwa number four on its 2012 best restaurant list, writing: "Though the menu speaks to the Aboriginal theme, Bear Robe wisely abandons the concept when the dish doesn't fall for it."[41] It also wrote, "We get it: Keriwa blends the traditional and the contemporary, the rustic and the urban."[42] Similar to how one Muckamuck review classified its décor as what one would expect of a Japanese eatery, calling the Keriwa Canadian reveals that the reviewers did not have a baseline of Indigenous restaurants with which to compare it, reinforcing the "foreignness" of First Nations cuisines in urban spaces.

In 2011 the *Globe and Mail* dabbled in the same cliché language as the articles covering the Muckamuck strike in the 1970s. "Many restaurants these days bandy about words such as 'sustainable' and 'local,'" writes Joanne Kates. "Indeed, these are the best new food-marketing buzzwords. But Keriwa, which to my knowledge is our first native restaurant, walks the walk, in moccasins."[43] Based on this start, it is not surprising that she wrote: "I had worried … that Keriwa might either fall victim to native kitsch (too many beads and feathers) or serve arcana such as dried corn or strange meats that sounded politically correct but were no fun to eat. Neither could be farther from the truth."[44] In light of this fear, the appetizers "in miniature dugout canoes made of burled wood" surprisingly charmed her. She described the restaurant as "where native tradition meets haute cuisine, a hybrid that produces a splendid combo platter."[45] Her expectation of "strange meats" reveals that she thought of an Indigenous restaurant in stereotypical terms. Like the *National Post* review, she anticipated that the menu would speak an ancient language rather than contemporary restaurant vernacular. This chef-versus-customer tension further exhibits the contrast between the appetites of critics for "traditional" foods and Indigenous chefs serving what they wish to cook.

Touching on representation, in May 2014, journalist Kathryn Blaze Carlson wrote, "Mr. Bear Robe says he never thought of himself as an 'aboriginal chef,' but rather a chef period. But when he opened Keriwa Cafe, customers with preconceived notions about aboriginal food complained. 'People commented it wasn't "aboriginal enough" or "traditional enough,"' he relayed,"[46] the same complaint Chief Chiniki Restaurant had heard. Who decides if something is Indigenous enough? The chef or the customer? Summarizing the scholarship around this point, Nicolas Maffei asserts, "The social construction of 'authenticity' has resulted from collaboration between consumer and entrepreneurs. Thus, 'authenticity' can be understood as a co-produced experience where the exotic is mitigated by the familiar."[47] Although I argue against evaluating food through the lens of authenticity, I, too, find that the meaning of a restaurant's dishes is formed by the merger of the kitchen's intentions with the customer's expectations. As historian Dorothea Weltecke asserts, foodways embody entangled history.[48] They are the result of a dialogue with and differentiation from "the other," and, thus, are interdependent. Cuisine, like all traditions, evolves through reinvention and renewal.

Bear Robe wished to showcase Indigenous ingredients and his own creativity without the responsibility of serving as a cuisine's ambassador or the enforced burden of cultural representation. A journalist quoted him as "eager to showcase not only his Aboriginal heritage ... but his interpretation of Canadian cuisine."[49] That said, complaints that the Keriwa Cafe was not Indigenous "enough" grant more power to the diner than to the chef. In the spirit of reinvention, Bear Robe decided to close the Keriwa Cafe and launch a private wine club.[50] In the second half of 2014, a South American eatery, Mata Petisco Bar, opened where Keriwa once stood, and since 2018, Islas Filipino BBQ and Bar has occupied 1690 Queen Street West.

## Claiming Dishes

In 2012 a journalist asked Bear Robe why there are not more Toronto restaurants offering Indigenous fare. "Well, because there aren't many Aboriginals in Canada. And generally, they are detached from mainstream society," he responded. "So I think being able to bring that to the forefront, and doing what we do in a little way to bring awareness is great ... The Aboriginal community is going through a revitalization now ... And I would love there to be more Aboriginal restaurants."[51] "Detached" flashes the ongoing legacies of historic segregation. It also flags the restaurant's role as a stage to present and to represent, as a contact zone. That same year, Bear Robe's wish came true. Tea-n-Bannock opened with a menu that couldn't be more different from his: by-the-book comfort food at an affordable price.

In Tea-n-Bannock's first year, the *Globe and Mail* profiled it with the headline "Bannock Tacos, Fried Baloney – This Is Aboriginal Cuisine?" More investigative reporting than restaurant criticism, the article probed how the menu at this new restaurant in town fitted the larger category of Indigenous cuisine. The article opened with "the kitchen staff are busy preparing affordable meals for a steady stream of native diners. They haven't come for wild meat or foraged vegetables. They're here for the deep-fried hot dogs wrapped in dough, fried baloney ... Are these highly processed foods really considered native cuisine?"[52] Never mind that Tea-n-Bannock could not serve wild game if it wanted to – owing to government regulations, the subject of Chapter 9 – the article presumes Indigenous fare is only hunted animals and foraged plants, an assumption Expo 67's La Toundra also made and that Lisa Myers drew attention to.

"Until recently, aboriginal restaurants were practically non-existent in Canada," points out the journalist; "you could only buy the cuisine at First Nations events or at the odd café on a reserve."[53] This frames Indigenous eateries as temporary and as non-urban. But by logging an absence, the *Globe and Mail* also identified a demand. The article quotes Janine Manning, then president of the Aboriginal Students' Association at York University: "Before, if you were in Toronto and you wanted to eat an Indian taco, or Kwik or baloney and bannock, you'd have to cook it or wait for the next powwow."[54] Manning believes that Tea-n-Bannock serves "true" Indigenous cuisine because the cooks use family recipes. Compared to its predecessors, it serves down-home, comfort food.

Despite bannock's leading role in the "Americanized trading post diet," Mihesuah recognizes that "Indian tacos are marketable to crowds looking to connect with Indian cultures."[55] Lewis seconds this, calling frybread "a goodwill ambassador to outside communities" and a "spokesperson" that is symbolic of the power in "breaking bread."[56] Bannock, to recall, signifies a cultural connection to Indigeneity for some, and restaurants like Tea-n-Bannock cater to this demand. Beyond the restaurant's name, "tea 'n' bannock" means chitchat. And just like Tea-n-Bannock's menu, chitchat is casual. However, this *Globe and Mail* review also employs the possessive, writing: "In the past couple years, half a dozen restaurants have opened specializing in native food. Each one faces the challenge of trying to explain the concept to non-aboriginal diners ... few have anything but a vague notion of *our* indigenous cuisine" (italics added). This problematically lays claim to Indigenous cuisine as Canada's, installing Indigenous culinary geography into the tight frame of Canadian cuisine as a national project.

Tea-n-Bannock's motto is "Where the past and present meet." These words decorate a chalkboard framed by birch branches. An illustrated bird soars between the restaurant's name and its motto. Below, a tepee stands tall and Toronto's tallest landmark taller still: the CN Tower. A literal visualization of the past meeting the present. Two crisscrossed paddles decorate the counter, and to its left is a table that doubles as a gift shop of books, teas, blueberry jam, and wild rice. The table sits in front of a wall-to-wall mural of birds coasting across a pastel lake at dusk. The other walls are red and peachy orange. The likes of art for sale, snowshoes, carvings, a miniature teepee, and moose antlers dress up the interior. The restaurant is small, thirteen tables for two, plus two love seats next to the window. Casual and eclectic, it does not serve alcohol, but it does serve "Labrador tea" (*Gaagigebak*) that is "hand picked in northern Canada" and "known for its health benefits."

In addition to listing dishes like "Elk-venison stew, "Three sisters soup," and "Wild-rice salad," the menu contains encyclopaedia-like texts about corn/maize, bannock, and Manoomin (wild rice).[57] It signs off with "Miigwetch/Thank you for dining here, please come again!" Miller, Tea-n-Bannock's owner, is not Indigenous.

The restaurant, however, is linked to the First Nation Church of Toronto and is Indigenous-staffed. The prints that decorate the bathrooms reveal this religious connection, and behind the door that leads downstairs to them hangs a map of Ontario that traces treaties, tribal councils, and nations. Colonial maps renamed lands and waters, erasing their Indigenous past and present. But this map undoes that, and the same one hangs in the Pow Wow Cafe.

Shawn Adler, the Pow Wow Cafe's owner, grew up in Orangeville, Ontario, trained at Stratford Chef School, and holds a BA in Native Studies. His mother is Anishinaabe and his father Jewish. In 2003, at the age of twenty-three, he opened his first restaurant in Peterborough, serving "Indigenous inspired cuisines," and called it his Ojibway name: Aasmaabik's Bakery and Bistro. Aasmaabik means "the face of the rock."[58] He then turned his attention to catering and made a name for himself slinging "Indian tacos" at music festivals, an idea he decided to turn into a restaurant. "In Toronto, there is a certain hipster crowd that is looking for something new. Foodies. And no one other than Indigenous people knew what an Indian taco is," he tells me.[59] Adler had perfected "Indian tacos" by the time he decided to open the Pow Wow Cafe in October 2016.

At festivals he hawks beef and veggie options (choosing beef over bison, venison, or elk because of the price) with cheddar cheese, tomato, lettuce, and cumin sour cream.[60] By adding cumin, Adler says he takes his liberties with the taco. "First of all, it is delicious," he affirms, "and it relates to South American cuisine and tacos, so it makes sense." The Pow Wow Cafe expanded his festival repertoire and serves other classics, like its "Scone dog with sage ketchup." Because "Indian tacos" were, and still are, unfamiliar to many Torontonians, the Pow Wow Cafe debuted with brunch as a safety net. "Toronto is full of freaks for brunch, so brunch could potentially save the business," Adler says. "It is kind of an introduction to a taco because it is two poached eggs on frybread." The Pow Wow Cafe serves comfort food to Indigenous customers and introduces non-Indigenous ones to pow wow classics.

The restaurant's name niggles some customers. As Adler reckons, most non-Indigenous people have never been to a pow wow and are not sure what it entails. He's asked: "Can you call your restaurant that? ... They think it is something negative. But a pow wow is a celebration, a community, a culture, its heart ... people don't realize that Indian is not a bad word. It is just a misnomer." This demonstrates settlers' general lack of exposure to Indigenous culture, as well as growing sensitivities about the misrepresentation of Indigenous names. It also demonstrates his restaurant's role in changing that by claiming dishes, like "Indian tacos," as Indigenous.

Adler considers frybread a survival food. He speaks of the diversity across Turtle Island before contact, of how many cuisines there were. Now, he thinks: "we have a pan-Canadian cuisine, or a pan-North American cuisine. Everyone makes frybread. Frybread is based on rations ... the five gifts of the white man – diabetes, basically."[61] Despite how ubiquitous frybread has become, Adler believes there is still immense regional variety. Nonetheless, he personally is not interested in fine dining. With so many farm-to-table restaurants, the competition is too high. "If you are just doing high end Indigenous cuisine you are really pigeon-holing yourself into a clientele," he tells me. Instead, Adler sticks to pow wow classics, claiming them as their own cuisine, but also reinventing them, one pinch of cumin at a time.

Adler is not afraid of the word fusion. He has served a "Jerk chicken taco with mango salsa," and considers it vital that the menu evolves. "I guess fusion is a bad word, or has been used as a bad word, culinary speaking ... There are things that work and things that don't in the landscape of fusion," he says. The Pow Wow Cafe supports local producers but does not restrict its menu geographically. "I know there are hyper local people in terms of cuisine," Adler admits, but that is not what he wants to do. "There has always been trade," he clarifies. "People have this notion of a cigar store Indian. People don't want Indians to be modern. The reality is that we live in the twenty-first century. Everything is available to us. I don't want to live without flour, pizza, pasta." Adler's example of a cigar store Indian returns to King's "Dead Indians." To cook with ingredients from around the world is the Pow Wow Cafe's way of claiming a contemporary Indigenous culinary identity. Like Wolfman, Adler finds freedom in fusion.

"Why Indigenous food now?" is another question Adler hears regularly. His answer begins with his own family: "Everyone went to residential school ... my mom speaks a bit of the language, but that was taken away. Numerous things have been taken away. But one thing that is hard to take away is somebody's food. It is one of the last connections that you can have to your culture." This explains why I differentiate restaurants that opened before the last residential school closed from ones that opened after. In *Food, Control and Resistance* Tamara Levi outlines how culinary knowledge is intergenerational. "Food also functions as a vehicle for the transfer of knowledge," she elucidates. "In addition to knowledge of traditional food sources and their uses, information on food preparation and ritual significance is passed on from one generation to the next." [62] As Adler makes obvious, the generation before his faced severe structural challenges. Although bits of the language have been forgotten, he remembers the food, and so do his mother and grandmother. Like other family heirlooms, a recipe passes down knowledge from one generation to the next. This often happens orally. It also returns to the significance of the end of the residential school era in Canada, in 1996. When the state forcibly separates children from parents and Elders, recipes and other forms of cultural knowledge do not circulate from one generation to the next.

Adler spent his summers on his mother's reserve over 1,300 kilometres away from where he grew up, Lac des Milles Lacs First Nation, just outside of Thunder Bay. He harvests cedar on his property just north of Toronto, and when I visited the restaurant a cook was boiling the branches to make soda. Adler might base his restaurant on pow wow fare, but he does not define Indigenous cuisines based on it alone. Layered between the beef and the frybread, between the cheese and the tomato, is the insistence on Indigenous culinary plurality.

## Reclaiming Ingredients

NishDish and Kūkŭm Kitchen aim to push Indigenous cuisine beyond bannock. NishDish offers baked bannock as a side, but not as a main feature. Instead, it promotes dishes with pre-contact ingredients, like "Elk with sweet cranberry coulis," "Roasted buffalo with house spices," and "Hominy corn soup." Similarly, Kūkŭm Kitchen casts bannock only in a supporting role. Its dishes span the "Arctic trio of beet cured salmon, seal tartare, and smoked rainbow trout," with bannock as a side, and, for mains, "Elk loin, baby carrots, beets, peas and Jerusalem artichoke velouté" and "Caribou, duchess potato, squash, foraged mushrooms with a braised onion purée." Out of Toronto's four Indigenous restaurants in 2017, Kūkŭm is the only fine-dining establishment and has the prices to match. Its dishes, with the exception of seal, the subject of the next chapter, resemble common fare in farm-to-table Canadian restaurants. The difference is that by plating these ingredients, Kūkŭm Kitchen reclaims them as Indigenous. The restaurant takes back ingredients that have been appropriated as Canadian. The same is true of NishDish. Like the You Are Welcome Food Truck, both restaurants aim to educate diners and to spread awareness of the original ingredients and peoples of the lands that are now called Canada.

NishDish's motto is "Your friendly neighbour since always" (Figure 7.1). Before debuting his storefront in 2017, Johl Whiteduck Ringuette had been running a catering company for over a decade.[63] He is Anishinaabe and Algonquin and grew up north of North Bay, where he picked blueberries and tapped maple syrup and his father hunted moose and deer. "I was six years old when my brother taught me how to skin a rabbit," he shares with me. His first job, at the age of fifteen, was as a catering waiter, but before opening NishDish he worked for Aboriginal Legal Services. He started his catering company in 2005, which he ran part-time, and, as of 2012, full-time, another example of how catering has propelled – and sustained – Indigenous chefs to open restaurants of their own.[64] The purpose of Ringuette's culinary work is to return Indigenous peoples "to optimal health, which is finding out what foods we should be eating."[65] To realize resurgence. That is one reason he limits bannock. "I actually try to dissuade most people from Indian tacos, which we don't make," he explains.[66] For Ringuette, bannock is a detour rather than the path forward.

Figure 7.1. "NishDish," 2019, Toronto, Ontario, photo by L. Sasha Gora.

I met Ringuette the year before he opened his restaurant. At the time, he was running a pop-up out of a shipping container turned market in Toronto's business district. "It is the high times of catering," he told me, attributing the change to the Truth and Reconciliation Commission. "A lot of people and groups want to serve Aboriginal food as part of honouring this new relationship between Aboriginal people and the government."[67] He noted that there are still plenty of hoops to jump through, yet notices a change. "There have been times where they have had galas and non-Aboriginal chefs cooking Aboriginal food, which is unacceptable. We want to see our people cook our food." There is a heightened awareness of the politics of who cooks what, of appropriation. And yet the hoops still stand. One concerns government regulations, such as it being illegal to serve wild game – the topic of Chapter 9.

NishDish doubles as a market. Ringuette sources ingredients from Indigenous communities, sweetgrass from the Six Nations and wild leeks from Beausoleil First Nation. For him, cooking is as much about land, knowledge, and culture as it is about the final dish. His approach is holistic and he is interested in "what it takes to sustain these foods." It is important to teach ceremonies around food. "I always make a spirit plate," he explains, "if there is an Elder at the location I do the spirit plate with them."[68] If a client does not have an Elder to smudge the food, Ringuette does it himself. As he says, "The whole journey has been learning what is ceremony with food. It is not a component. It is actually who we are."[69] Food is one part of the whole, which is also what makes it essential for resurgence. Ringuette considers it vital to talk about seeds, care, and relations, about rituals and lessons from one's ancestors, about how food entwines with relations, with kin. Language plays a central role in all of this.

Now most chefs and restaurants write Indigenous, but in 2016 Aboriginal and First Nations were the terms in circulation. Ringuette, at that point, called his cooking First Nations cuisine. He also calls it Anishinaabe. "Indigenous is not specific to Turtle Island," he clarifies. Language matters. Until this point, I have largely discussed Indigenous cuisine. Switching back and forth between the singular and the plural implies that multiple versions exist, which acknowledges regional and cultural variety. It prioritizes the possibilities of the plural over the stiffness of the singular. It also acknowledges time as an ingredient, how cuisines ebb and flow. Journalist Zoe Tennant, for example, notes that "The term 'Indigenous cuisine' in the singular, is hyper-generalized and rooted in a pan-Indigenous concept, the frame that conflates the diversity of hundreds of Indigenous nations across distinct geographies and millions of kilometres. There is no clear-cut definition of Indigenous cuisine because there is no *one* Indigenous cuisine. Rather, there are regionally specific Indigenous *cuisines*, in the plural."[70] That said, she also recognizes that for George Jr., for instance, "'Indigenous cuisine' makes sense."[71] This is because it crosses borders between different nations and regions to cook with Turtle Island's diverse ingredients.

With the You Are Welcome Food Truck, Wolfman served Anishinaabe dishes in Toronto. Vancouver's Muckamuck did not advertise "Native" food. Instead, it sought to represent "Native" foods of a particular region: the Pacific Northwest. And NishDish, as its name suggests, rallies for a more specific signifier.

## Mother Tongues

French was long the culinary world's dominant language. Chefs trained in French, diners ordered in French, and many dishes bore French names. Kuh writes about the shift in language on the menu for Le Cirque, which opened in New York in 1974: "to *insist* that it be Italian, was an act of semantic self-assertion that to customers may have meant very little, but for a man who … had had *presenter, découper, recomposer* drummed into him, it means the world."[72] To speak a language other than French introduced restaurant vernacular, opened up space for other languages. This gestures to something else that a menu does. Beyond listing options, a menu is a means of "semantic self-assertion." Names matter. Languages matter. To return to Haraway, it matters what restaurants are called and it matters which restaurants we think other restaurants with. Before the food or the décor, a restaurant's name makes its first impression. The name sets the scene and frames the story it tells. "The process of designing a restaurant," writes Ray, "can begin with the mere act of naming it."[73] For decades now, most restaurants in Canada have spoken English or French, borrowing an Italian, Thai, or Vietnamese term here or there, but these are languages from elsewhere.

The spelling of Kū-kŭm is not always the same. Sometimes a hyphen splits it in two; other times, it is a single word. Shawana's narrow restaurant is wedged between shops and eateries on a busy block of Mount Pleasant Road. Three horizontal panels of salvaged wood frame its entrance and bold white letters hang above the door: ᑯᑯᒼ x Kū-kŭm. Cree syllabics introduce the restaurant, followed by the Latin alphabet. James Evans, a Wesleyan Methodist missionary born in England, is credited with inventing Canadian

Aboriginal syllabic writing in the 1830s, first for Ojibway and then for Cree.[74] The restaurant may offer the name in the Latin alphabet, but no translation. Kū-kŭm means grandmother.[75]

Building on Mary Douglas's suggestion that ignorance of food's cultural significance is "explosively dangerous," literary scholar Meredith Abarca argues that "Since language, like food, expresses much about who we are, lack of critical judgment on the usage of language is also 'explosively dangerous.'"[76] ᑯᑯᐦ x Kū-kŭm: the words repeat on the window, with two more below: "indigenous kitchen." Sometimes, the restaurant drops the kitchen and the accents, as in a 2017 rave *Toronto Star* review. Despite its promise that this restaurant "will win you over with its Indigenous food," the critic writes Kukum and not Kūkŭm.[77] Others spell Kūkŭm differently. For example, Glenna Henderson from Sagkeeng First Nation named her Winnipeg restaurant Cookem Daisey's after her grandmother. And Josee Racicot named her now closed Dryden, Ontario, restaurant Kokom's Bannock Shack.[78] These spellings reflect regional varieties and personal choices, but they all assert a restaurant's chosen linguistic identity and the politics of returning Indigenous languages to urban spaces.

Tucked away in the basement, Kū-kŭm's bathroom doors repeat this language pattern: Cree syllabics, then the Latin alphabet – Skwew for women, and Napew for man. English comes last. The Cree syllabics are nearly the same size as the other two words combined. For anyone seeking a bathroom, these hand-drawn signs give pause.[79] To list only Cree – in syllabics or in the Latin alphabet – enforces a Cree-only space. The English is accommodating, generously so. The restaurant acknowledges diners first with Cree, and then accommodates them with English. Although Simpson does not write about cuisine, her analysis of aesthetics seamlessly applies to restaurants. "The use of Indigenous aesthetics in artistic practice," she writes, "is one mechanism Indigenous creators use to code their work, to 'disrupt the noise of colonialism,' to speak to multiple audiences, and to enact affirmative and generative forms of refusal."[80] Something as simple as a bathroom sign can simultaneously refuse a colonial language while still employing it to address diverse audiences. Asserting Indigenous languages in public spaces is, as Corntassel asserts, a daily act of renewal and, thus, "the foundations of resurgence."[81] This practice relates to efforts to reclaim Indigenous names, such as the Ogimaa Makana Project that is working to restore Anishinaabemowin place-names to the city's streets and avenues, paths and trails, as well as those who are calling the city by its original name of Tkaronto.

A few hours before dinner service, Shawana sits to the left of the bar where a mural of the three sisters – corn, squash, and beans – stretches across the wall. Norval Morriseau prints decorate the other walls. Shawana tells me about how he had cooked his way across Toronto, and in 2016, on National Indigenous Peoples Day, he hosted a one-off Indigenous-inspired dinner. The event sold out and so he proposed to his boss, Ben Castanie, that they do one every year.[82] The idea of an event shifted shape, expanding to take the form of an eatery, and that September he suggested they open a restaurant. At that point, Shawana didn't know of any other Indigenous restaurants. "It wasn't until people got wind that we were opening that all of these other Indigenous-owned restaurants started to contact us," he reveals. Other than the ones in Toronto, he heard of Salmon n' Bannock in Vancouver and La Traite in Wendake, Quebec. "But we are the only fine dining one," he says.

Shawana grew up eating moose, deer, rabbit, and fish. Now he cooks meats that were unfamiliar to him as a child, like elk and seal. He values curiosity and describes the restaurant's customers as coming in search of something they have never tried before. The restaurant purchases foraged ingredients from Forbes Wild Food: Most of their pickers are Indigenous in northern Ontario. For Shawana, like many other chefs, food is tangled with storytelling and education. You cannot separate one from the other. He describes his customers, either in Toronto or at one of his collaborative culinary events, as "coming for an experience to learn about cuisine, culture, heritage, and history." Shawana asserts that food is "our way of telling that story." He also emphasizes the range of these stories, mentioning the over six hundred First Nations, each with its own dialect or language. His reserve alone has three dialects, and on Manitoulin Island there are five other First Nations.[83] His band dries, seasons, and smokes fish differently from the others.

"Indigenous cuisine is not only a sole entity," he clarifies, "it is a collaboration of everyone around us." One dish, he believes, "can signify a vast variety of cuisines" from the Rockies and the Prairies and from the tundra to the Canadian Shield. Shawana's role as a chef is to promote and push Indigenous cuisine in the direction in which it can further grow in the future.

He also recognizes the importance of relearning. Similar to Audrey Logan's experience, at one of Shawana's events he stumbled upon a field of wild mustard. When he asked about it, no one could identify it. "Our own people don't know what we used to eat before grocery stores," he says. Relearning is part of reclaiming. His restaurant is a venue for relearning Indigenous plants and tastes, and for reclaiming their knowledge and stories. A culinary laboratory for Indigenous resurgence.

Some restaurants label their dishes as Indigenous and others reclaim their ingredients. Nestled between the two, the Keriwa Cafe highlighted Indigenous ingredients without the politics of Truth and Reconciliation. As Bear Robe made clear, he wanted to be seen as a chef, period. He did not wish to have to carry the responsibility of representing anything beyond his personal point of view. Nonetheless, in the eyes of the press he was an ambassador of Indigenous cuisine. Tea-n-Bannock and the Pow Wow Cafe mix Indigenous ingredients with post-contact dishes. Both have "Indian tacos": meat or veggie "Navajo/Indian Tacos" at Tea-n-Bannock and "Beef chili or Veggie chili tacos with cumin sour cream" at the Pow Wow Cafe. Although they sit side-by-side with traditional Indigenous ingredients (such as "Corn soup with smoked duck" at the Pow Wow Cafe, and bison, Arctic char, and wild rice at Tea-n-Bannock), the "Indian tacos" remain the main event. By serving them, both restaurants claim them as Indigenous. They disregard and move beyond the limits set by customers who expect "authentic" hunted and gathered ingredients – an example of the evolution of Indigenous restaurant politics. Tea-n-Bannock opened a couple of years before the Truth and Reconciliation era. The Pow Wow Cafe became Toronto's first Indigenous restaurant to open after the Commission concluded in 2015. Then NishDish and Kū-kŭm Kitchen opened, both aiming to present traditional ingredients in contemporary ways while relaying a more explicit pedagogical and political message.

Although I distinguish between restaurants that claim dishes versus ones that reclaim ingredients, this is not a hard cut. Both approaches share the same aim: to reinsert Indigenous peoples and their cultures in urban foodscapes. This brings up the politics of resurgence versus recognition, as well as cultural versus political resurgence. Glen Coulthard, a Yellowknives Dene scholar, rejects "the colonial politics of recognition."[84] In agreement, Simpson advocates for radical resurgence, arguing that the separation between cultural and political resurgence is artificial. "In the context of settler colonialism and neoliberalism," she writes, "the term *cultural* resurgence, as opposed to *political* resurgence, which refers to a resurgence of story, song, dance, art, language, and culture, is compatible with the reconciliation discourse ... or other depoliticized recovery-based narratives."[85] Although she notes that the Canadian state engages with cultural resurgence "because it is not concerned with dispossession" over political resurgence, which "is seen as a threat to settler sovereignty," according to Indigenous thought "the cultural and the political are joined and inseparable, and they are both generated through place-based practices – practices that require land."[86] An Indigenous restaurant is, thus, both a cultural and political project.

As a result of the COVID-19 pandemic – and the storm of challenges it wreaked on the restaurant industry – on 6 May 2020, NishDish announced that it was leaving 690 Bloor Street West. It reached out to its customers on social media, asking them to donate to its "COVID-19 contingency plan" as it weathered "this transitional phase to find a new home."[87] Local media mourned the loss of NishDish's storefront, commemorating the restaurant as "groundbreaking."[88] Although Toronto press praised the restaurant, it was its catering business that had kept its finances afloat. As soon as the pandemic hit, it knocked out NishDish's catering gigs. "It was devastating," Whiteduck Ringuette confessed. "They say there's a 70 per cent chance a restaurant will close within three years. Well, we made it. And then this hit."[89] The cost of running the restaurant was around $20,000 per month, out of which an estimated 50 to 60 per cent was food cost, and then $6,000 for rent. The *Toronto Star* reports that this food-cost percentage is "two or three times the industry standard," and that NishDish purchased from "small-scale, sustainable suppliers, many of them Anishinaabe or from other First Nations."[90] As Whiteduck Ringuette made clear about these ingredients, "A lot of them are wild. They're hard to grow, hard to find, and they're expensive. But we use them, because it's important."[91] Despite these challenges, Whiteduck Ringuette remained optimistic, writing that NishDish is "keeping the fires ready ... Remember our gratitude and our resilience as the people of this land."[92]

A year before, on 23 May 2019, Kūkŭm Kitchen announced it was closing and relocating to a larger, more central address. Two days earlier, however, a letter-sized sheet of paper blocked the front door: A "Notice to Terminate for Failure of Tenant to Pay Rent."[93] In April 2019, one month earlier, the restaurant was already listed for sale. And then, after seven years, the Pow Wow Cafe plated its last "Indian taco" on 28 May 2023, timed to match the end of its lease. Toronto's tally of Indigenous restaurants once again went back down to one: the now lone Tea-n-Bannock.

A month after NishDish closed, CBC Radio interviewed Shawana as part of the episode "How Indigenous leaders are changing the future of food." CBC introduced him as an advisor at Centennial College and the chair of the Indigenous Culinary of Associated Nations, a not-for-profit which he formed with other Indigenous chefs and stakeholders in 2019. Cree journalist Rosanna Deerchild noted that Kūkŭm Kitchen is currently closed and asked Shawana about what is next. His plan was to start it back up, after the pandemic, "but to also create a restaurant that's off of the beaten path ... on my reserve and open up my restaurant ... and serve our traditional foods and our traditional meats that we're not allowed to serve off reserve, right, so moose, deer, beaver, muskrat."[94] The following year he shared more details; his idea is to revive Kūkŭm on Manitoulin Island at Rainbow Ridge Golf Course, where he worked his first job. The question of what an Indigenous restaurant is both legally allowed and culturally expected to serve defined the restaurant's run in Toronto, and the next chapter zooms in on the debate its "Seal tartare" sparked.

chapter eight

# Seal Tartare

Plotted on a rectangular plate, on one end of the "Arctic Trio" are thin slices of maple-cured salmon, garnished with a pink nasturtium. A chunk of smoked trout, skin-on, is on the other. Between the salmon, trout, and toasted bannock is tartare. As dark as black rice and with a slight purple tint, the tartare is made from seal loin. It looks wet, glossy, and is topped with whitefish roe and a brightly shining quail egg. For $22, plus tax and tip, I ate seal for the first time at Kūkŭm Kitchen in Toronto. This was two thousand kilometres away from where the seal was hunted around Îles-de-la-Madeleine, Quebec, and similarly far from Inuit Nunangat – Canada's four Inuit regions, where seal is a quintessential food.[1] What sets Kūkŭm Kitchen apart from other establishments peddling the likes of roasted elk and pan-seared halibut is that chef Joseph Shawana opened it in June 2017 with the aim of serving Indigenous foods and, thereby, representing Indigenous cultures. According to Kūkŭm's menu, seal must be present to do so.

One month after I sampled seal, the American magazine *Food & Wine* published a profile of Kūkŭm Kitchen. "What Does Seal Taste Like?" it asked.[2] After having read it, Jennifer N. started an online petition: "Demand that Kūkŭm Kitchen in Toronto Ontario Take Seal Meat off Their Menu."[3] Aylan C. responded with the "Counter-Petition to Educate Anti-Seal Activist Jennifer N about Anti-Indigenous Behaviour and Colonialism. Support Kūkŭm Kitchen."[4] On the heels of both petitions and the media attention they stirred up, Shawana added "Seared seal loin with beets, watercress, and greens" to his menu, reaffirming seal's place on the table. By serving seal, Kūkŭm Kitchen challenges Canadian restaurant norms about what is edible, pushing the limits of palatability in Toronto – an example of restaurant politics.

Kūkŭm Kitchen is just one restaurant, and yet the debate orbiting its "Seal tartare" is much larger. It points toward the political aspects of Indigenous foods today, to how food is entangled in ideology and cultural expressions of what is food and for whom. Plates express power. What they code as dinner validates social and political agendas and hierarchies. Restaurants validate – or challenge – culinary norms. And by serving seal, a restaurant normalizes eating it. Disputes about seal's place on or off the menu, in other words, represent a clash of cultures. Through its discussion of seal as an (un)acceptable food, this chapter highlights the relationship between food and Indigenous sovereignty. It pushes the last chapters' themes, like language, further and demonstrates how restaurant dishes intervene in larger contestations about political and cultural sovereignty.

## Thin Ice

When the cold turns water to ice, seals must come to the surface to breathe and maintain holes to do so. On fresh ice the moisture in a seal's breath freezes, sculpting small lumps on the surface that trace and track the life beneath the ice. Seal breathing holes – *aglus* in Inuktitut – are moments of encounters. Crossroads between lives above and below the ice. *Aglus* are moments of contact between humans and non-humans, between hunters and seals, between life and death, and between Indigenous, Canadian, and European politics. The controversy provoked by Kūkŭm Kitchen's seal tartare is nothing new. Instead, the debate about whether a restaurant should serve seal – and whether humans should eat it – is the most recent chapter in an older and larger dispute: the seal hunt.

Seal has long been a symbol of animal rights activism. The anthropologist George Wenzel succinctly condenses the history of the anti-sealing campaign in a chapter in *Animal Rights Human*

*Rights: Ecology, Economy and Ideology in the Canadian Arctic* titled "The Seal Protest as Cultural Conflict." Discussions about eating animals express social, cultural, and personal beliefs about what kind of relationships humans should have with them. The decision to consider an animal food is consciously, or unconsciously, an expression of cultural beliefs. The difficulty in classifying seal, just like beaver, discloses Christian anxieties: both animals are aquatic mammals without fins and scales and thus have, according to the Old Testament, "unclean characteristics."[5] Hunger drives human appetites. Religions and cultural practices command what is considered acceptable to eat and for whom.

Discussions about eating animals reflect power structures, and in the sealing debate the voices of animal activists have been louder than those of the people who have lived with seals for centuries: the Inuit. Frustrated by this silencing, in 2016 filmmaker Alethea Arnaquq-Baril, who is from Iqaluit, Nunavut, released *Angry Inuk*, which recounts the conflict between Inuit and animal activists that has been betiding since the 1960s. In the documentary, Inuit eat – and enjoy – fresh seal meat. Some bits are raw and others boiled, as when a hunter swallows the still-warm brain and meat. It is tradition to use all parts, the blood, flesh, and organs as food, either for immediate consumption or fermented or frozen for later.[6] What remains is for clothing or tools.

The year 1955 marks the beginning of the anti-sealing campaign, when observers accused the hunt of being ecologically destructive and cruel.[7] The seal protest then gained momentum in the 1960s. Serge Deyglun, an entertainer from Montreal, made the 1964 documentary *Les Grands Phoques de la banquise*, and, one year later, *Massacre des innocents*. Then, in 1967, a "Save the Seals" campaign was launched and, for the first time, in 1971, the Canadian government imposed a quota for harp seals: the total allowable catch (TAC).[8] Every March the Ministry of Fisheries and Oceans and the Canadian Coast Guard announce an annual TAC (although the number of seals harvested is usually well below the quota).[9] Anti-sealing further peaked in 1977, when French film star Brigitte Bardot travelled to Newfoundland to pose with harp seal pups: whitecoats. Until then, the Save the Seals campaign was, as Greenpeace founder Robert Hunter described, "all blood and death." With Bardot's appearance, it was now "blood and death and sex."[10]

Although protests targeted the commercial hunt in Newfoundland – mainly harp seals and especially whitecoat pups – Inuit suffered the consequences. The Hudson's Bay Company started purchasing sealskins from Inuit in the mid-1950s. In 1976, a hunter could sell a skin, usually from a ringed seal, for $23. After Bardot's photo-op, the price dropped to less than $4.[11] Sheila Watt-Cloutier, an Inuk activist, officer of the Order of Canada, and former Canadian president of the Inuit Circumpolar Council, affirms: "And our hunters' pride and self-worth were damaged anew."[12] The seal hunt is not about economics alone; it is about culture, about worldmaking.

Six years later, in 1983, the European Community enforced a two-year ban on harp and hooded seal products. In *Angry Inuk*, Arnaquq-Baril calls 1983 "our great depression." Prices crashed again, and by the mid-1980s sealskin exports fell by nearly 97 per cent.[13] Historian Briton Cooper Busch refers to Inuit sealers as the boycott's "first real victims."[14] In response to the ban, in 1984 the Canadian government formed a Royal Commission on Seals and Sealing. But before it could report its findings, in 1985 the European Community renewed the ban. Nonetheless, the commission published its report the following year, recommending that the hunt for whitecoats and blueback seals should be banned. This became law in 1987. Hunting from large vessels was also banned. Yet the Commission still supported the seal hunt. Even the partial bans carried economic, cultural, social, and nutritional consequences, many for the worse. For instance, the market's collapse reduced Inuit hunters' cash incomes by two-thirds, which, in turn, caused poor nutrition.[15] As an example of how much seal contributes, in 2001, seals provided 1.5 million kilograms of meat for Inuit communities; it would require around $15 million to purchase an equivalent amount of food.[16] Yet, this data came too late, and the European bans were, like Bardot's trip to the ice, disastrous. Western Europe composed 80 per cent of the global trade of sealskin and so Inuit hunters lost access to their main market.[17]

The bans also spawned cultural consequences. Six different species of true seals live off Canada's Atlantic coast: grey, harbour, harp, and hooded seals, as well as ringed and bearded seals, which are more typical of the Arctic.[18] "Inuit believe that there is only one *nattiq* ... a ringed seal," writes Inuk politician Peter Irniq. "We Inuit do not refer to other seals, such as the harp seal ... as real 'seals.' The other seals each have a name of their own. Most of us don't even like to eat them."[19] Nattiq are the "fundamental food" of Inuit from Alaska and Canada to Greenland and Russia.[20] Other species swim in northern waters, but to say seal in the Arctic is to say nattiq. An eighteenth-century Greenlandic translation of the Lord's Prayer captures its magnitude.[21] The Norwegian missionary Hans Egede translated daily bread to seal.[22] Nonetheless, the nattiq hunt became entrapped in regulations that reacted to protests against the commercial hunt for Atlantic harp seals.

Seals are not a way of making a living in the Arctic: they are a way of life.[23] Their skin, oil, and meat prevent and counter sickness.[24] "The seal lies at the foundation of traditional Inuit society," details author David Pelly, "the complex of material, social, spiritual, and cultural values that define for many Inuit who they are."[25] The European Community bans on harp and hooded seal products posed a threat to Inuit culture, ideology, and sovereignty.

Protesters targeted an industry that turns the fur of harp seal pups into coats, but, historically, the demand for seal has not been all fur and leather. At different times seal has been as important for Europeans and settlers as it has been for Inuit. Seal oil was "the petroleum of its day" and once powered European street lamps.[26] Busch even argues that sealing made Newfoundland. Settlers in the northeast selected settlement locations based on seals, and sealing generated much of the capital's wealth.[27] In the early twentieth century, going "on the ice" to hunt seal was a rite of passage: a "test of manhood."[28] For Europeans and settlers, after the demand for oil dwindled, seal were popular for their hides and fur. But European policy focused on the history of seal as an animal that has been exploited for financial gain as opposed to its contemporary significance, both economically and culturally, to Inuit living on either side of the Atlantic.

In 2006 other celebrities added their voices to the debate, thus renewing the media's interest. Paul McCartney, of Beatles fame, and his then-wife Heather Mills were photographed petting a pup on the ice of the Gulf of the St. Lawrence. It was 2 March 2006 and the next day they were in New York City, where they spoke against the hunt on "Larry King Live." Together with Duane Smith, the president of ICC Canada, Watt-Cloutier, then-chair of the Inuit Circumpolar Council, penned a press release about what they called a stunt: "lying down on the sea ice and playing with seals is, frankly, silly, and it's also disrespectful to wildlife. Seals may look cute, but they are not pets – they are animals that live in the wild."[29] Smith and Watt-Cloutier suggested it was McCartney and Mills' behaviour that was inappropriate. After all, they were trespassing on the seals' ice. Watt-Cloutier calls "The McCartney media blitz" "a good reminder ... that the Arctic is better known for its wildlife than its people. Whether it's baby seals that need to be saved ... the world loves to focus on Arctic species that tug at the heartstrings of 'Southerners.'"[30] Like Wenzel, Watt-Cloutier raises the question of animal versus human rights.

In 2009 the European Union shifted its focus from harp and hooded seals and banned all seal products. The "EU Seal Regime" ban included an "Indigenous communities exception"; however, this applied only to Greenlandic Inuit. Canadian Inuit were excluded, an exception they challenged.[31] In 2014 the World Trade Organization ruled that this was discriminatory and unlawful.[32] The EU listened and, as of 2015, the Government of Nunavut qualified as an attestation body.[33] Three criteria must be met: the community has traditionally conducted the hunt; the hunt is not for commercial reasons and instead contributes to subsistence by providing food and income that supports sustainable livelihoods; and hunters consider animal welfare.[34] But the market has not yet recovered from 2009 because the public still believes that all seal products are illegal – or worse, immoral.[35] By introducing a ban, the EU reinforced negative associations around sealskin, which are not easy to reverse. The public campaigns and damaging media coverage had a lasting effect. Changing regulations is one thing. Changing cultural norms – and the stories they stand on, the storying that shores them – is another.

In 2018 the People for the Ethical Treatment of Animals (PETA) stated that it is not against Inuit subsistence hunting, insisting:

"Although indigenous people in Northern Canada hunt seals, PETA's campaign has always been against the commercial East Coast seal slaughter carried out by non-aboriginal fishers as an off-season cash grab. This slaughter accounts for about 97 percent of seals killed in Canada and has nothing to do with the Inuit hunt. The sealing industry tries to hide behind native people in a dishonest attempt to justify its actions."[36] This statement assumes that it is possible to separate Inuit from commercial hunting. It also sets forth the fallacy that there are two distinct hunts in Canada: a subsistence hunt for food in the Arctic and a commercial hunt for pelts in the Gulf of St. Lawrence. But, since the 1960s, both are intertwined in the same market. It is not possible to separate one from the other. As Arnaquq-Baril claims, it is difficult for both activists and politicians to understand that Inuit are part of the commercial market. Additionally, this does not imply that Inuit are no longer hunting for subsistence. Inuit require ammunition and snowmobiles, both of which must be purchased and maintained with money. Inuit use modern technology to uphold their traditions. "It is the Euro-Canadian contact history," explains Wenzel, "which makes the snowmobile a useful tool in modern Inuit harvesting."[37]

The Internet has allowed a wider audience to participate in the seal debate. When the comedian Ellen DeGeneres hosted the 2014 Academy Awards, she took a star-studded selfie, which, at the time, became the most retweeted post in history.[38] As a thank-you for the publicity, Samsung donated a million and a half dollars to a charity of her choice. She nominated the Humane Society of the United States, which runs a campaign against the Canadian seal hunt.[39] In 2005 it launched "Chef for Seals," in which grocery stores, restaurants, and food industry actors pledge to avoid "Some or all Canadian seafood until Canadian fishermen from Canada's east coast stop – once and for all – the commercial sea hunt."[40] It was not enough to boycott the seal hunt; the US Humane Society decided to boycott the entire Canadian seafood industry.

Inuit fought DeGeneres's selfie with "sealfies." People posted videos and photographs celebrating the connection between their cultures and seals.[41] Billy-Ray Belcourt describes "sealfies" as "a 'tongue-in-cheek protest' that sought to imagistically arrest the racial insensitives of animal rights activists who choose not to attend to how they are caught up in the coloniality of the world."[42] Less than two weeks after the Academy Awards, on 14 March, Tanya Tagaq, a throat singer from Iqaluktuutiaq, Nunavut, tweeted an image with the sealfie hashtag.[43] It has since been removed, but it showed her baby, cuddled up in blue, next to a dead grey seal that had coloured the rocks with blood. The picture predates the sealfie movement: "We went to an elders' camp ... and one of the hunters there came back with the seal ... and everyone was really happy ... It was just showing how much I appreciated the seal for giving its life so we could be happy and eat."[44] Before discussing reactions to this image, it is important to consider how the same picture can evoke dramatically different associations. Blood in one culture does not carry the same meaning in another. One person might see seal blood as the loss of life; another as life's continuation. "Many people in the South are sickened by pictures of animal blood on the ice," explains Watt-Cloutier, "but to Inuit, this blood represents a powerful cycle of giving life – an affirmation of life, not a confirmation of death."[45] For Tagaq, to sit her baby next to the seal was a gesture of respect. She was honouring her child and the death of a seal that allowed the community to eat. This was lost in translation. The online backlash was as personal as it was violent. One woman started a petition to have her baby taken away.[46] A man photoshopped a picture of her baby beaten under a hakapik, a Norwegian sealing club, and someone else did one of her baby being skinned.[47]

In her acknowledgments for *The Right to Be Cold*, Watt-Cloutier thanks country food for nourishing her "spiritually and physically."[48] To eat an animal, for her, is to respect it. She recounts a conversation with a filmmaker she hosted in Nunavut. Watt-Cloutier told him that she would get him to eat muktuk, the Arctic speciality of whale skin and blubber that La Toundra served in 1967, before heading home to California. "He quickly responded, 'Oh no, I can't do that. I have too much of an affinity for dolphins and whales to eat them.' Without a second thought, I responded, 'Ah, but we too have an affinity for whales, which is why we eat them.'"[49] For the filmmaker, not eating the animal was a sign of respect; for Watt-Cloutier, it was the opposite. "The animals that are our country food connect us to the water and the land, to the 'source' of our life, to God," Watt-Cloutier continues. "Often when I prepared country food, my hands fully covered in blood, I would think that those who garden in the South must feel the same, their hands covered in the soil in which their vegetables grow. Source is source, whether it is the blood of the animals we hunt and eat, or the soil in which we grow our food."[50] Her sentiment recalls a scene in *Angry Inuk* when a group of Inuit students are about to stage a counter-demonstration in Toronto against the International Day of Action against Seal Hunting.[51] On the bus, one confesses that she does not understand the protests. "They torture animals every day," she says of settlers, "and we don't." This paradoxical scene demonstrates how unfathomable it is to her that Inuit could be accused of abusing seals by a culture that breeds animals as disposable commodities.[52] At the Yonge Street protest, students chant, "What's the big deal? We eat seal!" Despite their casual declaration, eating seal continues to be a big deal.

Half a year after Tagaq's sealfie, she expressed a similar sentiment: "I don't understand the logic of protesting the hunting of a relatively small number of animals that are completely sustainable … as opposed to stopping indigenous, poverty-ridden people from being able to reap their own natural resources."[53] Her mention of natural resources is significant. The interest in the Canadian North has long been economic. As Wenzel argues: "Sealskins, in a northern world colonized and ruled by Euro-Canadians, provide a small measure of independence from mines and oil wells, bureaucracy and good intentions."[54] Wenzel claims, "the animal rights movement is itself a part of a continuing colonial process in the Canadian North."[55] What is at stake is who has the power to define relationships, which is to say who has the power to define how plants and animals and the environments from which they come should be used by whom.

*Angry Inuk* is not about seals. Instead, it is about people who live in northern environments and the foods that sustain them. Seven out of ten Inuit children go to school hungry, Arnaquq-Baril tells her audience, to make the case that "Hunting is still the best way to feed Inuit." She bolsters her point with trendy marketing labels: "Fresh, local, wild, organic seal." The debate is no longer solely concerned with whether people should wear sealskins and furs and whether seals should be hunted commercially. It has moved from the skin to the mouth. Should people eat seal? If so, who and where? These are the questions to which I now turn. Kūkŭm Kitchen is not the first restaurant in Canada to serve seal, but it is the first Indigenous-owned restaurant to throw its voice into the debate about what kind of culinary and, therefore, cultural relationships humans should have with seals.

## "Seal Is the New Black"

The 2018 dress code for *A Taste of the Arctic* was "Business casual & sealskin attire."[56] Organized by Ottawa-based Inuit Tapiriit Kanatami (ITK), an advocacy organization founded in 1971 that represents Inuit living across Canada, this fundraiser uses food to educate about Inuit culture. *A Taste of the Arctic* attracts a mixed crowd, ranging from the Ottawa Inuit community (with more than three thousand people, it has the largest Inuit population south of the Arctic) to politicians, professionals, and enthusiastic eaters.[57] Past dishes have been "Muskox meatballs with elderberry gravy," "Dried caribou jerky with caribou lichen, pickled spruce tips and crowberry compote," and a northern take on a Louisiana-style rice dish: "Seal Jambalaya." At the 2016 edition, a woman wore a black T-shirt: "SEAL is the new BLACK," its white letters announced.[58] Although the fundraiser is celebratory, there is a tension in serving gourmet dishes made with northern ingredients from regions where hunger is prevalent, just as there is tension between food as a human right and as a commodity. These tensions latch onto restaurant menus like footnotes – the fine print to read assiduously. They also point to the politics of Indigenous ingredients in Canada today.

Lauren Goodman, an ITK health and social development policy advisor, describes the dishes as comfort food for some and a new experience for others.[59] "Dried caribou jerky with caribou lichen, pickled spruce tips and crowberry compote" sounds like what one finds at Kūkŭm Kitchen in Toronto or even at Copenhagen's Noma.[60] This represents southern Canada's increasing interest in northern ingredients. Such a stake underlines Zona Spray's argument that trend-setting chefs are, in fact, replicating the techniques, formulas, and type of ingredients that Iñupiat women have long used. "At first glance," she acknowledges, "any connection between Arctic subsistence cuisine and modern culinary creations seems absurdly remote." And yet she compares contemporary restaurant tricks with tastes and temperatures to Arctic culinary traditions.[61]

But this southern appetite for northern fare comes at a cost. According to a 2017 study, "more than one-half (52%) of Inuit in Inuit Nunangat aged 25 and over lived in a household that experienced food insecurity in the previous 12 months."[62] In 2016 the Nunavut Food Price Survey reported that grocery store items cost up to three times as much as in southern Canada. The average price for a 796-millilitre can of tomatoes is $1.60.[63] In Nunavut the same can costs $5.32. ITK includes "not being able to eat culturally accepted foods" as part of food insecurity.[64] This includes not being able to access seal in cities like Ottawa, Toronto, and Vancouver.

In 1993 small-scale farmers and producers founded La Via Campesina – the peasants' way – an international organization which, in 1996, popularized the term "food sovereignty." Food sovereignty differs from food security in the sense that the latter means having enough food on the table – the ability to access food – while the former probes what food is and how it gets to the table.[65] Food sovereignty asserts that eating is as much about culture – and power – as it is about nutrition. To have a say is to enact food citizenship, to achieve food sovereignty. Or at least this is its academic definition: people working to become food sovereign often define it differently.[66] The term is recent but the concept is not. "In practice," Robin writes, "Indigenous food sovereignty has been visible in communities around the world for thousands of years."[67] Food activists might not explicitly call their goal "food sovereignty," although that is what they are working towards.

Accessing seal meat is an issue of both food security and sovereignty. Another definition of the latter is "the right of peoples to healthy and culturally appropriate food produced through ecologically sound and sustainable methods, and their right to define their own food and agricultural systems."[68] If there are culturally appropriate foods, then there are also culturally "inappropriate" foods, and food sovereignty advocates for communities to determine their own foodways. For Inuit and other communities, seal is a culturally appropriate food, and accessing it a right. Food sovereignty encompasses six pillars; it (1) focuses on food for people, (2) values food providers, (3) localizes food systems, (4) anchors control locally, (5) builds knowledge and skills, and (6) works with nature.[69] According to Food Secure Canada, there is a seventh: food is sacred.[70] In 2011 this non-profit rallied for a national food policy because "close to two and half million Canadians are food insecure."[71] This affects Indigenous peoples disproportionally. Studies estimate that food insecurity plagues somewhere between 25 and 70 per cent of Indigenous communities.[72] Therefore, "reclaiming indigenous food systems" represents the seventh pillar: "Indigenous food sovereignty understands food as sacred and part of a web of relationships with the natural world that sustains culture and community."[73] Food sovereignty, thus, recognizes Indigenous culinary sustainability.[74]

But Canada's first-ever federal food policy, announced in 2019, recognized food security rather than sovereignty.[75] Why? Yet another tension lies in balancing feeding the national population with economically depending on agriculture as a commodity export.[76] This entangles restaurants and the ingredients they can access. Food also opens the gates to sovereignty issues at large. "Efforts to foster food sovereignty tend to be supported or suppressed in direct relation to the level of discomfort they create for governments," assert Grey and Patel, "who see in (even limited) Indigenous self-determination a threat to national unity, territorial integrity, economic prosperity, and legitimate jurisdiction."[77] To spin this wording, food sovereignty returns to land. Tabitha Martens describes Indigenous food sovereignty as facilitating "a re-connection to land-based food and political systems" by addressing "issues such as land reform, treaty rights and obligations."[78] Food sovereignty, thus, enlists food in a broader political agenda.

Serving seal at a restaurant like Kūkŭm Kitchen is an act of resistance that, simultaneously, enacts Indigenous sovereignty and the politics of refusal in adhering to settler norms. Sovereignty's origins, however, are complicated. Audra Simpson traces the term's genealogy to "a Western European, monarchic right to kill – in a desire to secure jurisdiction over territory that appears to no longer matter in the world of today."[79] This is why she argues that sovereignty requires critique. It is critique that distinguishes "between sovereignty as western exceptionalism and dominance, and sovereignty as Indigenous belonging, dignity, and justice."[80] In Indigenous studies, sovereignty is shorthand for protecting territory and advocating for "justice, land, water, life, and dignity."[81] Sarah A. Nickel's definition – the process by which Indigenous people outline and execute their own political strategies, institutions, and customs according to local and historically specific circumstances – concurs.[82] And most importantly, Indigenous sovereignty predates European colonization.[83] How sovereignty is understood and practised sways, depending on the politics of the time. This makes sovereignty relational, as well as pluralist. Similar to how Simpson describes sovereignty as shorthand, in the Indigenous Arctic sovereignty is a historically contingent concept that is a part of the "long history of struggle to gain recognition and respect."[84] Reading the sealing debate in the context of sovereignty unveils that the conflict over sealing is a fight over authority and control. And in restaurants this manifests as which flora and fauna are accepted on the menu.

The "SEAL is the new BLACK" T-shirt harnesses a popular saying to claim seal as essential, a basic for some. But it also illustrates how for others seal is new and, potentially, trendy. Gwich'in and Haudenosaunee chef Rich Francis, whom I write about in the final chapter, sported this T-shirt while teaching a second-grade class how to make moose nose tacos at North Park Wilson School, Saskatoon.[85] On 20 February 2018, he posted a picture of a seal flipper, writing: "I use seal ... in what I do for many different reasons personal to myself ... I've done this from day 1 not because it is trendy (quite the opposite) which it is now starting to become[.] My fear is this: it's going to be exploited in the high end restaurants by chefs and consumers who have never honoured or respected our ways and will serve it for the sake of serving it."[86] Where is this fear coming from?

A few weeks before, Francis, together with Shane Chartrand, a member of the Enoch Cree Nation, and Winnipeg's Feast Bistro's Christa Bruneau-Guenther, who features in the next chapter, prepared "Seal tataki" for Vancouver's Dine Out festival.[87] Coincidentally, around the same time, I asked John Horne, the district executive chef of the Toronto restaurant Canoe, if he had served seal. "Yup," he confirmed. "I think that going forward you are going to start seeing more and more seal come back onto menus," he speculated. "It is controversial, but it is something that is becoming overpopulated ... they are going to have to start finding a market for it. And I don't think that it should be embarrassing for Canadians to eat seal. It is part of our heritage."[88] Yet Horne considers it challenging to whet a Torontonian's appetite for seal. "It is not easy to cook," he confesses. He has made pie with slow-braised seal and "wild Canadian ingredients like sumac or wild low bush cranberries to help cut the fattiness." One of his favourite ways was used at Chef Michael Städtlander's Wild Leek & Maple Syrup Festival at Eigensinn Farm in 2015.[89] Horne marinated the meat with soy, roasted it over hot coals, and served it with wild leek kimchi and flatbread made with wild leeks, yoghurt, and fresh day lilies. However, he told me: "Other than that I have not cooked it much. Guests are a little shy about seal."[90]

Horne is sensitive to what seal represents: "to cook seal in Toronto and make people want it is a tough thing. It is just so disconnected because it is not something they eat in their regular diet. And then you see these visuals of baby seals getting clubbed ... But that ... is not how you get seal. And you think about the people up north, without the seal ... how would they live? ... No one wants to buy the seal furs so they can't afford ... to buy anything ... We put them in a weird situation." He is aware that Inuit are a part of the commercial market, but also recognizes how little Canadians know about the seal hunt. Nonetheless, Horne believes some people will change their minds about eating seal. But the goal is not a McSeal. Instead, expanding urban settler constructions of edibility helps to secure seal as an essential Indigenous food. Restaurants normalize the edibility and, thus, palatability of particular flora and fauna. And so what a menu includes – alongside what it excludes – enacts restaurant politics.

Disgust is a barrier for some eaters to change their minds about seal. This is a reminder of Douglas's assertion that taboos reflect a culture's social structure.[91] Disgust works as a structuring mechanism. Folklorist Lucy Long, who coined the term "culinary tourism," revisits Douglas's work. "The realm of the *palatable* is an aesthetic rather than cognitive one," she argues."[92] This is a reminder that, other than for toxic or dangerous ingredients, edibility is a continually evolving category. "Disgust is the ultimate rule of belonging," believes Ray. "If you share my disgust then we're probably from the same community."[93] Just as eating seal can define a community or culture, so can not eating it.

Other settler chefs have already changed their minds, or never had a problem with eating seal. Montreal's Caribou Gourmand serves "Harp seal tataki with seaweed aïoli, root vegetable chips, and wild berries gastric."[94] Inès and Guillaume Paimparay, a couple from Normandy, France, opened it in 2016, and in 2018 it was one of thirteen Quebec restaurants participating in the culinary event Sealfest.[95] Manitoba is another Montreal restaurant that serves seal, offering "Seal, smoked butter, yarrow, mugwort, mint, raspberry leaf, and Labrador tea."[96] But neither was the first. Seal was already on the menu at Au Cinquième Péché, which closed after ten years in 2015. The restaurant made it into the *New York Times* in 2009.[97] "In order to write about seal on Montreal restaurant menus," confessed journalist Micheline Maynard, "I would have to try it. And I had misgivings … On the other hand, the Canadian hunt remains legal, the seals caught in the hunt are not endangered, and the seal meat I was about to eat at Au Cinquième Péché might have otherwise been discarded if Benoît Lenglet, the restaurant's chef, did not put it to culinary use."[98] Maynard tried a dish that was not on the menu. She sampled seal tartare, with seaweed, potato pancake, and smoked herring mousse, like Kūkŭm Kitchen's "Arctic Trio." But she preferred the other seal dishes. The French chef Benoit Lenglet, who ran Au Cinquième Péché with his brother Benjamin, briefly seared seal loin until just rare. Maynard names another Montreal eatery – Les Îles en Ville – that pan sears seal before roasting it in the oven and cushioning it with cranberry sauce. It offers six seal dishes, which the menu calls *Loup marin*.[99] The owner and chef Andrée Garcia has noticed a pattern: many of the customers ordering seal are from France.[100] For tourists, seal takes on the aura of something unique and Canadian.

And in some Canadian regions, seal has long been a food for settlers. The 1986 Royal Commission recounted that seal was popular in Atlantic Canada, with there being an estimated market for "the meat of at least 40,000 seals per year provided the prices are competitive and the quality good."[101] This heritage lives on today in Newfoundland, but feelings about it are ambiguous. "Flipper pie remains iconic," claimed folklorist Holly Everett in 2012, "not least as part of popular exoteric constructions of rural savagery."[102] She associates "rural savagery" with "brutality, poverty and simple-mindedness."[103] Everett argues that class plays a role in which Newfoundlanders are willing to accept seal flipper pie as representative of their local culture. Despite its "conspicuous absence" in provincial tourism marketing, flipper pie appears in regional cookbooks, as well as in song lyrics and poems. As Everett concludes, "Whether or not one actually consumes it, knowledge of the dish, and its significance in the province's history, is still a marker of identity. It may be viewed by younger generations as unpalatable, but not inedible."[104] Palatable or not, seal flipper pie is an insider food, a food for locals and not tourists, unlike the French tourists who order seal in Montreal. But seal is usually not available in Newfoundland restaurants, and so visitors have few opportunities to try it.[105]

A year after Everett's article, in 2013, Gail Shea, then federal minister of fisheries, announced that Ottawa would financially contribute to expanding the seal meat market.[106] In 2014, the celebrated Newfoundland restaurant chefs Jeremy Charles (of

Raymonds) and Todd Perrin (of Mallard Cottage) held a demonstration in St. John's to elevate the culinary range of seal beyond flipper pie.[107] Seal was a critical part of the winter diet because it contained vitamin C. And "Bottled seal" and "Flipper pie" are still found in the region.[108]

Seal also appears in European culinary histories. In *The Nordic Cookbook*, chef Magnus Nilsson points to the region's coasts, where different species have historically been food, but less so during modern times and now, in central Scandinavia, almost not at all.[109] His tome supplies three recipes: "Seal soup" (with pearl barley, onion, seal meat, blubber, and innards),[110] "Boiled seal intestines with blubber and crowberries,"[111] and "Annso's seal liver pâté." He introduces the pâté as "a truly excellent example of Danish influence having mingled with the deeply rooted food culture of Greenland and the products available there."[112] "Annso's seal liver pâté" shows how tastes change and how a traditional food can be interpreted in ways that reflect social and political transformations, as well as Danish colonial history.[113] Seals also have a culinary history in the Mediterranean. But the meat was not always liked. Galen, the Greek physician, for example, "considered it distasteful and slimy, not palatable except by common people, and only then with mustard and vinegar sauce."[114] Nonetheless, European doctors recommended seal up to the sixteenth century, believing that it aided in curing strokes, epilepsy, and giddiness.[115]

Despite Montreal restaurants that serve seal and its culinary heritage in Newfoundland, the same is not true of other provinces. Meat plays an important role in the Canadian culinary imagination, especially in terms of regional identity. The prairies are cattle country. Cod and lobster define the Atlantic. Salmon does the same for the Pacific. Quebec is largely imagined as Canada's gastronomic centre, one in which meat is bloodier and taste buds more promiscuous, which is perhaps why many of the restaurants that serve seal are in its largest city. Toronto goes by the nickname Hogtown because of its pork-processing history.[116] However, recognizing seal as food is still not common in most of the country.

## Culinary Compromises

In 2015 Montreal-based chef Derek Dammann published *True North: Canadian Cooking from Coast to Coast*. "Tundra" is its shortest chapter and reflects a growing interest in Northern ingredients. "Canadian chefs are recognizing how delicious caribou, ptarmigan, muskox and seal are," it begins.[117] To represent this deliciousness, it features three recipes, including "Seal mortadella" and *"Phoque Jésus."* Dammann describes "Seal mortadella" as a "user-friendly dish," but only after he explains that he believes the controversy surrounding the seal hunt is due to misinformation and "a lack of education."[118] This disclaimer assumes that readers will be sensitive about seal, and primes them by assuring them that the hunt is strictly regulated.[119] The recipe calls for skinless, boneless pork leg, pork belly, seal, pistachios, sweet smoked paprika, and apple brandy. Dammann offers a substitute – a culinary compromise – for seal: pork. Pork, too, is steeped in taboo and forbidden in two major religions. And yet, he sees pork as more accessible than seal. If one goes for a more "traditional" mortadella, Dammann recommends adding al dente macaroni and pimento-stuffed Manzanilla olives.[120] This version is no longer "Seal mortadella." It is simply mortadella. These names matter.

Kūkŭm's Arctic Trio spotlights "Seal tartare." "Names are the way we humans build relationships," emphasizes Robin Wall Kimmerer, "not only with each other but with the living world."[121] Calling raw seal tartare familiarizes seal meat. It integrates it into the European culinary canon. And this name has caught on. For example, *Niqiliurniq: A Cookbook from Igloolik* features a "Tartare" recipe, calling for "fresh seal fillet, without blood, fat, or muscle on it," "oil of your choice," green apple, Dijon mustard, green onions, savoury pickles, and pickled vinegar.[122]

Dammann adapts another European dish for his second seal recipe. "Traditionally a coarsely ground salami seasoned with red wine, spices and garlic is called a Petit Jésus," he explains. "It gets its name from the fact that it ages close to nine months and weighs about nine pounds. I discovered that seal meat paired nicely with the robust spicing. The name for my version is therefore a little tongue-in-cheek: *phoque* is French for seal."[123] "*Phoque Jésus*" assumes a European palette. Damman's recipes transform seal into Canadian dishes that draw from Euro-Canadian culinary traditions. Chef Eric Pateman's decision to sauce pasta with seal at his Vancouver restaurant Edible Canada further exemplifies this. "We wanted to do something in a Bolognaise ... that highlights the seal but also makes it understandable and approachable for the average consumer to try," he explains.[124]

But for some, not even pasta can familiarize seal meat. In January 2017 Pateman made headlines for serving "Seared seal loin" and "Seal pappardelle" as part of Dine Out Vancouver, one year before Francis cooked seal at the festival.[125] In response, the Vancouver Humane Society posted instructions to "Please tell this Vancouver restaurant to take baby seal meat off the menu," which included the contact details for Pateman and Dine Out Vancouver's coordinator.[126] Activists took to Facebook, leaving 2,400 one-star reviews.[127] Protesters did the same to Kūkŭm Kitchen, penning reviews for a restaurant they had never frequented. Although Edible Canada received threats and had to contact the police, no one started an online petition. Shawana received four threatening phone calls. "One ... told me that I better watch out because if you do that to a baby seal, just imagine what someone can do to your son."[128] But other than this one incident, business went on as usual. The petition did not affect the number of people coming in, nor was the restaurant a site for confrontation. Protests were confined to the Internet and Kūkŭm Kitchen continued to peddle seal. Even Greenpeace members dined there to show their support. Unlike PETA, Shawana explains that when the petitions hit the news, Greenpeace "sent us an email stating that they fully support us. They now see the repercussions of what they have done to the Inuit people in the past and they no longer support the protests against sealing." If anything, Shawana suggests the petition helped to boost business. People heard about the restaurant and visited it for the first time wanting to taste seal. But these violent reactions have contributed to keeping seal off the table at other restaurants. Because Inez Cook of Vancouver's Salmon n' Bannock, the subject of Chapter 10, had heard about restaurants receiving death threats, she decided not to serve seal. "If I had one Inuk person on staff I would fight the fight, but I need to keep my staff safe," she says.[129]

The taste for seal is about more than novelty. The same year as Charles and Perrin's cooking demonstration, *Modern Farmer* published an interview with Perrin, where he emphasizes just how much he likes seal: "We don't do it as a gimmick; if it wasn't a good viable product that I thought my customers would enjoy, we wouldn't be selling it ... We're doing it for culinary reasons, and it also just so happens to speak to our culture and speak to Newfoundland."[130] The reporter compares what Perrin is doing to Nordic chefs, like Nilsson at Fäviken and Redzepi at Noma, which is to say interpreting "the flavors and aromas and ingredients of Perrin's youth in a place he loves and still lives, but interpreted through the mind of a talented and innovative chef."[131] Perrin competed in the first season of "Top Chef Canada" in 2011, and cooked seal flipper.[132] Although the judges perceived the dish as daring, for Perrin "seal flipper was just something we ate."[133] Like the cooking demonstration with Charles, Perrin has been experimenting with ways to cook seal, and the most daring has been ice cream (which he admits was not the best).[134] He has also crafted terrines, sausages, carpaccio, and smoked seal meat, all dishes based on European culinary traditions.[135]

Kūkŭm Kitchen, in contrast, is the only Toronto restaurant to have regularly served seal. Its source is also part of the debate. Aylan Couchie, an artist from Nipissing First Nation who initiated the counter-petition, published a *Globe and Mail* opinion piece together with Ian Mosby on 12 October 2017. The two narrow in on the petition's argument that the seal Kūkŭm serves "comes from a commercial company called SeaDNA and therefore has nothing to do with the indigenous hunt." Couchie and Mosby clarify that "it's the Inuit who make up most of the commercial seal hunters and Inuit economies which are most dependent upon the commercial seal hunt."[136] They point out the petition's underlying lack of knowledge: "Also absent from these critiques is a real understanding of what Canadian colonialism really looks like: That Indigenous food ways have been, at best, simply tolerated in Canada and, at worst, actively suppressed."[137] The petition's oppressive logic is that it suggests it is okay if the seal came from an Indigenous hunt, but the Indigenous hunt cannot be a part of the commercial market.

Pateman of Edible Canada explains that seals are predominantly hunted for their pelts, "so the meat has typically been going to waste, so there is a primary sustainability issue there."[138] Although the Department of Fisheries and Oceans closely monitors the hunt, there is no record of how much meat is consumed. Nonetheless, Pateman exposes one of the seal debate's dilemmas. On the one hand, there are Inuit communities hunting seals for food and selling their pelts to secure cash that can be converted into ammunition and fuel so that they can continue to hunt. On the other, there is a hunting industry for pelts. This raises the question: what comes first, the tartare or the coat? Does an interest in seal in southern Canada mean less meat will be wasted as a by-product of the fur industry, or will there be an increase in the demand for seals? The answers are far from straightforward.

Based in Quebec City, SeaDNA has processing facilities for grey seals on the Magdalen Islands and for harp seals in Newfoundland. In response to the petition, Shawana clarified his decision to work with them: "It took me 4 months to find the supplier I loved to work with, they are federally regulated, and only met 15% of their quota that was set by the government last year. This countless research was done with every ingredient I use … as an avid hunter I was taught at a very young age to respect the animals as whole, we use every part of the animal because we respect it and thank the animal for the life it has given up for us to survive."[139] SeaDNA makes seal accessible. Shawana had never tried seal until shortly before opening Kūkŭm Kitchen in 2017. The Royal Bank of Canada invited him to do an event, which gave him his first taste of cooking Arctic foods: beluga whale, narwhale, caribou, and seal. He braised the flipper until the meat pulled apart. When he opened Kūkŭm, he wanted to have seal on the menu because of its significance as a northern Indigenous food.

SeaDNA's founder is from France. The company sells seal oil (an Omega-3 supplement), seal jerky flavoured with maple and chipotle, and twelve other products, including adult and "veal" loins, flippers, trims, burgers, sausages, merguez, smoked seal meat, péperettes, salami, terrines, and rillettes.[140] Similar to Dammann's, the charcuterie mixes seal with pork and the likes of plums, apples, oranges, spices, duck, beef, and wild cranberries. However, SeaDNA's charcuterie is only available in Quebec. SeaDNA targets non-Indigenous customers, but as Shawana argues, the company conducts itself in a way he respects. As of 2018, Off the Hook, a Toronto seafood store, carries its seal. When announcing this new supplier on its website, SeaDNA included a "Seal loin tataki" recipe and a sales pitch: "Seal is a true Canadian tradition that is sustainable, delicious and amazingly nutritious … It is also among the healthiest proteins on earth and one Canada should celebrate."[141] Not only does SeaDNA categorize seal as Canadian, it argues that it is a traditional food and part of the country's heritage.

Beyond the Canadian label, categorization is an issue. Because a seal lives in water, federally it is a fish. However, Quebec classifies it as a mammal and, therefore, a meat. SeaDNA argues that "This disagreement on seal product regulations has slowed down market development and responsible resource management for many years."[142] As should be clear, one seal species is not a substitute for another. SeaDNA once contacted Goodman at Inuit Tapiriit Kanatami because it had four hundred pounds of harp seal flippers to give away. Goodman asked some communities in Nunavut if they were interested, but they declined: they eat nattiq, and are not interested in harp seal.

Where should people eat seal? *A Taste of the Arctic* serves it in the nation's capital to spread awareness of Inuit culture. Restaurants that offer seal in urban Canada attract controversy, press, and protesters. But one of the most iconic moments someone ate seal was in 2009. Shortly after the European Union banned Canadian seal products, Michaëlle Jean, then governor general, was in Nunavut to celebrate its tenth anniversary. At a festival in Ranklin Inlet, she participated in skinning a seal with an *ulu*, and ate the animal's heart, raw.[143] Jean was called a Neanderthal in return, and gave the press plenty to talk about.[144] This moment, however, was symbolic. The governor general is the monarch's representative and carries out the monarch's ceremonial and constitutional duties. Mary Simon, then leader of Inuit Tapiriit Kanatami, called Jean's actions a show of support: "To us, this kind gesture is an acknowledgment by the Governor-General of our culture and our dependence upon our wildlife as an important resource for our communities today."[145] For eating seal heart, Peter MacKay, then federal defence minister, called Jean "Canada's new Braveheart."[146] For partaking in an Inuit feast, critics considered her a supporter of the commercial hunt. That this was considered a controversy further goes to show the settler logic trap that requires separating the Inuit hunt from the commercial one.

At Kūkŭm Kitchen, the table of two to my left also orders the "Arctic trio." "Could we get it without the seal?" asks the man. The woman nods and the waiter obliges. This raises Rebecca Spang's question of what this table is in relation to mine. "To the restaurateur they might be 'patrons' or 'customers,' and to a materialist they might be simply 'eaters,' but what were/are these people to each other?"[147] Even though we are seated next to each other, intimate neighbours, we are separated by tables of our own, a reminder of how eating out is publicly private. I watch their "Arctic trio" arrive. No longer a trio, its dishes are reduced from three to two. If restaurants are venues for cultural negotiation, requests for substitutions are compromises. The restaurant wants to serve a dish one way, but the diner wants it another.

By offering the pork-only option for "Seal mortadella," Dammann already anticipated resistance. He was prepared to offer a substitute, to accommodate. Some restaurants, like Momofuko, a New York City noodle bar with global outposts, do not allow substitutions, which I learned when my sister dared to request hot sauce. It is no coincidence that Momofuko's chef, David Chang, visited a Montreal institution with similar rules and pronounced it his "favourite place in the world."[148] Wilensky's Light Lunch has been serving a beef salami and bologna sandwich – the "Wilensky special" – since 1932. When Chang revisits he recalls a sign that read, "If you don't want mustard then we are going to charge you 10 cents." Sharon Wilensky explained that first it was five cents, then ten cents, and then they stopped doing it. "And I thought that was the most brilliant thing I've ever seen in any restaurant menu ever," whispered Chang with awe. Perhaps because Kūkŭm Kitchen was new, it was willing to bend the rules. Or perhaps because its staff recognized that seal is uncommon for many settlers. Either way, a culinary compromise is also a cultural one.

A year after I dined at Kūkŭm, Shawana replaced the "Arctic trio" with "Trio of tartare." For the same price, chinook salmon, seal loin, and bison tartare fan across the plate.[149] Preserved vegetables and bannock tag along as sides and, as a whole, as Shawana explains, "it is pretty much what we are known for now in the city, so we can't take it off the menu." Seal had become Kūkŭm's signature dish. Despite my neighbouring table's request, the tartare demonstrates the appetite of some diners to eat foods they never before had access to. By serving seal, Kūkŭm Kitchen positions Indigenous food sovereignty in the middle of Canada's metropolis. It visualizes the politics that restaurants enact, and seal holds an essential spot on the menu, Kūkŭm insists.

Why did I, a settler Canadian, order the "Arctic trio"? And why outside of the Arctic? I ate seal because thinking of seal as food matters. Like any living animal that is transformed into meat through an act of culinary imagination followed by killing and, often, cooking, seal is a way of life for some and a taboo for others. These cultural classifications become hierarchized through regulations and societal norms. The question of who can eat what is rooted in debates over to whom Canada's lands belong and how they are governed: debates about sovereignty.

The significance of settlers paying money to eat seal at an Indigenous-owned restaurant in Canada's largest city cannot be overstated. This chapter's intention has been to use Kūkŭm's seal tartare as a gateway to contour the debate's complexities and the wider political issues restaurants engage with. The discussion around seal as food is informed by concerns over economic opportunities, sustainability, and cultural appropriation. The petition against Kūkŭm Kitchen was not about seal; it was about what is and is not food. It was about ideals and worldviews. I have drawn attention to the entanglements surrounding a single restaurant dish, and this is what food history does best. Restaurants are venues for exchange and debate. The point is not to end with a conclusive "we should eat this, we should not eat that," but instead to draw connections between what people eat and how it reflects how they understand, construct, and interact with the worlds around them. Following this line of thinking, the next chapter travels to the Canadian capital and then turns back west to Winnipeg to further question the animals that appear on restaurant menus and the ones that don't.

chapter nine

# Where the Beaver and Buffalo Roam

It is lunchtime in August and Nikosi Bistro Pub's patio is beginning to fill up. The restaurant sits alongside the shores of the Gatineau River in Wakefield, Quebec, separated by a road aptly called Chemin Riverside. Named after a fur trader who drowned in its cold waters around 1683, the river rises north of the Baskatong Reservoir and flows 386 kilometres southeast to Canada's capital. It is here where the Gatineau joins the Ottawa River, separating the country's two oldest provinces: Quebec and Ontario. Formerly Lower and Upper Canada, they united as the Dominion of Canada together with New Brunswick and Nova Scotia in 1867. Ten years earlier, in 1857, Queen Victoria crowned Ottawa the capital.[1] It sits on the Ottawa River's south bank, on unceded Algonquin territory. To travel from Ottawa to Nikosi Bistro Pub, you drive thirty-five kilometres north on Autoroute 5. This highway shadows the Gatineau, mimicking the river's twists and turns.[2]

To map Canada is to map rivers and lakes. It is to map water. Waterways define the country's geography, and it is with waterways, and not by road or rail, that people navigated Canada for centuries both before and after it went by this name. Typical for North American restaurants, Nikosi serves water as cold as the river, free of charge. A pitcher of it with fresh cranberries, sprigs of mint, lemon wedges, and ice decorates each table. The restaurant's logo also evokes water: Two paddles flank a bear. The paddles represent the river location, as well as the partnership between knife and fork.

In addition to tap water, I drink an "ELECTRIC POW WOW," the first on Nikosi's Signature Cocktails menu: "Chic-Choc rum, blueberry maple kombucha, fresh lime, blueberries, mint." The name has a musical footnote. *Electric Pow Wow Drum* is the first song on A Tribe Called Red's 2012 debut album.[3] A blend of electronic and First Nations music, the DJ collective formed in Ottawa in 2008.[4] Like A Tribe Called Red's music, Nikosi's "ELECTRIC POW WOW" is a blend. It merges flavours and histories: Canadian spiced rum, a Quebec-made version of the alcohol that originated on seventeenth-century Caribbean sugar plantations; kombucha, a fermented tea that emerged in Northeast China around 200 BC and at Nikosi is brewed with blueberries and maple syrup; lime, which traces back to Southeast Asia; and mint, which is native to much of the world. Like Wolfman's Indigenous Fusion, Nikosi's menu mixes ingredients from near and far.

Top 40 hits play as I talk to Wapokunie Riel-Lachapelle.[5] Having grown up in Wakefield, at the age of eighteen she moved to BC, where she worked at the Fairmont Chateau Whistler. Although it only opened in 1989, the hotel is a disciple of the grand European chateau-inspired architecture that the Canadian Pacific Railway promoted. "I worked bottom up," she recounts.[6] Making her way from the kitchen to the dining room, she then graduated to restaurants in Vancouver and Toronto. She returned to Wakefield and opened Nikosi Bistro Pub on 19 January 2017. She first sketched the logo, which foreshadowed its name. "My nephew's name, Nikosi, means bear paw … bears in Indigenous culture represent our grandfathers, so it's like someone looking over you," she tells me.[7]

The menu is eclectic yet cohesive. It is a repertoire of flavours like maple syrup, wild mushrooms, berries, and "game." In addition to "Venison smoked meat," Nikosi offers options beyond Canada's usual suspects of beef, chicken, and pork – menu as menagerie. "It is really about educating people," Riel-Lachapelle says. "I try not to scare people away … You'll see that I have deer smoked meat on bannock. *Oh, it is smoked meat.* And you're eating Quebec deer … We do a twist with the bannock. Sometimes kale, or maybe cheddar and apple bannock. So we do fusion." At Nikosi Bistro Pub, fusion is a means of nudging diners to try something different. This approach is one part creative, one part accommodating. The menu features "Bannock grilled cheese with duck sausage," a "Boar burger," "Blueberry rabbit terrine," and "Spicy duck drumsticks." Meats like duck, boar, rabbit, and venison prop up Nikosi's fusion.

"Tagliatelle pasta 'à la Riel'" narrates a more personal history. The combination of "prawns, chorizo, cherry tomatoes, Kalamata olives, capers, fresh herbs, garlic infused olive oil and shaved parmesan" reviews her ancestry. "Louis Riel was my great, great, great, great-uncle," she explains. "This recipe I just love. There is not too much that is Aboriginal about it." This gives "à la Riel" a double meaning. She named the pasta after herself: *à la* indicates that this is her way of putting it together. Her family name traces her lineage to Riel: a symbolic figure as the Métis people's political leader, and a politician whom the Canadian government controversially convicted for high treason and executed in 1885.[8] A summer pasta with a historic footnote.

Nikosi Bistro Pub's proximity to Ottawa points to an important absence. Currently, there are no Indigenous restaurants in Canada's capital, although this was not always the case. Sweetgrass Aboriginal Bistro opened in the Byward Market in 2003, pronouncing itself Ottawa's first and, according to one guidebook, "purportedly Canada's second."[9] It closed in 2011.[10] Calling Sweetgrass Canada's second Indigenous restaurant overlooks earlier ones. The repetition of such "first" claims exposes the lack of public awareness that Indigenous restaurants are, in fact, not new.

Then husband and wife Phoebe and Warren Sutherland, who met at the New England Culinary Institute, opened Sweetgrass on 15 November 2003. She is Mistassini Cree, he is Jamaican, and together they compiled a menu of bison burgers and caribou sausages, of Arctic char and "Navajo fry bread with wild mushrooms and pine nuts." Artwork by Glenna Matoush, Benjamin Chee Chee, John Tenasco, and Doug Kakekagumick turned the restaurant's walls into a gallery.[11] Food writer Anne DesBrisay branded Sweetgrass "an original experiment: bringing First Nations cuisine to Ottawa … with a wee nod to Jamaica. Yes, Jamaica. Indeed. It's what makes Sweetgrass a quintessentially Canadian restaurant."[12] This description recalls culinary hybridity and Canadian creole. Although DesBrisay considered the décor cluttered, it matched "the modesty of the place, the convivial atmosphere and the affable service."[13]

A casual fine-dining restaurant, Sweetgrass offered "native teas," like crowberry, and wines only from countries with Indigenous populations, including Nk'Mip Cellars on the Osoyoos reserve in BC, alongside Jamaican Blue Mountain coffee and "Bounty rum bread pudding."[14] In 2005 the *Ottawa Citizen* published its recipes for "Maple sugar pie" and "Chipotle maple glaze Arctic char on wild rice-mushroom stir-fry."[15] Other dishes encompassed "Rabbit dumplings," "Smoked fish cakes," and "Wild boar chilli-rubbed back ribs with collard greens and scalloped potatoes."[16] In 2009, "Wild boar empanada stuffed with potatoes, cheddar with a mole sauce" with avocado salad made an appearance, another reminder of Latin American cuisines' Indigenous heritage.[17] In contrast to this wide culinary range, each table started their meal the same way: with a bowl of popcorn, long associated with movie theatres and paper bags. Sweetgrass reclaimed its Indigenous pedigree and served it as an appetizer. Popcorn set the stage for the rest of the dishes to come.

One dish spotlighted a bird that is frequently spotted on meadows, seashores, and winter coats, but rarely on restaurant menus: "A slow-roasted leg of Canada goose, the toothsome meat dripping off the bone into sautéed bitter greens, balanced with a sweetly-roasted root vegetable 'hash.'"[18] When food studies scholar Sarah Elton shared her plans to try Canada goose, people greeted her with looks "as if I'd said I was roasting a rat for dinner."[19] Together with the seagull and the pigeon, *Branta Canadensis* belongs to the trio of North America's most loathed birds.[20] This further touches on the concept of edibility and how the ubiquity of a particular food source does not necessarily whet a culture's appetite for it. In addition to roasting its leg and pairing it with bitter greens, Sweetgrass plated it alongside risotto, ginger, and apples.[21] Its decision to serve Canada goose challenged cultural biases and restaurants' standard meaty fare. By listing this "flying rat" on its menu,

Sweetgrass cooked outside of the box. This chapter fixes its focus on meat to further map how regulations – alongside conflicting imaginations of the edible – both influence and police which animals are game to eat. Here, regulations is shorthand for restaurant politics.

## Conflicting Imaginations of the Edible

Similar to the Canada goose, the beaver is a national icon, albeit a more beloved one. Since 1975 it has been an official emblem, which is to say an identity marker, a visual and material representation of the abstract idea of a nation. Because of the fur trade, the beaver was once over-trapped and reduced to scant numbers. This is no longer the case; however, the closest most Canadians get to eating beaver is a whole wheat, yeasted dough facsimile fried in oil and lathered with butter, cinnamon, and sugar. Grant and Pam Hooker gave this pastry an emblematic name when they opened their first stall in 1978.[22] BeaverTails (*Queues de Castor*) have since become a quintessentially Canadian food at home and abroad. But tails aside, to what extent is the beaver imagined as meat?

The beaver, according to cultural historian Jody Berland, can be studied as a living creature, as a commodity (fragments of a dead beaver, which this book does as food), and as a "material and semiotic object."[23] In 1941 anthropologist Marius Barbeau attempted to naturalize the beaver as a Canadian cultural symbol. His article was printed in the appropriately titled *The Beaver*.[24] Historian Joan Sangster argues that this publication, founded by the Hudson's Bay Company, created "an ideology of Canadian 'northerness' that promoted ideals of anthropological discovery, historical pride, and liberal tolerance for other cultures, while also reinforcing colonial images of Inuit and Native peoples."[25] *The Beaver* also reinforced the story of the "vanishing Indian" and, thus, as Fee details, "the imperative to salvage Indian culture."[26] That anthropologists were trying to document something that was vanishing, as opposed to in flux, reveals the limitations and cultural tensions surrounding Barbeau's representations of the beaver as a Canadian symbol.[27]

His article focuses on Indigenous art, and yet by framing his argument with the title "The Beaver in Canadian Art," he claims the art as Canadian, appropriating Indigenous peoples' visual history, similar to the tactic employed by the Canadian Pacific Railway.

The 2016 art project *oh-oh Canada*, organized by Leah Decter, called upon the tongue to challenge, to dissolve, this history. Artists used maple syrup, the country's culinary ambassador, to concoct eight candies, distributed to Parliament Hill crowds on Canada Day. Lisa Myers and Adrian Stimson, who appears in the Conclusion of this book, both contributed to the project. Michael Farnan crafted a beaver, inviting Canadians and tourists alike to put it in their mouths via a maple sweet. Importantly, he unspooled how beavers are symbolically associated with "the negative and enduring aspects of colonization."[28] Farnan transformed eating candy into a moment of critical reflection on how colonial history and popular culture have moulded cultural imaginations into perceiving the beaver as cute, as Canadian.

One reason the majority of Canadians do not consider the beaver as food is that its meat is often described as Indigenous, as "country food." This, however, erases the European history of beaver as meat. But, more importantly for *Culinary Claims*, government regulations render it difficult to access, which is true of game meat in general. Because it is illegal to buy and sell wild game in most of Canada, if one wants to eat beaver one has to trap it oneself. This point is crucial for considering a restaurant's ability to represent human relationships with animals and which ones are included in a cuisine.

The beaver as "country food" differentiates Indigenous fare from Canadian food by categorizing the former as what people ate and the latter as what people now eat. But beaver is not a universal food.[29] The beaver is absent in George Jr.'s *Modern Native Feasts: Healthy, Innovative, Sustainable Cuisine* (2013). However, there are two beaver recipes in his debut cookbook, first published in 1997 and then republished in 2010, the year of the Vancouver Olympics, as *A Feast for All Seasons: Traditional Native Peoples' Cuisine*. Both editions share the same recipes: "Smoked beaver meat" and "Boiled smoked beaver." "Beaver tail soup" was also part of

George Jr.'s winning menu at the 1992 Culinary Olympics.[30] Why are these dishes included in George Jr.'s first cookbook and not his second? *A Feast for All Seasons* features traditional cuisine, whereas the 2013 volume focuses on modern cooking.

Historian Alison Norman mentions that the Haudenosaunee ate beaver.[31] Brittany Luby mentions that Anishinaabeg in Treaty 3 Territory used beaver to encourage lactation.[32] Patricia Beeson's *Macdonald Was Late for Dinner* includes a section on Grey Owl based on stories from his relative through marriage – Madeline Theriault, a member of the Temagami First Nation. Recipes animate her stories, including one for "Roast beaver with raisins."[33] Eulogizing her great-grandmother's Christmas speciality, Theriault recounts that she "would make dough with raisins in it and put it in the beaver as the stuffing and roast it in the oven about two hours."[34]

But beaver's culinary predicament also exists within Indigenous communities. Recounting memories of family breakfast chatter, Myers recalls, "The conversation continued with stories of scone making, fried bologna, hunt camp meals of partridge soup with dumplings, and the unresolved controversy of whether a beaver tail cooked up like bacon or if it was just used to sharpen knives."[35] Weso agrees and describes beaver meat as palatable, though confessing his preference for rabbit or squirrel or bear.[36]

Despite modern narratives' associations with Indigenous foodways, Europeans and settlers consumed beaver meat for centuries. To list but a few examples, Catharine Parr Traill mentioned beaver as an option when "fresh meat is scarce" in her 1855 *The Female Emigrant's Guide*.[37] "Beaver Tail" was on the menu at an 1876 dinner in Ottawa hosted by Sandford Fleming, the engineer-in-chief of Canadian and Intercolonial Railways.[38] And Expo 67's La Toundra offered "Beaver tail broth" for seventy-five cents. By 1967, however, beaver had largely lost its reputation as a food. La Toundra's menu was about novelty, an attempt to serve "Canadian" dishes to the world. However, Expo 67 took place before the country promoted the beaver as its animal emblem in 1975.

As with cookbooks, restaurants, and events, television provides a medium through which to present and define cuisines. In "Moosemeat & Marmalade," which premiered on the Aboriginal

Peoples Television Network in 2015, beaver represents Indigenous food. The same network that aired "Cooking with the Wolfman," APTN provides a venue for Indigenous self-representation in the context of mainstream media. The premise of "Moosemeat & Marmalade" is that "two very different chefs" – Art Napoleon from West Moberly First Nations, a "seasoned hunter & bushcook," and Dan Hayes, a "classically trained French Chef" from the United Kingdom – "explore culture, culinary traditions and really good food."[39] Moosemeat, food that is hunted, signals Napoleon as an Indigenous "bushcook," while marmalade, food that is made in a kitchen with imported oranges, represents Hayes as a "chef."

The pilot is set in Napoleon's home of Moberly Lake, BC, where he takes Hayes beaver hunting. Napoleon is dressed all in green with an army cap, while Hayes dons a tweed jacket, tie, and knee-socks. As Napoleon explains the importance of respecting animals, Hayes responds that the British do not have such rituals, then chuckles about port wine. Not only do the men dress differently, they associate hunting with contrasting sentiments. With one shot the beaver is killed, and Napoleon gifts a tobacco offering to its spirit.[40] He explains that beaver was once a staple, "but these days most young people haven't even tried it. Hopefully, we can change this."[41] The meat's unpopularity is not connected to the animal's history as an over-trapped commodity. Instead, the focus is on people's lack of experience.

There are many ways to cook beaver. Napoleon turns a teepee into a smoker, seasons the meat with soy sauce, and cradles it in a metal net over the fire. The Indigenous "bushcook" prepares a dish the European "chef" has never tried. There is no mention of the history of beavers in the United Kingdom. By the twelfth century beavers were extinct in England and by the sixteenth century in the rest of the British Isles because of overhunting.[42] In 2009 beavers were reintroduced to Scotland and since 2013 have been spotted in England.[43] Today, the semi-aquatic, broad-tailed animal is classified as a rodent, something diners also associate with the Canada goose, but in the Middle Ages it was a fish. The Catholic Church followed Leviticus 11 from the Bible to classify the beaver as "primarily aquatic and therefore categorized as fish, as opposed to 'creatures which creapeth [sic] upon the land.'"[44] This granted permission to Catholics to eat it on Fridays, during fasts, and on holidays, including Lent. The history of beaver as fish challenges the narrative that beavers were hunted primarily for fur. Dolly Jørgensen clarifies that the distinction was not mammals versus fish and birds, but land versus water, which also applies to seal.[45] The beaver was a bifurcated creature. Both of land and water, its belly and tail were considered fish.[46] Because the animal passed as "fish" in Catholic doctrine, the history of beaver hunting is also one of food.

Hunting signifies status. It represents social hierarchies and cultural ideals regarding which animals are fit to eat and how they should be killed. It also communicates human relationships with animals in tandem with imaginations of ownership and property. Depending on the context, hunting can indicate wealth and nobility, or poverty and marginalization. Regarding Canada, John Ralston Saul writes, "Until well into the nineteenth century, hunting was a central source of wealth. Farming, a theoretically more advanced undertaking, was a recipe for poverty."[47] Hunting for profit is now illegal and yet still connects to social status and, most importantly, to issues related to land ownership and Indigenous sovereignty.

Driven by the seventeenth-century trend for felt hats, the quest for beaver led to settlement further and further west. It also led to tension among First Nation tribes that escalated in the Beaver Wars, also known as the Iroquois Wars, a series of conflicts between 1640 and 1701.[48] Many hats later, by the mid-1800s the species was nearing extinction.[49] The Cree artist Kent Monkman tells a similar story of the destruction caused by over-hunting and trapping in a 2015 exhibition at the Gardiner Museum, Toronto (Figure 9.1). The installation consists of a buffalo jump (a cliff formation used for hunting), a sculpture of the artist's alter ego, Miss Chief Eagle Testickle, two full-sized bison, and smashed ceramics that represent bone. *The Rise and Fall of Civilization* "references the near extinction of the American bison in the 1800s when humans killed approximately 50 million, reducing their numbers to the hundreds. The settlers killed the bison for their pelts, wastefully

Figure 9.1. Kent Monkman, *The Rise and Fall of Civilization*, 2015, mixed media installation, Gardiner Museum, photo by Jimmy Limit.

leaving the meat to rot."[50] Through casting the compacted bone as metaphor, the installation contrasts different approaches to hunting: one in which the entire animal was used and one in which single parts were exploited as commodities, largely discarding the rest and thus leading to the animal's near destruction. As Daschuk writes, "The demand for food created by the arrival of traders led to the commodification of bison as a commercial source of food."[51] With both bison and beaver, the pelt was the object of desire. The rest was secondary.

Monkman further alludes to the destruction of over-hunting in his 2011 painting *Les Castors du Roi* (Figure 9.2). The title does not name which king, but all signs point to France's King Henry IV, who seized the fur trade as an opportunity to solidify an empire in North America.[52] Nor does it warn about the massacre it depicts. Painted in a historical style that looks older than its production date, it depicts colonialism in the Americas as a bloody battle over beavers, one with both economic and symbolic stakes. It is

Figure 9.2. Kent Monkman, *Les Castors du Roi*, 2011, acrylic on canvas, 96 x 84 inches, Collection of the Montreal Museum of Fine Art, image courtesy of Kent Monkman.

an ironic story in the sense that killing beavers generated wealth and power, while also risking depleting the steady supply of beavers on which that wealth and power was based. Monkman offers a take on colonial history with the beaver as its victim. Canada's animal emblem is symbolic of the country's contradictory relationship to nature. "In many ways Canada is a country with a split personality," argues Glynnis Hood, "one that defines itself by the very wilderness it nearly destroyed."[53] Canada stories its nature as resource rather than kin.

Although traders valued pelts out of commercial interest, game meat was still important. Suman Roy and Brooke Ali touch on this in their cookbook *From Pemmican to Poutine: A Journey through Canada's Culinary History*. The authors identify game as one of the first available food sources to settlers and argue that hunting it was a way of expressing new rights to land: "It was also a measure of the new freedom available in the New World. In the 1600s, game hunting was a leisure activity for the wealthy and the nobility and it was forbidden to anyone but the high echelons of society. Settlers in the New World, however, were given the right to hunt the local game; a privilege that would have meant one was on par with the elite in the old country."[54] Hunting became a practice of freedom. This, however, dwindled in popularity once homesteads with cattle grew in size. Settlers "no longer needed to rely on the often unreliable practice of hunting for their protein."[55] Instead of a staple ingredient, game became a supplementary one.

Historian James E. McWilliams suggests otherwise. Although foodways differed from colony to colony, he describes consistent attitudes towards hunting: "As the English saw it, hunting may have served a purpose in rare times of need, but ultimately it was a sport, a diversion."[56] The British believed that "civilized" people relied on domesticated animals for their protein, and associated hunting with frontier foods.[57] This puts Hayes's reaction to Napoleon's description of the spiritual qualities of hunting into perspective. It also assumes that "produced" food is more valuable than "frontier food." Julia Roberts, however, finds the opposite true in her study of snipe in Canadian saloons. She affirms a connection between hunting and nobility.[58] To be sure, the historic, cultural, and political perceptions of hunting in Canada are complex because of differences in attitudes among the British, French, and other settlers. Regional differences in agriculture and foodways, and Indigenous food sovereignty, add to the complexity. Hunting implies relationships with the land and its non-human inhabitants that are different from animal husbandry. TallBear reflects on how hunters have "sets of relations with their prey."[59] These sets of relations recognize that humans, too, are prey. Furthermore, because of Indigenous practices of cultivating landscapes, hunting collapses a clear distinction between "wild" and "domesticated animals."

Yet, settlers associated domesticated animals with independence. By gaining "independence from wild meat," settlers distinguished themselves from Indigenous peoples, for whom hunting remained a cultural practice. Once a form of currency, wild meat became obsolete.[60] In turn, wild animals went from food to emblems. Today hunting is about more than subsistence.[61] When dinner does not depend on a hunt's success, the practice acquires different meanings. In a world where food is fragmented and commercialized, where an animal is one thing and meat – often boneless and skinless and smothered in plastic – another, hunting is a confrontational reminder that eating is about life and death.

## Restaurants and Regulations

Canada keeps hunting off the menu. Rules differ across the provinces and territories, but in most of the country it is illegal to buy and sell wild game.[62] Newfoundland and Nova Scotia are exceptions, and in Nunavut one can purchase game in supermarkets. British Columbia's Wildlife Act makes it unlawful to sell game meat, a fact of which some restaurant owners might not even be aware.[63] Under Ontario's Food Safety and Quality Act, hunted game that is not killed in a slaughterhouse is classified as "inedible material." In Ontario, and most of Canada, only meat that has been inspected and then slaughtered in a government-licensed facility is legal.[64] "If your local bistro peddles elk, duck ... venison, and even 'wild' boar," writes journalist Jacob Richler, "that animal grew up on a farm."[65] This is what enabled the Liliget Feast House in Vancouver to serve elk.[66] The same is true of Ottawa's Sweetgrass.

In Ontario there are hunting and trapping licences. Residents require an Outdoors Card and all applicable licences and tags, except for members of Indigenous nations with treaty hunting rights. "These hunters are not required to be in possession of an Outdoors Card," state the regulations, "provided they are hunting for food, social or ceremonial purposes within their traditional or treaty area."[67] This further raises issues of sovereignty and who can hunt where. Indigenous peoples can only hunt on their reserves. To hunt elsewhere requires a licence, which is to say official government approval.

Hunting regulations influence cuisine in the public realm, as the opportunity to consume wild game becomes a private affair. Richler calls it "an outrage that Canadian chefs cannot use their restaurants to showcase our own wild grouse, turkeys, deer ... For game is one of our great resources, and in keeping it out of the hands of real chefs who know what to do with it, and leaving it entirely to home cooks, who do not, we have defaulted on developing what might have been the cornerstone of our national cuisine."[68] He assumes that home cooks are less capable than trained chefs, even though the former, especially if they are hunters like Napoleon, are likely more experienced in preparing game. Governments, thus, have tremendous influence on regulating what is on and off the menu. One consequence is that Indigenous peoples who grow up learning to prepare game are not able to apply this knowledge to restaurants. Furthermore, Indigenous restaurants cannot represent their food cultures with wild meats, which Whiteduck Ringuette of Toronto's NishDish is critical of. "We can't get game from First Nations communities – this is a political restriction," he makes clear.[69]

Because of regulations, it is primarily hunters as well as Indigenous and risk-tasking chefs who know how to prepare game. Derek Dammann and Martin Picard are examples of the latter. In introducing a recipe for "Hare ravioli," Dammann refers to "the whole wild game thing in Canada" as "pretty strange."[70] He complains about not being able to legally serve moose and deer in

Quebec even though he can serve seal and hare. "It doesn't make any sense at all," he writes.[71] But that does not stop him from including recipes for "Moose tongue smoked meat" and "Smoked caribou carpaccio." Furthermore, some chefs find ways to skirt these regulations by hosting "private" dinners. For example, Louis Charest is the executive chef at the Office of the Secretary to the Governor General. In 2010, he prepared an Arctic-themed dinner that included whale, musk ox, seal, caribou, and walrus at Charlie's Burgers, a Toronto underground dinner club.[72] Richler writes about this loophole: "Where I live in Ontario, the only way for restaurants to serve real game is to arrange to have the meat donated for a designated event. Then the chef will prepare a special menu free of charge, while – nudge, nudge, wink, wink – billing their specially briefed customers $150 each for a bottle of mineral water or the use of a cloth napkin, all the while hoping no inspectors show up on a random check and complicate matters with questions about meat inspection certificates."[73] And so the same rules do not always apply.

A beaver recipe appears in another Montreal chef's cookbook: Martin Picard's 2012 *Au Pied de Cochon Sugar Shack*. Its six pages of instructions suggest that the dish is anything but everyday fare.[74] The beaver is stripped of its sacs and stuffed with its tail, which has been braised. The ingredient list assembles oyster and button mushrooms, pig's blood, cream, *foie gras*, and maple-smoked ham. It verges on extreme eating, food as spectacle or sport.[75] However, as Picard suggests, his recipe is not about shock value; it is about recognizing the culinary history of the beaver in Quebec and the animals he hunts at his sugar shack.[76] Still, tension remains with including a beaver recipe in a restaurant cookbook. The public cannot consume beaver at Au Pied de Cochon, nor at its sugar shack. If serving wild meat was legal, "Confederation beaver" could appear on Au Pied de Cochon's menu, but would it?[77]

A predecessor to Picard's dish appears in *The Northern Cookbook*, which includes a recipe for "Sweet pickled beaver." First published by the Canadian Department of Indian Affairs and Northern Development in 1967, this culinary handbook encouraged settlers to move to and eat well in the north. Here, the beaver is a local food with gourmet potential and part of a colonizing agenda. The recipe mixes beaver meat with ingredients that travel great distances, such as pineapple juice and lemon. As in the case of "Confederation beaver," one is left doubting the practicality of "Sweet pickled beaver."

Picard's "Confederation beaver" highlights that regulations make serving beaver meat in restaurants nearly impossible. Nonetheless, there is an emerging curiosity. As part of the 2015 gathering *Cook It Raw Alberta: The Shaping of a Culinary Frontier*, Edmonton-based chef Brayden Kozak cooked beaver. Founded by Italian food entrepreneur Alessandro Porcelli, the event brings chefs together to cook in the "wilderness." In a promotional video, Kozak stirs a beaver and carrot stew. "Beaver meat is obviously something extremely underutilized in cooking in Canada. Growing up, you learn a lot about the fur trade and how important beaver was to the pioneers," he says while stirring the stew. "So it kind of made sense to bring something that was so important to our nation's history."[78] It is because of beaver's historical importance that Kozak decides to cook it.

Although it is not explicitly stated in Kozak's description, there is an emphasis throughout *Cook It Raw Alberta* on what Toronto chef Jamie Kennedy calls the "Indigenous influence."[79] Porcelli names three ingredients that shape culinary identity – great people, talents, and products – and the method with which to execute it: tradition. "So what is tradition here?" he asks. "It's the Aboriginal people, it's the First Nations," Porcelli then answers. "All of the chefs here should be able to tap into this."[80] *Cook It Raw Alberta* shapes Canadian culinary identity based on Indigenous influences. However, only one of the fourteen chefs is Indigenous – Shane Chartrand, whom the Conclusion to this book discusses. Therefore, *Cook It Raw Alberta* also raises questions about who has the power to define culinary identity.

Beaver as a metaphor for Canadianness reveals a complex story about changing constructions of edibility. The beaver is cute and Canadian, and therefore an inappropriate edible. The Canada goose is its opposite – rat-like and appropriate for coats. Yet it, too, is incongruous for plates. These examples demonstrate how cultural imaginations frame what is appropriate restaurant fare. Returning to the Canadian capital, Sweetgrass offered meat representing Indigenous culinary traditions, yet still faced restrictions. "Everything that we get has to be commercial," explained Phoebe Sutherland in 2005, "so a lot of the stuff that we get is farm raised, so the moose meat that I would get back home I can't get here so I have to get deer to kind of replace it, or elk. The caribou still tastes the same because they run wild and they eat what they normally eat. But rabbit … does not taste the same … goose it's a little different."[81] The next chapter interrogates the distinction between wild and farmed. Here it is important to note the challenges such ongoing regulations impose.

Despite these restrictions, Sweetgrass was "a destination place to discover aboriginal traditions and artistic expressions."[82] A contact zone. According to Sutherland, Sweetgrass's settler diners "realize that Aboriginal people can be out there competing with four star restaurants."[83] She notes that customers come not just to eat: "They see art, they hear music, and [learn] a lot about our food, [because] our staff is able to explain where all this is from [and] … we use a lot of Aboriginal words in our menu and wording. So [those] kinds of thing teach them where this is from or what that word means … I think one of our main goals is to teach others about our culture."[84] A year after opening, the Greater Ottawa Chamber of Commerce crowned Sweetgrass "New Business of the Year." The award recognized its local engagement: from purchasing at local farmers' markets to making donations to organizations like Minwaashing Lodge Aboriginal Women's Support Centre.[85] In 2007 the *Ottawa Citizen* wrote that the city's "first and only aboriginal restaurant has evolved from a theme-eatery into one of Ottawa's reliably good restaurants." Later that year, it included it on its "Best Bites" list.[86]

The Sutherlands parted ways, and Phoebe continued to run Sweetgrass, together with chef Tim O'Connor.[87] In a July 2011 editorial in the *Nation*, a Cree magazine, she documented its beginnings: "the idea came about at a family dinner, the talk of 'what if' we one day opened a Native restaurant and served fine First

Nations Foods."[88] This idea fuelled her to pursue her culinary education, draft a business plan, apply for grants, and set her sights on Ottawa. "Sweetgrass Aboriginal Bistro is a restaurant like no other," Sutherland wrote. "It is a place where we showcase our Native foods in an upscale manner."[89] She listed customers, including "Chiefs, MPs, cabinet ministers, celebrities, hockey players, First Nation people and non-Aboriginals." Sutherland's editorial concluded by narrating the restaurant's end. She confessed her struggles to keep it – her "life's dream" – afloat, admitting to debt and the need for support, and ended with: "This restaurant is a Cree-owned business and I believe it has done our people proud."[90] In 2011 it closed.

To date, Sweetgrass has been Ottawa's only Indigenous restaurant. It operated in the second period I define, following the closure of Canada's last residential school but before the Truth and Reconciliation Commission. On the one hand, Sweetgrass tells the story of Canadian creole, a style committed to blending flavours and cultures rather than dabbling in fusion. It organically and unapologetically presented "Rum pudding," a Jamaican classic, alongside "Wild boar empanadas" and "Canada goose roasted in red wine." Despite the restaurant's promotion of an Indigenous agenda – exemplified by the ingredients it purveyed, the employees it hired, and the local communities with which it collaborated – and its exclusion of French wines in favour of ones from countries with Indigenous populations, Sweetgrass focused on the politics of representation rather than reconciliation. It served dishes with the intention of sharing Indigenous culture and spreading an awareness of it: Canada goose with a side of "What a unique dining experience." Kūkŭm and NishDish, on the other hand, serve their dishes with demands: they rally for resurgence. They want to revive Indigenous food systems. They want to take back what has been taken away: "Pine needle and citrus sorbet" with a side of historical accountability. As NishDish claims, it is Toronto's "friendly neighbour since always." Nonetheless, Sweetgrass highlights an acute challenge: keeping a restaurant open. To further discuss this point, I return to Winnipeg.

## Little Restaurant on the Prairie

Beef in most of Canada, and especially Western Canada, is a staple, and its place on the table an assumption. Not to offer it is to make a statement, something Christa Bruneau-Guenther does.[91] A member of the Peguis First Nation, Bruneau-Guenther opened Feast Cafe Bistro in December 2015 on Ellice Avenue in Winnipeg, a handsome corner restaurant accented with high ceilings and exposed beams. "The biggest decision was not to have beef on the menu," she tells me.[92] Instead, she found a source for local bison, which "is nearly double the price," but serving it, for Bruneau-Guenther, is non-negotiable. That beef is significantly cheaper and, therefore, easier for a restaurant to procure is witness to the history that Monkman's installation recites. Bison were driven off of the plains, replaced by cattle. But slowly they are coming back.

For nine years Bruneau-Guenther ran a daycare, where at mealtime she followed, first, the Manitoba food guide and then, as of 2007, Health Canada's freshly published *Food Guide for First Nations, Inuit and Métis*, which included beaver. The beaver, however, is not included in other government food guides, thus distinguishing between Indigenous foods and settler Canadian ones. Yet this guide sparked Bruneau-Guenther's interest in Indigenous vittles and she began to incorporate cooking lessons as a means of immersing kids in Indigenous cultures. "It is through food people identify," she believes. "Cooking is a lost skill in many Indigenous communities," she tells me, which is why she wants to bring it back. To cook is to reconnect.

With the exception of the *Food Guide*, Bruneau-Guenther found a dearth of information when she started studying Indigenous foods. One of the few cookbooks was by Dolly and Annie Watts. Like restaurants, cookbooks underrepresent Indigenous cuisines.[93] Elizabeth Driver's *Culinary Landmarks: A Bibliography of Canadian Cookbooks, 1825–1949* examines 2,276 Canadian titles and classifies only one as "Native."[94] But more and more Indigenous chefs and restaurateurs are expanding this genre. In the United States, for example, Sean Sherman's *The Sioux Chef's Indigenous Kitchen* took home the prestigious James Beard Foundation Book Award in the best American cookbook category in 2018. The same week the foundation announced its nominees, Sherman was on a book tour. In Los Angeles, he joked that he had to write this cookbook because there is no *The Joy of Native American Cooking*.[95] With limited print sources at the time, Bruneau-Guenther relied on seeds and soil to educate her about Indigenous foodways. Some years before opening Feast, she planted a garden with squash and mint, sage and basil, raspberry and beans. The garden grew in more ways than one, and, knowing that she wanted to work more with food, she closed the daycare and decided to open a restaurant where education and empowerment take centre stage.

The menu at Feast Cafe Bistro speaks with directness. Its ingredients and dishes are familiar, while still proudly Indigenous, the likes of Saskatoon berry vinaigrette and blueberry BBQ sauce, cranberries and squash, sunflower seeds, hazelnuts, pine nuts, elk and bison, pickerel and salmon. Bruneau-Guenther is committed to keeping prices accessible: "I want that a young Indigenous mother can come in and feel connected to her culture."[96] She sweetens the Saskatoon berry smoothie with maple syrup. The food spans "Bannock pizza" with Manitoba grass-fed bison sausage, cheddar, pine nuts, and maple chipotle sour cream, "Caesar salad with herbed bannock croutons," "Bison stew," "Vegan chili," and "Traditional 'tipi' tacos."[97] Feast offers a choice between bannock and gluten-free corn tortillas. As Bruneau-Guenther details, "Original bannock would have been gluten-free," made from corn, roots, or rice. But she recognizes the "spiritual and childhood connection to frybread" that many have, and, therefore, makes room for it on her menu. Nonetheless, she wants to use as many Indigenous foods as she can, explaining: "I want people to experience traditional foods. It is about reidentifying with who you are in your culture. The music, the art, the languages are coming back. And it is starting with food." Food is a gateway to revival, to resurgence.

In 2016 there was another Indigenous restaurant in town: Cookem Daisey's, run by Glenna Henderson, who secured a year-long lease and opened a downtown space with seats for twelve. When I met Henderson, she fed me a hearty bowl of soup with bannock on the side. "This is our hamburger soup. And if I showed you my invoices, I would say that at least a third of our orders are for hamburger soup and bannock," she told me.[98] Beyond catering events for local Indigenous businesses, Henderson served Justin Trudeau an "Indian taco" in June 2016, when he became the first sitting prime minister to do an interview at the Winnipeg-based APTN. It was evening when Henderson received a phone call: "Can you do hamburger soup and tacos for the prime minister's crew?" The next morning she hurried to the grocery store, prepared the food, and then, after the interview, passed him the taco to go.

Henderson's catering company, turned restaurant, turned once again catering company, offered pow wow fare, quite different from Feast Bistro's menu. But what is important here is impact. When Bruneau-Guenther opened Feast, catering sustained her business, and her finances felt a difference when Cookem Daisey's opened, which raises the question how many Indigenous restaurants Winnipeg can support. In 2017 Toronto had four, but is there room for more? What about Winnipeg? After all, Winnipeg has the largest urban Indigenous population in the country, 92,810 according to the 2016 census: 12.2 per cent of the city's population.[99]

When Feast Cafe Bistro opened, there were two other Indigenous restaurants in town. Robert Chartrand, a former country-rock singer and Manitoba Métis Federation's chairman, bought what was a Chinese restaurant at 967 Main Street in 1997. His wife, Connie Chartrand, had been working at Harman's drug store's lunch counter and was laid off. In his words, "I guess you could say I purchased my wife a new job."[100] As the *Winnipeg Free Press* recounts, "the Chartrands decided their menu should reflect their culture. An outdoor sign has read 'Proudly Aboriginal Owned and Operated' since Day 1 ... providing aboriginal people with a restaurant to call their own."[101] The menu played a diner's top hits – sandwiches and hamburgers – but sprinkled in Indigenous references, like pickerel and bannock. After more than twenty years in business, Connie's Corner Cafe closed in 2018.

Bison Berry, the second restaurant in town, operated out of Neechi Commons' top floor.[102] Louise Champagne is the president of

Neechi Foods Co-op Ltd., and, in 1989, the worker cooperative bought a space in the North End, where it opened an Indigenous grocery store. When the Teepee Restaurant closed, its baker came to Neechi. In March 2013 Neechi Foods expanded by moving from Dufferin Avenue to 865 Main Street. The new building cost eight million dollars, half of which they raised and half of which they took on as debt. Downstairs a painting of the three sisters – three women lined up in a row, one with corn in her hands, one with beans, and one with squash – decorates a wall. Beyond groceries – the likes of pickerel, fresh bannock, and wild blueberries, as well as the usual grocery store suspects – the complex housed Bison Berry, an Indigenous designer's co-op, a gallery, and a store showcasing art, crafts, clothing, and books.

Similar to the Teepee owner's description of Main Street, Champagne explains that it was once a thriving business street, but then newly built suburbs attracted its inhabitants away, emptying the area of its grocery stores.[103] "There are lots of people who come and work in these parts of the city, but then they leave and spend their money in the suburbs. Access to food in this neighbourhood is limited," she tells me, which is why Neechi fills a gap. Champagne solicited the community about what they wanted, and needed, in a space like Neechi Commons: a grocery store for people rather than profit. Jamie Cidro, Bamidele Adekunle, Evelyn Peters, and Tabitha Martens illustrate: "It is important to note that in Winnipeg Neechi Foods and Neechi Commons, an inner city Aboriginal cooperative enterprise, provides access to many of these foods, for example fish, bison, blueberries and wild rice."[104] Making Indigenous foods accessible in the thick of the city, Neechi is an example of urban Indigenous food sovereignty.

Bison Berry's menu gathers pickerel and bison burgers, pancakes and salads. There are "Wild rice croquettes," "Bannock French toast," and "La Boule," a Métis dish of meatballs, mashed potatoes, and gravy. "La Boule" also goes by its plural, "Les Boulettes," and as Cyr and Slater write in their study of traditional Métis foods, these are "usually only served during holiday gatherings due to the amount of work required to prepare the recipe."[105] Repetition matters. "Culture is what you do every day.

Food culture is what you eat every day," elucidates Champagne. "Everybody is buying food in one way or another and they are buying more than the food," which is a reminder that food choices make larger statements about culture and community. Bison Berry attracted Winnipeggers from other parts of town and provided a healthy place to eat in a neighbourhood marked by food apartheid. In Champagne's words, "We need to reclaim the economy and make it work for us in a way that supports our culture." Neechi served as an outlet for locally produced products.

Unfortunately, Neechi Commons did not survive its debt after failing to auction the building. It closed in June 2018. With forty payroll staff, it was the largest employer of First Nations and Métis people in Winnipeg.[106] Some restaurants cater to the well-to-do, but by selling fresh ingredients and affordable meals Neechi Commons made a crucial contribution to its local community as well as to Indigenous food sovereignty at large. Its closure is both a loss and an example of the ongoing trials of running a community grocery store and eatery, which manage government regulations, especially ones regarding meat, and access to ingredients alongside striking a balance between financially sustaining a business and offering prices that speak to local communities, their needs and their wants. This shows that despite an increasing interest in Indigenous foods, contemporary Indigenous eateries still face challenges in keeping their doors open. In contrast to Winnipeg and Ottawa, Indigenous restaurants have had the longest continual presence in Vancouver, the city to which the final chapter returns.

chapter ten

# Salmon and the F-Word

Inez Cook and Remi Caudron opened Salmon n' Bannock on West Broadway in Vancouver in 2010. She is Nuxalk but was adopted as a child by a family with Mennonite heritage, and he is French.[1] The two met as Air Canada flight attendants and worked together at a Lebanese restaurant. In 2009 Cook went on a trip to Kelowna, BC, where she stumbled upon a café with the slogan "Don't panic … We have bannock." She came home with an idea for a restaurant. "Can you believe it?" she asked Caudron. "There is a Native restaurant in Kelowna, but there's nothing in Vancouver," she reported. "The whole world is coming to Vancouver for the Olympics and there is no Native restaurant."[2] Through word of mouth, the two of them learned about a space whose owner was locked into a lease. Caudron and Cook took it over and opened Salmon n' Bannock on 15 February 2010, three years after the Liliget Feast House had closed.[3] In 2019, Inez became the sole owner and, today, all of its staff are Indigenous.

As other examples have shown, décor plays an important role in staging a restaurant's Indigeneity. Moreover, exhibiting art is a means to support Indigenous artists. At Salmon n' Bannock, the walls are deep red, a shade even darker than the wildest of salmon. "We knew that we could not have a First Nations restaurant in a blank space. We knew that we had to have some art," Caudron tells me. Someone recommended a Native health society that had been supporting a local artist.[4] When its director learned they were opening a restaurant, he gifted them a canoe to send them "on a good journey."

Although securing a space and even the art to fill it went smoothly, Caudron and Cook encountered other challenges. Caudron is not Indigenous and, as a survivor of the Sixties Scoop, Cook grew up outside of her culture. "We had to show a commitment and a desire to represent the culture with something that people could be proud of," Caudron clarifies. They had to prove their dedication to local Indigenous communities, an obvious change since Muckamuck's time. Today, not everyone can open an Indigenous restaurant. The power dynamics have changed.

Salmon n' Bannock's menu also demonstrates how Indigenous restaurants have evolved since the Muckamuck's 1971 debut. Although the Kekuli Cafe in Kelowna inspired Cook and Caudron, the Kekuli is more casual. Beyond the salmon and bannock its name implies, Salmon n' Bannock serves "Braised bison back ribs," "Pulled boar and elk burgers," and "Bannock bread pudding." There is also "Lazy hunter's bannock" (a vegetarian option), "Bannock with pemmican mousse," "House smoked braised duck wings," and "Maple coleslaw." Compared to Vancouver's earlier eateries, Salmon n' Bannock is most similar to the Liliget Feast House, as it features Indigenous ingredients prepared in contemporary ways. And like Ottawa's Sweetgrass, it pours glasses of merlot and pinot blanc from Turtle Island's first Indigenous winery, Nk'Mip Cellars.

Salmon n' Bannock accents its menu with seasonal specialties, from pickerel to herring roe on kelp and, up until January 2019, smoked oolichans. When I visited, Caudron explained that they offer oolichan grease and soapberry ice cream to those who ask, but do not print it on the menu. Both are traditional and honoured, and the restaurant does not want people to order them out of the desire to try something new, only to abandon them on their plates. This recalls the Muckamuck's chef, who dissuaded the owners from offering grease. But now, oolichans are not only off the menu but also off the table. Authorities informed the restaurant that it is no longer permitted to serve this "traditional fish traded in our communities like gold."[5] This is another example of the recurring theme of regulations, many of which still hinder Indigenous restaurants from featuring traditional foods. Sustainability, of course, is a concern, but regulations often reflect more than supply. They represent and reinforce the dominant culture's norms.

Salmon n' Bannock's motto is "We got game." But as the previous chapter unpacked, just how "wild" that game is is subject to regulations. "There are people who, when they think 'game,' apprehend a very strong taste," observes Caudron. Salmon n' Bannock's "Game sampler" platter provides bite-sized tastes of the likes of wild boar salami, air-dried bison, and elk served alongside doubled-smoked cheddar, pickles, sage-infused blueberries, cedar jelly, and baked bannock crackers. It changes based on availability, which regulations again influence. Moose, for example, is not commercially available, and caribou is sporadic. BC is not known for its game, and most of what Salmon n' Bannock peddles comes from the Prairies. "There is definitely a premium to pay," Caudron adds – it would be about 25 per cent cheaper to serve venison from Aotearoa New Zealand than from Quebec. There is deer closer to home, but laws keep it off the table. "This touches on food sovereignty, right?" Caudron says. "You could say that Native people have an entitlement to access their traditional foods. Now we are in a commercial setting so we have to serve things that are approved in a commercial facility." Two issues arise. First, a commercial setting influences a chef's ability to source and serve traditional foods and, thus, represent Indigenous culinary cultures. Second, traditional meat, because of government requirements, might be cheaper to purchase from another region, and thus shifts notions of what is local and for whom. For Vancouver this means that local is not always Canadian. Echoing King's point, Caudron explains: "There is technically in the Native world no border between Canada and the US. There is no border; it is all one territory. We do play with that, and go over the border." Salmon n' Bannock reflects an Indigenous view of Turtle Island and demonstrates that local foods cross and challenge settler borders. Accessing ingredients is but one of the challenges Indigenous restaurants in Canada continue to face today. If Salmon n' Bannock restricted itself to local fare, only fish would be on the menu.

A twenty-minute walk north of Salmon n' Bannock is Granville Market, Vancouver's central purveyor of salmon – fresh and smoked. "Wild chum salmon, sugar, salt, spice, maple flavour (water, propylene glycol, natural & artificial flavour, caramel colour, citric acid, sodium benzoate)": these are the ingredients in the "Premium Maple Smoked Indian Candy" I buy. A similar package is on sale at Toronto Pearson airport seasoned with pepper and "natural wood smoke." Boasting "100% Canadian maple syrup," its package is decorated with a colourful illustration of a woman tending a fire, with a baby bundled on her back. Produced by West Coast Select in British Columbia, the product is historicized by the package's back: "In early times while the Native women prepared the salmon for the smoke house this was given to the children as a treat. It is now a delicacy that is enjoyed by all. Maple Smoked Indian Candy is a gourmet treat as well as a perfect souvenir of Canada, combining both our most famous tastes, Canadian smoked salmon and pure maple syrup." Typical of all Canadian products, the label is in English and French: "Saumon fumé a l'erable a la façon Indienne." Neither company is Indigenous-owned.

Like seal and beaver, salmon is an animal and a food; however, salmon was neither taboo nor forgotten. Rather, salmon has become less and less of a fish and more and more a food, which is to say that it is a widely circulated commodity and one of Canada's greatest culinary hits. Smoked with or without maple syrup, it is a Canadian staple. Salmon is simply everywhere, but how? Unlike seal and beaver, humans farm salmon. Because of aquaculture, salmon went from special-occasion extravagance to affordable, a bagel with smoked salmon barely costing more than one without. Like bannock, salmon is sometimes Canadian, other times Indigenous, and sometimes both. Although Newman is sceptical about a single dish's ability to represent a nation, she believes that "salmon has a strong claim as national main course."[6] Anita Stewart calls salmon "*the* Canadian fish."[7] According to Newman, "Cod might have been the fish that founded Canada, but salmon is the fish that defined it."[8]

But at Montreal's Expo 67, salmon was not yet ubiquitously Canadian. La Toundra featured a handful of dishes from the sea:

"Oysters and clams from Atlantic shores," "Ojibway Kee Wee Sen," and "Baked dore Outaouais" as Cuisine Canadienne; "Northern lake trout," "Char Emavik," and "Rainbow trout Agnakuk" as part of La Toundra. And "Chilled shrimp cocktail," "Seafood vol au vent" (with halibut and dore), and "Canadian lobster a la Nage" as International Cuisine. "*The* Canadian fish " made only a single appearance: "Smoked salmon" as "a savoury appetizer" on the International Cuisine menu. International? Neither Indigenous nor Canadian? Was salmon too expensive at the time? By 1967 salmon farming had yet to reach Canada. Early attempts were underway in Norway, but only in the 1970s did these farms grow into an industry that made salmon affordable, even cheap.

Salmon is now the most popular fish on Canadian menus.[9] From smoked to poached and from pan-fried to grilled, it is a favourite for breakfast, lunch, and dinner. Salmon has been swimming along and has already surfaced several times throughout this book, from Sonny Assu's boxes of *Salmon Crisp* and *Salmon Loops* to Muckamuck's menu and, now, the name of Vancouver's Salmon n' Bannock. In this chapter, it takes the bait. In light of a growing awareness of Indigenous food cultures, when is salmon Indigenous and when is it Canadian? How did it go from a local Indigenous food to a pan-Canadian one? This chapter surveys the relationship between salmon and place, salmon "pluralities," how chef Rich Francis reclaims it as Indigenous, and what this means for restaurants.

## Wildly Farmed

Not one but many, there are one Atlantic, five Pacific, and two Asian Pacific salmon species, a total of eight across two genera.[10] The fish's habitat is vast. Because salmon feed in open oceans and then swim hundreds of miles to spawn in freshwater streams, William Cronon writes that "their lives integrate the ecologies of terrestrial and marine environments as few other organisms ever do."[11] Like beaver, salmon shape environments, as Richard Manning's apt title *The Forest That Fish Built* illustrates. Salmon transfer nitrogen and carbon – "life's basic elements" – from the ocean to inland ecosystems.[12] In the 1860s, when the canning industry was just developing on North America's west coast, there was only one kind of salmon, regardless of the different species: "the wild one."[13]

In addition to wind-drying and smoking, canning expanded the possibility of preserving, and thus commodifying, salmon. "Canning, along with meatpacking and grain processing," historian Anna Zeide explains, "was the original technique of processing food, yielding a product that emerged from the factory in a form quite different from what you would find in nature or on the farm."[14] Its origins lie in the French Revolutionary Wars, when Napoleon's government staged a competition for better methods of preserving food and, thus, provisioning for troops.[15] Nicolas Appert won the prize of 12,000 francs in 1809 for sealing food in glass jars. The following year he published *L'Art de conserver, pendant plusieurs années, toutes les substances animales et végétales*, and by 1815 moved away from glass and toward tinplate canisters – making him the "father of the canning industry."[16] In 1864 the Hume brothers set up a salmon cannery on California's Sacramento River, the West Coast's first.[17] During the late nineteenth and early twentieth century, coho (medium red) and sockeye (dark red) dominated the catch to the point that "salmon became synonymous with deep red."[18] Canned food's connection to war also continued. Between 1942 and 1946 British Columbia sent 80 per cent of its canned salmon to British troops.[19]

In Canada salmon is strongly associated with the West Coast. But the Atlantic and even the Great Lakes were also once home to industrial salmon fishing.[20] Writing about present-day Peterborough – not far from Lake Ontario, which is called Chi-Niibish, meaning "literally big water" – Simpson calls Michi Saagiig Nishnaabeg salmon people.[21] She recalls Elder Doug William's memories of the wild salmon that once called this lake home: "Doug tells me Chi'Niibish had its own resident population of salmon that migrated all the way to Stoney Lake to spawn."[22] The Michi Saagiig Nishnaabeg "witnessed the extirpation of salmon and eels from our territory."[23] Simpson insists on writing "are" salmon people rather than "were," even though the land has lost its native fish. Today coho salmon swim through Ontario, but this salmon was introduced.[24]

In response to dwindling numbers, the global aquaculture industry developed a second salmon: "the semi-wild fish born and raised in a hatchery and eventually released into rivers."[25] Then in the mid-1960s, salmon farmers in Norway began cultivating fish in floating pens. Born in the 1960s and the one that most people eat today, "the fish farm's domestic salmon" is the third.[26] Salmon farms were set up in Canada on both the Atlantic and the Pacific coasts in the early 1980s. Farming transformed a luxury into a widely available and affordable food. By 1986 Atlantic salmon made up 64 per cent of global consumption; by 2012, it jumped to 99 per cent.[27] Canada – the world's fourth-largest producer – propagates Atlantic (*Salmo salar*), King or Chinook (*Oncorhynchus tshawytscha*), and Coho (*Oncorhynchus kisutch*). Atlantic salmon, however, is its top aquaculture export, going largely to the US.[28] Most recently, there is a fourth: genetically modified salmon. In 1989 AquaBounty Technologies designed the AquAdvantage salmon, which debuted in Canada in 2017. The US Food and Drug Administration approved it in 2019.[29] Encompassing these multiple varieties, the label salmon is far from straightforward.

Farming has made salmon affordable. But, cheaper prices camouflage other costs. "Salmon breeding," to quote food historian Richard Warren Shepro, "breeds controversy."[30] Feed, which is about 60 per cent of the cost of growing salmon, is part of the controversy.[31] It contains antibiotics, growth hormones, and dye that colours the flesh a perky orange to meet consumer expectations, ingredients that contaminate the water. Wild salmon eat krill, which are an orange so fluorescent that it stains their flesh dark red. Farmed salmon, in contrast, eat feed pellets containing what the industry calls colourants rather than synthetic dye.[32] In 2003 the Swiss pharmaceutical company Hoffmann–La Roche designed the SalmoFan, in a range which Coates compares to "the paint charts available at decorating stores," of thirty-three shades of salmon, "from bold bubble-gum to a very subtle rose."[33] First salmon farmers learned to design the fish's colour, and now, as the AquAdvantage salmon models, they can engineer the entire fish. Farmed salmon are still great swimmers, and some escape. The runaways compete with their wild kin for habitat, food, and spawning grounds. Additionally, farmed salmon are more likely to carry and pass on viruses and parasites, which is why they're fed antibiotics. The environmental impacts and effects of climate change – extreme weather events and rising water temperatures – add further complexity to the salmon industry and its future.

Anthropologist Marianne Lien and sociologist John Law call salmon "newcomers to the farm."[34] Before the 1970s, the sea was a place for fishermen. The "blue revolution" made it one for farmers.[35] Calling the Atlantic salmon "an icon of wilderness,"[36] they address the close proximity between wild and farmed fish – from the waterways they occupy to their life cycles. But these relations change from place to place. "Fish pluralities," a concept developed by Métis anthropologist Zoe Todd, connects to what Lien and Law call "the salmon multiple."[37] Spanning both wild and farmed, it recognizes how the two entangle, but also that "wild" is relational. Without farmed salmon, there is no "wild." And before salmon became a newcomer to the farm, this fish was simply salmon, no adjective needed. Beyond this introduced binary, the practices of fixing salmon "also enact salmon as slippery, elusive, and as something other."[38] Slipperiness makes salmon, for some cultures, difficult to know. Salmon have multiple identities, some of which overlap to challenge the simple dichotomy of farmed versus wild. What does this mean for salmon as an Indigenous ingredient?

## A Salmon and Its River

Before salmon was canned, farmed, or designed, it was kin. And it still is. "The salmon is not just a salmon; the salmon is family to us," asserts Mi'qmaw scholar Fred Metallic. "And it's really hard to get people who speak the English language to appreciate that the salmon is not just a noun, not just an object."[39] Likewise, Todd considers fish teachers.[40] Recognizing how fish shape human identities, she defines "fish pluralities" as "multiple ways of knowing and defining fish."[41] Fish pluralities are slippery. They embrace "differing understandings and conceptualizations of fish, which were sometimes complementary and sometimes contradictory."[42] Following suit, I consider "salmon pluralities." Abiding by Todd's warning against assuming that "very local and specific forms of human-fish engagement" translate from one part of Canada to another,[43] I do not wish to risk generalizations in surveying salmon pluralities. Instead, I hope this slippery account highlights issues related to salmon, place, culture, and the making of a farmed fish-turned-souvenir.

Fish reflect human relationships to place. "When I look at a salmon," writes fisheries biologist Jim Lichatowich, "I don't just see a silver fish, I see the Northwest."[44] A 1993 *Vancouver Sun* article agrees. "First Feasts," which recommended both the Quilicum and Dolly Watts's catering company, recites that "In the beginning were the salmon, and an entire culture followed. To state the obvious, the food came first. Without salmon, there would be no totem poles, no masks, no rattles, no bentwood boxes, no monumental carvings in the University of B.C. Museum of Anthropology."[45] Salmon long anchored coastal Indigenous cultures in the Pacific Northwest.[46] The Columbia River, for example, was "a great table."[47] It formed a "table for both sides of the river," as one Elder explained in 1915.[48] A seasonal food that returned year after year, salmon also lent itself to preservation: dried, smoked, and "pounded into pemmican."[49] Just like the beaver's status as Canada's national emblem, in 2013 British Columbia crowned salmon the province's official fish.[50] Although "people of the salmon" and "salmon nations" usually conjures up the Pacific Northwest, other cultures – from northwestern Europe to the Siberian Far East – have also appointed salmon as a cultural symbol.[51]

The relationship most people have with salmon is a culinary one. Grey and Newman attribute settler appetites for salmon to their familiarity with the fish from European rivers.[52] But on Canada's West Coast, the taste for smoked salmon came only after the Second World War, a craving that increased as prices decreased. Beyond an interest in Indigenous traditions like smoked salmon, settlers developed "fusion dishes that incorporate salmon into immigrant cuisines."[53] This demonstrates adaptability and culinary exchange.[54] In addition to curries and sushi rolls, Newman lists smoked salmon's spot alongside maple syrup in souvenir shops, "both resulting from and further increasing its reputation as a traditional Canadian food."[55] Salmon built culture, but how do farmed salmon fit into this culture?

In her research with the Ahousaht and Namgis First Nations in BC, ethnohistorian Dorothee Schreiber argues that farmed salmon does not relay the same meaning as its wild prototype. Despite the ready availability of farmed fish, the Ahousaht and Namgis people continue to rely on "wild-caught, Pacific salmon," which attests to how they "both resist cultural assimilation and incorporate change."[56] Schreiber mentions one First Nation–owned salmon farm. Others, however, "feel that the growth of salmon farming represents yet another attempt to assimilate and colonize First Nations people and their lands."[57] Farmed salmon as another form of colonization.[58] Revisiting the connections between food, land, and control, farmed salmon represent how the Canadian government continues to intervene in Indigenous food systems. Lawrence Paul Yuxweluptun, a Coast Salish and Syilx artist, visualizes this in his 2014 painting *Fish Farmers They Have Sea Lice* (Figure 10.1) – "an indictment of the mismanaged fish farming industry in British Columbia."[59] Four men dressed in suits stand side by side. Their hair is neatly combed, but Coast Salish masks hide their faces. The title narrates a similar story to Monkman's *The Rise and Fall of Civilization*. And similar to the work of Sonny Assu, bright colours clash with grave concerns regarding land and the environment, Indigenous peoples and sovereignty.

Driven by voracious appetites for food and for profit, aquaculture has transformed relationships to salmon. On the Pacific coast, its commercial boom was driven "by the prospect of fortunes to be made."[60] But this sacrificed the guarantee of a safe passage for fish to return upstream. To further turn salmon into commodities, industrialists built salmon hatcheries.

"They thought they could make salmon without rivers," writes Kimmerer.[61] Is a salmon without a river still a salmon? The commercial fishing industry says yes, but in other circles this question yields contrasting answers. Hereditary Chief Stanley Larson from Hesquiaht, for instance, considers farmed salmon just another

Figure 10.1. Lawrence Paul Yuxweluptun, *Fish Farmers They Have Sea Lice*, 2014, acrylic on canvas, 162.6 x 244 cm, photo by Ken Mayer, courtesy of UBC Museum of Anthropology.

highly processed European food – like sugar, baloney, or bannock – that has damaged Indigenous health.[62] Farmed salmon has become another commodity food, and so to resist it, to insist on eating wild salmon instead, exercises Indigenous sovereignty.

This circles back to reconciliation. Although Todd problematizes its shortcomings, she returns to it in her writing about fish. "Ultimately, it is imperative to expand political notions ... such as reconciliation, beyond concepts of *human* redress," she insists. "Instead, we must acknowledge that people and fish, together, are important agents in both a) experiencing colonialism and b) dismantling colonialism."[63] Reconciliation, in other words, must be a multispecies project. Indigenous involvement in the salmon harvest differs in Atlantic and Pacific Canada, yet fishing regulations went hand in hand with Canadian assimilation policies. The government discouraged Indigenous peoples from participating in salmon fishing for both subsistence and commercial purposes, rather ironically, as part of a policy "forcing Native people to become more self-sufficient and individualistic."[64] Salmon long sustained Indigenous cultures, but the development of commercial salmon farming has changed what salmon mean, where they swim, and what this fish has become and is becoming.

## Salmon with Four Medicines

"Top Chef Canada" contestants dress in classic chef whites. Embroidery contributes splashes of colour. The show's name stretches across the uniform in yellow and grey, and a patch of dark red peeks out from the sleeve: the Canadian flag's maple leaf. In season 4, Rich Francis stitched the Haudenosaunee flag onto his uniform. Blue and white, it represents the Hiawatha wampum belt. A tree symbolizing peace stands in its centre and is flanked by two squares. On Francis's uniform, the Haudenosaunee flag hovers above the Canadian one. The eye goes to it first. Francis was the show's first Indigenous contestant, which he considers his only disappointment. "How could a Canadian show have zero representation of Indigenous foods or chefs?" he asked, only to answer himself: "But then again, why would it be different? Our food is relatively unknown."[65] Francis took advantage of this exposure to promote Indigenous cuisines, an example of gastrodiplomacy. Although he was a "Top Chef Canada" contestant, and even placed third, Francis made it clear that he was not representing Canada.

Francis is the owner of the Seventh Fire Hospitality Group, a catering company. He cooks "Braised shredded moose leg, wild rice, mushroom 'ragout,'" "Fire roasted deer ribs finished with a low bush cranberry muskeg 'bbq' sauce," and "Buffalo prime rib cooked and covered with buffalo sage and cinnamon bark." "There's nothing wrong with bannock," he declares, but he has a bone to pick with it – one about representation.[66] Or as he says:

"this kind of preconceived notion that it is Aboriginal cuisine."[67] Similar to Adler of the Pow Wow Cafe, Francis sees bannock as a symbol of survival. He states: "Our food is rooted in trauma. Bannock is a result of that." Although he recognizes that "Bannock still has that reputation of comfort," Francis wants to move on. He doesn't reject bannock completely. Francis grants bannock a supporting role, but it is never the star. Instead, he prioritizes pre-contact ingredients, reclaiming them as Indigenous.

From Fort McPherson in the Northwest Territories, Francis's mother is Haudenosaunee of the Tuscarora Nation and his father Gwich'in. He is based on the Six Nations of the Grand River, Ontario, but is often on the road. After having graduated from the Stratford Chef School, where Adler and Myers also trained, he worked in fine dining, only to switch to studying pre-contact ingredients. Since "Top Chef," Francis has been travelling across Canada, hosting dinners, participating in events, and teaching workshops.[68] In 2019 he co-starred in "Red Chef Revival: A Travel Series about Food & Reconciliation."[69]

Francis describes his cooking as "a candid journey toward Truth and Reconciliation using Indigenous foods to create a better understanding of pre-colonial Indigenous culture and the impact of colonization."[70] Although reconciliation is not his responsibility, he wishes to participate. "It is my contribution to the process of reconciliation within Canada. But how it started was for myself," he tells me. "I reconnected with who I was. Identifying again with where I come from ... that is where it has to start – within one's self before you can make it whole. And if you look at the word reconciliation it is essentially to make whole again. What exactly are we making whole? I think that is our mind, body, and spirit. Generational trauma. But it is a process. I don't think there is a finish line. It is a process. It is ongoing. I chose to make a contribution and I do it through food." For Francis, it is not possible to separate food from medicine and healing, from reclaiming who he is and his history. Cooking reconnected him to traditional foods and knowledge, which then realigned what he was cooking, how, for whom, and with what intention.

You can also call Francis's cooking "New Indigenous cuisine." Tradition informs his palette but does not dictate it. Instead, he reinvents what he cooks. "Our ancestral diets are boring," he laughs. But he recognizes that traditional foods served a purpose. For example, "diabetes did not exist then." Nonetheless, it is only now, Francis believes, that "We are now finding our culinary identity," one beyond bannock. No cuisine is static. Even ones anchored in tradition change, and this is what Francis celebrates. He considers existing definitions of Indigenous cuisines too parochial. Many overlook regionality. "It is not that it is unexplored. It is that people haven't noticed it and are only starting to notice it now," Francis elaborates. "But I think that our role as Indigenous chefs is that we are really bringing that to the forefront." He sees himself as a culinary ambassador.

To cook traditional ingredients requires relearning. Francis leads workshops with urban Indigenous students, many of whom have never tried such foods. "I cook a lot with medicines as flavour carriers. They identify with something, but they don't know what it is. I see it and I think that is our food DNA. That's the power food has," he tells me. The idea of food DNA relates to different genres of remembering, from body memory to inherited memory. Francis has cooked for Elders "who have literally broken down into tears … Because it really does bring them back to maybe the time before they were taken away to residential school."[71] Memory, according to environmental humanities scholar Katherine Wright, "is at the heart of decolonisation because the perceived legitimacy of settler colonial occupation of land and the denial of Aboriginal sovereignty depends on silence and amnesia."[72] To reclaim requires remembering. Because of this, as Jeff Corntassel sums up, "Within a colonial context, acts of remembrance are resurgence."[73] Food DNA draws a line between the mouth and the mind, between taste and memory.

Francis is adamant that what he is doing is not a trend. The 2017 CBC map of Indigenous restaurants flashed this word: "A new surge of Indigenous restaurants opening across the country has chefs finding innovative ways to serve up First Nations inspired selections. It's a trend that many note is long overdue."[74] The next year, CBC published a summary of "four emerging trends," with "First Nations food" ranked number three.[75] The article admits that Francis disagrees with the term trend and then quotes him: "It's not something you can all of a sudden latch onto. It has to be a way of life."[76] A trend, by definition, is short-lived, a fashion that is here today, gone tomorrow. For Francis, reclaiming traditional foodways and promoting Indigenous cuisine is a lifelong project. It is about continuity rather than temporality.

Similar to how his "Top Chef Canada" uniform waved the Haudenosaunee flag, Francis's cooking is not Canadian. "I think one of the biggest – or most annoying – questions I get is what is Canadian food," he confesses, "because I am still trying to define what Indigenous cuisine is." "There are so many different levels of Indigenous cuisine. We have to look at pre-contact, post-contact, pre-colonial, post-colonial, pre-residential school, post-residential … and people have this preconceived notion that we are a big melting pot of powwow food, which is bullshit. I think Canadian food is bastardized Indigenous food basically." This suggests that the national cuisine continues to mine and market Indigenous ingredients. Francis's cooking does not reject per se the idea of a Canadian creole, a diverse culinary pantry informed by immigrants the world over. After all, his cooking, like Wolfman's, is based on pre-contact ingredients but not monogamous to them. Chapter 3 considered "bastard cooking" as an alternative to fusion food, the cultural assumptions behind both regarding power structures, and who can borrow from whom, but here, Francis uses "bastardized" in a different sense. His definition of Canadian cuisine is a set of culinary practices that steals Indigenous ingredients without giving them credit, an example of cultural appropriation.

Francis's signature dish is "Salmon with the four flavours of the medicine wheel" (or "Medicine wheel salmon"). The name changes here and there, but as he puts it, "Salmon cured with sage, tobacco, sweetgrass, and cedar" is his "one go-to advertiser," his culinary calling card. He has served it again and again. What makes it his signature? The salmon? Food as medicine? The story? All three? "People don't have a reference for medicine, let alone for tasting medicines," Francis admits. "They don't have a flavour profile for it. So that is what makes it not only intriguing, but really impactful as well. There is that connection. I just can't throw a piece of salmon on a plate with a bunch of other shit and call it Indigenous food. There is no significance there. It doesn't tell a story." This is what, in many ways, Expo 67's La Toundra did. But names matter. They invoke relationships and responsibilities. Without referencing the medicine wheel, sage, tobacco, sweetgrass, and sage are simply flavours, a clutch of seasonings perking up a fillet of fish. The name of Francis's cured salmon is a reminder of food's potential to heal. This recalls what Kimmerer has learned from plants. They teach in the universal language of food, she writes, adding that "Plants know how to make food and medicine from light and water, and then they give it away."[77] "Medicine wheel salmon" follows this teaching, where food is remedy, where food is care.

Kimmerer's magnum opus is titled *Braiding Sweetgrass: Indigenous Wisdom, Scientific Knowledge, and the Teaching of Plants*, and although she writes about many plants, her words about sweetgrass connect closest to Francis's "Cooking for Reconciliation." Sweetgrass reminded Kimmerer "that it is not the land that has been broken, but our relationship to it."[78] This echoes what farmer Leah Penniman writes about contemporary Black agrarianism in the United States: "While the land was the 'scene of the crime,' she was never the criminal."[79] To restore land one must first restore relationships to it.[80] One way begins with recognizing "Land as sustainer. Land as identity. Land as grocery store and pharmacy. Land as connection to our ancestors. Land as moral obligation. Land as sacred. Land as self."[81] Francis's "Medicine wheel salmon" approaches land as grocery store and pharmacy, viewing flora and fauna and the environments from which they come and in which they live through the lens of relations rather than as resources. This dish seeks not only to eat from the land but to reconnect to it by acknowledging food as its expression. Perhaps even its breath.

In 2017, *East Coast Living* published Francis's "Medicine wheel salmon recipe." It calls for Atlantic salmon ("preferably organic"), brown sugar, kosher salt, juniper berries, fresh thyme, a cinnamon stick, three inches of braided sweetgrass ("available at Indigenous

Friendship Centres and some First Nations gift shops"), pepper, red beet, and buffalo or white sage.[82] You blend the ingredients, remove the skin, press the seasoning mixture onto the fillets, and then leave them to cure in the fridge for four to twelve hours. Francis has adopted this recipe for the home cook, specifically an East Coast one. A recipe in a West Coast publication would surely not suggest Atlantic salmon. Cedar and tobacco are missing. Did Francis predict that home cooks might have trouble finding them? Or is this recipe a culinary compromise, a soft introduction for Canadians who know little about the notion of cooking with medicines or Indigenous cuisines?

Cedar and tobacco are not common ingredients, but they are legal. However, there are also foods that Francis is not allowed to serve. On 13 November 2017 he posted an image on Facebook of muktuk – whale skin with its blubber – which La Toundra featured in 1967. "I'm exhausted, angry and frustrated from being told what I can and can't serve on my menus," Francis wrote. "In 2017 nothing has changed in over 150 years of colonialism and cultural genocide … I still have to 'hide' to serve Moose meat, muktuk, sea lion among other things. I face lengthy jail sentences and huge fine ($70,000.00) if I get caught. Am I criminal for doing this? … it's infuriating that still today I have to go in isolation privately or pull back from what was original to accommodate to the rules and regulations of the Canadian government … Food as a weapon is very real, if you control the food you control the people."[83] The rules that police food, in turn, also police Indigenous people. Francis posted the same content again on 19 August 2018, a reminder that the same rules still apply.[84] He added pictures of a moose heart and ribs and alerted his followers that, despite repeatedly being booked for events, he had been told he couldn't serve traditional Indigenous food. This returns to restaurant politics – who has the power to legally define what is on the menu and, therefore, on the table.

Francis's crucial complaint connects to Michael D. Wise's argument about the Indigenous food movement south of the border, which the Conclusion considers. "By framing access to food not only as a human right but also a treaty right," argues Wise, "Indian activists over the twentieth century reshaped political conversations over the significance of food in the process of settler colonialism."[85] What may come off at first as a wee grievance – what a menu can and cannot include – pools into colossal conflicts about land, power, and control. Cooking for Francis is a method for unsettling, for decolonizing diets, and for reconnecting with Indigenous traditions, knowledge, and lands. The dead ends he hits in his efforts to do so are reminders of the legal constraints still in place.

These restrictions also influence where Francis cooks. Although he has courted the idea of opening a restaurant, first in Saskatoon and then in Hamilton, he has decided to prioritize other projects instead. If you want to try his "Medicine wheel salmon," you have to sign up for one of his private events, or track down tobacco and cedar, sweetgrass and sage and make it at home. This raises the limitations of restaurants. I spoke to Francis when he was still going ahead with his plans to open his own eatery in Hamilton: "Up until this point, we were told what we could and could not serve in our restaurant … if we are going to reconcile, let's do it properly. If my time in court comes, I hope it will be a restaurant that will lead by example. I am not looking to be on the *EnRoute* Canada Top 10 list, I want to be a First Nations dining experience you have never experienced," he tells me.

There is another layer to Francis's decision to work with game. He describes how engineered food is, from fish to "chicken that aren't really chicken," but these are the ingredients that restaurant regulations allow. He wants to challenge this. "I cannot dull down my vision to accommodate the rules and regulations," he insists. Francis demonstrates the potential of food for surfacing difficult conversations, as well as the limitations of restaurants as a means of reconciliation. He is not interested in seeking settler permission to serve what he believes has a place on his menu. This taps into "the seemingly impossible decision (common in most resistance movements) of whether to work within a system to challenge it (thus recognizing the system as legitimate) or to refuse that system outright and [seek] change from the outside."[86] Not opening a restaurant, in this instance, refuses the settler state's authority over Indigenous peoples and their foodways.

## With the Addition of Salt

Many of the Indigenous restaurants this book profiles serve or have served salmon. Is it Atlantic or Pacific? Farmed or wild? And what stories do these dishes tell? Salmon is so central to Vancouver's Indigenous bistro that it even appears in its name. Salmon n' Bannock's menu doubles as an inventory of how to prepare salmon: gravlax and mousse, wild sockeye fillets and "Indian candy," soup and their signature burger: smoked wild sockeye on bannock with lemon aioli and house-made pickles.

Salmon n' Bannock serves only wild salmon: "No 'F' word."[87] In addition to selecting which fish to serve and how to prepare it, a chef must address seasoning, and with seasoning come cultural expectations. Reflecting on Vancouver's culinary scene, Caudron explains that diners are accustomed to spices and rich flavours, but "Aboriginal food is the ingredient as is. It is maybe smoked or cured, or it has been salted. It is very much pure as is." He gives their salmon soup as an example. Its broth is clear. It has potato, carrot, celery, salmon, and seaweed, "but for some people it just doesn't cut it in terms of flavour." This echoes Coates's description: "Coastal tribes ate their salmon plain but often garnished it with ritual in gratitude."[88] But these accounts come from non-Indigenous voices. Caudron also mentioned conflicting tastes over salmon's "doneness." Just as one person's salty is another's bland, one chef's just-right is a customer's over-cooked. "Medium or rare?" restaurants ask diners how they fancy their steak, but not their salmon – a reminder of how eateries continually negotiate between what they want to cook, and how, and what customers wish to eat. The politics of the customer's taste often trumps the chef's.

Muckamuck predates farmed salmon's triumphant takeover. It offered what was known then as salmon and now as "wild." Alongside courting local Indigenous producers, Muckamuck used classified ads in its effort to track down ingredients. In 1976 the restaurant ran an ad in the *Lake District News* in Burns Lake, a village around a thousand kilometres north of Vancouver. "Muckamuck Restaurant in Vancouver is in need of Labrador tea, soapberries, and wind-dried salmon," it read.[89] The Muckamuck, and then the Quilicium, served salmon as is, seasoned by wind or fire alone. Because it sourced ingredients from Indigenous communities, a customer might encounter a delivery, expected or not, a sight that would surely further flavour the flesh. A 1974 review recounts when "an Indian woman from the Interior walked in unannounced one day with a hundred pounds of dried sockeye salmon."[90] The same review identified the Muckamuck's speciality: "the most succulent pieces of the salmon, which happen to be the tail, the belly and the entire head."[91] But the head is divisive: "Not many people can eat the eyes," it quotes co-owner Jane Erickson. "I don't think I really can yet. But the cheeks are delicious – moist and smooth-tasting."[92] Muckamuck encouraged customers to taste salmon beyond its fillets and steaks, from head to tail, but even its co-owner stayed clear of the eyes. Eating an eye exceeded her culinary comfort zone, akin to the story of oolichan grease. The eyes were "too" authentic, but the cheeks "authentic enough," tracing when the collaboration between settler curiosity and palatability runs out.[93]

Vancouver's third Indigenous restaurant, the Liliget Feast House, also specialized in salmon. Decades before Dolly Watts opened her restaurant, her first job was at a cannery when she was eleven years old. "But I was tall for eleven," she laughs. It was summer and she was returning from residential school to visit her family. "I took the ferry and met my Dad and brother in Port Rupert. I asked where my mom was. My dad said to come with them, to work." Her father dropped her off at the Carlisle Cannery on the Skeena River.[94] "His instructions were to look for someone and say I'm looking for work," she remembers. "I didn't even need to say that. They saw me and brought me upstairs, and showed me what to do, how to use the metal cans. There were other young girls learning as well." Watts canned sockeye and spring salmon. When she was fourteen, she worked at another cannery.

Around half a century later, a speciality at her Vancouver restaurant was "Ha'gul jam." In 2005 the *Vancouver Sun* shared the recipe, which her cookbook also featured.[95] "'Hagul jam' means 'slow boil' in the Gitk'san language," Watts writes. "Traditionally, as long ago as the pre-contact era, the Gitk'san would prepare this by pouring cold water into a cedar box or tightly woven basket, placing a heated rock inside and then the salmon."[96] The other ingredients are potatoes, onions, and water, similar to Salmon n' Bannock's soup. As Watts recalls, "Late Louisa Watts, my mother-in-law, taught me how to preserve salmon in jars and smoke salmon in several different ways."[97] Her cookbook *Where People Feast* also includes a "Smoked salmon mousse" recipe that "is great to serve at any event or dinner party," which flexes the range of salmon at the Liliget Feast House: from an unadorned traditional soup to a creamy seasoned mousse ready for a party.[98]

As *Culinary Claims* maintains, what is off the menu is as important as what is on it. And in Toronto Aaron Joseph Bear Robe banned Canada's most popular fish from the Keriwa Cafe. He refused to play the country's biggest hit of a fish. As one review put it, the Keriwa "serves Saskatoon berry jelly, but not salmon."[99] In another interview, Bear Robe admits, "A large misconception is that there's some sort of 'pan Aboriginal' cuisine, that because I'm Aboriginal, I'm going to cook salmon, which for me, culturally doesn't make any sense, and as a restaurant being local and seasonal doesn't make any sense either."[100] He ordered bison from Alberta because it represented his land's traditional foods. Despite salmon's importance along Canada's coasts and some rivers and lakes in between, it did not carry the same meaning for Bear Robe. He resisted a fish many expect an Indigenous, or even Canadian, restaurant to feature. Instead, he represented his interpretation of Indigenous cuisine, prioritizing his own appetite.

Like the Keriwa Cafe, David Wolfman is from Toronto, but he grew up with stories from the Fraser River, "Salmon Valley," where his mother was from: the Xaxli'p First Nation.[101] "My mother's people love salmon in many forms; they love it so much they consider it a sacred food," he writes.[102] Wolfman remembers her telling him, "When the people heard a particular type of cricket sound (around the end of May or beginning of June), they knew they had two to three days to get down to the river and cast their salmon nets."[103] He recalls Elders who claimed it was the crickets that called the salmon: "Noticing their symphony was their way of listening to the land."[104] A multisensory and multispecies calendar.

Wolfman also writes about smoked salt. He introduces his "Cold-smoked alderwood salt" recipe with "Vikings are said to have evaporated seawater over wood fires of juniper, cherry, elm, beech and oak to produce flavoured sea salt a millennium ago. That may be true, but Indigenous peoples along the Pacific coast in Canada are big on wood-smoked salt too, and they use it regularly when cooking salmon – alder is a favourite."[105] This suggests that salmon's history as a traditional food in the Pacific Northwest is more complex than the stereotype that it was only served "plain." Wolfman's cookbook is rich in salmon recipes, the likes of "Baked Xaxli'p salmon on pea purée."[106] There are recipes for "Hot smoked salmon with sour cream and onion dip" (it calls for a fresh coho salmon fillet); "Cold-smoked juniper salmon" (it also calls for coho salmon); "White salmon pizza" (it calls for "fresh salmon"); and, "Dandelion and pepper stuffed salmon with clarified butter" (it calls for "salmon fillets").[107] Like his memory of his mom listening for the crickets, stories accompany the recipes, firmly anchoring them in family, culture, and place.

## Giftwrapped

The term "Indian candy" is a souvenir from an earlier time. This smoky-sweet snack once went by a more derogatory name – "Squaw candy" – and today salmon smoked with sugar or maple syrup is called "Salmon candy" or "Candied salmon." "Smoked salmon is a mainstay in tourist gift shops," Grey and Newman point out, "typically sold in cedar boxes adorned with Salish art, though seldom purchased from Salish peoples."[108] Yet the term "Indian candy" does acknowledge Indigenous foodways. It also maps the transition from acknowledgment to adaptation and assimilation. Early Canadian cookbooks tell a similar story. They mention "Indian corn," which later became "Canadian corn" or simply "corn."[109] The history of salmon in Canada starts with this fish as a foundation for diverse cultures shoring both the Atlantic and Pacific coasts, inland as well, and then becomes a story of its transformation into a commercial commodity. Smoked salmon is much older than farmed salmon and older still than the names

"Candied salmon" or "Indian candy." Yet, there is a tension between smoking salmon to preserve it and packaging it to sell, just as there is a tension between food as numinous and food as commodity, between relation and resource. But what matters is who is selling what and with which stories. And with whose stories.

Ellen Melcosky, a member of Esk'etemc First Nation, marinates salmon with spices and white wine and then slowly cold smokes it over woodchips, a technique she learned from her mother. Since 1996 she has been selling it under her Okanagan-based label: Little Miss Chief. Outfitted in a white and red headdress and with a wide smile, she stars in her business's logo. The grey label is one part photograph and two parts illustration. Below her picture is a drawing of an eagle: wings spread out, it scoops up a salmon (Figure 10.2). In contrast to the images decorating the Canadian Pacific Railway menus, Melcosky uses salmon for self-representation. She also uses it to financially support herself. When re-entering the workforce, she had limited access to funding and solicited family, friends, and the Women's Enterprise Society for support.[110] Since then she has won numerous awards, including the 2010 National Aboriginal Achievement Award. Her company aims to sustainably balance honouring salmon as a provider of food and culture with using salmon as a source of income.

Using only wild fish, Little Miss Chief started with sockeye, but because of environmental concerns over dwindling stocks, switched to chum (keta). Melcosky offers a range of packaging, including cedar boxes adorned with formline illustrations. Each box comes with a "Traditions and Legends" description that contextualizes the cultural meaning of the Thunder Bird, the Bear, the Salmon, the Raven, or the Eagle. Yes, this is a commercial product, but one that sustains Melcosky economically as well as culturally. As the growth of salmon farming has demonstrated, salmon contribute to the economic making of place. Salmon also contribute to a place's culinary making. But salmon's unseasonal making of place is destructive. These entanglements require eaters to be aware of how their appetites are entangled in environments near and far, how certain foods give back and others are greedier in what they take. As Melcosky's decision to switch from sockeye to chum shows, adaptability is vital.

Figure 10.2. "Little Miss Chief smoked salmon label," image from LittleMissChief.com.

Salmon defines many places, but sometimes borders get in the way. Once when I was visiting Vancouver, my sister, husband, and I drove to Seattle, a popular international day trip. American passport control accepted our two Canadian passports, but not my husband's German one. We parked the car. While we were waiting for him to collect a stamp, to get the green light to cross the line between the two countries, an American border agent exited the building. Waving a sturdy Ziploc-bag in his hand, he shouted at a group of officers: "Anyone want some home-smoked salmon?" Its burnt orange skin sparkled behind the plastic. Salmon the animal can swim across the US-Canada border. Commercially canned, frozen, or smoked salmon can also cross this border, but this bag of home-smoked salmon could not, even though the border agent's enthusiastic invitation made it clear that the salmon was good to eat.

Salmon roam far and wide, disregarding borders and boundaries alike. They join rivers and oceans, merging the local and the global. They connect rivers to vacuum-sealed bags and airport gift shops, kitchen tables and restaurants. Salmon connect aquaculture farms in Chile, a larger producer than Canada, to menus across the world. Salmon is a global food and yet intimately entangled with local imaginations of place. A menu that lists "salmon" does not say much, but the global appetite for salmon does. Even farmed salmon, whose relationship to rivers and saltwater and migratory routes industrial farmers have dramatically re-engineered, are caught up in imaginations of place. Take for instance "Organic Norwegian salmon." Organic is a sexier way to say farmed. But as Francis's "Salmon with four medicines" narrates, a salmon's story, the chef's intention, and the dish's connection to a culture's past and present all inform salmon's entanglement with competing claims over land.

Like many products, smoked souvenir salmon started somewhere and then spread. On Turtle Island it used to be only Indigenous and yet had different meanings from one place to the next. Now it has acquired new ones, many of which challenge its previous ones. Salmon crossed local, tribal, and regional borders to become a pan-Canadian food. By blurring biological boundaries, farming transformed salmon into a popular, affordable, and Canadian culinary souvenir. Before Cook opened Salmon n' Bannock, her job was in the sky; she worked as a flight attendant for thirty-three years, and for twenty-five of those years she was based out of Vancouver International Airport. On 19 December 2022, her work brought her back to the airport, where she opened her restaurant's second location, Salmon n' Bannock on the Fly, in the international departures area, post-security.[111] Smoked salmon packed in a cedar box is easy to transport. It is sealed and, as Little Miss Chief boasts, her wild Pacific salmon has a minimum shelf life of five years. Because salmon has become ubiquitous within Canada and smoked salmon is packaged and ready to take on a plane, it is an easy last-minute airport gift. In turn, I have ended with souvenir salmon as I depart Canada for global culinary considerations.

# Conclusion: The North

Covered by a glass dome, "*L'eclade*" arrives in a dramatic fashion. The menu describes the dish as "Mussels smoked in pine needles, pine ash butter," which is not just smoke and mirrors. The waiter lifts the dome, clouded with steam, to reveal a deep plate of mussels in their shells. One does not see the pine needles and ash; one smells them. I began this book with mussels, and with soup. "Soup is a harmony where multiple ingredients get together supporting each other," write the self-proclaimed bastard cooks Melasniemi and Tiravanija. "They let go of their individual characters and collaborate with each other to form new entities."[1] Although "*L'eclade*" is not a soup per se, the mussels come in a generous serving of pine-spiked broth that diners are invited to sip with a spoon or soak up with bread.

To contextualize how the history of Indigenous restaurants in Canada fits within global culinary changes, *Culinary Claims* concludes by pondering pine needles and restaurant fare in an expanded geography. First, I turn to Canada's neighbour: the United States. As Chapter 3 established, culinary trends south of the border prompted a revival in local foodways to its north. Unlike the smoked salmon a US customs agent confiscated, this conclusion crosses the border to look at other examples of Indigenous restaurants. It then returns to pine needles and "*L'eclade*" to consider how much of this history is specific to Canada and how much tells a global story. It ends by considering how an Indigenous restaurant is different from one peddling farm-to-table local, Canadian fare.

## South of the Border

A California "American Native food" eatery also offers a pine-based dish. Filmmaker Francis Ford Coppola opened Werowocomoco in November 2016 at his Virginia Dare Winery in Geyserville.[2] Named after a seventeenth-century Algonquin town, the vineyard's mother vine connects Sonoma to an early English settlement in North Carolina.[3] In the restaurant's words, its "heritage is steeped in American native myth and early American winemaking."[4] And its name is loaded with colonial history.[5] The menu, which Coppola developed, presents "Fry bread tacos," "Venison chilli," and "Pine ice cream made with lemon zest and estate-foraged pine needles." Its opening provoked discussions about culinary appropriation, raising questions about how to define Native American cuisines and the ingredients they share with what has become Californian and new American fare. Werowocomoco closed only one year after opening. Then, in April 2018, with much less press coverage, it reopened with a similar menu and shorter name: Wero.

This casual eatery, where you order at a counter, is tucked behind the winery. A deer stencilled on the sidewalk leads to the entrance. Prints of chiefs decorate one wall and a buckskin painting of a hunter on horseback another. The tasting room is one part wine bar, one part museum-style gift shop. Handmade baskets and Native American art catalogues are for sale. Neither the staff nor the menu mediates the food. The menu casually lists what's available, as if "Indian tacos" are common in California wine country. Wero is not about representation or negotiation or Indigenous food cultures. It reduces Indigenous culture to décor. Wero, instead, is a contemporary example of the Canadian Pacific Railway menus and La Toundra. As I ordered an "Indian taco," Bob Dylan's 1964 *Positively 4th Street* played in the background. "You've got a lotta nerve to say you are my friend / When I was down you just stood there grinnin' / You've got a lotta nerve to say you got a helping hand to lend / You just want to be on the side that's winnin'."

One wall in the gift shop, however, is food for thought. Bright blue waterways run across a brown landmass, composing a buckskin map of the United States. The land north of its border is off-white. Polar bears and bushy green trees roam its otherwise empty terrain. The map's focus is clearly the country to Canada's south. Pinned across its expanse are labels mapping Indigenous tribes, including the Pomo, Miwok, and Ohlone along what has become California's northern coast. The map, in other words, erases state lines and reimagines the United States as Indigenous.

California changed the way America eats. Bay area chefs, like Alice Waters, championed local ingredients. But local for whom? In 2018, Vincent Medina (Chochenyo Ohlone) and Louis Trevino (Rumsen Ohlone) opened Cafe Ohlone in Berkeley in response to this question. They cook dishes that carry on their ancestors' culinary traditions and that share stories not only about the Bay's Indigenous past but, most importantly, its present. Hidden behind a bookstore across from the University of California Berkeley campus, Cafe Ohlone began by serving tea on Tuesday, lunch on Thursday, weekend brunch, and Saturday night dinners.[6] The set menu shadows the seasons to feature the likes of acorn flour, foraged berries and greens, San Francisco Bay sea salt, and game meats.[7] The menu stretches from "Hazelnut milk chia porridge with blackberry and bay laurel sauce" to "Roasted salmon with duck fat heirloom potatoes and fiddleheads." Located on a leafy northern California terrace, the words "Ohlone Land" sprawl across the back fence.

Through language, Medina and Trevino became interested in food. Medina tells me that they use traditional culinary knowledge to "rebuild what we lost." He pauses. "Actually lost is not the right word," he corrects himself. "What was dormant and with the right effort ... those things that were dormant can reawaken."[8] Medina's great-grandmother was the last in his family to speak Chochenyo. Elders could recite lone words, but not enough to string together a sentence. Medina started studying linguist's John Peabody Harrington's collection of notes and realized there was enough documentation to revive the language. "Not just for formal speeches to have it a tokenism way, but to have it," which is to say to move it from short announcements and acknowledgments and back to conversations, to the everyday. The ideal would be, once again, to communicate in Chochenyo. He also realized "how much was there beyond the language." One page covers tenses, then the next recounts a joke or a story about food. Again and again he noticed references to food. Medina listened to 1920s recordings of Angela de los Colos, and one word stuck with him: mak-'amham, the Chochenyo word for our food. This word serves as the name of the umbrella project of which Cafe Ohlone is a part. "These food references are always connected to language," Medina makes clear.

Besides language revival, mak-'amham prioritizes representation. "There is a lot at stake in representation," Medina observes. He recounts growing up and not seeing "things that reflected my presence anywhere outside of my home. And that can be really harmful … it is damaging when you don't have things reinforcing that you exist, that your culture is valuable." Similarly, Oakland-based chef Crystal Wahpepah, a member of the Kickapoo tribe, realized at a young age that "We didn't have our food in restaurants."[9] Then when she was a teenager she ate at Loretta Barret Oden's restaurant in Santa Fe: "An elegant restaurant with pre-colonial foods. I had never seen this food in a nice restaurant." In 1993 Oden, a citizen of the Potawatomi Nation, opened the Corn Dance Café, similar to Kūkŭm Kitchen, offering polished plates of Indigenous ingredients.[10] Encountering Indigenous food in a fine-dining setting was a moment of pride that Wahpepah remembers. This is why urban Indigenous restaurants, including fine-dining ones, matter. They inspire younger generations to represent their personal culinary points of view and to claim a contemporary, cultural presence.[11] Indigenous restaurants counter, as Medina describes, the violence of erasure. They claim a seat at the table, which is to say they purposely take up space in urban foodscapes. They also demonstrate Leanne Betasamosake Simpson's assertion: "presence is our weapon."[12]

Years after dining at Santa Fe's Corn Dance Café, in 2012, Wahpepah set up a catering company, Wahpepah's Kitchen, and in November 2021 a restaurant with the same name. Similar to eateries across Canada, Cafe Ohlone and Wahpepah's Kitchen leverage food to reclaim an Indigenous presence in San Francisco's East Bay. The number of Indigenous food initiatives in the United States, as in Canada, continues to grow. In 1989 Winona LaDuke founded the White Earth Land Recovery Project, and in 2000, White Mountain Apache and Diné chef Nephi Craig established the Native American Culinary Association.[13] In 2016 Craig then opened Café Gozhóó in Whiteriver on the Fort Apache Indian Reservation in Arizona. Urban restaurants include Pueblo Harvest, opened in Albuquerque in 1976 by the nineteen tribes in New Mexico, and the Tiwa Kitchen in Taos, which opened in 1993 – both still operating today.[14] Lois Ellen Frank from the Kiowa Nation, whose four periods of Indigenous cuisine appeared in the Introduction, is the founder of Red Mesa Cuisine. She is also the author of the first Native American cookbook to have won a James Beard Award: *Foods of the Southwest Indian Nations*.[15] Her second cookbook, *Seed to Plate, Soil to Sky: Modern Plant-Based Recipes Using Native American Ingredients*, promotes what she calls a "Nativevore Diet."[16] When the National Museum of the American Indian opened on the National Mall in Washington, DC, in 2004, it premiered the Mitsitam Cafe, which means "let's eat" in the Picataway language.[17] Matt Chandra and Ben Jacobs of Osage Nation started Tocabe in Denver in 2008.[18] In 2016 the Slow Food Turtle Island Association was established.[19] Also in 2016, Conflict Kitchen – a public-art project initiated in Pittsburgh by two settler artists that serves the cuisines of countries the United States is in conflict with – presented the Haudenosaunee Confederacy edition. After having offered North Korean, Venezuelan, and Palestinian menus, Conflict Kitchen raised awareness of Indigenous sovereignty with dishes like "Wadesai'dö:ndak" ("Sweet maple baked beans with salt pork") and "Oshöwe" ("Crispy Iroquois white corn mush topped with root vegetable hash").[20] There is a podcast devoted to Indigenous foods – "Toasted Sister" – which Andi Murphy, a Diné journalist, launched in 2017. And in 2020, director Sanja Rawal released the documentary *Gather* – a portrait of the Native American food sovereignty movement that co-stars Craig.

In addition to publishing *The Sioux Chef's Indigenous Cookbook* in 2017, Oglala Lakota chef Sean Sherman established the North American Traditional Indigenous Food Systems and the Indigenous Food Lab in Minneapolis and opened a restaurant of his own in 2021: Owamni.[21] Sherman stars in American press coverage of the Indigenous food movement. But it was time in Mexico that sparked his interest in Indigenous foods. Burned out from long restaurant hours, he moved from the Midwest to the beach town of San Francisco in Nayarit. Witnessing the local Huichol people's culture, he realized, "I have been spending all of this time thinking about other cuisines all around the world without knowing much about my own Lakota ancestry."[22] A reminder of North America's history of "erase and replace" and its influence on culinary knowledge. Sherman recognizes the importance of supporting other Indigenous chefs across borders, and his cookbook has a chapter that features their recipes, including one from Rich Francis.

However, borders do not only exist in imaginations. There are laws about who or what may cross them. In the 1990s the Native American Student Association at the University of Iowa invited David Wolfman to perform a cooking demo. His menu sported pickled milkweed pods he had received from a friend, but on his way to Iowa he was questioned at the border. Wolfman had declared twelve jars of pickled milkweed pods on his customs form. "The agent looks at me: 'you're bringing pickled milkweed pods … those things that grow on the side of the highway?' I said 'Yes – it is a First Nation food' … 'When do you eat it?' 'With grilled cheese.' I am making this up, just trying to get through customs … He calls this guy … the darkest, Native looking guy I have ever seen … He said 'do you guys eat pickled milkweed pods with your grilled cheese?' … this guy with a Spanish accent says, 'I am not Indigenous. I am Mexican. We eat anything with anything.' The customs officer says, 'well, have a good trip' and stamps me to go. My heart is racing."[23] When Wolfman arrived at the event, an organizer introduced him as a "Native American chef." In response, he grabbed the microphone and said something he had not planned: "We didn't cross the border. The border crossed us." Wolfman was lucky to coax pickled milkweed pods across, but the moral of his story is that borders police bodies, plants, and animals. Because of regulations, changing a food culture also means breaking the law, as Francis makes clear. Indigenous chefs north and south of the border are proposing new ways to imagine places through food – to reclaim culture and land – but they are doing so within distinct national conversations.

By studying Canada, *Culinary Claims* has done the same. One could, therefore, accuse it of "methodological nationalism."[24] But by acknowledging the international influences and the multi-layered identities of Indigenous chefs across Turtle Island, I wish to highlight the constructed nature of national frameworks. I aspire to think about foodways above and below the nation state.[25] History, as Mary Jane McCallum points out, is "an exercise in nation building." I have been mindful of how using "the nation-state as an organizing principle subtly and unsubtly presents history and more particularly Canadian history as not the project of Aboriginal people and nonwhite people more generally."[26] At the same time, the border between Canada and the United States influences Indigenous cuisines and their narratives. After seeing Sherman speak in Los Angeles in 2017, I asked Claudia Serrato, who moderated the Q&A, about the conversation with which Indigenous cooking in the United States is in tune. Francis, for example, aligns himself with reconciliation, but this is specific to Canada. Serrato, an Xicana Indígena of Purépecha origin, is an anthropologist, chef, and co-founder of the Los Angeles Indigenous catering company Cocina Manakurhini. Her answer was "revitalization."[27] Why is this distinction relevant? Despite their similarities, conversations around the resurgence of Indigenous foodways differ in Canada and the United States.

The influence of international culinary shifts, exemplified by California's Chez Panisse and Copenhagen's Noma, demonstrates that the development of cuisines is not limited to an independent, national discourse. Although borders define cuisines, culinary history dissolves them. However, as the discussion in *Culinary Claims* of national regulations concerning game and other ingredients and its focus on chefs and restaurants that promote reconciliation have shown, national institutions yield great power. They have a decisive influence and create a regulatory framework and a spatial reference for the distinction of, to quote the *Globe and Mail*, "our Indigenous cuisine." Both global deterritorialization practices and efforts to cross and challenge Turtle Island's contemporary political borders add layers to the history of Indigenous restaurants, but they do not negate the national story.

To paraphrase Francis, reconciliation is to make something whole again. In Canada it means to restore the relationship of the Canadian government and settler society with Indigenous peoples. Reconcile is to fix, to put something back together. It begins with "conciliation" – the act of mediating between disputing groups. Revitalization is to give new life. The "re" marks a return, that something comes back and lives again. Revitalization is a part of reconciliation, and in Canada they go hand in hand. Reconciliation acknowledges and responds to the history of erasure, to the gap. Revitalization helps to remember, to fill it. Even though similar revitalization processes are playing out in the United States, because of the 2015 Commission and the country's distinct national conversation, in Canada they contribute to the work toward reconciliation.

Fittingly, a personal act of reconciliation takes place around a dining room table. For the 2019 inaugural Toronto Biennale, artists Adrian Stimson and AA Bronson collaborated on a performative installation. Stimson, a member of the Siksika Nation, is the great-grandson of Chief Old Sun. (Chef Bear Robe of the Keriwa Cafe is also Siksika.) Bronson is the great-grandson of Reverend John Williams Tims, Anglican missionary and founder of the Old Sun residential school on Siksika Nation, Alberta. Stimson's and Bronson's great-grandfathers were on opposing sides in the 1895 Siksika rebellion, a conflict sparked by food allowance cuts, among other tensions. Bronson's great-grandfather fled, but his son, Bronson's grandfather, later ran a residential school on another reserve. For the Toronto Biennale, Bronson revisited and reflected on his

Figure 11.1. AA Bronson, *A Public Apology to Siksika Nation*, and Adrian Stimson, *Iini Sookumapii: Guess Who's Coming to Dinner?*, 2019. Commissioned by the Toronto Biennial of Art, photo by Toni Hafkenscheid, courtesy of the Toronto Biennial of Art.

family history to craft *A Public Apology to Siksika Nation*: a book – which he calls a "public rehearsal" – and performance.[28]

In the exhibition space, Bronson presented research material that reconstructs the first years of the Siksika Reserve – 1883 to 1895 – alongside boxes of his apology (Figure 11.1). The collaboration's centrepiece is Stimson's *Iini Sookumapii: Guess Who's Coming to Dinner?*, an artwork that memorializes the experiences of residential school survivors (Figure 11.2).[29] A black and white painting hangs on the wall. Young students sit at neat rows of tables. You can see hunger in their eyes. The painting mirrors what Bronson writes in his apology about his great-grandfather: "Tims forbade [them] to speak their own language; to those children then, separated from their parents, partitioned from their own culture, forbidden to perform their own rituals or eat their own foods."[30] Crimes for which Bronson apologizes.

Figure 11.2. Adrian Stimson, *Iini Sookumapii: Guess Who's Coming to Dinner?*, 2019, mixed-media installation, dimensions variable, commissioned by the Toronto Biennial of Art, photo by Toni Hafkenscheid, courtesy of the Toronto Biennial of Art.

Stimpson matches the painting with a table dressed in white cloth and gold-rimmed plates. A bronze bison sculpture perches on each plate, a reminder of how the decimation of the bison forced the Siksika onto reserves (Figure 11.3). The table is set for a conversation between Bronson and the Siksika, a stage for Bronson's apology. Although Bronson concludes, "I have no excuse for the slaughter of the buffalo, nor the genocide of First Nations,"[31] the installation advocates for the need for intimate conversations, ones that tables host. Ben Miller, a writer and Bronson's research assistant for the project, describes *A Public Apology to Siksika Nation* as an act of "conciliation."[32] It is also an act of reconciliation. Conciliation builds harmony and peace. Reconciliation re-establishes relations.

The table is a place to reconcile. Restaurants are too. As contact zones, restaurants host both reconciliation and revitalization efforts. To reconcile and revitalize, one has to look back. But

Figure 11.3. Adrian Stimson, *Iini Sookumapii: Guess Who's Coming to Dinner?* (detail), 2019, mixed-media installation, dimensions variable, commissioned by the Toronto Biennial of Art, photo by Triple Threat, courtesy of the Toronto Biennial of Art.

looking back is equally about the present. "Most of us think that history is in the past," writes Thomas King. "It's not. History is the stories we tell about the past."[33] This point holds hands with Black studies scholar Christina Sharpe's conviction that "In the wake, the past that is not past reappears, always, to rupture the present."[34] Like a sink tasked to swallow more than it can hold, the past leaks and spills, pooling into the colonial present.

Just as the name "Salmon with the four flavours of the medicine wheel" lends the dish a restorative meaning, the name of Francis's culinary company does too: Seventh Fire Hospitality. Taking its name from the Anishinaabe Seven Fires prophecy, Francis aligns his cooking with its final phase: renewal. "The people of the Seventh Fire do not yet walk forward; rather," Kimmerer describes, "they are told to turn around and retrace the steps of the ones who brought us here. Their sacred purpose is to walk back along the red road of our ancestors' path and to gather up all the fragments that lay scattered."[35] The seventh phase looks back to move forward. As Francis makes clear, he does not cook traditional food; instead, he draws from tradition to craft contemporary dishes. What is the difference? Continuity is not about repetition alone. In step with Medina, Francis says, "Revitalization is huge. But nothing was ever lost. It was just forgotten."[36] Renewal is a means to remember.

## Eating Evergreens

The interest in revisiting traditional foods crosses the world. The internationally influential organization Slow Food – founded by Carlo Petrini in Italy in 1986 – runs a program titled Ark of Taste dedicated to rediscovering "forgotten foods."[37] Everywhere I travel, from Panama to Canada, this is evident. It is this same idea that guides Redzepi at Noma. The day before Christmas, in 2010, the *New York Times* published an online op-ed by Redzepi: "Evergreen, Ever Delicious." Accompanying it is the video "Asparagus and Spruce," shot between the field and the kitchen. Redzepi narrates: "The dish more or less consists of pine and asparagus. They live five meters apart and that is what we have on the plate" – grilled white asparagus, a sauce of green asparagus, a dollop of whipped cream, spruce shoots, and pine branches.[38] The video was filmed in a month other than December. The seasons for asparagus and Christmas trees do not overlap. In Europe asparagus is so much associated with spring that Redzepi calls it the season's king.[39] Green asparagus from Peru is available year-round, but because of its detachment from a particular season and the distance it travels, it clashes with Noma's philosophy: local foods in season or preserved – pickled, fermented, or rendered into powder, oil, or vinegar. You can, of course, pick pine tree needles outside of December, but then you are foraging as opposed to giving a Christmas tree a culinary afterlife. Redzepi's article does not bother with these details. It doesn't even mention asparagus, nor is it about Christmas trees. Instead, it is a think piece aimed at raising awareness that "Food is everywhere."[40]

Cooking with pine needles signifies distinction. "Foraging also enables chefs to differentiate themselves from their rivals and gain cachet," explains Goldstein.[41] The dish of mussels in a glass dome is not from Noma. It was served at Boralia, a Toronto restaurant. Wayne Morris, a chef with Métis heritage from Nova Scotia, and Evelyn Wu, who previously worked at the Fat Duck in Bray, England, with Heston Blumenthal, a British chef whose culinary calling card is digging deep into the gastronomic past to revisit historic recipes, opened Boralia on Ossington Avenue in 2014. Beyond the ingredients, the menu provides another detail about the dish: a date, "c. 1605." Following Blumenthal's interest in historic recipes, this too is Boralia's concept. "Boralia celebrates the historic origins of Canadian cuisine," its website states. "Our menu draws inspiration from traditional Aboriginal dishes, as well as the recipes of early settlers and immigrants of the 18th and 19th centuries."[42] Dishes with dates cite specific histories. Tea eggs tell the story of Chinese migration, pierogies – as at Bear Robe's Keriwa Cafe – Polish and Ukrainian immigrants. Dishes without dates – "'Pemmican' salad" and the "Venison liver & foie gras parfait" – Morris and Wu explain, are influenced by Canada's Indigenous heritage.[43]

A 2015 *Globe and Mail* review reveals the history of "*L'eclade*," explaining that it has the same origins as Samuel de Champlain: Charente on France's southwest coast. "With the traditional recipe, you arrange the mussels with their openings facing down and then smother them with flaming pine needles, which cooks and smokes them at once," it instructs.[44] Known as "the Father of New France," Champlain cooked the dish at Port Royal, a settlement established in 1605. More than four centuries separate when Champlain ate "*L'eclade*" on both sides of the Atlantic and when Boralia opened with its history-lesson menu. Boralia contributes to reimagining Canada and the stories the country tells about itself through food. The restaurant acknowledges Indigenous influences. However, Boralia parts ways from predecessors – such as the Tomahawk and La Toundra – to use food to narrate Canadian history in a way that recognizes Indigenous influence beyond décor and novelty. It presents Indigenous ingredients and history as a central part of

Canadian culture and cuisine. But it is not an Indigenous restaurant. It represents without appropriating.

My main course at Boralia was mussels with pine and, one year later, I ended my meal across town at Kūkŭm Kitchen with "Pine needle and citrus sorbet." Since then both restaurants have closed, but their aftertaste, like pine itself, lingers.[45] Unlike the mint colour of Wero's ice cream, Kūkŭm's sorbet was not green. It was the glossy, soft texture of ice slivered by hockey skates. Although pine and spruce are different evergreens, Redzepi used the terms interchangeably. Differences aside, ethnobotanist Mary Siisip Geniusz, of Cree and Métis descent, emphasizes pine's medicinal virtues and praises spruce for its vitamin C, with which its foliage is packed. Like all conifers – and green plants – spruce has vitamin C, but spruce releases the vitamin faster.[46] This makes spruce "the vehicle of choice" should one fall ill from a vitamin C deficiency. In Canada spruce is a local source, unlike the citrus, guava, and kiwi the national food guide recommends.[47]

Geniusz tells a story of another Frenchman: Jacques Cartier (1491–1557). Cartier lived before Champlain and claimed lands for the French crown. Both are protagonists in Canada's colonial history and both ate or drank conifers. When the St. Lawrence River held Cartier's ship hostage in its ice in 1535, supplies were limited. Cartier's crew depended on its onboard staples and the game they could barter from the local Iroquois. But by midwinter the men grew sick, a weakness Cartier did not want the Iroquois to know. One day Cartier spotted a man he had traded with, Dom Agaya, who had just been ill. As Geniusz details, "Cartier asked Dom Agaya how he had been cured, and the Iroquois obligingly sent two women off into the bush to bring Cartier the boughs of a tree ... As directed, Cartier cooked up a decoction of the foliage and bark of the tree and gave it to his sick sailors as a tea, while poulticing their wounds with the same plant material."[48] Despite the effectiveness of Dom Agaya's cure for scurvy, Geniusz writes that the tree has remained a mystery because no one recorded an accurate description of it.[49] She and other scholars believe it was spruce.

As I write this on Little Beausoleil Island in Ontario, I have to peek through a cluster of trees to see Georgian Bay's "Big" Beausoleil Island, which is now a national park. To the right, a spruce tree stands tall, and between it and the rocky shoreline are white pine, cedar, and maple. A postcard-perfect image of the Canadian Shield. It is early September and the maple leaves have started to blush as red as the country's flag, brightening my view of the island, which has a history so much older than Canada's. Ojibwa have called these lands and waters home for centuries. With the exception of the Christian Islands, the home of Beausoleil First Nation, of which Lisa Meyers is a member, in 1856 the rest of Georgian Bay's islands were surrendered or sold to the British Crown.[50] This included Little Beausoleil Island, where my family has a cottage.[51] It is here I conclude my research about the relationship between food, place, and stories in the lands now called Canada.

The liaison between food and land brings up the French notion of *terroir* – the idea that wine and food possess tastes unique to place. That a grape growing on one hill doesn't taste the same as one ripening on another. Anthropologist Amy Trubek unpacks the two terms that frame what she calls a "foodview," both of which have agrarian origins. "*Terroir* and *goût du terroir* are categories for framing and explaining people's relationships to the land," she writes, "be it sensual, practical, or habitual. This connection is considered essential, as timeless as the earth itself."[52] As categories, these concepts have been naturalized as ways of classifying a food's connection to place. However, *terroir* and *goût du terroir* do not describe the relationship between food and land; they describe how people perceive this relationship. Noma's focus on locality also relates to sociologists David Inglis and Debra Gimlin's point: "Far from destroying more local and specific senses of belonging, identity and affiliation, globalization processes may actually help reinvigorate, if not in fact *create*, these."[53] The global demand for regional identity succours in crafting it.

Food historian Ken Albala writes about the shift that happened in Europe between the late Middle Ages and the eighteenth century. Wild foods went from having an esteemed position on banquet tables to being replaced by cultivated plants and domesticated animals, a shift he attributes to changes in population and geography but also culture.[54] He extrapolates that changing views of wild foods were rooted in changing views of nature. Being dependent on wild foods means being at nature's mercy. Relying instead on domesticated animals and plants granted humans a stronger sense of mastery. Today the situation has once again changed. As Noma exemplifies, contemporary fine dining celebrates local foods. But, more importantly, home cooks embrace local foods as a reaction to globalized food systems, defining a revitalized interest in eating wildly.[55] Around the world there is an ever-increasing interest in Indigenous foods. From Māori chef Monique Fiso in Aotearoa New Zealand and Bundjalung chef Mark Olive in Australia to Sean Sherman and Crystal Wahpepah in the United States, chefs across the world are cooking to tell stories that reimagine and reclaim Indigenous heritage.[56] This is also happening outside of Indigenous communities, as Copenhagen's Noma exemplifies. But in a settler colonial context it takes on a specific texture. For Indigenous chefs, this shift – or let's call it a return – means something else.

## The Stories Are the Spice

Restaurants represent culturally specific eating practices that taxonomize plants and animals. They are venues for storytelling. "For me food is a totally painless way of awakening people," writes Alice Waters, "and sharpening their senses."[57] Pain in Canada's colonial history has been acute, and the move towards reconciliation acknowledges this. Wolfman and the Mississaugas of the Credit took a similar approach with the You Are Welcome Food Truck. With food they endeavoured to awaken Torontonians to the city's Indigenous history and present. They also realize Brittany Luby's point that "If we accept that boundaries are performed, that to occupy space is to claim space, then the performance of daily life, at root, is an act of sovereignty."[58] Cooking Indigenous foods is an act of sovereignty, as is serving these foods in restaurants.

Conclusion: The North 301

What does the You Are Welcome Food Truck tell about Canada and changing imaginations of it? What stories do restaurants tell? Indigenous chefs demonstrate how ingredients – from ones that have been appropriated as Canadian to ones that are controversial for settlers, like seal, and for Indigenous chefs, like bannock – narrate stories about Turtle Island's history, its present, and its future. Some stories, like foods, are easier to swallow than others, but all are important. Taken together, the fifty years of restaurant history this book spotlights have traced the emergence of Indigenous cuisines as a distinct style of dining and the negotiations chefs and restaurateurs have made with pre-existing imaginations – settler storying and colonial traps – while resisting these outsider imaginations.

Indigenous restaurants cannot be reduced to a specific set of characteristics, but there are certain themes that run through the examples I have gathered. These histories, however, defy a neat distillation, as Indigenous restaurants do not come in one form. From ingredients to décor, there are sometimes commonalities, but they are also diverse and distinct. Some serve bannock, while others reject it. Some focus on comfort food, while others reclaim local ingredients. Some, like NishDish, represent Anishinaabe foodways, while others, like Winnipeg's Cookem Daisy's, celebrate pow wow food's greatest hits. Indigenous restaurants do not have the same significations for customers as for owners. Many attract diverse clientele, Indigenous peoples and settlers alike. Thus, I demur at the idea that Indigenous restaurants intend to symbolize a particular ethnicity to non-Indigenous groups and that they are mainly for Indigenous consumption. The diversity of Indigenous restaurants, their growing numbers across the country, and Canadians' openness to them represent a shift away from the Imaginary "Indians" on the Canadian Pacific Railway menus and a step towards re-learning, re-telling, and reconciliation. At a minimum, urban Indigenous restaurants signal a change in attitude. For example, Salmon n' Bannock's menu opens with a land acknowledgment of "the Traditional Coast Salish Territories of the Musquem, Squamish and Tsleil Waututh First Nations."[59] The menu educates diners about politics and Indigenous history, in addition to listing the restaurant's fare. A colonial GPS. And reminder that we are all treaty people.

Restaurants are venues for expressing personal culinary points of view and culturally based traditions. Some chefs speak for themselves and others for their communities. By reimagining ingredients, some Indigenous restaurants expose what was erased but, as Medina and Francis say, never truly gone. What these restaurants serve is not exclusively historic. Instead, restaurants demonstrate what Indigenous cuisines have become, are becoming, and will become. Although it has not taken on the task of defining Indigenous cuisines, *Culinary Claims* has tracked how their interpretations and representations have evolved across time and terrain, from "Indian tacos" to "Seal tartare" and from "Elk with sweet cranberry coulis" to "Salmon with four medicines."

It would be easy to conclude that these early Indigenous restaurants, especially those with lifespans similar to a one-off exposition's, failed. But to evaluate success based on longevity alone would dismiss the valuable culinary and cultural contributions these eateries made. It would overlook their efforts in claiming a presence in Canada's urban restaurantscape, in reclaiming ingredients as Indigenous, and in visualizing the politics that punctuate even the shortest of menus. Despite the media's tendency to label Indigenous restaurants as "new" and, thus, muddy the history of earlier examples, these first entrepreneurs have led the way so that contemporary chefs can cook outside of settler storying, which is to say make their own foods, tell their own stories. Restaurants, as this book has shown, manifest how food is at the absolute heart of the struggle over Indigenous representation.

With its settler owners, in many ways the Muckamuck picked up where La Toundra had left off. It also went one step further by hiring Indigenous employees who, in turn, challenged their working conditions, maintained a three-year-long picket line, and, eventually, reopened the space as an Indigenous co-owned restaurant. This exemplifies the first period I identify: 1971 to 1996. During this era, diners and critics viewed restaurants like Winnipeg's Bungees and Edmonton's Tribes as novel, as unique. Their menus generally adhered to pow wow hits and Canadian classics. In the second period, after the last residential school closed but before the Truth and Reconciliation Commission, restaurants such as Ottawa's Sweetgrass and Toronto's Keriwa Cafe further challenged diners' expectations of an Indigenous restaurant, but without the politics and shift in national conversation that the Truth and Reconciliation Commission kindled. By embracing cooking styles that check the box of fusion, these restaurants aimed to narrate personal culinary points of view: Feast Cafe Bistro, NishDish, and Nikosi Bistro Pub in Winnipeg, Toronto, and Wakefield, in Manitoba, Ontario, and Quebec. These restaurants share the current period, though in different provinces with different laws. All three opened after the advent of the Truth and Reconciliation Commission and serve stories that support Indigenous resurgence, that demand reconciliation, that renegotiate restaurant politics. These restaurants are, of course, all infused with Indigenous histories but, equally important, are manifestations of the Indigenous present. They challenge settler storying that confines Indigenous cuisines to the past or even to the lost, the disappeared.

In concluding *Speaking in Cod Tongues*, Newman writes, "It should be clear by this point that much of Canadian cuisine is Indigenous, though it is seldom recognized as such, but the emergence of Indigenous dishes and restaurants represents a first halting step in recognizing how critical Indigenous culinary traditions have been to our cuisine."[60] The evolution of these eateries further echoes Newman and Grey's discussion of the scholarship that chronicles the progress of food in a settler colonial state: "initially the destruction of Indigenous food systems as a tool of war (conquest), followed by forced conversion to a Settler diet (assimilation), before the revalorization of Indigenous gastronomy for Settler consumption (appropriation). Indigenous cuisines are thus gentrified, reoriented toward the demographic that originally sought their eradication."[61] The last step is when those who wanted to destroy Indigenous food systems reorient these systems for themselves. Settlers turned their noses up at wild foods, which, a century later, became sought out at high-end restaurants. However, the end of this progression eats its tail. "Authentic" cuisine does not exist, as Newman and Grey write, "since gastronomy is neither a static practice nor a timeless product. The irony here is that 'traditional' Indigenous cuisines are creative responses to a wide complex of colonial forces, including government rations, enclosure, and the suppression of traditional knowledge."[62] Restaurants represent these creative responses and are venues in which Indigenous cuisines respond, adapt, and resurge, in which Indigenous cuisines challenge settler stories and where chefs cook back. To pick up Lien and Law's framing of salmon, like *villaks*, the category of Indigenous cuisine is relational and is in part defined in contrast to the settler majority culinary culture. This is what defines restaurant politics.

Shane Chartrand, the tattooed, Harley-riding executive chef at SC Restaurant at River Cree Resort and Casino in Enoch, Alberta, collaborated with Francis and Bruneau-Guenther on a 2018 Dine Out Vancouver dinner. A member of the Enoch Cree Nation, he was the only Indigenous chef to participate in "Cook It Raw Alberta."[63] The following year, in February 2016, Chartrand spoke in Edmonton at Redx Talks about what he calls "progressive Indigenous Cuisine." For him, Indigenous cuisine is "ultimately Canadian cuisine": "[young Aboriginal chefs] need to take on that responsibility of making it Canadian cuisine. First Nations, Aboriginal cuisine is a big, big part of who we are. It is a big part of the food and beverage world, of the culinary arts world. But why does it really matter? Some people will come up to me and say you're not saving lives. But the thing is we are saving lives because food is medicine. Food changes our attitude. Food changes who we are ... I believe that we have a platform to take a moment to think about our food ... and say maybe this is Canadian cuisine, this is what it's all about, it's the spirituality and the way we eat it."[64] Like Waters, Chartrand sees food as a means of awakening the senses. By suggesting that Indigenous cuisine is Canadian, Chartrand further reclaims what is Indigenous, alongside their relations, their ecological kin.

Chartrand's words return to the question of what differentiates an Indigenous restaurant from a farm-to-table one serving local Canadian fare. As is clear, the two are entangled. They mesh, shift, and define each other. From the ingredients to the finished plate, the food might not be different, but the stories are. "The stories," as Wolfman says, "are the spice." Navajo chef Freddie Bitsoi agrees. "But what's notable about Indigenous recipes," he writes, "isn't so much what we cook or how we cook it, but our relationship with it."[65] It is not just the food that matters, but what the food represents and the relationships it sustains.

Unlike in 1974 when Canadian newspapers claimed the Muckamuck's menu as "real Canadian food," today Indigenous chefs are taking back ingredients to tell their own stories, to determine their own foodways. Even though Indigenous cuisines are still underrepresented in eateries across the country, the fact that more Indigenous restaurants continue to open shows how their chefs and restaurateurs are reclaiming foodways, ingredients, and a contemporary urban presence. Historical policies prohibited Indigenous peoples from participating in commercial food production and the restaurant industry. Indigenous chefs – such as Francis with his "Cooking for Reconciliation" and Wolfman with his You Are Welcome Food Truck – cast food as a tool of resistance and resurgence. Food is a means to reclaim culture, tradition, identity, language, health, and power. Through opening eateries of their own, Indigenous chefs have made more people aware of their foods and their cultures, and of their lands. Cooking and restaurants are, thus, means to restore and reconcile. From chef to chef and from city to city, the foods may change, but their power to narrate stories remains constant.

In telling these stories, my intention has not been to index every Indigenous restaurant in Canada, but to demonstrate their diversity and their relevance to contemporary conversations about how food imagines, represents, and constructs place. To map the many worlds these restaurants story. Restaurants track how culinary values shift. As new restaurants open, others close, which reflects both the nature of the industry and the ongoing challenges of regulations and financing, ingredients and appetites. Nonetheless, the presence of more Indigenous restaurants – and Canadians' openness to them – represents a step towards pluralizing stories about Turtle Island. A chef's decision to feature foraged, local ingredients also relates to shifts in food availability and ethics, including animal welfare and concerns about healthy bodies and environments.

Some chefs work only with pre-contact ingredients and others dabble with fusion. Many of the restaurants I have discussed aim for both Indigenous consumption and sharing a personal story about land, communities, and Indigeneity with settler diners. Restaurants can restore cultural connections. For Inez Cook, a Sixties Scoop survivor, opening Salmon n' Bannock reconnected her with her family. Chartrand, who was adopted as a child, tells a similar story, how while cooking at a restaurant he met a cousin and learned he was from the Enoch Nation.[66]

Indigenous restaurants, in short, are as much about stories as they are about food. There is no one-size-fits all for either. Indigenous restaurants in Canada warrant further research attention, both to fill gaps in the academic literature about Canada's restaurant history and to illuminate regional examples, especially from the Maritimes and northern territories. Catering companies do too. The restaurants this book has chronicled are commercial businesses that aim to diffuse different stories, and sometimes even foods, to reposition plants, humans, and animals in relationships that differ from the extractive model of owner and resource. The foods it has studied are commercial – foods that are for sale. But as historian Alex Ketchum's research about feminist restaurants exemplifies, a commercial eatery can challenge capitalist norms and promote alternative systems.[67] Restaurants can share overlooked stories, and even though this happens through the commodification of food in a venue engaged with consumer culture, Indigenous restaurants engage with these dynamics on their own terms.

In 2012 I was visiting New Delhi, where a friend told me he wanted to eat "First Nations food" the next time he was in Toronto. "Where can I try it?" he asked. "What is Native food?" he quickly followed up. "And are there Native restaurants?" In between sips of chai, I paused, only to realize I had no idea. When I was a kid, I learned the word Indian, then the words Native, First Peoples, and First Nations. When I started the research for this book, Aboriginal was the common term, and halfway through, Indigenous replaced it. It felt ironic – but also somehow auspicious – that it was in India where I was first asked the question that prompted this project, a reminder of the power of names, including misnomers, and the interconnections of places.[68]

# Acknowledgments

Some say it takes a village. As a Torontonian (without a driver's licence no less), I don't know a lot about villages, but I do know how many people it takes to put together a meal. So thank you to everyone who has helped *Culinary Claims* make it to the table. A thousand thanks to everyone named here and so many others who are not.

It means the world to publish with a hometown press. Many thanks to the Culinaria series editors, to Robert Davidson, H. Rosi Song, and Jo Sharma, for believing in this book, and to the University of Toronto Press, especially to Len Husband for guiding this manuscript through peer review and revision, the willingness to dial international country codes, and a perfect sense of humour. Enric Bou, I owe you my gratitude for introducing me to Bob (and for teaching me how much cherries offer gazpacho). Janice Evans, thank you for turning a Word document bursting at its seams into a book, and Judy Williams, thank you for your exacting editing. Annika Feldmeier, *danke sehr* for your enthusiasm in navigating these many pages and for finely crafting its index.

Thank you so much to the reviewers who pushed me to roll up my sleeves and edit, edit, edit. Thank you for your careful readings and generous engagement, for your sharp suggestions. What you read here is my attempt to improve this manuscript, as well as to improve as a scholar. Of course any mistakes that remain are my responsibility and – to quote the wise historian Brittany Luby – are, I hope, an opportunity to grow.

To have made it from Germany back to Turtle Island again and again I am beholden to the Bavarian American Academy, LMU Munich's Graduate Center and Amerika-Institut, the Rachel Carson Center, the DAAD, and the Association of Canadian Studies in German-Speaking Countries. I am particularly thankful to have participated in the LMU-UCB Research in the Humanities partnership, which was funded by LMU Munich's Institutional Strategy LMUexcellent within the framework of the German Excellence Initiative. Thank you for the chance to become a Berkeley Bowl regular. At Cal, my biggest thanks go to Lok Siu and the Ethnic Studies Department and Canadian Studies Program teams.

In Munich I am thankful that Christof Mauch took me on as a doctoral candidate even though my application proposed three ideas, none of which I wrote about. Thank you for encouraging me to teach, the one thing I love as much as writing. (And almost as much as eating.) I am indebted to my secondary supervisor, Julia Herzberg, who has nudged me to think about food beyond the lens of culture and to further venture into its myriad discourses. I am also grateful for Charlotte Lerg, whose advice always performs the same magic as a splash of olive oil in a bowl of soup.

Many thanks to the RCC and AI communities – my colleagues and friends who have been kind with their words, time, and support. Special thanks to Elena, Ruhi, and Sarah. Thank you for always being up for sharing ideas, G&Ts, and the energy to pick myself up (both literally and figuratively). Sarah, your sageness, your wit, and your largesse have saved me more than once. Thank you for CL nights, B.A. memes, and for always being up for one last round. Also, I owe a squinty-eye-I-promise-I'm-not-going-to-cry thank you to my students at the Amerika-Institut and the RCC. Thank you for trusting me that menus are worth your attention, tolerating my jokes, and doing (most of) the reading.

To everyone who listened to me try my best to speak within my time limit at conferences, workshops, and talks, thank you for your attention, for your feedback. To the editors I worked with while nurturing this manuscript, thank you for making me a better writer. Great editors are like salt – they bring out the best of an ingredient, making writing taste sharper, brighter, more like itself.

Thank you for your just-right pinches. Versions of some of the ideas in this book have surfaced in other texts. I am most grateful to Taylor and Francis, Prospect Books, and McGill-Queen's University Press for their permission to revisit my earlier missives here. I first shared bits of Chapter 1's "Sad ol' mush" subsection in *Childhood in the Past*, volume 15, issue 2, 2022, titled "Childhood and Food: Literary-Historical Perspectives (c. 19–20th Centuries)" (available at https://www.tandfonline.com/journals/ycip20/special-issues). I rehearsed parts of Chapter 4 and Chapter 9 in my contributions to Prospect Books' *Proceedings of the Oxford Symposium on Food and Cookery 2019, Food & Power* (2020) and *Proceedings of the Oxford Symposium on Food and Cookery 2016, Offal: Rejected and Reclaimed Food* (2017) (c) Equinox Publishing Ltd. I also presented earlier parts of Chapter 9 in *Canadian Culinary Imaginations*, published by McGill-Queen's University Press.

*Culinary Claims* has taken me many places and, in turn, I have taken it with me as I have moved from one position and place to the next. It was, first, in Venice that this research grew up, and for that I would like to thank the Center for the Humanities & Social Change at Ca' Foscari University. Thank you for gifting me a city free of tourists, one equally foggy as delightfully salty. Many thanks to Shaul Bassi, Barbara del Mercato, Valentina Bonifacio, Francesca Tarocco, Renata Sõukand and the ethnobotany team, especially Baiba Pruse (I cannot wait to go beaver hunting), the Ocean Space Family, and to my colleagues, who all look so dashing in masks. Thanks to Ifor Duncan for always being up for shop talk, spritz, and Tonolo. No one models *aqua alta* waders as well as you. To Marco Bravetti, thank you for teaching me the many meanings of *tocia* and that lunch is an activity that lasts all day. Thank you, Giorgia Aquilar, for helping me to apartment hunt even from afar, for answering my calls from *la Questura*, for translating and interpreting, and for everything else. To Elisabetta, *grazie mille* for making Monday and Thursday evenings so fun – even when the heating didn't work and the mosquitos were on a mission. While writing a book in my mother tongue, it was humbling to have to start from scratch in another language. Thank you, Pietro Consolandi, for always keeping me in the loop about what's new on the Rialto.

Back in Germany, I have Munich (again), Essen, and, now, Augsburg to thank as the next cities and communities that supported me as this book further matured. Because rewriting is much more work than writing, my thanks go to everyone who guided me and cheered me on. Thank you, Tae Cimarosti, for Thursday afternoon coffee dates and for surprise croissant deliveries. Tamar Blickstein, thank you for speedy train station walks and for encouraging me to try and try again. I'm grateful for our V.B. sisterhood. Thanks to Carmel Finley for your wisdom about celebrating small victories. Thank you, Jonatan Palmblad, for your dedication to the Oxford comma. Pauline Kargruber, thank you for reacting so quickly when I electrocuted myself and for calling an ambulance.

Thank you to everyone who shared advice about writing and revising (and life, really, when I think of it), especially Nicole Seymour, Petra Dolata, Thomas Lekan, Arielle Helmick, Ursula Münster, Astrid Schrader, Alessandro Rippa, Melissa Petrou, Kris Decker, Alexandra Irmia, Verena Kick, and Krishnendu Ray. Thank you, Anna Antonova, for becoming a Billy's regular and for booking conference hotels with saunas. And a forever thank you to Amanda Boetzkes. I sure won the lottery with my first art history course. Simone Müller, *vielen, vielen Dank* for welcoming me to Augsburg, for seeing the potential of my ideas when my exhaustion fogged my own vision, and for limitlessly sharing your experience, your time, your support. And thank you to Penelope Volinia and Philine Schiller for joining me in growing "Off the Menu" into the research team I could have only dreamed of.

Although my time in London was far too short, I am chuffed to have had the privilege of joining Delfina Foundation's *Politics of Food* family. Special thanks to Aaron Cezar, Salma Tuqan, Viviana Checchia, Erin Li, Maya Marshak, and Derek Tumala, as well as Cooking Sections and Gaia Art Foundation. Also, a big thank you to Ruhi and Martin for letting this manuscript crash your wedding. It was wonderful to celebrate your love and your families and to allow myself to be distracted by impala and guinea fowl while penning my final edits.

In addition to everyone who graciously took the time to meet and speak, thank you to those who housed me as I travelled: Shirin and Petrina in Vancouver, Ali King who found me a place to stay in

Winnipeg, Steve McCullough and Denise Catherine for loaning me their house, Terry Macleod and Ellen MacDonald for cooking me dinner (to celebrate their anniversary, no less), and Finn for loaning me his parents. Corinna, thank you for sharing your Ottawa home (and for yelling "go girl go" out the window the morning I realized my meeting at Rideau Hall was at 6:30 a.m. and not p.m.). Warm thanks to Shruti for hosting me in Helsinki. And thank you, Freda, for the weekend at Bear's Inn.

I was not able to include quotes from everyone I interviewed, but am most grateful for those who have shared their words and have trusted me with their stories. Your tales have further shaped my thinking about restaurants and foodways across Turtle Island. Also, thank you to Anthony Walsh, Justin Cournoyer, Derek Dammann, David McMillan, and Court Desautels. Many thanks to Elizabeth Driver, Ian Mosby, Jeffrey Pilcher, Nelson Graburn, Trisha Cusak, and Dan Philippon for giving me feedback along the way.

And thank you, thank you, thank you to all of the artists and organizations who have generously gifted this book their images: Kent Monkman, Dana Claxton, Sean Griffin, Sonny Assu, Lawrence Paul Yuxweluptun, Little Miss Chief, ReMatriate Collective, Lisa Myers, AA Bronson, and, especially, Adrian Stimson for letting the cover dress up in your artwork. Special thanks to the Toronto Biennale of Art, to Teresa Sudeyko and the Morris and Helen Belkin Art Gallery, and to Annie Watts. Also, it is with gratitude that I acknowledge that this book was printed with support of the Association for Canadian Studies in German-speaking Countries (GKS). Many thanks to the GKS for covering the reproduction fees of images. And a thousand thanks to the Elite Network of Bavaria and the University of Augsburg for their support.

A thank you to my friends for their charm, their love, and their giggles, especially Erica, Julie, Anna, Arwed, Jena, Kate, Nadia, and Alina. Camilla, thank you for keeping me company in libraries, sending the best postcards, hunting for obscure culinary titles in second-hand bookshops, and sharing your love of words and Al Pacino (plus your pashmina scarf when libraries blast their air conditioning).

To the Goras, Sitarskis, Blakes, Morrows, and Kemps, thank you for raising me with an interest in the places we come from and the stories we tell about them. To Carolyn, thank you for teaching me that good writing is rewriting (and the importance of reading the washing instructions on clothing labels, and that yellow kiwis are better than green, and to always pack a comb to the beach, and for everything, really). Thank you for eating at many of these restaurants, driving us there, and graciously picking up the bill. I'm glad we made it to Ottawa and had macaroons to snack on while we waited for the tow truck. Blake, thank you for letting me choose where to eat and for tolerating my strategy of making you taste something again and again until you like it. To Babcia and Dziadzia, thank you for always being my audience. Dziadzia for teaching me to take breakfast seriously (and for driving across the GTA in rush-hour traffic to pick up the city's best blintzes), and Babcia for teaching me to take all meals seriously, but never so seriously that laughter doesn't have a place to the table. Mike, thank you for making sure there is always something sweet (and often chocolatey) on the counter and that the water is always cold.

To the best-looking Blake, this is for you. Your stories influenced me more than you knew. Thank you for sharing your memories of learning history in a one-room Prairie classroom in the 1930s. Although that history was spoiled with colonial bias, you encouraged me to listen, to write, and to always be curious. Also, thank you for sharing your love of evening whiskey, sky-blue pink, and not giving a shit for Tread.

And, finally, thank you, Toby. Thank you for cooking buttered endives and for always doing the dishes. Thank you for planning our vacations based on places to eat. For listening to me for hours, in cars, on trains, and at home, talk about food and stories and the world. For adding salt to everything I write. For reminding me to enjoy the view. And for accepting that I am now the Historian in the Gora-Federkeil household.

# Notes

**Introduction: You Are Welcome**

1. Peterson, "Why Toronto Should Get Excited about the Pan Am Games."
2. Ibid.
3. Ibid.
4. Indigenous Service Canada and Indigenous Relations and Northern Affairs Canada, "Toronto Purchase, No. 13."
5. Edwards, "Shrugs Greet Historic $145M Toronto Land Claim Settlement."
6. Ibid.
7. DeMontis, "Celebrating Aboriginal Cuisine with Recipes from Chef David Wolfman." At the time of the Pan Am Games, the official name was The Mississaugas of the New Credit First Nation. In 2019, they dropped the "new."
8. Bain, "First Nations Food Truck Welcomes Pan Am Patrons."
9. For example, a Toronto blog wrote: "We like to think of ourselves as foodies, but it recently donned [sic] on us that we're pretty unfamiliar with Aboriginal cuisine. Sure, we've all had game meat dishes like buffalo burgers and elk roasts, and we've heard of bannock, but that about sums up our experience." *She Does the City*, "Wanna Try Aboriginal Cuisine?"
10. As of 31 July 2018, the City of Toronto's Public Health Program had tallied 17,243 food-serving institutions. Toronto Restaurants.
11. City of Toronto, "Dine Safe."
12. Robin, Dennis, and Hart, "Feeding Indigenous People in Canada," 8.

13 LaDuke, "Seeds of Our Ancestors, Seeds of Life." Kaitlyn S. Patterson provides an example of the relationships between people and the living entities that become food. Reflecting on the Algonquin food system, she writes: "In my education as a dietitian, I understood why I needed to learn about the composition and 'utility' of food – how to use it and how it helps our bodies. However, I failed to learn about the *who* behind our food sources. *Who* are the cattails? Who makes up their relations? Why are these relations crucial to their wellbeing? Instead of constantly asking myself (situated within my position in dietetics), what can this 'food' do for me/my body, I needed to shift to: what can I do for this being to ensure that our reciprocal relationship with one another is maintained?" Patterson, "Who Are the Cattails?," 25–6.
14 Fee, *Literary Land Claims*, 1.
15 The aphorism to which they refer is "Dis-moi ce que tu manges, je te dirai ce que tu es" from *The Physiology of Taste*, the 1825 magnum opus of the French lawyer and politician Jean Anthelme Brillat-Savarin. Brillat-Savarin, *The Physiology of Taste*, 13. Bell and Valentine, *Consuming Geographies*, 3. Priscilla Ferguson writes that the obvious comparison to this aphorism "is the well-known German adage 'Mann ist, was er ißt,' which Americans personalize as 'You are what you eat.'" She clarifies that "What sounds like a proverb was formulated well after Brillat-Savarin by the material philosopher Ludwig Feuerbach in *Die Naturwissenschaft und die Revolution* of 1850, as 'Der Mensch ist, was er isst.' M.F.K. Fisher in her (1949) translation ... states the connection between being and eating was not original to Feuerbach, but provides no anterior citation other than Brillat-Savarin." Stateside, Victor Lindlahr's 1942 book *You Are What You Eat: How to Win and Keep Health with Diet* popularized this expression. Ferguson, *Accounting for Taste*, 31, 216.
16 Maffei, "Surveying the Borders," 211.
17 For a definition of settler societies, see Stasiulis and Yuval-Davis, "Introduction," 3.
18 Poulain, *The Sociology of Food*, 9.
19 Ibid., 12.
20 Middell and Naumann, "Global History and the Spatial Turn," 152.
21 Solnit, *Storming the Gates of Paradise*, 1.
22 Ibid.
23 Gabaccia, *We Are What We Eat*, 8.
24 The others are: Land Is Life; Language Is Power; Freedom Is the Other Side of Fear; and, Change Happens One Warrior at a Time. Alfred and Corntassel, "Being Indigenous," 612–13.

25 Robin, "Responsibilities and Reflections," 11.
26 Bruni, "Nordic Chef Explores Backyard."
27 Ibid.
28 Years after opening Noma, Redzepi also entertained this question: "We're still figuring out what it means to be a cook in this part of the world. Our original idea to use only local products eventually started to collapse under the weight of new questions: When is an ingredient truly local? What makes it belong here? What does it take for an ingredient to be integrated to the point where you think, *Now I can put it on the menu? Now it makes sense?* If you go far enough back in time, you'll find that almost everything in your everyday pantry actually came from somewhere else. Over time, we began to understand that an ingredient like cardamom has a thousand-year-old history in the region. Why deprive ourselves of it?" He concludes with: "The way I see things today, if something grows here, it belongs here." Redzepi, "If It Does Well Here, It Belongs Here," 88, 90.
29 In 2021 Caldwell First Nation announced plans to open an Indigenous restaurant: Three Fires. Hamel-Charest, "Qu'y a-t-il dans une assiette autochtone?" This 2022 article discusses contemporary examples rather than the historic ones that *Culinary Claims* spotlights.
30 In 2022 Tawnya Brant competed on the tenth season of "Top Chef Canada," becoming the show's fourth Indigenous contestant. Rich Francis was the first, having appeared in season four in 2014. See Chapter 10, "Salmon and the F-Word." Stephane Levac, of M'Chigeeng First Nation, and Siobhan Detkavich, who is Hawaiian and Cowichan, both contended on the ninth season in 2021.
31 The heritage of its owner, however, has raised some questions. She identifies as Métis. See Maracle, "Menu and Decor at Manitou Bistro 'Reprehensible' Some Kitigan Zibi Members Say."
32 There are also other Indigenous culinary businesses, including catering companies and food trucks, such as Vancouver's Mr. Bannock Indigenous Cuisine (founded by Paul Natrall of the Squamish Nation in 2018); BigHeart Bannock Catering, which ran from 2017 to 2023 in Vancouver and included a spell as BigHeart Bannock Cultural Café; Native Delights in Edmonton (a food cart that launched in January 2013, transformed into a restaurant, and then went back to a food truck in 2016); Winnipeg's Bannock Food Truck; and Regina's The Bannock House. Although this was not a food business, in 2012 Althea Guiboche, known as the Bannock Lady, started distributing homemade bannock and soup to Winnipeggers without housing.

33 Williams-Forson, "Foreword," xvii–xviii. She quotes Adichie, "The Danger of a Single Story."
34 Martens, Cidro, Hart, and McLachlan, "Understanding Indigenous Food Sovereignty through an Indigenous Research Paradigm," 24.
35 Absolon and Willett, "Aboriginal Research," 5.
36 Reder, "Introduction: *Position*," 7. I also identify as an ally based on literary scholar Sam McKegney's definition. "An ally, in my understanding, is one who acknowledges the limits of her or his knowledge, but neither cowers beneath those limits nor uses them as a crutch," he writes. "An ally recognizes the responsibility to gain knowledge about the cultures and communities whose artistic creations she or he analyzes before entering the critical fray and offering public interpretations. An ally privileges the work of Native scholars, writers, and community members – not as political gesture, but as a sincere attempt to produce the most effective criticism – yet she or he does not accept their work uncritically; she or he recognizes that healthy skepticism and critical debate are signs of engagement and respect, not dismissal." McKegney, "Strategies for Ethnical Engagement," 63–4.
37 Chen, "Speaking Nearby," 87.
38 Szanto, "Is It Hot in Here, or Is It Just Me?" 6.
39 Hargreaves, "The Lake Is the People and Life That Come to It," 109.
40 King, *The Truth about Stories*, 9.
41 Ibid., 10.
42 Greenblatt, *The Rise and Fall of Adam and Eve*, 2.
43 Jørgensen, "Extinction and the End of Futures," 2.
44 Demuth, *Floating Coast*, 15.
45 Kimmerer, *Braiding Sweetgrass*, 7.
46 Ibid., 9.
47 Johl Whiteduck Ringuette, email to author, 8 August 2016.
48 See Robin, "Responsibilities and Reflections," 10. For storytelling as a critical methodology in Indigenous cultures, see also Patterson, "Who Are the Cattails?," 22. For the purpose of tribal stories, see Mihesuah, *So You Want to Write about American Indians?*, 64.
49 I owe this realization to reading about what Weston calls the "great gay migration" in "Get Thee to a Big City."
50 As literary scholar Abigail Manzella puts it, "the United States was founded on the displacement of peoples." The same is true of Canada. Manzella, *Migrating Fictions*, 7.
51 Hunt and Starblanket, *Storying Violence*, 14.

52 Ibid., 10–11.
53 King, *The Inconvenient Indian*, xv–xvi.
54 Ferguson, *Accounting for Taste*, 2–3.
55 Kyla Wazana Tompkins proposes a framework for studying eating beyond gastronomy, writing: "My goal in making this shift from food to eating – a shift to a framework we might call *critical eating studies* – implicitly entails the examination of the field of food studies' unconscious investments in the commodity itself." Tompkins, *Racial Indigestion*, 2.
56 Spray, "Alaska's Vanishing Arctic Cuisine," 40. Spray cites "Personal Interview with Giuliano Bugialli, April 1989."
57 Ferguson, "Eating Orders," 689. Spang, *The Invention of the Restaurant*, 186. I address this in "Today's Special."
58 Here I draw inspiration from Le Guin, *The Carrier Bag Theory of Fiction*.
59 Simpson, *As We Have Always Done*, 195. In Canada 53 per cent of Indigenous people live in urban centres. This number increased 13 per cent between 1961 and 2006. Skinner, Pratley, and Burnett, "Eating in the City," 1, 3.
60 Simpson, *As We Have Always Done*, 173.
61 Operated by the Roman Catholic church, the Kamloops Indian residential school opened in 1890 and closed in 1978. Enrolling up to five hundred students, it was Canada's largest. Lindeman, "Canada."
62 Wilson et al., "Reflections on the Role and Responsibilities of Food Studies in Canada, Indigenous Territories, and Beyond – 2020–21," 6.
63 Grey and Newman, "Beyond Culinary Colonialism," 717.
64 Morris, "*Kai* or Kiwi?"; Morris, "The Politics of Palatability."
65 Morris, "The Politics of Palatability," 6–7.
66 Ibid., 19.
67 Ibid.
68 Ibid., 14.
69 In *Seeing Red*, Anderson and Robertson call the newspaper Canada's "most ubiquitous agent of popular education." As their study of English-language newspaper representations of Indigenous peoples in Canada from 1869 to 2009 illustrates, "the news constitutes a kind of national curriculum, which emerges organically as if nothing were more natural." This makes it essential to read newspaper sources critically. However, the authors do not include any restaurant coverage and only limited accounts of food. Anderson and Robertson, *Seeing Red*, 3, 8.
70 Here I am indebted to titles such as Sarah Carter's *Lost Harvests*, James Daschuk's *Clearing the Plains*, and Ester Reiter's *Making Fast Food*.

Regarding Indigenous foodways, scholarship tends to focus on the relationships between tradition and territory, often with an emphasis on health and nutrition. Examples include Mary-Ellen Kelm's *Colonizing Bodies*, Maureen K. Lux's *Medicine That Walks* and the volume edited by Robidoux and Mason, *A Land Not Forgotten*.

71 Powers and Stewart, eds., *Northern Bounty*; Cooke, ed., *What's to Eat?*; and Iacovetta, Korinek, and Epp, eds., *Edible Histories, Cultural Politics*.

72 To date, there are few books about Canadian restaurant history. Focusing on colonial taverns, Julia Roberts's *In Mixed Company* lays down the groundwork for interpreting public eateries as colonial contact zones. And although she focuses on Burger King, Reiter's *Making Fast Food* has a chapter about "The Restaurant Industry in Canada" that begins to map this overlooked history. Steve Penfold's *The Donut* also focuses on fast food, and Janet Thiessen's *Snacks: A Canadian Food History* profiles industrial food companies. Powers and Stewart's *Northern Bounty* has a chapter about the emergence of Canadian restaurants, but is not academic in its approach. Lily Cho's *Eating Chinese* is an important contribution, but focuses only on Alberta. All of these texts focus on Canadian settlers and newcomers. In 2023 journalist Gabby Peyton published *Where We Ate*, which she describes as a "love letter" to the country's eateries. Peyton lists 150 restaurants from pre-Confederation Canada to the present, the most recent having opened in 2013. Although she does not disclose her selection criteria, she argues that the restaurants she chronicles have "impacted the way we eat," which is to say the way Canada eats, not just what, but also where. Peyton, *Where We Ate*, 6, 3.

73 Freedman, *Ten Restaurants That Changed America*, xxxix.

74 Historians Katie Rawson and Elliott Shore write that "the modern Western restaurant" was born in Paris but that the "first restaurants did not begin there. They began in twelfth-century China." They locate the first restaurants in Kaifeng, which was the capital of the Song Dynasty until 1127. However, the word restaurant did not yet exist, and the authors do not provide the Chinese term for these eateries. How would this term have been translated into French, or English, before the word restaurant was in use? Therefore, I consider these twelfth-century Chinese eateries early predecessors of restaurants, as opposed to the "first restaurants." Rawson and Shore, *Dining Out*, 10, 25.

75 Freedman, *Ten Restaurants That Changed America*, xli.

76 Spang, *The Invention of the Restaurant*, 2.

77 Ibid.

78 Writing about nineteenth-century Boston, historian Kelly Erby acknowledges this exclusivity, clarifying that "not every restaurant welcomed women, African Americans, or immigrants." Yet, she points out that although many eateries refused them as customers, they frequently hired them as employees. Erby, *Restaurant Republic*, xix. See also Kwate, *Burgers in Blackface*.
79 Roberts, *In Mixed Company*, 8.
80 Ibid., 2.
81 Reiter writes, "The first commercial eating places in North America were associated with inns located on travel routes." Reiter, *Making Fast Food*, 22.
82 Peyton, *Where We Ate*, 12. Her chapter "Before Confederation" lists inns and hotels, which their individual names further underline: Auberge Saint-Gabriel; Old Angel Inn (Niagara-on-the-Lake, Ontario, 1789–present): l'Hôtel de la Nouvelle Constitution (Quebec City, Quebec, 1792); King's Head Inn (Burlington Bay, Ontario, 1794–1813), Toronto Coffee House (Toronto, Ontario, 1801–6); Restaurant Compain (Montreal, Quebec, 1847–91); Windsor House Hotel (Ottawa, Ontario, 1850s–1957); Six Mile Pub (Victoria, British Columbia, 1855–present); Stewart's Dining Room & Oyster Saloon (Halifax, Nova Scotia, 1857–65) and Pioneer Hotel (Cameronton, British Columbia, 1864–70). The first eatery in her book to identify itself as a restaurant by its name is Restaurant Compain.
83 CBC Radio, "The Restaurant." The Wheatsheaf Tavern temporarily closed for renovation in 2019 and then reopened in 2020. Its sign reads "Toronto's oldest bar." Its legacy, however, is rather quiet. In contrast, Montreal's Joe Beef's is as loud as the most festive of happy hours. Charles McKiernan, born in Cavan County, Ireland, in 1835, gained the nickname "Joe Beef" during the Crimean War because of his "talent for providing food and shelter." He followed his brigade to Canada, left the army in 1868, and opened the Crown and Sceptre Tavern, known as "Joe Beef's Cantine." It was a popular watering hole for working men. In addition to accommodation and alcohol, Joe Beef supplied simple meals of cheese, bread, and meat. But it also sparked moral debates. As archivist Peter DeLottinville writes, "Middle-class Montreal saw this tavern as a moral hazard to all who entered and a threat to social peace." McKiernan died in 1889, and by 1893 his tavern, too, was gone. But in 2005 chefs Frédéric Morin and David McMillan opened a restaurant in Montreal called Joe Beef: "An homage to Charles 'Joe-Beef' McKiernan, 19th century innkeeper and Montreal working class hero." McKiernan was the inspiration and namesake of a world-renowned eatery known

for its customers' gluttonous appetites. By naming their restaurant after this tavern keeper, Morin and McMillan further canonized McKiernan's tavern in Canada's restaurant history. Reiter, *Making Fast Food*, 23. DeLottinville, "Joe Beef of Montreal," 12, 10, 14. McMillan parted ways with the restaurant in 2021. Joe Beef is one of the few Canadian restaurants to have gained international recognition; in 2015, it made the world's one hundred best restaurants list, at number 81. *Restaurant Magazine*, "The World's 50 Best Restaurants." Canadian restaurants rarely make this list. See Akhtar, "Why Canadian Restaurants Rarely Make the World's 50 Best List." The restaurant appeared on Anthony Bourdain's television programs twice, and it was at Joe Beef's sister restaurant next door, Liverpool House, that Barack Obama and Justin Trudeau dined on oysters, spaghetti lobster, halibut with morels, asparagus, steak, and strawberry shortcake in 2017. BBC News, "Obama and Trudeau Meet Up for Dinner in Montreal."

84 South of the border, the first restaurants in the United States opened in the 1820s and 1830s. Haley, *Turning the Tables*, 11–12. Freedman considers Delmonico's in New York City "the first real restaurant in the United States." Opened in 1827 by two brothers from Italian-speaking Switzerland, Delmonico's became a culinary destination. There are also earlier examples, ones Freedman calls rudimentary, like Boston's Julien's Restorator, which Jean Baptiste Gilbert Payplat dis Julien opened in 1793, but Delmonico's set the American restaurant standard for a small section of the public. Freedman, *Ten Restaurants That Changed America*, xxv–xliv, 3. For Julien's Restorator, see Smith, *The Oxford Companion to American Food and Drink*, 550, and Erby, *Restaurant Republic*, 5.

85 Reiter, *Making Fast Food*, 23.
86 Ibid.
87 Ibid.
88 Ibid., 21.
89 Ibid., 26. In *First Nations Cuisines*, Sebastian Schellhaas studies the professionalization of Indigenous gastronomy in Canada without taking into consideration how this fits into the larger history of Canadian culinary professionalization. As this section demonstrates, restaurants in Canada are relatively recent, and, therefore, the country's "restaurantscape" should not be taken as a given, but, instead, approached as a historical development.
90 Reiter, *Making Fast Food*, 44.
91 Ibid., 45.

92 Ibid., 15. Brittany Luby makes an important critique of post-war Canadian affluence. Writing about her book *Dammed*, she states: "This book makes clear that Indigenous Peoples did not form part of Canada's affluent society after 1945. Instead, it demonstrates how federal and provincial actors removed resources from Indigenous communities and reduced the income-generating potential of Indigenous families specifically to benefit Anglo-settlers generally. Postwar Canada was not an affluent society; it was (and it remains) a colonial one." Luby, *Dammed*, 26
93 Restaurants Canada, "Canada's Restaurant Industry Infographic."
94 Ibid. The COVID-19 pandemic has had immense consequences for the restaurant industry. See Mintz, *The Next Supper*.
95 Anthropologist Marilyn Strathern taught Haraway that "it matters what ideas we use to think other ideas (with)." Haraway, *Staying with the Trouble*, 12.
96 Bird, "What We Want to Be Called," 2.
97 Alfred and Corntassel, "Being Indigenous," 597.
98 Simpson, "On Ethnographic Refusal," 69.
99 Here I follow historian Sarah A. Nickel's lead, who writes: "Recognizing the difficulties of labelling Indigenous communities according to geopolitical organization and socio-political realities, I will use the terms *Indigenous communities* and *bands* somewhat interchangeably. I acknowledge the politically and culturally problematic nature of equating Indigenous communities with settler-state-determined 'bands,' and, wherever possible, I avoid the latter term. In some cases, where Indigenous peoples used the term *band* or where the political structures of band membership are explicitly discussed, I will default to this term for clarity. I take the same approach to *reserves* and typically use the term *community* to refer to these geopolitical spaces." Nickel, *Assembling Unity*, 176.
100 Dreyer, *Dreyer's English*, 75. I replicate original sources when it comes to accents. Otherwise, I follow the French spelling.
101 Sky Woman is sometimes two words and other times one. See King, *The Truth about Stories*; Kimmerer, *Braiding Sweetgrass*; and Hoover, *The River Is in Us*.
102 Gómez-Peña, "The New World Border," 750.
103 Twitty, *The Cooking Gene*, 7.
104 For food and gender, see Shapiro, *Perfection Salad*; Williams-Forson, *Building Houses Out of Chicken Legs*; Agg, *I Hear She's a Real Bitch*; and Contois, *Diners, Dudes, and Diets*.

105 Quoted in McComb Sanchez, "Balance and a Bean," 44–5. Original source: Lois Ellen Frank, "The Discourse and Practice of Native American Cuisine: Native American Chefs and Native American Cooks in Contemporary Southwest Kitchens" (PhD diss., University of New Mexico, 2011), 5–11. Frank also introduces these four periods in *Seed to Plate, Soil to Sky*, 7–13.
106 Douglas, *Purity and Danger*.

## 1. Agricultural Flagpoles

1 Twitty, *The Cooking Gene*, 6.
2 A settler Canadian, Donati lives in Australia, which is her text's subject. Donati's "gastro nullius" is similar to what journalist Zoe Tennant calls "*terra nullius* on the plate." Donati, "From Gastro Nullius to 'Nourishing Terrain.'" Tennant, "*Terra Nullius* on the Plate."
3 Carolyn King, interview by the author, 9 September 2018.
4 Weso, *Good Seeds*, 54. This also connects to historian Michael D. Wise's reading of the farm: "As a lens for seeing the agricultural landscape, the farm also signified a heteronormative set of expectations that identified white, land-owning men (and their able-bodied and virile sons) as the land's primary economic actors, a way of seeing that pushed the visibility of other labor – waged, unwaged, or enslaved – into the background." Wise, *Native Foods*, 11.
5 Kimmerer, *Braiding Sweetgrass*, 129.
6 Worster, *An Unsettled Country*, 10.
7 Knobloch, *The Culture of Wilderness*, 1.
8 Ibid., 4.
9 Matties, "Unsettling Settler Food Movements."
10 See Hoover, *The River Is in Us*, Luby, "From Milk-Medicine to Public (Re)Education Programs," and Luby, *Dammed*, especially Chapter 3, "Power Lost and Power Gained," 84–112.
11 Whyte, "The Dakota Access Pipeline, Environmental Injustice, and U.S. Colonialism," 158.
12 For "settler time," see Rifkin, *Beyond Settler Time*.
13 Wolfe, "Settler Colonialism and the Elimination of the Native," 388.
14 Ibid.
15 Simpson, "The Sovereignty of Critique," 687.
16 Wise, *Native Foods*, 7.
17 Ibid., 9.

18 Here I use the word "naked" in reference to Rebecca Earles's seminal *The Body of the Conquistador*. With these words, in the 1570s the royal cosmographer Juan López de Velasco described what the land looked like prior to the arrival of the Spanish. "Almost everywhere the land was untended, and so little cultivated that, naked as it was, it produced only those plants and seeds that nature itself brought forth," he wrote. As Earle details, the story the Spanish empire told itself was that "it had elevated this naked, virgin land from its savage state and was rewarded with abundant harvests of Spanish crops." Earle, *The Body of the Conquistador*, 79. More specifically, she focuses on how food sculpted the body, distinguishing between Europeans and "Amerindians" and, thus, was central to Spain's colonial endeavour. Ibid., 2, 3, 183.
19 Wise, *Native Foods*, 9.
20 Wolfe, "Settler Colonialism and the Elimination of the Native," 395.
21 Simpson, *As We Have Always Done*, 43.
22 Kimmerer, *Braiding Sweetgrass*, 17.
23 Carter, *Lost Harvests*, ix.
24 King, *The Inconvenient Indian*, 70.
25 Carter, *Lost Harvests*, 157.
26 Kaplan, "Manifest Domesticity," 582–4.
27 Carter, *Capturing Women*, xiv, xiv.
28 Hill, "Seeds as Ancestors, Seeds as Archives," 93.
29 Ibid., 95. Also see LaDuke, "Seeds of Our Ancestors, Seeds of Life." The opposite of this was, of course, settler efforts to spread seeds. Historian Coll Thrush describes this in his study of culinary encounters on the Northwest Coast from 1774 to 1804, writing: "Crews planted not just flags but produce, leaving peas, parsley, strawberries, and more as proof of their passing, as succor to those Europeans who would follow, and as ritualized claiming through cultivation. Often, this was among a crew's very first tasks upon landing." Thrush, "Vancouver the Cannibal," 4.
30 Bodirsky and Johnson, "Decolonizing Diet."
31 Writing about US American "dietary assimilation," Pretty Gadhoke and Barrett P. Brenton make clear that "It is difficult to separate this type of dietary assimilation from the parallel strategies used to suppress expressions of their language, religion, and culture." Gadhoke and Brenton, "Erasure of Indigenous Food Memories and (Re)Imaginations," 208. For "milk colonialism," see Cohen, "Animal Colonialism," 36.
32 Luby, *Dammed*, 188.
33 Pratt, "The Advantages of Mingling Indians with Whites," 260.

34 Johnston, *Indian School Days*, 58.
35 Bodirsky and Johnson, "Decolonizing Diet."
36 Johnston, *Indian School Days*, 72–3.
37 Kelm, *Colonizing Bodies*, 71.
38 Truth and Reconciliation Commission of Canada, *Honouring the Truth, Reconciling for the Future*, 75.
39 Although he focuses on 1942–52, Mosby concludes that these experiments continued beyond this period. Mosby, "Administering Colonial Science." See also Walters, "A National Priority."
40 Miller, "Residential Schools in Canada."
41 Operated by the Roman Catholic church, the Kamloops Indian residential school opened in 1890 and closed in 1978. Enrolling up to five hundred students, it was Canada's largest. Austen, "Horrible History."
42 Simpson, *As We Have Always Done*, 43.
43 Basil, *Be My Guest*, 54.
44 Miller, "Residential Schools in Canada." Original reference: Department of Indian Affairs 1893, 174.
45 Lindeman, "Canada."
46 Hewitt, "Educating Priscilla," 12–13.
47 Johnston, *Indian School Days*, 19.
48 Ibid., 12.
49 Ibid., 87.
50 Ibid., 95.
51 Ibid., 96.
52 Ibid., 32.
53 Ibid., 32.
54 Ibid., 40.
55 Wagamese, *Indian Horse*, 60, 78.
56 Johnston, *Indian School Days*, 137.
57 Ibid.
58 Ibid.
59 Ibid., 142.
60 Ibid.
61 Ibid., 143.
62 Ibid.
63 Ibid., 144.
64 The genre has shifted from representing school experiences to its legacies. *Indian School Days* belongs to a literary sub-genre that Renate Eigenbrod has titled "residential school literature." Ranging from poetry and plays to memoirs and fiction, it recreates "the school experience through the

literary imagination." Writers create a record that combines historical experiences with literary craft. "Survivors express a sense of survivance," notes Eigenbrod, "which may also be understood in terms of agency and 'imaginative sovereignty.'" The first example is Cree author Jane Willis's *Geniesh* (1973), published during the so-called Indigenous Renaissance. Addressing this period, Eigenbrod says: "In tandem with the general marginalization of Native literature in English in the 1970s and 1980s, Indigenous survivors' stories were hardly noticed and not many were published." Eigenbrod, "'For the Child Taken, for the Parent Left Behind,'" 277, 278.

65 Truth and Reconciliation Commission of Canada, *Honouring the Truth, Reconciling for the Future*, 57.
66 Grey and Patel, "Food Sovereignty as Decolonization," 438.
67 They distinguish their use of the term from the work of other scholars: "This differs from Heldke's (2001, 78) 'culinary colonialism,' which refers to a gastronomic 'culture-hopping' accomplished through consuming the cuisines of primarily Third World cultures, 'motivated by a deep desire ... somehow to own an experience of an Exotic Other to make [oneself] more interesting.' It also differs from Mehta's (2009) 'culinary colonization,' in which the imposition of Western values renders (in her case, Caribbean) food cultures inferior, even hated, inspiring feelings of shame in cultural insiders." Grey and Newman, "Beyond Culinary Colonialism," 719.
68 Brotherton, "Object of the Week."
69 Baxley, "Sonny Assu."
70 Johnston, *Native Children and the Child Welfare System*.
71 Audrey Logan, interview by the author, 10 September 2016. In 2019 Logan published a zine about her gardening and food knowledge: *Out to Dry*.
72 Hill, "Seeds as Ancestors, Seeds as Archives," 98.
73 Anna Sigrithur, interview by the author, 10 September 2016.
74 Weso, *Good Seeds*, 19.
75 Roberts, "The Snipe Were Good and the Wine Not Bad," 58. One example is Samuel de Champlain's 1606 *L'Ordre de bon temps* (The Order of Good Cheer) in Port Royal, Nova Scotia, a gastronomic society whose "purpose was to prevent the mysterious 'land sickness' (scurvy), thought to be caused by ill-temper, idleness, and discontent." Powers and Stewart, *Northern Bounty*, 235.
76 Collingham, *The Hungry Empire*, xvii. Her book's title flags this point. Interestingly, this connects to Thrush's writing about culinary colonial

326  Notes to pages 46–8

encounters in the Northwest: "In fact, many Coast Salish language words for the newcomers are variations on a word that means 'hungry people' – xwenitem at the mouth of the Fraser River, slwa'-ne'htum among the Klallam who briefly thought Vancouver was a cannibal." Thrush, "Vancouver the Cannibal," 12.
77 Collingham, *The Hungry Empire*, xviii.
78 For the decimation of the bison, see Colpitts, *Pemmican Empire*.
79 Alfred and Corntassel, "Being Indigenous," 598.
80 A striking example is wine. Historian Erica Hannickel argues that in the nineteenth century because of wine's important standing in Western culture, as exemplified by ancient Greece and Rome, "grape culture was more explicitly expansionist than other agricultural products." Wine isn't just for drinking and toasting. In addition to the ingredients of grapes and time, wine contains ideas about where and how to live, about civilization and about conquest. And, in North America and elsewhere, about geographic expansion. Hannickel, *Empire of Vines*, 7.
81 Smith and Wiedman, "Fat Content of South Florida Indian Frybread," 582.
82 Arreak et al., *Niqiliurniq*, 102.
83 These images come from two festivals: the Flin Flon Trout Festival and the Trappers Festival. A mining town, Flin Flon straddles the Manitoba-Saskatchewan border and since the 1950s has been hosting an annual Trout Festival in July. Its activities have changed over time, but a 1955 program previews events such as the "Gold Rush Canoe Derby" and "Bathing Beauty Contest," a "Flour Packing Competition" (Robin Hood Flour has an advertisement in its program), and the derogatory and segregated "Squaw Races." This is the context in which this photograph must be interpreted. Similarly, the Northern Manitoba Trappers' Festival has organized itself under various names since 1916, with breaks in between.
84 Wolfman's "Wild blueberry bannock" calls for all-purpose flour, two teaspoons of sugar, salt, baking powder, wild blueberries (or dried, depending on the season), vegetable shortening (or butter), one egg, and 2 per cent milk.
85 In *Niqiliurniq* the authors suggest adding "flaked and cooked Arctic char and fresh herbs to the batter." Arreak et al., *Niqiliurniq*, 109. For an impressive inventory of just some types of bannock and frybread, see Phillipps and Skinner, "Bannock," 60.
86 Dana Vantrease writes about the FDPIR, the US government's Food Distribution Program on Indian Reservations. "The FDPIR foods are commonly called 'commodity foods' or 'commods' because the foods

come from government purchases of surplus agricultural commodities." Vantrease, "Commod Bods and Frybread Power," 55. Another example is the picture book by legal scholar and member of the Seminole Nation of Oklahoma Kevin Noble Maillard, *Fry Bread*.
87 Mihesuah, "Decolonizing Our Diets by Recovering Our Ancestors' Garden," 823.
88 Tompkins, *Racial Indigestion*, 71.
89 Edmund Searles writes how bannock became a staple for Inuit in Canada as of the 1950s. Searles, "Food and the Making of Modern Inuit Identities." Also, *Niqiliurniq* gives bannock as an example of how food traditions have changed based on the introduction of new ingredients, like flour. It instructs that melted blubber can be swapped for the oil. Arreak et al., *Niqiliurniq*, 1. Nutritionist Janell Smith and anthropologist Dennis Wiedman describe frybread as both a "relatively new addition to the Native diet" and "a universal food among American Indians, First Nations, Alaska Native and Inuit persons in North America." Smith and Wiedman, "Fat Content of South Florida Indian Frybread," 582. For frybread and "the impacts of the forces of assimilation," see Gadhoke and Brenton. "Erasure of Indigenous Food Memories and (Re)Imaginations." This history links to what Alfred Crosby called the "Columbian Exchange." See Crosby, *The Columbian Exchange*.
90 It appears twice in Margaret Fraser's "Canada's Breadbasket: Decades of Change," once in "Ontario Cooking: Cuisines in Transitions" by Dorothy Duncan, and then three times in Skye's "Traditional Cree and Iroquois Foods." Fraser, "Canada's Breadbasket," 52, 59. Duncan, "Ontario Cooking," 104. Skye, "Traditional Cree and Iroquois Foods," 113, 116, 117.
91 Bell, "Bannock and Canada's First Peoples."
92 Blackstock, "Bannock Awareness."
93 Thurton, "Bannock Recipe." CBC also reports that Indigenous peoples originally made bannock from a paste crafted from lichen. And ethnobiologist Nancy Turner names another pre-contact version made from cama bulbs. CBC Radio, "Bannock."
94 Ironically, Gabaccia points out that food rations usually excluded corn: "While domestic scientists saw corn-eating as a way to Americanize new immigrants, they seemed eager to wean Native Americans off cornmeal, and onto white wheat flour and baking powder breads." Gabaccia, *We Are What We Eat*, 130. For parallel examples in Australia and the US, also see Levi, *Food, Control and Resistance*.
95 Erdrich, *Original Local*, 96.
96 Dennis and Robin, "Healthy on Our Own Terms," 4.

97 Erdrich, *Original Local*, 96.
98 Tennant writes about how Oji-Cree Winnipeg-based artist KC Adams refuses to eat bannock. Adams eats a "hunter-gatherer" diet, which means no flour, sugar, milk, or lard/butter, and so no bannock, which she does not consider Indigenous. Her 2011 installation, *The Gift That Keeps on Giving*, which was exhibited in Meyers's *Best Before*, however, did consume these ingredients. Adams crafted ceramic pots that were balanced between rocks. The pots were unfired, permeable and porous, and more sensitive to the materials they held. Adams added milk, flour, sugar, salt, and lard, which all left their marks on the ceramic pots and thus became a metaphor for how colonial foods impact Indigenous bodies. Tennant, "Breaking Bread." Schellhaas also mentions this in "Gastronomical Indians," 196.
99 Mihesuah, "Indigenous Health Initiatives, Frybread, and the Marketing of Nontraditional 'Traditional' American Indian Foods," 46. Potawatomi chef Loretta Barrett Oden, who appears in the Conclusion of this book, agrees. "Think of Indian food," she writes, "and fry bread is often the first thing that comes to mind. But fry bread is *not* Indigenous, and it certainly isn't traditional." She continues: "A plate-sized disk of lard-fried white-flour dough is, in fact, delicious; yet its history is brutal, an example of profit over a people's health." She concludes that "fry bread is a food of survival and resilience" before sharing a recipe for "Loretta's cornmeal fry bread." Oden and Dooley, *Corn Dance*, 165.
100 Lewis, "Frybread Wars," 427.
101 Mihesuah, "Indigenous Health Initiatives, Frybread, and the Marketing of Nontraditional 'Traditional' American Indian Foods," 46.
102 Ibid.
103 Ibid., 48.
104 Ibid., 54.
105 Ibid., 57. Lewis, however, spells out the negative consequences of attempts to ban frybread in the name of health. Writing about "the great frybread war" in Detroit when the American Indian Health and Family Services attempted to ban it, Lewis calls this "yet another chipping away at Native identity and Native symbols of strength by the US federal government and the larger settler-colonial society." Lewis, "Frybread Wars," 429.
106 Cyr and Slater, "Honouring the Grandmothers through (Re)membering, (Re)learning, and (Re)vitalizing Métis Traditional Foods and Protocols," 55.
107 Lewis, "Frybread Wars," Dennis Kelly conjures frybread in what he calls "the semiotics of resistance." He ends his essay with "For What

It's Worth: My Frybread Recipe." It requires six steps. The penultimate is: "Fry in the oil one at a time until golden brown, flipping once halfway through." And the last: "Think about the resilience of American Indians and First Nations people and what they have endured to keep their traditions alive." Kelley, "The Semiotics of Resistance," 207.
108 Chrystos, "Really Delicious Fry Bread," 9. For "commods" as "the basis of jokes, songs, and other cultural expressions," see Vantrease, "Commod Bods and Frybread Power," 64.
109 The Anglican Church operated this school from 1873 to 1970.
110 Myers, "Straining and Absorbing."
111 Wilson-Sanchez, "Exhibition Review," 357.
112 Ibid., 358.
113 Berton, *The National Dream*, 7.
114 Ibid., 6.
115 Ibid.
116 Daschuk, *Clearing the Plains*, xxi.
117 Ibid.
118 Robin, "Protecting Indigenous Women and Two-Spirit Peoples as Food System Revitalization." See also McCallum, "Starvation, Experimentation, Segregation, and Trauma," 98.
119 Collingham, *The Hungry Empire*, 223. However, it was only in 1896 that growing wheat for Britain became economically viable. Ibid. See also Müller, "Still Feeding the World?"
120 Although its reign was short-lived, when the Royal York Hotel opened in 1929 it was the tallest building in the British Empire until 1931. Today a poster in the lobby remembers this history.
121 For the history of CPR dining cars, see Viaud, "Dining Railway-Style in North America." The Canadian Railway Museum published this cookbook, which contains ninety recipes from Canada's three major railway companies: Canadian Pacific Railway, CN, and VIA Rail Canada.
122 Kvill, "Ordering off Western Canada's Menu," 58. Kvill addresses the difficulties in studying CPR menus: "There do not appear to be any menus surviving or accessible from CPR dining cars prior to the 1910s. Additionally, records related to employees of the CPR are not available to the public, which makes it impossible to determine who the chefs for the dining cars were." Ibid., 74. She analyses a different set of menus. For a discussion of one from circa the 1920s that uses Indigenous imagery to attract tourists, see her Chapter 4, "The CPR and the Creation of a Western Canadian Identity," 59–83. Kvill also points out

that CPR menus in the 1920s represent a moment in which Canada was trying to craft a separate identity from that of Imperial Britain. Ibid., 41. And Corser mentions the CPR's "colonist cars" that transported millions of immigrants across Canada between the 1880s and 1930s. Corser, "Sockeye Salmon and Saskatoon Pie," 168–9.
123 As Hunt and Starblanket spell out, "new settler identities have a tendency to 'borrow' Indigenous motifs and symbols for the creation of their own cultural identity," in what Hunt terms "'settler replacement narratives' that simultaneously appropriate symbols of Indigeneity while disavowing Indigenous peoples' active social and political existences and, indeed, our futures." Hunt and Starblanket, *Storying Violence*, 54–5.
124 Spang, *The Invention of the Restaurant*, 192–3.
125 Cho, *Eating Chinese*, 57.
126 Canadian Pacific Railway Menu, "Before the Canadian Pacific," Box 47, Menus, Folder 47, Ephemera Collection, Thomas Fisher Rare Books Library, Toronto, Ontario, Canada. Despite the generous efforts of Exporail, the Canadian Railway Museum, I unfortunately did not receive permission from the Canadian Pacific Kansas City railroad company to include images of these menus.
127 I base this on the folder in which I found the menu in the archives.
128 Francis, *The Imaginary Indian*, 3.
129 Ibid., 7.
130 This romantic coupling is an example of "the ecological Indian," a term popularized by Shepard Krech III's book of the same name. Although Vine Deloria considered this book "anti-Indian," Kim TallBear uses the book to rethink academic assumptions of the past. Krech, *The Ecological Indian*. TallBear, "Shepard Krech's *The Ecological Indian*."
131 For examples of the Canadian National Railways' Colonization Department, see Hunt and Starblanket, *Storying Violence*, 21–9.
132 Ibid., 24.
133 Experimental farms supplied much of the produce for railway dining cars. And by 1914, this meant produce for up to six thousand meals a day aboard the CPR. Corser, "Sockeye Salmon and Saskatoon Pie," 174, 172–3.
134 Canadian Pacific Railway Menu, "An Indian Chief," 1943, Box 47, Menus. Folder 16, Ephemera Collection, Thomas Fisher Rare Books Library, Toronto, Ontario, Canada.
135 Bell, "Voyageur Re-presentations and Complications," 100.
136 Ibid., 101. Bell references Tobin, *Picturing Imperial Power*, 1.

137 Stevens, "Tomahawk," 485.
138 Wolfe, "Settler Colonialism and the Elimination of the Native," 389.
139 Parenteau, "Care, Control and Supervision," 28.
140 Ibid., 29.
141 "The Royal York Hotel's August 20, 1956 menu," Box 114. Folder 11, Ephemera Collection, Thomas Fisher Rare Books Library, Toronto, Ontario, Canada. The Royal York Hotel, regrettably, did not grant me permission to include an image of this menu. Their Marketing Department was concerned about the "messaging" it would communicate. The absence of this image, I believe, speaks louder than its presence would, illustrating that many Canadian institutions are still hesitant about acknowledging – not to mention atoning for – their colonial pasts and presents. For more about the Toronto Purchase's ongoing cultural relevance, see A Treaty Guide for Torontonians, "By These Presents: 'Purchasing' Toronto," "an absurdist examination of the Toronto 'Purchase'" that blends dance, puppetry, and humour into a thirty-minute video originally commissioned by the Toronto Biennale of Art in 2019.
142 Toronto comes from the Mohawk *Tkaronto*, meaning "where there are trees standing in the water." Careless, "Toronto."
143 Canadian Pacific Railway Menu, "Canadian Pacific Dining Car Service. February 1959 – Breakfast," Box 114, Folder 4, Ephemera Collection, Thomas Fisher Rare Books Library, Toronto, Ontario, Canada.
144 "Squaw" is a derogatory term for Indigenous women. See Mihesuah, *So You Want to Write about American Indians?*, 18. For the equally offensive "squaw man," see Carter, *Capturing Women*, 184.
145 Drees, "'Indians' Bygone Past," 8. However, the festival became annual only in 1912. Mason, "The Banff Indian Days Tourism Festival," 79.
146 Drees, "'Indians' Bygone Past," 7.
147 Mason, "The Banff Indian Days Tourism Festival," 79.
148 Ibid., 83.
149 As early as 1913 organizers banned participants dressed in modern attire from joining the parade. Ibid., 84.
150 Drees, "'Indians' Bygone Past," 8.
151 Mason, "The Banff Indian Days Tourism Festival," 79.
152 Drees, "'Indians' Bygone Past," 4–6.
153 Ibid., 13.
154 Ibid. A similar dynamic appears in Thomas King's novel *Green Grass, Running Water*. In the fictional town of Blossom, Alberta, one plot revolves around The Dead Dog Café. King later adapted this storyline for a CBC

332  Notes to pages 63–71

Radio show. King describes the café in the novel's dialogue: "'Nice to have a real Indian restaurant in town.' People come from all over the world to eat at the Dead Dog Café. 'She sells hamburger and tells everyone that it's dog meat.' Germany, Japan, Russia, Italy, Brazil, England, France, Toronto. 'Everybody comes to the Dead Dog.' The Blackfoot didn't eat dog. 'It's for tourists.'" King, *Green Grass, Running Water*, 59.
155 Daschuk, *Clearing the Plains*, xxi.
156 Drees, "Indians' Bygone Past," 20.

## 2. From Trains to Tundra

1 The year 1967 is significant for another reason. On 30 September, the Great Canadian Oil Sands opened their facility north of Fort McMurray, Alberta. For resource extractivism and settler colonialism see Preston, "Racial Extractivism."
2 "Restaurants Review Expo 67, An official publication," 1, 1967, RG71-G, R869, Volume/box 42, file ARC-71/42/5, Library and Archives Canada, Ottawa, Ontario, Canada.
3 Ibid., 1.
4 Ibid., 5.
5 Mills, "Missing Teeth, and Relatives."
6 "Restaurants Review Expo 67," 22. Surprisingly, Peyton's *Where We Ate* overlooks La Toundra but features another Expo 67 restaurant: the Russian Pavilion's Moskva.
7 "Menu of La Toundra Restaurant, Canada pavilion, Expo 67," 1967, P573/Do2, M2004.156.2 C285 / B1.1, Box 3, Fonds Gilberte Christin de Cardaillac, McCord Museum, Montreal, Canada.
8 Kenneally also discusses the dishes. She focuses on their relationship to universal expositions, and Expo 67's emphasis on modernism. My aim here differs: it is to show how Expo 67 appropriates Indigenous ingredients and how this continues the history of the erasure and colonization of Indigenous foodways. Kenneally, "The Cuisine of the Tundra."
9 Ibid., 289.
10 It is not clear who illustrated the menu.
11 "Restaurants Review Expo 67," 20.
12 Ibid., 22.
13 *Gazette*, "La Toundra Advertisement," 17 May 1967.
14 "Restaurants Review Expo 67," 22.
15 Kenneally "The Cuisine of the Tundra," 297.
16 Ibid., 289.

17 Ibid.
18 Ibid., 297.
19 "Restaurants Review Expo 67," 1.
20 Small, "Fiddleheads."
21 Freedman, *Ten Restaurants That Changed America*, 343.
22 Ibid., 341.
23 Ibid., 326.
24 Ibid., 343.
25 "Restaurants Review Expo 67," 1.
26 The Ontario Pavilion housed five restaurants: Birch Room, Cartwright Lounge, Yorkville, The Clearing, and International Café. The fine-dining Birch Room served one dish with an obvious Indigenous reference: "Algonquin Saddle of Venison 'Windsor' with Celery and Chestnuts." "Restaurants Review Expo 67," 24.
27 Kenneally, "The Cuisine of the Tundra," 299. For the culinary history of whale meat in the United States, see Shoemaker, "Whale Meat in American History." Previously there were "two novel attempts to normalize whale meat in the American diet" in the twentieth century. The first was a reaction to fears of wartime food shortages during the First World War and the second was the promotion of "Capt. Seth's Frozen Tenderloin Norwegian Whale Steak," among other whale products, in the 1950s. Shoemaker, "Whale Meat in American History," 280–2.
28 La Toundra spelled it muktuk, but other spellings include maktaaq and maktak.
29 "Restaurants Review Expo 67," 20.
30 Ibid., 24.
31 Kenneally, "The Greatest Dining Extravaganza in Canada's History," 31.
32 "La Toundra Cocktail Menu, Canada Expo67," Item 0224, Collection MSG 1269 – Menu Collection, McGill Archival Collections.
33 *Gazette*, "New Ideas Displayed at Lounge."
34 *Gazette*, "Gourmet Guide."
35 *Gazette*, "Indian Room Advertisement."
36 "Indian Room Menu," P573/Do2, C285/B1,1, Menus, Restaurants montréalais (1951–), Fonds Gilberte Christin de Cardaillac, McCord Museum, Montreal.
37 Mills, "Missing Teeth, and Relatives," 39.
38 Kenneally, "The Greatest Dining Extravaganza in Canada's History," 31. For pictures of the Queen's visit to Expo 67 (which unfortunately do not include any of her dining at La Toundra), see "Queen Elizabeth II," Expo 67: A Virtual Experience, Library and Archives Canada.

39 Cronon, *Changes in the Land*, 178.
40 Ibid., 137.
41 Just because a food came from elsewhere doesn't mean that it does not become important. Take for example Mihesuah's writing about pigs, which "were brought to the Southeast by Hernando de Soto when he landed at the Atlantic Coast of Florida in 1539. But similar to Apache groups, who have stories that say horses were always a part of those cultures, and Navajos, who have similar stories about sheep, Chahtas have stories that imply pigs and hogs were always with them. The story tells of how important the animals and food sources quickly became to the tribes." Mihesuah, "Decolonizing Our Diets by Recovering Our Ancestors' Garden," 814.
42 "Restaurants Review Expo 67," 20.
43 Wilmshurst, "How to Eat Like a Canadian."
44 The 1960s was also a time when Canada asserted a culinary identity in cookbooks. See Kenneally, "There *Is* a Canadian Cuisine, and It Is Unique in the World."
45 Myers, "Best Before," 3.
46 Ibid.
47 Ibid., 5–6.
48 Ibid., 2.
49 Ibid., 5.
50 Ibid., 6–7. Cyr and Slater make a similar point about imaginations of Indigenous foodways, writing: "The rhetoric surrounding *traditional foods*, while important, is flawed. The literature suggests that traditional foods are solely cultivated from the land, which fails to acknowledge food and recipes that have evolved into traditional meals throughout generations, mainly with the incorporation of bartered or purchased ingredients." Cyr and Slater, "Honouring the Grandmothers through (Re)membering, (Re)learning, and (Re)vitalizing Métis Traditional Foods and Protocols," 66 For more about the necessity of approaching the term tradition with caution see Cidro et al., "First Foods as Indigenous Food Sovereignty," 30.
51 For an overview of this history, see Royal Commission on Aboriginal Peoples, *The High Arctic Relocation*, and Grant, *"Errors Exposed."*
52 Ray, *The Ethnic Restaurateur*, 194. He writes: "The use of the term 'ethnic restaurant' peaked in the 1970s, slowly declining into the 2000s, for which *The New York Times* index identifies only eleven records in 2010, and none at all in 2013. It appears that the era of 'ethnicity' as a catch-all category between race and nation may be ending among high-status

journalists, which is precisely the time to take a look back and its half-century-long career in defining the American relationship to gustatory difference." Ibid., 73.
53 hooks, "Eating the Other."
54 Long, "Culinary Tourism," 20–1.
55 Ray, "Taste, Toil and Ethnicity," 112.
56 A powerful example of this is Susan Orlean's 1996 *New Yorker* article "The Homesick Restaurant" about Centro Vasco in Miami's Little Havana. She writes, "there might have been no other place in the world so layered with different people's pinings – no other place where you have had a Basque dinner in a restaurant from Havana in a Cuban neighbourhood of a city in Florida in a dining room decorated with yodeling hikers and little deer." The article unfolds in two parts, the first in Centro Vasco in Miami's Little Havana and the second in Centro Vasco in Havana, where only the writer is able to travel, not the regulars or the restaurateur. As Orlean describes, "There has never been anything in my life that I couldn't go back to if I really wanted to," unlike those that frequent this Little Havana eatery. Orlean, "The Homesick Restaurant," 286, 288. For food and migration see, for example, Diner, *Hungering for America*.
57 Lu and Fine, "The Presentation of Ethnic Authenticity," 548. See also Heldke, *Exotic Appetites*, xvi.
58 Siu, "Chino Latino Restaurants," 162.
59 Zelinsky, "The Roving Palate," 54. But an ethnic restaurant does not necessarily sell "ethnic" food. See Kuh, *The Last Days of Haute Cuisine*, 178–9, and Cho, *Eating Chinese*.
60 Weso, *Good Seeds*, 93.
61 Cho, *Eating Chinese*, 51.
62 Ibid.
63 King, *The Inconvenient Indian*, xii.
64 Ibid., 61.
65 Deloria, *Custer Died for Your Sins*, 2.
66 King, *The Inconvenient Indian*, 62.
67 Ibid.
68 Wolfe, *Settler Colonialism and the Transformation of Anthropology*, 163.
69 King, *The Inconvenient Indian*, 65. The Land O' Lakes butter logo is one of King's "favourite Dead Indian products." Founded in 1921, this Minnesota-based Dairy Co-op cast an "Indian Maiden in a buckskin dress on her knees holding a box of butter at bosom level" as its corporate identity. However, in 2020, it quietly redesigned its label, leaving the background of bushy trees and lake water, and removing

336   Notes to pages 84–8

the "Indian Maiden." Ibid., 57. This is one example of a racist marketing campaign. Another is Aunt Jemima, which Quaker Oats decided to retire in June 2020 – after 131 years – in light of the Black Lives Matter movement.
70   Ibid., 65.
71   Ibid., 68. King cites the 2006 census, which estimated the number of Indigenous people to be 1.2 million. Ten years later, the 2016 census reported a population of 1,673,785. Statistics Canada, "2016 Census Topic: Aboriginal Peoples." This is, however, only an estimate. Nonetheless, the Indigenous population is growing. According to Statistics Canada, the growth rate between 2006 and 2016 of the Indigenous population was "more than four times the growth rate of the non-Aboriginal population over the same period." Statistics Canada, "Aboriginal Peoples in Canada."
72   Stevenson and Troupe, "From Kitchen Tables to Formal Organization," 309.
73   Nickel, *Assembling Unity*, 51.
74   Ibid., 47.
75   King, *The Inconvenient Indian*, 69.
76   Ibid., 65.

## 3. Restaurants and Representation

1   City of Vancouver, "First Nations Art and Totem Poles."
2   Thorni, "Tomahawk Barbecue Evolves with the Times." The Tomahawk also makes Peyton's list of the 150 restaurants that have shaped how, what, and where Canadians eat. Peyton, *Where We Ate*, 84.
3   Moore, "Dining."
4   Ibid.
5   Tomahawk Restaurant, "Tomahawk History."
6   Ibid.
7   In dialogue with André Malraux's conviction that "art" requires "metamorphosis" to become "art," anthropologist Shelly Errington distinguishes between *"art by appropriation* (rather than by metamorphosis) and *art by intention*." As she spells out: "Art by intention was made *as* art, created in contexts that had a concept of art approximating what we now hold: paradigmatically, the kinds of objects created in the Italian renaissance as art. Art by appropriation consists of the diverse objects that became 'art' with the founding of public art museums at the end of the 18th century." Errington, "What Became Authentic Primitive Art?" 202–3.

8 Stevens, "Tomahawk," 481.
9 Ibid.
10 Ibid.
11 *OhMore Story*, "91 Years of Breakfast with the Community at the Tomahawk."
12 Tomahawk Restaurant, "The Legendary Tomahawk Menu."
13 Ibid.
14 O'Higgins, "On the Trail of the Best Burgers for Your Buck."
15 *OhMore Story*, "91 Years of Breakfast with the Community at the Tomahawk."
16 Thorni, "Tomahawk Barbecue Evolves with the Times."
17 *OhMore Story*, "91 Years of Breakfast with the Community at the Tomahawk."
18 Fischer, *Cattle Colonialism*, 5–6.
19 As Kelm writes: "Milk drinking was a central part of the residential school health education programs. But the First Nations have almost always treated drinking cow's milk with disdain. Glorian Cranmeer Webster remembers being told not to feed her children cow's milk. The elder who advised her said, 'Have you ever looked at cows, they are really stupid animals and your baby will be like that if you feed it cow's milk.' There is more to this attitude, of course, than a prejudice against cows; many Aboriginal people simply cannot digest cow's milk, and it causes them extreme discomfort. Researchers have found that Aboriginal people on the northwest coasts show a high rate of lactase deficiency and consequent lactose intolerance ... among thirty healthy west coast Aboriginal people, 63.3 percent were lactose intolerant. For First Nations people, then, milk was hardly the miracle food of contemporary Euro-Canadian public health tracts." Kelm, *Colonizing Bodies*, 37. For colonial control and health, also see Lux, *Medicine That Walks*.
20 Fischer, *Cattle Colonialism*, 8. For the United States, see also Specht, *Red Meat Republic*.
21 For the potlatch ban, see Cole and Chaikin, *An Iron Hand upon the People*.
22 Dagenais, "THE DISH."
23 Ibid.
24 *Scout Vancouver*, "Tomahawk."
25 Brant, "Cultural Appropriation of Indigenous Peoples in Canada."
26 Ibid.
27 Ray discusses this in relation to "culinary misappropriation," which is his term for what Williams-Forson calls "culinary malpractice" as exemplified by "the homogenization of black taste into fried chicken and black-eyed peas" in the United States. He compares this to

Indigenous food cultures. "In contrast, the American attitude toward Native American culinary culture is not misappropriation but forced assimilation via land colonization, physical displacement, and the imposition of a war-refugee diet of cheap carbohydrates (a pattern that can be found in other settler-colonial cultures, such as Australia, New Zealand, etc.)." Ray, "Culinary Difference Makes a Difference," 153–4.

28 Poke is a Hawaiian dish consisting of cubes of raw fish seasoned with seaweed, salt, and ground kukui nut. On the US mainland, poke refers to a sort of sushi bowl: rice or grains topped with raw fish (or tofu), avocado, mango, or crispy onions and various sauces, like white peach and wasabi dressing. In other words, poke means something else on the mainland than it does in Hawaii.

29 Ho, "The Chicago Poke Chain That Tried to Stop Hawaiian Businesses from Using the Word 'Aloha.'"

30 *Oxford Dictionaries*, s.v. "authentic."

31 For example, anthropologist David Sutton writes: "Each time, literally each day that one cooks, one sets out to make *something*. In doing so, that category, moussaka, for example, *is put at risk* as a multiple of contingencies, material resistances, and potential improvisations come into play in determining the eventual outcome of the dish." Sutton, "Cooking in Theory," 90.

32 See Ragavan, "Authenticity in Food," and Giuffrida, "Venice Bans Kebab Shops to 'Preserve Decorum and Traditions' of City."

33 Johnston and Baumann, *Foodies*, 69–70.

34 Ibid., 70.

35 Ibid., 197.

36 Ku, *Dubious Gastronomy*, 6.

37 Ibid., 4.

38 Bendix, "Diverging Paths in the Scientific Search for Authenticity," 103.

39 Literary scholar Meredith E. Abarca prefers the word "original" over authentic. After surveying the dangers of essentialism and cultural hijacking, she argues: "the word original diminishes the possibility for encompassing colonizing attitudes, and therefore for operating under stereotypes." She asserts that "original underwrites the power relations implicit in 'authentic' on at least two accounts": first, it allows for those physically preparing a recipe to define it, and, second, "it fosters a dialogue to exchange experiences without placing them in a hierarchy paradigm that measures this value." Abarca, "Authentic or Not, It's Original," 19–20.

40 David Wolfman, interview by the author, 6 September 2016.

41 Wolfman and Finn, *Cooking with the Wolfman*, 1. Since 1994 he has been a Chef Professor at Toronto's George Brown College and from 1999 to 2012 he starred in eight seasons of "Cooking with the Wolfman" on the Aboriginal Peoples Television Network (APTN).
42 Food Trucks, "You Are Welcome Food Truck."
43 Luo and Stark, "Only the Bad Die Young."
44 Ibid.
45 But food trucks have also become popular sui generis. See Siu, "Twenty-First Century Food Trucks."
46 The Canadian Imperial Bank of Commerce (CIBC) was the Pan Am Game's sponsor. The Mississaugas, however, had received sponsorship from the Bank of Montreal (BMO) and had to remove their sign. They also experienced restrictions regarding placing their logo on printed material.
47 See Baloy, "Our Home(s) and/on Native Land," and Sidsworth, "Aboriginal Participation in the Vancouver/Whistler 2010 Olympic Games."
48 One year after Wolfman handed out "Blueberry bannock" and "Nish kabobs" while Toronto hosted the Pan Am Games, the Toronto District School Board – Canada's largest and North America's fourth largest – took a step in acknowledging that the city is on treaty land. It added a land acknowledgment to school morning announcements. Martin, "TDSB Schools Now Play Daily Tribute to Indigenous Lands They're Built On." However, a land acknowledgment is far from straightforward. Jesse Thistle, a Métis-Cree historian, believes that Toronto's acknowledgment should not include the Métis. Although historically Métis did live here, Toronto was never their homeland. Thistle believes that to suggest otherwise "disempowers the Haudenosaunee or the Anishinaabe, who do have a rightful claim." Jesse Thistle quoted in Marche, "Canada's Impossible Acknowledgement."
49 The You Are Welcome Food Truck is just one example of a project that uses food to reconnect to Indigenous territory. Another was initiated by Kerry Muswagon, the cultural awareness teacher in Cross Lake, Manitoba, a Cree Nation that has struggled with an epidemic of youth suicide, who took his students goose hunting in an effort to reunite them with their culture and, thus, raise their spirits and confidence. And another example from Manitoba is "Food is our language – Reconnecting Youth to Culture through Indigenous Food Sovereignty: An exploration into the role of youth engaging in traditional food and cultural skills impacts cultural identity & self esteem" – led by Jaime Cidro,

Department of Anthropology at the University of Winnipeg, Neechi Commons, and Garden City Collegiate, started in 2013.
50 Frank, *Seed to Plate, Soil to Sky*, 70.
51 For Korean tacos and cultural hybridity see Kinney, "Riding Shotgun with an LA Son."
52 Goldstein, *Inside the California Food Revolution*, 23.
53 Ibid., 316.
54 Ibid.
55 Morris, "The Politics of Palatability," 26.
56 Siu, "Twenty-First Century Food Trucks," 243.
57 Kramer, "Introduction," 23.
58 Melasniemi and Tiravanija, *Bastard Cookbook*, 40.
59 Ibid.
60 They title their Introduction "Identity as Exchange." Capatti and Montanari, *Italian Cuisine*.
61 A comparable example is found in literary scholar Courtney Thorsson's summary: "radical Black culinary writing refuses the metaphor of melting pot (ingredients blend beyond recognition) in favor of gumbo (each ingredient is distinct)." Nettles-Barcelón et al., "Black Women's Food Work as Critical Space," 44.
62 Newman, *Speaking in Cod Tongues*, 83.
63 Grey and Newman, "Beyond Culinary Colonialism," 717.
64 Gabaccia, *We Are What We Eat*, 5.
65 In 2016, 46.1 per cent of Toronto's population was foreign-born. Ontario Ministry of Finance, "2016 Census Highlights." And 37.4 per cent of all immigrants to Canada live in Toronto. Statistics Canada, "Immigration and Ethnocultural Diversity in Canada."
66 Toronto also hosts a few restaurants called The Hungry Thai.
67 Rasta Pasta, "Menu."
68 Wolfman and Finn, *Cooking with the Wolfman*, 4.
69 For decolonizing foodways, see Calvo and Esquibel, *Decolonize Your Diet*.
70 Greer, "Thanksgiving Favourites Trace Origins to First Nations Foods."
71 Bain, "First Nations Food Truck Welcomes Pan Am Patrons."
72 Armstrong, "Emphasize People Not Spice, Culinary Arts Professor Tells Young Chefs."
73 Glasner, "From Seal Tartare to Bison on a Bun, Indigenous Chefs Are Reclaiming Their Heritage One Plate at a Time." Tennant stages a similar opening in "*Terra Nullius* on the Plate." She writes: "On any given night in a Canadian city, it is possible to eat at restaurants offering a wide variety of cuisines – from Moroccan to Vietnamese, from French

to Sri Lankan. However, it is almost impossible to go to a restaurant that serves Indigenous cuisines." Tennant, *"Terra Nullius* on the Plate," 77. Tennant also argues that "The invisibility of Indigenous cuisines in Canada's restaurant landscape ... can be understood as a continuation of a history of erasure, appropriation, and colonial blindness." This "colonial blindness" is "informed by concepts like *terra nullius* (or 'empty land')." Ibid., 78. Her chapter makes an important contribution to drawing attention to how few Indigenous restaurants there are in Canada. My argument here, however, differs. As opposed to arguing that the invisibility of Indigenous restaurants is a continuation of colonial history, I aim to add texture to this history by charting how Indigenous restaurants have changed over time and to spotlight these restaurants as sites of resurgence.

74 Ibid.
75 For Kekuli Cafe's menu, see Schellhaas, "Gastronomical Indians."
76 Glasner, "From Seal Tartare to Bison on a Bun."
77 Allan, "Guide to Winnipeg Could Become Local Best-Seller."
78 Ibid.
79 Ibid.
80 Ibid. Although this article is not concerned with sketching out the history of "hot-rock or stone-boiling," Annie Turner outlines the method: "This technique involved gathering the rocks found in creeks or in river beds that would not crack when exposed to tremendous heat. Rocks would be heated by placing them in the hot embers of the fire. They would then be removed from the fire using wooden tongs, rinsed of grit and ashes, and placed into cooking vessels that were filled with water. This process of heating the rocks and placing them in the container would be repeated until the water boiled and the food cooked." Turner, "Delicious Resistance, Sweet Persistence," 69.
81 Simmel, "The Sociology of the Meal," 346.
82 From the layout, typeface, and size, at the beginning of the nineteenth century menus resembled newspapers and, as the historian Rebecca Spang argues, became their own genre of literary text. Because menus predate the 1830s and 1880s print-technology revolution, producing them was expensive. Restaurants printed them in large quantities and listed everything they might serve – a welter of edible possibilities. Spang, *The Invention of the Restaurant*, 185, 189.
83 Kuh, *The Last Days of Haute Cuisine*, 27. See also Gora, "Today's Special."
84 Portnoy and Pilcher, "Roy Choi, Ricardo Zárate, and Pacific Fusion Cuisine in Los Angeles," 150.

85 His restaurants earned more than thirty Michelin stars over the course of his career and the guide Gault Millau crowned him "Chef of the Century" in 1989. Gopnik, "What Joël Robuchon Meant for French Cooking."
86 Ibid.
87 Freedman, *Ten Restaurants That Changed America*, xxxiv.
88 For French cuisine's history and its former global dominance, see Steinberger, *Au Revoir to All That*.
89 Waters, *Chez Panisse Menu Cookbook*, x.
90 Guthman, "Fast Food/Organic Food," 48.
91 Freedman, *Ten Restaurants that Changed America*, 323. See also Kuh, *The Last Days of Haute Cuisine*.
92 Guthman, "Fast Food/Organic Food," 52.
93 Kuh, *The Last Days of Haute Cuisine*, 169.
94 Ibid.
95 Noma has reinvented itself several times, which has included relocating to cities such as Tulum and Kyoto. On 9 January 2023, the *New York Times* broke the news that it was closing for regular service at the end of 2024. But a closure is not an ending. Its next life will be as a full-time laboratory that supplies its online shop, Noma Projects, and an occasional host for pop-ups. Nonetheless this announcement – alongside Redzepi's verdict that fine dining is "unsustainable" – landed with a thud in the food media. And its timing did not go unnoticed. Only a couple of months prior, Noma had just started paying its interns, which reveals how the math behind fine dining relies on unpaid labour. Moskin, "Noma, Rated the World's Best Restaurant, Is Closing Its Doors."
96 Skyum-Nielsen, "The Perfect Storm," 11.
97 Mares and Peña, "Environmental and Food Justice," 198. Also, what they call "AlterNative" refers to "the sense of the deeply rooted practices of Native peoples that *alter* and challenge the dominant food system." 201. See also O'Brien and Wogahn, "Bringing a Berry Back from the Land of the Dead."
98 Powers and Stewart, *Northern Bounty*, xi.
99 Eve Johnson, "Historical Influences on West Coast Cooking," in Powers and Stewart, *Northern Bounty*, 10.
100 Ibid., 12.
101 Newman, *Speaking in Cod Tongues*, 9.
102 Caira, "The Evolution of Canadian Cuisine in Restaurants," 135.
103 Cho, *Eating Chinese*.

104 Located on the fifty-fourth floor of the Toronto Dominion Centre, it describes itself as being "inspired by Canada's raw, rich land." Canoe, "About."
105 Caira, "The Evolution of Canadian Cuisine in Restaurants," 135.
106 Turner, Philip, and Turner, "Traditional Native Plant Foods in Contemporary Cuisine in British Columbia."
107 Gilbride, "Eat Canadian."
108 Ibid.
109 Ibid.
110 Ibid.
111 Ibid.
112 The editors of *Edible Histories, Cultural Politics* organize the first part around contact zones: "Cultural Exchanges and Cuisines in the Contact Zone." Iacovetta, Korinek, and Epp, *Edible Histories, Cultural Politics*, 29–82.
113 Pratt, "Arts of the Contact Zone," 33.
114 Anthropologist James Clifford applies Pratt's "contact zones" to museums, writing, "The organizing structure of the museum-as-collection functions like Pratt's frontier. A center and periphery are assumed: the center a point of gathering, the periphery an area of discovery." Clifford, *Routes*, 192–3.
115 Spang, *The Invention of the Restaurant*, 52.
116 *Dictionnaire de L'Académie Française*, n.p.
117 Government of Canada, "Truth and Reconciliation Commission of Canada: Official Mandate," Schedule N of the Settlement Agreement.
118 Ibid.
119 Ibid.
120 CBC News, "Truth and Reconciliation Chair Says Final Report Marks Start of 'New Era.'"
121 Simpson, *As We Have Always Done*, 46.
122 Belcourt, "Political Depression in a Time of Reconciliation."
123 Tuck and Yang, "Decolonization Is Not a Metaphor," 35.
124 Corntassel, "Re-envisioning Resurgence," 91–2.
125 Truth and Reconciliation Commission of Canada, *Honouring the Truth, Reconciling for the Future*, 2.
126 Corntassel, "Re-envisioning Resurgence," 93.
127 *Oxford Dictionaries*, s.v. "reconcile."
128 The Dominion of Canada's Department of Indian Affairs annual report for 1894 mentions a restaurant at Onion Lake Agency, Saskatchewan. "There is a restaurant where the Indians take their meals when working at the mill or when visiting the agency." Library and Archives Canada,

"Dominion of Canada Annual Report of the Department of Indian Affairs for the Year Ended 30th June 1894," 197.
129 For the Kekuli Cafe, see Mihesuah, "Indigenous Health Initiatives, Frybread, and the Marketing of Nontraditional 'Traditional' American Indian Foods," 59; and Schellhaas, "Gastronomical Indians." Also, caterer Hiawatha Osawamick, from Wiikwemkoong Unceded Territory, had plans to open the first Indigenous restaurant in Sudbury in 2020, which local media had previewed in 2019, but because of the COVID-19 pandemic her "restaurant never got to see the light of day." Hiawatha's, Facebook, 26 September 2020. Rutherford, "Sudbury to Get New Restaurant Serving Indigenous Cuisine."

## 4. An Edible Exhibition

1 City of Vancouver Archives, "Muckamuck Restaurant: Northwest Coast Native Indian food." Pamphlet collection. AM1519– : 2011–045.1 Box: 632–A–02. Vancouver, British Columbia, Canada.
2 Some newspapers report that the restaurant opened in 1972, but others, as well as Nicol, state that it was in 1971. Nicol, "Unions Aren't Native." Schellhaas incorrectly identifies the Muckamuck as having opened in 1974. Schellhaas, "Gastronomical Indians," 190. Schellhaas, *First Nations Cuisines*, 217. Schellhaas, "Changing Tides," 69.
3 Nicol, "Unions Aren't Native," 236. Nicol spells Doug Chrismas's last name with a *t*, as do some articles. However, according to the United States Bankruptcy Court, it is spelled without the *t*.
4 *Ottawa Journal*, "Muck-a-Muck House Serves 'Just Plain Good Food.'" Other newspapers also ran this article: *Brandon Sun*, "Muck-a-Muck House Now a Work of Culinary Art"; and *Leader-Post*, "Gallery Patrons Sample Authentic Indian Foods."
5 *Ottawa Journal*, "Muck-a-Muck House Serves 'Just Plain Good Food.'"
6 Ibid.
7 Ibid.
8 It is not clear when the hyphens and word house disappeared.
9 *Ottawa Citizen*, "Come to the Muckamuck." The *Gazette* and the *Calgary Herald* published the same article.
10 Douglas James Chrismas was born in Vancouver in 1944. Having dropped out of high school, at the age of sixteen he opened a frame shop. One year later, in 1961, he bought and took over the New Design Gallery, renaming it the Ace. McKenna, "The Ace Is Wild." The artist Douglas Coupland describes Chrismas as a "mild-looking Canadian art dealer." Coupland, "Ace in the Hole," 43.

11 Macrae, "Warhol."
12 Blackbridge, "The Chrismas Connection."
13 Powell and Sullivan, "Chinook Wawa."
14 McCook, "Eat Your Oolichan – And Enjoy It." The *Nanaimo Daily Press* published McCook's article, but under the title "Muck-a-Muck Truly Unique" (6F). This article also ran in the 4 May 1975 issue of *Statesman Journal* (22), but with a new opening paragraph and without the author's name. It is attributed to Lillie Madsen, *Statesman* travel editor. It was also published on 15 June 1975 in the *Times Herald* (63) without an author and with the title "Muck-a-Muck Indian Restaurant a Real Treat."
15 *Oxford Dictionaries*, s.v. "muckamuck."
16 Powell and Sullivan, "Chinook Wawa."
17 *Ottawa Journal*, "Muck-a-Muck House Serves 'Just Plain Good Food.'"
18 Ibid.
19 *Ottawa Citizen*, "Come to the Muckamuck."
20 Ibid.
21 Nicol, "Unions Aren't Native," 237.
22 *Ottawa Journal*, "Muck-a-Muck House Serves 'Just Plain Good Food.'"
23 Ibid.
24 Ibid.
25 Ibid.
26 McCook, "Eat Your Oolichan – And Enjoy It."
27 Barber, "$15 (Each) Will Buy Sumptuous Meals."
28 Bitsoie and Fraioli's *New Native Kitchen* includes a recipe for "Steamed Indian corn pudding" – Bitsoie's version of "pioneer pudding." As he explains: "I've adopted this dish from a recipe first made popular by English settlers in the colonial era of the U.S. It's a traditional American dessert with Native American roots. The English, craving the sweetened porridge they called hasty pudding, began using Native American cornmeal (which they called Indian meal) to create a similar porridge sweetened with milk and molasses." 268.
29 McCook, "Eat Your Oolichan – And Enjoy It."
30 Ibid.
31 Ibid.
32 Barber, "$15 (Each) Will Buy Sumptuous Meals."
33 McCook, "Eat Your Oolichan – And Enjoy It."
34 *Ottawa Citizen*, "Come to the Muckamuck."
35 McCook, "Eat Your Oolichan – And Enjoy It."
36 *Ottawa Citizen*, "Come to the Muckamuck."
37 By 1977, George Ross was the head cook. Barber, "$15 (Each) Will Buy Sumptuous Meals."

38 *Ottawa Citizen*, "Come to the Muckamuck."
39 Ibid.
40 McCook, "Eat Your Oolichan – And Enjoy It."
41 Ibid.
42 *Ottawa Citizen*, "Come to the Muckamuck."
43 *Vancouver Sun*, "Muck-a-Muck House Advertisement."
44 Barber, "$15 (Each) Will Buy Sumptuous Meals."
45 United States Department of Agriculture, "Cape Perpetua Scenic Area."
46 Government of Canada, "First Nations in Canada."
47 CBC News, "5 Vancouver Island Native Bands Get Commercial Fishery."
48 From the Royal British Columbia Museum Archives, "The North American Indian" by Edward S. Curtis; Volume 11; Plate No. 374; Nootka method of spearing, 1915.
49 Gidley, "The Making of Edward S. Curtis's *The North American Indian*."
50 Ibid., 319.
51 Ibid., 328.
52 The photographer might have more power than the person in front of the camera, but this does not diminish the subject's sway. By pointing out how romanticized Curtis's photograph is, I do not wish to diminish the agency of the fisherman it depicts.
53 Arrivé, "Beyond True and False?" 4–5.
54 Ibid., 6.
55 Errington, "What Became Authentic Primitive Art?" 201.
56 Myers, "'Primitivism,' Anthropology, and the Category of 'Primitive Art,'" 267. The term peaked in popularity, at the same time that its period ended, with the Museum of Modern Art's 1984 exhibition *"Primitivism" in 20th Century Art*, which unleashed a public debate about the word and it supposed "authenticity." Errington, "What Became Authentic Primitive Art?" 203.
57 Anderson and Robertson, *Seeing Red*, 7.
58 British Columbia Ministry of Forest, Lands, and Natural Resource Operations, "2019–2021 Freshwater Fishing Regulations Synopsis." See "Province-wide regulations, definitions, and licensing information," "Region 1 – Vancouver Island," and "Region 2 – Lower Mainland."
59 Dominion of Canada, *Annual Report of the Department of Fisheries, Dominion of Canada, For the Year 1888*.
60 Parenteau, "Care, Control and Supervision," 11.
61 Brown, "The Muckamuck." The 1972 advertisement did, however, provide a phone number "For reservations," which suggests that the restaurant stopped taking them at some point.

62 Ibid.
63 Peyton, *Where We Ate*, 125.
64 Comparelli, "Indian Cooks, Waiters Battle Restaurant's White Managers."
65 *Ottawa Citizen*, "Come to the Muckamuck."
66 Barber, "$15 (Each) Will Buy Sumptuous Meals."
67 McCook, "Eat Your Oolichan – And Enjoy It."
68 Ibid.
69 Dickenson, "Vancouver's Spark."
70 McCook, "Eat Your Oolichan – And Enjoy It."
71 Brown, "The Muckamuck."
72 Ibid.
73 In 1977, Barber's column in the *Province* reported that word of the Muckamuck had even made it to Tokyo: "The Japanese here talk about Vancouver with some affection. The Muckamuck, they say with a smile, firstly because Muckamuck sounds a little weird in Japanese, but mainly because they have memories of it as an honest restaurant." Barber, "'Honest' Restaurant Is Hard to Find," 37.
74 Trumbull, "What's Doing in Vancouver."
75 *Atlanta Constitution*, "My Best Recipe."
76 Barber, "$15 (each) Will Buy Sumptuous Meals."
77 Ibid.
78 *Minneapolis Star*, "Muckamuck."
79 Ibid.
80 Pacific Tribune Photograph Collection, "Muckamuck strikers march, downtown Vancouver," 12 August 1978, MSC160–396_03, Simon Fraser University Digitized Collections.
81 Nicol, "Unions Aren't Native," 235.
82 Ibid., 237. The union's history, including the Muckamuck strike, is the subject of historian Julia Smith's "An 'Entirely Different' Kind of Union." This article is based on her Master's thesis: Smith, "Organizing the Unorganized."
83 Watson, "Muckamuck."
84 Ibid.
85 Ibid.
86 Ibid.
87 Nicol, "Unions Aren't Native," 235.
88 Ibid.
89 Ibid., 236.
90 Ibid., 235.

91 Ibid., 238.
92 Ibid.
93 Ibid., 236.
94 Ibid., 240.
95 Ibid., 237.
96 Ibid., 236 and 242.
97 See Nickel, *Assembling Unity*, 33.
98 *Kinesis*, "Muckamuck Worker Ethel Gardner on the Dispute."
99 Johnson, "The Impact He Made on Vancouver's Art Scene."
100 Sotheby's, "Contemporary Art Evening Auction."
101 Bill Reid's *The Spirit of Haida Gwaii* graced Canadian twenty-dollar bills printed between 2004 and 2012. Coupland, "Ace in the Hole," 45. Macrae, "Warhol."
102 Macrae, "Warhol."
103 Smith, "An 'Entirely Different' Kind of Union," 57. Nicol, "Unions Aren't Native," 242.
104 SORWUC, "All the Questions You've Wanted to Ask about Muckamuck."
105 Nickel, *Assembling Unity*, 116. She further details: "Many point to the 1961 creation of the National Indian Youth Council (NIYC) – a breakaway group form the more conservative National Congress of American Indians (NCAI) – as a pivotal moment for the Red Power movement, with the term *Red Power* first used by NIYC members in 1964 and by Vine Deloria Jr. in 1966. The Puget Sound fish-ins of the mid-1960s and mid-1970s are, then, generally considered part of the Red Power movement, as tribes centred around the Nisqually River drew on the terms of the western Washington treaties signed in the mid-1800s as proof of their continued right to fish, undisturbed, in their traditional territories." Ibid., 116–17. See also Deloria, *Custer Died for Your Sins*.
106 Nickel, *Assembling Unity*, 116.
107 Nicol, "Unions Aren't Native," 236.
108 Lane, "Tsilhqot'in (Chilcotin)."
109 *Province*, "Muckamuck Goes Cowboy in Bid to Beat Strike."
110 Comparelli, "Cowboys Lasso Muckamuck."
111 Ibid.
112 *Times Colonist*, "Indians, Cowboys Same to Strikers."
113 University of British Columbia Archives, *S.O.R.W.U.C. Newsletter* (Fall 1978), Service, Office, and Retail Workers Union of Canada fonds, Folder 6-3, Victoria, Canada.
114 Differ et al., "Letter to the Editor."

115 Ibid.
116 Boyle, "Both Sides' Failings Victimize Muckamuck."
117 Ibid.
118 Prince, "Letters to the Editor."
119 Ibid.
120 University of British Columbia Archives, *S.O.R.W.U.C. Newsletter* (December 1978), Service, Office, and Retail Workers Union of Canada fonds, Folder 6–3, Victoria, Canada.
121 Ibid.
122 *Vancouver Sun*, "Muckamuck Owners Claim to Be in Debt." For the history of the Union of BC Indian Chiefs, see Nickel, *Assembling Unity*.
123 *Vancouver Sun*, "Muckamuck Owners Claim to Be in Debt."
124 Comparelli, "Cowboys Lasso Muckamuck."
125 Ibid.
126 *Vancouver Sun*, "Restaurant Management Now Willing to Bargain."
127 Thompson, "Muckamuck Stew Is Back at the LRB." In October 1987, SORWUC supporters distributed leaflets about the strike outside of his gallery in Venice, California. *Kinesis*, "New Development in the Muckamuck Strike." On 10 December 1980, strikers organized a demonstration in front of his Vancouver gallery. *Vancouver Sun*, "Union Members Picket Gallery."
128 Ibid.
129 Nicol, "Unions Aren't Native," 249.
130 Smith "An 'Entirely Different' Kind of Union," 64.
131 Gardner, "Letter."
132 Nicol "Unions Aren't Native," 239.
133 Woodward, "Still on Strike at Muckamuck."
134 Nicol, "Unions Aren't Native," 239.
135 Eatmon et al., "Muckamuck."
136 Belkin Art Gallery, *Beginning with the Seventies*. At the time of writing, in 2022, the collective is no longer active.
137 White, "Seed Rematriation."
138 The 2019 inaugural Toronto Biennale also exhibited this work.

## 5. One Address, Three Restaurants

1 University of British Columbia Archives, *S.O.R.W.U.C. Newsletter* (December 1983).
2 Nicol, "Unions Aren't Native," 249.
3 Pynn, "Former Strikers Replace Muckamuck."

4 Ibid.
5 Chatelin, "Native Indian Feast Returns at Quilicum."
6 Ibid.
7 Hewitt, "Quilicum," 131.
8 Pynn, "Former Strikers Replace Muckamuck."
9 *Vancouver Sun*, "Opening Delayed." Incorrectly, Schellhaas states that the Quilicum opened in 1986. Additionally, he writes, "This time, the operation was all-Indigenous with some of the former Muckamuck employees among the owners." This omits McSporran. Schellhaas, "Changing Tides," 69.
10 Pynn, "Former Strikers Replace Muckamuck." Another article called it the "Bellacoola" language. *Asheville Citizen-Times*, "Parris."
11 Pynn, "Budget Gourmet."
12 Fournier, "Quilicum Offers Authentic Native Food in Artistic Surroundings."
13 Pynn, "Former Strikers Replace Muckamuck."
14 Pynn, "Budget Gourmet."
15 Ibid.
16 One review says that Bolton was Ross's uncle and another that he was Ross's cousin. Lasley and Harryman, "Dining Highlights in and near Vancouver." Cardozo and Hirsch, "Quilicum."
17 Lasley and Harryman, "Dining Highlights in and near Vancouver." One year before, another paper reported: "The speciality of the house, however, is the barbecued fish and seafood. (It's grilled over mesquite, which gives food a delicious flavor. But not so many years ago, fish in the Pacific Northwest was grilled over native alder wood, which has a special taste of its own. When the mesquite trend passes, perhaps the alder tradition will be rediscovered.)" This suggests that the restaurant had switched from mesquite to alder wood. Pennington, "Fine Fare in Vancouver."
18 Lasley and Harryman, "Dining Highlights in and near Vancouver."
19 Pynn, "Former Strikers Replace Muckamuck."
20 Chatelin, "Native Indian Feast Returns at Quilicum."
21 The review pointed out that, although the ferns are shipped frozen from the other side of the country, "they're packed by natives back in the province of New Brunswick." Cardozo and Hirsch, "Quilicum."
22 Pennington, "Fine Fare in Vancouver."
23 Ibid.
24 One critic pronounced the salad "iffy" for not including the wild herbs the menu promised. Johnson, "Native Past Recaptured, but Stick to the Seafood."

25 Lasley and Harryman, "Dining Highlights in and near Vancouver."
26 Johnson, "Native Past Recaptured, but Stick to the Seafood."
27 Fournier, "Quilicum Offers Authentic Native Food in Artistic Surroundings."
28 Cardozo and Hirsch, "Quilicum."
29 Ibid.
30 Pennington, "Fine Fare in Vancouver."
31 Lasley and Harryman, "Dining Highlights in and near Vancouver."
32 *Province Magazine*, "Ice Cream."
33 MacDonald, "A Taste of Life with an Indian Flavor."
34 Johnson, "Native Past Recaptured, but Stick to the Seafood."
35 MacDonald, "A Taste of Life with an Indian Flavor."
36 Ibid.
37 Chatelin, "Native Indian Feast Returns at Quilicum."
38 Ibid.
39 Pennington, "Fine Fare in Vancouver."
40 Pynn, "Budget Gourmet."
41 Johnson, "Native Past Recaptured, but Stick to the Seafood."
42 Lasley and Harryman, "Dining Highlights in and near Vancouver."
43 Johnson, "Native Past Recaptured, but Stick to the Seafood."
44 Ibid.
45 *Atlanta Constitution*, "Hard to Find, Easy to Enjoy."
46 *Philadelphia Inquirer*, "In British Columbia, a Revival of Interest in Indian Culture."
47 Ibid.
48 *Philadelphia Inquirer*, "True Contender for the 'Most Beautiful.'"
49 Hewitt, "Quilicum," 132.
50 Lasley and Harryman, "Dining Highlights in and near Vancouver." Likewise, McSporran is absent in Johnson's 1990 review.
51 Fournier, "Quilicum Offers Authentic Native Food in Artistic Surroundings."
52 At this point, Thorne's twenty-year-old son Clint was one of the cooks, together with Doris Dick, from the Lil'wat Nation. Ibid.
53 *Financial Post Magazine*, "Snapshot."
54 *Philadelphia Inquirer*, "True Contender for the 'Most Beautiful.'"
55 *Los Angeles Times*, "EXPO."
56 O'Leary, "Expo 86."
57 Hauka, "A World of Good Food."
58 Ibid.
59 He enrolled in the Vancouver Vocational Institute in 1983 and graduated in 1985. In 2010, George Jr. was the head chef at the Vancouver Olympic's

Four Host First Nations Pavilion. See George Jr. and Gairns, *A Feast for All Seasons*, 11.
60 Ibid., xv–xvi. Navajo chef Freddie Bitsoie also addresses such discriminatory biases, writing: "North America is not, and has never been, a monolith. Just like Europe, it's an expansive continent that's incredibly diverse in terms of language, geography, culture, and more. But European countries like France and Spain are praised for their food traditions, which are taught in elite culinary schools; Indigenous cuisines, with similarly sourced ingredients and finessed preparations, unfortunately don't get that same attention. My aim is to change that." Bitsoie, and Fraioli, *New Native Kitchen*, 8.
61 Eulachon is another spelling. Ibid., xvi.
62 Carlson, "George Jr. Is a Cut Above," A3.
63 Lillicrap, "Hall Feeds Expo's Masses."
64 Kettner, "Coast Indian Dishes."
65 Ibid.
66 Ibid.
67 Lillicrap, "Hall Feeds Expo's Masses."
68 Ibid.
69 Chandwani, "Expo 86."
70 Riches, "Folk Art of All Kinds Provides Calm Contrast."
71 Burklo, "Expo '86 Was a Taste-ful Event."
72 Matthews, "First Nations' Does Its Bannock Right."
73 Ibid.
74 Lillicrap, "Hall Feeds Expo's Masses." Another article tallies two hundred seats. Kettner, "Coast Indian Dishes."
75 Lillicrap, "Hall Feeds Expo's Masses."
76 Chandwani, "Expo 86."
77 Kettner and Hauka, "Good Native Fare and a Bit of '86."
78 Kettner, "Coast Indian Dishes."
79 Kettner and Hauka, "Good Native Fare and a Bit of '86."
80 Matthews, "First Nations' Does Its Bannock Right."
81 Armstrong, "Expo Offers Muskox Burgers, Prehistoric Ice."
82 Kettner and Hauka, "Good Native Fare and a Bit of '86."
83 Matthews, "First Nations' Does Its Bannock Right."
84 Ibid.
85 Kettner and Hauka, "Good Native Fare and a Bit of '86."
86 Matthews, "First Nations' Does Its Bannock Right."
87 Burklo, "Expo '86 Was A Taste-ful Event."
88 Ibid.

89  Polson, "Reindeer Ragout."
90  Ibid.
91  Kettner, "Coast Indian Dishes." Although distinct, "Indian ice cream" also brings to mind "Inuit ice cream," which is sometimes called "Indian Dream Whip": "animal fat mixed with mammal oil and a filling," such as berries. Arreak et al., *Niqiliurniq*, 52.
92  Polson, "Reindeer Ragout."
93  Kettner and Hauka, "Good Native Fare and a Bit of '86."
94  Ibid.
95  *Edmonton Journal*, "Expo 86 at a Glance."
96  Chandwani, "Expo 86."
97  *Richmond Review*, "One of 60 on Site."
98  Kettner and Hauka, "Good Native Fare and a Bit of '86."
99  Lillicrap, "Hall Feeds Expo's Masses."
100  Chandwani, "Expo 86."
101  Armstrong, "Expo Offers Muskox Burgers, Prehistoric Ice."
102  Polson, "Reindeer Ragout." Budgen, "Get Early Start to Make Most of Expo Nightlife."
103  Armstrong, "Expo Offers Muskox Burgers, Prehistoric Ice."
104  Polson, "Reindeer Ragout."
105  Ibid.
106  Ibid.
107  Budgen, "Get Early Start to Make Most of Expo Nightlife."
108  *Vancouver Sun*, "Your Guide to Expo Eating."
109  Budgen, "Get Early Start to Make Most of Expo Nightlife."
110  Ibid.
111  Ibid.
112  Pennington, "Fine Fare in Vancouver."
113  Lillicrap, "Hall Feeds Expo's Masses."
114  The spelling of Toody Ni ranges and sometimes a hyphen connects the two words. I have followed the spelling in George's cookbook. George Jr. and Gairns, *A Feast for All Seasons*, 13.
115  Ibid., 17. Tennant, however, describes the restaurant as being "located on a quiet strip of East Hastings Street." Tennant, "First Course."
116  Carlson, "George Jr. Is a Cut Above."
117  *Province*, "Dining Choice Varied."
118  Faulder, "Aboriginal Cuisine Basic with 'Amazing' Flavours."
119  George Jr. and Gairns, *A Feast for All Seasons*, 17.
120  Ibid. According to his cookbook, Toody Ni did not receive government support. However, according to a 1992 *Times Colonist* article, it received

loans from the United Native Nations (UNN), which became part of a debate about how loans are distributed. "Three top executive members of the UNN – president Dan Smith, Mayer and Wong, along with Ron George – own shares in Toody-Ni." Ron George's nephew Andrew George Jr. is quoted as saying: "I always get dragged into political battles whenever there is mud slinging against Ron. All I'm trying to do is start a business. Everybody ties me and Ron George together. I've been audited by the UNN. He has 2 1/2 shares worth $2,500. The others have a couple of shares. I own 49 and the rest are for sale. I'm struggling out of my own pocket and am waiting for funding from the Canadian Aboriginal Economic Development Strategy [a federal program]." The article continues: "George said secretary-treasurer Sandy Wong provided loans from the UNN to cover his payroll in 1991. They totalled $1,400, according to the auditor's report. 'That was it. I have all the records. I paid them back within days.'" *Times Colonist*, "Public Funds Funnelled to Friends as Easy Loans, Say Native Critics."
121 A 1991 article names George Jr.'s business partner at Toody Ni: George Seiff. However, Seiff's involvement rarely comes up in other news clippings, and George's cookbooks do not mention him. *Vancouver Sun*, "In the Spirit." Employing different spelling, Schellhaas writes that, "together with George Seipp," Andrew George Jr. opened the Toody Ni Grill and Catering Company. He also writes that George and "Seipp" attended the Vancouver Vocational Institute together. Schellhaas, *First Nations Cuisines*, 222.
122 George Jr. and Gairns, *A Feast for All Seasons*, 18.
123 Tennant, "First Course."
124 *Windspeaker*, "Toody Ni Advertisement."
125 *Windspeaker*, "About" section.
126 *Anishinabek News*, "Native Culinary Team Wins Gold."
127 George in a 2016 interview, quoted in Schellhaas, *First Nations Cuisines*, 222.
128 George Jr. and Gairns, *A Feast for All Seasons*, 37.
129 Schellhaas writes that Toody-Ni had a different clientele from the Quilicum and that the location of both restaurants is the best indicator for this. The Quilicum was downtown near the English Bay, beloved by tourists and locals, whereas Toody-Ni was in the Vancouver Aboriginal Friendship Centre Society at 1607 East Hastings Street, the centre of the city's "Downtown East Side." According to Schellhaas, George described his core clientele as "professionals working in the neighbourhood." Schellhaas, *First Nations Cuisines*, 223. However,

although Davie Street and East Hastings do not physically meet, history connects them. As literary scholar Jes Battis writes, "Up until the late 1980s, Davie Street was one of the centres of Vancouver's sex trade, and served as a gathering space for queer and trans sex workers, as well as IV-drug users." In 1984 Vancouver issued an expulsion of sex workers from the West End. A kilometre away from the Muckmuck, another part of Davie Street became known as "Davie Village," Vancouver's gay village, in 1999. Battis continues, "The Vancouver Police Department gradually pushed these marginalized groups out of the West End, forcing them to concentrate in the embattled Downtown Eastside neighbourhood. This purge was what made Davie Street a destination for gay men with disposable income, but the gentrification process also pushed rents up steadily, making it an inaccessible space for many." Battis, "Breaking Bread," 331. The 1984 documentary *Hookers on Davie* profiles the history of sex workers in this neighbourhood and city efforts to "clean up the street."

130 Garber, "Boris and Bubba's Best."
131 Carlson, "George Jr. Is a Cut Above."
132 Tennant, "First Course." *Anishinabek News*, "Native Culinary Team Wins Gold." In 2019 Tennant reports: "there are very few restaurants serving Indigenous cuisine. And these restaurants represent a vast increase in numbers over time – when George set out for the Olympics in 1992, Indigenous cuisine was almost invisible." However, as *Culinary Claims* demonstrates, there were Indigenous restaurants before 1992. Furthermore, Indigenous ingredients featured at events like Montreal's Expo 67 and Vancouver's Expo 86. The difference is that Indigenous chefs were not always behind these menus. At the time the Native Haute Cuisine Team was coming together for the Culinary Olympics, Wolfman was "Head Chef with Marriott Management Services in Toronto." *Anishinabek News*, "Native Culinary Team Wins Gold." The other team members were Bertha Skye (Ahtahkakoop First Nation, Cree), Arnold Olson (Cree), and Bryan Sappier (Wolastoqiyik). For more about the Native Haute Cuisine Team at the Culinary Olympics, see Schellhaas, "Changing Tides," and Turner, "Delicious Resistance," 82–91.
133 Hawthorn, "Our Chefs Are Tops."
134 *Anishinabek News*, "Native Culinary Team Wins Gold."
135 Turner, "Delicious Resistance," 83. Turner interviewed Medina in 2005.
136 Schellhaas, "Changing Tides," 67.
137 Smith, "What a Delicious *Feast!*"

138 *Lakes District News*, "Feast! A Cookbook for All Seasons – Literally." In a 2016 interview George Jr. explains that he had to close Toody Ni because the Friendship Centre increased the rent. Schellhaas, *First Nations Cuisines*, 223.
139 *Lakes District News*, "Feast! A Cookbook for All Seasons – Literally."
140 Ibid.
141 Smith, "What a Delicious *Feast!*"
142 In 2010 Arsenal Pulp Press republished this cookbook with a new name: *A Feast for All Seasons: Traditional Native Peoples' Cuisine*. Both editions have the same recipes.
143 *Houston Today*, "Glitzy, but Not Too Gourmet, Feast Is a Cookbook with Taste as Well as Style." The same article was published in *Lakes District News* with the title "Feast! A Cookbook for All Seasons – Literally."
144 Smith, "What a Delicious *Feast!*"
145 Ibid.
146 *Houston Today*, "Glitzy, but Not Too Gourmet, Feast Is a Cookbook with Taste as well as Style."
147 Johnson, "First Feasts."
148 Duffy, "Women Overcoming Odds."
149 Lane, "Feast on These First Nations Recipes."
150 Dolly Watts (McRae), phone interview, 28 June 2019.
151 Watts and Watts, *Where People Feast*, vi.
152 Watts, interview.
153 Parry, "Town Talk." Peyton incorrectly identifies Liliget Feast House as "the first First Nations restaurant in North America." Peyton, *Where We Ate*, 236. Earlier in the book, she acknowledges "the conspicuous lack of Indigenous restaurants" as "part of our restaurant history," calling it "a consequence of systemic racism towards Indigenous people in Canada ranging from prohibitive game laws to forced assimilation." Ibid., 6.
154 Watts and Watts, *Where People Feast*, vii.
155 Watts, interview.
156 Parry, "Trade Talk."
157 Liliget Feast House.
158 I have not been able to confirm when the Quilicum closed.
159 Lin, "The Taste of Home Can Be Found Downtown," 12.
160 *Vancouver Sun*, "Critic's Choice."
161 *Vancouver Sun*, "Liliget Feast House Brings First Nation Cuisine to Vancouver."
162 Chatelin, *The Seattle & Vancouver Book*, 230.

163 *Vancouver Sun*, "Liliget Feast House Brings First Nation Cuisine to Vancouver."
164 Townshend, "Destination Vancouver."
165 Ibid. *Vancouver Sun*, "Critic's Choice."
166 *Edmonton Journal*, "National Aboriginal Achievement Awards 2001."
167 Stainsby, "Canadian Content."
168 Ibid.
169 Banff National Park launched its "Plains bison reintroduction" in 2017. Banff National Park, "Plains Bison Reintroduction."
170 Watts and Watts, *Where People Feast*, 19.
171 Watts, interview.
172 Ibid.
173 *Vancouver Sun*, "Liliget Feast House Brings First Nation Cuisine to Vancouver." Stainsby, "Canadian Content." Annie Watts has also shared a video on YouTube, in which head chef Felix Parnell prepares the Liliget feast platter. Watts, "Liliget Feast House." A second video narrates the restaurant's history: Watts, "Food Business."
174 Stainsby, "Canadian Content." Liliget Feast House, "2006 Menu."
175 Liliget Feast House, "2006 Menu."
176 McRae, *My Name Is Dolly*, vii–viii.
177 Lin, "The Taste of Home Can Be Found Downtown," 12.
178 Goethe, "Carte Blanche."
179 She won with her take on spawn – also known as herring eggs – on kelp, a popular ingredient in Japan, and beat chef Hidekazu Tojo, who is credited with inventing the California roll. McRae, *My Name Is Dolly*, 32.
180 Colombara, "Restaurant Reviews 1999."
181 Carmichael, "What's Doing in Vancouver."
182 Gill, "Native Exposure."
183 *Edmonton Journal*, "National Aboriginal Achievement Awards 2001," G7.
184 McRae, *My Name Is Dolly*, 32.
185 Gill, "Native Exposure."
186 Watts and Watts, *Where People Feast*, vii.
187 For example, listed under "Secret Aboriginal Attractions," a 2003 Vancouver guidebook identified Felix Parnell, from Haida Gwaii, as the chef. Appelbe, *Secret Vancouver*, 14.
188 Watts and Watts, *Where People Feast*, v.
189 Parry, "Trade Talk."
190 Ibid.
191 Lane, "Feast on These First Nations Recipes."

192 Watts, interview. For more about the history of Indigenous labour and how it intersects with gender, see McCallum, *Indigenous Women, Work, And History*.
193 Watts, interview.
194 Ibid.
195 Stainsby, "Nature's Supermarket."
196 Ibid.
197 Ibid.
198 Ibid.
199 Watts was born in 1935.
200 Parry, "Trade Talk."
201 Watts, interview.
202 Parry, "Town Talk." Since retiring, Watts returned to Port Alberni where she married and became Dolly McRae, and published poetry collections and a memoir. I have used Watts throughout this book, since this was her last name during her restaurateur period. Her daughter Annie also returned to Port Alberni, where she runs ALW Publishing, which released a book about her mother's experience at residential school. Shaw, "Storytelling a Key Part of the Business Mix in Port Alberni."
203 The cookbook was one part of the restaurant's afterlife; the second was a line of sweet vodka beverages, Liliget Firewater. The restaurant had also offered a signature cocktail, Firewater, a blend of cranberry juice, sopalali puree, ginger ale, and Red Tassel vodka. Moore, "Cocktail of the Week."
204 Lane, "Feast on These First Nations Recipes."
205 Blackstone, "Aboriginal Celebration of Northwest Bounty."
206 The Alberni Residential School, which Watts attended, closed in 1973.

## 6. A Meal for a Chief

1 *National Post*, "The Restaurant." Plans to create an Indigenous restaurant in Winnipeg started in the 1970s when the Indian and Métis Friendship Centre offered cooking classes with the intention of later opening an eatery. Moore and Thiessen, *mmm ... Manitoba*, 196.
2 Ibid., 197–8.
3 Ibid., 196.
4 Ibid., 200.
5 *National Post*, "The Restaurant."
6 Moore and Thiessen, *mmm ... Manitoba*, 200.

7 *Leader-Post*, "Native Women Obstructed in Business Community." Born in 1940 in Camperville, Manitoba, Richard moved to Winnipeg, where she trained and worked as a hairdresser before taking on leadership roles at Indigenous organizations. She died in 2010. Moore and Thiessen, *mmm … Manitoba*, 199.
8 Tefft, "Groups Help Native Enterprises Get Off on the Right Foot." This article calls her Yvonne Black, and Moore and Thiessen's account calls her Yvonne Monkman.
9 Ibid.
10 Ibid.
11 Stevenson and Troupe, "From Kitchen Tables to Formal Organization," 303.
12 Ibid., 304.
13 Tefft, "Groups Help Native Enterprises Get Off on the Right Foot."
14 Ming Court.
15 *Calgary Herald*, "A Calgary Herald Advertising Feature."
16 Ibid.
17 Ibid. Zickerfoose, "Officials Await Report on Chief Chiniki Fire."
18 Richardier, "Country-Dining Spot's Nice Way to End Drive."
19 *Calgary Herald*, "A Calgary Herald Advertising Feature."
20 Ibid.
21 Carter, *Capturing Women*, 188.
22 *Calgary Herald*, "A Calgary Herald Advertising Feature."
23 Ibid.
24 Ibid.
25 *Calgary Herald*, "Chiniki Village Co-op Feast."
26 Richardier, "Chiniki Restaurant Offers Pleasant Food, Service."
27 Ibid.
28 Ibid.
29 Ibid.
30 Ibid.
31 Willet, "Offerings a Mix of Old, New."
32 Willet, "History in the Making."
33 Willet, "Offerings a Mix of Old, New."
34 Ibid.
35 *Edmonton Journal*, "Familiar Foods in Native Dress Featured at Tribes Restaurant."
36 Ibid.
37 Ibid.

38 Ibid. *Edmonton Journal*, "Native Restaurant Would Face Obstacles."
39 *Edmonton Journal*, "Familiar Foods in Native Dress Featured at Tribes Restaurant."
40 Ibid.
41 Ibid.
42 Morash, "Cookbooks Bring Native Cuisine to the Kitchen." The first article mentions *Spirit of the Harvest: North American Indian Cooking* by Beverley Cox and Martin Jacobs; *Foods of the Southwest Indian Nations: Native American Cooking* by Lois Ellen Frank (the order of title and subtitle is reversed in the article); *Indian Givers* by Jack Weatherford; and *Native Harvests: Recipes and Botanicals of the American Indian* by Barrie Kavasch. *Edmonton Journal*, "Native Restaurant Would Face Obstacles."
43 *Edmonton Journal*, "Native Restaurant Would Face Obstacles."
44 Ibid.
45 Ibid.
46 Ibid.
47 Yelp, "Chief Chiniki Menu."
48 CBC News, "John Gilchrist Reviews Chiniki Restaurant."
49 Ibid.
50 Ibid.
51 Heldke, *Exotic Appetites*, xxiv.
52 Basil, *Be My Guest*, 17–18.
53 Derrida, "Hostipitality," 3.
54 Rosanna Deerchild begins a radio episode about Food Is Our Language, a school program in Winnipeg that uses food to reconnect urban Indigenous youth to their cultures, by revealing that although most people consider maple syrup French Canadian, "it is actually an Indigenous food." CBC Radio, "Tapping into a History That Connects Maple Syrup to First Nations." There is still only a handful of Indigenous-owned maple syrup companies in Canada. These include Awazibi, which is Kitigan Zibi Anishinabeg–run and based in Quebec, Wabanaki Maple, a female-owned company on Neqotkuk (Tobique First Nation) in New Brunswick, Giizhigat Maple Products on the Six Nations of the Grand River in Ontario, and Kleekhoot Gold Bigleaf Syrup, run by members of the Hupacasath First Nation on Vancouver Island.
55 CBC News, "John Gilchrist Reviews Chiniki Restaurant."
56 Ibid.
57 Morris, "The Politics of Palatability," 16.
58 Zickerfoose, "Chief Chiniki Restaurant May Be Rebuilt after Blaze," B1.

59 The man arrested was Nocian Twoyoungmen of the Stoney First Nation, and the police charged an additional three minors. Hudes, "Chief Chiniki Restaurant Set to Rise from the Ashes."
60 Ibid.
61 Ibid.
62 Ibid.
63 *Cochrane Today*, "Future of Chiniki Restaurant Unknown."
64 Clarke, "Chiniki Cultural Centre and Stones Restaurant Closes."
65 Robertson, "His Menu Is a Bit 'Wild,'" 10.
66 Ibid., 10.
67 Silverthorn, "A South-Regina Landmark No More," A1.
68 Robertson, "His Menu Is a Bit 'Wild.'"
69 City of Regina Photographs Collection, "Gold West Inn at 4150 Albert Street, which later became the Landmark Inn," c. 1975, Item CORA-A-0885.
70 This is based on a 1977 classified advertisement: Landmark Inn, "Part-Time Waiters-Waitresses" in *Leader-Post*.
71 Piche, "Big Band Sound Is Live Saturday at Regina's Landmark Inn." Ad in *Leader-Post*, "You Will Stop Smoking on June 2nd ..."
72 *Star-Phoenix*, "Regina's Landmark Inn Latest Victim of Economy."
73 In fall 1993 an investment company, Cryptic Ventures Inc., headed by Vancouver businessman Robert Ferguson, purchased the Inn's common shares from Gerald McCullough, while Royal Fund investors owned its preferred shares. The *Leader-Post* sums up Gerald McCullough's involvement: "It was 1994 when fraud investigators with the RCMP and Regina police began probing Royal Fund Investment Inc. and fund manager Hamilton-based INET Corp., which was controlled by McCullough. The fund had raised nearly $5 million from 34 offshore shareholders from Asia and the Middle East under the federal immigrant investor program. It was designed to attract business people and their capital to Canada, allowing wealthy investors who ponied up $150,000 to qualify for an immigrant visa. The fund's most tangible asset was the Landmark Inn, a Regina hotel into which $2 million was poured." Pacholk, "The $1,000,00 Pay-Back." In 2000 Robert Ferguson was tried for fraud for siphoning $120,000 "of immigrant investor money" out of the Landmark Inn. O'Connor, "Businessman a 'Minnow Swimming with Sharks.'"
74 Silverthorn, "Landmark Inn Staying Open until Friday."
75 Robertson, "His Menu Is a Bit 'Wild.'"
76 Ibid.
77 Ibid.

78  Ibid.
79  Ibid.
80  Ibid.
81  Ibid.
82  Ibid.
83  Reports of the number of rooms vary between 186, 187, and 188. Landmark Inn, "Advertisement." Silverthorn, "A Landmark No More" and "A South-Regina Landmark No More."
84  *Leader-Post*, "Landmark Has Tasty Menu."
85  Ibid.
86  Ibid.
87  Ibid.
88  Ibid.
89  Ibid.
90  Silverthorn, "Landmark Inn Staying Open until Friday."
91  Silverthorn, "A South-Regina Landmark No More."
92  CBC News, "First Nation Checks Out of the Hotel Business."
93  Ibid.
94  Silverthorn, "A Landmark No More."
95  *Saskatoon Star-Phoenix*, "Wanuskewin Restaurant Named One of Canada's Tastiest Indigenous Dining Spots."
96  DK Eyewitness Travel, *Canada*, 377.
97  CBC News, "Saskatoon Chef Ryan Young Creates Diabetic-Friendly Menu."
98  Wanuskewin, "Story of the Northern Plains."
99  *Star Tribune*, "Passport Is Not Required, but Some ID Is."
100  Wanuskewin, "Appointment."
101  Ibid.
102  Wanuskewin, "Restaurant Manager."
103  Wanuskewin Heritage Park, "Ad," 11.
104  Lessard, "Who I Am." Hill, "Jenni Lessard Brings Diverse Experience to Wanuskewin."
105  Nightingale, "Bringing Millennia of Culinary History to Life in the 21st Century."

## 7. Culinary Resurgence

1  In the 1960s the Iroquois Coffee Shop on Toronto Island occupied what once was the park superintendent's house. Presumably, it was similar to Montreal's The Indian Room in that its name was the most Indigenous

thing about it. Architectural photographs taken in the 1970s do not provide further details about it or its history. City of Toronto Archives, "Iroquois coffee shop, Toronto Island," 1961 and 1962, Fonds 220, Series 316, Files 205, 726, 727, 736, 756, 758. "Park Superintendent's House at Petunia Island," Fonds 1047, Series 872, File 15, City of Toronto Archives, Ontario, Canada. Harris, "Ring of Fun around Toronto."
2 Black, "A Kind of Cheers on the Web."
3 *Toronto Star*, "A Taste of First Nations."
4 Ibid.
5 Ibid.
6 Ibid.
7 Ibid. That said, one journalist writes that Eureka Continuum is "remembered less for its ground-breaking grub than for one of it's [sic] bouncers murdering a customer and disposing the body in a bathtub of Javex." Davey, "Original Aboriginal."
8 Bain, "A Pretty Fancy Powwow."
9 Ibid.
10 Ibid.
11 Ibid.
12 Ibid.
13 Ibid.
14 Jermanok, "Toronto Doesn't Get More Native Than This." Mallet, "Restaurant Review" and "Dine by Design." Kates, "At Keriwa, Local Food Goes Native with Stunning Results." *Toronto Life*, "Best New Restaurants 2012."
15 Davey, "Original Aboriginal."
16 Kates, "At Keriwa, Local Food Goes Native with Stunning Results." Although Keriwa did not make Peyton's list of 150 restaurants, she mentions it in her summary of the 2010s: "Indigenous restaurants started to grow in number as Indigenous chefs showcased their traditional recipes and ingredients on luxe tasting menus such as that at the Keriwa Cafe, as well as via food trucks and family eateries." Peyton, *Where We Ate*, 263.
17 Chu, "Get to Know a Chef."
18 Born in Lubeck, Germany, Michael Stadtländer moved to Canada in 1980.
19 Jermanok, "Toronto Doesn't Get More Native Than This," 6.
20 Davey, "Original Aboriginal."
21 Jermanok, "Toronto Doesn't Get More Native Than This." Kates, "At Keriwa, Local Food Goes Native with Stunning Results."
22 *Toronto Life*, "Best New Restaurants 2012." Cyr and Slater report something similar in their discussion of Métis foodways: "Several

participants discussed how their grandmothers 'borrowed' recipes from their neighbors or married into lineages that would introduce them to recipes from other heritages, typically European. This was the result of settler immigration to Manitoba from predominantly European countries and living in close settlements in the Red River Valley. Participants who grew up in St. Laurent reported that holiday celebrations with community members included various Polish and Ukrainian dishes such as perogies and holopchi." Cyr and Slater, "Honouring the Grandmothers through (Re)membering, (Re)learning, and (Re)vitalizing Métis Traditional Foods and Protocols," 61.
23 Mallet, "Restaurant Review." Kates, "At Keriwa, Local Food Goes Native with Stunning Results."
24 Jermanok, "Toronto Doesn't Get More Native Than This."
25 Mallet, "Restaurant Review."
26 Kates, "At Keriwa, Local Food Goes Native with Stunning Results."
27 Examples include Lovell Springs Trout Farm and Vicki's Veggies. Chu, "Get to Know a Chef."
28 Knight, "The Morning After." For the cultural politics of brunch, see Micallef, *The Trouble with Brunch*.
29 Mallet, "Restaurant Review."
30 Kates, "At Keriwa, Local Food Goes Native with Stunning Results."
31 Jermanok, "Toronto Doesn't Get More Native Than This."
32 Kates, "At Keriwa, Local Food Goes Native with Stunning Results."
33 Mallet, "Dine by Design."
34 Ibid.
35 Ibid. For the history of pemmican see Colpitts, *Pemmican Empire*.
36 Mallet, "Dine by Design."
37 See the "Vegandale" debate: Ngabo, "Is It Parkdale or Vegandale?"
38 Jermanok, "Toronto Doesn't Get More Native Than This."
39 *EnRoute*, "8: Keriwa Cafe, Toronto."
40 Krader, "An Insider's Guide to Toronto."
41 *Toronto Life*, "Best New Restaurants 2012."
42 Ibid.
43 Kates, "At Keriwa, Local Food Goes Native with Stunning Results."
44 Ibid.
45 Ibid,
46 Carlson, "What Lies Ahead for Aboriginals."
47 Maffei, "Surveying the Borders," 211.
48 Weltecke, "Essen und Fasten in interreligiöser Abgrenzung, Konkurrenz und Austausch," 12.

49 Chu, "Get to Know a Chef."
50 Whiteduck Ringuette told me that the "Keriwa Cafe did really well and then it had to close because of a flood for a month and when it reopened, no one came back." However, I have not been able to confirm this in any newspaper articles, and although I contacted Bear Robe, I did not hear back. Johl Whiteduck Ringuette, interview by the author, 18 September 2016. The Wine Club, where Bear Rob is the managing partner, launched in 2016.
51 Chu, "Get to Know a Chef."
52 Efron, "Bannock Tacos, Fried Baloney – This Is Aboriginal Cuisine?"
53 Ibid.
54 Ibid.
55 Mihesuah, "Indigenous Health Initiatives, Frybread, and the Marketing of Nontraditional 'Traditional' American Indian Foods," 49, 57.
56 Lewis, "Frybread Wars," 442.
57 Wild rice is a sacred ingredient and has already made several appearances throughout this book. For the spiritual, cultural, and colonial lives of wild rice, see, for example, Gross, "Harvesting Wild Rice," Luby, *Dammed*, Cooke, "Stories of Rice Lake," Zilberstein, "Inured to Empire," and Chapter 6 of Moore and Thiessen, *mmm ... Manitoba*.
58 Shawn Adler, interview by the author, 11 September 2017. In her 2005 summary of Indigenous culinary arts in Canada, Annie Turner writes: "Although his restaurant does not feature exclusively Aboriginal cuisine, he does offer some occasional Aboriginal specials, and also does catering for the Native Studies program at Trent University and for weddings and other gatherings at reserves in the surrounding area." Turner, "Delicious Resistance," 94.
59 Adler, interview.
60 When Adler was a kid, there was no sour cream. "At pow wows, as far as I can tell, sour cream was added ten or fifteen years ago," he reckons.
61 The so-called "five gifts of the white man" are flour, salt, sugar, milk, and lard.
62 Levi, *Food, Control and Resistance*, 8. Although this important study overlooks both Canada and restaurants, Levi compares the similar foundations of food rations in the United States and Australia: "Both governments desired greater access to lands occupied by indigenous peoples; however, straightforward exile or extermination did not fit with prevailing national ideologies encompassing humanitarian thought and Christian duty. As a means of achieving their goals, the governments developed indigenous policies in which the control of food played a crucial role." Ibid., 6–7.

63 At one point chef Rich Francis worked for him. Whiteduck Ringuette was also the co-subject of the documentary *The Edible Indian*, in which he further expands on his relationship between food and land. Gardiner, *The Edible Indian*.
64 His first client was Ryerson (now Toronto Metropolitan) University's Aboriginal Student Services. The University of Toronto regularly hires him, and so does the imagineNATIVE Film + Media Arts Festival.
65 Gardiner, *The Edible Indian*.
66 Ibid.
67 Ringuette, interview.
68 Gardiner, *The Edible Indian*.
69 Ibid.
70 Tennant, "*Terra Nullius* on the Plate," 78.
71 Tennant, "First Course." Michael D. Wise also opts for the singular cuisine. Wise, *Native Foods*.
72 Kuh, *The Last Days of Haute Cuisine*, 192.
73 Ray, *The Ethnic Restaurateur*, 39.
74 *Dictionary of Canadian Biography*, "Evans, James." Evans is a problematic figure who was accused of initiating sexual relations with young Indigenous girls.
75 Shawana is Odawa and his wife is Cree.
76 Abarca, "Authentic or Not, It's Original," 2.
77 Pataki, "Kukum Kitchen Will Win You Over with Its Indigenous Food."
78 CBC News featured both eateries on its 2017 Indigenous restaurant map.
79 This practice relates to code switching. For a prominent example, as well as the relationship between language, colonialism, and borders, see Anzaldúa, *Borderlands*.
80 Simpson, *As We Have Always Done*, 200.
81 Corntassel, "Re-envisioning Resurgence," 89.
82 Joseph Shawana, interview by the author, 5 September 2018.
83 Shawana's family originally came from the Minnesota-Wisconsin area and migrated to Manitoulin Island around four hundred years ago.
84 Coulthard, *Red Skin, White Masks*, 3.
85 Simpson, *As We Have Always Done*, 49.
86 Ibid., 49–50.
87 NishDish, 6 May 2020 Instagram post.
88 Carlberg, "Toronto's Groundbreaking Indigenous Restaurant Is Shutting Down."
89 Rubin, "Nishdish, Closed for Good by COVID-19, Served Up Anishinaabe Cuisine and History."

90 Ibid.
91 Ibid.
92 NishDish, "Restaurant."
93 Carlberg, "One of Toronto's Favourite Indigenous Restaurants Shut Down by Landlord."
94 CBC Radio, "How Indigenous Leaders Are Changing the Future of Food."

## 8. Seal Tartare

1 The four Inuit regions are Inuvialuit Settlement Region (the northwestern part of the Northwest Territories), Nunavut, Nunavik (Quebec), and Nunatsiavut (Labrador).
2 Landsel, "What Does Seal Taste Like?"
3 Jennifer N., "Demand That Kukum Kitchen in Toronto Canada Take Seal Meat off Their Menu."
4 Aylan C., "Counter-Petition to Educate Anti-Seal Activist Jennifer N about Anti-Indigenous Behaviour and Colonialism." At the time of writing, April 2018, the anti-seal petition had 6,698 signatures, the pro-seal petition 5,412. 19 April 2018. Both petitions attracted a plethora of media attention: Bailey, "Quebec Company Touts Seal Meat as 'Canadian Superfood.'" McGillivray, "It's Who We Are." Whalen, "Seal Meat on the Menu at Toronto Restaurant Sparks Duelling Petitions, Online Debate." Gignac, "Petition Asks That Seal Meat Be Removed from Toronto Restaurant's Menu." Beaumont, "Animal Rights Activists Target Indigenous Restaurant for Serving Seal Meat." Randhawa, "Animal Rights Activists and Inuit Clash over Canada's Indigenous Food Traditions."
5 Leviticus 11:9–12.
6 Spray was born above the Arctic Circle in Shungnak. Addressing the Inupiat and Yupik Eskimos in Alaska, she elaborates: "The word 'Eskimo' refers here to Alaska's Arctic Eskimo and is the term the elders prefer." "Alaska's Vanishing Arctic Cuisine," 40. Her work is important, as there is little scholarly work about Arctic cuisines. "On the surface Eskimo food appears too primitive for culinary investigation. However, native women created an extensive and complex repertoire of dishes, preparing hundreds of indigenous foods according to specific techniques." Ibid., 30. Spray writes about how women turned seal blubber into oil, a practice that is less common today. "Seal touched nearly every food, either in its preparation, as a preservative during storage, or as a final seasoning." Ibid., 32. Seal oil was once "the Eskimo's salt and pepper." Ibid., 32.

Other dishes she mentions that have lost popularity include "Fermented Ugruk flippers," "Fermented Ugruk intestines," and "Soured seal livers." Ibid., 38.

7 Wenzel, *Animal Rights Human Rights*, 46.
8 Ibid., 47.
9 Fisheries and Oceans Canada, "Management Decision."
10 Robert Hunter, quoted in Zelko, *Make it a Green Peace!*, 267.
11 Pelly, *Sacred Hunt*, 110.
12 Watt-Cloutier, *The Right to Be Cold*, 69.
13 Dickenson, *Seal*, 158.
14 Busch, *The War against Seals*, 249.
15 Malouf, *Seals and Sealing in Canada*, 32.
16 Pelly, *Sacred Hunt*, 112.
17 Malouf, *Seals and Sealing in Canada*, 43.
18 Fisheries and Oceans Canada, "Seals and Sealing." Along with the northern elephant seal, there are three other species of eared seals in Pacific waters: the northern fur seal, northern sea lion, and California sea lion.
19 Peter Irniq, "Foreword," viii.
20 Pelly, *Sacred Hunt*, 2.
21 For more about the relationship between Inuit and seal, see Pelly, *Sacred Hunt*.
22 Dickenson, *Seal*, 135. This translation recalls what Earle reports from her sources in Spanish America: A 1634 Nahuatl translation of the Lord's Prayer replaces "daily bread" with "daily tortillas." Earle, *The Body of the Conquistador*, 150.
23 Anthropologist Kristen Borré, for example, discusses the importance of fatty seal meat and its connection to warmth and good health in the Arctic. Borré, "Seal Blood, Inuit Blood, and Diet." The anthropologist Jean L. Briggs surveys the distinction made between "Inuit" (wild) food and "*Qallunaaq*" (store-bought, Euro-Canadian) food. Briggs, "From Trait to Emblem and Back," 229. See also Searles, "Inuit Identity in the Canadian Arctic" and "Food and the Making of Modern Inuit Identities."
24 Borré, "The Healing Power of the Seal."
25 Pelly, *Sacred Hunt*, 114.
26 Dickenson, *Seal*, 119. Arendt, "Caribou to Cod," 88.
27 Dickenson, *Seal*, 41.
28 Ibid., 57.
29 Watt-Cloutier, *The Right to Be Cold*, 246.
30 Ibid., 247.

31 Hennig and Caddell, "On Thin Ice?," 298.
32 Ibid., 299.
33 Ibid., 313.
34 Fakhri, "Gauging US and EU Seal Regimes in the Arctic against Inuit Sovereignty," 229.
35 Ibid., 231
36 PETA, "8 Things You Need to Know about Canada's Seal Slaughter."
37 Wenzel, *Animal Rights Human Rights*, 184.
38 Luckerson, "These Are the 10 Most Popular Tweets of All Time."
39 Humane Society of the United States, "Protect Seal."
40 Humane Society of the United States, "Chefs for Seal." Anthony Bourdain spoke out against this campaign, tweeting, "I'm all for protecting seals, but a total ban dooms the indigenous people above arctic circle to death or relocation." (@Bourdain, 28 October 2013). This made Canadian news: Hui, "U.S. Celebrity Chefs Boycotting Canadian Seafood Draw Backlash."
41 CBC News, "Inuit Gather in Iqaluit for Pro-Sealing, Anti-Ellen #sealfie." Dean, "We Spoke to the Inuit Woman behind 'Sealfies.'"
42 Belcourt, "Coda," 235.
43 Kennedy, "Tanya Tagaq Takes Shot at PETA Even Though It's Not against Inuit Seal Hunt."
44 Dean, "Tanya Tagaq's Cute Sealfie Pissed Off a Lot of Idiots."
45 Watt-Cloutier, *The Right to Be Cold*, 247.
46 CBC News, "Tanya Tagaq #sealfie Provokes Anti-Sealing Activists."
47 APTN National News, "Animal Rights Group Puts Nunavut Musician in Cross Hairs over Seal Pelt Debate."
48 Watt-Cloutier, *The Right to Be Cold*, 327.
49 Ibid., 248.
50 Ibid., 137.
51 The International Day of Action against Seal Hunting was cancelled when the organization found out about the counter-protest. "We need to have a better relationship with animal rights groups," Arnaquq-Baril argues. "Believe it or not, we're on the same side."
52 This connects to a point TallBear makes: "I was raised implicitly, not explicitly, to understand that nonhumans have their own life trajectories. And I felt very averse to the ways that humans mess with nonhuman life paths, and that includes breeding them and making them too dependent on us." TallBear, "Being in Relation," 59. Belcourt also brings this up in his discussion of animal activism: "It is paradox that allows us to negate what Kim TallBear describes as the ethical superiority that activists

assume when attempting to steward 'the lives of those that are less than they are.' TallBear insists that these activists don't think about animals as relations." Belcourt, "Coda," 238.
53 Tagaq, "Eating Seal Meat Is a Vital Part of Life in My Community."
54 Wenzel, *Animal Rights Human Rights*, 3–4.
55 Ibid., 8.
56 Inuit Tapiriit Kanatami, "A Taste of the Arctic."
57 Payne, "Ottawa's Urban Inuit Renaissance." However, Statistics Canada's numbers are incomplete. Pfeffer, "'Woefully Inaccurate' Inuit Population Data Overwhelming Local Agencies."
58 Rose, "Seal Meat and Caribou Offer a Taste of Canada's Inuit Identity." The Nunavut Arts and Crafts Association sold these T-shirts at a 2014 Ottawa trade fair. Dickenson, *Seal*. 159.
59 Lauren Goodman, interview by the author, 29 August 2017.
60 Redzepi has cooked a fair bit with lichen. One example is "Crispy reindeer moss, cep powder and *crème fraîche*." Redzepi, *A Work in Progress*, 50.
61 Spray Starks, "Arctic Foodways and Contemporary Cuisine," 41, 42, 45.
62 Statistics Canada, "Food Insecurity among Inuit Living in Inuit Nunagat."
63 Government of Nunavut, Bureau of Statistics, "Prices."
64 Inuit Tapiriit Kanatami, "What We Do."
65 La Via Campesina, "Who We Are." Grey and Patel argue that the term "invites contestation." They refer to Marc Edelman's work that shows the Spanish term – *soberanía alimentaria* – predates the English and was coined by the Mexican government for their National Food Program. Grey and Patel, however, distinguish between Food Sovereignty, associated with its Mexican origins, and food sovereignty, as advocated by La Via Campesia, and follow the latter's example by not capitalizing the term. Grey and Patel, "Food Sovereignty as Decolonization," 431.
66 Hoover, "You Can't Say You're Sovereign If You Can't Feed Yourself."
67 Robin, "Our Hands at Work," 87. She chronicles a wide range of Indigenous food sovereignty projects – from greenhouses to school gardens and from traditional foods education initiatives to market garden cooperatives – but does not include restaurants.
68 Nyéléni, *Nyéléni 2007: Forum for Food Sovereignty*, 9.
69 Ibid., n.p.
70 For a discussion of the food sovereignty movement in Canada, see Desmarais and Wittman, "Farmers, Foodies and First Nations."
71 Food Secure Canada, *Resetting the Table*, 1.
72 Agriculture and Agri-Food Canada, *A Food Policy for Canada*, 10.

73 Food Secure Canada, *Resetting the Table*, 1.9. See also Cidro et al., "First Food as Indigenous Food Sovereignty," 28.
74 For Indigenous culinary sustainability, see Gora, "From New York's Silverbird to Santa Fe's Corn Dance Café."
75 Agriculture and Agri-Food Canada, *"Everyone at the Table!"*
76 Canada's agriculture and agri-food system accounts for 6.7 per cent of its GDP. Agriculture and Agri-Food Canada, *An Overview of the Canadian Food System 2017*.
77 Grey and Patel, "Food Sovereignty as Decolonization," 440.
78 Martens et al., "Understanding Indigenous Food Sovereignty through an Indigenous Research Paradigm," 18, 21.
79 Simpson, "The Sovereignty of Critique," 686.
80 Ibid.
81 Ibid., 687.
82 Nickel, *Assembling Unity*, 147.
83 Ibid., 148.
84 Fakhri, "Gauging US and EU Seal Regimes in the Arctic against Inuit Sovereignty," 204.
85 Trembath, "A Feast of Culture."
86 Francis, Facebook, 20 February 2018.
87 Bellrichard, "Famed Indigenous Chefs Team Up for Vancouver Dinner Series."
88 John Horne, phone interview by author, 17 January 2018.
89 Stadtländer's annual Wild Leek & Maple Syrup Festival in Singhampton, Ontario, costs $165 and includes collaborations with Toronto chefs.
90 Horne also said: "I think I offended a lot more people with the horse than with seal."
91 Douglas, *Purity and Danger*.
92 Long, "Culinary Tourism," 33.
93 Melasniemi and Tiravanija, *Bastard Cookbook*, 22.
94 Caribou Gourmand, "Menu."
95 "Phoque Fest."
96 Restaurant Manitoba, "Menu."
97 Maynard, "Canadian Chefs Serve Seal, with a Side of Controversy" and "When Seal Is on the Menu."
98 Ibid.
99 Les Iles en Ville, "Menu."
100 Maynard, "When Seal Is on the Menu."
101 Malouf, *Seals and Sealing in Canada*, 43.
102 Everett, "Food, Class and the Self," 74.

103 Ibid., 91.
104 Ibid., 87. Peyton chronicles one of the few "'nice places' in St. John's to take a date on a Friday night or for a special occasion meal": The Candlelite, which opened in 1955 and closed in 1976. Steak and milkshakes shared a menu alongside fresh lobster and "seal flipper pie dinners." Peyton, *Where We Ate*, 135.
105 Everett, "Food, Class and the Self," 91.
106 Bailey, "Government to Fund Development of Seal Products for Canadian Grocery Store."
107 CBC News, "St. John's Chefs Push Benefits of Seal Meat."
108 Newman, *Speaking in Cod Tongues*, 162. Caribou liver and whale skin are also rich in vitamin C. Arreak et al., *Niqiliurniq*, 10.
109 Nilsson, *The Nordic Cookbook*, 248.
110 Ibid., 259.
111 Ibid.
112 Ibid., 440.
113 Ibid., 111. Other northern residents, such as those of Uist Island, Shetland, ate seal during Lent because it was classified as a fish, just like beaver.
114 Galenus, *De alimentorum facultatibus libri iii*, cited in Johnson and Lavigne, "Monk Seals in Antiquity," 36. Cited in Dickenson, *Seal*, 111.
115 Dickenson, *Seal*, 117.
116 My great-aunt once packaged pork in a Toronto factory.
117 Dammann and Johns, *True North*, 92.
118 Ibid.
119 Ibid.
120 Ibid.
121 Kimmerer, *Braiding Sweetgrass*, 208.
122 Arreak et al., *Niquiliurniq*, 44.
123 Dammann and Johns, *True North*, 99.
124 Johnson, "Newfoundland Seal Featured on Vancouver Menu."
125 Mijure, "Vancouver Eatery Serves Up Controversy with Newfoundland Seal Dish." Slattery, "PETA to Hold 'Bloody' Protest against Seal Dish at Edible Canada Restaurant." Brend, "Seal Meat May Turn Some Stomachs, but Inuit Country Food Is Smart." In fact, the seal dishes were popular and sold the most. The runner-up in terms of sales was lamb heart. As one review writes, "Editor's note: lamb heart comes from a very cute, baby animal, but strangely there were no protests about that." *The Truth about Fur*, "Eating Seal Meat."
126 Fricker, "Please Tell This Vancouver Restaurant to Take Baby Seal Meat off the Menu."

127 "Edible Canada," Facebook.
128 Joseph Shawana, interview by the author, 5 September 2018.
129 Stainsby, "First Nations Food Gaining Wide Appeal."
130 Nosowitz, "Seal Meat."
131 Ibid.
132 "Top Chef Canada," season 1, episode 1, "Getting to Know You."
133 Nosowitz, "Seal Meat."
134 Ibid.
135 Knight, "Seals Are Delicious, So Let's Kill and Eat Them."
136 Couchie and Mosby, "Anti-Seal Hunt Rhetoric Ignores Facts and Suppresses Indigenous Culture."
137 Ibid.
138 Mijure, "Vancouver Eatery Serves Up Controversy with Newfoundland Seal Dish."
139 Whalen, "Seal Meat on the Menu at Toronto Restaurant Sparks Duelling Petitions, Online Debate."
140 SeaDNA, "Seal Cuts."
141 SeaDNA, "Market in Ontario."
142 SeaDNA, "Seal Cuts."
143 Newman, *Speaking in Cod Tongues*, 58.
144 Potter, "Row Erupts over Governor General's Seal Taste."
145 Galloway, "Governor General Applauded, Denounced for Eating Raw Seal."
146 CBC News, "Governor General's Seal Snack Sparks Controversy."
147 Spang, *The Invention of the Restaurant*, 79.
148 "Mind of a Chef Sneak Peek with comedian Aziz Ansari."
149 Kūkŭm Kitchen, "Menu."

## 9. Where the Beaver and Buffalo Roam

1 Saul argues that this was not the case: "If you were to ask most Canadians how Ottawa came to be our capital, they would reply that Queen Victoria chose it. The fact that she didn't seems to be irrelevant. That her role was no more than that of any constitutional monarch or Governor General, who follows the advice of their ministers, is brushed aside." As he argues, Macdonald, Cartier, and Sir Edmund Head, the governor general at the time, "had pretty much settled on Ottawa," prepared a list of five candidate cities and asked the queen to choose. However, Saul states, "In reality she was given no choice" and "Ottawa was the only choice." Saul, *A Fair Country*, 244–6.

2 Although Wakefield is in Quebec, the town speaks English. It is one of the villages that compose the municipality of La Pêche, which in 2011 had a population of 7,619. It is small, but not insignificant. Lester B. Pearson, Canada's fourteenth prime minister (1963–8), is buried here. It is also one of the locations where the 1999 film *Grey Owl* was shot, which tells the story of controversial Archibald Belaney. He claimed Anishinaabe identity, only to have it come out after his death that he was British. See Chapter 6, "They Taught Me Much," in Fee, *Literary Land Claims*, 147–80.

3 The name references A Tribe Called Quest, formed in 1985 and a protagonist of alternative hip-hop.

4 One of the characters in Tommy Orange's novel *There There* listens to A Tribe Called Red, commenting, "It's the most modern, or most postmodern, form of Indigenous music I've heard that's both traditional and new-sounding. The problem with Indigenous art in general is that it's stuck in the past. The catch, or the double bind, about the whole thing is this: If it isn't pulling from tradition, how is it Indigenous? And if it is stuck in tradition, in the past, how can it be relevant to other Indigenous people living now, how can it be modern? So to get close to but keep enough distance from tradition, in order to be recognizably Native and modern-sounding is a small kind of miracle these three First Nations producers made happen." Orange, *There There*, 77.

5 Restaurants frequently play music to set the mood, but to also camouflage background noise. Haley mentions music's rocky journey to becoming a feature of restaurants in *Turning the Tables*.

6 Wapokunie Riel-Lachapelle, interview by the author, 26 August 2017.

7 Brown, "Wakefield's Nikosi Bistro-Pub Promotes Rustic French Cooking with Indigenous Influences."

8 Strangely, one of the few historic menus featuring Indigenous foods before Expo 1967 is from a 1919 "Annual Campfire Banquet of the 1866–'70 and '85 Veterans, the Red River Settlers, and the Trail-Blazers of the Canadian North-west." This time period covers Canadian Confederation (1867), the Red River Rebellion, which Riel led (1869–10), the year Manitoba joined Canada (1870), and, finally, the year Riel was hanged for treason (1885). Celebrating those who defeated the political leader of the Métis people, the dinner took place on 24 April 1919, and included "Pemmican," "Mock rump moose," "Succotash," "Kildonan bannocks," "Assiniboine fruits," "Saskatoon berries," "Red River tea," and "Norway House pudding." Province of Manitoba Archives, "2015/008/18: Unidentified banquet." L.E. Wilson's records related to the Hudson's Bay

Company's 250th anniversary celebrations, HB2015/008, Province of Manitoba Archives, Winnipeg. For Riel's legacy see Braz, *The False Traitor*.

9 DesBrisay, *Capital Dining*, 209. The *Ottawa Citizen* also claimed that the owners' "dream was to see a second aboriginal restaurant open in Canada, the first being in British Columbia." Cook, "Aboriginal Cooking Debuts in Market."
10 Bite Burger House now stands in its place, which, unlike Sweetgrass, offers many a burger but none with bison.
11 DesBrisay, *Capital Dining*, 209. Sweetgrass Aboriginal Bistro, "Frequently Asked Questions."
12 DesBrisay, "Sweetgrass Delights."
13 Ibid.
14 This meant "no French" wine. *National Post*, "Canada's Best Restaurants."
15 Cook, "Maple Syrup Adds Golden Touch."
16 *Ottawa Citizen*, "Recently Recommended." Desbrisay, "Best Bites of 2007."
17 Laffrey, "72 Hours in Ottawa, Ontario."
18 DesBrisay, *Capital Dining*, 210.
19 Elton, "My First Helping of Canada Goose."
20 Ibid. This aversion is not a Canadian phenomenon. Lisa Ma's art project "Invasive" responds to Ghent, Belgium's 2013 campaign to "humanely" kill the "invasive" Canadian geese. As an alternative to poisoning the birds, Ma proposed that residents eat the geese as a way of managing them, and prepared an "invasive species" dish for the city's mayor. Ma, "Invasive Species."
21 *Ottawa Citizen*, "Recently Recommended."
22 According to Bill Casselman, there was already a dough dish with this name. He cites Frank Russell's 1896 *Explorations in the Far North*: "If the traveler has no frying pan the bread is baked in a *beaver tail*. Such a loaf is long and narrow and is exposed to the fire upon a stick." Casselman, "Canadian Food Words."
23 Berland, "The Work of the Beaver," 25.
24 *The Beaver: Canada's History Magazine* changed its name in 2010 to *Canada's History*. CBC News, "The Beaver Gets a New Name."
25 Sangster, "'The Beaver' as Ideology," 191.
26 Fee, "Rewriting Anthropology and Identifications on the North Pacific Coast," 19.
27 The 1928 film *Beaver People*, made by the National Parks branch of the Department of the Interior, features the controversial figure Grey Owl and his relationship with beavers. See chapter 5, "Ecologist," of Poliquin's *Beaver*.

28 *Oh-oh Canada*, "Michael Farnan."
29 Poliquin, *Beaver*, 181–2. Beaver also comes up in Cyr and Slater's review of Métis foodways: "Wild game such as moose, muskrat, venison, and rabbit were reported as traditional as were water fowl such as duck, geese, and muskrat [sic] because of their presence in participants' diets. Three participants reported also eating beaver, however, their responses suggested that beaver was not necessarily a desirable meat and was consumed when other game was unavailable." Cyr and Slater, "Honouring the Grandmothers through (Re)membering, (Re)learning, and (Re)vitalizing Métis Traditional Foods and Protocols," 56.
30 George Jr. and Gairns, *A Feast for All Seasons*, 21.
31 Norman, "Fit for the Table of the Most Fastidious Epicure," 34.
32 Luby, *Dammed*, 177. Beaver recipes also appear in twentieth- and twenty-first-century Indigenous cookbooks, such as Fox, *Nishnabe Delights*, People of 'Ksan, *Gathering What the Great Nature Provided: Food Traditions of the Gitksan*, Lovesick Lake Native Women's Association, *The Rural and Native Heritage Cookbook: The Gathering*, and Kurtness, *Pachamama: Cuisine des Premières Nations*.
33 Beeson, *Macdonald Was Late for Dinner*, 168–74.
34 Ibid., 175.
35 Myers, "Best Before," 1.
36 Weso, *Good Seeds*, 38.
37 Cooke and Lucas, *Catharine Parr Traill's The Female Emigrant Guide*, 162.
38 Driver, "Regional Differences in the Canadian Daily Meal?," 211–12.
39 "Moosemeat & Marmalade," "About the Show."
40 Simpson shares a memory of Long Lake '58 First Nation: "An elder told me that he didn't always have enough money to purchase tobacco when he went out hunting. Instead of tobacco, he would gift the animal whatever he had with him of value, which oftentimes, he explained, was a piece of baloney sandwich. He felt that the animal spirit would understand his intent and accept this gift in the spirit it had been intended." This story illustrates the continuity of tradition, and the importance of intent over the material details of what a hunter offers the animal's spirit. Simpson, *As We Have Always Done*, 139.
41 "Moosemeat & Marmalade," season 1, episode 1, "Beaver and the Boys."
42 Poliquin, *Beaver*, 17, 164.
43 Jørgensen, "Beavers Are Back in England."
44 Campbell-Palmer et al., *The Eurasian Beaver*, 24. This is from Leviticus 11:46. See also "The Abominations of Leviticus" in Douglas, *Purity and Danger*, 42–58.

45 Jørgensen, "Beaver for Lent."
46 Poliquin, *Beaver*, 22.
47 Saul, *A Fair Country*, 46.
48 Parrott and Marshall, "Iroquois Wars." The beaver trade shaped the politics of the region and is one example that Adelman and Aron give of how North American "borderlands" became "border lands." Adelman and Aron, "From Borderlands to Borders."
49 Boonstra, "Beaver."
50 Gardiner Museum, "Kent Monkman." For more about *The Rise and Fall of Civilization* and its connection to the eradication of bison, see Barnard, "The Bison and the Cow." There is also a connection between beavers and bison on the Prairies, which Wise details: "Beaver bundles were perhaps the most famous of these Blackfoot medicine bundles. As one of the most powerful members of the nonhuman world, beavers were believed to exert control over bison. If properly utilized in association with the correct ritual practices, a beaver bundle would enable its bearer to summon the beaver's help in controlling where bison would move and how they would behave when hunters sought to drive them." Wise, *Native Foods*, 104.
51 Daschuk, *Clearing the Plains*, 27. This commodification of bison continues today with the booming health food industry's interest in bison bars. See Noble, "Bison Bars Were Supposed to Restore Native Communities and Grass-Based Ranches."
52 Government of Canada, "Official Symbols of Canada." For Monkman's engagement with the genre of history painting, see Reder and McCall, "Indigenous and Postcolonial Studies," 4, 11.
53 Hood, *The Beaver Manifesto*, 40.
54 Roy and Ali, *From Pemmican to Poutine*, 43.
55 Ibid.
56 McWilliams, *A Revolution in Eating*, 8.
57 Ibid.
58 Roberts, "The Snipe Were Good and the Wine Not Bad," 62.
59 TallBear, "Being in Relation," 61.
60 Colpitts, *Game in the Garden*, 64.
61 See Cartmill, *A View to a Death in the Morning*.
62 Richler, "Wild about Eating Game."
63 CBC News, "Illegal Hunting Starting Early This Season."
64 Ontario Regulations, Food Safety and Quality Act.
65 Richler, "Wild about Eating Game."
66 One review, however, claims that the authors stray too far from the restaurant: "Furthermore, the book barely mentions Liliget itself. Skip

the introduction and you might never know the Wattses ran a restaurant. While its recipes are excellent, Where People Feast misses the opportunity to be much more than just a recipe collection." *Quill and Quire*, "Reviews."
67 Ontario Regulations, Food Safety and Quality Act, 2001, S.O. 2001, c. 20.
68 Richler, *My Canada Includes Foie Gras*, 113.
69 Whiteduck Ringuette, interview.
70 Dammann and Johns, *True North*, 49.
71 Ibid.
72 Louis Charest, interview by the author, 30 August 2017.
73 Richler, "Wild about Eating Game."
74 Humphreys, "Controversial Montreal Chef Martin Picard's New Book Includes Recipes for 'Squirrel Sushi' and 'Confederation Beaver.'"
75 For extreme eating, see Goodyear, *Anything That Moves*.
76 Panetta, "Martin Picard's Squirrel Sushi and Braised Beaver in New Cookbook."
77 Picard is also responsible for giving Anthony Bourdain, who happens to be the author of the preface to Picard's first cookbook, his first taste of beaver in a 2013 episode of "Parts Unknown." Bourdain's show is often about extreme eating, but Picard did not serve "Confederation beaver"; instead, he prepared a simple stew, forgoing the foie gras. Bourdain's verdict was "Absolutely delicious." "Anthony Bourdain," "Quebec." Noma has also experimented with beaver, which Jesper Schytte hunts in Sweden and delivers to the Copenhagen restaurant. Jesper Schytte, email to the author, 17 July 2016.
78 Salminen, "Cook It Raw Alberta and the Art of Slowing Down."
79 Salminen, "Hunting for the Future at Cook It Raw Alberta."
80 Salminen, "Cook It Raw Alberta and the Art of Slowing Down."
81 Turner, "Delicious Resistance," 105.
82 Ibid., 119.
83 Ibid., 98.
84 Ibid.
85 *Ottawa Citizen*, "Greater Ottawa Chamber of Commerce 2004 Business Achievement Award Winners."
86 *Ottawa Citizen*, "Recently Recommended." DesBrisay, "Best Bites of 2007."
87 Warren Sutherland moved on to other Ottawa kitchens. Eade, "Omnivore's Ottawa."
88 Sutherland, "Sweetgrass on the Verge."
89 Ibid.
90 Ibid.

91 For beef's cultural and economic importance, see Korinek, "Meat Stinks/ Eat Beef Dyke!"
92 Christa Bruneau-Guenther, interview by the author, 12 September 2016.
93 For cookbooks as a medium for storytelling and an index of cultural, social, and political shifts, see Appadurai, "How to Make a National Cuisine," Bower, "Bound Together," and Neuhaus, *Manly Meals and Mom's Home Cooking*.
94 Driver lists "self-taught ethnologist" Frederick Wilkerson Waugh's 1916 *Iroquis* [sic] *Foods and Food Preparation*, which the Canadian Department of Mines published. Driver, *Culinary Landmarks*, 545–6. In another text she divides the evolution of "Canada's culinary literature" into three stages: the first fifty years, 1825–76; "the emergence of new types," 1877–1900; and "the proliferation of cookbooks in the twentieth century." For historical context, the two first cookbooks published in Canada were not unique. The first, *La cuisinière bourgeoise* (Quebec City, 1825), reproduced an eighteenth-century French volume, and the second, *The Cook Not Mad* (Kingston, 1831), an American one. Driver, "Canadian Cookbooks (1825–1949)," 27.
95 *The Joy of Cooking* is an American classic that has been in print since 1936 and has sold over eighteen million copies. Rombauer and Rombauer Becker, *The Joy of Cooking*. Sherman repeats this in Mihesuah and Hoover, eds., *Indigenous Food Sovereignty in the U.S.*, 44–8.
96 Bruneau-Guenther, interview.
97 Feast Cafe Bistro makes Peyton's list of 150 restaurants in Canada. The book also shares its recipe for "Indigenous Traditional Bison Tacos." Peyton, *Where We Ate*, 284–5. It calls for oil, onion, ground bison or beef, garlic, kosher salt, chili powder, smoked paprika, cumin powder, black pepper, tomato sauce, maple syrup, honey, or brown sugar, frozen corn kernels, turtle beans (black beans), and fry bread tacos. Shredded lettuce, diced red onions, shredded cheddar cheese, salsa, sour cream, and chopped cilantro are all listed as optional toppings. After acknowledging bison's complicated history, Peyton says: "Dishes like Indian tacos – bannock topped with Tex-Mex ingredients – are something that" Bruneau-Guenther wanted to focus on when she opened her restaurant. "Bannock is a major culinary component for Feast Cafe Bistro chef and owner Christa Bruneau-Guenther," writes Peyton. "Before the colonial introduction of white sugar and flour, her ancestors used cattail or wild rice flour, sweetening it with berries or maple syrup and frying it in animal fats, but these days, she chooses the easier modern methodology and views Bannock as a sign of resilience, survival and creativity." Ibid., 284.

98  Glenna Henderson, interview by the author, 13 September 2016.
99  Statistics Canada, "National Indigenous Peoples Day ... by the Numbers."
100 Sanderson, "Métis Island."
101 Ibid.
102 Bison Berry first went by the name Tansi Café, and Talia Syrie, the chef and owner of the Winnipeg restaurant the Tallest Poppy, developed the eatery.
103 Louise Champagne, interview by the author, 7 September 2016.
104 Cidro et al., "Beyond Food Security," 29.
105 Cyr and Slater, "Honouring the Grandmothers Through (Re)membering, (Re)learning, and (Re)vitalizing," 57.
106 Neechi, "About."

## 10. Salmon and the F-Word

1  A Sixties Scoop survivor, Cook penned a children's book about her experience. Additionally, it is through the restaurant that she reconnected with her family. CBC Radio, "Indigenous Cuisine Reconnected a Sixties Scoop Survivor with Family, Community and Culture."
2  Remi Caudron, interview by the author, 16 February 2016. Gora, "Vancouver's Only Aboriginal Restaurant's Got Game." Salmon n' Bannock also features in Peyton's "love letter" to Canadian restaurants. Peyton, *Where We Ate*, 266.
3  There was also a temporary restaurant in Vancouver: The Wild Salmon Restaurant on the Vancouver Community College campus, which students in the Aboriginal Culinary Arts Class ran.
4  Winnipeg's Feast supported an artist in a similar way. Glowacki, "He's Taught Me So Much."
5  Salmon n' Bannock Bistro, Facebook.
6  Newman, *Speaking in Cod Tongues*, 98.
7  Ibid.
8  Ibid.
9  The study reports that 5 per cent of Canadians prefer farmed and 46 per cent prefer wild. This also tells a geographical and generational story: 69 per cent of British Columbians prefer wild to farmed salmon, whereas in Quebec the number is only 35 per cent. Canadians over the age of sixty are more likely to prefer wild salmon – perhaps they remember when salmon was only wild. Coletto, Di Francesco, and Morrison, "Seafood Survey," 3, 8. For Canadian culinary tourism, see Hashimoto and Telfer, "Selling Canadian Culinary Tourism."

10 *Salmo salar* is Atlantic salmon. The Pacific species are *Oncorhynchus tschawytscha* (King, Spring, and Chinook); *Oncorhynchus nerka* (Sockeye); *Oncorhynchus gorbuscha* (Pink); *Oncorhynchus kisutsch* (Coho, Medium red, Silver); and, *Oncorhynchus keta* (Chum, Dog). The two Asian Pacific species are *Oncorhynchus masou* and *Oncorhynchus rhodurus*.
11 Cronon, "Foreword," xi.
12 Coates, *Salmon*, 55.
13 Ibid., 85.
14 Zeide, *Canned*, 3.
15 Ibid., 13. Coates, *Salmon*, 69.
16 Ibid. Zeide, *Canned*, 13.
17 Coates, *Salmon*, 69.
18 Ibid., 74–5.
19 Ibid., 160.
20 Fisheries and Oceans Canada, "Wild Atlantic Salmon in Eastern Canada," 4.
21 Simpson, *As We Have Always Done*, 2.
22 Ibid., 3.
23 Ibid., 99. She also mentions the destruction of wild rice beds.
24 Government of Ontario, "Chinook Salmon." It was once possible to fish for salmon in Toronto. Beeson quotes the 1793 diary of Elizabeth Simcoe (the wife of Ontario's first lieutenant governor) about her Toronto harbour fishing trip: "At 8 this dark evening we went in a boat to see salmon speared." Beeson, *Macdonald Was Late for Dinner*, 113.
25 Coates, *Salmon*, 85.
26 Ibid.
27 Shepro, "The Rhetoric of Salmon," 349.
28 Fisheries and Oceans Canada, "Farmed Salmon." Somewhat confusingly, Atlantic salmon is also farmed in the Pacific. The Canadian industry employs three methods – land-based hatcheries, saltwater net pens with some land-based systems, and land-based – in five provinces: Newfoundland and Labrador, Prince Edward Island, Nova Scotia, New Brunswick, and British Columbia – the largest. As of 2012, three Norwegian companies controlled 92 per cent of British Columbia's salmon farms. Schreiber and Brattland, "Introduction," 6. From 2011 to 2015, the annual average "farm-gate" value of Canada's salmon culture was $735.2 million, with BC's production contributing 60 per cent. Ibid.
29 Bloch, "AquAdvantage, the First GMO Salmon, Is Coming to America."
30 Shepro, "The Rhetoric of Salmon," 347.
31 Lien and Law, "Emergent Aliens," 72.

32  Coates, *Salmon*, 100.
33  Ibid.
34  Lien and Law, "Slippery," 12.
35  Lien, *Becoming Salmon*, 2.
36  Lien and Law, "Emergent Aliens," 65–6.
37  Ibid., 70.
38  Lien and Law, "Slippery," 3.
39  Metallic and Metallic, "A Mi'qmaq Perspective on Wild Salmon Management and the Salmon Farming Industry," 19.
40  Todd, "Fish, Kin and Hope," 97. This also connects to Luby's notion of "presence-ing." She writes: "Receiving gifts or learning from plant and animal teachers requires relationship building, which depends on careful attention over time, a process that I call presence-ing." This reinforces "the interconnectedness of all living things." Luby, *Dammed*, 28.
41  Todd, "Fish Pluralities," 217.
42  Ibid., 219.
43  Ibid., 225.
44  Lichatowich, *Salmon without Rivers*, 23.
45  Johnson, "First Feasts."
46  For salmon in the Pacific Northwest, see Newell, *Tangled Webs of History*; Roche and McHutchison eds., *First Fish, First People*; and Harris, *Fish, Law, and Colonialism*.
47  Coates, *Salmon*, 11.
48  O'Brien, "Of Coyotes and Culverts," 53.
49  Newman, *Speaking in Cod Tongues*, 99.
50  CBC News, "'Pacific Salmon' Named B.C.'S Official Fish."
51  Coates, *Salmon*, 12.
52  Grey and Newman, "Beyond Culinary Colonialism," 723.
53  Newman, *Speaking in Cod Tongues*, 101.
54  Together with distinction and competition, Weltecke describes adaptability and culinary exchange as one of the three forms of entangled food history. Weltecke, "Essen und Fasten in interreligiöser Abgrenzung, Kokurrenz und Austausch," 20.
55  Newman, *Speaking in Cod Tongues*, 101.
56  Schreiber, "Our Wealth Sits on the Table," 361.
57  Ibid., 362.
58  Ibid., 376.
59  Boyd and Barenscott, "Introduction," in Barenscott and Boyd, *Canadian Culinary Imaginations*, 17.
60  Kimmerer, *Braiding Sweetgrass*, 246.

61 Ibid.
62 Schreiber, "Our Wealth Sits on the Table," 366.
63 Todd, "Fish Pluralities," 231.
64 Parenteau, "Care, Control and Supervision," 34.
65 Rich Francis, phone interview by author, 10 September 2018.
66 Lynn, "Former Top Chef Canada Finalist Wants to Redefine Aboriginal Cuisine."
67 Ibid.
68 One example is the "Cooking for Truth and Reconciliation" dinner with Chef Vikram Vij at My Shanti in Surrey, BC, in January 2018.
69 The other two chefs that *Red Chef Revival* features are Cezin Nottawa (Algonquin) and Shane Chartrand (Cree). Danny Berish, *Red Chef Revival*.
70 Seventh Fire.
71 Francis is aware of the extent to which food can heal. Before "Top Chef Canada" and the exposure it gave him, he "lost his soul" in Vancouver's downtown east side. "I was a chef at the time and was clean and sober. I had a day off and one day I blew it. I didn't know it at the time, one block at the time from east Hastings. I was going to go to Chinatown, I looked down the street, on the left hand side, I can see it so clearly in my head. I was like, what is down there. And I went and checked it out. East Hastings, I had no idea. A few months later I literally lost everything. I called my mom and I don't know how I made it out of that situation or that time of my life alive, but it was food that got me up. It got me on my feet and I decided I had to give life another shot. So it is Indigenous food that have saved my life more times than I care to admit."
72 Wright, "In the Shadow of a Willow Tree," 82. Winnipeg-based chef Steven Watson, a member of Peguis First Nation, counters historical erasure with his project "1491" – asking "how Indigenous food might have developed over 500 years without colonialism." Moore and Thiessen, *mmm ... Manitoba*, 207.
73 Corntassel, "Re-envisioning Resurgence," 91.
74 Glasner, "From Seal Tartare to Bison on a Bun, Indigenous Chefs Are Reclaiming Their Heritage One Plate at a Time."
75 Coppolino, "Food-Ordering Apps, More Veggies and Playing with Food Are the New Trends."
76 Ibid.
77 Kimmerer, *Braiding Sweetgrass*, 129, 10.
78 Ibid., 336.
79 Penniman, *Farming While Black*, 8.
80 Kimmerer, *Braiding Sweetgrass*, 338.

81 Ibid., 337.
82 Francis, "Medicine Wheel Cured Salmon."
83 Francis, Facebook, 13 November 2017.
84 Francis, Instagram.
85 Wise, *Native Foods*, 128.
86 Nickel, *Assembling Unity*, 153.
87 Salmon n' Bannock, Facebook.
88 Coates, *Salmon*, 149.
89 *Lakes District News*, "Classified Ads."
90 *Ottawa Citizen*, "Come to the Muckamuck."
91 Ibid.
92 Ibid.
93 Lu and Fine discuss the balance that customers expect "ethnic" restaurants to achieve between "too American" (so not exotic enough) and "too" authentic. Lu and Fine, "The Presentation of Ethnic Authenticity," 547.
94 Watts remembers that the cannery was Japanese-owned, which I have not been able to confirm.
95 Stainsby, "Canadian Content."
96 Watts and Watts, *Where People Feast*, 92.
97 McRae, *My Name Is Dolly*, 30.
98 Watts and Watts, *Where People Feast*, 78.
99 Davey, "Original Aboriginal."
100 Chu, "Get to Know a Chef."
101 Wolfman remembers a public appearance where the moderator incorrectly introduced him as from the bear clan; his last name is Jewish.
102 Wolfman and Finn, *Cooking with the Wolfman*, 45.
103 Ibid., 164.
104 Ibid.
105 Ibid., 30.
106 Ibid., 164–6.
107 Ibid., 45–7, 48–9, 89, 170.
108 Grey and Newman, "Beyond Culinary Colonialism," 724.
109 For example, Parr Traill writes "Indian corn" in her 1855 guide. Cooke and Lucas, *Catharine Parr Traill's The Female Emigrant Guide*, 116. Additionally, Beeson published a recipe for corn bread from the Queen's Royal Hotel at Niagara-on-the-Lake. Included in the hotel's "old handwritten ledgers," the recipe dates to the 1860s and calls for "Indian meal." To clarify, Beeson writes "cornmeal" in square brackets in 1993. Beeson, *Macdonald Was Late for Dinner*, 62. In contrast, *The Maple*

*Leaf Canadian Recipe Book*, issued by the director of Canadian Trade Publicity at the British Columbia House in London in the 1930s, calls corn "Canadian." The book targeted "the British housewife," with the intention of providing "more links in the chain of distribution between the Canadian producer and the British consumer." He includes recipes for "Canadian corn soup" (which calls for "1 can Canadian corn"), but still uses the term "Indian meal" for "cornmeal mush." Bowker, *The Maple Leaf Canadian Recipe Book*, 29. Moving to the United States, Zogry's survey of "early selected non-indigenous perspectives on corn and Indigenous botanical and cultivation knowledge," also illustrates how corn became American. Zogry, "Introduction," 7. However, chef Bitsoie reclaims corn as "Indian corn" in his "Sweet summer corn broth" recipe, which calls for "6 fresh ears sweet Indian Summer corn, kernels removed and cobs reserved." Bitsoie and Fraioli, *New Native Kitchen*, 52. Wise takes corn as an example to argue that, in part, "the inconspicuousness of Native American food and agriculture is discursive, explained by patterns of language that first emerged with the colonial appropriation of North America by Europeans more than five centuries ago. The word *corn*, for instance – a generic English term for any type of edible grain that could be harvested and stored – leapt from the lips of colonists who were too impatient to consider more precise distinctions for the novel vegetable grown by Native farmers in an array of colors and cultivars. The linguistic act of encoding corn as *corn* reduced those complexities and helped to make it recognizable as an English possession." Wise, *Native Foods*, 3. The word, he explains, was especially used for barley. Ibid., 28.

110 Little Miss Chief, "The Little Miss Chief Story."
111 Bhat, "Salmon n' Bannock Expands to YVR, the First Indigenous Restaurant to Open in a Canadian Airport."

**Conclusion: The North**

1 Melasniemi and Tiravanija, *Bastard Cookbook*, 63.
2 Coppola explained the impetus for a Native American–inspired restaurant in a *San Francisco Chronicle* opinion piece: "More reading and study led to my desire to resurrect this early American wine brand at the site of the former Geyser Peak winery in Geyserville. As the purchase of the property brought with it a permit allowing the development of a visitor center and restaurant, I began to imagine that we could feature Native American ambience and food that would highlight ingredients

of America as it once had been." He is honest in stating: "I confess that I used my own imagination and creative powers to bring this project to life much in the way that I would have in making a film." The text's objective is to quiet any concerns about cultural appropriation, and it ends with an economic promise: "The Virginia Dare Winery, a family-owned company, will donate 5 percent of its pretax profits to America's Native People." The following day, Jonathan Kauffman wrote: "Werowocomoco appears at a time when publications like the New York Times and the Atlantic are profiling American Indian chefs, yet only a handful of restaurants serving indigenous North American cuisines are operating across the country." Coppola, "Coppola's New Restaurant." Kauffman, "Questions of Cuisine and Culture Surround Coppola's New Restaurant."

3 Hannickel's description of the Catawba grape – "early Ohio's most popular and profitable wine grape, a natural hybrid of American and European vines" – tells a similar story, and she argues that it was cultivated to accentuate a deeper heritage of the grape: "acknowledging its native appellations, not its colonial ones." Hannickel, *Empire of Vines*, 136–8.

4 Truder, "Why Is Francis Ford Coppola Opening an 'American Native' Restaurant?"

5 For Virginia Dare's meaning, see Hannickel, *Empire of Vines*, 144.

6 Because of COVID-19, University Press Books closed and Cafe Ohlone thus lost its host. But then on 1 September 2022, Cafe Ohlone opened in a new location: the University of California Berkeley's Phoebe A. Hearst Museum of Anthropology.

7 The acorn was a vital pre-contact food in what is now California. See Jacknis, ed., *Food in California Indian Culture* and Clarke, "Bringing the Past to the Present."

8 Vincent Medina, interview by the author, 7 March 2019.

9 Crystal Wahpepah, interview by the author, 15 April 2019.

10 For the history of the Corn Dance Café, see Gora, "From New York's Silverbird to Santa Fe's Corn Dance Café" and Oden and Dooley, *Corn Dance*. After closing her restaurant, Oden later became "the Indigenous food consultant" at Thirty Nine Restaurant, which is hosted by Oklahoma City's First American Museum. Oden and Dooley, *Corn Dance*, 10.

11 Siu provides a different example of how restaurants are sometimes the only cultural institutions representing particular communities. Siu, "Chino Latino Restaurants," 162.

12 Simpson, *As We Have Always Done*, 6. This also connects to Luby's concept of "passive resistance," which she defines in dialogue with Simpson's work, as well as the work of Taiaiake Alfred. Luby, *Dammed*, 35.

13 See Mihesuah, "Nephi Craig."
14 Moving to drink, in 2016 Shyla Sheppard from the Fort Berthold Reservation in North Dakota opened the Bow & Arrow Brewing Co. in Albuquerque together with Missy Begay, from the Navajo Nation. Gora, "Indigenous Cuisine Revitalization."
15 The cookbook was published in 2002 and took home the award in 2003.
16 Frank, *Seed to Plate, Soil to Sky*, 15.
17 Bitsoie, *New Native Kitchen*, 236. See also Hetzler, *The Mitsitam Cafe Cookbook*. For more about Indigenous foodways in the United States, see Wilson, *Buffalo Bird Woman's Garden*, Berzok, *American Indian Food*, Mihesuah and Hoover, eds., *Indigenous Food Sovereignty in the United States*, Nabhan, *Enduring Seeds*, Pesantubbee and Zogry, eds., *Native Foodways*, Powers and Powers, "Metaphysical Aspects of an Oglala Food System," and Wise, *Native Foods*.
18 The restaurant that Jacob's family had opened in 1989 to feature recipes from the Osage Nation inspired them to open their own.
19 There are also organizations such as the Cultural Conservancy' Native Foodways program in San Francisco (formed in 1995). Also, Martin Reinhardt ran the Decolonizing Diet Project at the Northern Michigan University Center for Native American Studies from 2010 to 2014.
20 Conflict Kitchen, "Haudenosaunee."
21 Rao, "The Movement to Define Native American Cuisine." See also Gora, "From New York's Silverbird to Santa Fe's Corn Dance Café."
22 Sherman, "Tasting and Talk."
23 Wolfman, interview. The racial assumptions of this story and how they relate to Indigeneity and identity in Mexico are worth unpacking.
24 Middell and Naumann, "Global History and the Spatial Turn," 155.
25 I model this approach after Gabaccia, "Is Everywhere Nowhere?," 1117.
26 McCallum, "Indigenous Labor and Indigenous History," 534.
27 Claudia Serrato, interview by the author, 17 March 2018. Future work should also compare Canada and the United States to Mexico. Pilcher tells a similar story in his chapter "The Blue Corn Bonanza." Pilcher, *Planet Taco*, 189–220.
28 Bronson, *A Public Apology to Siksika Nation*, 7.
29 The installation's subtitle replicates the title of a 1967 American film about an interracial marriage at a time when such legal romantic unions were illegal in seventeen states. For the majority of the film, the parents of the married-couple-to-be express colossal doubt, only for this to fade in the very last scene as they all trail into the dining room, ready to eat together.
30 Bronson, *A Public Apology to Siksika Nation*, 19–20.
31 Ibid., 25.

32 Miller, "Determined to Keep Up Their Dances," 79.
33 King, *The Inconvenient Indian*, 2–3.
34 Sharpe, *In the Wake*, 19.
35 Kimmerer, *Braiding Sweetgrass*, 367. For the Seven Fires creation story, see Simpson, *Dancing on Our Turtle's Back*, 31–49 and *As We Have Always Done*, 20–1, 211.
36 Francis, interview.
37 Slow Food, "Terminology."
38 *New York Times*, "Asparagus and Spruce."
39 Redzepi, *NOMA*, 41.
40 Redzepi, "Evergreen, Ever Delicious."
41 Goldstein, *Inside the California Food Revolution*, 311.
42 Boralia.
43 Evelyn Wu and Wayne Morris, interview by the author, 31 August 2016.
44 Nuttall-Smith, "Boralia." Loretta Barrrett Oden's debut cookbook features a similar recipe for "Mussels and Chanterelles Simmered with Pine Needles," which calls for "1 small pine branch" alongside "1 cup dry white wine or ocean water." As she explains, "This recipe is the happy result of an afternoon foraging mussels along the Santa Cruz Coast with Chef Michel Nischan for one of our PBS episodes." Oden and Dooley, *Corn Dance*, 101. Released as five episodes in 2006, her PBS TV series "Seasoned with Spirit" won an Emmy. Oden also has a recipe for "Pine Needle Ice Cream," calling for "1/2 cup spruce or Douglas fir needles." Ibid., 183.
45 After a four-year run, Boralia closed in November 2018. The arrival of the owners' second child plus "ever-increasing rent" led them to close. Boralia, Instagram.
46 Geniusz, *Plants Have So Much To Give Us, All We Have To Do Is Ask*, 99.
47 "Vitamin C," Health Canada.
48 Geniusz, *Plants Have So Much to Give Us, All We Have to Do Is Ask*, 101.
49 Ibid., 101–2.
50 Parks Canada, "Georgian Bay Islands National Park."
51 For more about settler colonial politics in Ontario's "cottage country," see Drew Hayden Taylor's play and book *Cottagers and Indians* and Peter A. Stevens's scholarship about Canadian cottage culture, including "Decolonizing Cottage Country." See also Stevens, "A Little Place in the (Next) Country."
52 Trubek, *The Taste of Place*, 18.
53 Inglis and Gimlin, "Food Globalizations," 8.
54 Albala, "Wild Food," 9.

55  For the growing interest in wild foods, see La Cerva, *Feasting Wild*.
56  Since 2016 Fiso has hosted the pop-up dining series Hikai, which combines Māori ingredients and traditions with her knowledge of working in Michelin-starred kitchens in New York City. In 2020 she published her first cookbook: *Hiakai*.
57  Waters, *Chez Panisse Menu Cookbook*, xi.
58  Luby, *Dammed*, 137.
59  Salmon n' Bannock Bistro, "Menu."
60  Newman, *Speaking in Cod Tongues*, 236.
61  Grey and Newman, "Beyond Culinary Colonialism," 719.
62  Ibid., 720.
63  In 2015 Chartrand came in second on season 2 of "Chopped Canada."
64  Chartrand, "Art Is the Medicine."
65  Bitsoi and Fraioli, *New Native Kitchen*, 54.
66  Shane Chartrand, born Shane John Gordon, went into foster care when he was a year and a half old. Belinda and Dennis Chartrand adopted him when he was nearly seven. Years later, when he was working at Dante's Bistro in Edmonton, a man recognized him, and Chartrand learned that they were cousins. Chartrand and King, *tawâw*, 2, 9.
67  Ketchum, "Memory Has Added Seasoning," "The Place We've Always Wanted to Go but Never Could Find," and *Ingredients for Revolution*.
68  In 2014 the *Food Republic* ran the headline "New York's First Native American Restaurant Was Run by an Indian-American Chef." Rahul Akerkar worked at Silverbird's, which was owned by a half-Apache and half-Navajo man named Silverbird together with his German wife. In recalling his time cooking there, he recounts: "We'd cook buffalo and possum, rattlesnake, rabbit, gator, all in the traditional way. We didn't use black pepper, we used spices that were indigenous to the U.S., like pollen and sage." Kapadia, "New York's First Native American Restaurant Was Run by an Indian-American Chef." See Gora, "From New York's Silverbird to Santa Fe's Corn Dance Café."

# Bibliography

## Archival Collections

### City of Regina Photographs Collection

"Gold West Inn at 4150 Albert Street, which later became the Landmark Inn." c. 1975, Item CORA-A-0885.

### City of Toronto Archives, Ontario

"Iroquois coffee shop, Toronto Island," 1961 and 1962. Fonds 220, Series 316, Files 205, 726, 727, 736, 756, 758.
"Park Superintendent's House at Petunia Island." Fonds 1047, Series 872, File 15.
"Whale meat shipment at North Toronto Station," December 1918. Item 1939. Fonds 1244, Williams James family fonds.

### City of Vancouver Archives, Vancouver, British Columbia

"Muckamuck Restaurant: Northwest Coast Native Indian food." AM1519-: 2011-045.1 Box: 632-A-02. Pamphlet collection.

### Library and Archives Canada, Ottawa, Ontario

"Restaurants Review Expo 67, An official publication," 1967. RG71-G, R869, Volume/box 42, file ARC-71/42/5.

"Dominion of Canada Annual Report of the Department of Indian Affairs for the Year Ended 30th June 1894." Ottawa: Dominion of Canada, 1895. Item number: 9745.

"Two Aboriginal women reading a Canada's Food Guide posted in the Community Health Workers Training Program, Coqualeetza, British Columbia," n.d. Online MIKAN no. 4322469.

### McCord Museum, Montreal, Quebec

Fonds Gilberte Christin de Cardaillac, P573/Do2.

### McGill Archival Collections, Montreal, Quebec

MSG 1269 – Menu Collection.

### Province of Manitoba Archives, Winnipeg, Manitoba

"2015/008/18: Unidentified banquet. Probably the annual campfire banquet of the 1866–'70 and '85 veterans, the Red River Settlers and the trailblazers of the Canadian North-west." HB2015/008. L.E. Wilson's records related to the Hudson's Bay Company's 250th anniversary celebrations.

"Bannock Baking Contest, Flin Flon Trout Festival," n.d. SA-2-57. GR10030. Government photographs.

"Trappers Festival, Bannock Baking," 1963.63-744. GR0201. Government photographs.

### Royal British Columbia Museum Archives, Victoria, British Columbia

"The North American Indian" by Edward S. Curtis; Volume 11; Plate No. 374; Nootka method of spearing, 1915. D-08321.

### Simon Fraser University Archives, Vancouver, British Columbia

Pacific Tribune Photograph Collection. Digitized Collections.

### Thomas Fisher Rare Books Library, University of Toronto, Ontario

Canadian Pacific Railway Menu, "Before the Canadian Pacific," n.d. Box 47, Menus. Folder 47. Ephemera Collection.

Canadian Pacific Railway Menu, "Canadian Pacific Dining Car Service. February 1959 – Breakfast." Box 114. Folder 4. Ephemera Collection.
Canadian Pacific Railway Menu, "An Indian Chief," 1943. Box 47, Menus. Folder 16. Ephemera Collection.
"The Royal York Hotel's August 20, 1956 menu." Box 114. Folder 11. Ephemera Collection.

### *University of British Columbia Archives, Vancouver, British Columbia*

Service, Office, and Retail Workers Union of Canada fonds.

## Personal Interviews

Adler, Shawn. Owner of the Pow Wow Cafe. Toronto, Ontario. 11 September 2017.
Bruneau-Guenther, Christa. Owner of Feast Cafe Bistro. Winnipeg, Manitoba. 12 September 2016.
Caudron, Remi. Co-owner of Salmon n' Bannock. Vancouver, British Columbia. 16 February 2016.
Champagne, Louise. President of Neechi Foods Co-op Ltd. Winnipeg, Manitoba. 7 September 2016.
Charest, Louis. Executive Chef at the Office of the Secretary to the Governor General. Ottawa, Ontario. 30 August 2017.
Francis, Rich. Owner of Seventh Fire Hospitality Group. Six Nations of the Grand River, Ontario. Phone interview. 10 September 2018.
Goodman, Lauren. Senior Policy Advisor at Inuit Tapiriit Kanatami. Ottawa, Ontario. 29 August 2017.
Henderson, Glenna. Owner of Cookem Daisey's. Winnipeg, Manitoba. 13 September 2016.
Horne, John. Chef at Canoe. Toronto, Ontario. Phone interview. 17 January 2018.
King, Carolyn. Elder and Former Chief of the Mississaugas of the Credit First Nation. Toronto, Ontario. 9 September 2018.
Logan, Audrey. Gardener. Winnipeg, Manitoba. 10 September 2016.
Medina, Vincent, and Louis Trevino. Owners of Cafe Ohlone. Berkeley, California. 7 March 2019.
Riel-Lachapelle, Wapokunie. Owner of Nikosi Bistro Pub. Wakefield, Quebec. 26 August 2017.

Ringuette, Johl Whiteduck. Owner of NishDish. Toronto, Ontario. 18 September 2016.
Sault, Gary. Elder. Toronto, Ontario. 9 September 2018.
Serrato, Claudia. Co-founder of Cocina Manakurhini. Los Angeles, California. 17 March 2018.
Shawana, Joseph. Chef at Kūkům Kitchen. Toronto, Ontario. 5 September 2018.
Sigrithur, Anna. Chef and Podcast Host. Winnipeg, Manitoba. 10 September 2016.
Wahpepah, Crystal. Owner of Wahpepah's Kitchen. Oakland, California. 15 April 2019.
Watts (McRae), Dolly. Owner of Liliget Feast House. Port Alberni, British Columbia. Phone interview. 28 June 2019.
Wolfman, David. Culinary Arts Professor. Toronto, Ontario. 6 September 2016.
Wu, Evelyn, and Wayne Morris. Owners of Boralia. Toronto, Ontario. 31 August 2016.

## Sources

Abarca, Meredith E. "Authentic or Not, It's Original." *Food and Foodways* 12, no. 1 (2004): 1–25.
Absolon, Kathy, and Cam Willett. "Aboriginal Research: Berry Picking and Hunting in the 21st Century." *First Peoples Child & Family Review* 1, no. 1 (2004): 5–17.
Adamson, Joni. "Medicine Food: Critical Environmental Justice Studies, Native North American Literature, and the Movement for Food Sovereignty." *Environmental Justice* 4, no. 4 (December 2011): 213–19.
Adelman, Jeremy, and Stephen Aron. "From Borderlands to Borders: Empires, Nation-States, and the Peoples In Between in North American History." *American Historical Review* 104, no. 3 (June 1999): 814–41.
Adichie, Chimamanda. "The Danger of a Single Story." TEDGlobal 2009 Conference, Oxford, UK, 21–4 July 2009. https://www.ted.com/talks/chimamanda_ngozi_adichie_the_danger_of_a_single_story.
Agg, Jen. *I Hear She's a Real Bitch*. Toronto: Penguin Random House Canada, 2016.
Agriculture and Agri-Food Canada. *"Everyone at the Table!" Government of Canada Announces First-Ever Food Policy for Canada*. Press Release. 17 June 2019. https://www.canada.ca/en/agriculture-agri-food/news/2019/06/everyone-at-the-table-government-of-canada-announces-the-first-ever-food-policy-for-canada.html.

- *A Food Policy for Canada: Report on the Standing Committee on Agriculture and Agri-Food*. By Pat Finnigan. Ottawa: the House of Commons, December 2017.
- *An Overview of the Canadian Food System 2017*. Last modified 10 November 2017. http://www.agr.gc.ca/eng/about-us/publications/economic-publications/an-overview-of-the-canadian-agriculture-and-agri-food-system-2017/?id=1510326669269.

Akhtar, Khalil. "Why Canadian Restaurants Rarely Make the World's 50 Best List." CBC News, 14 June 2016. https://www.cbc.ca/news/canada/why-canadian-restaurants-rarely-make-the-world-s-50-best-list-1.3633392.

Albala, Ken. "Wild Food: The Call of the Domestic." In *Wild Food: Proceedings of the Oxford Symposium on Food & Cookery 2004*, edited by Richard Hoskings, 9–19. Totnes, Devon: Prospect Books, 2006.

Aldred, Jessica. "Scotland Wild Beaver Reintroduction Trial 'An Outstanding Success.'" *Guardian*, 14 May 2014. https://www.theguardian.com/environment/2014/may/14/scotland-wild-beaver-reintroduced-knapdale.

Alfred, Taiaiake, and Jeff Corntassel. "Being Indigenous: Resurgences against Contemporary Colonialism." *Government and Opposition* 40, no. 4 (2005): 597–614.

Allan, Ted. "Guide to Winnipeg Could Become Local Best-Seller." *Winnipeg Free Press*, 3 December 1975.

Anderson, Mark Cronlund, and Carmen L. Robertson. *Seeing Red: A History of Natives in Canadian Newspapers*. Winnipeg: University of Manitoba Press, 2011.

*Angry Inuk*. Directed by Alethea Arnaquq-Baril. Montreal: National Film Board of Canada and EyeSteelFilm, 2016.

*Anishinabek News*. "Native Culinary Team Wins Gold." 5, no. 1 (January 1993): 3.

"Anthony Bourdain: Parts Unknown," season 1, episode 4, "Quebec." CNN, 5 May 2013.

Anzaldúa, Gloria. *Borderlands: La Frontera*. San Francisco: Aunt Lute Book Company, 1987.

Appadurai, Arjun. "How to Make a National Cuisine: Cookbooks in Contemporary India." *Comparative Studies in Society and History* 30, no. 1 (January 1988): 3–24.

Appelbe, Alison. *Secret Vancouver: The Unique Guidebook to Vancouver's Hidden Sites, Sounds & Tastes*. Oakville: ECW Press, 2003.

Appert, Nicolas. *L'Art de conserver, pendant plusieurs années, toutes les substances animales et végétales*. Paris: 1810. https://gallica.bnf.fr/ark:/12148/bpt6k202755q.pdf.

APTN National News. "Animal Rights Group Puts Nunavut Musician in Cross Hairs over Seal Pelt Debate." 7 April 2014. http://aptnnews.ca/2014/04/07/animal-rights-group-puts-nunavut-musician-cross-hairs-seal-pelt-debate/.
Arendt, Beatrix. "Caribou to Cod: Moravian Missionary Influence on Inuit Subsistence Strategies." *Historical Archaeology* 44, no. 3 (2010): 81–101.
Armstrong, Julian. "Expo Offers Muskox Burgers, Prehistoric Ice." *Gazette*, 18 June 1986, E4.
Armstrong, Nigel. "Emphasize People Not Spice, Culinary Arts Professor Tells Young Chefs." *Guardian*, 4 March 2010. www.theguardian.pe.ca/Living/2010-03-04/article-1298064/Emphasize-people-not-spice-culinary-arts-professor-tells-young-chefs/1.
Arreak, Micah, Annie Désilets, Lucy Kappianaq, Glenda Kripanik, and Kanadaise Uyarasuk. *Niqiliurniq: A Cookbook from Igloolik*. Iqaluit and Toronto: Inhabit Media, 2019.
Arrivé, Mathilde. "Beyond True and False? The Artificial Authenticity of Edward S. Curtis: Response and Reactions." *Études photographiques* 29 (2012): 1–30.
*Asheville Citizen-Times*. "Parris." 17 January 1990, 8A.
*Atlanta Constitution*. "Hard to Find, Easy to Enjoy." 31 July 1994, K6.
– "My Best Recipe: Bread Fit for Fish." 13 April 1978, 10F.
Auberge Chez Denis. "Menu." Accessed 2 May 2018. https://www.aubergechezdenis.ca/resto.html.
Austen, Ian. "'Horrible History': Mass Grave of Indigenous Children Reported in Canada." *New York Times*, 28 May 2021. https://www.nytimes.com/2021/05/28/world/canada/kamloops-mass-grave-residential-schools.html.
Bailey, Sue. "Government to Fund Development of Seal Products for Canadian Grocery Store." Global News, 6 December 2013. http://globalnews.ca/news/1015153/government-to-fund-development-of-seal-products-for-canadian-grocery-stores/.
– "Quebec Company Touts Seal Meat as 'Canadian Superfood.'" CBC News, 16 November 2017. http://www.cbc.ca/news/canada/montreal/quebec-seal-meat-company-super-food-1.4406270.
Bain, Jennifer. "First Nations Food Truck Welcomes Pan Am Patrons." *Toronto Star*, 14 July 2015. www.thestar.com/life/food_wine/2015/07/14/first-nations-food-truck-welcomes-pan-am-patrons.html.
– "A Pretty Fancy Powwow." *Toronto Star*, 30 November 2005.
Bajada, Simon. *The New Nordic: Recipes from a Scandinavian Kitchen*. Melbourne: Hardie Grant, 2015.

- *Nordic Light: Lighter, Everyday Eating from a Scandinavian Kitchen.* Melbourne: Hardie Grant, 2015.
Baloy, Natalie J.K. "Our Home(s) and/on Native Land: Spectacular Re-Visions and Refusals at Vancouver's 2010 Winter Olympic Games." *Streetnotes* 25 (2016): 194–211.
Banff National Park. "Plains Bison Reintroduction." Last modified 2 August 2018. https://www.pc.gc.ca/en/pn-np/ab/banff/info/gestion-management/bisons.
Barbeau, Marius. "The Beaver in Canadian Art." *The Beaver* (September 1941): 14–18.
Barber, James. "$15 (Each) Will Buy Sumptuous Meals." *Province*, 13 May 1977, 25.
- "'Honest' Restaurant Is Hard to Find." *Province*, 23 May 1977, 37.
Barenscott, Dorothy, and Shelley Boyd. *Canadian Culinary Imaginations.* Montreal and Kingston: McGill-Queen's University Press, 2020.
Barnard, John Levi. "The Bison and the Cow: Food, Empire, Extinction." *American Quarterly* 72, no. 2 (2020): 377–401.
Basil, Priya. *Be My Guest: Reflections on Food, Community and the Meaning of Generosity.* Edinburgh: Canongate, 2019.
Battis, Jes. "Breaking Bread: Queer Foodways and the Non-Human." In *Canadian Culinary Imaginations*, edited by Shelley Boyd and Dorothy Barenscott, 311–32. Montreal and Kingston: McGill-Queen's University Press, 2020.
Baxley, Crystal. "Sonny Assu." *Contemporary North American Indigenous Artists*, 31 May 2011. http://contemporarynativeartists.tumblr.com/post/6030123932/sonny-assu-laich-kwil-tach-kwakwakawakw.
BBC News. "Obama and Trudeau Meet Up for Dinner in Montreal." 7 June 2017, https://www.bbc.com/news/world-us-canada-40190393.
Beaumont, Hilary. "Animal Rights Activists Target Indigenous Restaurant for Serving Seal Meat." *VICE*, 11 October 2017. https://news.vice.com/en_ca/article/d3x4ym/animal-rights-activists-target-indigenous-restaurant-for-serving-seal-meat.
Beeson, Patricia. *Macdonald Was Late for Dinner: A Slice of Culinary Life in Early Canada.* Peterborough: Broadview Press, 1993.
Belcourt, Billy-Ray. "Coda: Thinking Paradoxically." In *Messy Eating: Conversations on Animals as Food*, edited by Samantha King, R. Scott Carey, Isabel Macquarrie, Victoria Niva Millious, and Elaine M. Power, 233–41. New York: Fordham University Press, 2019.
- "Political Depression in a Time of Reconciliation." *Active History*, 15 January 2016. http://activehistory.ca/2016/01/political-depression-in-a-time-of-reconciliation/#_ftnref3.

Bell, Alison. "Bannock and Canada's First Peoples." *Food Day Canada*. Accessed 1 October 2018. http://fooddaycanada.ca/articles/bannock-canadas-first-peoples/.

Bell, David, and Gill Valentine, eds. *Consuming Geographies: We Are Where We Eat*. London and New York: Routledge, 1997.

Bell, Gloria Jane. "Voyageur Re-presentations and Complications: Frances Anne Hopkins and the Métis Nation of Ontario." *Wicazo Sa Review* 28, no. 1 (Spring 2013): 100–18.

Bellrichard, Chantelle. "Famed Indigenous Chefs Team Up for Vancouver Dinner Series." CBC News, 24 January 2018. http://www.cbc.ca/news/indigenous/indigenous-chefs-dinner-vancouver-1.4502384.

Bendix, Regina. "Diverging Paths in the Scientific Search for Authenticity." *Journal of Folklore Research* 29, no. 2 (1992): 103–32.

Berish, Danny. *Red Chef Revival*, 2019. https://www.youtube.com/playlist?list=PLojTmuIpQn4tP6dbLv7ikACbl4FZo3khS.

Berland, Jody. "The Work of the Beaver." In *Material Cultures in Canada*, edited by Thomas Allen and Jennifer Blair, 25–50. Waterloo: Wilfrid Laurier University Press, 2015.

Berton, Pierre. *The National Dream: The Great Railway 1871–1881*. Toronto: Anchor Canada, 1970.

Berzok, Linda Murray. *American Indian Food*. Westport, CT, and London: Greenwood, 2005.

Bhat, Priya. "Salmon n' Bannock Expands to YVR, the First Indigenous Restaurant to Open in a Canadian Airport." CBC News, 16 December 2022. https://www.cbc.ca/news/canada/british-columbia/salmon-bannock-indigenous-restaurant-yvr-airport-vancouver-1.6689601.

Bitsoie, Freddie, and James O. Fraioli. *New Native Kitchen: Celebrating Modern Recipes of the American Indian*. New York: Abrams, 2021.

Black, Shannon. "A Kind of Cheers on the Web." *National Post*, 2 March 2001, A17.

Blackbridge, Persimmon. "The Chrismas Connection: An Artist's Impression." *Kinesis*, August 1979.

Blackstock, Michael. "Bannock Awareness." British Columbia Forest Service. 21 June 2000. https://www.for.gov.bc.ca/rsi/fnb/fnb.htm.

Blackstone, Renee. "Aboriginal Celebration of Northwest Bounty." *Province*, 3 June 2007, C19.

Bloch, Sam. "AquAdvantage, the First GMO Salmon, Is Coming to America." *New Food Economy*, 11 March 2019. https://newfoodeconomy.org/fda-aquabounty-gmo-salmon-seafood-restriction-market/.

Bodirsky, Monica, and Jon Johnson. "Decolonizing Diet: Healing by Reclaiming Traditional Indigenous Foodways." *Cuizine: The Journal of*

*Canadian Food Cultures/Cuizine: Revue des cultures culinaires au Canada* 1, no. 1 (2008).

Boonstra, Rudy. "Beaver." *The Canadian Encyclopedia*. Last modified 22 March 2015. https://www.thecanadianencyclopedia.ca/en/article/beaver.

Boralia. Accessed 1 August 2016. http://boraliato.com/.

– Instagram. 22 October 2018. https://www.instagram.com/p/BpPbcD2gnqR/.

Borré, Kristen. "The Healing Power of the Seal: The Meaning of Inuit Health Practice and Belief." *Arctic Anthropology* 31, no. 1 (1994): 1–15.

– "Seal Blood, Inuit Blood, and Diet: A Biocultural Model of Physiology and Cultural Identity." *Medical Anthropology Quarterly* 5, no. 1 (March 1991): 48–62.

Bower, Anne L. "Bound Together: Recipes, Lives, Stories, and Readings." In *Recipes for Reading: Community Cookbooks, Stories, Histories*, edited by Anne L. Bower, 1–14. Amherst: University of Massachusetts Press, 1997.

Bowker, Kathleen K. *The Maple Leaf Canadian Recipe Book*. London: Canadian Department of Trade and Commerce, 1930.

Boyle, Eleanor. "Both Sides' Failings Victimize Muckamuck." *Vancouver Sun*, 13 October 1978, C5.

*Brandon Sun*. "Muck-a-Muck House Now a Work of Culinary Art." 12 July 1972, 21.

Brant, Jennifer. "Cultural Appropriation of Indigenous Peoples in Canada." *The Canadian Encyclopedia*. Last modified 18 April 2018. https://www.thecanadianencyclopedia.ca/en/article/cultural-appropriation-of-indigenous-peoples-in-canada.

Braz, Albert. *The False Traitor: Louis Riel in Canadian Culture*. Toronto: University of Toronto Press, 2003.

Brend, Yvette. "Seal Meat May Turn Some Stomachs, but Inuit Country Food Is Smart." CBC News, 14 January 2017. http://www.cbc.ca/news/canada/british-columbia/seal-meat-indigenous-foods-traditional-hunt-elk-beaver-muskrat-caribou-1.3929734.

Briggs, Jean L. "From Trait to Emblem and Back: Living and Representing Culture in Everyday Inuit Life." *Arctic Anthropology* 34, no. 1 (1997): 227–35.

Brillat-Savarin, Jean Anthelme. *The Physiology of Taste*. Translated by Anne Drayton. London: Penguin Books, 1970.

British Columbia Ministry of Forest, Lands and Natural Resource Operations. "2019–2021 Freshwater Fishing Regulations Synopsis." Accessed 28 May 2019. http://www.env.gov.bc.ca/fw/fish/regulations/#Synopsis.

Bronson, AA. *A Public Apology to Siksika Nation*. New York: Mitchell-Innes & Nash, 2020.
Brotherton, Barbara. "Object of the Week: Breakfast Series." *Seattle Art Museum Blog*, 13 October 2018. http://samblog.seattleartmuseum.org/2017/10/breakfast-series-sonny-assu/.
Brown, Dave. "The Muckamuck: Gargantuan Meals Challenge the Biggest of Appetites." *Ottawa Journal*, 3 June 1978, 28.
Brown, Sarah. "Wakefield's Nikosi Bistro-Pub Promotes Rustic French Cooking with Indigenous Influences." *Ottawa Magazine*, 5 April 2017. https://ottawamagazine.com/eating-and-drinking/wakefields-bustling-nikosi-bistro-pub-promotes-rustic-french-cooking-with-indigenous-influences/.
Bruni, Frank. "Nordic Chef Explores Backyard." *New York Times*, 6 July 2010. https://www.nytimes.com/2010/07/07/dining/07chef.html?pagewanted=all.
Budgen, Mark. "Get Early Start to Make Most of Expo Nightlife." *Financial Post*, 3 May 1986, S5.
Burklo, Barbara. "Expo '86 Was a Taste-Ful Event." *Santa Cruz Sentinel*, 22 October 1986, C3.
Busch, Briton Cooper. *The War against Seals: A History of the North American Seal Fishery*. Kingston and Montreal: McGill-Queen's University Press, 1985.
C., Aylan. "Counter-Petition to Educate Anti-Seal Activist Jennifer N about Anti-Indigenous Behaviour and Colonialism. Support Kukum Kitchen." *The Petition Site*. Accessed 12 October 2017. https://www.thepetitionsite.com/de/takeaction/655/465/418/.
Caira, Rosanna. "The Evolution of Canadian Cuisine in Restaurants." In *Northern Bounty: A Celebration of Canadian Cuisine*, edited by Jo Marie Powers and Anita Stewart, 135–41. Toronto: Random House of Canada, 1995.
*Calgary Herald*. "A Calgary Herald Advertising Feature: New Morley Restaurant Honors Chief." 24 July 1981, A17.
– "Chiniki Village Co-op Feast." 16 May 1984, F2.
Calvo, Luz, and Catriona Rueda Esquibel. *Decolonize Your Diet: Plant-Based Mexican-American Recipes for Health and Healing*. Vancouver: Arsenal Pulp Press, 2015.
Campbell-Palmer, Róisín, Derek Gow, Robert Needham, Simon Jones, and Frank Rosell. *The Eurasian Beaver*. Exeter, UK: Pelagic Publishing, 2015.
Canoe. "About." Accessed 12 January 2018. https://www.canoerestaurant.com/about/.

Capatti, Alberto, and Massimo Montanari. *Italian Cuisine: A Cultural History.* New York: Columbia University Press, 2003.

Cardozo, Yvette, and Bill Hirsch. "Quilcum: At This Native American Restaurant, the Cook Keeps It Simple." *Seattle Times,* 22 July 1990. http://community.seattletimes.nwsource.com/archive/?date=19900722&slug=1083629.

Careless, James Maurice Stockford. "Toronto." *The Canadian Enyclopedia,* 17 March 2013. Last updated 6 November 2018, https://www.thecanadianencyclopedia.ca/en/article/toronto.

Caribou Gourmand. "Menu." Accessed 20 April 2018. http://docs.wixstatic.com/ugd/ee491a_8c50e309fd2c4ecd9fbc3e5b24ab5ea1.pdf.

Carlberg, Amy. "One of Toronto's Favourite Indigenous Restaurants Shut Down by Landlord." *Blog TO,* 25 May 2019. https://www.blogto.com/eat_drink/2019/05/kukum-toronto-closed/.

– "10 Restaurants You Could Buy in Toronto Right Now." *Blog TO,* 9 April 2019. https://www.blogto.com/eat_drink/2019/04/restaurants-for-sale-toronto-april-2019/.

– "Toronto's Groundbreaking Indigenous Restaurant Is Shutting Down." *Blog TO,* 20 May 2020. https://www.blogto.com/eat_drink/2020/05/toronto-indigenous-restaurant-shutting-down/.

Carlson, Kathryn Blaze. "What Lies Ahead for Aboriginals." *Globe and Mail,* 9 May 2014. https://www.theglobeandmail.com/news/national/what-lies-ahead-for-aboriginals/article18587968/.

Carlson, Paula. "George Jr. Is a Cut Above." *Interior News,* 4 April 2007, A3.

Carmichael, Suzanne. "What's Doing in Vancouver." *New York Times,* 28 April 1996. https://archive.nytimes.com/www.nytimes.com/library/travel/whatsdoing/wd960428.html.

Carter, Sarah. *Capturing Women: The Manipulation of Cultural Imagery in Canada's Prairie West.* Montreal and Kingston: McGill-Queen's University Press, 1997.

– *Lost Harvests: Prairie Indian Reserve Farmers and Government Policy.* Montreal and Kingston: McGill-Queen's University Press, 1990.

Cartmill, Matt. *A View to a Death in the Morning: Hunting and Nature through History.* Cambridge, MA: Harvard University Press, 1996.

Casselman, Bill. "Canadian Food Words." Accessed 26 January 2016. http://www.billcasselman.com/canadian_food_words/cfw_five.html.

CBC News. "The Beaver Gets a New Name." 12 January 2010. http://www.cbc.ca/news/canada/manitoba/the-beaver-gets-a-new-name-1.865851.

– "First Nation Checks out of the Hotel Business." 18 October 2001. https://www.cbc.ca/news/canada/first-nation-checks-out-of-the-hotel-business-1.269180.

- "5 Vancouver Island Native Bands Get Commercial Fishery." 30 January 2014. https://www.cbc.ca/news/canada/british-columbia/5-vancouver-island-native-bands-get-commercial-fishery-1.2517444.
- "Governor General's Seal Snack Sparks Controversy." 26 May 2009. http://www.cbc.ca/news/canada/governor-general-s-seal-snack-sparks-controversy-1.833274.
- "Illegal Hunting Starting Early This Season." 11 September 2015. http://www.cbc.ca/news/canada/british-columbia/illegal-hunting-starting-early-this-season-1.3224570.
- "Inuit Gather in Iqaluit for Pro-Sealing, Anti-Ellen #sealfie." 27 March 2014. http://www.cbc.ca/news/canada/north/inuit-gather-in-iqaluit-for-pro-sealing-anti-ellen-sealfie-1.2589012.
- "John Gilchrist Reviews Chiniki Restaurant." 16 September 2016. https://www.cbc.ca/news/canada/calgary/programs/eyeopener/john-gilchrist-reviews-chiniki-restaurant-1.3765904.
- "'Pacific Salmon' Named B.C.'s Official Fish." 16 March 2013. https://www.cbc.ca/news/canada/british-columbia/pacific-salmon-named-b-c-s-official-fish-1.1395379.
- "Saskatoon Chef Ryan Young Creates Diabetic-Friendly Menu." 16 February 2015. https://www.cbc.ca/news/canada/saskatoon/saskatoon-chef-ryan-young-creates-diabetic-friendly-menu-1.2958328.
- "St. John's Chefs Push Benefits of Seal Meat." 8 December 2014. http://www.cbc.ca/news/canada/newfoundland-labrador/st-john-s-chefs-push-benefits-of-seal-meat-1.2863700.
- "Tanya Tagaq #sealfie Provokes Anti-Sealing Activists." 2 April 2014. http://www.cbc.ca/news/canada/north/tanya-tagaq-sealfie-provokes-anti-sealing-activists-1.2595250.
- "Truth and Reconciliation Chair Says Final Report Marks Start of 'New Era.'" 15 December 2015. https://www.cbc.ca/news/politics/truth-and-reconciliation-final-report-ottawa-event-1.3365921.

CBC Radio. "Bannock: A Brief History." 29 January 2016. http://www.cbc.ca/radio/unreserved/bannock-wild-meat-and-indigenous-food-sovereignty-1.3424436/bannock-a-brief-history-1.3425549.
- "How Indigenous Leaders Are Changing the Future of Food." 11 June 2020. https://www.cbc.ca/radio/unreserved/how-indigenous-leaders-are-changing-the-future-of-food-1.5605180.
- "Indigenous Cuisine Reconnected a Sixties Scoop Survivor with Family, Community and Culture." 6 October 2017. https://www.cbc.ca/radio/unreserved/how-food-brings-indigenous-communities-together-1.4327345/indigenous-cuisine-reconnected-a-sixties-scoop-survivor-with-family-community-and-culture-1.4330568.

- "The Restaurant: A Table Divided." 26 February 2019. https://www.cbc.ca/radio/ideas/the-restaurant-a-table-divided-1.4669493.
- "Tapping into a History That Connects Maple Syrup to First Nations." 24 March 2016. https://www.cbc.ca/radio/unreserved/lost-found-and-the-journey-of-self-discovery-1.3504360/tapping-into-a-history-that-connects-maple-syrup-to-first-nations-1.3506255.

Chandwani, Ashok. "Expo 86: A Whirlwind Guide." *Gazette*, 31 May 1986.

Chartrand, Shane. "Art Is the Medicine." REDx Talks. Uploaded 28 May 2016. https://vimeo.com/168471494.

Chartrand, Shane M., and Jennifer Cockrall-King. *tawâw: Progressive Indigenous Cuisine*. Toronto: Ambrosia, 2019.

Chatelin, Ray. "Native Indian Feast Returns at Quilicum." *Province*, 14 June 1985, 46.

- *The Seattle & Vancouver Book*. Woodstock, VT: Countryman Press, 2005.

Chen, Nancy N. "'Speaking Nearby': A Conversation with Trinh T. Minh-Ha." *Visual Anthropology Review* 8, no. 1 (Spring 1992): 82–91.

Cho, Lily. *Eating Chinese: Culture on the Menu in Small Town Canada*. Toronto: University of Toronto Press, 2010.

Chrystos. "Really Delicious Fry Bread." In *My Home as I Remember*, edited by Lee Maracle and Sandra Laronde, 8–9. Toronto: Natural Heritage Books, 2000.

Chu, Natalie. "Get to Know a Chef: Aaron Joseph Bear Robe, Keriwa Cafe." *BlogTO*, 17 May 2012. https://www.blogto.com/people/2012/05/get_to_know_a_chef_aaron_joseph_bear_robe_keriwa_cafe/.

Cidro, Jamie, Bamidele Adekunle, Evelyn Peters, and Tabitha Martens. "Beyond Food Security: Understanding Access to Cultural Food for Urban Indigenous People in Winnipeg as Indigenous Food Sovereignty." *Canadian Journal of Urban Research* 24, no. 1 (2015): 24–43.

Cidro, Jamie, Tabitha Robin Martens, Lynelle Zahayko, and Herenia P. Lawrence. "First Foods as Indigenous Food Sovereignty: Country Foods and Breastfeeding Practices in a Manitoban First Nations Community." *Canadian Food Studies* 5, no. 2 (2018): 25–43.

City of Toronto. "Dine Safe." Accessed 1 August 2018. https://www.toronto.ca/health/dinesafe/.

City of Vancouver. "First Nations Art and Totem Poles." Accessed 25 September 2018. https://vancouver.ca/parks-recreation-culture/totems-and-first-nations-art.aspx.

Clarke, Gerald. "Bringing the Past to the Present: Traditional Indigenous Farming in Southern California." In *Indigenous Food Sovereignty in the United States*, edited by Devon A. Mihesuah and Elizabeth Hoover, 253–75. Norman: University of Oklahoma Press, 2019.

Clarke, Paul. "Chiniki Cultural Centre and Stones Restaurant Closes." *Rocky Mountain Outlook*, 1 November 2018. https://www.rmotoday.com/business-news/chiniki-cultural-centre-and-stones-restaurant-closes-1573251.

Clifford, James. *Routes: Travel and Translation in the Late Twentieth Century*. Cambridge, MA: Harvard University Press, 1997.

Coates, Peter. *Salmon*. London: Reaktion Books, 2006.

*Cochrane Today*. "Future of Chiniki Restaurant Unknown." 9 March 2017. https://www.cochranetoday.ca/local-news/future-of-chiniki-restaurant-unknown-1453272.

Cohen, Mathilde. "Animal Colonialism: The Case of Milk." In *Studies in Global Animal Law*, edited by Anne Peters, 35–44. Berlin: Springer, 2000.

Cole, Douglas, and Ira Chaikin. *An Iron Hand upon the People: The Law against the Potlatch on the Northwest Coast*. Vancouver: Douglas and McIntyre, 1990.

Cole, Janis, and Holly Dale. *Hookers on Davie*. 1984.

Coletto, David, Lydia Di Francesco, and Jaime Morrison. "Seafood Survey: Public Opinion on Aquaculture and a National Aquaculture Act." 16 May 2011. Canadian Aquaculture Industry Alliance. http://www.aquaculture.ca/news-releases/2011/6/6/majority-of-canadians-eat-seafood-but-frequency-doesnt-meet-health-guidelines.

Collingham, Lizzie. *The Hungry Empire: How Britain's Quest for Food Shaped the Modern World*. London: Bodley Head, 2017.

Colombara, Michael. "Restaurant Reviews 1999." *Pacific Rim Magazine*. http://kevinmc.info/prm2017/1999/food/from-chinese-noodles-to-west-coast-fare-three-stories-of-gastronomic-proportions/.

Colpitts, George. *Game in the Garden: A Human History of Wildlife in Western Canada to 1940*. Vancouver: University of British Columbia Press, 2002.

– *Pemmican Empire: Food, Trade, and the Last Bison Hunts in the North American Plains, 1780–1882*. New York: Cambridge University Press, 2015.

Comparelli, Peter. "Cowboys Lasso Muckamuck." *Vancouver Sun*, 11 October 1978, 1.

– "Indian Cooks, Waiters Battle Restaurant's White Managers." *Vancouver Sun*, 22 May 1978, B16.

Conflict Kitchen. "Haudenosaunee." Accessed 5 January 2021. https://www.conflictkitchen.org/past/haudenosaunee/.

Contois, Emily. *Diners, Dudes, and Diets: How Gender and Power Collide in Food Media and Culture*. Chapel Hill: University of North Carolina Press, 2020.

Cook, Gay. "Aboriginal Cooking Debuts in Market." *Ottawa Citizen*, 14 January 2004. B6–B7.

- "Maple Syrup Adds Golden Touch." *Ottawa Citizen*, 30 March 2005, E2.
Cooke, Nathalie. "Stories of Rice Lake – Stewards, Settlers, and Storytellers." In *Food and Landscape: Proceedings of the Oxford Symposium on Food and Cookery 2017*, edited by Mark McWilliams, 99–109. London: Prospect Books, 2018.
–, ed. *What's to Eat? Entrées in Canadian Food History*. Montreal and Kingston: McGill-Queen's University Press, 2009.
Cooke, Nathalie, and Fiona Lucas. *Catharine Parr Traill's The Female Emigrant Guide: Cooking with a Canadian Classic*. Kingston and Montreal: McGill-Queen's University Press, 2017.
Coppola, Francis Ford. "Coppola's New Restaurant: Menu with a Story to Tell." *San Francisco Chronicle*, 3 November 2016. https://www.sfchronicle.com/opinion/openforum/article/Coppola-s-new-restaurant-menu-with-a-story-to-10592174.php.
Coppolino, Andrew. "Food-Ordering Apps, More Veggies and Playing with Food Are the New Trends." CBC News, 13 January 2018. https://www.cbc.ca/news/canada/kitchener-waterloo/andrew-coppolino-food-trends-1.4485584.
Corntassel, Jeff. "Re-envisioning Resurgence: Indigenous Pathways to Decolonization and Sustainable Self-Determination." *Decolonization: Indigeneity, Education & Society* 1, no. 1 (2012): 86–101.
Corser, Judy. "Sockeye Salmon and Saskatoon Pie: Regional Foods on Canada's Long-Distance Railways." In *Food on the Move: Dining on the Legendary Railway Journey of the World*, edited by Sharon Hudgins, 159–88. London: Reaktion Books, 2019.
Couchie, Aylan, and Ian Mosby. "Anti–Seal Hunt Rhetoric Ignores Facts and Suppresses Indigenous Culture." *Globe and Mail*, 12 October 2017. https://www.theglobeandmail.com/opinion/anti-seal-hunt-rhetoric-borne-of-long-legacy-of-suppression-of-indigenous-food/article36565128/.
Coulthard, Glen Sean. *Red Skin, White Masks: Rejecting the Colonial Politics of Recognition*. Minneapolis: University of Minnesota Press, 2014.
Coupland, Douglas. "Ace in the Hole." *Vancouver Magazine*, June 1987, 42–8.
Cox, Beverley, and Martin Jacobs. *Spirit of the Harvest: North American Indian Cooking*. New York: Stewart, Tabori & Chang, 1991.
Cronon, William. *Changes in the Land: Indians, Colonists, and the Ecology of New England*. New York: Hill and Wang, 2003 [1983].
– "Foreword: On the Saltwater Margins of a Northern Frontier." In *The Fishermen's Frontier: People and Salmon in Southeast Alaska*, edited by David F. Arnold, ix–xiv. Seattle: University of Washington Press, 2008.

– "A Place for Stories: Nature, History, and Narrative." *Journal of American History* 78, no. 4 (March 1992): 1347–76.
Crosby, Alfred W., Jr. *The Columbian Exchange: Biological and Cultural Consequences of 1492*. Westport, CT, and London: Praeger, 2003 [1972].
Cyr, Monica, and Joyce Slater. "Honouring the Grandmothers through (Re)membering, (Re)learning, and (Re)vitalizing Métis Traditional Foods and Protocols." *Canadian Food Studies* 6, no. 2 (2019): 51–72.
Dagenais, Chris. "THE DISH: Storied Norgate Diner Steeped in History." *North Shore News*, 8 November 2016. https://www.nsnews.com/lifestyle/taste/the-dish-storied-norgate-diner-steeped-in-history-1.2537577.
Dammann, Derek, and Chris Johns. *True North: Canadian Cooking from Coast to Coast*. Toronto: HarperCollins, 2015.
Daschuk, James. *Clearing the Plains: Disease, Politics of Starvation, and the Loss of Indigenous Life*. Regina: University of Regina Press, 2013.
Davey, Steven. "Original Aboriginal." *Now Magazine*, 20 October 2011. https://nowtoronto.com/food-and-drink/food/original-aboriginal/.
Dean, Dave. "Tanya Tagaq's Cute Sealfie Pissed Off a Lot of Idiots." *VICE*, 9 April 2014. https://www.vice.com/en_ca/article/4w7awj/tanya-taqaqs-cute-sealfie-pissed-off-a-lot-of-idiots.
– "We Spoke to the Inuit Woman behind 'Sealfies.'" *VICE*, 31 March 2014. https://www.vice.com/en_ca/article/3b47x8/we-spoke-to-the-inuit-women-behind-sealfies.
Deloria, Vine, Jr. *Custer Died for Your Sins: An Indian Manifesto*. Norman: University of Oklahoma Press, 1988 [1969].
DeLottinville, Peter. "Joe Beef of Montreal: Working-Class Culture and the Tavern, 1869–1889." *Labour/Le Travailleur* 8, no. 9 (Autumn/Spring 1981–2): 9–40.
DeMontis, Rita. "Celebrating Aboriginal Cuisine with Recipes from Chef David Wolfman." *Toronto Sun*, 15 July 2015. www.torontosun.com/2015/07/14/celebrating-aboriginal-cuisine-with-recipes-from-chef-david-wolfman.
Demuth, Bathsheba. *Floating Coast: An Environmental History of the Bering Strait*. New York: W.W. Norton & Company, 2019.
Dennis, Mary Kate, and Tabitha Robin. "Healthy on Our Own Terms: Indigenous Wellbeing and the Colonized Food System." *Journal of Critical Dietetics* 5, no. 1 (2020): 4–11.
Derrida, Jacques. "Hostipitality." *Angelaki: Journal of the Theoretical Humanities* 5, no. 3 (2000): 3–18.
DesBrisay, Anne. "Best Bites of 2007." *Ottawa Citizen*, 30 December 2007, B7.
– *Capital Dining: Anne DesBrisay's Guide to Ottawa Restaurants*. Toronto: ECW Press, 2004.

– "Sweetgrass Delights." *Ottawa Citizen*, 25 March 2007, B8.
Desmarais, Annette Aurélie, and Hannah Wittman. "Farmers, Foodies and First Nations: Getting to Food Sovereignty in Canada." *Journal of Peasant Studies* 41, no. 6 (2014): 1–21.
Deur, Douglas, and Nancy J. Turner, eds. *Keeping It Living: Traditions of Plant Use and Cultivation on the Northwest Coast of North America*. Seattle: University of Washington Press, 2005.
di Cintio, Marcello. "Farming the Monsoon: A Return to Traditional Tohono O'oodham Foods." *Gastronomica* (Summer 2012): 14–17.
Dickenson, Thelma. "Vancouver's Spark: The Contrasts." *National Post*, 22 June 1974, 20.
Dickenson, Victoria. *Seal*. London: Reaktion Books, 2016.
*Dictionary of Canadian Biography*. "Evans, James." Accessed 4 March 2019, http://www.biographi.ca/en/bio/evans_james_7E.html.
Differ, Florence, Doris Olney, Matthew Jacob, and Doreen Harry. "Letter to the Editor: No Exploitation Say Native Staff." *Richmond Review*, 10 November 1978, 5.
Diner, Hasia R. *Hungering for America*. Cambridge, MA: Harvard University Press, 1991.
DK Eyewitness Travel. *Canada*. London: Penguin Random House, 2016.
Dominion of Canada. *Annual Report of the Department of Fisheries, Dominion of Canada, For the Year 1888*. Ottawa, 1889.
Donati, Kelly. "From Gastro Nullius to 'Nourishing Terrain': Preliminary Reflections on Decolonising Gastronomy in Australia." Institute of Australian Geographers Conference, 11 July 2019.
Douglas, Mary. *Purity and Danger: An Analysis of Concepts of Pollution and Taboo*. London and New York: Routledge, 1966.
Drees, Laurie Meijer. "'Indians' Bygone Past': The Banff Indian Days, 1902–1945." *Past Imperfect* 2 (1993): 7–28.
Dreyer, Benjamin. *Dreyer's English: An Utterly Correct Guide to Clarity and Style*. New York: Random House, 2019.
Driver, Elizabeth. "Canadian Cookbooks (1825–1949): In the Heart of the Home." *Petits Propos Culinaires* 72 (2003): 19–39.
– *Culinary Landmarks: A Bibliography of Canadian Cookbooks, 1825–1949*. Toronto, Buffalo, London: University of Toronto Press, 2008.
– "Regional Differences in the Canadian Daily Meal? Cookbooks Answer the Question." In *What's to Eat? Entrées in Canadian Food History*, edited by Nathalie Cooke, 197–212. Montreal and Kingston: McGill-Queen's University Press, 2009.
Duffy, Andrew A. "Women Overcoming Odds." *Times Colonist*, 5 October 2004, C1.

Duncan, Dorothy. *Canadians at Table: A Culinary History of Canada: Food, Fellowship, and Folklore*. Toronto: Dundurn Press, 2006.
– "Ontario Cooking: Cuisines in Transition." In *Northern Bounty: A Celebration of Canadian Cuisine*, edited by Jo Marie Powers and Anita Stewart, 102–12. Toronto: Random House of Canada, 1995.
Eade, Ron. "Omnivore's Ottawa." *Ottawa Citizen*, 27 April 2011, E3.
Earle, Rebecca. *The Body of the Conquistador: Food, Race and the Colonial Experience in Spanish America, 1492–1700*. Cambridge: Cambridge University Press, 2012.
Eatmon, Sandra, Ethel Gardner, Nat Girvan, Rob Hunt, Vikki Peters, Bonnie Thorne, Christina Prince, Sam Bob, and Rick Terry. "Muckamuck: A Strike for Indian Self Determination." *Kinesis*, July 1980.
Edible Canada. Facebook. Accessed 2 May 2018. https://www.facebook.com/ediblecanada/.
*Edmonton Journal*. "Expo 86 at a Glance." 15 February 1986, C12.
– "Familiar Foods in Native Dress Featured at Tribes Restaurant." 2 September 1982, C10.
– "National Aboriginal Achievement Awards 2001. Dolly Watts. Gitksan – Business and Commerce." 14 March 2001, G7.
– "Native Restaurant Would Face Obstacles." 2 October 1991, C2.
Edwards, Peter. "Shrugs Greet Historic $145M Toronto Land Claim Settlement." *Toronto Star*, 8 June 2010. www.thestar.com/news/gta/2010/06/08/shrugs_greet_historic_145m_toronto_land_claim_settlement.html.
Efron, Sarah. "Bannock Tacos, Fried Baloney – This Is Aboriginal Cuisine?" *Globe and Mail*, 17 July 2012. http://www.theglobeandmail.com/life/food-and-wine/food-trends/bannock-tacos-fried-baloney-this-is-aboriginal-cuisine/article4424044/.
Eigenbrod, Renate. "'For the Child Taken, for the Parent Left Behind': Residential School Narratives as Acts of 'Survivance.'" *ESC* 38, no. 3–4 (2012): 277–97.
Ellis, Eleanor. *The Northern Cookbook*. Ottawa: Canadian Department of Indian Affairs and Northern Development, 1967.
Elton, Sarah. "My First Helping of Canada Goose." *Atlantic*, 19 October 2011. https://www.theatlantic.com/health/archive/2011/10/my-first-helping-of-canada-goose/246881/.
*EnRoute*. "8: Keriwa Cafe, Toronto." November 2012, 92.
Erby, Kelly. *Restaurant Republic: The Rise of Public Dining in Boston*. Minneapolis: University of Minnesota Press, 2016.
Erdrich, Heid E. *Original Local: Indigenous Foods, Stories, and Recipes from the Upper Midwest*. St. Paul: Minnesota Historical Society Press, 2013.

Errington, Shelly. "What Became Authentic Primitive Art?" *Cultural Anthropology* 9, no. 2 (1994): 201–26.
Everett, Holly. "Food, Class and the Self: Seal Flipper Pie and Class Conflict." In *Food for Thought: A Multidisciplinary Discussion*, edited by Robert Scott Stewart and Susan A. Korol, 71–97. Sydney, NS: Cape Breton University Press, 2012.
Fakhri, Michael. "Gauging US and EU Seal Regimes in the Arctic against Inuit Sovereignty." In *The European Union and the Arctic*, edited by Nengye Liu, Elizabeth A. Kirk, and Tore Henriksen, 200–35. Leiden: Brill, 2017.
Faulder, Liane. "Aboriginal Cuisine Basic with 'Amazing' Flavours." *Edmonton Journal*, 9 October 2013, E2.
Fee, Margery. *Literary Land Claims: The "Indian Land Question" from Pontiac's War to Attawapiskat*. Waterloo: Wilfrid Laurier University Press, 2015.
– "Rewriting Anthropology and Identifications on the North Pacific Coast: The Work of George Hunt, William Beynon, Franz Boas, and Marius Barbeau." *Australian Literary Studies* 25, no. 4 (2010): 17–32.
– "Stories of Traditional Aboriginal Food, Territory, and Health." In *What's to Eat? Entrées in Canadian Food History*, edited by Nathalie Cooke, 55–78. Montreal and Kingston: McGill-Queen's University Press, 2009.
Ferguson, Priscilla Parkhurst. *Accounting for Taste: The Triumph of French Cuisine*. Chicago: University of Chicago Press, 2004.
– "Eating Orders: Markets, Menus, and Meals." *Journal of Modern History* 77 (2005): 679–700.
*Financial Post Magazine*. "Snapshot: Vancouver." 20 June 1991, 50.
Fischer, John Ryan. *Cattle Colonialism: An Environmental History of the Conquest of California and Hawai'i*. Chapel Hill: University of North Carolina Press, 2015.
Fisheries and Oceans Canada. "Farmed Salmon." Last modified 15 March 2017. http://www.dfo-mpo.gc.ca/aquaculture/sector-secteur/species-especes/salmon-saumon-eng.htm.
– "Management Decision." Accessed 8 May 2018. http://www.dfo-mpo.gc.ca/fm-gp/seal-phoque/management-decision-gestion-eng.htm.
– "Seals and Sealing: Identify a Species." Accessed 8 May 2018. http://www.dfo-mpo.gc.ca/fisheries-peches/seals-phoques/species-especes/index-eng.html.
– "Wild Atlantic Salmon in Eastern Canada: Report on the Standing Committee on Fisheries and Oceans." By Scott Simms. January 2017. http://publications.gc.ca/collections/collection_2017/parl/xc51-1/XC51-1-1-421-5-eng.pdf.
Fiso, Monique. *Hiakai*. Auckland: Random House New Zealand, 2020.

Food Secure Canada. *From Patchwork to Policy Coherence: Principles and Priorities of Canada's National Food Policy*. May 2017. https://foodsecurecanada.org/patchwork-policy-coherence-principles-and-priorities-canadas-national-food.
– *Resetting the Table: A People's Food Policy for Canada*. Toronto, 2011. http://peoplesfoodpolicy.ca/policy/resetting-table-peoples-food-policy-canada.
– "What We Do." Accessed 2 July 2018. https://foodsecurecanada.org/who-we-are/what-we-do.
Food Trucks. "You Are Welcome Food Truck." 13 July 2015. http://torontofoodtrucks.ca/you-are-welcome-food-truck-toronto.
Fournier, Suzanne. "Quilicum Offers Authentic Native Food in Artistic Surroundings." *Province*, 13 July 1990, 35.
Fox, Mary Lou. *Nishnabe Delights*. Serpent River Indian Reserve, Cutler, Ontario: Woodlands Studio, 1975.
Francis, Daniel. *The Imaginary Indian: The Image of the Indian in Canadian Culture*. Vancouver: Arsenal Pulp Press, 2011.
Francis, Rich. Facebook. 20 February 2018. https://www.facebook.com/7thFire.
– Facebook. 13 November 2017.
– Facebook. 15 June 2017.
– Instagram. 19 August 2018. https://www.instagram.com/p/BmpwxIQgpmP/?hl=en&taken-by=seventhfire.
– "Medicine Wheel Cured Salmon." *East Coast Living*, 17 October 2017. http://eastcoastliving.ca/recipes/medicine-wheel-cured-salmon/.
Frank, Lois Ellen. *Foods of the Southwest Indian Nations: Contemporary Native American Recipes*. Berkeley: Ten Speed Press, 2002.
– *Seed to Plate, Soil to Sky: Modern Plant-Based Recipes Using Native American Ingredients*. New York: Hachette Books, 2023.
Fraser, Margaret. "Canada's Breadbasket: Decades of Change." In *Northern Bounty: A Celebration of Canadian Cuisine*, edited by Jo Marie Powers and Anita Stewart, 50–61. Toronto: Random House of Canada, 1995.
Freedman, Paul. *Ten Restaurants That Changed America*. New York: Liveright, 2016.
Freeman, Victoria. *Distant Relations: How My Ancestors Colonized North America*. Toronto: McClelland & Stewart, 2000.
Fricker, Peter. "Please Tell This Vancouver Restaurant to Take Baby Seal Meat off the Menu." *Vancouver Humane Society*, 10 January 2017. http://www.vancouverhumanesociety.bc.ca/please-tell-vancouver-restaurant-take-baby-seal-meat-off-menu/.

Gabaccia, Donna R. "Is Everywhere Nowhere? Nomads, Nations, and the Immigrant Paradigm of United States History." *Journal of American History* 86, no. 3 (December 1999): 1115–34.
– *We Are What We Eat: Ethnic Food and the Making of Americans.* Cambridge, MA, and London: Harvard University Press, 1998.
Gadhoke, Pretty, and Barrett P. Brenton. "Erasure of Indigenous Food Memories and (Re)Imaginations." In *Food Cults: How Fads, Dogma, and Doctrine Influence Diet,* edited by Kima Cargill, 205–18. Lanham, MD: Rowman & Littlefield, 2017.
Galloway, Gloria. "Governor General Applauded, Denounced for Eating Raw Seal." *Globe and Mail,* 26 May 2009. https://www.theglobeandmail.com/news/politics/governor-general-applauded-denounced-for-eating-raw-seal/article4292531/.
Garber, Anne. "Boris and Bubba's Best: The Vancouver Summit, from Borscht to Barbecue and Beans." *Province Preview,* 2 April 1993, B29.
Gardiner, Cassandra. *The Edible Indian.* 2013. https://vimeo.com/68448478.
Gardiner Museum. "Kent Monkman: The Rise and Fall of Civilization." Accessed 3 February 2016. http://www.gardinermuseum.on.ca/exhibition/kent-monkman-the-rise-and-fall-of-civilization.
Gardner, Ethel. "Letter." *Union of BC Indian Chiefs Newsletter,* June 1978, 11.
Gaudry, Adam. "Métis." *The Canadian Encyclopedia.* Last modified 16 November 2016. https://www.thecanadianencyclopedia.ca/en/article/metis.
*Gazette.* "Gourmet Guide: Dining at the Indian Room." 28 November 1961, 4.
– "Indian Room Advertisement." 27 January 1951, 2.
– "La Toundra Advertisement." 17 May 1967, B2.
– "New Ideas Displayed at Lounge." 6 March 1962, 10.
Geniusz, Mary Siisip. *Plants Have So Much to Give Us, All We Have to Do Is Ask: Anishinaabe Botanical Teachings.* Minneapolis: University of Minnesota Press, 2015.
George Jr., Andrew. *Modern Native Feast: Healthy, Innovative, Sustainable Cuisine.* Vancouver: Arsenal Pulp Press, 2013.
George Jr., Andrew, and Robert Gairns. *Feast! Canadian Native Cuisine for All Seasons.* Toronto: Doubleday Canada, 1997.
– *A Feast for All Seasons: Traditional Native Peoples' Cuisine.* Vancouver: Arsenal Pulp Press, 2010.
Gidley, Mick. "The Making of Edward S. Curtis's *The North American Indian.*" *Princeton University Library Chronicle* 67, no. 2 (Winter 2006): 314–29.

Gignac, Julien. "Petition Asks That Seal Meat Be Removed from Toronto Restaurant's Menu." *Toronto Star*, 11 October 2017. https://www.thestar.com/news/gta/2017/10/11/petition-asks-that-seal-meat-be-removed-from-toronto-restaurants-menu.html.

Gilbride, Neil. "'Eat Canadian': Canadian Restaurants Stress Native Dishes." *Ottawa Citizen*, 27 August 1973, 9.

Gill, Alexandra. "Native Exposure." *Globe and Mail*, 10 September 2003. https://www.theglobeandmail.com/life/native-exposure/article772254/.

Giuffrida, Angela. "Venice Bans Kebab Shops to 'Preserve Decorum and Traditions' of City." *Guardian*, 5 May 2017. https://www.theguardian.com/world/2017/may/05/venice-bans-kebab-shops-preserve-decorum-traditions-city.

Glasner, Eli. "From Seal Tartare to Bison on a Bun, Indigenous Chefs Are Reclaiming Their Heritage One Plate at a Time." CBC News, 9 June 2017. https://www.cbc.ca/news/multimedia/from-seal-tartare-to-bison-on-a-bun-indigenous-chefs-are-reclaiming-their-heritage-one-plate-at-a-time-1.4147016.

Glowacki, Laura. "'He's Taught Me So Much': Winnipeggers Raise Funds for Homeless Artist's Funeral." CBC News, 9 August 2019. https://www.cbc.ca/news/canada/manitoba/daniel-james-martin-1.5240974.

Goethe, Jurgen. "Carte Blanche." *Vancouver Sun*, 30 December 1995, D12.

Goldstein, Joyce. *Inside the California Food Revolution: Thirty Years That Changed Our Culinary Consciousness*. Berkeley: University of California Press, 2013.

Gómez-Peña, Guillermo. "The New World Border." In *The Mexico Reader: History, Culture, Politics*, edited by Gilbert M. Joseph and Timothy J. Henderson, 750–5. Durham, NC: Duke University Press, 2003.

Goodyear, Dana. *Anything That Moves: Renegade Chefs, Fearless Eaters, and the Making of a New American Food Culture*. New York: Penguin, 2013.

Gopnik, Adam. "What Joël Robuchon Meant for French Cooking." *New Yorker*, 6 August 2018. https://www.newyorker.com/culture/postscript/what-joel-robuchon-meant-for-french-cooking.

Gora, L. Sasha. "Beaver as Offal: The Presence and Absence of Beaver in Canadian Cuisine." In *Proceedings of the Oxford Symposium on Food & Cookery 2016: Offal*, edited by Mark McWilliams, 200–10. London: Prospect Books, 2017.

– "From Meat to Metaphor: Beavers and Reimagining the Edible in Canadian Cuisine." In *Canadian Culinary Imaginations*, edited by Dorothy Barenscott and Shelley Boyd, 93–113. Montreal and Kingston: McGill-Queen's University Press, 2020.

– "From New York's Silverbird to Santa Fe's Corn Dance Café: Sustaining Indigenous Restaurants." In *Chefs, Restaurants, and Sustainability*, edited

by Carole Counihan and Susanne Højlund. Fayetteville: University of Arkansas Press, 2024. (Forthcoming).
- "Indigenous Cuisine Revitalization: Best Places to Sample Traditional Foods." *Lonely Planet*, 27 September 2019. https://www.lonelyplanet.com/articles/indigenous-food-restaurants-north-america.
- "The Muckamuck: Restaurants, Labour, and the Power of Representation." In *Proceedings of the Oxford Symposium on Food & Cookery 2019: Food & Power*, edited by Mark McWilliams, 104–14. London: Prospect Books, 2020.
- "'Sad ol' mush': The Poetics and Politics of Porridge in Residential Schools in Canada." *Childhood in the Past* (18 July 2022).
- "Today's Special: Reading Menus as Cultural Texts." In *Food Studies: Matter, Meaning, Movement*, edited by David Szanto, Amanda Di Battista, and Irena Knezevic. Montreal: Rebus, 2022.
- "Vancouver's Only Aboriginal Restaurant's Got Game." *MUNCHIES: Food by Vice*, 25 March 2016. https://munchies.vice.com/en_us/article/aea85k/vancouvers-only-aboriginal-restaurants-got-game.
- "The Visual Representation of New Nordic Food and the North in the Cookbook *NOMA: Time and Place in Nordic Cuisine*." *Graduate Journal of Food Studies* 3, no. 2 (November 2017).
Government of Canada. "First Nations in Canada." Last modified 2 May 2017. https://www.rcaanc-cirnac.gc.ca/eng/1307460755710/1536862806124.
- "Official Symbols of Canada." Last modified 12 January 2016. http://canada.pch.gc.ca/eng/1444070816842.
- "Truth and Reconciliation Commission of Canada: Official Mandate." Last modified 2 February 2019. https://www.rcaanc-cirnac.gc.ca/eng/1450124405592/1529106060525.
Government of Nunavut Bureau of Statistics. "Prices." Accessed 8 May 2018. https://assets.documentcloud.org/documents/2900528/2016-Nunavut-Food-Price-Survey-Comparison.pdf.
Government of Ontario. "Chinook Salmon." Last modified 29 March 2019. https://www.ontario.ca/page/chinook-salmon.
Grant, Shelagh D. *"Errors Exposed": Inuit Relocations to the High Arctic, 1953–1960*. Calgary: Documents on Canadian Arctic Sovereignty and Security No. 8, 2016.
Greenblatt, Stephen. *The Rise and Fall of Adam and Eve*. New York and London: W.W. Norton & Company, 2017.
Greer, Susan. "Thanksgiving Favourites Trace Origins to First Nations Foods." CTV News, 9 October 2014. http://www.ctvnews.ca/lifestyle/thanksgiving-favourites-trace-origins-to-first-nations-foods-1.2046425.

Grey, Sam, and Lenore Newman. "Beyond Culinary Colonialism: Indigenous Food Sovereignty, Liberal Multiculturalism, and the Control of Gastronomic Capital." *Agriculture and Human Values* 35, no. 3 (September 2018): 717–30.

Grey, Sam, and Raj Patel. "Food Sovereignty as Decolonization: Some Contributions from Indigenous Movements to Food System and Development Politics." *Agriculture and Human Values* 32, no. 3 (2015): 431–44.

Griffin, Kevin. "In Vancouver: Andy Warhol, Celebrity Artist." *Vancouver Sun*, 16 March 2012. https://vancouversun.com/news/staff-blogs/in-vancouver-andy-warhol-celebrity-artist.

Gross, Lawrence. "Harvesting Wild Rice." In *Native Foodways: Indigenous North American Religious Traditions and Foods*, edited by Michelene E. Pesantubbee and Michael J. Zogry, 99–107. Albany: SUNY Press, 2021.

Guthman, Julie. "Fast Food/Organic Food: Reflexive Tastes and the Making of 'Yuppie Chow.'" *Social & Cultural Geography* 4, no.1 (2003): 45–58.

Haley, Andrew P. *Turning the Tables: Restaurants and the Rise of the American Middle Class, 1880–1920*. Chapel Hill: University of North Carolina Press, 2011.

Hamel-Charest, Laurence. "Qu'y a-t-il dans une assiette autochtone? Réflexion sur la restauration autochtone au Canada et seas enjeux." *Anthropology of Food* [online] (23 March 2022).

Hannickel, Erica. *Empire of Vines: Wine Culture in America*. Philadelphia: University of Pennsylvania Press, 2013.

Haraway, Donna. "Situated Knowledges: The Science Question in Feminism and the Privilege of Partial Perspective." *Feminist Studies* 14, no. 3 (Autumn 1988): 575–99.

– *Staying with the Trouble: Making Kin in the Chthulucene*. Durham, NC, and London: Duke University Press, 2016.

Hargreaves, Allison. "'The Lake Is the People and Life That Come to It': Location as Critical Practice." In *Approaching Indigenous Literatures*, edited by Deanne Reder and Linda M. Morra, 107–10. Waterloo: Wilfrid Laurier University Press, 2016.

Harris, Douglas C. *Fish, Law, and Colonialism: The Legal Capture of Salmon in British Columbia*. Toronto: University of Toronto Press, 2001.

Harris, John. "Ring of Fun around Toronto." *Boston Globe*, 21 July 1968, 2A.

Hashimoto, Atsuko, and David J. Telfer. "Selling Canadian Culinary Tourism: Branding the Global and the Regional Product." *Tourism*

*Geographies: An International Journal of Tourism Space, Place and Environment* 8, no. 1 (2006): 31–55.
Hauka, Don. "A World of Good Food." *Province*, 7 February 1986, 27.
Hawthorn, Tom. "Our Chefs Are Tops: Gold at Culinary Olympics." *Province*, 18 October 1992, A8.
Health Canada. *Eating Well with Canada's Food Guide: First Nations, Inuit and Métis.* Ottawa, 2007.
– "Vitamin C." Last modified 22 January 2019. https://www.canada.ca/en/health-canada/services/nutrients/vitamin-c.html.
Heidenreich, C.E. "Huron-Wendat." *The Canadian Encyclopedia*. Last modified 10 October 2018. https://www.thecanadianencyclopedia.ca/en/article/huron.
Heldke, Lisa. *Exotic Appetites: Ruminations of a Food Adventurer.* New York and London: Routledge, 2003.
Hennig, Martin, and Richard Caddell. "On Thin Ice? Arctic Indigenous Communities, the European Union and the Sustainable Use of Marine Mammals." In *The European Union and the Arctic*, edited by Nengye Liu, Elizabeth A. Kirk, and Tore Henriksen, 296–341. Leiden: Brill, 2017.
Hetzler, Richard. *The Mitsitam Cafe Cookbook: Recipes from the Smithsonian Museum of the American Indian.* Golden, CO: Fulcrum Publishing, 2010.
Hewitt, Priscilla. "Educating Priscilla." *Canadian Woman Studies/Les Cahier de la Femme* 9, no. 3–4 (1988): 12–14.
– "Quilicum: A West Coast Indian Restaurant." *Canadian Woman Studies/Cahier de la Femme* 10, no. 2–3 (1989): 131–2.
Hiawatha's. Facebook. 26 September 2020. https://www.facebook.com/HiawathasCatering.
Hill, Angela. "Jenni Lessard Brings Diverse Experience to Wanuskewin." *Star Phoenix*, 31 January 2020. https://thestarphoenix.com/life/bridges/jenni-lessard-brings-diverse-experience-to-wanuskewin.
Hill, Christina Gish. "Seeds as Ancestors, Seeds as Archives: Seed Sovereignty and the Politics of Repatriation to Native Peoples." *American Indian Culture and Research Journal* 41, no. 3 (2017): 93–112.
Ho, Soleil. "The Chicago Poke Chain That Tried to Stop Hawaiian Businesses from Using the Word 'Aloha.'" *New Yorker*, 10 August 2018. https://www.newyorker.com/culture/annals-of-gastronomy/the-chicago-poke-chain-that-tried-to-stop-hawaiian-businesses-from-using-the-word-aloha.
Hood, Glynnis. *The Beaver Manifesto.* Toronto: Rocky Mountain Books, 2011.
hooks, bell. "Eating the Other: Desire and Resistance." In *Black Looks: Race and Representation*, 21–39. Boston: South End Press, 1992.

Hoover, Elizabeth. *The River Is in Us: Fighting Toxics in Mohawk Country*. Minneapolis: University of Minnesota Press, 2017.

– "'You Can't Say You're Sovereign If You Can't Feed Yourself': Defining and Enacting Food Sovereignty in American Indian Community Gardening." In *Indigenous Food Sovereignty in the United States: Restoring Cultural Knowledge, Protecting Environments and Regaining Health*, edited by Devon A. Mihesuah and Elizabeth Hoover, 57–93. Norman: University of Oklahoma Press, 2019.

*Houston Today*. "Glitzy, but Not Too Gourmet, Feast Is a Cookbook with Taste as well as Style." 19 November 1997, 16.

Hudes, Sammy. "Chief Chiniki Restaurant Set to Rise from the Ashes." *Calgary Herald*, 16 July 2015, A3.

Hui, Ann. "U.S. Celebrity Chefs Boycotting Canadian Seafood Draw Backlash." *Globe and Mail*, 29 October 2013. http://www.theglobeandmail.com/news/national/boycott-of-canadian-seafood-ill-considered-says-anthony-bordain/article15133191/.

Humane Society of the United States. "Chefs for Seal." Accessed 3 May 2018. http://www.humanesociety.org/issues/seal_hunt/facts/stars_and_chefs.html.

– "Protect Seal." Accessed 3 May 2018. http://www.humanesociety.org/issues/seal_hunt/.

Humphreys, Adrian. "Controversial Montreal Chef Martin Picard's New Book Includes Recipes for 'Squirrel Sushi' and 'Confederation Beaver.'" *National Post*, 2 March 2012. http://news.nationalpost.com/news/canada/controversial-montreal-chef-martin-picards-new-book-includes-recipes-for-squirrel-sushi-and-confederation-beaver.

Hunt, Dallas, and Gina Starblanket. *Storying Violence: Unraveling Colonial Narratives in the Stanley Trial*. Winnipeg: ARP Books, 2020.

Iacovetta, Franca, Valerie Korinek, and Marlene Epp, eds. *Edible Histories, Cultural Politics: Towards a Canadian Food History*. Toronto: University of Toronto Press, 2012.

Indigenous Service Canada and Indigenous Relations and Northern Affairs Canada. "Toronto Purchase, No. 13." Accessed 1 October 2018. https://www.aadnc-aandc.gc.ca/eng/1370372152585/1370372222012#ucls13.

Inglis, David, and Debra Gimlin, "Food Globalizations: Ironies and Ambivalences of Food, Cuisine and Globality." In *The Globalization of Food*, edited by David Inglis and Debra Gimlin, 3–44. London: Bloomsbury Academic, 2010.

Inuit Tapiriit Kanatami. "A Taste of the Arctic." Accessed 2 May 2018. https://itk.ca/atota/#about.
- "What We Do." Accessed 3 May 2018. https://www.itk.ca/what-we-do/.
Irniq, Peter. "Foreword." In *Sacred Hunt: A Portrait of the Relationship between Seals and Inuit*, by David Pelly, viii–x. Vancouver: Greystone Books, 2001.
Jacknis, Ira, ed. *Food in California Indian Culture*. Berkeley: Phoebe Hearst Museum of Anthropology, University of California Berkeley, 2004.
Jacobs, Hersch. "Structural Elements in Canadian Cuisine." *Cuizine: The Journal of Canadian Food Cultures/Cuizine: Revue des cultures culinaires au Canada* 2, no. 1 (2009).
Jermanok, Steve. "Toronto Doesn't Get More Native Than This." *Chicago Tribune*, 31 March 2013, 6.
Joe Beef. Accessed 12 March 2019, http://www.joebeef.ca/.
Johnson, Eve. "First Feasts." *Vancouver Sun*, 25 August 1993, D6.
- "Historical Influences on West Coast Cooking." In *Northern Bounty: A Celebration of Canadian Cuisine*, edited by Jo Marie Powers and Anita Stewart, 9–15. Toronto: Random House of Canada, 1995.
- "The Impact He Made on Vancouver's Art Scene." *Vancouver Sun*, 19 April 1986, D3.
- "Native Past Recaptured, but Stick to the Seafood." *Vancouver Sun*, 4 April 1990, C3.
- "Tomahawk: Old-fashioned Eatery that Survived the City." *Vancouver Sun*, 16 March 1988, F3.
Johnson, Lisa. "Newfoundland Seal Featured on Vancouver Menu." CBC News, 9 January 2017. http://www.cbc.ca/news/canada/british-columbia/newfoundland-seal-vancouver-menu-1.3927668.
Johnston, Basil H. *Indian School Days*. Norman: University of Oklahoma Press, 1988.
Johnston, Josée, and Shyon Baumann. *Foodies: Democracy and Distinction in the Gourmet Foodscape*. New York and London: Routledge, 2010.
Johnston, Patrick. *Native Children and the Child Welfare System*. Ottawa: Lorimer, 1983.
Jørgensen, Dolly. "Beavers Are Back in England." *The Return of Native Nordic Fauna*, 1 April 2015. http://dolly.jorgensenweb.net/nordicnature/?p=2153.
- "Beaver for Lent." *The Return of Native Nordic Fauna*. 19 April 2014. http://dolly.jorgensenweb.net/nordicnature/?p=1568.
- "Extinction and the End of Futures." *History and Theory* 61, no. 2 (June 2022): 209–18.

Kapadia, Jess. "New York's First Native American Restaurant Was Run by an Indian-American Chef." *Food Republic*, 23 April 2014. https://www.foodrepublic.com/2014/04/23/new-yorks-first-native-american-restaurant-was-run-by-an-indian-american-chef/.

Kaplan, Amy. "Manifest Domesticity." *American Literature* 70, no. 3 (September 1998): 581–606.

Kates, Joanne. "At Keriwa, Local Food Goes Native with Stunning Results." *Globe and Mail*, 9 September 2011. https://www.theglobeandmail.com/life/food-and-wine/restaurant-reviews/at-keriwa-local-food-goes-native-with-stunning-results/article629689/.

Kauffman, Jonathan. "Questions of Cuisine and Culture Surround Coppola's New Restaurant." *San Francisco Chronicle*, 4 November 2016. https://www.sfchronicle.com/bayarea/article/Questions-of-cuisine-and-culture-surround-10594199.php#photo-11747691.

Kavasch, Barrie E. *Native Harvests: American Indian Wild Foods and Recipes*. Mineola, NY: Dover Publications, 2005 [1977].

Kelley, Dennis. "The Semiotics of Resistance: On the Power of Frybread." In *Native Foodways: Indigenous North American Religious Traditions and Foods*, edited by Michelene E. Pesantubbee and Michael J. Zogry, 195–209. Albany: SUNY Press, 2021.

Kelm, Mary-Ellen. *Colonizing Bodies: Aboriginal Health and Healing in British Columbia, 1900–50*. Vancouver: University of British Columbia Press, 1999.

Kenneally, Rhona Richman. "The Cuisine of the Tundra: Towards a Canadian Food Culture at Expo 67." *Food, Culture & Society* 11, no. 3 (2008): 287–313.

– "'The Greatest Dining Extravaganza in Canada's History': Food, Nationalism, and Authenticity at Expo 67." In *Expo 67: Not Just a Souvenir*, edited by Rhona Richman Kenneally and Johanne Sloan, 27–46. Toronto: University of Toronto Press, 2010.

– "'There *Is* a Canadian Cuisine, and It Is Unique in the World': Crafting National Food Culture during the Long 1960s." In *What's to Eat? Entrées in Canadian Food History*, edited by Nathalie Cooke, 167–96. Montreal and Kingston: McGill-Queen's University Press, 2009.

Kennedy, John R. "Tanya Tagaq Takes Shot at PETA Even Though It's Not against Inuit Seal Hunt." Global News, 23 September 2014. https://globalnews.ca/news/1578299/tanya-tagaq-takes-shot-at-peta-even-though-it-supports-inuit-seal-hunt/.

Ketchum, Alex. *Ingredients for Revolution: A History of American Feminist Restaurants, Cafes, and Coffeehouses*. Montreal: Concordia University Press, 2022.

- "Memory Has Added Seasoning: The Legacy of Feminist Restaurants in the United States." *Anthropology of Food* (18 April 2019).
- "'The Place We've Always Wanted to Go but Never Could Find': Finding Woman Space in Ontario's Feminist Restaurants and Cafes 1974–1982." *Feminist Studies* 14, no. 1 (2018): 126–52.

Kettner, Bonni Raines. "Coast Indian Dishes." *Province*, 30 April 1986, 48.

Kettner, Bonni Raines, and Don Hauka. "Good Native Fare and a Bit of '86." *Province*, 8 June 1986, 69.

Kimmerer, Robin Wall. *Braiding Sweetgrass: Indigenous Wisdom, Scientific Knowledge, and the Teaching of Plants*. Minneapolis: Milkweed Editions, 2013.

Kinesis. "Muckamuck Worker Ethel Gardner on the Dispute." July 1978
- "New Development in the Muckamuck Strike." October 1978, 3.

King, Thomas. *Green Grass, Running Water*. New York: Bantam Books, 1993.
- *The Inconvenient Indian: A Curious Account of Native People in North America*. Toronto: Anchor Canada, 2013.
- *The Truth about Stories: A Native Narrative*. Minneapolis: University of Minnesota Press, 2003.

Kinney, Rebecca J. "Riding Shotgun with an LA Son: Narratives of Race, Place, and Mobility in Roy Choi's Culinary Autobiography." *Food, Culture & Society* 20, no. 1 (March 2017): 59–75.

Knobloch, Frieda. *The Culture of Wilderness: Agriculture as Colonization in the American West*. Chapel Hill: University of North Carolina Press, 1996.

Knight, Ivy. "The Morning After: Brunch at Keriwa Cafe." *Toronto Star*, 14 December 2011. https://www.thestar.com/life/food_wine/restaurants/2011/12/14/the_morning_after_brunch_at_keriwa_caf.html
- "Seals Are Delicious, So Let's Kill and Eat Them." *MUNCHIES: Food by Vice*, 17 December 2013. https://munchies.vice.com/en/articles/seals-are-delicious-so-lets-kill-and-eat-them.

Koc, Mustafa, Jennifer Sumner, and Anthony Winson. *Critical Perspectives in Food Studies: Second Edition*. Oxford: Oxford University Press, 2016.

Korinek, Valerie J. "'Meat Stinks/Eat Beef Dyke!' Coming Out as a Vegetarian in the Prairies." In *Edible Histories, Cultural Politics: Towards a Canadian Food History*, edited by Franca Iacovetta, Valerie J. Korinek, and Marlene Epp, 326–48. Toronto: University of Toronto Press, 2012.

Krader, Kate. "An Insider's Guide to Toronto." *Food & Wine*, 31 March 2015. https://www.foodandwine.com/articles/an-insiders-guide-to-toronto.

Kramer, Lola. "Introduction: Bastards Beware." In *Bastard Cookbook: The Odious Smell of Truth*, edited by Antto Melasniemi and Rirkrit Tiravanija, 19–28. New York: Garret Publication and Finnish Cultural Institute, 2019.

Krech, Shepard, III. *The Ecological Indian: Myth and History*. New York and London: W.W. Norton & Company, 1999.

Ku, Robert Ji-Song. *Dubious Gastronomy: The Cultural Politics of Eating Asian in the USA*. Honolulu: University of Hawai'i Press, 2013.

Kuh, Patric. *The Last Days of Haute Cuisine: The Coming of Age of American Restaurants*. New York: Penguin Books, 2001.

Kuhnlein, Harriet V., and Nancy J. Turner. *Traditional Plant Foods of Canadian Indigenous Peoples: Nutrition, Botany, and Use*. Philadelphia: Gordon and Breach, 1991.

Kūkŭm Kitchen. "Menu." Accessed 15 January 2019. http://www.kukum-kitchen.com/menu/.

Kurtness, Manuel Kak'wa. *Pachamama: Cuisine des Premières Nations*. Quebec City: Les Editions du Boreal, 2009.

Kvill, Kesia Theresa. "Ordering off Western Canada's Menu: Public Dining in Alberta, 1880s–1920s." Master's thesis, University of Calgary, 2016.

Kwate, Naa Oyo A. *Burgers in Blackface: Anti-Black Restaurants Then and Now*. Minneapolis: University of Minnesota Press, 2019.

La Cerva, Gina Rae. *Feasting Wild: In Search of the Last Untamed Food*. Vancouver: Greystone Books, 2020.

LaDuke, Winona. *All Our Relations: Native Struggles for Land and Life*. Minneapolis: Honor the Earth, 1999.

– "Seeds of Our Ancestors, Seeds of Life." TEDx Talks. Uploaded 5 March 2012. https://www.youtube.com/watch?v=pHNlel72eQc.

Laffrey, Mary Lu. "72 Hours in Ottawa, Ontario." *Dispatch*, 10 May 2009, F6.

*Lakes District News*. "Classified Ads." 25 February 1976, 14.

– "Feast! A Cookbook for All Seasons – Literally." 19 November 1997, 8.

– "Feast! Local Chef Andrew George Jr. Puts Out Native Cuisine Cookbook." 2 July 1997, 8.

Landmark Inn. "Advertisement." *Leader-Post*, 31 January 1981, 30.

– "Part-Time Waiters-Waitresses." *Leader-Post*, 1 November 1977, 38.

Landsel, David. "What Does Seal Taste Like?" *Food and Wine*, 2 October 2017, http://www.foodandwine.com/travel/what-does-seal-taste.

Lane, Judith. "Feast on These First Nations Recipes." *Georgia Straight*, 18 July 2007. https://www.straight.com/article-102009/feast-on-these-first-nations-recipes.

Lane, Robert B. "Tsilhqot'in (Chilcotin)." *The Canadian Encyclopedia*. Last modified 5 November 2018. https://www.thecanadianencyclopedia.ca/en/article/chilcotin-tsilhqotin.

Lasley, Paul, and Elizabeth Harryman. "Dining Highlights in and near Vancouver." *San Francisco Examiner*, 19 April 1987, T10.

La Via Campesina. "Who We Are." Accessed 2 July 2018. https://viacampesina.org/en/who-are-we/.
*Leader-Post.* "Gallery Patrons Sample Authentic Indian Foods." 10 July 1972, 13.
– "Landmark Has Tasty Menu." 8 December 1999, A5.
– "Native Women Obstructed in Business Community." 11 January 1985, 25.
– "You Will Stop Smoking on June 2nd …" 5 May 1987, A8.
Le Guin, Ursula K. *The Carrier Bag Theory of Fiction.* London: Ignota Books, 2020 [1986].
Les Iles en Ville. "Menu." Accessed 2 May 2018. http://www.lesilesenville.com/menu.html.
Lessard, Jenni. "Who I Am." Accessed 9 December 2023. https://www.jennilessard.com/inspired-by-nature.
Levi, Tamara. *Food, Control and Resistance: Rations and Indigenous Peoples in the United States and South Australia.* Lubbock: Texas Tech University Press, 2016.
Lévi-Strauss, Claude. *The Raw and the Cooked.* Translated by John and Doreen Weightman. Chicago: University of Chicago Press, 1969.
– *Totemism.* Translated by Rodney Needham. London: Merlin Press, 1964.
Lewis, Courtney. "Frybread Wars: Biopolitics and the Consequences of Selective United States Healthcare Practices for American Indians." *Food, Culture & Society* 21, no. 4 (2018): 427–48.
Lichatowich, Jim. *Salmon without Rivers: A History of the Pacific Salmon Crisis.* Washington, DC and Covelo, CA: Island Press, 1999.
Lien, Marianne. *Becoming Salmon: Aquaculture and the Domestication of a Fish.* Oakland: University of California Press, 2015.
Lien, Marianne Elisabeth, and John Law. "'Emergent Aliens': On Salmon, Nature, and Their Enactment." *Ethnos* 76, no. 1 (March 2011): 65–87.
– "Slippery: Field Notes on Empirical Ontology." *Social Studies of Science* 43, no. 3 (June 2012): 1–14.
Liliget Feast House. Accessed 1 June 2019. http://www.liliget.com/.
– "2006 Menu." Accessed 1 June 2019. http://www.anniewatts.com.
Lillicrap, Bill. "Hall Feeds Expo's Masses." *Chilliwack Progress,* 4 June 1986, B10.
Lin, Brian. "The Taste of Home Can Be Found Downtown." *Raven's Eye* 5 (2001): 12. https://ammsa.com/publications/ravens-eye/taste-home-can-be-found-downtown.
Lindeman, Tracey. "Canada: Remains of 215 Children Found at Indigenous Residential School Site." *Guardian,* 28 May 2021. https://www.theguardian.com/world/2021/may/28/canada-remains-indigenous-children-mass-graves.

Lindlahr, Victor H. *You Are What You Eat: How to Win and Keep Health with Diet*. Hollywood: Newcastle, 1942.
Little Miss Chief. "The Little Miss Chief Story." Accessed 24 July 2019. https://littlemisschief.com/the-little-miss-chief-story/.
Logan, Audrey. *Out to Dry: An Urban Bushwoman's Guide to the Traditional Art and Science of Food Dehydration*. Winnipeg: Dehydration Nations, 2019.
Long, Lucy M. "Culinary Tourism. A Folkloristic Perspective on Eating and Otherness." In *Culinary Tourism*, edited by Lucy M. Long, 20–50. Lexington: University of Kentucky, 2004.
*Los Angeles Times*. "EXPO: Restaurant Menu." 17 August 1986, 8, 20.
Lovesick Lake Native Women's Association. *The Rural and Native Heritage Cookbook: The Gathering*. Selwyn, ON: Lovesick Lake Native Women's Association, 1985.
Lu, Shun, and Gary Alan Fine. "The Presentation of Ethnic Authenticity: Chinese Food as a Social Accomplishment." *Sociological Quarterly* 36, no. 3 (Summer 1995): 535–53.
Luby, Brittany. *Dammed: The Politics of Loss and Survival in Anishinaabe Territory*. Winnipeg: University of Manitoba Press, 2020.
– "From Milk-Medicine to Public (Re)Education Programs: An Examination of Anishinabek Mothers' Responses to Hydroelectric Flooding in the Treaty #3 District, 1900–1975." *Canadian Bulletin of Medical History* 32, no. 2 (2015): 363–89.
Luckerson, Victor. "These Are the 10 Most Popular Tweets of All Time." *Time*, 11 April 2017. http://time.com/4263227/most-popular-tweets/.
Luo, Tiano, and Philip B. Stark. "Only the Bad Die Young: Restaurant Mortality in the Western US." October 2014. https://arxiv.org/ftp/arxiv/papers/1410/1410.8603.pdf.
Lux, Maureen K. *Medicine That Walks: Disease, Medicine, and Canadian Plains Native People, 1880–1940*. Toronto: University of Toronto Press, 2001.
Lynn, Josh. "Former Top Chef Canada Finalist Wants to Redefine Aboriginal Cuisine." CBC News, 27 August 2016. http://www.cbc.ca/news/canada/saskatoon/saskatoon-rich-francis-cuisine-1.3728625.
Ma, Lisa. "Invasive." Accessed 5 January 2020. http://www.lisama.co.uk/works.
MacDonald, Susan. "A Taste of Life with an Indian Flavor." *Province*, 14 June 1985, 47.
Macrae, Scott. "Warhol: He Came, He Saw, and He Said Nowt." *Vancouver Sun*, 26 November 1976, 5A.
Maffei, Nicolas P. "Surveying the Borders: 'Authenticity' in Mexican-American Food Packaging, Imagery and Architecture." In *Designed Worlds: National Design Histories in an Age of Globalization*, edited by Kjetil Fallan and Grace Lees-Maffei, 211–25. New York: Berghahn Books, 2016.

Maillard, Kevin Noble. *Fry Bread: A Native American Family Story*. New York: Roaring Book Press, 2019.
Mallet, Gina. "Dine by Design." *National Post*, 22 October 2011, TO4.
– "Restaurant Review: Pemmican Pursuits." *National Post*, 27 August 2011, TO4.
Malouf, Albert H. *Seals and Sealing in Canada: Reports of the Royal Commission: Volumes I and II*. Ottawa: Canadian Government Publishing Centre, 1986.
Manzella, Abigail G.H. *Migrating Fictions: Gender, Race, and Citizenship in U.S. Internal Displacements*. Columbus: Ohio University Press, 2018.
Maracle, Candace. "Menu and Decor at Manitou Bistro 'Reprehensible' Some Kitigan Zibi Members Say." CBC News, 8 August 2023. https://www.cbc.ca/news/indigenous/manitou-bistro-kitigan-zibi-1.6919989.
Marche, Stephen. "Canada's Impossible Acknowledgement." *New Yorker*, 7 September 2017. https://www.newyorker.com/culture/culture-desk/canadas-impossible-acknowledgment.
Mares, Teresa M., and Devon G. Peña. "Environmental and Food Justice: Toward Local, Slow, and Deep Food Systems." In *Cultivating Food Justice: Race, Class, and Sustainability*, edited by Alison Hope Alkon and Julian Agyeman, 197–219. Cambridge, MA: MIT Press, 2011.
Martens, Tabitha, Jaime Cidro, Michael Anthony Hart, and Stéphane McLachlan. "Understanding Indigenous Food Sovereignty through an Indigenous Research Paradigm." *Journal of Indigenous Social Development* 5, no. 1 (2016): 18–37.
Martin, Shannon. "TDSB Schools Now Play Daily Tribute to Indigenous Lands They're Built On." CBC News, 22 September 2016. https://www.cbc.ca/news/canada/toronto/tdsb-indigenous-land-1.3773050.
Mason, Courtney W. "The Banff Indian Days Tourism Festival." *Annals of Tourism Research* 53 (2015): 77–95.
Matthews, Judith. "First Nations' Does Its Bannock Right." *Richmond Review*, 24 August 1986, 12.
Matties, Zoe. "Unsettling Settler Food Movements: Food Sovereignty and Decolonization in Canada." *Cuizine: The Journal of Canadian Food Cultures /Cuizine: Revue des cultures culinaires au Canada*, 7, no. 2 (2016).
Maynard, Micheline. "Canadian Chefs Serve Seal, with a Side of Controversy." *New York Times*, 30 June 2009. https://www.nytimes.com/2009/07/01/dining/01seal.html?_r=1&ref=dining.
– "When Seal Is on the Menu." *New York Times Diner's Journal*, 30 June 2009. https://dinersjournal.blogs.nytimes.com/2009/06/30/when-seal-is-on-the-menu/.
McCallum, Mary Jane Logan. "Indigenous Labor and Indigenous History." *American Indian Quarterly* 33, no. 4 (2009): 523–44.

- *Indigenous Women, Work, and History: 1940–1980.* Winnipeg: University of Manitoba Press, 2013.
- "Starvation, Experimentation, Segregation, and Trauma: Words for Reading Indigenous Health History." *Canadian Historical Review* 98, no. 1 (2017): 96–113.

McComb Sanchez, Andrea. "Balance and a Bean: Revitalizing *Himdag* through Traditional Farming and Sacred Knowledge." *Native Foodways: Indigenous North American Religious Traditions and Foods*, edited by Michelene E. Pesantubbee and Michael J. Zogry, 33–50. Albany: SUNY Press, 2021.

McCook, Sheila. "Eat Your Oolichan – And Enjoy It." *Daily Independent Journal*, 19 April 1975, M13.

McGillivray, Kate. "'It's Who We Are': Indigenous Chef Joseph Shawana Stands by Decision to Serve Seal." CBC News, 11 October 2017. http://www.cbc.ca/news/canada/toronto/joseph-shawana-seal-meat-kukum-kitchen-1.4350357.

McKegney, Sam. "Strategies for Ethical Engagement: An Open Letter Concerning Non-Native Scholars of Native Literature." *Studies in American Indian Literatures* 20, no. 4 (Winter 2008): 55–67.

McKenna, Tine. "The Ace Is Wild." *LA Weekly*, 9 October 2003. https://www.laweekly.com/news/the-ace-is-wild-2137131.

McRae, Dolly. *My Name Is Dolly.* Port Alberni, BC: ALW Publishing, 2014.

McWilliams, James E. *Just Food: Where Locavores Get It Wrong and How We Can Truly Eat Responsibly.* New York: Back Bay Books, 2009.

- *A Revolution in Eating: How the Quest for Food Shaped America.* New York: Columbia University Press, 2005.

Melasniemi, Antto, and Rirkrit Tiravanija. *Bastard Cookbook: The Odious Smell of Truth.* New York: Garret Publication and Finnish Cultural Institute, 2019.

Metallic, Fred, and Isaac Metallic. "A Mi'qmaq Perspective on Wild Salmon Management and the Salmon Farming Industry." In *Salmon Cultures: Indigenous Peoples and the Aquaculture Industry*, edited by Dorothee Schreiber and Camilla Brattland, 13–20. *RCC Perspectives* 4 (2012).

Micallef, Shawn. *The Trouble with Brunch: Work, Class and the Pursuit of Leisure.* Toronto: Coach House, 2014.

Middell, Matthias, and Katja Naumann. "Global History and the Spatial Turn: From the Impact of Area Studies to the Study of Critical Junctures of Globalization." *Journal of Global History* 5, no. 1 (March 2010): 149–70.

Mihesuah, Devon A. "Decolonizing Our Diets by Recovering Our Ancestors' Gardens." *American Indian Quarterly* 27, no. 3–4 (Summer–Autumn 2003): 807–39.

- "Indigenous Health Initiatives, Frybread, and the Marketing of Nontraditional 'Traditional' American Indian Foods." *Native American and Indigenous Studies* 3, no. 2 (Fall 2016): 45–69.
- "Nephi Craig: Life in Second Sight." In *Indigenous Food Sovereignty in the United States*, edited by Devon A. Mihesuah and Elizabeth Hoover, 300–19. Norman: University of Oklahoma Press, 2019.
- *Recovering Our Ancestors' Gardens: Indigenous Recipes and Guide to Diet and Fitness*. Lincoln: University of Nebraska Press, 2006.
- *So You Want to Write about American Indians? A Guide for Writers, Students, and Scholars*. Lincoln and London: University of Nebraska Press, 2005.

Mihesuah, Devon A., and Elizabeth Hoover, eds. *Indigenous Food Sovereignty in the U.S.: Restoring Cultural Knowledge, Protecting Environments, and Regaining Health*. Norman: University of Oklahoma Press, 2019.

Mijure, Ben. "Vancouver Eatery Serves Up Controversy with Newfoundland Seal Dish." CTV News Vancouver, 10 January 2017. https://bc.ctvnews.ca/vancouver-eatery-serves-up-controversy-with-newfoundland-seal-dish-1.3235046.

Miller, Ben. "Determined to Keep Up Their Dances." In *A Public Apology to Siksika Nation*, by AA Bronson, 77–108.

Miller, J.R. "Residential Schools in Canada." *The Canadian Encyclopedia*. 2 September 2020. https://www.thecanadianencyclopedia.ca/en/article/residential-schools.

Mills, Win. "Missing Teeth, and Relatives." *Ottawa Citizen*, 13 June 1968, 39.

"Mind of a Chef Sneak Peek with Comedian Aziz Ansari." PBS. Uploaded 8 November 2012. https://www.youtube.com/watch?v=cek6rK5F4EA.

Ming Court. Accessed 1 June 2019. https://www.mingcourt.ca/.

*Minneapolis Star*. "Muckamuck: Indian Fare Finds Favor in Vancouver." 12 July 1978, 4C.

Mintz, Corey. *The Next Supper: The End of Restaurants As We Know Them*. New York: PublicAffairs, 2021.

Mississaugas of the New Credit First Nation. "The History of the Mississaugas of the New Credit First Nation." April 2018. http://mncfn.ca/wp-content/uploads/2018/04/The-History-of-MNCFN-FINAL.pdf.

Moore, Kerry. "Cocktail of the Week." *Province*, 12 November 2004, A48.
- "Dining." *Province*. 8 May 1983, 14.

Moore, Kimberley, and Janis Thiessen. *mmm ... Manitoba*. Winnipeg: University of Manitoba Press, 2024.

"Moosemeat & Marmalade." "About the Show." Accessed 10 October 2016. http://moosemeatandmarmalade.com/about-the-show/.
- Season 1, episode 1, "Beaver and the Boys," APTN, 7 July 2015.

Morash, Gordon. "Cookbooks Bring Native Cuisine to the Kitchen." *Edmonton Journal*, 2 October 1991, C2.
Morris, Carolyn. "*Kai* or Kiwi? Māori and 'Kiwi' Cookbooks and the Struggle for the Field of New Zealand Cuisine." *Journal of Sociology* 49, no. 2–3 (2013): 210–23.
– "The Politics of Palatability: On the Absence of Māori Restaurants." *Food, Culture and Society* 13, no. 1 (2010): 5–28.
Morris and Helen Belkin Art Gallery. "Beginning with the Seventies: Collective Acts." Exhibition 4 September 2018–2 December 2018. https://belkin.ubc.ca/exhibitions/beginning-with-the-seventies-collective-acts/.
Morrissette, Suzanne. "Press Text: *Blueprints for a long walk*." Urban Shaman Gallery, Winnipeg, 30 May to 29 June 2013. https://www.suzannemorrissette.com/blueprints-for-a-long-walk/.
Mosby, Ian. "Administering Colonial Science: Nutrition Research and Human Biomedical Experimentation in Aboriginal Communities and Residential Schools, 1942–1952." *Histoire sociale/Social History* 46, no. 91 (May 2013): 145–72.
Mosby, Ian, and Tracey Galloway. "'The Abiding Condition Was Hunger': Assessing the Long-Term Biological and Health Effects of Malnutrition and Hunger in Canada's Residential Schools." *British Journal of Canadian Studies* 30, no. 2 (September 2017): 147–62.
Moskin, Julia. "Noma, Rated the World's Best Restaurant, Is Closing Its Doors." *New York Times*, 9 January 2023. https://www.nytimes.com/2023/01/09/dining/noma-closing-rene-redzepi.html.
Müller, Birgit. "Still Feeding the World? The Political Ecology of Canadian Prairie Farmers." *Anthropologica* 50, no. 2 (2008): 389–407.
Myers, Fred. "'Primitivism,' Anthropology, and the Category of 'Primitive Art.'" In *Handbook of Material Culture*, edited by Christopher Tilley, Webb Keane, and Patricia Spyer, 267–84. London: Sage, 2006.
Myers, Lisa Rose. "Artist Statement." Accessed 25 September 2018. https://lisarosemyers.com/home.html.
– "Best Before: Recipes and Food in Contemporary Aboriginal Art." Master's thesis, OCAD University, 2011.
– "Straining and Absorbing." Accessed 25 September 2018. https://lisarosemyers.com/artwork/3830492_straining_and_absorbing.html.
N., Jennifer. "Demand That Kukum Kitchen in Toronto Canada Take Seal Meat off Their Menu." *The Petition Site*. Accessed 12 October 2017. https://www.thepetitionsite.com/de/704/964/589/demand-that-kukum-kitchen-in-toronto-ontario-take-seal-meat-off-their-menu/.

Nabhan, Gary Paul. *Enduring Seeds: Native American Agriculture and Wild Plant Conservation*. Tucson: University of Arizona Press, 2002 [1989].

National Inquiry into Missing and Murdered Indigenous Women and Girls. *Reclaiming Power and Place: The Final Report of the National Inquiry into Missing and Murdered Indigenous Women and Girls*. 24 May 2019. https://www.mmiwg-ffada.ca/wp-content/uploads/2019/06/Final_Report_Vol_1a-1.pdf.

*National Post*. "Canada's Best Restaurants: Ontario." 28 October 2006, WP15.

– "The Restaurant." 1 May 1982, 171.

Neechi. "About." Accessed 6 September 2016. https://neechi.ca/about/.

Nettles-Barcelón, Kimberly D., Gillian Clark, Courtney Thorsson, Jessica Kenyatta Walker, and Psyche Williams-Forson. "Black Women's Food Work as Critical Space." *Gastronomica* 15, no. 4 (Winter 2015): 34–49.

Neuhaus, Jessamyn. *Manly Meals and Mom's Home Cooking: Cookbooks and Gender in Modern America*. Baltimore and London: Johns Hopkins University Press, 2003.

Newell, Dianne. *Tangled Webs of History: Indians and the Law in Canada's Pacific Coast Fisheries*. Toronto: University of Toronto Press, 1993.

Newman, Lenore. *Speaking in Cod Tongues: A Canadian Culinary Journey*. Regina: University of Regina Press, 2017.

*New York Times*. "Asparagus and Spruce." 23 December 2010. https://www.nytimes.com/video/multimedia/1248069481544/asparagus-and-spruce.html?action=click&contentCollection=Opinion&module=RelatedCoverage&region=Marginalia&pgtype=article.

Ngabo, Gilbert. "First Nations Food Truck Greets Pan Am Visitors in Toronto." *Metro News*, 12 July 2015. http://www.metronews.ca/news/toronto/2015/07/12/first-nations-food-truck-greets-pan-am-visitors-in-toronto.html.

– "Is It Parkdale or Vegandale? Fight Intensifies over Neighbourhood's Identity." *Toronto Star*, 2 August 2018. https://www.thestar.com/news/gta/2018/08/02/is-it-parkdale-or-vegandale-fight-intensifies-over-neighbourhoods-identity.html.

Nickel, Sarah A. *Assembling Unity: Indigenous Politics, Gender, and the Union of BC Indian Chiefs*. Vancouver and Toronto: UBC Press, 2019.

Nicol, Janet Mary. "'Unions Aren't Native': The Muckamuck Restaurant Labour Dispute Vancouver, B.C. (1978–1983)." *Labour/Le Travail* 40 (Fall 1997): 235–51.

Nightingale, Tom. "Bringing Millennia of Culinary History to Life in the 21st Century." *Restobiz*, 7 March 2022. https://www.restobiz.ca/bringing-millennia-of-culinary-history-to-life-in-the-21st-century/.

Nilsson, Magnus. *Fäviken*. London: Phaidon, 2012.
– *Nordic Cookbook*. London and New York: Phaidon, 2015.
NishDish. Instagram Post. 6 May 2020. https://www.instagram.com/p/B_1EsjQgvKG/.
– "Restaurant." Accessed 4 January 2021. https://www.nishdish.com/restaurant.
Noble, Marilyn. "Bison Bars Were Supposed to Restore Native Communities and Grass-Based Ranches. Then Came Epic Provisions." In *The Best American Food Writing 2019*, edited by Samin Nosrat, 162–72. Boston and New York: Mariner Books, 2019.
Norman, Alison. "'Fit for the Table of the Most Fastidious Epicure': Culinary Colonialism in the Upper Canadian Contact Zone." In *Edible Histories, Cultural Politics: Towards a Canadian Food History*, edited by Franca Iacovetta, Marlene Epp, and Valerie Korinek, 31–51. Toronto: University of Toronto Press, 2009.
Nosowitz, Dan. "Seal Meat: Veal of the Ocean?" *Modern Farmer*, 17 November 2014. http://modernfarmer.com/2014/11/seal-meat-next-big-thing/.
Nuttall-Smith, Chris. "Boralia: A History Lesson in Canadiana That Tastes Unforgettably Good." *Globe and Mail*, 13 March 2015. http://www.theglobeandmail.com/life/food-and-wine/restaurant-reviews/borealia-a-history-lesson-in-canadiana-that-tastes-unforgettably-good/article23455376/.
Nyéléni. "*Nyéléni 2007: Forum for Food Sovereignty*." February 2007. https://nyeleni.org/DOWNLOADS/Nyelni_EN.pdf.
O'Brien, Suzanne Crawford. "Of Coyotes and Culverts: Salmon and the People of the Mid-Columbia River." In *Native Foodways: Indigenous North American Religious Traditions and Foods*, edited by Michelene E. Pesantubbee and Michael J. Zogry, 51–72. Albany: SUNY Press, 2021.
O'Brien, Suzanne Crawford, and Kimberly Wogahn. "Bringing a Berry Back from the Land of the Dead." In *Native Foodways: Indigenous North American Religious Traditions and Foods*, edited by Michelene E. Pesantubbee and Michael J. Zogry, 137–65. Albany: SUNY Press, 2021.
O'Connor, Kevin. "Businessman a 'Minnow Swimming with Sharks.'" *Leader-Post*, 22 June 2000, A8.
Oden, Loretta Barrett, and Beth Dooley. *Corn Dance: Inspired First American Cuisine*. Norman: University of Oklahoma Press, 2023.
O'Higgins, Nancy. "On the Trail of the Best Burgers for Your Buck." *Province*, 6 September 1981, B4.

*OhMore Story*. "91 Years of Breakfast with the Community at the Tomahawk." 4 August 2017. https://www.youtube.com/watch?v=NxB9FwAgLb8.

*oh-oh Canada*. "Michael Farnan." Accessed 10 October 2016. http://ohohcanada.ca/michael-farnan.

O'Leary, Kim Patrick. "Expo 86." *The Canadian Encyclopedia*, 7 February 2016, last edited March 4, 2015. https://www.thecanadianencyclopedia.ca/en/article/expo-86.

Ontario Ministry of Finance. "2016 Census Highlights: Factsheet 8." Accessed 4 June 2019. https://www.fin.gov.on.ca/en/economy/demographics/census/cenhi16-8.html.

Ontario Regulation. Food Safety and Quality Act, 2001, S.O. 2001, c. 20. Last modified 1 July 2014. https://www.ontario.ca/laws/regulation/050031.

Orange, Tommy. *There There*. New York: Penguin Random House, 2019.

Orlean, Susan. "The Homesick Restaurant." In *Secret Ingredients: The New Yorker Book of Food and Drink*, edited by David Remnick, 283–96. New York: Modern Library, 2007.

Oster, Richard T., Angela Grier, Rick Lightning, Maria J. Mayan, and Ellen L. Toth. "Cultural Continuity, Traditional Indigenous Language, and Diabetes in Alberta First Nations: A Mixed Methods Study." *International Journal for Equity in Health* 13, no. 92 (2014): 1–11.

*Ottawa Citizen*. "Come to the Muckamuck: It Means Food. Real Canadian Food." 4 May 1974.

– "Greater Ottawa Chamber of Commerce 2004 Business Achievement Award Winners." 4 December 2004, H3.

– "Recently Recommended." 1 April 2007, B9.

*Ottawa Journal*. "Muck-a-Muck House Serves 'Just Plain Good Food.'" 11 July 1972, 29.

Pacholk, Barb. "The $1,000,00 Pay-Back." *Leader-Post*, 5 May 2012, G1.

Panetta, Alexander. "Martin Picard's Squirrel Sushi and Braised Beaver in New Cookbook." *Huffington Post*, 3 January 2012. http://www.huffington post.ca/2012/03/01/martin-picard-squirrel-sushi_n_1313474.html.

Parenteau, Bill. "'Care, Control and Supervision': Native People in the Canadian Atlantic Salmon Fishery, 1867–1900." *Canadian Historian Review* 79, no. 1 (March 1998): 1–35.

Parker, Arthur C. *Iroquois Uses of Maize and Other Food Plants*. London: Forgotten Books, 2017 [1910].

Parks Canada. "Georgian Bay Islands National Park: Cultural Heritage." Accessed 6 September 2019. https://www.pc.gc.ca/en/pn-np/on/georg/decouvrir-discovers/natcul3.
Parrott, Zach, and Tabitha Marshall. "Iroquois Wars." *The Canadian Encyclopedia*. Last modified 31 July 2019. https://www.thecanadianencyclopedia.ca/en/article/iroquois-wars.
Parry, Malcolm. "Town Talk." *Vancouver Sun*, 22 August 1995, B2.
– "Trade Talk." *Vancouver Sun*, 18 November 2004, D5.
Pataki, Amy. "Kukum Kitchen Will Win You Over with Its Indigenous Food: Review." *Toronto Star*, 25 July 2017. https://www.thestar.com/life/food_wine/2017/07/25/kukum-kitchen-will-win-you-over-with-its-indigenous-food-review.html.
Patterson, S. Kaitlyn. "Who Are the Cattails? Stories of Algonquin Anishinaabe Food Systems." *Canadian Food Studies* 8, no. 1 (2021): 22–8.
Payne, Elizabeth. "Ottawa's Urban Inuit Renaissance." *Ottawa Citizen*, 17 April 2015. http://ottawacitizen.com/news/local-news/ottawas-urban-inuit-renaissance.
Pelly, David F. *Sacred Hunt: A Portrait of the Relationship between Seals and Inuit*. Vancouver: Greystone Books, 2001.
Penfold, Steve. *The Donut: A Canadian History*. Toronto: University of Toronto Press, 2008.
Penniman, Leah. *Farming While Black: Soul Fire Farm's Practical Guide to Liberation on the Land*. White River Junction, VT: Chelsea Green Publishing, 2018.
Pennington, Gail. "Fine Fare in Vancouver." *St. Louis Post-Dispatch*, 28 May 1986, D7.
People of 'Ksan. *Gathering What the Great Nature Provide: Food Traditions of the Gitksan*. Seattle: University of Washington Press, 1980.
Perreaux, Les. "Quebec Lets Select Restaurants Put Hunted Wild Game on Menu." *Globe and Mail*, 24 February 2014. http://www.theglobeandmail.com/news/national/quebec-puts-wild-game-back-on-menu/article17076775/.
PETA. "8 Things You Need to Know about Canada's Seal Slaughter." *Canada's Shame*. Accessed 27 April 2018. https://www.canadasshame.com/features/8-things-you-need-to-know-about-canadas-seal-slaughter/.
Peterson, David. "Why Toronto Should Get Excited about the Pan Am Games." *Globe and Mail*, 10 July 2014. http://www.theglobeandmail.com/opinion/why-toronto-should-get-excited-about-the-pan-am-games/article19543736/.

Peyton, Gabby. *Where We Ate: A Field Guide to Canada's Restaurants, Past and Present*. Toronto: Appetite by Random House, 2023.
Pfeffer, Amanda. "'Woefully Inaccurate' Inuit Population Data Overwhelming Local Agencies." CBC News, 12 November 2017. http://www.cbc.ca/news/canada/ottawa/woefully-inaccurate-inuit-population-ottawa-1.4391742.
*Philadelphia Inquirer*. "In British Columbia, a Revival of Interest in Indian Culture." 8 March 1987, 14R.
– "True Contender for the 'Most Beautiful.'" 12 June 1994, T11.
Phillipps, Breanna, and Kelly Skinner. "Bannock: Using a Contested Bread to Understand Indigenous and Settler Relations and Ways Forward within Canada." In *Recipes and Reciprocity: Building Relationships in Research*, edited by Hannah Tait Neufeld and Elizabeth Finnis, 55–78. Winnipeg: University of Manitoba Press, 2022.
Phoque Fest. Accessed 20 April 2018. https://phoquefest.ca/en/.
Picard, Martin. *Au Pied de Cochon Sugar Shack*. Montreal: Au Pied du Cochon, 2012.
Piche, Ron. "Big Band Sound Is Live Saturday at Regina's Landmark Inn." *Leader-Post*, 24 November 1983, B1.
Pilcher, Jeffrey. "Culinary Infrastructure: How Facilities and Technologies Create Value and Meaning around Food." *Global Food History* 2, no. 2 (2016): 105–31.
– *Planet Taco: A Global History of Mexican Food*. Oxford: Oxford University Press, 2012.
Poliquin, Rachel. *Beaver*. London: Reaktion Books, 2015.
Polson, Dorothee. "Reindeer Ragout: Canada's Expo 86 Offers a Taste of the Northwest." *Arizona Republic*, 3 August 1986, S43.
Portnoy, Sarah, and Jeffrey Pilcher. "Roy Choi, Ricardo Zárate, and Pacific Fusion Cuisine in Los Angeles." In *Global Latin America*, edited by Matthew Gutmann and Jeffrey Lesser, 146–62. Berkeley: University of California Press, 2015.
Potter, Mitch. "Row Erupts over Governor General's Seal Taste." *Toronto Star*, 26 May 2009. https://www.thestar.com/news/canada/2009/05/26/row_erupts_over_governor_generals_seal_taste.html.
Poulain, Jean-Pierre. *The Sociology of Food: Eating and the Place of Food in Society*. Translated by Augusta Dörr. London and New York: Bloomsbury, 2017.
Powell, J.V., and Sam Sullivan. "Chinook Wawa." *The Canadian Encyclopedia*. Last modified 26 October 2017. https://www.thecanadianencyclopedia.ca/en/article/chinook-jargon.

Powers, Jo Marie, and Anita Stewart, eds. *Northern Bounty: A Celebration of Canadian Cuisine*. Toronto: Random House of Canada, 1995.

Powers, William K., and Marla M.N. Powers. "Metaphysical Aspects of an Oglala Food System." In *Food in the Social Orders: Studies in Food and Festivities in Three American Communities*, edited by Mary Douglas, 40–96. London and New York: Routledge, 1973.

Pratt, Mary Louise. "Arts of the Contact Zone." *Profession* 91 (1991): 33–40.

Pratt, Richard H. "The Advantages of Mingling Indians with Whites." In *Americanizing the American Indians: Writings by the "Friends of the Indian" 1880–1900*, edited by Francis Paul Prucha, 260–71. Cambridge, MA: Harvard University Press, 1973.

Preston, Jennifer. "Racial Extractivism: Neoliberal White Settler Colonialism and Tar Sands Extraction." PhD dissertation, York University, 2017.

Prince, Christina. "Letters to the Editor: Union Wasn't Spoiling for a Fight." *Vancouver Sun*, 21 October 1978, A5.

*Province*. "Dining Choice Varied." 16 August 1984, 20.

– "Muckamuck Goes Cowboy in Bid to Beat Strike." 11 October 1978, 44.

*Province Magazine*. "Ice Cream." 30 June 1985, 10.

Puglisi, Christian F. *Relæ: A Book of Ideas*. Emeryville, CA: Ten Speed Press, 2014.

Pynn, Larry. "Budget Gourmet: Now for Something Different." *Vancouver Sun*, 6 December 1985, F11.

– "Former Strikers Replace Muckamuck." *Vancouver Sun*, 3 May 1985, A17.

"Queen Elizabeth II. Expo 67: A Virtual Experience, Library and Archives Canada." Accessed 1 July 2018. collectionscanada.ca/expo/0533020 403_e.html.

*Quill and Quire*. "Reviews: *Where People Feast: An Indigenous People's Cookbook* by Annie Watts and Dolly Watts." 2007. https://quillandquire.com/review/where-people-feast-an-indigenous-people-s-cookbook/.

Ragavan, Surekha. "Authenticity in Food: What Is It and Does It Matter?" *Time Out Kuala Lumpur*, 30 August 2016. http://www.timeout.com/kuala-lumpur/restaurants/authenticity-in-food-what-defines-it-and-does-it-matter.

Randhawa, Selena. "Animal Rights Activists and Inuit Clash over Canada's Indigenous Food Traditions." *Guardian*, 1 November 2017. https://www.theguardian.com/inequality/2017/nov/01/animal-rights-activists-inuit-clash-canada-indigenous-food-traditions?CMP=share_btn_fb.

Rao, Tejal. "The Movement to Define Native American Cuisine." *New York Times*, 16 August 2016. http://www.nytimes.com/2016/08/17/dining/new-native-american-cuisine.html?_r=0.

Rasky, Frank. "The Wondrous Fair: The Tastes." *Montreal Gazette*, 17 June 2007, 9
Rasta Pasta. "Menu." Accessed 2 October 2018. https://eatrastapasta.ca/menu/.
Rawal, Sanjay. *Gather*. Illumine Group, 2020.
Rawson, Katie, and Elliott Shore. *Dining Out: A Global History of Restaurants*. London: Reaktion Books, 2019.
Ray, Krishnendu. "Culinary Difference Makes a Difference." In *You and I Eat the Same: On the Countless Ways Food and Cooking Connect Us to One Another*, edited by Chris Ying, 151–9. New York: Artisan, 2018.
– *The Ethnic Restaurateur*. London and New York: Bloomsbury, 2016.
– "Taste, Toil and Ethnicity: Immigrant Restaurateur and the American City." *Ethnologie française* 44, no. 1 (2014): 105–14.
Reder, Deanne. "Introduction: *Position*." In *Approaching Indigenous Literatures*, edited by Deanne Reder and Linda M. Morra, 7–17. Waterloo: Wilfrid Laurier University Press, 2016.
Reder, Deanne, and Sophie McCall. "Indigenous and Postcolonial Studies: Tensions and Interrelationships, Creative, and Critical Interventions." *Ariel: A Review of International English Literature* 51, no. 2–3 (2020): 1–25.
Redzepi, René. "Evergreen, Ever Delicious." *New York Times*, 24 December 2010. http://www.nytimes.com/2010/12/25/opinion/25redzepi.html?mcubz=0.
– "If It Does Well Here, It Belongs Here." In *You and I Eat the Same: On the Countless Ways Food and Cooking Connect Us to One Another*, edited by Chris Ying, 87–95. New York: Artisan, 2018.
– *NOMA: Time and Place in Nordic Cuisine*. London and New York: Phaidon, 2010.
– *A Work in Progress: Noma Recipes*. London and New York: Phaidon, 2013.
Reiter, Ester. *Making Fast Food: From the Frying Pan into the Fryer*. Montreal and Kingston: McGill-Queen's University Press, 1991.
*Restaurant Magazine*. "The World's 50 Best Restaurants." Accessed 12 March 2019. https://www.theworlds50best.com/blog/News/the-worlds-50-best-restaurants-51-100-list-highlights-in-pictures.html.
Restaurant Manitoba. "Menu." Accessed April 20, 2018. http://restaurantmanitoba.com/?lang=en.
Restaurants Canada. "Canada's Restaurant Industry Infographic." June 2018. https://www.restaurantscanada.org/wp-content/uploads/2018/06/Canada_ENG_Infographic_June_2018.pdf.
– "Ontario's Restaurant Industry." June 2018. https://www.restaurantscanada.org/wp-content/uploads/2018/06/Ontario_Infographic_June2018.pdf.

Richardier, Kathy. "Chinki Restaurant Offers Pleasant Food, Service." *Calgary Herald*, 7 August 1987, E2.
– "Country-Dining Spot's Nice Way to End Drive." *Calgary Herald*, 7 June 1989, F4.
Riches, Hester. "Folk Art of All Kinds Provides Calm Contrast." *Vancouver Sun*, 28 April 1986, C1.
Richler, Jacob. *My Canada Includes Foie Gras: A Culinary Life*. Toronto: Viking, 2012.
– "Wild about Eating Game." *Maclean's*, 28 October 2012. http://www.macleans.ca/society/life/wild-about-game/.
*Richmond Review*. "One of 60 on Site: A Restaurant 'First.'" 12 February 1986, 17A.
Rifkin, Mark. *Beyond Settler Time: Temporal Sovereignty and Indigenous Self-Determination*. Durham, NC, and London: Duke University Press, 2017.
Roberts, Julia. *In Mixed Company: Taverns and Public Life in Upper Canada*. Vancouver: University of British Columbia Press, 2009.
– "'The Snipe Were Good and the Wine Not Bad': Enabling Public Life for Privileged Men." In *Edible Histories, Cultural Politics: Towards a Canadian Food History*, edited by Franca Iacovetta, Valerie Korinek, and Marlene Epp, 52–69. Toronto: University of Toronto Press, 2012.
Robertson, Paul. "His Menu Is a Bit 'Wild.'" *Regina Sun*, 24 October 1999, 10.
Robidoux, Michael A., and Courtney W. Mason, eds. *A Land Not Forgotten: Indigenous Food Security and Land-Based Practices in Northern Ontario*. Winnipeg: University of Manitoba Press, 2017.
Robin, Tabitha. "Our Hands at Work: Indigenous Food Sovereignty in Western Canada." *Journal of Agriculture, Food Systems, and Community Development* 9, no. 2 (2019): 85–89.
– "Protecting Indigenous Women and Two-Spirit Peoples as Food System Revitalization." Presentation at *Food Relatives: Decolonizing and Indigenizing the Global Food System*, UC Berkeley. 1 April 2022.
– "Responsibilities and Reflections: Indigenous Food, Culture, and Relationships." *Canadian Food Studies* 5, no. 2 (2018): 9–12.
Robin, Tabitha (Marten), Mary Kate Dennis, and Michael Anthony Hart. "Feeding Indigenous People in Canada." *International Social Work* (2020): 1–11.
Roche, Judith, and Meg McHutchison, eds. *First Fish, First People: Salmon Tales of the North Pacific Rim*. Vancouver: UBC Press, 1998.
Rombauer, Irma S., and Marion Rombauer Becker. *The Joy of Cooking: The American Household Classic Newly Revised*. New York: Scribner, 1975.

Rose, Nick. "Seal Meat and Caribou Offer a Taste of Canada's Inuit Identity." *MUNCHIES: Food by Vice*, 9 March 2016. https://munchies.vice.com/en_us/article/gvk9yb/seal-meat-narwhal-and-inuit-identity.

Roy, Suman, and Brooke Ali. *From Pemmican to Poutine: A Journey through Canada's Culinary History*. Toronto: Key Publishing House, 2010.

Royal Commission on Aboriginal Peoples. *The High Arctic Relocation: A Report on the 1953–55 Relocation*. Ottawa: Minister of Supply and Services Canada, 1994.

Rubin, Josh. "Nishdish, Closed for Good by COVID-19, Served Up Anishinaabe Cuisine and History." *Toronto Star*, 25 May 2020. https://www.thestar.com/business/2020/05/25/nishdish-closed-for-good-by-covid-19-served-up-anishnaabe-cuisine-and-history.html.

Rutherford, Kate. "Sudbury to Get New Restaurant Serving Indigenous Cuisine: Hiawatha's." CBC, 18 October 2019. https://www.cbc.ca/news/canada/sudbury/indigenous-cuisine-restaurant-hiawatha-sudbury-1.5325374.

Salminen, Edith. "Cook It Raw Alberta and the Art of Slowing Down." *MUNCHIES: Food by VICE*, 15 September 2015. https://munchies.vice.com/en/articles/cook-it-raw-alberta-and-the-art-of-slowing-down.

– "Hunting for the Future at Cook It Raw Alberta." *MUNCHIES: Food by VICE*, 16 November 2015. https://munchies.vice.com/en/articles/hunting-for-the-future-at-cook-it-raw-alberta.

Salmon n' Bannock. Facebook. 1 July 2019. https://www.facebook.com/SalmonNBannockBistro/.

– "Menu." Accessed 1 July 2019. https://www.salmonandbannock.net/DINNER_MENU_Feb_2019_DS3.pdf.

Sanderson, David. "Métis Island." *Winnipeg Free Press*, 16 February 2008, F3.

Sangster, Jane. "'The Beaver' as Ideology: Constructing Images of Inuit and Native Life in Post–World War II Canada." *Anthropologica* 49, no. 2 (2007): 191–209.

*Saskatoon Star-Phoenix*. "Wanuskewin Restaurant Named One of Canada's Tastiest Indigenous Dining Spots." 16 May 2016. https://thestarphoenix.com/news/local-news/wanuskewin-restaurant-named-one-of-canadas-tastiest-indigenous-dining-spots.

Saul, John Ralston. *A Fair Country: Telling Truths about Canada*. Toronto: Viking Canada, 2008.

Schellhaas, Sebastian. "Changing Tides: Indigenous Chefs at the Culinary Olympics and the Gastronomic Professionalization of Aboriginal Cooking." In *Canadian Culinary Imaginations*, edited by Shelley Boyd

and Dorothy Barenscott, 57–76. Montreal and Kingston: McGill-Queen's University Press, 2020.
– *First Nations Cuisines: Wandel und Professionalisierung indigener Ernährungskulturen in British Columbia, Kanada*. Bielefeld: Transcript Verlag, 2020.
– "Gastronomical Indians: Indigene Gastronomie als kulturelle Selbstimmung in Kanada." In *Kulinarische Ethnologie: Beiträge zur Wissenschaft von eigenen, fremden und globalisierten Ernährungskulturen*, edited by Daniel Kofahl and Sebastian Schellhaas, 167–206. Bielefeld: Transcript Verlag, 2018.
Schreiber, Dorothee. "Our Wealth Sits on the Table: Food, Resistance, and Salmon Farming in Two First Nations Communities." *American Indian Quarterly* 26, no. 3 (Summer 2002): 360–77.
Schreiber, Dorothee, and Camilla Brattland. "Introduction." In *Salmon Cultures: Indigenous Peoples and the Aquaculture Industry*, edited by Dorothee Schreiber and Camilla Brattland, 5–10. *RCC Perspectives* 4 (2012).
*Scout Vancouver*. "Tomahawk." 22 April 2013. http://scoutmagazine.ca/2013/04/22/vancouver-lexicon-tomahawk/.
SeaDNA. "Market in Ontario." Accessed 20 April 2018. https://www.seadna.ca/new-market-in-ontario/.
– "Seal Cuts." Accessed 20 April 2018. https://www.seadna.ca/seal-cuts-phoconailles/.
Searles, Edmund. "Food and the Making of Modern Inuit Identities." *Food and Foodways* 10 (2002): 55–78.
– "Inuit Identity in the Canadian Arctic." *Ethnology* 47, no. 4 (Fall 2008): 239–55.
Seventh Fire. Accessed 24 January 2018. https://seventhfire.ca/seventh-fire/.
Shapiro, Laura. *Perfection Salad: Women and Cooking at the Turn of the Century*. Berkeley: University of California Press, 1986.
Sharpe, Christina. *In the Wake: On Blackness and Being*. Durham, NC: Duke University Press, 2016.
Shaw, Rob. "Storytelling a Key Part of the Business Mix in Port Alberni." *Vancouver Sun*, 23 September 2014, C2.
*She Does the City*. "Wanna Try Aboriginal Cuisine? The #YouAreWelcome Food Truck Is Coming to Toronto!" 8 July 2015. www.shedoesthecity.com/wanna-try-aboriginal-cuisine-the-youarewelcome-food-truck-is-coming-to-toronto.
Shepro, Richard Warren. "The Rhetoric of Salmon: The War of Words, Images and Metaphors in the Battle of Wild-Caught vs. Farmed Salmon." In *Food & Communication: Proceedings of the Oxford Symposium on Food*

*and Cookery 2015*, edited by Mark McWilliams, 347–62. London: Prospect Books, 2016.
Sherman, Sean. "Tasting and Talk: Native Cuisines with Sean Sherman of The Sioux Chef." Hauser & Wirth, Los Angeles, 17 March 2018.
Sherman, Sean, and Beth Dooley. *The Sioux Chef's Indigenous Kitchen*. Minneapolis: University of Minnesota Press, 2017.
Shoemaker, Nancy. "Whale Meat in American History." *Environmental History* 10 (April 2005): 269–94.
Sidsworth, Robin. "Aboriginal Participation in the Vancouver/Whistler 2010 Olympic Games: Consultation, Reconciliation and the New Relationship." Master's thesis, University of British Columbia, 2010.
Silva, Nikki, and Davia Nelson. *Hidden Kitchens: Stories, Recipes, and More from NPR's The Kitchen Sisters*. Emmaus, PA: Rodale Books, 2005.
Silverthorn, Colleen. "A Landmark No More." *Leader-Post*, 15 January 2002, A10.
– "Landmark Inn Staying Open until Friday." *Leader-Post*, 23 October 2001, B3.
– "A South-Regina Landmark No More." *Leader-Post*, 18 October 2001, A1.
Simmel, Georg. "The Sociology of the Meal." Translated by Michael Symons in Michael Symons, "Simmel's Gastronomic Sociology: An Overlooked Essay." *Food and Foodways* 5, no. 4 (1994): 333–51.
Simpson, Audra. "On Ethnographic Refusal: Indigeneity, 'Voice' and Colonial Citizenship." *Junctures*, 9 December 2007, 67–80.
– "The Sovereignty of Critique." *South Atlantic Quarterly* 119, no. 4 (2020): 685–99.
Simpson, Leanne Betasamosake. *As We Have Always Done: Indigenous Freedom through Radical Resistance*. Minneapolis: University of Minnesota Press, 2017.
– *Dancing on Our Turtle's Back: Stories of Nishnaabeg Re-Creation, Resurgence, and a New Emergence*. Winnipeg: Arbeiter Ring Publishing, 2012.
Siu, Lok. "Chino Latino Restaurants: Converging Communities, Identities, and Cultures." *Afro-Hispanic Review* 27, no. 1 (Spring 2008): 161–71.
– "Twenty-First Century Food Trucks: Mobility, Social Media, and Urban Hipness." In *Eating Asian America: A Food Studies Reader*, edited by Robert Ko, Martin Manalansan, and Anita Mannur, 231–44. New York: NYU Press, 2013
Skinner, Kelly, Erin Pratley, and Kristin Burnett. "Eating in the City: A Review of the Literature on Food Insecurity and Indigenous People Living in Urban Spaces." *Societies* 6, no. 7 (2016): 1–17.
Skye, Bertha. "Traditional Cree and Iroquois Foods." In *Northern Bounty: A Celebration of Canadian Cuisine*, edited by Jo Marie Powers and Anita Stewart, 113–19. Toronto: Random House of Canada, 1995.

Skyum-Nielsen, Rune. "The Perfect Storm." In *NOMA: Time and Place in Nordic Cuisine*, edited by René Redzepi. London: Phaidon Press, 2010.

Slattery, Jill. "PETA to Hold 'Bloody' Protest against Seal Dish at Edible Canada Restaurant." Global News, 20 January 2017. https://globalnews.ca/news/3193812/peta-seal-protest-vancouver-restaurant/.

Slow Food. "Terminology." Accessed 29 August 2019. https://www.slowfood.com/about-us/slow-food-terminology/.

Small, Ernest. "Fiddleheads." *The Canadian Encyclopedia*. Last modified 23 March 2015. https://www.thecanadianencyclopedia.ca/en/article/fiddleheads.

Smith, Andrew F. *The Oxford Companion to American Food and Drink*. Oxford: Oxford University Press, 2007.

Smith, Janell, and Dennis Wiedman. "Fat Content of South Florida Indian Frybread: Health Implications for a Pervasive Native-American Food." *Journal of the American Dietetic Association* 101, no. 5 (May 2001): 582–4.

Smith, Julia. "An 'Entirely Different' Kind of Union: The Service, Office, and Retail Workers' Union of Canada (SORWUC), 1972–1986." *Labour/Le Travail* 73 (Spring 2014): 23–65.

– "Organizing the Unorganized: The Service, Office, and Retail Workers' Union of Canada (SORWUC), 1972–1986." Master's thesis, Simon Fraser University, 2007.

Smith, Susan. "What a Delicious *Feast!* A Wet'suwet'en Chef Has Written a One-of-a-Kind Cook Book." *Interior News*, 26 November 1997, C1.

Solnit, Rebecca. *Storming the Gates of Paradise: Landscapes for Politics*. Berkeley: University of California Press, 2007.

SORWUC. "All the Questions You've Wanted to Ask about Muckamuck." *Kinesis*, August 1980.

Sotheby's. "Contemporary Art Evening Auction. Andy Warhol, *The American Indian (Russell Means)*." Accessed 22 May 2019. https://www.sothebys.com/en/auctions/ecatalogue/2019/contemporary-art-evening-auction-n10069/lot.20.html.

Spang, Rebecca L. *The Invention of the Restaurant: Paris and Modern Gastronomic Culture*. Cambridge, MA, and London: Harvard University Press, 2000.

Specht, Joshua. *Red Meat Republic: A Hoof-to-Table History of How Beef Changed America*. Princeton and Oxford: Princeton University Press, 2019.

Spray, Zona. "Alaska's Vanishing Arctic Cuisine." *Gastronomica* 2, no. 1 (Winter 2002): 30–40.

Spray Starks, Zona. "Arctic Foodways and Contemporary Cuisine." *Gastronomica* 7, no. 1 (Winter 2007): 41–9.

Stainsby, Mia. "Canadian Content." *Vancouver Sun*, 30 June 2005, C21.
– "First Nations Food Gaining Wide Appeal." *Province*, 10 May 2018, 37.
– "Nature's Supermarket." *Vancouver Sun*, 20 August 2008, C3.
*Star-Phoenix*. "Regina's Landmark Inn Latest Victim of Economy." 5 February 1990, A6.
*Star Tribune*. "Passport Is Not Required, but Some ID Is." 2 May 1999, 94.
Stasiulis, Davia, and Nira Yuval-Davis. "Introduction: Beyond Dichotomies – Gender, Race, Ethnicity and Class in Settler Societies." In *Unsettling Settler Societies: Articulations of Gender, Race, Ethnicity and Class*, edited by Davia Stasiulis and Nira Yuval-Davis, 12–38. London: SAGE Publications, 1995.
Statistics Canada. "Aboriginal Peoples in Canada: Key Results from the 2016 Census." Last modified 25 October 2017. https://www150.statcan.gc.ca/n1/daily-quotidien/171025/dq171025a-eng.htm.
– "Food Insecurity among Inuit Living in Inuit Nunagat: Insights on Canadian Society." 1 February 2017. http://www.statcan.gc.ca/pub/75-006-x/2017001/article/14774-eng.htm.
– "Immigration and Ethnocultural Diversity in Canada." Accessed 4 June 2019. https://www12.statcan.gc.ca/nhs-enm/2011/as-sa/99-010-x/99-010-x2011001-eng.cfm.
– "National Indigenous Peoples Day ... by the Numbers." Last modified 20 June 2018. https://www.statcan.gc.ca/eng/dai/smr08/2018/smr08_225_2018.
– "2016 Census Topic: Aboriginal Peoples." Last modified 21 June 2018. https://www12.statcan.gc.ca/census-recensement/2016/rt-td/ap-pa-eng.cfm.
Steinberger, Michael. *Au Revoir to All That: The Rise and Fall of French Cuisine*. London: Bloomsbury, 2010.
Stevens, Peter A. "Decolonizing Cottage Country." *Active History*, 22 February 2018. http://activehistory.ca/2018/02/decolonizing-cottage-country/#more-23121.
– "A Little Place in the (Next) Country: Negotiating Nature and Nation in 1970s Ontario." *Journal of Canadian Studies* 47, no. 3 (Fall 2013): 42–66.
Stevens, Scott Manning. "Tomahawk: Materiality and Depictions of the Haudenosaunee." *Early American Literature* 53, no. 2 (2018): 475–511.
Stevenson, Allyson, and Cheryl Troupe. "From Kitchen Tables to Formal Organization: Indigenous Women's Social and Political Activism in Saskatchewan to 1980." In *Compelled to Act: Histories of Women's Activism in Western Canada*, edited by Sarah Carter and Nanci Langford, 301–46. Winnipeg: University of Manitoba Press, 2020.

Sutherland, Phoebe. "Sweetgrass on the Verge." *Nation*, 15 July 2011. http://www.nationnews.ca/sweetgrass-on-the-verge/.

Sutton, David E. "Cooking in Theory: Risky Events in the Structure of the Conjuncture." *Anthropological Theory* 18, no. 4 (September 2017): 81–105.

Sweetgrass Aboriginal Bistro. "Frequently Asked Questions." Accessed 23 November 2023. http://www.sweetgrassbistro.ca/faq.htm.

Szanto, David. "Is It Hot in Here, or Is It Just Me? On Being an Emotional Academic." *Canadian Food Studies* 3, no. 1 (April 2016): 4–8.

Tagaq, Tanya. "Eating Seal Meat Is a Vital Part of Life in My Community." *MUNCHIES: Food by Vice*, 28 June 2017. http://munchies.vice.com/articles/eating-seal-meat-is-a-vital-part-of-life-in-my-community.

TallBear, Kim. "Being in Relation." In *Messy Eating: Conversations on Animals as Food*, edited by Samantha King, R. Scott Carey, Isabel Macquarrie, Victoria Niva Millious, and Elaine M. Power, 54–67. New York: Fordham University Press, 2019.

– "Shepard Krech's *The Ecological Indian*: One Indian's Perspective." *Ecological Indian Review* (September 2000): 1–5.

Taylor, Drew Hayden. *Cottagers and Indians*. Vancouver: Talonbooks, 2019.

Tefft, Marianne. "Groups Help Native Enterprises Get Off on the Right Foot." *Financial Post*, 23 February 1985, S3.

Tennant, Zoe. "Breaking Bread: Bannock's Contentious Place in Aboriginal Cuisine." *Walrus*, 20 May 2016. https://thewalrus.ca/breaking-bread/.

– "First Course." *Granta*, 6 February 2019. https://granta.com/first-course/.

– "*Terra Nullius* on the Plate: Colonial Blindness, Restaurant Discourse, and Indigenous Cuisines." In *Canadian Culinary Imaginations*, edited by Shelley Boyd and Dorothy Barenscott, 77–92. Montreal and Kingston: McGill-Queen's University Press, 2020.

Thiessen, Janet. *Snacks: A Canadian Food History*. Winnipeg: University of Manitoba Press, 2017.

Thompson, Joey. "Muckamuck Stew Is Back at the LRB." *Province*, 14 May 1980, A4.

Thorni, Stephen. "Tomahawk Barbecue Evolves with the Times." *Vancouver Sun*, 15 January 2016, C10.

Thrush, Coll. "Vancouver the Cannibal: Cuisine, Encounter, and the Dilemma of Difference on the Northwest Coast, 1774–1804." *Ethnohistory* 58:1 (Winter 2011): 1–35.

Thurton, David. "Bannock Recipe: How to Make a Northern Staple." CBC News, 13 June 2015. http://www.cbc.ca/news/canada/north/bannock-recipe-how-to-make-a-northern-staple-1.3112436.

*Times Colonist*. "Indians, Cowboys Same to Strikers." 11 October 1978, N.

– "Public Funds Funnelled to Friends as Easy Loans, Say Native Critics." 28 November 1992, A1 and A8.

Tobin, Beth Fowkes. *Picturing Imperial Power: Colonial Subjects in Eighteenth-Century British Painting*. Durham, NC: Duke University Press, 1999.
Todd, Zoe. "Fish, Kin and Hope: Tending to Water Violations in Amishkwaciwaskahikan and Treaty Six Territory." *Afterall* (Spring/Summer 2017): 95–9.
– "Fish Pluralities: Human-Animal Relations and Sites of Engagement in Paulatuuq, Arctic Canada." *Etudes/Inuit/Studies* 38, no. 1–2 (2014): 217–38.
Tomahawk Restaurant. "The Legendary Tomahawk Menu." Accessed 26 September 2018. http://www.tomahawkrestaurant.com/menu.html.
– "Tomahawk History." Accessed 26 September 2018. http://www.tomahawkrestaurant.com/history.html.
Tompkins, Kyla Wazana. *Racial Indigestion: Eating Bodies in the 19th Century*. New York: New York University Press, 2012.
"Top Chef Canada," season 1, episode 1, "Getting to Know You," Food Network Canada, 11 April 2011.
Toronto Biennale of Art. "A Public Apology to Siksika Nation." Accessed 1 October 2019. https://torontobiennial.org/programs/apology-to-siksika-nation/.
*Toronto Life*. "Best New Restaurants 2012: No. 4. Keriwa." 27 March 2012. https://torontolife.com/food/restaurants/best-new-restaurants-2012/.
Toronto Restaurants. Accessed 1 August 2018. http://torontorestaurants.com/.
*Toronto Star*. "A Taste of First Nations." 28 June 2000, F6.
Townshend, Don. "Destination Vancouver." *Sydney Morning Herald*, 3 October 1999, 209.
Treaty Guide for Torontonians, A. "By These Presents: 'Purchasing' Toronto (2019)." Accessed 23 November 2023. https://talkingtreaties.ca/about/talking-treaties/purchasing-toronto.
Trembath, Sean. "A Feast of Culture: First Nations Cuisine on the Rise." *Saskatoon Star-Phoenix*, 31 March 2017. http://thestarphoenix.com/life/bridges/a-feast-of-culture-first-nations-cuisine-on-the-rise.
Trubek, Amy. *The Taste of Place: A Cultural Journey into Terroir*. Berkeley and Los Angeles: University of California Press, 2008.
Truder, Stefanie. "Why Is Francis Ford Coppola Opening an 'American Native' Restaurant?" *San Francisco Eater*, 24 October 2016. https://sf.eater.com/2016/10/24/13385456/francis-ford-coppola-werowocomoco-virgina-dare-winery-geyserville-sonoma.
Trumbull, Robert. "What's Doing in Vancouver." *New York Times*, 5 June 51977, XX7.
*Truth about Fur, The*. "Eating Seal Meat: Vancouver Chef Puts Seal on Menu." 2 February 2017. http://www.truthaboutfur.com/blog/eating-seal-meat-vancouver-chef-puts-seal-on-menu/.

Truth and Reconciliation Commission of Canada. *Honouring the Truth, Reconciling for the Future: Summary of the Final Report of the Truth and Reconciliation Commission of Canada*. 23 July 2015. http://www.trc.ca/websites/trcinstitution/File/2015/Honouring_the_Truth_Reconciling_for_the_Future_July_23_2015.pdf.
– *Truth and Reconciliation Commission of Canada Calls to Action*. Winnipeg, 2015. http://trc.ca/assets/pdf/Calls_to_Action_English2.pdf.
Tuck, Eve, and K. Wayne Yang. "Decolonization Is Not a Metaphor." *Decolonization: Indigeneity, Education & Society* 1, no. 1 (2012): 1–40.
Turner, Annie. "Delicious Resistance, Sweet Persistence: First Nations Culinary Arts in Canada." Master's thesis, Carleton University, 2005.
Turner, Nancy J. *Ancient Pathways, Ancestral Knowledge: Ethnobotany and Ecological Wisdom of Indigenous Peoples of Northwestern North America*. Montreal and Kingston: McGill-Queen's University Press, 2014.
– *Food Plants of Interior First Peoples*. Vancouver: University of British Columbia Press, 1997.
Turner, Nancy J., Sinclair Philip, and Robert D. Turner. "Traditional Native Plant Foods in Contemporary Cuisine in British Columbia." In *Northern Bounty: A Celebration of Canadian Cuisine*, edited by Jo Marie Powers and Anita Stewart, 23–30. Toronto: Random House of Canada, 1995.
Twitty, Michael. *The Cooking Gene: A Journey through African American Culinary History in the Old South*. New York: Amistad, 2017.
United States Department of Agriculture, Forest Service. "Cape Perpetua Scenic Area – Historical Richness." Accessed 17 May 2019. https://www.fs.usda.gov/detail/siuslaw/specialplaces/?cid=fsbdev7_007177.
*Vancouver Sun*. "Critic's Choice: Restaurant Guide: Liliget Feast House." 7 August 1997, C6.
– "In the Spirit." 18 December 1991, B9.
– "Liliget Feast House Brings First Nation Cuisine to Vancouver." 27 October 2001, E5.
– "Muck-a-Muck House Advertisement." 19 May 1972, 43A.
– "Muckamuck Owners Claim to Be in Debt." 13 June 1979, C2.
– "Opening Delayed." 4 May 1985, H8.
– "Restaurant Management Now Willing to Bargain." 26 April 1980, A12.
– "Union Members Picket Gallery." 10 December 1980, H3.
– "Your Guide to Expo Eating." 10 May 1986, H3.
Vantrease, Dana. "Commod Bods and Frybread Power: Government Food Aid in American Indian Culture." *Journal of American Folklore* 126 (2013): 55–69.

Viaud, Jean-Paul. "Dining Railway-Style in North America." In *100 Years of Canadian Railway Recipes*, edited by Marie-Paul Partikian and Jean-Paul Viaud, 9–21. Saint-Constant QC: Exporail Canada, 2014.

Visser, Margaret. *The Rituals of Dinner: The Origins, Evolution, Eccentricities and Meaning of Table Manners*. Toronto: HarperCollins, 1991.

Wagamese, Richard. *Indian Horse*. Madeira Park, BC: Douglas and McIntyre, 2013.

Walters, Krista. "'A National Priority': Nutrition Canada's *Survey* and the Disciplining of Aboriginal Bodies, 1964–1975." In *Edible Histories, Cultural Politics: Towards a Canadian Food History*, edited by Franca Iacovetta, Valerie Korinek, and Marlene Epp, 433–51. Toronto: University of Toronto Press, 2012.

Wanuskewin. "Appointment." *Star-Phoenix*, 11 May 1992, 4.

– "Restaurant Manager." *Leader-Post*, 14 November 1992, 25.

– "Story of the Northern Plains." Accessed 9 December 2023, https://wanuskewin.com/.

Wanuskewin Heritage Park "Ad."

Wanuskewin Restaurant. "Thank You Dairy Producers." *Star-Phoenix*, 30 October 1993, 11.

Waters, Alice. *Chez Panisse Menu Cookbook*. New York: Random House, 1982.

– *Coming to My Senses: The Making of a Counterculture Cook*. London: Hardie Grant Books, 2017.

Watson, Catherine. "Muckamuck: Where the Food Is Intriguing." *Minneapolis Tribune*, 11 May 1980, 4E.

Watt-Cloutier, Sheila. *The Right to Be Cold: One Woman's Fight to Protect the Arctic and Save the Planet from Climate Change*. Minneapolis: University of Minnesota Press, 2018 [2015].

Watts, Annie L. "Food Business." YouTube, 28 September 2103. https://www.youtube.com/watch?v=Ihef0sqakdE&t=296s.

– "Liliget Feast House." YouTube. 12 November 2014. https://www.youtube.com/watch?v=oa-nArGEC7M&t=9s.

Watts, Dolly, and Annie Watts. *Where People Feast: An Indigenous People's Cookbook*. Vancouver: Arsenal Pulp Press, 2007.

Waugh, Frederick Wilkerson. *Iroquis* [sic] *Foods and Food Preparation*. Ottawa: Canadian Department of Mines, 1916.

Weatherford, Jack. *Indian Givers: How the Indians of the Americas Transformed the World*. New York: Bellantine Books, 1989.

Weltecke, Dorothea. "Essen und Fasten in interreligiöser Abgrenzung, Konkurrenz und Austausch – einleitende Bemerkungen." In *Essen und Fasten in interreligiöser Abgrenzung, Konkurrenz und Austauschrpozesse*, edited by Dorothea Weltecke, 7–22. Cologne, Weimar, and Vienna: Böhlau Verlag, 2017.

Wenzel, George. *Animal Rights Human Rights: Ecology, Economy and Ideology in the Canadian Arctic*. Toronto and Buffalo: University of Toronto Press, 1991.

Werowocomoco. "Menu." Accessed 4 December 2016. https://www.virginiadarewinery.com/en/visit-us/restaurant.

Weso, Thomas Pecore. *Good Seeds: A Menominee Indian Food Memoir*. Madison: Wisconsin Historical Society Press, 2016.

Weston, Kath. "Get Thee to a Big City: Sexual Imaginary and the Great Gay Migration." *GLQ* 2 (1995): 253–77.

Whalen, Julia. "Seal Meat on the Menu at Toronto Restaurant Sparks Duelling Petitions, Online Debate." CBC News, 10 October 2017. http://www.cbc.ca/news/canada/toronto/seal-meat-debate-kukum-1.4347858.

White, Rowen. "Seed Rematriation." *Sierra Seeds*, 19 March 2018. http://sierraseeds.org/seed-rematriation/.

Whyte, Kyle Powys. "The Dakota Access Pipeline, Environmental Injustice, and U.S. Colonialism." *Red Ink* 19, no.1 (Spring 2017): 154–69.

– "Food Sovereignty, Justice and Indigenous People: An Essay on Settler Colonialism and Collective Continuance." *The Oxford Handbook of Food Ethics*, edited by Anne Barnhill, Mark Budolfson, and Tyler Doggett, 345–66. Oxford: Oxford University Press, 2018.

Wilensky. "Menu." Accessed 7 May 2018. http://top2000.ca/wilenskys/ENG_TABLE_Menu.htm. Accessed May 7, 2018.

Willet, Cynny. "History in the Making." *Calgary Herald*, 23 April 1995, B8.

– "Offerings a Mix of Old, New." *Calgary Herald*, 23 April 1995, B8.

Williams-Forson, Psyche. *Building Houses out of Chicken Legs: Black Women, Food, and Power*. Chapel Hill: University of North Carolina Press, 2006.

– "Foreword." In *Vibration Cooking: Or, The Travel Notes of a Geechee Girl*, by Vertamae Smart-Grosvenor, xi–xxxii. Athens and London: University of Georgia Press, 2011.

Willis, Jane. *Geniesh: An Indian Girlhood*. Toronto: New Press, 1973.

Wilmshurst, Sara. "How to Eat Like a Canadian: Centennial Cookbooks and Visions of Culinary Identity." *Cuizine: The Journal of Canadian Food Cultures/Cuizine: Revue des cultures culinaires au Canada* 4, no. 2 (2013).

Wilson, Amanda, Meredith Bessey, Jennifer Brady, Michael Classens, Kirsten Lee, Charles Z. Levkoe, Jennifer Marshman, Tabitha Martens, Sarah-Louise Ruder, Phoebe Stephens, and Tammara Soma. "Reflections on the Role and Responsibilities of Food Studies in Canada, Indigenous Territories, and Beyond – 2020–21." *Canadian Food Studies* 8, no. 3 (2021): 5–10.

Wilson, Gilbert L. *Buffalo Bird Woman's Garden: Agriculture of the Hidatsa Indians*. Minneapolis: Minnesota Historical Society Press, 1987 [1917].

Wilson-Sanchez, Maya. "Exhibition Review: *Blueprints.*" *The Senses and Society* 11, no. 3 (November 2016): 357–62.
*Windspeaker.* "Toody Ni Advertisement." 8 June 1992, 13.
– "Windspeaker." 8 June 1992, "About" section, 4.
Wise, Michael D. *Native Foods: Agriculture, Indigeneity, and Settler Colonialism in American History.* Fayetteville: University of Arkansas Press, 2023.
Wolfe, Patrick. "Settler Colonialism and the Elimination of the Native." *Journal of Genocide Research* 8, no. 4 (2006): 387–409.
– *Settler Colonialism and the Transformation of Anthropology: The Politics and Poetics of an Ethnographic Event.* London and New York: Cassell, 1999.
Wolfman, David, and Maureen Finn. *Cooking with the Wolfman: Indigenous Fusion.* Madeira Park, BC: Douglas and McIntyre, 2017.
Woodward, Joan. "Still on Strike at Muckamuck." *Kinesis*, July–August 1978.
Worster, Donald. *An Unsettled Country: Changing Landscapes of the American West.* Albuquerque: University of New Mexico Press, 1994.
Wright, Katherine. "In the Shadow of a Willow Tree: A Community Garden Experiment in Decolonising, Multispecies Research." *Cultural Studies Review* 24, no. 1 (2018): 74–101.
Yellow Bird, Michael. "What We Want to Be Called: Indigenous Peoples' Perspectives on Racial and Ethnic Identity Labels." *American Indian Quarterly* 23, no. 2 (Spring 1999): 1–21.
Yelp. "Chief Chiniki Menu." 24 June 2011. https://www.yelp.ca/biz_photos/chief-chiniki-restaurant-morley-2?select=HNKHDYVBeJSxPAF1MB8GcQ.
Zeide, Anna. *Canned: The Rise and Fall of Consumer Confidence in the American Food Industry.* Oakland: University of California Press, 2018.
Zelinsky, Wilbur. "The Roving Palate: North America's Ethnic Restaurant Cuisines." *Geoforum* 16, no. 1 (1985): 51–72.
Zelko, Frank. *Make It a Green Peace! The Rise of Countercultural Environmentalism.* Oxford: Oxford University Press, 2013.
Zickerfoose, Sherri. "Chief Chiniki Restaurant May Be Rebuilt after Blaze." *Calgary Herald*, 22 August 2022, B1.
– "Officials Await Report on Chief Chiniki Fire." *Calgary Herald*, 23 August 2012, B3.
Zilberstein, Anya. "Inured to Empire: Wild Rice and Climate Change." *William and Mary Quarterly* 72, no. 1 (2015): 127–58.
Zogry, Michael J. "Introduction." In *Native Foodways: Indigenous North American Religious Traditions and Foods*, edited by Michelene E. Pesantubbee and Michael J. Zogry, 1–31. Albany: SUNY Press, 2021.

# Index

Aasmaabik (the face of the rock), 200
"Aboriginal cuisine," emergence of, 79
Absolon, Kathy, 12
Ace Gallery, 119, 134
Adams, KC, 78
Adichie, Chimamanda, 10
Adler, Shawn, 200
Adrià, Ferran, 105
*aglus* (seal breathing holes), 213
Ahtahkakoop Cree Nation, 109
Akwesasne Mohawk Nation, 59
Alfred, Taiaiake, 7, 25, 46
Ali, Brooke, 248
"Alice Waters diaspora," 105
Allan, Ted, 101
Aloha Poke Stop, 91
*Along the Tracks* (Myers), 52
"Alsea fisherman" (Curtis), 125
AlterNative food movement, 106–7
American Indian Resource Corporation, 151
*Andy Warhol: The American Indian Series*, 134
anti-sealing campaign, 214. *See also* Save the Seals
Arctic Trio, 212. *See also* Kūkŭm Kitchen
*Arizona Republic*, 153, 155
Arnaquq-Baril, Alethea, 214

artists, Indigenous: Adams, KC, 78; Assu, Sonny, 42; Belcourt, Billy-Ray, 112, 218; Chrystos, 51; Claxton, Dana, 139; Douglas, Keesic, 78; Gómez Peña, Guillermo, 25; L'Hirondelle, Cheryl, 78; Monkman, Kent, 245–8, 255, 269; Morin, Peter, 78; Morrissette, Suzanne, 78; Myers, Lisa, 52; Pudlat, Elijah, 70; Reid, Bill, 134; ReMatriate Collective, 139–40; Saggiak, Kumukuluk, 70; Stimson, Adrian, 292; Yuxweluptun, Lawrence Paul, 269
artworks, Indigenous: *Along the Tracks* (Myers), 52; *Beginning with the Seventies: Collective Acts* (Claxton), 139; *Best Before* (Myers), 78–9; *Blueprints* (Myers), 52–4; *Breakfast Series* (Assu), 42–4; *Fish Farmers They Have Sea Lice* (Yuxweluptun), 269; *Iini Sookumapii: Guess Who's Coming to Dinner?* (Stimson), 293; *Les Castors du Roi* (Monkman), 246; *The Rise and Fall of Civilization* (Monkman), 245
Assu, Sonny, 42
*Atlanta Constitution*, 129, 147

authenticity, 92; paradox of, 93; primitive, 127; repressive (Wolfe), 84, 102, 183; social construction of, 197

Ballantyne, Jennifer, 10
Banff Indian Days, 61–3, 131; bison over beef, 62–3, 135
bannock, 47–50; limiting of, 203; pre-contact, 49; symbolism of, 199
ban-wich, 164
Barbeau, Marius, 241
Basil, Priya, 37, 182
bastard cooking, 97–8, 274
bastardized, 97, 274
Baumann, Shyon, 92
Bear Robe, Aaron Joseph, 191, 193–4, 196–8, 209, 280, 292, 297
Beausoleil First Nation, 52, 205, 299
*Beaver, The* (Barbeau), 241
beaver meat, 241–3; accessibility of, 242; in Catholic doctrine, 244; culinary imaginations of, 242–3; recipes, 251–2; wars, 245
beef, 255; Banff Indian Days, 62–3; imperial history of, 89; replacing of, 36, 255
Beeson, Patricia, 243
*Beginning with the Seventies: Collective Acts* (Claxton), 139
Belcourt, Billy-Ray, 112, 218
Bell, David, 5
Bell, Gloria Jane, 58
Bendix, Regina, 93
*Best Before* (Myers), 78–9
bison: *see* buffalo
Bison Berry, 257–8
Bistro on Notre Dame, 9
Bjornson, Teresa, 119
Blackstock, Michael, 49
blueberries, 52, 121, 238, 258, 262
*Blueprints* (Myers), 52–4
Blumenthal, Heston, 297
Bocuse, Paul, 103
Bolton, Art, 143
Boralia, 297–8

*Braiding Sweetgrass: Indigenous Wisdom, Scientific Knowledge and the Teachings of Plants* (Kimmerer), 275
Brandon, Gerry, 9
Brant, Tawnya, 9
*Breakfast Series* (Assu), 42–4
Bronson, AA, 292–3
Bruneau-Guenther, Christa, 225, 255
buffalo, 245–6, 294
Buffalo smokies, 164
Bugialli, Guiliano, 15
Bungees, 172–3
Burklo, Barbara, 153

Caira, Rosanna, 108
*Calgary Herald*, 176, 178–9
Canadian Creole, 97–8, 254, 274
Canadian culinary guides: *Northern Bounty* (Powers and Stewart), 49, 107–9; *Speaking in Cod Tongues: A Canadian Culinary Journey* (Newman), 97, 108; *Where to Eat in Canada* (Hardy), 124
Canadian Pacific Railway (CPR), 55, 57; de Grandmaison, Nicholas Raphael, 58; menu, 57–8; menu illustration, 58
Canadian Restaurant Association, 23, 109, 110
Canoe, 107
Capatti, Alberto, 97
Cardinal, Curtis Red-Rokk, 9
Carter, Sarah, 33, 177
Caudron, Remi, 260
CBC, 100–1, 182, 188, 211, 273–4; CBC Radio, 211
Chamberlain, Chick, 87–8
Chamberlain, Chuck, 87
Chandra, Matt, 289
Charlie's Burgers, 251
Chartrand, Robert, 257
Chartrand, Shane, 225, 252, 304
chefs, Indigenous: Adler, Shawn, 200; Ballantyne, Jennifer, 10; Bear Robe, Aaron Joseph, 191, 193–4, 196–8, 209, 280, 292, 297;

Brandon, Gerry, 9; Brant, Tawnya, 9; Bruneau-Guenther, Christa, 225, 255; Chartrand, Shane, 225, 252, 304; Condo, Norma, 114; Craig, Nephi, 289; Francis, Rich, 224, 264, 271, 290; Frank, Lois Ellen, 95, 289; George Jr., Andrew, 149, 150, 156–61, 183, 193, 205, 242–3; Houle, Helen, 176; Lasard, Jenni, 189; Medina, Vincent, 287; Napoleon, Art, 244; O'Connor, Tim, 253; Ross, George, 144; Sherman, Sean, 256, 290–1, 300; Skye, Brian, 192; Trevino, Louis, 287; Wahpepah, Crystal, 288, 300; Wilson, Mary, 124; Wolfman, David, 4, 7, 50, 93, 280, 290
chefs, non-Indigenous: Adrià, Ferran, 105; Bocuse, Paul, 103; Dammann, Derek, 229, 234, 250, 311; Escoffier, George Auguste, 103; Garcia, Andrée, 227; Goldstein, Joyce, 96; Hayes, Dan, 244; Kennedy, Jamie, 252; Kozak, Brayden, 252; Lenglet, Benoit, 226–7; Puck, Wolfgang, 96; Redzepi, René, 105–6, 232, 296, 298; Robuchon, Joël, 104; Yorke, Tom, 178
Chez Panisse, 104–5, 107, 116, 141, 291
*Chicago Tribune*, 193
Chief Chiniki Restaurant, 175–9, 181–4, 190
Chilcotin Bar Seven, 135–6
*Chilliwack Progress*, 151
Chi-Niibish (literally big water), 265
Chiniki, John, Chief, 176
Chiniki Cultural Centre and Stones Restaurant, 184
Chippewas of Nawash Unceded First Nation, 38
Cho, Lily, 56, 83
Chrismas, Doug, 119, 130
Chrystos, 51
Cidro, Jaime, 12
Claxton, Dana, 139

Cocina Manakurhini, 291
Collingham, Lizzie, 46
colonial imaginations, 58–9, 61
comfort food, 158
conciliation, 292, 294. *See also* reconciliation
Condo, Norma, 114
Confederation Beaver, 151–2
contact zone, 111, 114, 176, 198; and reconciliation, 113, 294
Cook, Inez, 230, 260, 306
cookbooks, Indigenous: *Feast! Canadian Native Cuisine for All Seasons* (George Jr., Gairns), 160; *Foods of the Southwest Indian Nations* (Frank), 289; *Modern Native Feasts: Healthy, Innovative, Sustainable Cuisine* (George Jr.), 242; *Niquiliurniq: A Cookbook from Igloolik* (Arreak), 229; *Original Local: Indigenous Foods, Stories and Recipes from the Upper Midwest* (Erdrich), 50; *Seed to Plate, Soil to Sky: Modern Plant Based Recipes Using Native American Ingredients* (Frank), 289; *The Sioux Chef's Indigenous Kitchen* (Sherman), 255, 290; *Where People Feast: An Indigenous People's Cookbook* (Watts), 169, 280
cookbooks, non-Indigenous: *Au Pied de Cochon Sugar Shack* (Picard), 251; *Bastard Cookbook: The Odious Smell of Truth* (Melasiemi and Tiravanija), 97; *From Pemmican to Poutine: A Journey through Canada's Culinary History* (Roy and Ali), 248; *The Nordic Cookbook* (Nilsson), 228; *The Northern Cookbook* (Canadian Department of Indian Affairs and Northern Development), 251; *True North: Canadian Cooking from Coast to Coast* (Dammann), 229
Cookem Daisey's, 207, 256–7
Coppola, Francis Ford, 286

Corntassel, Jeff, 7, 25, 46, 112, 208, 273
country food, 219–20, 242
Craig, Nephi, 289
Cree syllabics, 206
creolization, 97–8
Cronon, William, 77, 264
cuisine, 15; Canadian, 124–5, 274; *classique*, 103; definition, 15; and ethnic labelling, 80–3; *grande*, 103; *nouvelle*, 103, 120; *post-nouvelle*, 104
culinary: appropriation, 54, 90, 204; branding, 110; confirmation, 96; identity, 252, 273; knowledge, 113, 202, 287; tourism, 81
culinary imagination, 228, 235; of beaver, 241–2
Culinary Olympics, 159–60
cultural appropriation, 91, 235; changing power dynamics, 261; copy and commodify, 91
Curtis, Edward S., 125
Cyr, Monica, 51

Dammann, Derek, 229, 234, 235, 250, 311
Deerchild, Rosanna, 211
Deloria, Vine, 84
*denii ne'aas* (people coming together), 161
Derrida, Jacques, 182
Deyglun, Serge, 214
Dickens, Charles, 39
dietary assimilation, 37–8, 40, 44
Differ, Florence, 136
disgust, 226
dish, definition, 15
documentaries: *Angry Inuk*, 214–15, 220; *Gather*, 290; *Les Grands Phoques de la banquise*, 214; *Massacre des innocents*, 214
Donati, Kelly, 29
Douglas, Keesic, 78
Drees, Laurie Meijer, 61
Driftpile Cree Nation, 112

*East Coast Living*, 275
*Edmonton Journal*, 154, 167, 179, 180

el Bulli, 105
Elders: King, Carolyn, 30, 94; Logan, Audrey, 3, 44; Sault, Gary, 30; Thomas, Mary, 50; William, Doug, 265
Enoch Cree Nation, 225, 304
*EnRoute*, 195, 277
Erdrich, Heid E., 50–1
Erickson, Jane, 119, 279
Escoffier, George Auguste, 103
Esk'etemc First Nation, 282
Essaunce, Vance, 52
Eureka Continuum, 191–2
Expo 67, 64–5; program, 78. *See also* La Toundra; Best Before
Expo 86, 149; First Nation Restaurant, 149, 151–6; Hall, Bob, 150–51; Harvest Restaurant, 156; Icicles, 155–56; Vogel, Gunnar, 150

Feast Cafe Bistro, 255–6
Fedorick, Joy, 172
festivals: Sealfest, 226; Vancouver Dine Out Festival, 225; Wild Leek & Maple Syrup Festival, 225
fiddleheads, 73, 116, 172–3
*Financial Post*, 148, 173
*Financial Post Magazine*, 148, 172
Fine, Gary Alan, 82
fine dining, 92, 103–4
*Fish Farmers They Have Sea Lice* (Yuxweluptun), 269
fish pluralities, 267
fishery regulations, 128, 271
flipper pie, 227–8
food, 5, 15; culturally appropriate, 223; frontier vs. produced, 248; and language, 205, 288; as medicine, 274–5; traditional vs. cultural, 50, 196–7; value shifts of, 107, 168; wild, 168–9, 299–300
"food adventurers" (Heldke), 182
*Food & Wine*, 196, 212
food apartheid, 175
food DNA, 273

*Food Guide for First Nations, Inuit, and Métis* (Health Canada), 255
food sovereignty, 223; Indigenous, 137, 222–3, 235; and regulations, 217, 295; vs. security, 222–4
"foodview" (Trubek), 299
Forbes Wild Food, 208
Foucault, Suzette, 10
Francis, Daniel, 56
Francis, Rich, 224, 264, 271–7, 290
Frank, Lois Ellen, 95, 289
Freedman, Paul, 22, 73
fry bread, 48, 199, 201; duality of, 51
fusion, 95–6, 98

*gaagigebak* (Labrador Tea), 199
Gabaccia, Donna, 6, 98
Gairns, Robert, 160
Garcia, Andrée, 227
Garden River First Nation Reserve, 53
Gardner, Ethel, 119, 134
"gastro nullius" (Donati), 29
*Gazette*, 77, 119
Geniusz, Mary Siisip, 298
George, Denton, 188
George Jr., Andrew, 149, 150, 156–61, 183, 193, 205, 242–3
Gish Hill, Christina, 48, 59
Gitksan First Nation, 168
Glasner, Eli, 101
*Globe and Mail*, 3, 166, 193, 196, 198–9, 231, 292, 297
Gold, Jonathan, 96
Goldstein, Joyce, 96
Gómez Peña, Guillermo, 25
*goût de terroir* (Trubek), 299
Grey, Sam, 18, 41, 97
Guthman, Julie, 104

*hagul jam* (slow boil), 279
Hall, Bob, 150–1
hamburgers: buffalo, 156, 158, 177; on menus, 88–9, 193, 258, 261; non-beef, 89–90, 232–3
Haraway, Donna, 24
Hardy, Anne, 124

Hart, Michael Anthony, 12
Hayes, Dan, 244
Heldke, Lisa, 182
Herkert, Dean, 9
Hewitt, Priscilla, 148
Ho, Soleil, 91
Hochelaga, 77
"hole-in-the-wall," 93
hooks, bell, 81
hostipitality (Derrida), 182
Houle, Helen, 176
hunting, 245–8; and relationship, 249; licences, 250; regulations of, 249
Hyndford, Doug, 189

*Iini Sookumapii: Guess Who's Coming to Dinner?* (Stimson), 293
*ilkalu* (Arctic char), 73
Indian, 56; dead/alive, 83–6; legal, 85
Indian Act, 33, 35, 85, 174
Indian and Métis Friendship Centre, The, 102, 172
Indian candy, 263, 281–2
Indian ice cream, 122, 174
Indian Room, The, 75, 77
"Indian Taco," 178; demand for, 94, 222, 257; reclaiming of, 201, 209; refusal to serve, 203
Indigeneity/Indigenousness, 24–5, 84; romanticization, 10, 56–7; Simpson, Audra, 25, 32; staging of, 62, 131, 176, 261; Yellow Bird, Michael, 24–5
Indigenous cuisine, 26–7, 79, 274, 304; continuity vs. plurality, 273–4; New, 273
Indigenous Food Lab (Sherman), 290
Indigenous Food Movement, 7, 276–7
Indigenous restaurants: evolution of, 170, 26–7; politics of, 83, 137, 170–1, 186, 276–7
Indigenous sovereignty, 224, 235
Indigenous winery, 261

industrial salmon fishing, 265–7
Inuit Circumpolar Council, 215, 217
Inuit Tapiriit Kanatami (ITK), 221

Jacobs, Ben, 289
Johnson, Eve, 147
Johnston, Basil, 36, 38
Johnston, Josée, 92
Just Like Grandma's Bannock, 161–2

Kaplan, Amy, 33
*katimavik* (meeting place), 72
Kee Wee Sen, 80
Keeshig, Zack, 10
Kekuli Cafe, 101, 114
*kelalugak* (beluga whale), 74
Kelly, J.D., 60
Kelowna's Red Fox Club, 114
Kenneally, Rhona Richman, 70
Kennedy, Jamie, 252
*keriwa* (eagle), 194
Keriwa Cafe, 191, 193, 195–7, 209
Kiju's, 101
Kimmerer, Robin Wall, 13, 31, 33, 229, 269, 275, 295
*Kinesis*, 138–9
King, Carolyn, 30, 94
King, Thomas, 13, 83, 295
Kiowa Nation, 289
Knobloch, Frieda, 31
Kokom's Bannock Shack, 101, 207
Kozak, Brayden, 252
Ku, Robert Ji-Song, 93
Kuh, Patric, 103
*kŭ-kŭm* (grandmother), 207
Kŭkŭm Kitchen, 202–3, 211–3, 221
Kvill, Kesia, 55
Kwakwaka'wakw Nations, 42

L'Autochtone, 9
L'eclade, 285, 297
La Boule, 291
La Sagamité, 101
La Toundra, 65; and appropriation, 77–9; and settler storying, 73; décor, 70–1; drinks, 74–5; menu, 72–4; menu graphics, 66–70; romanticization, 77, 80
La Traite, 101
Lac des Milles Lacs First Nation, 202
LaDuke, Winona, 5, 289
LaForme, Bryan, 4
LaForme, Maurice, 3
*Lake District News*, 278
land, 5; access to, 30; and cattle, 89, 102–3; claims to, 3–4, 31; dispossession of, 33, 37; disputes, 42; and pigs, 77; ownership, 245, 248; reclaiming of, 45, 51, 94, 112–13, 223–4, 273; relationship with, 13, 16, 29, 189, 249, 275; and settler colonialism, 32–3, 47, 54, 57, 59, 79, 210, 269, 200. *See also* Oka crisis
Landmark Inn, 184–7
Larson, Stanley, 269
Lasard, Jenni, 189
Lax-kw'alaams First Nation, 144
*Leader-Post*, 173, 187
Lenglet, Benoit, 226–7
*Les Castors du Roi* (Monkman), 246
Levi, Tamara, 202
Lewis, Courtney, 51
L'Hirondelle, Cheryl, 78
*liliget* (where people feast), 161
Liliget Feast House, 161–7
Little Chief Hotel Restaurant, 114
Little Miss Chief, 282–3
Logan, Audrey, 13, 44
Long, Lucy, 81, 226
Lu, Shun, 82
Luby, Brittany, 243, 300

Maffei, Nicolas P., 5–6, 197
*mak-'amham* (our food), 288
manifest domesticity (Kaplan), 33
Manitou Bistro, 10
Manoomin, 10
*manoomin* (wild rice), 199
Manuel, George, 38, 137
Mares, Teresa M., 106
Martens, Tabitha Robin, 7, 12

Matties, Zoe, 31
McSporran, Malcolm, 143
Means, Russell, 134
Mearns, Debbie, 130, 136
Medicine wheel salmon, 274–5
Medina, Danielle, 160
Medina, Vincent, 287
Melasniemi, Annto, 97
Melcosky, Ellen, 282
Membertou First Nation, 101
memory, 273
Menominee Indian Nation, 30, 51, 82
menus: agency of, 83; and bilingualism, 72–3, 199; and borders, 56; dishes vs. ingredients lists, 120, 209; as semantic self-assertion, 260; as textual trace, 103; and time, 73, 102–3
Metallic, Fred, 267
Métis Nation, 189
Meyer, Claus, 8
Middell, Matthias, 6
Mihesuah, Devon, 51
*Miigwetch* (thank you), 199
*Minneapolis Star*, 129
*Minneapolis Tribune*, 130, 133
Miqmak Catering Indigenous Kitchen, 9, 114
Mississaugas of the Credit, 3–4, 12, 30, 94, 300
*Modern Farmer*, 231
molecular gastronomy, 105
Monkman, Kent, 245–8, 255, 269
Monkman, Yvonne, 172
Montanari, Massimo, 97
Morin, Peter, 78
Morris, Carolyn, 31
Morris, Wayne, 334
Morrissette, Suzanne, 78
Muckamuck, 116, 119–21; and authenticity, 120, 124; décor, 128–9; menu, 118, 122–3; strike 145–7; using local ingredients, 121
*muckamuck* (a lot of food), 119–20
Muck-a-Muck House, 119
*muktuk* (whale skin and blubber), 74

Murphy, Andi, 289–90
Myers, Lisa, 52

Naagan, 10
Nabhan, Gary, 13
Nakoda First Nation, 176
Napoleon, Art, 244
*Nation*, 253
National Inquiry into Missing and Murdered Indigenous Women and Girls, 18
*National Post*, 129, 193, 195–6
Native American Culinary Association, 289
Native Delights, 101
"Nativevore Diet" (Frank), 289
*nattiq* (ringed seal), 216
Naumann, Katja, 6
Neechi Foods Co-op Ltd., 257–8
neo-traditional foods, 65
new Nordic cuisine, 105–6; food movement, 7–8, 106. *See also* Noma
*New York Times*, 129, 166, 226, 296
Newman, Lenore, 18, 21, 97, 108
Nickel, Sarah, 85
Niheu, Kalamaokaaina, 91
*nikosi* (bear paw), 238
Nikosi Bistro Pub, 101, 237–9
Nipissing First Nation, 231
NishDish Marketeria, 191, 202–3, 205
Nk'Mip Cellars, 261
Noma, 8–9, 11, 105–6, 300
North American Traditional Indigenous Food Systems (Sherman), 290
*Now Magazine*, 193
Nuu-Chah-Nulth Nation, 143

Ochapowace First Nation, 187
O'Connor, Tim, 253
Ogimaa Makana Project, 208
Ojibwa First Nation, 4
Oka Crisis, 159
oolichan, 123
Opaskwayak Cree Nation, 10

Origins Restaurant, 193
Osage Nation, 289
Oshöwe, 289
ostrich fern, 73
*Ottawa Citizen*, 109, 240, 253
*Ottawa Journal*, 119–20, 129, 133

*Pacific Rim Magazine*, 166
Painted Pony Cafe, 101
Pākehā (non-Māori), 18
palatability, 214, 226; beaver, 252–3; Canada goose, 240–1, 252–3; of Māori foods, 18; salmon, 279; seal, 226–7, 230
pass system, 62, 177
Patel, Raj, 41
Peguis First Nation, 255
pemmican, 195
Peña, Devon G., 106
*Philadelphia Inquirer*, 147, 149
Picard, Martin, 250–1
Pilcher, Jeffrey, 203
popcorn, 240
Porcelli, Alessandro, 251
pork chops Hochelaga, 77
Pörksen, Uwe, 93
porridge, 36–9
Portnoy, Sarah, 103
positionality: about, 12; Absolon, Kathy, 12; Cidro, Jaime, 12; Freeman, Victoria, 12; Hart, Michael Anthony, 12; McLachlan, Stéphane, 24; Minh Hà, Trịnh Thị, 12; Reder, Deanne, 12; Willets, Cam, 12
Potawatomi Nation, 31, 288
potlatch, 90
Poulain, Jean-Pierre, 6
Pow Wow Cafe, 101, 191, 200–1
Powderface, Frank, Chief, 176
Powers, Jo Marie, 49, 107
Powys Whyte, Kyle, 31
primitivity, 125–7
Prince, Christina, 130–1
*Province*, 138, 148, 153, 158
*Province Preview*, 158
*Province's Magazine*, 146

*Public Apology to Siksika Nation, A* (AA Bronson), 293
Puck, Wolfgang, 96
Pudlat, Elijah, 70

Quilicum, 119, 143–8

Rama First Nation, 78
Ray, Krishnendu, 81, 91
"Really Delicious Fry Bread" (Chrystos), 52
reconciliation, 111, 292; critique of, 112; and Indian residential schools, 111–12; and restaurants, 294
Red Mesa Cuisine, 289
Redbird, Duke, 191
Redzepi, René, 8, 105–6, 232, 296, 298
*Regina Sun*, 186
Reid, Bill, 134
Reiter, Ester, 23
ReMatriate Collective, 139–40
rematriation, 140
residential schools, 34; Alberni Residential School, 167; Carlisle Indian School, 35; and food, 40–1; Gordon Indian Residential School, 40; Kamloops Indian School, 37; Marieval Indian School, 37; Mohawk Institute, 35, 38; Nova Scotia Shubenacadie School, 41; Portage La Prairie School, 41; Qu'Appelle North West Territories Industrial School, 37; St. Eugene's Mission School, 37; St. Peter Claver School, 38
*Restaurant Magazine*, 8
restaurants: about, 21–4; and cultural negotiation, 234–5; and cultural presence, 82, 288, 302; culture, 16; lifespan of, 94; as places for reconciliation and resurgence, 112–13; politics, 16, 19, 174; regulations, 261–2
restaurants, Indigenous, USA: Café Gozhóó, 289; Cafe Ohlone, 287;

Conflict Kitchen, 289; Corn Dance Café, 289; Mitsitsam Cafe, 289; Owamni, 290; Pueblo Harvest, 289; Tiwa Kitchen, 289; Tocabe, 289; Wahpepah's Kitchen, 289
restaurateur's room, 22
resurgence: cultural vs. political, 210; and memory/remembrance, 273; and restaurants, 112; US vs. Canada, 291–2; vs. recognition, 210
revitalization, 7, 292, 294
Richard, Mary, 172
*Richmond Review*, 136
Riel-Lachapelle, Wapokunie, 238
Ringuette, Johl Whiteduck, 191, 203
*Rise and Fall of Civilization, The* (Monkman), 245
Roberts, Julia, 22, 46, 248
Robuchon, Joël, 104
Ross, George, 144
Roundhouse Café, 101
Roy, Suman, 248
Royal York Hotel, 60
rural savagery, 227
Ryan, John, 89

Saddle Lake Cree Nation, 179
Saggiak, Kumukuluk, 70
Sagkeeng First Nation, 207
SalmoFan, 266
salmon, 263–5; canned, 265; edibility of, 279; genetically modified, 266; and kinship, 267–8; local vs. global, 284; semi-wild, 266; and wildness, 267
salmon farming, 266; controversies around, 266–7; as form of colonization, 269; and Indigenous sovereignty, 270; relationship transformation, 268–9
Salmon n' Bannock, 260–2
Salteaux soup, 172
*San Francisco Examiner*, 146, 148
*Santa Cruz Sentinel*, 153
Saugeen First Nation, 191
Sault, Gary, 30
Sauvé, Claude, 65

Save the Seals campaign, 214–15
Schafaff, Jörn, 97
SeaDNA, 231–3
Seafood Chowder Toody Ni, 158
seal: absence at Expo 67, 74; Au Cinquième Péché, 226–7; and blood, 219; categorization of, 233; Edible Canada, 230; edibility of, 226–7; in Europe, 228; Les Îles en Ville, 227
seal hunting, 213–14; ban of, 215, 217; consequences of ban, 215–16; subsistence vs. commercial, 218, 232
seal mortadella, 229, 234
seal tartare 212; edibility of, 212–13; petitions against, 212
sealfies, 218–9
Seattle Art Museum, 42
seed sovereignty, 34, 140
Selbst, Suzzy, 130
servers, 123
settler appetites, 108
settler colonialism, 31–3; erase and replace ethos, 32, 50, 91; and gendered experiences, 174. See also dietary assimilation
Seven Fires prophecy, 295
Seventh Fire Hospitality Group, 295
Shawana, Joseph, 191, 212
Sherman, Sean, 256, 290–1, 300
Shirt, Eric, 179
Sigrithur, Anna, 45
Siksika Nation, 191, 292–3
Simmel, Georg, 103
Simpson, Leanne Betasamosake, 16, 33, 288
"single story" (Adichie), 10
Siu, Lok, 82, 97
Sixties Scoop, 44
Skowkale First Nation, 150
Skwah First Nation, 131
Skye, Bertha, 109, 192
Skye, Brian, 192
Skyum-Nielsen, Rune, 106
Slater, Joyce, 51
Slow Food Turtle Island Association, 289

smoked salt, 281
soapberries, 122, 154
Solnit, Rebecca, 6
SORWUC (Service, Office, and Retail Workers' Union of Canada), 130
Spang, Rebecca, 22
spirit plate, 205
Spray, Zona, 15, 222
spruce, 298
*St. Louis Post-Dispatch*, 156
Stainsby, Mia, 168
*Star-Phoenix*, 188–9
Stevens, Scott Manning, 54, 88
Stevenson, Allyson, 84, 174
Stewart, Anita, 49, 107, 263
Stimson, Adrian, 229, 242, 292, 311
Stoney Nakoda Nation, 183
stories, 13–14; and food, 52, 208
"storying" (Hunt and Starblanket), 14; settler colonial, 32, 57
Stratford Chefs School, 52
Sweetgrass Aboriginal Bistro, 239–41, 254
*Sydney Morning Herald*, 163

Tahltan Nation, 78
Tagaq, Tanya, 219
Taste of the Arctic, A (ITK), 221
taverns, 22; Auberge Saint-Gabriel, 23; Wheatsheaf, 23
tea 'n' bannock (chitchat), 199
Tea-n-Bannock, 101, 191, 198–200, 209
Tee Pee Treats, 9
Teepee Restaurant and Lounge, 173–74. *See also* Bungees
television shows: "Cook It Raw Alberta: The Shaping of the Culinary Frontier," 252, 304; "Diners, Drive-Ins and Dives," 93; "Moosemeat & Marmalade," 243–4; "Red Chef Revival: A Travel Series about Food & Reconciliation," 272; "Top Chef Canada," 231, 271
Temagami First Nation, 243
Theriault, Madeline, 243

Thomas, Mary, 50
Thorne, Bonnie, 143
three sisters, 30–1, 208, 258
Thunderbird Cafe, 101
*Times Colonist*, 135
Tiravanija, Rikrit, 97
*Tkaronto* (Toronto), 12, 60
"Toasted Sister" (Murphy), 289
Tobin, Beth Fowkes, 58
tomahawk, 88
Tomahawk Barbeque, 87–8; hamburgers, 88–90
Tompkins, Kyla Wazana, 48
*toody ni* (where the hill faces the river), 156
Toody Ni Grill and Catering Company, 156–7
*Toronto Life*, 193, 196
*Toronto Purchase, The* (Kelly), 60
*Toronto Star*, 192–3, 207, 211
Trevino, Louis, 287
Tribe Called Red, A, 238
Tribes, 179–81
Troupe, Cheryl, 84, 174
Trubek, Amy, 299
Truth and Reconciliation Commission (TRC), 18, 41, 111, 113–14; and calls to action, 113; report of, 26; Sinclair, Justice Murray, 36, 112
Tsi Kiontonhwentsison (creation story), 25
Tsilhqot'in (people of the red river), 135
Tsuut'ina Nation, 114
Turgeon, Laurier, 88
Turtle Island, 25
Tuscarora Nation, 272
Twitty, Michael, 25, 29, 109

*Union of B.C. Indian Chiefs Newsletter*, 138
urban Indigenous revival, 147–8

Valentine, Gill, 5
Vancouver Aboriginal Friendship Centre, 174

*Vancouver Sun*, 124, 134–6, 138, 161–2, 164, 166, 169, 268, 279
Vogel, Gunnar, 150

Wadesai'dö:ndak, 289
Wagamese, Richard, 39
Wahpepah, Crystal, 288, 300
Waleau, Raymond, 65
*wanuskewin* (seeking peace of mind), 188
Wanuskewin Heritage Park, 101, 188–9
Waters, Alice, 287
Watt-Cloutier, Sheila, 215
Watts, Dolly, 161, 166–8, 279
Werowocomoco, 286
Weso, Thomas Pecore, 30, 45
White, Rowen, 140
White Earth Land Recovery Project (LaDuke), 289
White Paper, 85
wild meat, 208; and settlers, 249; regulating of, 249–50, 261–2
wilderness, 60
Willett, Cam, 12

William, Doug, 265
Williams-Forson, Psyche, 10
Wilson, Mary, 124
Wilson-Sanchez, Maya, 53
*Windspeaker*, 157
Wine, Cynthia, 101
*Winnipeg Free Press*, 101, 257
Wise, Michael D., 32, 276
Wolfe, Patrick, 32
Wolfman, David, 4, 7, 50, 93, 280, 290
Worster, Donald, 31
Wu, Evelyn, 297

Xaxli'p First Nation, 4, 99, 280

Yawékon, 9
Yellow Bird, Michael, 24
Yorke, Tom, 178
You Are Welcome Food Truck, 4, 93–5, 300–1
Yuxweluptun, Lawrence Paul, 269

Zelinsky, Wilbur, 82

www.ingramcontent.com/pod-product-compliance
Lightning Source LLC
Chambersburg PA
CBHW052006070526
44584CB00016B/1645